Women in Pastoral Office

WOMEN IN PASTORAL OFFICE

The Story of Santa Prassede, Rome

MARY M. SCHAEFER

OXFORD
UNIVERSITY PRESS

OXFORD
UNIVERSITY PRESS

Oxford University Press is a department of the University of Oxford.
It furthers the University's objective of excellence in research, scholarship,
and education by publishing worldwide.

Oxford   New York
Auckland   Cape Town   Dar es Salaam   Hong Kong   Karachi
Kuala Lumpur   Madrid   Melbourne   Mexico City   Nairobi
New Delhi   Shanghai   Taipei   Toronto

With offices in
Argentina   Austria   Brazil   Chile   Czech Republic   France   Greece
Guatemala   Hungary   Italy   Japan   Poland   Portugal   Singapore
South Korea   Switzerland   Thailand   Turkey   Ukraine   Vietnam

Oxford is a registered trademark of Oxford University Press
in the UK and certain other countries.

Published in the United States of America by
Oxford University Press
198 Madison Avenue, New York, NY 10016

© Oxford University Press 2013

All rights reserved. No part of this publication may be reproduced, stored in a
retrieval system, or transmitted, in any form or by any means, without the prior
permission in writing of Oxford University Press, or as expressly permitted by law,
by license, or under terms agreed with the appropriate reproduction rights organization.
Inquiries concerning reproduction outside the scope of the above should be sent to the
Rights Department, Oxford University Press, at the address above.

You must not circulate this work in any other form
and you must impose this same condition on any acquirer.

Library of Congress Cataloging-in-Publication Data
Schaefer, Mary M. (Mary Martina)
Women in pastoral office : the story of Santa Prassede, Rome / Mary M. Schaefer ; edited by
Joyce Rilett Wood.
pages cm
Includes bibliographical references and index.
ISBN 978–0–19–997762–8 (alk. paper)—ISBN 978–0–19–997763–5 (ebook)
1. Women clergy—History.   2. S. Prassede (Church : Rome, Italy)—History.   3. Rome
(Italy)—Church history.   4. Liturgics.   I. Rilett Wood, Joyce Louise, editor of
compilation.   II. Title.
BV676.S28 2013
282'.45632—dc23
2013004448

1 3 5 7 9 8 6 4 2
Printed in the United States of America
on acid-free paper

In memory of my parents
Paul Schaefer
and
Carolyn (Keseberg) Schaefer
Conservers of nature and heritage
Writers of books in their sunset years

Contents

Preface	xi
Editor's Note	xvii
Abbreviations	xix
1. Saints, Setting, and Context	1
2. Iconography and Sources of S. Prassede's Decorative Cycles	52
3. Women's Pastoral Offices in Churches Outside Rome	112
4. Women's Pastoral Offices in the Church of Rome	169
5. Ordination Rites: For Men Only? For Women Too!	239
6. A Second Look at Myth, History, and Monument	313
Afterword	375
Bibliography	381
Index of Authors	435
Index of Sources	439
Index of Subjects	447

Permission to reprint Figure 6.1 was granted by Gregory J. MacNeil, Roderick J. MacNeil, Jerry MacNeil Architects Limited, Halifax, Nova Scotia.

Preface

THIS BOOK HAD its beginnings toward the end of a memorable six-month Roman sabbatical in 1990–1991. It had been my custom to attend the Saturday evening liturgy celebrated in the ninth-century church of Santa Prassede, accessible from a side street some ninety meters from St. Mary Major's atop Rome's Esquiline hill. The hour of liturgical gathering was the one assured time during the week when the apse, together with apsidal and triumphal arches, were lit continuously. The intricate beauties of this best preserved of Roman parish mosaic programs prior to 1200 could be contemplated in keeping with the original intent of the structure, to serve as environment for the action of the Roman mass. With the aid of a worn New Testament, questions gradually formed: Given the schemes of presbyterium decoration known in the city's churches from the fifth century, why did this program contain so many unique and unexplained features, including the apparent attempt to balance female and male imagery? The jewel of Santa Prassede is the Zeno Chapel, which opens off the basilica's east aisle. No thoroughgoing hypothesis had yet been put forward to connect these two contemporary and nearly intact pictorial cycles. Did the pope who commissioned the church intend that the Zeno Chapel and its decoration be independent of the presbyterium program?

As my time in Rome drew to its close I perused the bulging pilgrim's guide to Santa Prassede published in 1725 by its Benedictine prior Dom Benigno Davanzati, stumbling upon references to the church's patron Praxedes made in 1655 by the priest-scholar and Roman antiquarian Fioravante Martinelli. Martinelli asserted, with Davanzati following him, that Praxedes had been a *presbytera*, head of an early Christian house-church on the site of the present church. As elsewhere in Rome, more awaited investigation here than first met the appreciative eye.

Edward J. Kilmartin, SJ (1923–1994), my doctoral adviser at the University of Notre Dame, was now professor ordinarius at the Pontifical Oriental Institute across the piazza from Santa Maria Maggiore. When I informed him of Martinelli's and Davanzati's belief that Saint Praxedes had been a woman presbyter of the early Roman church, he said in characteristic fashion, "Don't waste your time. They will have destroyed the evidence." Shortly afterward I returned to Canada by way of an eight-day stopover in Romania in search of eucharistic imagery in Orthodox churches. Sent north to "the Romanian Athos," I was welcomed to the Basilian Orthodox community of Varatec by its abbess, Reverend Mother Nazaria Nita Natalia. Varatec consists of three monastic villages set amidst peasant farms dotting a Carpathian mountainside. Mother Nazaria's abbatial responsibilities are described at the end of chapter five.

This book searches out the implications of the foundation myth underlying Pope Paschal I's rebuilding of Santa Prassede and that of its sister-church down the hill, Santa Pudenziana. Chapter one recounts the popular hagiographical story of the two sisters Praxedes and Pudentiana and their model Christian senatorial family during the apostolic and post-apostolic periods in Rome. It reviews their *vita*'s early Christian context and rehearses what is known of Pope Paschal I (817–824). Chapter two explores the iconography of the mosaics of Santa Prassede's presbyterium apse, triumphal arch, and Zeno Chapel, making the case for the thematic importance of the book of Revelation and the Easter lectionary. This chapter also introduces a topic that other authors have not considered: the male and female imagery. Initiated by discussion of the mosaic bust of Theodora episcopa that ends the second chapter, and utilizing categories and data established by Ute Eisen's epigraphical survey *Women Officeholders in Early Christianity*, the third chapter surveys women's official ecclesiastical ministries in the Christian world outside Rome. Chapter four turns to Rome. Dom Davanzati, for sixteen years prior of Santa Prassede, was familiar with scholarship about Eastern ordination rites and speculation regarding women's ministries in the early churches, and he drew on these sources to explicate the presbyteral office attributed to Praxedes. Can evidence be produced to support the abbot's claim? Epigraphy, ecclesiastical texts, and works of art indicate that women exercised various pastoral offices in Rome, the church believed to be the recipient of chapter 16 of Paul's letter to the Romans.

Chapter five reviews significant aspects of installation in church office and analyzes relevant ordination rituals deputing women for pastoral office in some of the churches of East and West. The prayer for the making of a diacona introduced into the papal Gregorian Sacramentary in 682–683 and the *Hadrianum*'s role in transmitting this prayer to Charlemagne's realm are discussed. Rituals for making diaconas and for ordaining canonical and monastic abbesses, and parallels with ordination rites for men, are analyzed to throw light on ecclesiastical offices brought forward in chapters three and four. Information on the diaconal office available within women's religious houses in the fourteenth and later centuries closes this chapter. Chapter six summarizes the place Paschal made for women in his life and art commissions. The sisters' story of house-church leadership, as recounted in their *vita*, is analyzed for aspects of early church governance. Reconstruction of the dedication ritual of Santa Prassede's relic-altar clarifies the church's dating. Paintings and frescoes corroborate their story. Exploration of Praxedes' "meaning" within the stational liturgies of Holy Week and in the lectionaries ties together themes developed earlier.

A Roman sabbatical in 1990–1991, granted by the Board of Governors of Atlantic School of Theology, Halifax, Nova Scotia, acquainted me with the churches on the Esquiline hill, libraries, and selected catacombs. Research has been carried forward in subsequent visits to the Eternal City. I am especially indebted to the librarians and staffs of the following institutions: In Rome, the Biblioteca Apostolica Vaticana and its former Prefect, Leonard Boyle, OP; the Pontificio Istituto Orientale and its former Librarian, James Dugan, SJ; the Pontificio Istituto di Archeologia Cristiana; the Pontificio Istituto di San Anselmo; Biblioteca Vallicelliana; the Hertziana; the Deutsches Archäologisches Institut; in Grottaferrata, the Librarian of its Monastic Library, Alessandro Caboni; in Switzerland, the St. Gall Bibliothek and Fribourg University Library; in Toronto, the Pontifical Institute of Mediaeval Studies; in Ottawa, Saint Paul University; in Washington, DC, Dumbarton Oaks. Last, but by no means least, the library staff of Atlantic School of Theology have been unfailingly helpful, speedily tracking down whatever was needed.

An academic is indebted to her teachers and mentors. This book could not have been written without introduction to the Middle Ages, its art and culture, at the University of Toronto and the University of St. Michael's College. As a fledgling graduate student, I participated in the daunting seminar on early Christian and Byzantine architecture offered by Richard Krautheimer (1897–1994) at the Institute of Fine Arts, New York University. His archeological investigations of early Christian and medieval churches in Rome have no equal. Krautheimer spent his last years in Rome reconstructing its culture through study of its buildings. In his broad perspective the East was always in view, as was the truism that churches were built for liturgy, to be "read" by making the connections between material structure, ritual use, and spiritual aspiration, a task he urged on his students.

Formal liturgical studies began with the Benedictines of Saint John's Abbey, Collegeville, Minnesota. Edward Kilmartin, adviser of many graduate students at the University of Notre Dame, taught me what I know about theology of worship as he developed the discipline. Kilmartin's love of the Church of Rome and of the whole *oikoumene* fueled his studies in patristic theology and sacraments as well as his construction of a contemporary theology of Trinitarian worship open to the ecumenical reality. He would gladly have died in Rome. A long-time member of Orthodox and Oriental dialogues in the United States and secretary to the former, Kilmartin never tired of bringing the texts and theologies of the East into play with those of the West. Robert F. Taft, SJ, has never shrunk from speaking truth. Indefatigably he has studied the prayer texts of the Eastern churches, showing his special students, others like myself at greater remove, and the churches at large how very much the Christian East has to teach the West. His method and work continue to enrich and challenge liturgical and ecumenical scholarship. These three great teachers have approached study of the churches of East and West as spiritually, if not always institutionally, in communion, diverse yet united in those beliefs that matter most. I hope that the story of Praxedes and her church presented here is not entirely unworthy of these mentors.

I am grateful to the many persons who have listened to and encouraged my exposition of the subject along the way. These include the international congresses of Societas Liturgica in Toronto (1991) and Dresden (2005), the theology students of Montreal's Concordia University (1996), and in abbreviated form the Patristics Congress on the diaconate held at Rome's Augustinianum (2009). Special thanks go to two friends in Rome, the liturgical scholars Elena Velkovska and Stefano Parenti; and to Jutta Dresken-Weiland and Albrecht Weiland, scholars of antiquity and early Christian archeology who first saw possibilities for this research. Scholars and colleagues over the years have assisted at important junctures, among them Gary Macy, Carmella Vircillo Franklin, Pamela Bright, Tom McIllwraith, Cettina Militello, Eileen Schuller, OSU, Reverend Sue Walters, Trudi Bunting, Tom S. Abler, Christine Mader, Ged Blackmore, Gregory J. MacNeil, and Roderick J. MacNeil of Jerry MacNeil Architects.

From Atlantic School of Theology students I have learned much about ecumenical collaboration and dedication to ministry. Sister Ada Samson, OSA, and the nuns of Santa Lucia, Rome, and Our Lady of Grace Monastery, Nova Scotia, have supported me by prayer, as have untold others. Friends like Enid Rubin have offered encouragement however long the work went on. Strangers in Roman restaurants have vowed to read this book.

Without the constant support and dedicated assistance of Anne Moynihan the first draft would not have been completed, and she has offered many valued ideas. Kevin Moynihan has played an irreplaceable role in technical matters and accompanied me with friendship. Lloyd Melanson has been indispensable in finalizing the manuscript. Deep thanks go to Joyce Rilett Wood, biblical scholar, writer, editor, and unflagging critic. Whatever richness the book contains comes from the observations and annotations of many persons who, in manuscript and in print, have shared their views on Saint Praxedes and perceptions of her church over the centuries. What errors are found in the story's telling are all my own.

Mary M. Schaefer
Halifax, Nova Scotia
October 27, 2012

Editor's Note

MARY MARTINA SCHAEFER died on March 27, 2013, during Holy Week, in Halifax, Nova Scotia, and within days of entering the final production stages of her manuscript. Mary was an avid mountain climber, the apt metaphor for the challenges she faced in finishing her book on women clergy and the story of Santa Prassede. It takes physical strength and courage to reach a summit. It takes will and wisdom for a successful climb under dire circumstances. In the months leading up to her death, Mary focused on all the steps to reach her goal. With joyful spirit and steely determination, she revised her text several times, and in March she was preparing for the arrival of the first set of proofs.

The completion of Mary Schaefer's book has depended on the collaborative effort of individuals and institutions. Cynthia Read, executive editor at Oxford University Press, played a big part in speedily processing the manuscript through its review stage. Charlotte Steinhardt, assistant editor at OUP, offered advice and support and discussed with Mary the design of her book. Cammy Richelli, production editor, was gracious and helpful in providing professional and technical expertise. Katherine Ulrich, copyeditor, was my conversation partner in commenting on the manuscript, and she updated my research on the bibliography and documentation by reconciling the two. Lloyd Melanson generously provided editorial and technical assistance and reviewed the tables he constructed. Anne and Kevin Moynihan took charge of the illustrations and checked their accuracy. Diane Barrington carefully prepared the indices. To these and others we are indebted in bringing Mary's legacy to fruition.

Joyce Rilett Wood
Toronto, Ontario
August 15, 2013

Abbreviations

AA.SS.   Acta sanctorum quotquot toto orbe coluntur
AB   Analecta Bollandiana
ACC   Alcuin Club Collections
ACW   Ancient Christian Writers
AJA   American Journal of Archaeology
AT   Apostolic Tradition
ATR   Anglican Theological Review
BAV   Bibliotheca Apostolica Vaticana
BHL   Bibliotheca hagiographica latinae antiquae et mediae aetatis
BHLns   Bibliotheca hagiographica latina antiquae et mediae aetatis, novum supplementum
BZ   Byzantinische Zeitschrift
CA   Cahiers archéologiques
CARB   Corso di cultura sull'arte ravennate e bizantina
CBCR   Krautheimer, Richard. *Corpus Basilicarum Christianarum Romae*
CCCM   Corpus Christianorum Continuatio Medievalis
CCSL   Corpus Christianorum Series Latina
CNRS   Centre national de la recherche scientifique
CSEL   Corpus Scriptorum Ecclesiasticorum Latinorum
CTSA   Catholic Theological Society of America
DACL   Dictionnaire d'archéologie chrétienne et de liturgie
EL   Ephemerides liturgicae
EM   Encyclopedia of Monasticism
EME   Early Medieval Europe
EO   Ecclesia orans
fol.   folio; r = recto (right-hand page), v = verso (left-hand page)

Hefele	C.-J. Hefele, *Histoire des conciles d'après les documents originaux*
HBS	Henry Bradshaw Society
HTR	*Harvard Theological Review*
ILCV	*Inscriptiones Latinae Christianae Veteres*, ed. E. Diehl.
JB	*Jerusalem Bible* (1966)
JECS	*Journal of Early Christian Studies*
JEH	*Journal of Ecclesiastical History*
JFSR	*Journal of Feminist Studies in Religion*
JRH	*Journal of Religious History*
JSNT	*Journal for the Study of the New Testament*
JTS	*Journal of Theological Studies*
KL	Kalends, Calends (the first day of the Roman month)
LMD	*La Maison-Dieu*
LP	*Liber Pontificalis*
LThK	*Lexikon für Theologie und Kirche*
LXX	Septuagint
Mansi	J. D. Mansi, *Sacrorum conciliorum nova et amplissima collectio*
MEFRA	*Mélanges de l'école française de Rome*
MGH	Monumenta Germaniae historica
MR	*Martyrologium Romanum*; Roman Martyrology
ms.	manuscript
MS	*Mediaeval Studies*
MT	Masoretic Text
NCE	*New Catholic Encyclopedia* (1967 and 2003 editions)
NDSW	*New Dictionary of Sacramental Worship*
NTS	*New Testament Studies*
OCA	*Orientalia Christiana Analecta*
OCP	*Orientalia Christiana Periodica*
OR	Andrieu, Michel. *Ordines romani du haut moyen*
Qd	Quaestiones disputatae
PBSR	*Papers of the British School at Rome*
PCAS	Pontificia Commissione di Archeologia Sacra
PIAC	Pontificio Istituto di Archeologia Cristiana
PIO	Pontificio Istituto Orientale
PL	Jacques Paul Migne, *Patrologiae cursus completus, series Latina*
PRG	*Pontifical Romano-Germanique du dixième siècle*

RAC	*Rivista di archeologia cristiana*
RB	*Revue bénédictine*
REDF	Rerum ecclesiasticarum documenta. Fontes
RGP X	Romano-Germanic Pontifical of the Tenth Century
RLAC	*Reallexikon für Antike und Christentum*
RP XII	Roman Pontifical of the Twelfth Century
RQ	*Römische Quartalschrift für christliche Altertumskunde und Kirchengeschichte*
RSR	*Revue des sciences religieuses*
S.	Sanctus, San; Sancta, Santa (Latin or Italian masculine and feminine singular for Saint)
Sacr. grég.	*Sacramentaire grégorien*, ed. Jean Deshusses. 3 vols.
SC	*Sources chrétiennes*
SP	*Studia Patristica*
SS.	Sancti, Santi; Sanctae, Sante (Latin or Italian feminine plural for Saints)
SSL	Spicilegium sacrum lovaniense
ST	Studi e Testi
SWR	Studies in Women and Religion
TDNT	*Theological Dictionary of the New Testament*
TRE	*Theologische Realenzyclopädie*
TJT	*Toronto Journal of Theology*
TS	*Theological Studies*
VC	*Vigiliae Christianae*
VetChr	*Vetera Christianorum*
VG	Vulgate
ZNW	*Zeitschrift für die neutestamentliche Wissenschaft*

Women in Pastoral Office

I
Saints, Setting, and Context

IT WAS WEDNESDAY the 20th day of July of the year 819 and the vigil of St. Praxedes' feast when Pope Paschal I (817–824) buried the bones of nearly 2,300 saints under the altar of the newly built church of S. Prassede (Fig. 1.1).[1] All was in readiness for the dedication of Paschal's new church on Praxedes' *natale*, her heavenly birthday, on 21 July. Who was the woman Praxedes, patron of this beautiful church designed to imitate Old Saint Peter's across town?[2] In the first of the "historical" martyrologies of the Latin church, the Venerable Bede (d. 735) had listed for 19 May the virgin St. Potentiana, who 120 years later would be identified with Praxedes' older sister St. Pudentiana. In his second edition, for 21 July Bede added, after the prophet Daniel, the virgin St. Praxedes. Circa 825, Florus of Lyons, active during the second quarter of the ninth century, added the presbyter

---

1. 20 July 817 is the year traditionally given for the relic deposition and dedication of S. Prassede, the date coming from an inscription on the two-piece marble plaque embedded in the pier between the church's side entrance and the Zeno Chapel. In subsequent chapters the author will resolve the discrepancy between the usual date given for the dedication and the one proposed here, pursue themes set out in this chapter, and offer solutions to controverted issues involving the church of Santa Prassede and its patron.

2. Prassede is the Italian translation of Praxedes (Greek) or Praxedis (Latin), connoting action, deed. Greek speakers formed the majority of Roman Christians in the first two centuries, and Praxedes is used throughout this study as congruent with that Greek culture. Praxedes' feastday is found in the Bollandists' *Acta Sanctorum* (*AA.SS.*), ed. Johannes Bolland, Jean Baptiste Carnandet, and Godefridus Henschenius (Paris: V. Palmé, 1866), Julii V, 130–32 (vol. 32, 1868). The standard account is interleaved with that of her older sister Potentiana (Pudentiana) in *AA.SS.*, Maii IV, 295–301 (vol. 17, 1866); also Boninus Mombritius, *Sanctuarium seu Vitae sanctorum*, ed. Monks of Solesmes (2 vols.; Paris: Fontemoing, 1910, repr. Hildesheim, New York: Georg Olms Verlag, 1978), 2:353–54. See also Agostino Amore, *I martiri di Roma* (Rome: Antonianum, 1975), 68–69; David Hugh Farmer, *The Oxford Dictionary of Saints* (2nd ed.; Oxford; New York: Oxford University Press, 1987), 362–63. The name but not the gender of the saint is remembered in the novels of Andrew Greeley (the parish of St. Praxides the male forester), *Confessions of a Parish Priest: An Autobiography* (New York: Simon and Schuster, c1986).

FIGURE 1.1 Rome, S. Prassede. Nave and presbytery (817–819). Photo © Adrian Fletcher www.paradoxplace.com.

and martyr Simmetrius with twenty-two others "whom blessed Praxedes buried."[3]

A few years before Florus compiled his martyrology, the Council of Aachen (817) had legislated that reading from the martyrology be done by clerics and monastics at the hour of Prime.[4] But many days of the church year were *vacans*; besides, many saints were barely distinguishable one from another. Archbishop Ado of Vienne (d. 875) set out to remedy this defect, composing

---

3. A martyrology gives the anniversary dates of the death (*natale*) of saints (originally martyrs, blood-witnesses to the faith) with the place of cult and title. Venerable Bede invented the "historical" martyrology which gave a glimpse, often anecdotal, of their stories. See Jacques Dubois, *Les martyrologes du moyen âge latin* (Turnhout: Brepols, 1978), 13–14. The entries of the 1st and 2nd recensions of the martyrologies of Bede, the Anonymous of Lyons, and the 1st and 2nd recensions of Florus are available in Jacques Dubois and Geneviève Renaud, *Édition pratique des martyrologes de Bède, de l'Anonyme lyonnais et de Florus* (Paris: Éditions du Centre national de la recherche scientifique, 1976), 90, 95, and 132.

4. Already the practice in some monasteries in the mid-8th century, it was extended to the secular clergy by canon 36 of the Council of Aachen. See Pierre Salmon, *Les manuscrits liturgiques latins de la Bibliothèque vaticane* (5 vols.; Vatican City: BAV, 1971), 4:xi.

around 855 a vastly augmented historical martyrology. Ado introduced material from sources that included the Scriptures and *Liber Pontificalis*.[5] He added *gesta and passiones* composed in the fifth and sixth centuries that even he knew were long, and tampered with dates.[6] Between his first and second editions Ado composed the *Parvum romanum* to mislead critics.[7] His was the most popular of the historical martyrologies whose heyday fell in the period from 800 to around 860. Ado's notice for the younger of the sisters reads:

> At Rome Saint Praxedes virgin. This one with her blessed sister Potentiana or Pudentiana, by the most holy father Pudens who was educated in faith by the apostle Paul, trained in all chastity and the divine law, after the parent's death having unceasing leisure for vigils and prayers and fastings, with the aforesaid blessed sister at once gave out all her patrimony in support of the poor and the saints of Christ. Indeed in the *titulus* that their father Pudens dedicated in the name of blessed Pastor, with the counsel of blessed Pius bishop of the apostolic see, the one sister and herself taking pains to construct a baptismal font that their household might be baptized on the holy day of Easter. Blessed Pius washed clean with saving water those manumitted, to the number of 96.

---

5. *Le Liber pontificalis: texte, introduction et commentaire* by Louis Duchesne, with Latin text and notes in 2 vols., 1886–1892; republished by Cyrille Vogel, with a third volume on the history of *LP*, including additions, corrections, and indices since Duchesne's edition (2nd ed.; 3 vols.; Paris: E. de Boccard, 1955–1957; repr.; of 1955–1957 edition; Paris: E. de Boccard, 1981), 3:54–68 (hereafter referred to as *LP*). *LP* is translated with introduction and commentary by Raymond Davis, *The Book of Pontiffs (Liber Pontificalis): The Ancient Biographies of the First Ninety Roman Bishops to AD 715* (rev. ed.; Liverpool: Liverpool University Press, 2000); *The Lives of the Eighth-Century Popes (Liber Pontificalis): The Ancient Biographies of Nine Popes from AD 715 to AD 817* (Liverpool: Liverpool University Press, 1992); *The Lives of the Ninth-Century Popes (Liber Pontificalis): The Ancient Biographies of Ten Popes from AD 817–891* (Liverpool: Liverpool University Press, 1995). Davis' English edition of *LP* is used throughout this study. *LP* was compiled about 530 and continued by a second editor before 546. Much material before the 6th century is fictitious. About 640 *LP* was revised and continued (*Book of Pontiffs*, xlvi–xlviii). The biographies of the later popes contain details suggesting authorship by officials within the papal chancellery.

6. Ado, Archbishop of Vienne (ca. 800–875), *Le martyrologe d'Adon: Ses deux familles, ses trois recensions, texte et commentaire*, ed. Jacques Dubois and Geneviève Renaud (Paris: CNRS Éditions, 1984), xx–xxix.

7. St. Gall, Stiftsbibliothek cod. 454, fol. iv–p. 23. The "Shorter Roman Martyrology" or *Parvum Romanum* is a falsified document because Ado composed it himself but claimed that it was written by a pope and loaned to him during a visit to Italy. This early version of the story did not mention the *titulus* of Praxedes.

> Whence after innumerable works of piety, after the burial of many martyrs—among whom she buried with her own hands near the aforesaid *titulus* blessed Simmetrius the presbyter with another 22,—who passed to the heavenly realms through the palm of martyrdom, this same most blessed virgin departed to the Lord, to receive the crown of justice, XII. Kal. Aug. Buried in the cemetery of Priscilla, Via Salaria, placed next to her sister and holy father Pudens.[8]

This overview of Praxedes' pious life followed on similar notices for her sister Potentiana and friend Novatus excerpted from the *vita*.[9] Along with a few other ninth-century manuscripts, these notices provide the earliest accounts of this pious, early Christian family.

In his martyrology, written between 843 and 854, hence shortly before Ado's, the archbishop of Mainz Rabanus Maurus (d. 857) highlighted the episode of Simmetrius and the other twenty-two martyrs from Praxedes' *vita*:

> At Rome the virgin Saint Praxedes, who was sister of Potentiana, and out of her means assisted many Christians at the time of emperor Antoninus. But when it had been divulged to emperor Antoninus that there would be an assembly in Praxedes' *titulus*, he sent and had many taken into custody. Among those arrested was Simmetrius the presbyter with another twenty-two persons, whom he ordered to be punished by the sword without interrogation in that same *titulus*. By night on the seventh day of the Kalends of July [26 June] blessed Praxedes gathered up and buried the bodies in Priscilla's cemetery. Then constrained by affliction, blessed Praxedes mourned, and prayed to the Lord that she might be taken from this world. Her prayers and tears having come before the Lord Jesus Christ after the martyrdom and crowning of the

---

8. St. Gall, Stiftsbibliothek cod. 454, p. 183 for XII KL AUG (21 July). Ms. 454 may be the only 9th-century manuscript of Ado's augmented martyrology.

9. On Potentiana/Pudentiana, see St. Gall, Stiftsbibliothek cod. 454, p. 135 for XIIII KL JUN (19 May). Her father Pudens, after whom she is named in Latin style, is mentioned on the same day and from the same source. Novatus was introduced by Ado and placed by him on the date exactly halfway between the feasts of Potentiana and Praxedes (Novatus, XII KL IUL [20 June 20]), p. 163; Dubois and Renaud, *Martyrologe d'Adon*, 163–64).

aforementioned saints, the sacred virgin departed to the Lord on the twelfth day of the Kalends of August [21 July].[10]

The two archbishops' versions show that the story was known in centers as far distant as Lyons and Mainz. Usuard of Saint-Germain-des-Prés (d. 875) abridged the first recension of Ado's martyrology (ca. 855), omitting what he judged to be false or without foundation, but making contributions of his own.[11] His text was followed closely by the Roman martyrology in use from 1584 until 1969, which stated succinctly: "At Rome Saint Praxedes, Virgin, well versed in all that concerned chastity and the divine law, who after passing her life assiduously in vigil, praying and fasting, fell asleep in Christ, and was buried near her sister Pudentiana on the Via Salaria."[12] While the martyrology edited under Benedict XIV (1740–1758) retained her feastday, the commission he entrusted with revision of the Roman breviary declared her life a fable and the calendar revision of 1969 finally suppressed the feast. But the church bearing her name remains the most intact, the most virginal, of all the early Christian and medieval churches of the Eternal City, claiming a significance that defies any hierarchical efforts to erase the story about two women of the early church, Praxedes and her older sister Potentiana or Pudentiana. Situated a mere ninety meters from the great basilica of S. Maria Maggiore on the Esquiline hill, Praxedes' church, the most notable architectural achievement of Paschal's relatively brief pontificate, was rebuilt on a site said to be only slightly removed from that of the old *titulus*.[13]

---

10. *Rabani Mauri Martyrologium*, ed. John McCulloh (Turnhout: Brepols, 1979), 69–70.

11. Jacques Dubois, *Le martyrologe d'Usuard: texte et commentaire* (Brussels: Société des Bollandistes, 1965).

12. *Martyrologium romanum:Gregorii Papae XIII jussu editum Urbani VIII et Clementis X*, ed. Benedict XIV (Rome: Vatican Polyglot Press, 1913), 137, hereafter cited as *MR*. Its modern state was little changed from that achieved at the hands of Usuard of Saint-Germain, ca. 858 (Dubois, *Martyrologe d'Usuard*, 250). Only the notices of Bede and the "anonyme lyonnais" predate Paschal's pontificate. Taken all together the martyrologies attest to the wide diffusion of the story of the Pudens family north of the Alps by the mid-9th century. Usuard gives "Potentiana." Both Potentiana and Pudentiana (Italian Pudenziana) are found, with Potentiana predominating earlier. A St. Potentiana appears about the same time as the sisters' *acta* in some recensions of the Roman martyrology and as the patron of a stational church in the 8th-century *capitulare evangeliorum* of Würzburg. The church is called Santa Pudenziana. Throughout this study the spelling found in the source is followed.

13. A traditional definition of a Roman *titulus* is immovable church property, a building held in the name or "title" of a private citizen. Twenty-five of these community centers existed in the 4th and 5th centuries, and a few more were added to total 29. *Tituli* differed

The papal complex at the far end of the Lateran district, on the other side of town from St. Peter's, was separated from the old city by a greenbelt of vineyards and orchards harboring several monasteries. To the northwest of the pope's seat, far enough away to allow for a respectable procession, was the fifth-century basilica of St. Mary Major, forming the center of its own group of *tituli, diaconiae* (social service centers), and monasteries.[14] The old *titulus Praxedis*, part of this grouping, was referred to in 491 in an epitaph of Argyrius in the cemetery of S. Ippolito. S. Prassede's presbyters signed in at the Roman synod of 499, and a century later at the synod of 595, Deusdedit and Aventius signed as presbyters *tituli sanctae Praxedis*, "canonizing" her by prefixing to the founder's name the honorific "saint."[15] Then the *titulus Praxedis* vanishes from the record until it replaces SS. Nereus and Achilleus as a Roman station for the Lenten liturgy sometime during the eighth century. This probably led to its restoration by Hadrian I in 783–784.[16]

---

from juridically autonomous parishes in being non-territorial and serving the unity of the city-church. Most were designated as "stational" churches when pope and clergy converged with the devout laity to celebrate a feast. For the standard liturgical account, see John F. Baldovin, *The Urban Character of Christian Worship: The Origins, Development, and Meaning of Stational Liturgy* (Rome: Pontifical Oriental Institute, 1987), 105–18. A *titulus* may be viewed primarily in terms of its ecclesiastical function or as a civil entity. It has been defined as a church accompanied by a self-supporting patrimony that limits episcopal disposition of the property; see Julia Hillner, "Families, Patronage, and the Titular Churches of Rome, c.300–c.600," in Kate Cooper and Julia Hillner, eds., *Religion, Dynasty, and Patronage in Early Christian Rome, 300–900* (Cambridge: Cambridge University Press, 2007), 225–61.

14. The Liberian basilica, completed by Pope Sixtus III (432–440), was dedicated to *sancta Maria* around the time of the Council of Ephesus (431). For descriptions of Rome and its early churches I am indebted to Richard Krautheimer, *Rome: Profile of a City, 312–1308* (Princeton, NJ: Princeton University Press, [1980] 2000), which gathers the fruits of his lifelong labors in the field of Christian architecture. During our period neither the monasteries of S. Agnese ad Duo Furna (Duas Furnas) nor of S. Praxedes, staffed by Greek monks, served St. Mary Major's as a basilical monastery responsible for choir duty. See Guy Ferrari, *Early Roman Monasteries: Notes for the History of the Monasteries and Convents at Rome from the V through the X Century* (Vatican City: PIAC, 1957), 370; see also Louis Duchesne, "Les monastères desservants de Sainte-Marie-Majeure," *Mélanges d'archéologie et d'histoire* 27 (1907): 479–94.

15. A. de Waal, "Der Titulus Praxedis," *RQ* 19 (1905): 169–80.

16. Herman Geertman, *More Veterum: il Liber Pontificalis e gli edifici ecclesiastici di Roma nella tarda antichità e nell'alto medioevo* (Groningen: H. D. Tjeenk Willink, 1975), 164. Geertman notes that SS. Nereo ed Achilleo lost its stational status on Holy Monday and became a deaconry (social service center) sometime between 600 and 776. Hadrian I (772–795) rebuilt and restored much in the city; *LP* gives the year 783–784 for the renewing of St. Praxedes' *titulus* "which was partly ruinous" (Davis, *Lives of Eighth-Century Popes*, 97.78).

Beyond and well below the apse of St. Mary Major's, in the valley formed by the Esquiline slope and the rising Viminal hill, on the ancient Vicus Patricius in the Patrician quarter, stands the basilica of S. Pudenziana. Its foundations and fabric date from the second and subsequent centuries.[17] This basilica has been identified as part of a Roman baths complex, probably taken over by a Christian congregation as its community center. Notices of clergy attached to this community center are extant from 384 and 499. Its renovation, begun under popes Damasus (366–384) and Siricius (384–399), was completed under Innocent I (401–417). The church's façade rises across what is now a forecourt sunk three meters below the level of the present Via Urbana. Nine meters below the basilica's floor are the remains of a large two-story private dwelling, accessible as late as the ninth century, whose foundations can be dated by brick stamps to 123–139 CE. This dwelling was identified as the *titulus Pudentis*, a two-story private house named for the scion of a senatorial family thought to have flourished during the first and second Christian centuries.[18] In reviewing the hagiographical and archeological data, the archeologist Federico Guidobaldi identifies at least three persons named Pudens who can be associated with this site from 166 CE. Guidobaldi has sought authentic aspects of the sisters' story, identifying Potentiana as a saint venerated from the beginning of the fifth century, attested in some versions of the Hieronymian martyrology.[19] Seventh-century pilgrim itineraries name her as buried with her sister Praxedes in the Priscilla cemetery. The shallow apse of the church at the northwest displays the oldest monumental Christian mosaic in Rome, commissioned during Innocent I's pontificate (Fig. 1.2).The majestic Christ dominating the mosaic holds on his lap a book bearing the words DOMINUS CONSERVATOR ECCLESIAE PUDENTIANAE, literally "The Lord protector of Pudens' faith-assembly."[20] This mosaic has played a central role in the "history" of our sisters.

---

17. A *vicus* was a city district with a certain number of inhabitants overseen by civic officials. On the building and its history, see Richard Krautheimer, "S. Pudenziana," in Krautheimer, *Corpus basilicarum Christianarum Romae: Le basiliche cristiane antiche di Roma* (sec. IV–IX) = *The Early Christian Basilicas of Rome* (IV–IX Cent.) (5 vols; Vatican City: PIAC, 1967), 3:277–302 (hereafter cited as *CBCR* 3).

18. An early, inventive account is that of John Henry Parker, "The House of Pudens in Rome," *Archaeological Journal* 28 (1871): 40–49.

19. Federico Guidobaldi, "Osservazioni sugli edifici romani in cui si insediò l'Ecclesia Pudentiana," in Federico Guidobaldi and Alessandra Guiglia Guidobaldi, eds., *Ecclesiae urbis: Atti del congresso internazionale di studi sulle chiese di Roma (IV–X secolo), Roma, 4–10 settembre 2000* (3 vols.; Vatican City: PIAC, 2002), 2:1040–65.

20. Pudentiana is the adjectival form meaning "of Pudens." At first *ecclesia* referred to the congregation, "those who are called by God," and later to the community's place of assembly.

FIGURE I.2 Rome, S. Pudenziana. Apse mosaic with Christ enthroned among the Twelve and two female figures (ca. 401–417). Photograph by Mary M. Schaefer.

Recent scholarship has sorted out the various literary genres of late antiquity that contain fictionalized lives. Late second- and early third-century apocryphal writings featuring Peter, Mary Magdalene, the "hidden lives" of the holy family (*Protoevangelium of James*), and so on were a type of postbiblical literature that attempted to supply, sometimes in great detail, information and a storyline about which the canonical gospels were silent.[21] The alternative lifestyle of chastity for women leading to a romantic triangle between a spurned sexual partner, the woman, and the ascetic apostle was typical.[22] Early hagiography, whose intent was to edify and inspire devotion toward the saints, took several forms. The Bollandist

---

A *basilica* is an oblong Roman building type, often with interior colonnade, which Christians adapted to suit processions by placing its apse at the far short end.

21. *Neutestamentlichen Apokryphen*, ed. Wilhelm Schneemelcher (rev. ed.; Tübingen, 1959–1997) in English translation, *The New Testament Apocrypha I: Gospels and Related Writings*, ed. R. McL. Wilson (2 vols.; Cambridge: James Clarke & Co., 1991); *The Apocryphal New Testament: A Collection of Apocryphal Christian Literature in an English Translation*, ed. J. K. Elliott; trans. Montague Rhodes James (rev. ed.; New York: Oxford University Press, [1924] 1993); *The Other Gospels: Non-Canonical Gospel Texts*, ed. Ron Cameron (Philadelphia: Westminster, 1982); *The Complete Gospels: Annotated Scholars Version*, ed. Robert J. Miller (rev. ed.; Sonoma, CA: Polebridge, [1992] 1994); *The Apocryphal Jesus: Legends of the Early Church*, ed. J.K. Elliott (Oxford: Oxford University Press, 1996).

22. Virginia Burrus, *Chastity as Autonomy: Women in the Stories of the Apocryphal Acts* (Lewiston, NY: Edwin Mellen, 1987).

Hippolyte Delehaye (1859–1941) identified four categories: (1) official records or eyewitness accounts; (2) edited versions of the same; (3) historical romance; (4) imaginative romance.[23] Delehaye took the position that the Roman legendary, a compilation of saints' lives to be read, hence its name *legenda*, includes only the third type, the "historical romance." Suiting Delehaye's category of the imaginative romance, the *gesta martyrum*, composed in the fifth to seventh centuries, exhibited features of their historical period while intending to supply for the lost pre-Constantinian acts of the Roman martyrs. Kate Cooper discusses their romantic and novelistic character, noting that "the *Gesta* lent literary weight to the ascetic vocation by assimilating it to an earlier tradition of literature and to the increasingly powerful martyr cult."[24] Clare Pilsworth defines the *gesta* as a "cycle of post-Constantinian Latin hagiographical romances centred on legendary martyr heroes and heroines of pre-Constantinian Rome."[25] Recent scholarship has looked "behind" the text of the various literary forms for further interpretation. The story of the Pudens clan does not well fit the *gesta martyrum* template, differing in its narrative simplicity, historical references, and lack of miraculous events.

1. *The Story and Family Genealogy*

The *vita* of the two sisters Potentiana/Pudentiana and Praxedes used to be dated not earlier than the later fifth or sixth century, in the period between the extant notices of the Roman synods of 499, whose archpresbyter and presbyter styled themselves clergy of the *titulus Praxidae*, and 595, when the presbyters Deusdedit and Aventius signed for the *titulus sanctae Praxedis*. Modern hagiographers judged the story of the Pudens

---

23. Hippolyte Delehaye, *Les Légendes hagiographiques* (Brussels, 1905), an English translation of 1955 4th edition, Delehaye, *The Legends of the Saints*, trans. Donald Attwater (New York: Fordham University Press, 1962), 3, 8, 86–92.

24. Kate Cooper, *The Virgin and the Bride: Idealized Womanhood in Late Antiquity* (Cambridge, MA: Harvard University Press, 1996), 117; Cooper, "The Martyr, the Matrona and the Bishop: the Matron Lucina and the Politics of Martyr Cult in Fifth- and Sixth-Century Rome," *EME* 8 (1999): 297–318, esp. 305–8.

25. Clare Pilsworth, "Dating the *Gesta martyrum*: A Manuscript-Based Approach," *EME* 9 (2000): 310. Pilsworth (p. 313) discusses the unresolved problems in the dating of the *gesta*, the diversity of the collections found in the manuscripts, and the lack of critical editions. A salutary warning about the difficulties of locating and interpreting *gesta martyrum* comes from Gregory the Great himself, who searched the papal archives and libraries of Rome to find only one such collection.

clan to be entirely legendary, the two sisters figuring in an etiological explanation of two ancient *tituli* close to St. Mary Major's, their *vita* serving as a foundation myth for the renovated S. Pudenziana (ca. 400) and the beautifully appointed church (817–819) purpose-built by Paschal I to honor St. Praxedes.[26] Their *vita* was popular throughout the Middle Ages.[27] The number of family members and friends who came to be included in the Roman martyrology meant that the story was retold frequently in church and refectory during the spring and summer months.

The sisters' *vita*, composed of two letters and a narrative appendix, form the "acts of Pudentiana and Praxedes," less commonly entitled the "acts of Pastor and Timothy." The first letter is addressed by a presbyter named Pastor to a presbyter Timothy, and the second purports to be Timothy's reply to Pastor. In the appendix, Pastor again takes up the narrative. The grandfather, Punicus Pudens, scion of a senatorial family, had extended hospitality to the apostle Peter and was baptized by him.[28] A second Pudens ("Junior"), son of Punicus Pudens and husband of Sav(b)inella, has two daughters named Potentiana (or Pudentiana) and Praxedes.[29] On his wife's

---

26. On the legend of the Pudens clan, see Basile Vanmaele, "Potenziana (Pudenziana) e Prassede, vergini sante, martiri di Roma," *Bibliotheca Sanctorum* 10 (1968): 1062–72; Amore, *I martiri*, 68. Delehaye (*Légendes hagiographiques* [1905], 129) termed stories such as this one "historical romance" from which can be reclaimed only the name of the saint, existence of a sanctuary, and date of the feast. See also Albert Dufourcq, *Étude sur les Gesta martyrum romains* (4 vols.; Paris: Albert Fontemoing, 1900–1910), 1:84, 127–30. "Foundation myth" is a term used by Peter Brown, *The Cult of the Saints: Its Rise and Function in Latin Christianity* (Chicago: University of Chicago Press, 1981), 97.

27. In his dissertation, Basile Vanmaele (*L'église Pudentienne de Rome (Santa Pudenziana): contribution à l'histoire de ce moment insigne de la Rome Chrétienne ancienne IIe au XXe siècle* [Averbode: Praemonstratensia, 1965]) listed 151 codices: 3 from the 9th century, 9 from the 10th, 21 (11th), 40 (12th), 30 (13th), 14 (14th), 20 (15th), 2 (17th), and 2 of unknown date. These have been distinguished as *acta* (which treat the story integrally) and *passiones* (which present the stories discretely for the martyrology). The multiple recensions, identified by *incipit* in manuscripts catalogued in Bollandist publications, e.g., *Bibliotheca Hagiographica Latina antiquae et mediae aetatis*, ed. Socii Bollandiani [Brussels: Société de Bollandistes, 1898–1901, 1911, 1949; novum supplementum, ed. Heinricus Fros, 1986], can now be accessed at http://bhlms.fltr.ucl.ac.be. See "Pudentiana" and "Praxedis v. Romana."

28. Two churches built over Roman houses of appropriate vintage, S. Prisca on the Aventine hill and S. Pudenziana on the Viminal, were associated with this senator, taken to be the Pudens mentioned in 2 Tim 4:21. His wife Priscilla owned the extensive villa whose grounds would be developed into the Priscilla cemetery on the Via Salaria Nova.

29. Josef Wilpert, "Eine mittelalterliche Tradition über die Bekehrung des Pudens durch Paulus," *RQ* 22 (1908): 172–77. Cardinal Cesare Baronius (1538–1607), in *Annales ecclesiastici*, I (12 vols.; Rome: Ex typographica Vaticana, 1588–1607), an. 159, had inferred that there were two generations. Already attested in the mss., such extended life spans led scholars to propose a three-generation chronology. Citing manuscripts, the Roman priest-scholar

death he donates his house in the patrician quarter (*vicus Patricius*) for use as a Roman house-church bearing Pastor's name.[30] Christians are constrained to use their homes for worship because Emperor Antoninus Pius (138–161) has prohibited public assemblies.[31] Upon their father's death his daughters consecrate themselves to God and the service of the church and devote their wealth to the poor. A baptistry is built and consecrated by Pius I, bishop of Rome (140–155 or 145–157?) and close friend of the family, in time for use in ninety-six Easter baptisms, when slaves are manumitted.[32] The elder sister Potentiana dies after a life devoted to ministry.[33] A man named Novatus (Timothy's sibling), who owns a bath building no longer

---

Fioravante Martinelli (1599–1667) (*Primo Trofeo della santissima Croce eretto in Roma nella via lata da S. Pietro apostolo* [Rome: Nicolangelo Tinassi, 1655], 41–44) critiqued assumptions of earlier scholars, situated the baths of Timothy and Novatus on the Esquiline hill (p. 45), accurately transcribed the inscription on the marble plaque, "un antichissimo marmo" (46–47), reflected on the family's identification with known historical persons (47–52), and deduced that the daughters, born around the years 66/67 CE, with their mother Sabina were baptized by Paul (48). Dom Benigno Davanzati (1670–1676), rector of S. Prassede for 16 years, then elected abbot of the Vallombrosan Benedictines who had staffed the church since the 13th century, published a panegyric of 544 pages about S. Prassede and its patron. Davanzati (*Notizie al pellegrino della Basilica di S. Prassede* [Rome: Antonio de'Rossi, 1725], 125 and *passim*) claims all possible prerogatives for S. Prassede. Davanzati called it the *titulus* of Pudens and the first Christian basilica erected in Rome 44/45 CE, where Peter preached and celebrated the sacraments (p. 62). Davanzati was not uninformed about S. Pudenziana, for he had earlier served as rector there.

30. This is irregular for the earliest centuries, since the immovable properties given over to church use kept the name of their founder. In the 6th and 7th centuries, this place of Christian assembly in the Viminal was known as *titulus Pastoris*, the most perplexing of its titles (Amato P. Frutaz, "Titolo di Pudente: denominazione successive, clero e cardinali titolari," *RAC* 40 [1964]: 55). Could the *vita* have occasioned the renaming of the *titulus*?

31. The story has it backward. During the 2nd century, gathering in private not public assemblies was counted as inimical to the public religion of the state and to good order. In conscience Christians could not join in the public civil religion. W. H. C. Frend (*Martyrdom and Persecution in the Early Church: A Study of a Conflict from the Maccabees to Donatus* [Oxford: Blackwell, 1965]) does not know of an ordinance against assemblies during the reigns of Antoninus Pius and the early years of Marcus Aurelius. Frend (237) characterizes the church during 135–165 CE as enjoying "general quiet" and "lenient administration of the existing law."

32. Freeing of slaves at baptism in the Pudens *titulus* evokes the imprisoned Paul's recommendation regarding Onesimus, expressed in his letter to Philemon, the leader of a domestic church, and especially Rom 16:10, 11; see Peter Lampe, *From Paul to Valentinus: Christians at Rome in the First Two Centuries*, trans. Michael Steinhauser; ed. Marshall D. Johnson (Minneapolis, MN: Fortress, 2003), 359.

33. Davanzati (*Notizie al pellegrino*, 113–14; see *BHL* 6988–6989, *AA.SS.* Maii IV, 299) discusses Potentiana's supposed death at the tender age of 16 and writes it off as scribal error. The text could also be understood as indicating "after sixteen years of ministry." Boninus Mombritius (*BHL* 6991, "Vitae sanctae Potentianae virginis," *Sanctuarium seu Vitae Sanctorum*, 391) gives "mense decimo et annis duobus," two years and ten months.

in use, visits Praxedes to comfort her. He takes ill and dies, bequeathing his property to Praxedes and Pastor.

In the second letter Timothy agrees to the inheritance of Novatus' property by Praxedes and Pastor and gives them full power to dispose of it. Praxedes takes full charge of the bequest; she requests that Pius dedicate the bath building of Novatus as a community worship space (*ecclesia* is the word used) under the name of the blessed Potentiana.[34] Pastor informs the reader that a *titulus* has been established in the Lateran quarter in Praxedes' name. There on 13 May another baptistry is consecrated.[35] After two years, a persecution begins. "Fervent in the Holy Spirit," Praxedes hides many Christians, whom she nourishes both with earthly food and the word of God. Information about the holding of forbidden assemblies in Praxedes' house-church reaches the emperor, who has the presbyter Simmetrius and twenty-two persons found with him summarily beheaded.[36] The mourning Praxedes buries the bodies in Priscilla's cemetery and, heartbroken, dies in her house-church on 21 July. The presbyter

---

34. Doubtless popular devotion effected the identification of Pudentiana with "her" *ecclesia pudentiana* (the adjectival form meaning "of Pudens" is the title in the book held open by Christ in the apse mosaic of ca. 410) and the martyr Potentiana named by the 7th-century pilgrim itineraries. The five-syllable spellings were readily interchangeable. S. Potentiana rested close to "Praxidis" in the Priscilla catacomb. The 5th-century *vita* presented them as sisters. The Roman synod of 595 called the virgin-sisters saints, the Roman Council of 745 referring to the church as S. Potentiana. Their story satisfactorily explained the conversion of an early Christian *titulus* in the patrician quarter into a Christian basilica, as is implied in "titulum Pudentis, id est ecclesia sanctae Pudentianae" in the life of Hadrian I (Davis, *Lives of Eighth-Century Popes*, 97.76, for the years 782–783). Under Leo III (*LP* 98) the titular status of the parent's property was applied to the church honoring the eldest daughter ("titulo sanctae Pudentianae" or "titulo beatae Pudentiane," Davis, *Lives of Eighth-Century Popes*, 98.37, 112); only once is the archaic "titulo Pudentis" revisited (Davis, *Lives of Eighth-Century Popes*, 98.74).

35. Initially Christian initiation in the city was celebrated by the bishop at the Lateran baptistry built ca. 315 by Constantine. By the late 4th century the popularity of baptism at the shrines of the martyrs led to the addition of baptistries at St. Peter's and S. Lorenzo's. The 5th century saw the redecoration of the Lateran font and the inclusion of baptistries in the building projects of old and new city churches (Krautheimer, *Rome*, 54–58; Krautheimer, *Three Christian Capitals: Topography and Politics* [Berkeley: University of California Press, 1983], 110–12). The story preserves the recollection of adult baptisms at Easter and explains the presence of fonts in some *tituli*, among them S. Pudenziana. There is no factual information for S. Prassede.

36. There is no historical documentation for such a persecution under Antoninus Pius. In this incident all are killed, whereas the second edict of Valerian (258) a century later mandated that "bishops, priests, and deacons should be executed 'on the spot'" (Ludwig Hertling and Engelbert Kirschbaum, *The Roman Catacombs and Their Martyrs* [Milwaukee, WI: Bruce, 1956], 45 and n. 14 citing Cyprian, *Ep.* 80.1). The fateful discovery in 258 of Pope Sixtus II (257–258) with four of his deacons and a large crowd of laity celebrating eucharist at the Callistus catacomb ended with only the bishop and deacons martyred (ibid., 44–46).

Pastor buries her next to her father in her grandmother Priscilla's cemetery. Praxedes, meriting honor thanks to her long life of dedicated service to the church, must have been in her eighties when she died circa 156 at the end of Pius' episcopate.[37]

When these pseudo-"pastoral letters" were read at Nocturns of the Roman liturgy of the hours on the vigils of feastdays, the hearers were edified by the story of a pious family whose three generations spanned much of the early Roman apostolic, subapostolic, and post-apostolic ages.[38] An eighteenth-century papal commission and twentieth-century hagiographers were skeptical; however, scholars of the sixteenth and seventeenth centuries as well as some ranking archeologists of the nineteenth and early twentieth centuries took the story at face value. With the rediscovery and excavation of Priscilla's cemetery by Giovanni Battista de Rossi in the last third of the nineteenth century, the Punicus Pudens gens regained its fascination for ecclesiastical scholars such as the Benedictine Ildefonso Schuster (1880–1954), abbot of St. Paul's Outside the Walls.

Punicus Pudens' hospitality to Peter, leading to the householder's conversion at the start of the apostle's twenty-five-year Roman ministry, explained the multiple Petrine references claimed for Priscilla's cemetery. According to Acts 28:16, Paul arrived in Rome in chains circa 61 and lived for two years under house arrest. Paul's baptism of Savinella and her children in the mid-sixties, just prior to his martyrdom, further undergirded the story of this fervent senatorial family.[39] Their genealogy in conjunction with the "histories" of their close friends and associates takes this shape (Table 1.1)

Patriarch of the first generation, Punicus Pudens was identified by some scholars with Quintus Cornelius Pudens, supposedly baptized

---

37. According to Davanzati (*Notizie del pellegrino*, 124), an ancient lectionary gives Prassede's death as the year 156: "[I]o trovo in uno de' Lezzionarj antichi, che si conservano nel Monastero di Vallombrosa, e che si credono cavati di Monastero di S. Prassede di Roma...."

38. Perhaps as early as the time of Pope Hadrian I (772–795) and certainly before 850, an *ordo* giving directions concerning the antiphons and responsories to be used at the liturgy of the hours, written by a Frankish scribe who knew Roman customs well, informs us, "The passions of the saints or their acts (*gesta*) were read only there where the church of that very saint or title was. Nevertheless, in his time [Hadrian] himself prescribed renewal and established that the readings be done in St. Peter's church." See Michel Andrieu, *Les ordines romani du haut moyen âge*, vol. 2: *Les textes* (Louvain: Spicilegium sacrum Lovaniense, 1960), XII.25, 466.

39. Despite his own remonstrations that he was an evangelizer not a baptizer (with two exceptions: Crispus and Gaius, and the household of Stephanus, 1 Cor 1:14–17), Paul supposedly baptized Savinella and her children.

14   WOMEN IN PASTORAL OFFICE

Table 1.1 Genealogy of the Pudens clan

Evangelized by Peter				
grandparents	Punicus Pudens (disciple of Peter)	+ Priscilla		
Evangelized by Paul				
parents	Pudens "Junior" [feast 19 May]	+ Sav(b)inella (Sabina)		
	(husband, disciple of Paul)	(wife, baptized by Paul)		
siblings	Potentiana/ Pudentiana [feast 19 May]	Praxedes [feast 21 July]	Novatus [feast 20 June]	Timothy [feast 24 Jan]
	(daughters of Pudens Junior & Savinella)		(brothers, identified by *MR* as siblings of Pot & Prax)	
friends	Bishop Pius I [feast 11 July]	Pastor, brother of Pius I [feast 11 May, Ado; 26 July, *MR*]	Simmetrius [feast 26 May]	
	(Roman bishop, ca. 140–155)	(Roman presbyter)	(martyred under one of the Antonines)	

by Peter while the apostle lived in the senator's house on the Aventine. A portion of the wooden portable altar, claimed as that on which Peter celebrated mass, preserved as a relic in the chapel of St. Peter terminating S. Pudenziana's left aisle, can be classified as a family heirloom. The cemetery of Priscilla on the Via Salaria Nova, which *LP* identifies as burial place of seven popes, contains a number of the best-known and most enigmatic paintings of catacomb art, carried out in a painterly impressionistic style of superior quality. The great archeologist G. B. de Rossi reconstructed the family relationships, connecting the Priscilla cemetery across town with the Aventine and Viminal churches.[40] Pudens

---

40. Orazio Marucchi's popular handbook *Guide des catacombes romaines* (2nd French ed. [Paris: Desclée, Lefebvre & Cie, 1902], 381–472, at 381–87) promulgated De Rossi's intuitions.

("Junior") and his wife Sav(b)inella constituted the second generation. Later legend had Pudens enter the clerical *gradus* as lector on the death of his wife. Ado of Vienne (d. 875) introduced Pudens into the martyrology.[41] The epitaph "Sabinae beatae" marks a *loculus* (shelf-grave) in the Priscilla cemetery.[42]

The third generation consists of two sets of siblings. Potentiana/Pudentiana and Praxedes are daughters of Pudens Junior and Savinella. The Hieronymian Martyrology makes them sisters of two brothers, Novatus and Timothy, who figure largely in the story; later hagiography takes this up. Later still the question is raised whether all are related by blood or are sisters and brothers in the Lord. Ado places "Pudentiana or Potentiana" ahead of the other saints of the day, knows her as the daughter of Pudens and Sabinella, and names her sister Praxedes and her friend blessed Pius, bishop of the city.[43] Corresponding to her sister's entry, Bede's second recension puts in the second place, after the prophet Daniel, "Natale sanctae Praxedis virginis." Although Praxedes is clearly a virgin not a martyr, she is awarded the latter title in the biography of Paschal I.[44]

A lengthy notice by Ado styles Novatus "brother of Timothy the apostle," calls him "man of God" and saint, and adds the pertinent part of the *passio*.[45] The entry for XII KL Iulii in Ado's concise "Shorter Roman Martyrology" reads, "At Rome Novatus brother of the apostle Timothy, who were taught by the apostles."[46] Usuard corrects Ado by refusing to name the presbyter Timothy an apostle but terms Novatus a saint. Some editions of the Hieronymian martyrology make the two sisters and two

---

41. Dubois and Renaud, *Martyrologe d'Adon*, 163–64.

42. Henri Leclercq, "Priscille (Cimetière de)," in *Dictionnaire d'archéologie chrétienne et de liturgie*, 14/2 (1948), 1799–1874, at 1828, fig. 10538; henceforth cited as *DACL*. Yet another interpretation queries whether Claudia (named with Pudens and Linus, 2 Tim 4:21) was Pudens' wife, a widow, or a deaconess. Is this Linus (in the reading of Irenaeus and Augustine) the first bishop (67–76 CE) to succeed the Roman church's founders Peter and Paul? (Davis, *Book of Pontiffs*, 2).43. St. Gall, Stiftsbibliothek cod. 454, 135–36. Bede's first recension read simply "Natale sanctae Potentianae virginis." The lengthy text attributed to Bede (*PL* 94, 919–21) may represent a later scribe's extensive copying from the *vita*. Florus provided a eulogy.

44. Davis, *Lives of Ninth-Century Popes*, 100.9.

45. St. Gall, Stiftsbibliothek cod. 454, 163; Dubois and Renaud, *Martyrologe d'Adon*, 199–200. Amore (*I martiri*, 68) erroneously labels the Novatus of our story a presbyter.

46. "Romae novati fratris timothei apostoli, qui ab apostolis eruditi sunt" (St. Gall, Stiftsbibliothek cod. 454, 12).

brothers siblings. The Pastoral Letters, purportedly written by the apostle Paul as he nears death, address Timothy by name (1 Tim 1:2, 18; 6:20 and 2 Tim 1:2).[47] Second Timothy 1:17 suggests the letter's origin in Rome, where Paul is captive. Paul's second letter to Timothy 4:21 extends greetings from Pudens, Linus, Claudia, and all the brothers and sisters.[48] Ado has made Timothy a primary disciple of Paul, thus cementing the Pudens clan's familial relationship with the apostle to the Gentiles. Tradition holds that the relics of Timothy, martyred first bishop of Ephesus, were translated to the Church of the Holy Apostles, Constantinople, in 356.

The family friends named in the *vita* gradually make their way into the martyrologies. On Pudens' death, the house where the Christian community (*ecclesia Pudentiana*) had assembled was put in the name of a presbyter called Pastor ("Shepherd"). (*Titulus Pastoris* was its actual legal title for only the sixth and seventh centuries, after which it reverted to *titulus Pudentis*.) The story casts the two sisters as the real leaders of this house-church (*domus ecclesiae*). Pastor initiates their story with his letter and reappears chiefly for burials; his personality is two-dimensional.[49] However, the Muratorian Fragment (ca. 200) and the *Liberian Catalogue*, included in a compilation by the Chronographer of 354, identified Pius' brother as Hermas, the author of the popular noncanonical *Shepherd* perhaps written in two periods, about 100 and 150 CE.[50] In the eighth century, Pastor is a title for St. Peter as in the oratory dedicated to "St. Pastor the

---

47. A Timothy is also named in Acts 16:1; Rom 16:21; 1 Cor 16:10; 2 Cor 1:1, 19; Phil 1:1, 2:19–24; Col 1:1; 1 Thess 1:1; 2 Thess 1:1; Phlm 1; Heb 13:23. Phil 2:22 reads, "You know what Timothy's worth is, how as a son with a father, he has served with me in the gospel." See Bruce Malina, *Timothy: Paul's Closest Associate* (Collegeville, MN: Liturgical Press, 2008).

48. Luke Timothy Johnson, *The First and Second Letters to Timothy* (Anchor Bible 35A; New York: Doubleday, 2001) takes Paul for the author of the Pastorals while laying out the hermeneutical options on issues involving women's roles in the Christian community.

49. Amore (*I martiri di Roma*, 34) mentions a martyr Pastor as having been buried by a presbyter Giovanni, who figures in several *passiones* as a burier of martyrs. Pimenius, supposedly presbyter of Pastor's *titulus* at the time of Constantine (ibid., 230–31), is sometimes named as Pastor's alter ego. We may ask whether both are not "straw" characters who facilitate stories about "real" people. On the multiple "personalities" of Pastor, see Claudia Angelelli, *La basilica titolare di S. Pudenziana: nuove ricerche* (Vatican City: PIAC, 2010), 19–24.

50. The *Liberian Catalogue*, the earliest version of *LP*, contains an early list of popes which identifies "Hermas" as brother of Pius. So does an Epitome of *LP*'s 1st ed. (Davis, *Book of Pontiffs*, no.11, p. 98). Although they may be assumed, our *vita* does not take up these identifications. On Hermas author of *Shepherd*, see Lampe, *From Paul to Valentinus*, 218–36. Following a Vulgate variant, Ado cites Romans 16:14 that "they" claim the Hermas named there to be author of the *Shepherd* (Martyrology of Ado, St. Gall, Stiftsbibliothek cod. 454, 38, feastday 11 May).

martyr" in Old St. Peter's.[51] In this cryptic fashion, the story connects the church of S. Pudenziana with Peter, supposed catechist and houseguest of the senator Pudens Senior. The Roman martyrology in use until 1969 continues the fiction (*Romae sancti Pastori, cujus nomine Titulus exstat in Viminali, apud sanctam Pudentianam*) understanding the *titulus* and S. Pudenziana as separate buildings.[52]

Liber Pontificalis (hereafter *LP*) identifies Pius I as born in Aquileia; he was bishop of Rome for about nineteen years.[53] "Pius, natione Italus, ex patre Rufino, frater Pastoris, de civitate Aquilegia, sedit ann. XVIIII m. IIII d. III. Fuit autem temporibus Antonini Pii, a consolatu Clari et Severi" is found (fol. 2v) among the summary list of popes near the beginning of Vatican ms. lat. 3764, an eleventh- or twelfth-century *liber pontificalis* from Cava or Farfa, which had been in the care of the seventeenth-century priest-antiquarian Fioravante Martinelli (fl. 1650). The more noteworthy personage is Hermas, here not specifically identified with Pastor: "In [Pius'] episcopacy, Hermas wrote a book in which he includes the order that an angel of the Lord imposed on him when he came to him in shepherd's apparel, and instructed him that Easter be celebrated on a Lord's day." If Pastor was Pius' brother, this is never the reason given for the bishop's frequenting the *titulus* on the Viminale. Rather, his friendship with the sisters appears to occasion the sacramental visits. The claim that Pius I was martyred under Marcus Aurelius is made by the Roman martyrology. The final family friend to be listed in the Roman martyrology is the martyr Simmetrius, added by Ado.[54] Skeptical of Ado's listings, Usuard includes neither Pastor nor Pius but retains Simmetrius.[55]

---

51. Davis, *Lives of Ninth-Century Popes*, 105.43, n. 72, and Sible de Blaauw, *Cultus et decor: liturgia e architettura nella Roma tardoantica e medievale* (2 vols.; Vatican City: BAV, 1994), 1:571.

52. *Martyrologium Romanum: Gregorii Papae XIII jussu editum, Urbani VIII et Clementis X auctoritate recognitum, ac deinde anno MDCCXLIX Benedicti XIV opera ac studio emendatum et auctum* (5th ed.; Turin: Marietti, 1949), 222.

53. On Pius, see J. N. D. Kelly and Michael Walsh, *The Oxford Dictionary of Popes* (2nd ed.; Oxford: Oxford University Press, 2010), 6–7.

54. St. Gall, Stiftsbibliothek cod. 454, p. 139, stating that he was martyred with 20 (not 22) others in the *titulus* of Pudens; cf. Praxedes (ibid., p. 184). Ado does not know a Praxedes *titulus*.

55. Cf. Dubois and Renaud, *Martyrologe d'Adon*, 169 and Dubois, *Martyrologe d'Usuard*, 235.

A. Topographical Questions and a Recent Challenge

The story of the Pudens gens gained an additional air of realism when archeologists of the nineteenth and twentieth centuries excavated the second-century house foundations nine meters below the floor of the present church of S. Pudenziana and carried out investigations of its fabric. The integrated *Acta SS. Pudentianae et Praxedis*, which inspired the archeologists' deductions, had been published by the Bollandist Daniel Papebroch (1628–1714) in *Acta Sanctorum*'s fourth volume for the month of May.[56] Papebroch inserted into his life of Pius I a gloss found in *LP* manuscripts from Cava or Farfa (now Vat. ms. lat. 3764, written in the same hand as the main entry), and Florence (Laurenziana LXVI, 35): "Here [Pius] at the request of blessed Praxedes dedicated the baths of Novatus as a church in the Patrician quarter, in honor of her Sister holy Potentiana, where he also offered many gifts; where often he ministered offering the Lord's sacrifice."[57] The text added by Papebroch to the *Acta Sanctorum* entry, where it is indicated between brackets, reads, "in the Patrician quarter. However, he also dedicated another in the name of the blessed Virgin Praxedes."[58] His readers would immediately think of the two separate churches of S. Pudenziana at the base of the Viminale and S. Prassede on the Esquiline, by the Carolingian period nicely distinguished. S. Pudenziana was said to utilize for its church assembly a thermae hall identified as that of Novatus, a large and spacious building (*aedificium magnum...et spatiosum*), situated on the *vicus Patricius*. Most commentators have followed the *Acta Sanctorum* with its *LP* gloss.[59]

---

56. *AA.SS.*, Maii IV (1866), 298–99.

57. In his critical edition of *LP*, Louis Duchesne (*LP*, 1:133, n. 8) noted the passage in question, interpreting it as depending on the *acta*. It reads, "Hic [Pius] ex rogatu beate Praxedis dedicavit aecclesiam thermas Novati in vico Patricii, in honore Sororis suae sanctae Potentiane, ubi et multa dona obtulit; ubi saepius sacrificium Domino offerens ministrabat," transcribed from Vat. ms. lat. 3764, fols.111r–v.

58. Inserted between "sub nomine beatae Virginis Potentiane" and "infra urbem Romam" and indicated by brackets the text reads "in vico Patricius. Dedicavit autem et aliam sub nomine sanctae Virginis Praxedis" (*AA.SS.*, Maii IV [1886], 299D).

59. Richard Krautheimer ("S. Prassede," *CBCR* 3:234, n. 3) asserted, "The legendary foundation by pope Pius I (142?–157?) of the *titulus* of S. Pudenziana in the thermae of Novatius and of that of S. Prassede in the vicus Lateranus cannot be substantiated," adding that the entire *passio* is pious fiction, the passage inspired by the sisters' *vita* inserted into the *LP* biography of Pius at a later date. He follows *LP*'s hierarchical reading of events, which attributes foundations to one or another pope rather than to the lay benefactors in whose names *tituli* were held. However, Davis believes that this gloss may contain authentic material.

Proposing corrective readings to the topographical, archeological, and documentary record, Federico Guidobaldi challenges the prevailing interpretations of the foundation stories of the churches of S. Pudenziana and S. Prassede.[60] S. Pudenziana, the older of the two churches, was located in an area populated by patrician families in the second century. By the fourth century the neighborhood had been transformed into multistoried structures and commercial establishments. Rather than originating in the great hall of a bath, Guidobaldi shows that S. Pudenziana was renovated from a private or commercial building with an open courtyard containing such shallow pools that it could not have been a bath building. He repudiates the reading that situates the church dedicated to St. Pudentiana in the renovated baths of Novatus in the *vicus Patricius*. Instead he proposes that the Praxedes *titulus* utilizes baths "of Novatus" located in the Lateran quarter, in which is located its assembly hall, the *ecclesia Pudentianae*.[61] Guidobaldi points out that it is not untypical for *tituli* to have more than one title or dedication, keeping the owner's "title" for the *domus ecclesiae* and that of the honored patron for the church proper. After all, many *tituli* started out as privately owned buildings that included living quarters. Private baths would have served for baptistries. In our case the community center would be named for Praxedes, the assembly hall within it for Pudentiana. The *titulus Praxedis* disappeared from the record after 599, perhaps continuing as a minor community center until its restoration by Hadrian I.[62] Misled by the apse inscription reading DOMINUS CONSERVATOR ECCLESIAE PUDENTIANAE, the *titulus* of Pudens, in Pastor's name only in the fifth and sixth centuries, acquires its own saint, Potentiana or Pudentiana. The unified *acta* with its late eleventh-century interpolation, Guidobaldi continues, has adapted its reading to suit the Carolingian

---

60. Guidobaldi, "Osservazioni," 2:1033–71.

61. Guidobaldi ("Osservazioni," 2:1045, n. 32) cites the priest-antiquarian F. Martinelli (*Roma ricercata nel suo sito* [Rome: 1653] 46 and 286) and F. Nardini in 1818. However, he does not mention the separate recensions for Praxedes' feastday, e.g. *Martyrology of Ado* (St. Gall, Stiftsbibliothek cod. 454, late 9th century, 183–84). A Saint Gall collection of *passiones* (Saint Gall, Stiftsbibliothek cod. 577, 9th–10th centuries), reads for S. Prassede, "Quod placuit sancto pio episcopo et dedicavit ecclesiam termas novati, in nomine beatae virginis praxedis, in urbe roma, in vico qui appellatur laterici (267)." Vat. Pal. lat. 846 (109r, 10th century) states that Praxedes had been living in the *titulus* of her sister Potentiana. Vat. Barb. lat. 586 (21r, 11th–12th centuries), places the thermae of Novatus dedicated in Praxedes' name in the Lateran quarter, as does the elaborated narrative of Vat. lat. 1191 (100v, end 12th century), which does not know an ecclesia in Pudentiana's name.

62. Guidobaldi, "Osservazioni," 2:1038–39.

profiles of two distinct, well-known churches, both of which by that period served as Lenten stational churches.[63]

2. Early Church Life and the "Age of the Martyrs"

The sisters' story begins in the formative years of Roman Christianity, whose shape has recently been the subject of much critical study. Scholars agree that a Jewish-Christian community with converts from Palestine or Syria existed in Rome prior to the arrival of Peter in the fifties. Many Jews were expelled from Rome in approximately 49 CE by the Edict of Claudius and their property expropriated. Likely the influential couple Prisca and Aquila, whose profession was tent-making, fled Rome for Corinth where they were joined in their home about 51 by the apostle Paul and later traveled with him to Ephesus.[64] When Paul wrote the letter to the Romans circa 57–58 he was hoping to visit Rome. Paul arrived in Rome around 61 as a prisoner under house arrest. For about two years he was able to carry on the evangelization and instruction of the Roman community in his own rented living quarters (Acts 28:16). If indeed Romans 16 is an integral part of that letter and was written to Rome, Prisc[ill]a and Aquila had already returned to the capital where once again they hosted a house-church (Rom 16:3–5).[65] In Romans 16 Paul seeks to prepare the way for his own ministry by greeting the individuals, families, and Christian leaders with whom he has already come into contact in the Christian mission.

---

63. The unified account claims that a bath building is renovated for S. Prassede and a baptistery built. No documentary or archeological evidence has been found for a baptistery. Krautheimer (*CBCR* 3:240) suggests that a curved fragment of concrete vaulting discovered in S. Prassede's forecourt or atrium may be a remnant of a Roman bath building.

64. Prisca and Aquila were partners in the Pauline mission (Acts 18:2, 26; Rom 16:3; 1 Cor 16:19; 2 Tim 4:19); of their deaths scripture tells us nothing. On the interchangeable names Prisca/Priscilla, see Amore, *I martiri*, 66–67. Jerome Murphy-O'Connor ("Prisca and Aquila: Travelling Tentmakers and Church Builders," *Bible Review* 8 [1992]: 40–51, 62) explains that, while Prisca/Priscilla is usually named first indicating that she was the leader of the pair, the diminutive form Priscilla is always used by Luke (Acts 18:2, 18, 26). Paul prefers the mature form Prisca (Rom 16:3–5; 2 Tim 4:19; cf. 1 Cor 16:19). This couple established Christian communities in Corinth (Acts 18:3), Ephesus (Acts 18:26–27) and Rome (Rom 16:5, ca. 55 CE); see Marie Noël Keller, *Priscilla and Aquila: Paul's Coworkers in Christ Jesus* (Collegeville, MN: Liturgical Press, 2010). They figure in Ado's martyrology on 8 July (St. Gall, Stiftsbibliothek cod. 454, 13 and 177; Dubois and Renaud, *Martyrologe d'Adon*, 219).

65. Much scholarly opinion, supported by the early manuscript tradition, again favors this position. The trajectory of this chapter is Rome—Ephesus (Lampe, *From Paul to Valentinus*, 153–86.)

The great fire of Rome, starting 19 July 64, led to the scapegoating of Christians and their relentless persecution by the emperor Nero, who died by suicide 9 June 68. The writer Tacitus (*Ann.* 15.44) details the atrocities Nero decreed for a "huge multitude" of the Christian sect.[66] According to Tertullian, for whose statements no firm material proof has so far been adduced, Peter was crucified in the circus of Nero on the Vatican Hill just south of Old St. Peter's about the year 64 or 65 CE; Paul was beheaded circa 67.[67] Tradition speaks of Peter and Paul as jointly founding the Roman church by the shedding of their blood.

Information about the growth of the Roman church in the second and third centuries is sparse; until at least the second half of the second century it was governed by a presbyteral council rather than a single bishop (the so-called "monarchical episcopacy"). Presbyter-bishops were termed elders or overseers/supervisors according to their function: counseling, instructing, and ordering the church's internal life, or overseeing (*episcope*) the distribution of charity.[68] The Roman church solemnly commemorated the martyrdom of its bishop-rulers (and only them) by a city-wide celebration at their place of burial. From the middle of the third century and construction of the papal crypt by Pope Fabian (235–250), this could be done at the catacomb of Callistus.[69] The compilation by the Chronographer of 354 lists these commemorations.[70] Any existing lists of less memorable but no less heroic blood-witnesses for the faith were lost in the first two centuries, in the intermittent persecutions of the third century, and especially in the chaotic times of Diocletianic persecution (303–305).

---

66. Cf. 1 Clement to Corinth 5, 5–6, in *Early Christian Fathers*, trans. and ed. Cyril C. Richardson, with Eugene R. Fairweather et al. (New York: Macmillan, 1970), 45–46.

67. Tertullian, *De praescriptione hereticorum* 36, ca. 200, in *Traité de la prescription contre les hérétiques: Tertullien*, ed. R. F. Refoulé; trans. P. de Labriolle (Paris: Cerf, 1957). Hard evidence does not exist for the presumed martyrdoms of Peter and Paul. Eusebius of Caesarea (d. ca. 340; *Eccles. Hist.* 2:25) carefully qualifies his statement that "Paul is therefore said to have been beheaded at Rome, and Peter to have been crucified under [Nero]. And this account is confirmed by the fact that the names of Peter and Paul still remain in the cemeteries of that city even to this day." See Eusebius Pamphilus of Caesarea, *The Ecclesiastical History of Eusebius Pamphilus*, trans. C. F. Cruse (London: George Bell, 1876; repr., Grand Rapids, MI: Baker Book House, 1955).

68. Peter Lampe, *From Paul to Valentinus*, 399–400.

69. Hertling and Kirschbaum, *Roman Catacombs and Their Martyrs*, 36–48.

70. M. R. P. McGuire, "Chronographer of 354," *NCE* 3 (2003): 569–70.

The Roman church was slower than Asia Minor (in the second century) and North Africa (before the mid-third century) to develop a cult of martyrs who were not bishops. Finally rank-and-file Christians, heroes of both sexes and all ages, children, women and men, single and married, lay and ecclesiastic, with many among them who had freely chosen to remain virgins, began to be commemorated by the Roman church on their *natale,* the date of their death and heavenly birth.[71] Impetus was provided in the fourth century by pilgrimages and in the fifth and sixth by the development of spurious "acts" of these martyrs to replace those records that had been destroyed.[72] Until then, bishops of Rome who remained steadfast in the faith and died for it constituted the "calendar" of saints. Authentic stories of individual and communal heroism, of avoidance through bribery or of outright disloyalty provoked by fear, cajoling, or torture, are lost to history. Even the particularities of imperial attitudes and official policy toward Christians are cloaked in obscurity. For those holy persons, including the Virgin Mary, who were not martyrs or confessors, recognition of their saintly status by inclusion in the Roman calendar would have to await the seventh century.

The *vita* of Potentiana and Praxedes is set within the "age of the martyrs" prior to the Peace of the Church. From the mid-nineteenth century the beginnings of scientific excavation of catacombs in the Roman suburbs by eager explorers like G. B. de Rossi (1822–1894) fueled speculation about this period. Ecclesiastical authors like H. D. M. Spence-Jones set out to recreate that age in which the faith held by a small transplanted sect centered on a crucified Savior was sown and became rooted in the

---

71. The distinction between lay person and ecclesiastic is not found in the Jesus-movement. In Rome at the end of the 1st century, the author of 1 Clement twice uses the Greek *laikos* in an argument utilizing the model of the Temple priesthood. The term reappears a century later in Clement of Alexandria and Tertullian; see Alexandre Faivre, *The Emergence of the Laity in the Early Church,* trans. David Smith (New York: Paulist Press, 1990), 15–25.

72. Only official court proceedings ("minutes") can properly be called *acta martyrum* ("acts of the martyrs"), although *acta* was used for the Pudentiana and Praxedes story in older literature. J. Quasten cites as an actual record only the court process of Justin Martyr (d. ca. 165). See also G. W. Bowersock, *Martyrdom and Rome* (Cambridge: Cambridge University Press, 1995). Quasten's second category, that of eyewitness or contemporary accounts of martyrdoms (*passiones, martyria*), has occasionally been used of Pudentiana's story, although she does not die a martyr. Like Delehaye's types, Quasten's third category, that of the legend, either fantastic with an admixture of truth or purely imaginary, does not on the face of it fit the content of the Potentiana and Praxedes story, which is linked to historical personages and topographical sites. See Johannes Quasten, *Patrology,* vol 1: *The Beginnings of Patristic Literature* (4 vols.; Utrecht-Antwerp: Spectrum, [1950] 1966), 176–78, 183–84. Vita is used throughout this study as a generic term.

center of the greatest pagan empire.[73] The beginnings of repressive policies against Christians are dated to the final years of Emperor Hadrian's reign and the end of the Jewish war, 134/135. Of special interest for our story is the period following Hadrian's death (d. 138) when the two Antonines reigned, Hadrian's adopted son Antoninus Pius (138–161), followed by Marcus Antoninus Aurelius (161–180), the latter's adopted son. Both were outstanding rulers and both figure in some recensions of the *vita*. Antoninus was styled "Pius" by the Roman Senate, apparently for his unstinting care of Hadrian during the latter's declining years. Spence-Jones refers to this "almost flawless life" of "unfeigned devotion to the ancient Roman religion, the reputation of Antoninus for justice and wisdom, for clemency and sobriety, his stern morality, the high example he ever set in his private and public life."[74] How could such a person persecute a religion that preached love, compassion, forgiveness of enemies? Marcus Antoninus Aurelius, philosopher-author of the *Meditations*, was treated as divine on his death.[75] He was also the author of "fierce and deliberate" persecutions throughout the empire.[76] Practicing the prescribed rituals with devotion, Marcus truly believed in the power of the ancient gods. Other persecutors during the third century—Decius, Aurelian, and Diocletian—likewise were devoted to the Roman civil religion. Spence-Jones summarizes, "Christianity was utterly incompatible with the ancient traditions of Rome." But whatever the actual numbers of martyrs and the intensity of the persecutions, our story leads up to an anticipated climax, that of blood-witness in a period of sporadic persecution.[77]

Roman law required that corpses be buried *extra muros*, outside the city. Around 200 CE cremation started to give way to inhumation among

---

73. H. D. M. Spence-Jones, *The Early Christians in Rome* (London: Methuen, 1910).

74. Spence-Jones, *Early Christians in Rome*, 85.

75. *Marcus Aurelius and His Times: The Transition from Paganism to Christianity*, with an introduction by Irwin Edman (New York: Walter J. Black, 1945), 2–133. In *Meditations* 11.3, making his sole reference to Christians, Marcus judges that their choice of death over life is irrationally obstinate.

76. *Marcus Aurelius*, 94.

77. *Marcus Aurelius*, 97. For a balanced judgment, see Hertling and Kirschbaum, *Roman Catacombs and Their Martyrs*, 87–107; for cautions on numbers of martyrs and authentic data about them, see Felice Lifshitz, "The Martyr, the Tomb, and the Matron: Constructing the (Masculine) 'Past' as a Female Power Base," in *Medieval Concepts of the Past: Ritual, Memory, Historiography*, eds. Gerd Althoff, Johannes Fried, and Patrick J. Geary (Washington, DC: German Historical Institute and Cambridge University Press, 2002), 311–41.

pagans.[78] Cemeteries held as private properties bearing the name of the owner served the extended family: immediate family members, freedmen and freedwomen employed in its service, and slaves who might be manumitted on the owner's death. A family vault could be the nucleus out of which a cemetery or catacomb for the burial of members of the Christian community developed.[79] Believing in the resurrection of the body, Christians practiced inhumation. These burials are found in the ground (*formae*), *loculi* (shelves in catacomb walls), *arcosolia* (tombs dug into stone with a frescoed stone arch), or *cubicula* ("little bedrooms," underground burial chambers for the wealthy), often with symbols indicating that the deceased was a Christian. As the Christian faithful grew in numbers, wealthier members provided places of interment for those less favored with material goods. The bodies of brothers and sisters *in Christo* populated the loculi or shelf-graves that, sprinkled with lime and sealed with a slab, filled catacomb corridors top to bottom until another layer was excavated underneath. High, long, irregular corridors led to family areas where wealthier members or persons reputed for holiness were interred, becoming centers of devotion preferred for burials. Like their wealthy patrons, persons who died witnessing to the Christian faith might be interred in cubicula. Where the place of rest of the ordinary deceased was marked out by a pottery lamp or glass vial, those singled out for special notice or veneration could be identified by fresco, stucco decoration, sarcophagus, sometimes by name, and often by prayer-graffiti. The earliest catacomb paintings date from around 200 and sculpted sarcophagi from around 230.

Some authors claimed that Priscilla's cemetery on the Via Salaria Nova was the first of the great Christian cemeteries to be rediscovered (in 1578) and one of the oldest.[80] It occupies the extended grounds of a country villa that speculation, especially that of G. B. de Rossi, connected with the Pudens gens and its grandmother Priscilla.[81] Although

---

78. J. M. C. Toynbee, *Death and Burial in the Roman World* (London: Thames & Hudson, 1971).

79. A "proscribed religion or association could not acquire property or enjoy any of the rights granted to the religious or funerary corporations recognized by the law." George La Piana, "The Roman Church at the End of the Second Century," *HTR* 18 (1925): 201–77, at 254–55.

80. However, that discovery has been shown to be the catacomb of the Jordani, also on the Via Salaria Nova a little closer to town.

81. Because early medieval itineraries list the Priscilla cemetery as the burial place of the martyr Prisca, often mistaken for Paul's coworker, and the lives of Hadrian I and Leo III

the extensive Christian cemetery with its regular "fishbone" pattern of burials on the second (lower) level dates from the fourth century, separate constructions of a private nature preceded it: sand pits transformed into places of burial; the hypogaeum of the Acili (an underground room whose inscriptions relate to that senatorial family); a nymphaeum and two water storage areas sometimes claimed as "baptismal fonts"; a cryptoporticus; and the third-century "Greek chapel." In the fourth century a small basilica above ground dedicated to the martyrs SS. Felix and Philip became the burial place of Roman bishops.[82] Earlier generations of scholars were fascinated by burial inscriptions in Priscilla's oldest sector and speculated about family connections, especially the consular family of M. Acilius Glabrio and the Pudens gens.[83] The first level of the Priscilla complex is outstanding for the quantity and quality of extant inscriptions and paintings, of which an unusual number feature women. The Petrine resonances that led Orazio Marucchi to propose Priscilla as Peter's "seat" and the place where he baptized explained, in his view, the otherwise unusual choice of this cemetery as a papal burying ground. Papal connections were paramount: the basilica of St. Sylvester on the grounds, burial place of no less than seven popes, replaced the Vatican necropolis and then the Callistus catacomb, where the earliest bishops had been interred.[84] The modern author Ruth Hoppin has revived speculation about connections between the Priscilla cemetery and the Pudens family legend, including a

---

in *LP* refer to the *titulus* on the Aventine as that of Prisca and Aquila, a familial relationship was also presumed with them. If a freedwoman, the evangelist Prisc[ill]a of Paul's letters could have borne the aristocratic Priscilla's name. Archeologists of the first "scientific" age—G. B. de Rossi and the Commission of Sacred Archaeology whose campaigns of excavation took place in the Priscilla cemetery in 1863 and 1887, and De Rossi's disciple Orazio Marucchi—pointed to archeological "coincidences" that tied the Pudens gens to both S. Prisca and S. Pudenziana, giving to the legends a "certain foundation of truth" (Marucchi, *Guide des catacombes romaines*, 381–87, at 385). Older speculations, especially those of G. B. de Rossi, are summarized and critiqued by H. Leclercq in *DACL* 1/1 (1907), 775–848 ("Agape"); 2/2 (1910), 2084–2106 ("Cappella Greca"); 6/1 (1924), 1259–1274 ("Glabrion, Manius Acilius"); 14/2 (1948), 1799–1874 ("Priscille, Cimetière de").

82. Francesco Tolotti, *Il cimitero di Priscilla: studio di topografia e architettura* (Vatican City: PIAC, 1970).

83. A beautifully carved tablet reads M. ACILIUS.../C.V./PRISCILLA C.... A Priscilla living in the second half of the second century may have made the villa property available for Christian burials.

84. Marucchi, *Guide des catacombes romaines*, 386, 456. The popes are Marcellinus, Marcellus, Sylvester, Liberius, Siricius, Celestinus, and Vigilius.

house of Pudens on the Aventine whose remnants are said to lie under the church of S. Prisca.[85]

3. The Second- and Third-Century Roman Church

Grounded in the early life of the city-church of Rome, the story of Potentiana and Praxedes held special status through close association with the two princes of the apostles, even though this device of hagiographical genre was scarcely restricted to the Pudens family. For a story judged by twentieth-century hagiographers to be entirely legendary, the apostolic connections of an early Christian family constructed from a few names mentioned in genuine Christian epistles or associated with Roman cemeteries was beyond compare. Did the apostolic pedigree of this edifying story inspire Pope Hadrian's rebuilding of a *titulus* in disrepair, and Paschal's rebuilding on a new site?

Pius I (ca. 140–155?), the only assuredly historical character among the family's close associates, is by most counts the ninth successor of Peter, although listed as the tenth or eleventh bishop in *LP*.[86] During his episcopate Pius would have confronted the notable heresies of Marcion and Valentinus, but these doctrinal controversies did not engage the interest of the *LP* compiler.[87] Instead, *LP* calls Pius brother of Pastor and alludes to the *Shepherd*, a noncanonical apocalypse authored by a certain Hermas and much favored in the East. Was this the Hermas referred to by Paul in Romans 16:14? This identification is now dismissed. The Muratorian Fragment (traditionally of Roman origin and dated to the second or third century) identifies Pius as brother of the author Hermas: "We also receive the Apocalypse of John and that of Peter although some of us do not want this read in church. But Hermas wrote the *Shepherd* very recently, in our own time, in the city of Rome when his brother, Bishop Pius, was sitting in the chair of the Church of Rome. And therefore it too should be read but it must not be read publicly to the people in church."[88] Since Hermas

---

85. Ruth Hoppin, *Priscilla's Letter: Finding the Author of the Epistle to the Hebrews* (Fort Bragg, CA: Lost Coast Press, 1997), 89–98.

86. The Liberian Catalogue lists Hyginus (138–149 CE), Anicetus (150–153), and Pius (146–161) as overlapping bishops nos. 10, <12>, and 11 (Davis, *Book of Pontiffs*, 98).

87. Eusebius, *Eccles. Hist.* 4:11.

88. Quasten, *Patrology*, 1:92; 2:208. *LP* calls "Pastor" the brother of Pius. Since Pastor means shepherd in Latin, the temptation presents itself to identify the Pastor of our *vita* with Hermas. But it does not take that step.

was a slave, it can be inferred that Pius was also enslaved. The *Liberian Catalogue* by the Chronographer of 354 says tersely of Pius: "In his episcopacy his brother Hermas wrote a book in which is included the order that an angel of the Lord imposed on him when he came to him in shepherd's apparel."[89] According to the long text of *Le Liber pontificalis*, "Hermas wrote a book in which he includes the order that an angel of the Lord imposed on him when he came to him in shepherd's apparel, and instructed him that <holy> Easter be celebrated on a Lord's day."[90] Since *Shepherd* is written in the first person singular, Hermas receives the order. But the *LP* entry adds the content of the order: that Easter be celebrated on Sunday.[91] In the context of its "biographies," the order regarding the celebration of Easter on Sunday could only be carried out by Pius.[92] Until the mid-second century in Rome there was no annual celebration of Easter; every Sunday was a celebration of the Lord's resurrection. To Pius is attributed the Roman custom of annually celebrating the resurrection on Sunday. There is more secure, but not as early, evidence that Pius' successor the Syrian (?) Anicetus (155?–166) introduced the annual celebration to Rome, following a visit from the aged bishop Polycarp of Smyrna (d. ca. 155) in the year of his martyrdom to confer regarding that issue.[93] They agreed to accept each region's customs: Rome would celebrate Easter on Sunday and the churches of Asia Minor on fourteenth Nisan, the day following the first day of Passover, which could fall on any day of the week.[94] These divergent customs soon evoked a bitter dispute, one of the outstanding

---

89. Davis, *Book of Pontiffs*, Liberian Catalogue, no. 11, p. 98.

90. <[H]oly> is an insertion in the *LP* biography of Pius; Davis, *Book of Pontiffs*, xlvii–xlviii, (no. 2). The whole of no. 4 (the dedication of the church in honor of St. Pudentiana in the baths of Novatus on the Vicus Patricius) is also an interpolation and is marked "< >."

91. Vat. ms. lat. 3764 reads, "Sub huius episcopatum Hermis librum scripsit in quo mandatum continet quod ei praecepit angelus Domini, cum venit ad eum in habitu pastoris; et praecepit ei ut Pascha die dominico celebraretur" (fol. 11r). Cf. *Shepherd of Hermas*, Vision 5, no. 25, where there is no command pertaining to Easter; see *The Apostolic Fathers: Greek Texts and English translations*, ed. and rev. Michael W. Holmes (3rd ed.; Grand Rapids, MI: Baker Books, 1999), 373–75.

92. An Epitome (Davis, *Book of Pontiffs*, 99–100, no. 15, 2) is the only text to name Pius: "[Victor] decreed like Pius that the holy Easter...3. He held a council and questioning took place on Easter or on the first day with Theophilus bishop of Alexandria about the moon."

93. On Anicetus and Easter, see E. G. Weltin, "Anicetus, St. Pope," *NCE* (2003), 1:455.

94. Eusebius, *Eccles. Hist.* 4:14. Paul F. Bradshaw ("The Origins of Easter," in Paul F. Bradshaw and Lawrence A. Hoffman, eds., *Passover and Easter: Origin and History to*

controversies in the later second century. Bishop Victor (ca. 189–199), perhaps of African origin, attempted to impose Roman custom by threatening to excommunicate all the churches of Asia. *Le Liber pontificalis* claims quite a lot for Victor: "He decreed like Eleuther...after a discussion with priests and bishops and after holding an assembly to which Theophilus bishop of Alexandria had been invited, that the holy Easter should be kept on the Lord's day from the fourteenth to the twenty-first of the first lunar month."[95] The centrality of the Easter feast to the leaders of the Roman church in the second century will, it seems, be reflected in Paschal's project at S. Prassede.

When read with discernment, Hermas' *Shepherd* can offer additional insight into leadership models and the second-century church. Carolyn Osiek has applied social analysis to the symbolic female figure of woman-church who is the Revealer in Visions 1–4 in *Shepherd*. The old woman (*presbytis*) on a white *cathedra* (Visions 1.2–3 [1.2–3]) reappears the following year as a younger *presbytera* reading a book; her message is to be sent to the other churches, to the widows and orphans, and to the *presbyteroi* who preside over the local church (Visions 2.5, 6.2–3 [2:5–6]).[96] Finally, thanks to *metanoia*, the conversion through which the church is regenerated, she appears as a radiantly young woman (Vision 3).[97] Traces of Wisdom tradition are present: "the female figure of the church in *Pastor Hermae* is not spousal, nor maternal, but a seemingly independent wisdom figure."[98] In Similitude (Parable) 9.12.2 [9:89], the Shepherd explains,

---

Modern Times [Notre Dame, IN: University of Notre Dame Press, 1999], 81–82) proposes that the Quartodeciman celebration was original, noting that "the celebration of Easter on a Sunday...was not adopted at Rome until about 165, although it may have emerged in Alexandria and Jerusalem somewhat earlier."

95. Davis, *Book of Pontiffs*, 15.2, 3. But *LP* makes no Easter claims for the previous pope, Eleuther (175–189). On calendrical questions, the Passover and the Quartodeciman dispute, see M. Richard, "La question pascale au IIe siècle," *L'orient syrien* 6 (1961): 179–212; Allen Brent, *Hippolytus and the Roman Church in the Third Century: Communities in Tension before the Emergence of a Monarch-Bishop* (Leiden: E.J. Brill, 1995), 63–68. The first part of Brent's study is given over to analysis of the so-called statue of Hippolytus at the entrance to the Vatican Library: the made-over figure of Themista/*Sophia* alludes to the Logos-christology of the Hippolytan philosophical school and its interest in the calculation of the date of Easter.

96. The numbers in brackets refer to the edition of *The Shepherd* in Holmes, *Apostolic Fathers*, 328–527.

97. Carolyn Osiek, "The Social Function of Female Imagery in Second Century Prophecy," *VetChr* 29 (1992): 55–74.

98. Osiek, "Social Function," 60.

"The Son of God is far older than all his creation, with the result that he was the Father's counselor in his creation," a characteristic second-century christology (Prov. 8:22–31).

A recent interpretation of the shadowy figure of Pastor by Steve Young casts Hermas the author of *Shepherd* in the roles of paterfamilias (patron) and pastor of a Christian house-church in second-century Rome.[99] As Hermas acknowledges his past failure effectively to manage his household (namely, to lead his community), he grows in his resolve to bear his pastoral responsibilities in a manly way. In Revelation 5.1–2 [25:1–2], his guide and revealer ceases to be a woman, symbol of the church, and is replaced by the visionary figure of the Shepherd. With this turn, Hermas accepts the challenge of woman-church, "Act like a man, Hermas" (Vision 1.4, 3) [1.4]. Hermas has grown into his pastoral identity. Do Pudentiana's death and Praxedes' move to her own independent *titulus* allow Pastor to assume a manly role as leader at the *domus ecclesiae* on the Viminale, which in the sixth and seventh centuries will bear his name?

As manuscripts of the sisters' *vita* multiplied, the foundation-myth gaining currency presented the community, overseen by Potentiana and Praxedes, as a "domestic" or house-church of second-century Rome.[100] But there were no longer house-churches when the story received its final editing. Did the leadership model in the faith community of Potentiana and Praxedes appeal as an ideal to those who handed on the story? In third-century house-churches, authority appears to have been held by a presbyteral council and leadership was exercised jointly according to gifts and social prestige.[101] The sisters' *vita* was framed as a series of "pastoral" letters written in the genre of the Pastorals—1 and 2 Timothy and Titus— omitting the Pastorals' negative attitudes toward women. "Household codes" and other features of the dominant male culture that control

---

99. Steve Young, "Being a Man: The Pursuit of Manliness in *The Shepherd* of Hermas," *JECS* 2 (1994): 237–55.

100. Noële Maurice-Denis Boulet, "Titres urbains et communauté dans la Rome chrétienne," *LMD* 36 (1953): 14–32; Joan M. Petersen, "House Churches in Rome," *VC* 23 (1969): 264–72; Petersen, "Some Titular Churches at Rome with Traditional New Testament Connections," *Expository Times* 84 (1973): 277–79; Raymond E. Brown and John P. Meier, *Antioch and Rome: New Testament Cradles of Catholic Christianity* (New York: Paulist Press, 1983), esp. Part 2; Vincent P. Branick, *The House Church in the Writings of Paul* (Wilmington, DE: Glazier, 1989), 66–71; Harry O. Maier, *The Social Setting of the Ministry as Reflected in the Writings of Hermas, Clement and Ignatius* (Waterloo, ON: Wilfrid Laurier University Press, 1991), esp. 55–86.

101. Lampe, *From Paul to Valentinus*, 397–403.

women, children, and slaves in the deutero-Pauline letters and 1 Peter do not constrain the liberty of the daughters and sons of God as depicted in this ideal household.[102] The relatively egalitarian and participatory role of women in the life of the Christian community was no doubt inspired by their sharing, during the age of the martyrs, in blood-witness for the Christian faith.[103]

In *Hippolytus and the Roman Church in the Third Century*, Allen Brent presents a nuanced interpretation of the sparse evidence about Christian communities in second- and third-century texts and archeological sources. He points to indications that at least some of these communities (for example, the one that met in Justin Martyr's house "over the bath of Martin son of Timothy") were "house-schools" representing the various philosophical groups in the city. Brent delineates the transformation of such schools, led by a single *proestos* (presider). Some were house-churches having a plurality of leaders, since the two offices of the *presbyteroi-episcopoi* were not yet clearly separated.[104] Many of the *tituli* (of which five had foundation-stories or "etiological legends" produced to explain their origins, while the other twenty had such venerable origins that no such story was required) developed out of "domestic" faith-communities, including those of Pudentiana and Praxedes.[105] Brent suggests that, in this early period before specific functions were restricted to certain offices, a presbyter "might be called a bishop" when he was exercising *episcope*, that is, overseeing material

---

102. Many scholars consider 1–2 Tim and Titus to be among the latest works of the Christian scriptures and "post-Pauline." For a clear statement respecting women's issues, see Joanna Dewey, "1 Timothy," "2 Timothy," "Titus," in Carol Ann Newsom and Sharon H. Ringe, eds., *Women's Bible Commentary* (exp. ed.; Louisville, KY: Westminster John Knox, 1998), 444–52. For our purposes it is useful to presume, as did commentators of earlier centuries, that these letters were written by Paul at the end of his life. The leadership style of the Pastorals' householder is investigated by David C. Verner, *The Household of God: The Social World of the Pastoral Epistles* (Chico, CA: Scholars Press, 1983).

103. On studying *gesta* from the perspective of women readers, see Felice Lifshitz, "Gender and Exemplarity East of the Middle Rhine: Jesus, Mary and the Saints in Manuscript Context," *EME* 9 (2000): 325–43.

104. If we follow Justin Martyr's account of the Sunday eucharist, ca. 150, the single presider was assisted by deacons. One presider sits on the *cathedra* in Hermas in Mand 11, 1 and 12 (Brent, *Hippolytus and the Roman Church*, 431), but cf. the "presiding presbyters" of Vision 2, 4 (ibid., 451).

105. Brent, *Hippolytus and the Roman Church*, 399–400; Federico Guidobaldi, "L'inserimento delle chiese titolari di Roma nel tessuto urbano preesistente: osservazioni ed implicazione," in Philippe Pergola, ed., *Quaeritur inventus colitur: miscellanea in onore di Padre Umberto Maria Fasola, B.* (2 vols.; Vatican City: PIAC, 1989), 1:383–96.

relief to widows, orphans, and the poor.[106] Another aspect invites consideration. Nine of the twenty-five Roman *tituli* named in the synods of 499 and 595 were private properties held by women. Some recent scholarship considers it likely that women householders were presidents of their worshiping communities and, in that role, led the prayers of thanksgiving (eucharist).[107]

4. A Political Interpretation of Our Story

More than three decades ago Peter A. B. Llewellyn argued for a political reading of the Potentiana/Praxedes story, proposing that it represents in narrative form tensions that surfaced during the Laurentian schism of 498–507.[108] During this time, bishops were usually elected from among deacons, presbyters, and laity of senatorial rank. Laurentius, probably archpresbyter of S. Prassede, was elected anti-pope with the support of the senatorial party against the Sardinian deacon Symmachus (498–514), who was supported by most of the clergy.[109] In such an environment, the celebration of Easter by Symmachus in 501 following the old Roman computations was a symbolic

---

106. Brent, *Hippolytus and the Roman Church*, 430. For his argument Brent uses Pius I, the *Shepherd* of Hermas, the Muratorian Canon, "Hippolytus," and the legend of the Novatian presbyter created by Pope Damasus.

107. Hans-Bernhard Meyer, *Eucharistie: Geschichte, Theologie, Pastoral* (Regensburg: Pustet, 1989), 79; Edward J. Kilmartin in a private communication. Raymond E. Brown (*The Churches the Apostles Left Behind* [New York: Paulist Press, 1984], 33) has pointed out that nothing in the Pastoral Letters suggests that presbyter-bishops presided at baptism or the eucharist in the early second century. Rather, these elder-overseers were responsible for preserving intact the "household of the church," its faith, doctrine, and traditions.

108. Peter A. B. Llewellyn, "The Roman Church during the Laurentian Schism: Priests and Senators," *Church History* 45 (1976): 417–27. For a critique, see Hillner, "Families, Patronage, and Titular Churches," 227–30. Davis (*Book of Pontiffs*, 103–5) gives the text of the Laurentian Fragment. On the anti-pope Lawrence, elected 22 November 498, see Kelly and Walsh, *Oxford Dictionary of Popes* (2010), 49.

109. The first documented reference to *titulus Praxedis* dates from 491, in an epitaph for a cleric. At the Roman synod of 499 Caelius Laurentius as archpresbyter and Petrus as presbyter signed for S. Prassede. Since the pretender Laurentius had taken control of the Lateran palace and Symmachus was displaced from it, the latter (pope 498–514) set up his episcopal curia at St. Peter's and introduced chapels and furnishings imitating those at the Lateran. St. Peter's became a papal center as well as martyrium and covered cemetery. See Sible de Blaauw, *Cultus et decor*, 2:506–7; Judson Emerick, "Altars Personified: The Cult of the Saints and the Chapel System in Pope Paschal I's S. Prassede (817–819)," in Judson J. Emerick and Deborah M. Deliyannis, eds., *Archaeology in Architecture: Studies in Honor of Cecil L. Striker* (Mainz: P. von Zabern, 2005), 50–52.

statement that he represented the true church.[110] Llewellyn pointed out the many fifth-century "markers" in the Potentiana/Praxedes tale: its distinctiveness when compared to other *gesta martyrum* and *passiones* of the period and the uncharacteristic foundation legends that flew in the face of the clericalism of Pope Gelasius I's decrees.[111] Can the *acta*—with its detailed account of legal title to lay-held and controlled properties—not be read, Llewellyn asked, as a claim by leading laity to juridical independence from church control for the twenty-five Roman *tituli*, and by extension, an argument for lay participation in church affairs and governance?[112] What Llewellyn failed to note is the two-dimensionality of the male characters; Pastor does not play the role of paterfamilias but appears to be at most administrator of a house-church located in the sisters' home. The sisters are the central characters in leading the faith community.

5. Background to Paschal I's Building Campaign

During the Carolingian era, Rome held exceptional interest for Western emperor, liturgical scholar, and pilgrim-tourist alike. Its classical monuments recalled the past glories of Roman imperial power. In the early centuries, the historical construction by Irenaeus, bishop of Lyons (d. 202), that Peter and Paul had been martyred in Rome after founding and establishing the church, was of greater import for the exercise of papal office than was Christ's commission conferring on Peter the power to bind and loose (Matt 16:18–19).[113] By virtue of occupying the seat founded on

---

110. Llewellyn ("Roman Church during Laurentian Schism," 420) calculates the intervals between Novatian's feastday (27 June or 29 June, the latter the feast of Peter and Paul) and other festal days, above all Easter.

111. B. de Gaiffier, "Un prologue hagiographique hostile au Décret de Gélase?," AB 82 (1964): 341–53. But now the "Gelasian Decretals" are considered to be Gallican, and later than Gelasius' reign (492–496). See Clare Pilsworth, "Dating the *Gesta martyrum*," 315, n. 27; Hillner, "Families, Patronage, Titular Churches," 248–57.

112. Kate Cooper ("Martyr, Matrona and Bishop," 297–318) reads Llewellyn's interpretation of Novatus' role in the *vita Praxedis* as that of the central character "standing in for the schismatic Novatian." Novatian (Gr. Novatus) was a presbyter, secretary of the Roman presbyteral college, perhaps ordained irregularly by Pope Fabian (235–250). After Fabian's martyrdom Novatian contested the papal election which Cornelius (251–253) had won. A schismatic community formed around Novatian. The political reading by Llewellyn suggests that Novatus was the black sheep of the Pudens family.

113. Francis Dvornik, *Byzantium and the Roman Primacy* (New York: Fordham University Press, 1966), 41–42. The popular tendency to regard Peter and Paul as equals was endorsed by intellectuals of the late 4th century and manifest in the building of the grand St. Paul's

the blood-witness of the apostles to the Jews (Peter) and Gentiles (Paul), Rome's bishop, styled patriarch of the West and *vicarius Petri* from Leo I's pontificate (440–461) on, claimed to possess apostolic authority in questions of dogma vis-à-vis the patriarchs of the East. The communion of East and West was such that from 640 until 752, of twenty popes thirteen were Dalmatians, Sicilians, Greeks, or Syrians; others, from Campania, were Greek-educated. Only in the mid-eighth century did this change, the popes being chosen from Roman aristocracy. At home, the vacuum left in social services when the Roman civil service departed with Emperor Constantine for New Rome (Constantinople) in 330 had been gradually filled by the Roman bishop and his ecclesiastics.[114] Over time, abetted by the people's love for a revered pastor like Gregory the Great (590–604) and by the role of ancient Rome in governance, the see of Peter claimed special status in secular as well as religious spheres.

A. The Roman Pilgrimages

Pilgrimages formed a significant part of any pope's pastoral oversight. Pilgrims had to be welcomed, housed, bathed, and fed. City of emperors and martyrs, Rome was the chief tourist attraction of the West during the first millennium.[115] The Roman pilgrimage peaked during the sixth and seventh centuries. The city was irresistible, whether to barbarian plunderers or to pious Christians in search of relics. Written guides to the holy sites were followed by eager pilgrims within and outside the walls of Rome. The earliest surviving guides are seventh century, two predating 650; they assisted the pilgrim-tourist in visiting all those places where martyrs rested.[116] If headed for the main catacombs south of town (Praetextatus, Callistus), the pilgrim passed through the city wall close to St. John Lateran to follow the Appian Way. To the southwest was St. Paul's Outside the Walls with a secondary shrine to a certain Timothy. Inside

---

Outside the Walls in ca. 380 to rival Old St. Peter's. Papal policy from the late 6th century onward gave Peter hegemony (Krautheimer, *Rome*, 42).

114. Thomas F. X. Noble (*The Republic of St. Peter: The Birth of the Papal State, 680–825* [Philadelphia: University of Pennsylvania Press, 1984], 230–34) outlines the social service contributions of the popes from the 5th century on, especially in the *diaconiae* or welfare centers.

115. Peter Llewellyn, *Rome in the Dark Ages* (London: Faber & Faber, 1971), 173–98.

116. John Osborne, "The Roman Catacombs in the Middle *Ages*," *PBSR* 53 (1985): 278–328.

the walls on the Aventine hill were the *tituli* of S. Sabina and S. Prisca.[117] To the west was the chief goal of the pilgrimage, the basilica dedicated to Peter with its attendant monasteries and pilgrim hostels. To the north and moving east of the city the pilgrim encountered in turn the catacomb of St. Valentine on the Flaminian Way and the Priscilla cemetery on the Via Salaria, where the martyr St. Potentiana was honored along with "Praxidis" and Simmetrius.[118] Farther east was the catacomb of St. Agnes on the Nomentana. All of these places and names figured in the guides and nourished the foundation-myth that inspired Pope Paschal's rebuilding of S. Prassede, the first of his three churches dedicated to women, the others being S. Cecilia in Trastevere and the *diaconia* S. Maria in Domnica.

The guide *Notitia ecclesiarum urbis Romae* (ca. 625–649) directed pilgrims to the martyrs sleeping outside the walls of old Rome in Priscilla's cemetery:

> Afterwards ascending by that same route to the church of Saint Sylvester; there a multitude of saints sleep: first Saint Sylvester pope and confessor, and at his feet pope Saint Siricius...and a large number of saints under the main altar; and in a cave the martyr Crescentius, and in another the martyr Saint Prisca; and Fimitis sleeps in the little chamber when you go out, and in another the martyr Saint Potentiana and Praxidis.[119]

The *Notitia* dignifies with the titles of saint and martyr both Prisca and Potentiana. In the later seventh century, both churches were papal stations, which gained for their patrons the title of saint. In time every patron of a *titulus* was raised to the status of sainthood. Since the Praxedes *titulus*

---

117. The *LP* entry for Leo III (795–816) uses the archaic term *titulus* for S. Sabina, elegant example of the Sistine renaissance (422–32; Davis, *Lives of Eighth-Century Popes*, 98.4) and S. Prisca, the "titulo beatis Aquile et Priscae" (ibid., 98.73) or "titulus Priscae." The latter refers to a supposed martyr St. Prisca (Henri Leclercq, "Prisque (Sainte)," *DACL* 14/2 [1948], 1883–85; Amore, *I martiri*, 66–67). By the 6th century Sabina is considered a martyr from outside Rome. A virgin Sabina appears in the mosaic procession at S. Apollinare Nuovo, Ravenna, dated ca. 568 (Amore, *I martiri*, 304–6).

118. Vincenzo Fiocchi Nicolai, "'Itinera ad sanctos': Testimonianze monumentali del passaggio dei pellegrini nei santuari del suburbio Romano," in *Atti del XII congresso internazionale di archeologia cristiana, Bonn 22–28 settembre 1991* (2 vols.; Vatican City: PIAC, 1995), 2:763–75.

119. *Itineraria et alia geographica*, ed. Paul Geyer, et al. (2 vols.; CCSL, 175–176, Turnholt: Brepols, 1965), CCSL 175, no. 10, 306.

did not serve as a station until midway in the eighth century, initially no saintly designation was bestowed on her. In *De locis sanctis martyrum* (ca. 635–645), the group resting in the catacomb of Priscilla is "canonized": S. Potentiana, S. Praxidis, S. Prisca, and S. Simmetrius, possibly reflecting the usage of an early recension of the Gregorian Sacramentary, the first liturgical tradition to show St. Praxedes' church as a papal station.[120]

B. An Early Fifth-Century Apse and Eighth-Century Restoration Work

Paschal's rebuilding and dedication of S. Prassede (817–819) would follow on restoration work by Hadrian I (772–795), who in 782–783 had also "freshly restored Pudens' *titulus*, which is St. Pudentiana's church, which had reached ruin."[121] Paschal had no hand in restoring S. Pudenziana; however, both churches would share the theme of Christ in majesty in heavenly Jerusalem, the older expressing late antique classicism in full flower and Paschal's new church displaying a Roman medieval style with some Byzantine influence. The early fifth-century apse of S. Pudenziana has been called Rome's greatest example of Theodosian classicism.[122] This beautiful mosaic marks a penultimate stage of classical illusionism.[123] The magisterial bearded Christ, holding in his lap the title DOMINUS CONSERVATOR ECCLESIAE PUDENTIANAE ("The Lord protector of the faith-assembly of Pudens"), is enthroned in the midst of the apostolic college garbed as senators; all are seated in front of a curved portico. Christ exercises

---

120. *Itineraria et alia geographica*, CCSL 175, no. 24, 320. The same four are named, without the prefix saint, by the 12th-century writer William of Malmesbury (no. 5, 326).

121. Davis, *Lives of Eighth-Century Popes*, 97.76. Krautheimer names as probable additions by Hadrian the Lamb and Dove in the 1595 drawing by Ciacconio (Vat. cod. 5407; cf. ms. Barb. lat. 4423, f. 63) made before the outer perimeter of the mosaic was cropped by further renovations (Geir Hellemo, *Adventus Domini: Eschatological Thought in 4th-Century Apses and Catecheses*, trans. Elinor Ruth Waaler [Leiden: E.J. Brill, 1989], illus. 14–16 and 117, n. 122), and the Eclissi copy ca. 1630 in Windsor, Royal Library (Krautheimer, *CBCR* 3: fig. 248).

122. Krautheimer (*Rome*, 40) judges this apse mosaic, heavily restored on the right side, to be "the earliest figural representation to survive in, and presumably one of the first to be designed for, a Roman church." Fredric W. Schlatter ("The Text in the Mosaic of Santa Pudenziana," *VC* 43 [1989]: 156) dates it between 402–417, proposing that it expresses gratitude to God for the church's preservation during the pillage of Rome in 410 (ibid., 161–63).

123. The monumental, strongly modeled naturalistic figures at Sts. Cosmas and Damian on the Via Sacra (526–530) in the lineage of *Traditio legis* are still inspired by the Roman classical heritage.

sovereignty within a stately ancient setting.[124] Behind him on the central axis a golden, bejeweled trophy of the cross stands on a mount (Golgotha? the Mount of Olives?); on either side spreads a realistic cityscape (Rome? Jerusalem?).[125] Christ is king of the cosmos, shown by the four living creatures (Ezek 1:5–10, cf. Ezek 10:8–22; Rev 4:6) hovering in a sky streaked with luminous clouds.[126] Doubtless the creatures are meant to bear the firmament while symbolizing the earth's four corners.[127] Two female figures

---

124. Hellemo, *Adventus Domini*, 39–56. The basic composition of Christ enthroned in the midst of the apostolic college has precedents in catacomb painting (catacomb of Domitilla) and early apse mosaics (Milan, S. Aquilino).

125. Eusebius had dared to identify Revelation's New Jerusalem with Constantine's newly restored city (*Vita Constantini*, III.33). Theories about the architecture depicted include Constantinian Jerusalem, the heavenly Jerusalem using neighborhood buildings, or the Roman Viminal district. Hellemo (*Adventus Domini*, 51–53) makes the compelling case for Jerusalem architecture, while emphasizing the ambiguity of symbolism in this period. The octagonal and square buildings may depict with some historical accuracy the holy places in Constantine's recently reconstructed Jerusalem: the Anastasis rotunda at the Holy Sepulchre and the Church of the Ascension on the Mount of Olives (John Wilkinson, *Egeria's Travels to the Holy Land* [rev. ed.: Jerusalem: Ariel, 1981], 39–53). Simultaneously these buildings symbolize the New Jerusalem coming down from above. Based on Jerome's commentary on Ezekiel 40–48, Fredric W. Schlatter ("A Mosaic Interpretation of Jerome, In Hiezechielem," *VC* 49 [1995]: 64–81, at 68, 76) proposes Jerome's idealized *Romam factam Hierosolymam*.

126. Frederic W. Schlatter ("Interpreting the Mosaic of Santa Pudenziana," *VC* 46 [1992]: 276–95 at 279–80, 285–86) develops an uncalled-for trinitarian proposal for the enthroned figure (God the Father), the gold cross (symbol of Christ), and the rosy clouds (the Holy Spirit). Thomas F. Mathews (*The Clash of Gods: A Reinterpretation of Early Christian Art* [Princeton: Princeton University Press, 1993], 92–114) explains convincingly the iconography of divinity symbolized in the bearded and enthroned Christ, which is integrated with the iconographic type of philosopher and disciples. Frederick Van der Meer (*Maiestas Domini: Théophanies de l'apocalypse dans l'art chrétien: Étude sur les origines d'une iconographie spéciale du Christ* [Vatican City: PIAC, 1938], 220–229) had already presented the patristic exegesis which favored interpretation of the Enthroned One of the Revelation visions as the Eternal Word, and explained the function of the living creatures within the theophany. However, Schlatter's theory ("Interpreting the Mosaic of Santa Pudenziana") about the influence of Jerome's Ezekiel commentary on the apse mosaic serves the evidence well.

127. Hellemo (*Adventus Domini*, 56–63) discusses the change in meaning of the four living creatures from their early function as cosmic symbols to symbols of the four evangelists. At S. Pudenziana the animals "of human form" appear in the sky in the order human, lion, ox, eagle, given in Ezek 1:10. The four creatures of this vision, each a composite with four faces and four wings (tetramorph), do not lend themselves to translation into visual imagery. But aspects of their physiognomy are melded with the six-winged, chanting seraphs of Isa 6:2–3 to provide, in the final biblical generation, Revelation's four separate animals, each with six wings (Rev 4:8). S. Pudenziana's two-winged creatures, each wing distinguished by three prominent feathers stretched upward, have their visual source in the Revelation text but their order from Ezekiel will later become adopted in manuscript illumination. When the winged human, lion, ox, and eagle hold gospel books, they symbolize Matthew, Mark, Luke, and John.

standing behind the balding Paul and curly-haired Peter offer wreaths to the enthroned one or more, likely to the apostolic princes.[128] The magisterial Christ, the colorful sky with its four living creatures, and the two women will figure in S. Prassede's apse and apsidal arch.

The sisters' popularity reached its apogee under Carolingian popes. After having restored Pudentiana's church in 782–783, Hadrian completely renewed Praxedes' *titulus*, "which was partly ruinous," in 783–784.[129] In whatever way the Praxedes *titulus* had functioned, and wherever it was located, Hadrian's restorations had a short life. The new church of Praxedes was built "in alio non longe demutans loco," Krautheimer speculating that the remains of the original *titulus Praxedis* may be preserved in the tenement buildings adjacent to the atrium.[130] He infers that it had functioned as a community center.[131]

---

128. Johann Peter Kirsch (*Die römischen Titelkirchen im Altertum* [Paderborn: Schöningh, 1918], 61–67) identified the two women presenting or holding *coronae* in the Pudenziana apse as Potentiana and Praxedes, the historically grounded mosaic images inspiring the sisters' legendary *vita*. A favorite interpretation has compared them to the two standing female figures in mosaic on the inside entrance wall of S. Sabina (422–432), titled *Ecclesia ex circumcisione* and *Ecclesia ex gentibus*. Fredric W. Schlatter ("The Two Women in the Mosaic of Santa Pudenziana," *JECS* 3 [1995] 1–24), propounding the theory of an Hieronymian source for the S. Pudenziana mosaic, explains the women by Jerome's commentary on Ezek 44 (Jerome, *Commentariorum in Hiezechielem* (libri 1–14), ed. F. Glorie [Turnhout: Brepols, 1964], 13.44.22). Schlatter reviews Jerome's exegesis of pairs of Old Testament women who signify the preexistence of the church in Jewish and Gentile forms, the reunion of the twelve tribes of Israel, and the restoration of Jerusalem and Israel in the church. The text explicating the S. Pudenziana apse, Schlatter proposes, is found in Ezekiel's description of "priestly functions in the New Jerusalem." Levitical priests serving in the eschatological temple shall marry only "a virgin of the stock of the house of Israel, or a widow who is the widow of a priest" (Ezek 44:22). Schlatter ("Two Women," 21) says, "[O]ne represents the inherited riches of the Jewish tradition now revealed in the New Testament, the other the valid insights Gentile wisdom has achieved." The *virgo* embodies the sapiential wisdom found in the Wisdom books, but this applies also to the priestly *vidua*. Through its priests the church teaches this wisdom. Thus women symbolize the priestly teaching function. How this identification squares with the adjacent male figures (Christ as ruler, the college of senator-apostles not of priests) is unexplained.

129. Davis, *Lives of Eighth-Century Popes*, 97.76, 78. Pope Leo III (795–816) donated a textile in 801 and a silver crown in 807 to S. Praxedes (ibid., 98.37 and 98.74), neither gift indicative of a significant site.

130. Krautheimer, *CBCR* 3:258.

131. In Krautheimer's *Rome* (313, 376) S. Prassede is categorized with the *tituli* S. Martino ai Monti and SS. Nereo ed Achilleo, both of which were listed as *diaconiae* during the pontificate of Leo III. Activities attributed to Praxedes' leadership of the house-church characterized both *tituli* headed by presbyters and *diaconiae* administered by lay superintendents. Successors in function and sometimes in location to imperial welfare centers, the earliest *diaconiae* were lay foundations in the mid-7th century. By the later 8th century, the 18 *diaconiae*

C. The Life of Paschal I

Constructed under a single patron over a brief time span, S. Prassede is a homogeneous, remarkably intact project of the Roman Carolingian renaissance. Paschal brought to the commissioning of S. Prassede the gifts of an artistically sensitive patron. He was elected pope on 25 January 817, one day after the death of Stephen IV (22 June 815–24 January 817).[132] Raymond Davis judges that the *LP* entry for Paschal, modeled on that of his patron Leo III, is of slipshod composition.[133] Several of the chief political events of Paschal's checkered career go unrecorded. Independent accounts of relations with Carolingian rulers suggest cooperation at times, and at other times suspicion and jockeying for power by those who occupied the two rival offices.[134] Other sources inform us that Paschal's harsh policies and suspected assassinations, not out of character for the bishop

---

were under church administration, with spiritual needs attended to by lay monks or small monastic communities, not deacons. There food was stored and distributed, baths were available, pilgrims taken in, and the sick and aged cared for (J. Lestocquoy, "Administration de Rome et diaconies du VIIe au IXe siècle," *RAC* 7 [1930]: 261–95; Ferrari, *Early Roman Monasteries*, 355–61; Krautheimer, *Rome*, 77–82). A small chapel on the premises symbolized the Christian presence. However, hers was a community center (*domus ecclesiae*).

132. As priest, Paschal was named abbot of the monastery behind the apse of St. Peter's which served pilgrims. S. Stefano degli Abessini is closest in design to S. Prassede. Following Krautheimer's older theory (since discarded), Davis (*Lives of Ninth-Century Popes*, 100.2, n. 6) presents S. Stefano as a model for S. Prassede. Richard Krautheimer (*Studies in Early Christian, Medieval, and Renaissance Art* [New York: New York University Press, 1969], 218–19 and postscript, 255) revised his judgment that S. Stefano was built under Leo III with Paschal, the probable *praepositus* and the dating to 850 (Leo IV).

133. Davanzati (*Notizie al pellegrino*, 383) calls Paschal "figliuolo di Massimo Bonoso Nobile Cittadino Romane, e di Teodora nata di pari Natali." On the political aspects of Paschal's papacy, see Davis, *Lives of Ninth-Century Popes*, 1–4; L. Duchesne, *The Beginnings of the Temporal Sovereignty of the Popes A.D. 754–1073*, trans. Arnold Harris Mathew (London: Kegan Paul, Trench, Trübner, 1908), 125–35; J. N. D. Kelly and Michael Walsh, "Paschal I, St.," in *The Oxford Dictionary of Popes* (2010), 98–99.

134. Krautheimer (*Rome*, 109–22) colorfully summarizes the papal and imperial politics affecting building programs in the city of Rome at this period. Noble (*Republic of St. Peter*, 263) comments on the "bond of love and devotion and peace" that was pledged between pope and Carolingian monarch (first Pepin, then Charlemagne, then Louis the Pious) by respective popes, witnessed to by the *Pactum Ludovicianum* dating from Stephen IV's pontificate (816–817) and enjoyed by Paschal. Davis (*Lives of Eighth-Century Popes*, p. 232) lists the territories over which the pact gave the pope governance. The political situation and relationships are detailed in Caroline J. Goodson, *Rome of Pope Paschal I: Papal Power, Urban Renovation, Church Building and Relic Translation, 817–824* (Cambridge: Cambridge University Press, 2010).

of Rome at this period, earned him bitter enemies.[135] On his death the belligerence of the Roman populace and the turmoil in the streets were such that Paschal's corpse could not be buried in the chapel of Sts. Processus and Martinian he had constructed at St. Peter's.[136] His successor Eugene II (824–827) probably interred his predecessor's corpse in S. Prassede.[137] In 1969 Paschal I was officially removed from the Roman calendar of saints.

The political record does not square with Paschal's comportment in the worlds of devotion and art. Chapter 1 of *LP* reads in part: "From his earliest youth [Paschal] was bound over to the worship of God, and at the holy church's patriarchate he was imbued with the study of God's saving Scripture...elegant, and perfect in all goodness, he was made subdeacon and afterwards honourably consecrated priest.... [H]e frequently applied himself to talking of the things of God with religious and holy monks as an unremitting duty by day and night."[138] The testimony in *LP* to Paschal's ecclesiastically formed piety and his habit of spending whole nights in church in meditation and discussion with the monks can account for the coherence of S. Prassede's design (plan, nave, and mosaics of the arches, apse, and martyrium-mausoleum).

The stereotypical description of Pope Paschal's amiable character and exceptional piety is modeled on the first two chapters of Leo III's lengthy *LP* biography. As with Leo, Paschal's entry evinces much interest in architectural foundations and artistic commissions, which are somewhat less open to criticism than political decisions. Such a selective approach saves the chronicler

---

135. When accused of the murder of two of his own high civil servants, Paschal sent a delegation to Louis, while by solemn oath he declared his innocence before an episcopal synod in Rome (Duchesne, *Beginnings of Temporal Sovereignty of Popes*, 127–28; Noble, *Republic of St. Peter*, 249–49, 309–12).

136. On this chapel, see Davis (*Lives of Ninth-Century Popes*, 100.5, 6, 23; 105.36). Its vault was carried by four columns and decorated with mosaic; the altar with crypt contained the bones of Sts Processus and Martinian (Gillian Mackie, *Early Christian Chapels in the West: Decoration, Function, and Patronage* (Toronto: University of Toronto Press, 2003), 80; Mackie, "The Zeno Chapel: A Prayer for Salvation," *PBSR* 57 (1989), 172–99, at 198, n. 117).

137. Duchesne (*Beginnings of Temporal Sovereignty of Popes*, 128–35) shows how Leo III's and Paschal I's weakness in temporal government led to more immediate oversight of the Roman church by Louis the Pious and to election of the pope by lay nobility and clergy together. Uncertainty about the date of Eugene II's (disputed?) election and ordination affect the dating of the disturbances before (?) or after (?) Paschal's death and the circumstances of Paschal's interment. Lothar's *Constitutio Romana* aimed to restore order by enforcing stronger connections between the papal court and the empire (Davis, *Lives of Ninth-Century Popes*, 31–38).

138. Davis, *Lives of Ninth-Century Popes*, 100.1–3.

from providing information about a career that might not be judged kindly. The final sentence of Paschal's eulogy in chapter 3 is both typical of the genre and indubitably true: "He was a devotee, a restorer and in every way a most devout adorner of all God's churches."[139]

Besides adding chapels at St. Peter's early in the seven years of his pontificate, and, near its end, rebuilding the papal throne in the presbyterium of S. Maria Maggiore, he relocated and rebuilt S. Prassede and had it decorated with the most important ninth-century mosaics in Rome, built the church of S. Cecilia in Trastevere close to the Tiber, and rebuilt the church of S. Maria in Domnica on the Celian hill, decorating the apses and apsidal arches of these latter churches with somewhat less expansive mosaic programs.[140] The pope's portrait, seemingly a likeness, appears in the last three.[141]

The gesture of *introductio* or *praesentatio* of the chief saints made by the "patrons" Peter and Paul to the Lord coming in glory is typical of early Roman apse compositions.[142] Earlier examples follow a standard pattern; Paschal's apses, on the other hand, are unique. S. Prassede's apse displays an engaging familiarity between the princes of the apostles and the two sisters. On the viewer's left, Paul has his arm around Praxedes' shoulders; Peter bestows the same gesture on Pudentiana at the right (Fig. 1.3). Cettina Militello notes that Roman apses are the only ones to contain female figures other than the Virgin. She concludes that gestures of *introductio* suggest an important role, exceeding that of patronage, for women in Rome, as do liturgical garments such as the dalmatics worn by some of them. By any century's standards, such intimate gestures speak to a collaboration and close relationship of men and women that is central to our story. Paschal, whose portrait with rectangular blue halo shows him

---

139. Davis, *Lives of Ninth-Century Popes*, 100.3. Paschal also commissioned numerous works of art, two of which, silver-gilt or gold and enamel cross-reliquaries with inscriptions naming the donor, have survived (see chapter two).

140. *LP* tells us that Paschal was visited by St. Cecilia in a dream. She asked him to find her body and place it in the church built on the foundations of her home in the Trastevere district (Davis, *Lives of Ninth-Century Popes*, 100.15). For discussion of Paschal's building projects, see Goodson, *Rome of Pope Paschal I*.

141. For comparisons of the portraits, see Krautheimer, *Rome*, 127–28, figs. 98–100; Gerhart B. Ladner, *Die Papstbildnisse des Altertums und des Mittelalters*, vol. 1: *Bis zum Ende des Investiturstreits* (Vatican City: PIAC, 1941), 130–41.

142. SS. Cosma e Damiano (526–530), S. Lorenzo's triumphal arch (578–590), S. Teodoro (ca. 600). See Christa Belting-Ihm, *"Sub matris tutela," Untersuchungen zur Vorgeschichte der Schutzmantelmadonna* (Heidelberg: Carl Winter, 1976), 27 and n. 65.

FIGURE 1.3 Rome, S. Prassede. Apse detail: Paschal I, St. Praxedes, St. Paul. Scala/Art Resource, NY.

to be a contemporary figure, occupies the far left side of the apse next to Praxedes.

6. *S. Prassede: The Building*

Chapter 8 of *LP* treats of Paschal's benefactions during *Indictio* XI (817–818).[143] The commencement of the S. Prassede building campaign is then described. The pope, "often being on watch there" and noting the ruined state of the old church dedicated to St. Praxedes, determines to relocate it a short distance away. The apse and triumphal arch are decorated with mosaic

---

143. Herman Geertman (*More Veterum*, 81) has deduced that the chronological system governing the *LP* biographies from Hadrian I through Stephen V (885–891) is that of indictions, as found in the curial registers. An indiction was a fiscal period on a 15-year cycle instituted by Constantine in 313 for the assessment of property tax.

work. Paschal's translation to his new church of the actual bodies of saints (and not *brandea*, cloth relics that had been the currency of relic veneration, exchange, and traffic at the time of Gregory I) on a scale never before envisioned, is described in chapter 9 of *LP*, where he refers also to the building of an adjacent monastery for a group of Greek monks and the construction of the Zeno Chapel.[144]

On ceremonial occasions churchgoers pass through a small porch from a narrow street, the Via di S. Martino ai Monti, and climb a broad, dimly lit staircase flanked by apartments evocative of the private dwelling signaled by S. Prassede's titular status to enter a small, bright atrium (Fig. 1.4).[145] The approach, façade, and outer walls of S. Prassede evoke the simple exterior of church buildings of the early Roman Christian period even to the brickwork technique. Double relieving arches surmount round-headed windows. The church's façade has an early Christian profile similar to that of Old St. Peter's, the basilica built circa 336 that was destroyed in the rebuilding of the present St. Peter's (1505–1608). Study of the entry, façade elevation, plan, and dimensions shows that S. Prassede imitates, in layout, proportions, and later renovations, the cemeterial basilica on the Vatican hill dedicated to Peter by the Emperor Constantine. The three-aisled basilica of S. Prassede with transept and annular crypt is a smaller version of the five-aisled St. Peter's erected over the *memoria* (shrine) of the apostle at his presumed burial site.[146] The simple exterior

---

144. Two monasteries in the vicinity of St. Mary Major's, S. Agnes ad Duo Furna and S. Praxedes, were in close proximity (Ferrari, *Early Roman Monasteries*, 3–10). If Paschal incorporated the oratory of St. Agnes, which seems to have been on an upper floor, into his new monastery as the second phase of this institution (4–6), the presence of the Roman favorite Agnes with the two sisters on the upper wall of the Zeno Chapel as well as on the triumphal arch is readily explicable (Davis, *Lives of Ninth-Century Popes*, 100.9–11).

145. Krautheimer (*CBCR* 3:258, and on the Roman structures, 239–40) suggests that the *titulus* was located in this tenement area. The term *ecclesia* used in the *LP* biographies of Leo III and Paschal I could refer to a large inner room in an insula (tenement) that was dedicated to congregational use.

146. Krautheimer (*Studies in Early Christian, Medieval, Renaissance Art*, 218–19) describes S. Prassede's plan as "a nave, two aisles, a semicircular apse, and a continuous transept.... An annular crypt extends underneath the apse. The nave is bounded by columns which are surmounted by an architrave; windows with double arches pierce the clerestory, each corresponding to the axis of one intercolumniation. The architect of Santa Prassede...strove for the neat purity of the simple basilica plan with its clear contrasts...between the plainness of the structure, the bareness of the exterior, and the sumptuous wealth of the interior decoration." The interior space measures 46 x 26 meters. The present three diaphragm arches are supported by piers that may hide the original columns. The nave murals date from the 16th century. S. Cecilia in Trastevere, also by Paschal, shares many features but omits the transept (ibid., 221).

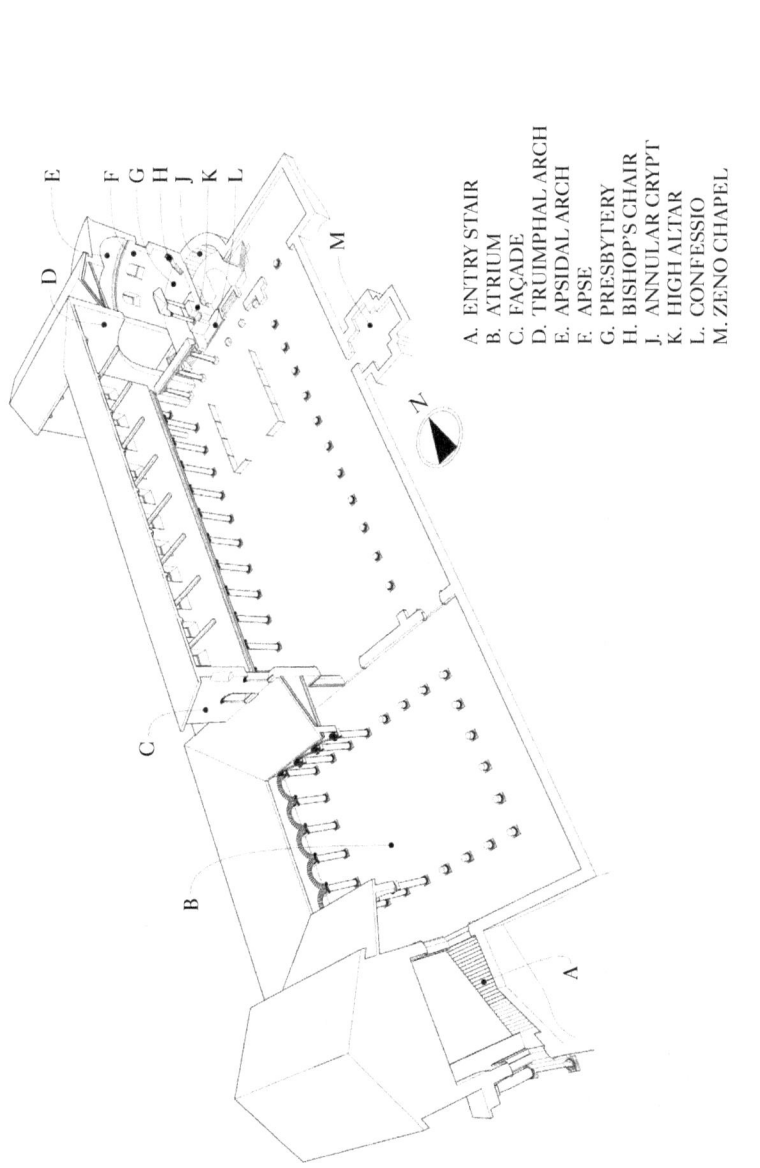

FIGURE 1.4 Rome, S. Prassede. Building information model (BIM) for imaging and visualization. By permission of Gregory J. MacNeil, Roderick J. MacNeil, Jerry MacNeil Architects Limited, Halifax, Nova Scotia.

A. ENTRY STAIR
B. ATRIUM
C. FAÇADE
D. TRUIMPHAL ARCH
E. APSIDAL ARCH
F. APSE
G. PRESBYTERY
H. BISHOP'S CHAIR
J. ANNULAR CRYPT
K. HIGH ALTAR
L. CONFESSIO
M. ZENO CHAPEL

conceals a well-lit interior of fine marble revetment. In the mind's eye the later diaphragm arches and coffered ceiling should be replaced by an open timber roof, the Renaissance murals above the nave colonnade "subtracted" along with all chapels except the Zeno. Inside the door and marked in the modern cosmatesque pavement (in 1914 replacing brick) is the well where, so the story goes, Praxedes poured the blood of the martyrs slain in her house-church. S. Prassede represents the most complete "copy" of Old St. Peter's made in Rome since St. Paul's Outside the Walls was erected by Theodosius I (ca. 380).[147]

A. The Zeno Chapel

Continuing in a northerly direction, halfway up the nave and drawn by the mosaics which shimmer from the triumphal and apsidal arches and apse, a small chapel opens to the east (see Gen 2:8). The Zeno Chapel has been called *hortus paradisi*, garden of paradise. Its façade hints at beauties within. The doorway is framed by columns carrying an antique entablature; above it a large third-century funerary urn dominates the round-headed aperture. The rectangular area above the entrance is a portrait gallery in mosaic, with roundels arranged in two roughly concentric arcs. On the outer arc against a blue ground are busts of Christ blessing and the twelve apostles. Mary Theotokos with Christ-child, accompanied by a deacon, a presbyter, and eight crowned women garbed in gold, occupy the inner golden horseshoe. Who are these women, whose presence balances the men?

In the small southern wing accessible from inside the Zeno Chapel stands a portion of the reputed column of the flagellation, brought from Constantinople in 1223 by S. Prassede's titular cardinal.[148] The column was the

---

147. For the classic presentation of his theory, see Richard Krautheimer, "The Carolingian Revival of Early Christian Architecture," *Art Bulletin* 24 (1942): 1–38. For S. Prassede's place within 8th- and 9th-century Rome, see Krautheimer, *Rome*, 123–27. A counter-position is presented by Valentino Pace, "La 'Felix culpa' di Richard Krautheimer: Roma, Santa Prassede e la 'rinascenza carolingia,'" in *Ecclesiae urbis: Atti del congresso internazionale di studi sulle chiese di Roma (IV–X secolo): Roma 4–10 settembre 2000*, ed. Federico Guidobaldi and Alessandra Guiglia Guidobaldi (3 vols.; Vatican City: PIAC, 2002), 1:65–72. See also Caroline Goodson, "Revival and Reality: The Carolingian Renaissance in Rome and the Case of S. Prassede," in Siri Sande and Lasse Hodne, eds., *Continuatio et Renovatio* (Acta ad archaeologiam et artium historiam pertinentia, 20 [n.s. 6]; Rome: Bardi Editore, 2006), 163–92.

148. Was this thought to be the column in Sion Church, which Antoninus of Pisa (ca. 570) reported as bearing the impression of Christ's chest and hands? Or even, according to the slightly earlier pilgrim Theodosius, his face? See Ernst Kitzinger, "The Cult of Images in the Age before

object of so much devotion that by 1714, and for some time before, the Zeno Chapel and its alcove had been off-limits to women "under pain of excommunication," except for the Sundays of Lent.[149] The first nave pier north of the entrance to the Zeno Chapel, in close proximity to the side entrance from Via di S. Prassede, carries a repaired two-piece marble plaque. In clear capitals its lengthy epigraphic inscription lists names and numbers of saints whose relics were interred in the church and monastery, to a total of 2,251. The plaque identifies the chapel as the place "where reposes the body of Paschal's very kindly mother, namely the lady Theodora *episcopa*," and Zeno with "two others."[150]

B. The Mosaic Program of the Church's Presbytery

The iconographic themes embellishing the presbytery end of the church are thoroughly Roman, of earlier Christian ancestry. In the presbytery the liturgical action is concentrated at lectern and altar. Here presider and people listen to God's word and, at the altar, pray for and anticipate the coming of Christ, participating in the eucharistic "bread from heaven."[151] This high-point of the interior, marked by triumphal arch, apsidal arch, and apse, with the crypt, might be designated the "(conventional) east end." Indeed the Zeno Chapel is oriented eastward in readiness for Christ's return in glory. However, the main body of the church is oriented to the north with, as Krautheimer notes, a slight lean toward the west, not much different from that of S. Maria Maggiore and other neighborhood churches.[152] Thanks to

---

Iconoclasm," in Ernst Kitzinger, *The Art of Byzantium and the Medieval West: Selected Studies*, ed. W. Eugene Kleinbauer (Bloomington: Indiana University Press, 1976), 91–156 at 104–5.

149. Davanzati (*Notizie al pellegrino*, 230–31) gives the text on a small sign above the door: "In questa Santa Cappella non possono entrare Donne sotto pena di scomunica." The chapel of Sts. Processus and Martinian in St. Peter's, also constructed by Paschal, shared this dubious threat (Davis, *Lives of Ninth-Century Popes*, 100.5, n. 15). It is not known in either case how ancient was the prohibition against women's entering.

150. Lines 36 to 39 read: "...Quocirca et in ipso ingressu basilicae manu dextra ubi utique benignissimae suae genetricis, scilicet domnae Theodorae episcopae, corpus quiescit...."

151. On the relation of the subject-matter of triumphal and apsidal arch programs to the mass as celebrated in the Roman rite, above all the Preface, Sanctus, and Roman canon, see Ursula Nilgen, "Die Bilder über dem Altar: Triumph- und Apsisbogenprogramme in Rom und Mittelitalien und ihr Bezug zur Liturgie," in Nicolas Bock, et al., eds., *Kunst und Liturgie im Mittelalter: Akten des Internationalen Kongresses der Bibliotheca Hertziana und des Nederlands Instituut te Rome, Rom, 28.-30. September 1997* (Munich: Hirmer, 2000), 75–90. Nilgen's perceptive reading of the eucharist better suits the late antique Roman liturgy when the iconographic formulae were developed than the Carolingian mass and its more remote presider.

152. Krautheimer, *CBCR* 3:238. Eastward orientation of churches is not characteristic of Rome, although theories about liturgical practice are still being promulgated based on this

numerous windows now closed up, the decorative ensembles of Paschal's church enjoyed much better natural lighting than at present.[153] The intricate mosaic program required a person of artistic sensitivity and theological acumen to guide the project from start to finish.

(i) Triumphal arch

The triumphal arch demarcating nave and presbytery was the first to be built in Rome since the fourth century. In the upper register mosaics show the heavenly city Jerusalem with people streaming toward it; in the spandrels, youths wave branches. What might be the pictorial sources? Catacomb depictions of the deceased banqueting with a few others in the celestial Jerusalem are known, while the walled cities of Bethlehem and Jerusalem, symbols of the mysteries of Christ's incarnation, death, and resurrection, are frequent fillers for the awkward lower space in apsidal arch spandrels. But the ambitious subject-matter of the S. Prassede triumphal arch is novel in this position and in its narrative character. On the top register, from far left and right, led by two magnificent angels with wings unfurled, two groups of people approach the walls of Jerusalem the golden whose open gates more angels guard. Walls built of precious stones surround the standing figure of Christ flanked by angel attendants. From the left come five apostles led by Paul and John the Baptist, all carrying crowns, with the interceding Theotokos in front. Daringly and uniquely, the interceding patron Praxedes leads Peter and the remaining apostles who converge from the right. In the plane behind this apostolic procession stand two male figures and a red-robed angel. Proportionally larger figures of Peter with key and Paul with *rotulus* are placed between the right-hand gate and the oncoming crowd. On the spandrels forming a

---

misconception. Like Greek temples before them, Constantinian basilicas were occidented. Sible de Blaauw (*Cultus et decor* 1:96) notes that later Roman churches are oriented in every direction. Many Roman churches have north-facing apses to allow, in my view, the rays of the rising and setting sun to illuminate the mosaics of apse and arches to best advantage during mass and vespers. S. Prassede is described as occidented by Judson J. Emerick, "Focusing on the Celebrant: the Column Display inside Santa Prassede," in *Mededelingen van het Nederlands Instituut te Rome* 59 (2001): 129–59 at 153, n. 5. However, this last strategy is confusing. Northward orientation allowed for the best possible lighting of the mosaics in the presbyterium and symbolic lighting from the east of the Zeno Chapel. The slight westward lean may be a nod to the westward orientation of Old St. Peter's and other Constantinian basilicas.

153. Krautheimer, *CBCR* 3:250.

lower register, interrupted by the sweep of the arch, white-robed youths on a gold ground wave martyrs' palms and acclaim Christ's theophany.[154]

Various explanations of this novel subject-matter have been proposed.[155] Among them is the actual translation of the bones of nearly 2,300 martyrs, brought by Paschal from various cemeteries around Rome and interred with his own hands.[156] Similarly, Joseph Dyer proposes as sources Old Roman antiphons sung at the burial of relics during the dedication of a church.[157] Entry into the heavenly city by Paschal and the Carolingian emperor and empress with their people to celebrate the heavenly liturgy; or, conversely, an image of heavenly Jerusalem representing Pope Paschal's assertion of the reign of the triune God as already realized in the church of Rome and confronting the power of the Carolingian emperor, have been quasi-political explanations.[158] But surely these are the leaders, patrons, and members of our two second-century house-churches who hasten toward the new Jerusalem.

(ii) Apsidal arch

The triumphal arch, which for the lay spectator forms the foreground plane with its expansive picture of the heavenly Jerusalem, frames the second plane consisting of the apsidal arch on the chord of the apse. The symbols of heavenly Jerusalem displayed here represent the liturgy of heaven. The Lamb as protagonist lies majestically enthroned (Rev 7:17) amid seven candlesticks, the four living creatures, and seven angelic spirits. With the

---

154. Tabernacles for the display of relics, dating from St. Carlo Borromeo (1538–84, titular cardinal from 1564), have mutilated the lower mosaic panels, the part with the youths.

155. A predecessor to portions of S. Prassede's triumphal arch is the fresco of the "Crucifixion with seraphs, angels and the blessed of all nations" on the upper wall above the apse of S. Maria Antiqua. See Per Jonas Nordhagen, *The Frescoes of John VII (A.D. 705–707) in S. Maria Antiqua in Rome*, ed. Hans Peter L'Orange and Hjalmar Torp; Institutum Romanum Norvegiae. Acta ad archaeologiam et artium historiam pertinentia 3 (Rome: Bretschneider, 1968), 43–54 and pl. 153. Other aspects are found in Carolingian and Ottonian mss. (51).

156. Giovanni Severano, *Memorie sacre delle sette chiese di Roma* (Rome: Giacoma Mascardi, 1630). Marchita B. Mauck ("The Mosaic of the Triumphal Arch of S. Prassede: A Liturgical Interpretation," *Speculum* 62 [1987]: 813–28) proposes the funerary antiphon *In paradisum* and imperial *adventus* ceremonial as sources.

157. Joseph Dyer, "Prolegomena to a History of Music and Liturgy at Rome in the Middle Ages," in Graeme M. Boone, ed., *Essays on Medieval Music in Honour of David G. Hughes* (Cambridge, MA: Harvard University Press, 1995), 87–116, at 94–99.

158. Rotraut Wisskirchen, *Das Mosaikprogramm von S. Prassede in Rom: Ikonographie und Ikonologie* ([Münster Westfalen: Aschendorff, 1990], 124–25) explores iconographic sources.

twenty-four elders in the spandrels, the symbols display serene aspects of the book of Revelation. The Bible's final book recapitulates its beginning, promising for the faithful a part in the new creation and, for food and drink, fruit of the tree of life and the water of eternal life. Roman church walls prominent in the early fifth century—the façade of Old St. Peter's and the triumphal arch of St. Paul's—had displayed key elements of this vision: angels, candlesticks, the four living creatures functioning as a code for the heavenly liturgy of Revelation's visions (Rev 4, 5, 7, 14, and 19). What more suitable subject-matter could surround the altar at which the church celebrates the earthly liturgy?

Until the renovations inaugurated in 1729, the apsidal arch framed a Carolingian altar and canopy much smaller than the present one commissioned by Cardinal Ludovico Pico della Mirandola, who bore the title of Cardinal of Santa Prassede from 1728–1731 and was responsible for maintaining the church's fabric.[159] In the middle of the presbytery the altar rose above an annular crypt inspired by Gregory the Great's design for St. Peter's presbyterium.[160] Like the altar at Old St. Peter's, the one at S. Prassede was almost certainly screened in a fastigium arrangement by the six delicately carved antique columns now engaged in the presbytery's side walls. The "Petrine"-style crypt, filled in around 1450 and only rediscovered in 1729, is now mostly intact but for the shaft under the altar containing the relics collected from many cemeteries. From the evening of 2 January 1729, into early May of 1730 the altar and the burial-crypt beneath it were dismantled under the aegis of Pope Benedict XIII Orsini (29 May 1724–21 February 1730) and Cardinal Ludovico Pico della Mirandola (titular 1728–1731).

(iii) Apse

From any vantage point in the nave, Cardinal Pico della Mirandola's altar ciborium partially hides the apse mosaic. Nevertheless, viewers making their way through the church cannot fail to identify the culmination of the

---

For illustrations, see Wisskirchen, "Die Mosaiken der Kirche Santa Prassede in Rom," *Antike Welt: Zeitschrift für Archäologie und Kulturgeschichte*, Jahrgang 23, Sondernummer; Mainz am Rhein: Phillip von Zabern, 1992.

159. Sheltered from the elements, remnants of Paschal's canopy are now attached to the wall above the stairs that give entry to the atrium. For details, see Goodson, *Rome of Pope Paschal I*, 129.

160. While still papal secretary, Gregory I (590–604) may have devised this ingenious solution to the disruption of liturgical services, crowding, and relic-snatching caused by pilgrims (Krautheimer, *Rome*, 86 and fig. 70). For reconstruction of the Old St. Peter's martyrium area in its 2nd-century Constantinian and Gregorian phases, see Jocelyn Toynbee and John Ward Perkins, *The Shrine of St. Peter and the Vatican Excavations* (London: Longmans, Green,

artistic program. As the shallow apse does for the building's exterior, so the apsidal mosaic, framed as it is by richly decorated triumphal and apsidal arches, functions as the visual and conceptual high point to proclaim the building's raison-d'être. Its message was one reiterated in Roman church apses from the time figural decoration was introduced into the earliest Roman patriarchal basilicas. The risen Christ giving the law to Peter and Paul is an iconographic scheme originating in imperial circles around the year 350 that became a popular one for apses in Rome and Latium from circa 400. Many partial small-scale copies suggest its famous prototype to be the apse mosaic of Old St. Peter's. There the Lord's imperial gesture of *adlocutio* evokes an acclamatory response from Paul (in the place of honor at the Lord's right hand), while Peter on the left is handed a scroll symbolizing the Law. This positioning of Paul and Peter was the iconographic pattern in Rome until the thirteenth century. The subject is not that of Christ conferring papal primacy on Peter but rather the bestowal of collaborative leadership ministry on the two apostolic princes, apostles to Gentiles and Jews respectively, whose martyrdoms in Rome were the charter-event that founded the church at Rome. The iconography arose in the relatively brief period when popular devotion linked the two apostles in the mission of spreading the gospel.[161]

The naturalistic apse mosaic of SS. Cosma e Damiano beside the Forum, a consular audience hall renovated around 528, changes the no-longer-meaningful juridical *Traditio legis* iconography of Old St. Peter's into a gesture of simple acclamation by the apostolic princes, who introduce the crown-carrying healers to the Lord coming on the clouds.[162] We saw that S. Prassede's apse mosaic takes this iconography in a daringly affectionate

---

1956). Besides inspiring similar arrangements north of the Alps, the design survives in Rome in a well-preserved "copy" at S. Pancrazio on the Via Aurelia, built by Honorius I (625–638); Krautheimer, *CBCR* 3:153–74.

161. Krautheimer (*Rome*, 40, 205) avers that St. Peter's *Traditio legis* apse mosaic, originally "unadorned gold ground," was late 4th century and that the early 5th-century apses of the Lateran and S. Paolo displayed this same theme. S. Paolo's triumphal arch, after an earthquake or fire in 441, carried the 24 elders offering their wreaths to Christ. See C. Davis-Weyer, "Das Traditio-Legis Bild und seine Nachfolge," *Münchner Jahrbuch der bildenden Kunst* 12 (1961): 7–45. W.N. Schumacher ("'Dominus legem dat,'" *RQ* 54 [1959]: 1–39) emphasizes the imperial content of the "handing on of the Law" iconography and its close connection with the Easter liturgy. Hellemo (*Adventus Domini*) treats the mystagogical meaning of these early iconographic schemes.

162. SS. Cosma e Damiano affords the earliest surviving monumental *Traditio legis*–based iconography in Rome, modified so that the apostolic princes present saints to Christ.

direction. Instead of acclaiming Christ, the two prince-apostles, each with an arm about the shoulders of the two women saints Praxedes and Pudentiana, introduce them to the arriving Lord.[163] The living pope and his attendant deacon (Timothy, Zeno, or most likely Stephen, proto-deacon of Jerusalem) stand at either end.[164] Lambs approaching the Lamb, and the Jordan River, are formulaic elements. At S. Prassede the traditional date palms are remnants of imperial symbolism; a phoenix symbolizes the resurrection.[165] In a paradisal landscape, the four rivers flow into the mystical Jordan, *fluvium aquae vitae* (Rev 22:5) and symbol of baptism. From the cities of Bethlehem and Jerusalem, twelve lambs symbolizing the "twelve apostles of the Lamb" (Rev 21:14) process to the Lamb standing on Mount Zion (Rev 14:1).

Conclusion

What moved Paschal to commission this first church of his pontificate, which displayed, next to S. Maria Maggiore's mosaics, the most extensive Christian Roman mosaic program prior to 1200? Walking from the entrance portico on the Via di S. Martino up the steps and through the atrium to the door, then traversing the thirty-six-meter-long nave, has brought the observant visitor of the present day from a space evocative

---

163. The next stage in this iconographical notion is found in the artistically weaker S. Cecilia mosaic, also commissioned by Paschal. Uniformly gaunt apostles present themselves while Cecilia, one arm affectionately about the shoulders of Paschal, presents the pope! For Cecilia's predilection for Paschal, see the dream-episode recounted in the papal biography (Davis, *Lives of Ninth-Century Popes*, 100.15–17, 19–21).

164. Davanzati (*Notizie al pellegrino*, 314) attributed to Clement I the legislation that no pope (as a bishop) celebrates without a deacon. Krautheimer (*Rome*, 126) identified the deacon garbed in a dalmatic embellished with Maltese crosses as Praxedes' "brother" Timothy. But if this saint serves as deacon to the reigning pontiff opposite, can he be the presbyter Timothy of our story? Likewise Zeno, a Roman martyr whose relics were brought from the Praetextatus catacomb, was presbyter not deacon. The proto-deacon Stephen was proposed by Margo Pautler Klass, "The Chapel of S. Zeno in S. Prassede in Rome" (Ph.D. thesis, Bryn Mawr College, 1972), 17. Paschal had been abbot of the monastery and pilgrim hostel dedicated to St. Stephen behind St. Peter's (Davis, *Lives of Ninth-Century Popes*, 100.2, n. 6). Llewellyn (*Rome in the Dark Ages*, 137) had noted the popularity of Stephen, proto-martyr and proto-deacon, as patron of churches and monasteries in the 7th and 8th centuries, and the contemporary development of *diaconiae*. See also Bowersock, *Martyrdom and Rome*, 75–76, and esp. Marios Costambeys and Conrad Leyser, "To Be the Neighbour of St. Stephen: Patronage, Martyr Cult, and Roman Monasteries, c. 600–c. 900," in Cooper and Hillner, *Religion, Dynasty, and Patronage*, 262–87, at 277–85. The essay treats the *Revelatio Stephani* and Augustine (see *City of God* 22.8 and 9) on the power of St. Stephen's relics in the context of miracles wrought by martyrs.

165. Hellemo, *Adventus Domini*, 75.

of the early Christian house-church through the era of the Constantinian Petrine basilica and into a careful Carolingian "imitation" of Christianity's golden ages. As the visitor walks toward the front, he or she approaches the great heavenly communion of saints signaled by the triumphal arch above and the innumerable bones once buried in the crypt. In the presbytery, the altar with its canopy, framed by the apsidal arch, highlights the intimate relationship of earthly and heavenly liturgies. Finally, the goal of the earthly pilgrimage is given visual expression in the majestic depiction of the risen and triumphant Christ, returning as eschatological judge at the end of the ages. At the heart of this triumphal scene are two women, Praxedes and Pudentiana, protagonists in the formation of faith during the age of the martyrs in Rome.

Erwin Panofsky, in his classic study of the iconography of the visual arts, distinguishes primary or natural subject matter (factual and expressional, constituting the world of artistic motifs) and secondary or conventional subject-matter (constituting the world of images, stories, and allegories) as strata pointing to their intrinsic meaning, the world of "symbolical" values. According to Panofsky, the interpreter falls back on "synthetic intuition, (familiarity with the essential tendencies of the human mind), conditioned by personal psychology and *Weltanschauung*" to understand the original creation.[166] In sifting through those factors that contributed to Paschal's *Weltanschauung*, the scholar's intuition plays a role, as does painstaking retrieval of all the "information" that contributes to the religious mentality of a person of a certain formation and role in a particular place and historical period. Retrieval of the cultural, spiritual, and cultic elements that shaped Paschal's mindset as commissioner of this remarkable building, as well as the factual underpinnings that help to account for the longevity and relevance of S. Prassede's foundation myth, are goals of the following chapters.

---

166. Erwin Panofsky, *Studies in Iconology: Humanistic Themes in the Art of the Renaissance* (New York: Oxford University Press, 1939), 14–15.

2

Iconography and Sources of S. Prassede's Decorative Cycles

WITH ITS IMPOSING fifth-century neighbor S. Maria Maggiore, the church of S. Prassede provides the richest of all intact figural cycles in Rome prior to 1200. Subjects drawn from the book of Revelation, which decorate the apses and arches of many Roman churches prior to 1300, have been given an especially complex treatment in S. Prassede's apse and apsidal and triumphal arches. As well, the thematically related upper parts of the gleaming Zeno Chapel, at once martyrs' shrine and mausoleum, have survived mostly unscathed.

The iconoclastic movement, by those who opposed the use of images in religious worship, impacted S. Prassede's extensive mosaic programs.[1] Iconoclastic controversy had convulsed Byzantium in 726–786 but lain dormant after the Council of Nicaea II in 787 reversed the stance of the iconoclastic council of 754. During the first iconoclastic period, Byzantine monks fled to Rome where they were received into existing Greek monasteries.[2] In 767 an encyclical from the East condemning the iconoclasts had been sent to

---

1. James R. Payton, Jr., "Iconoclasm (Controversy)," *Encyclopedia of Monasticism* (Chicago: Fitzroy Dearborn, 2000), 1:633–34; Gerhart B. Ladner, "Origin and Significance of the Byzantine Iconoclastic Controversy," *MS* 2 (1940): 127–49; Jaroslav Pelikan, *The Christian Tradition*, Vol. 2: *The Spirit of Eastern Christendom (600–1700)* (Chicago: University of Chicago Press, 1974), 91–145; John Julius Norwich, *A Short History of Byzantium* (London: Penguin, 1998); Kenneth Parry, *Depicting the Word: Byzantine Iconophile Thought of the Eighth and Ninth Centuries* (Leiden: E. J. Brill, 1996) (Leiden; New York; Cologne: E. J. Brill, 1996). For texts, see Cyril Mango, *The Art of the Byzantine Empire 312–1453* (Englewood, NJ: Prentice-Hall, 1972), 149–77; Daniel J. Sahas, trans., *Icon and Logos* (Toronto: University of Toronto Press, 1986); Crispino Valenziano, "Iconismo e aniconismo occidentale postniceno: dai Libri Carolini al secolo XIII," *EO* 13 (1996): 11–42; "Iconismo e aniconismo occidentale postniceno: il 'caso serio' della croce nel secolo XIII," *EO* 13 (1996): 185–206.

2. F. Antonelli, "I primi monasteri di monaci orientali in Roma," *RAC* 5 (1928): 105–21; H. Marrou, "L'origine orientale des diaconies romaines," *MEFRA* 57 (1940): 95–142; Ferrari, *Early Roman Monasteries*, 39, 355–61.

Iconography and Sources 53

Pope Paul I and read at a Lateran council in 769. Together with the Eastern patriarchates of Alexandria, Antioch, and Jerusalem, Rome sided with the icon-lovers. The letters of Pope Hadrian I (772–795) had represented the Roman doctrine on images to the Byzantine empress Irene and to the patriarch.[3] Iconoclasm was again revived in less severe form in Constantinople between 813 and 843. Paschal I was the recipient of correspondence from Theodore (759–826), abbot of the Stoudite monastery in Constantinople and staunch defender of images. It had been intended for Pope Leo III (795–816), but Leo died in 816 and Paschal occupied the see in 817.[4] The revival of the art of mosaic by Roman craftspeople surely received impetus from the icon-debates with the East. Like Paul I (757–767) before him, Paschal provided asylum to refugee Eastern monks.[5] In this, the less severe persecution, the monastery of S. Prassede was built by Paschal for these refugees, and the church of SS. Stefano e Cassiano, near St. Lawrence's Outside the Walls, was handed over to be staffed by Greek monks.[6]

In the same period, the Carolingian rulers, themselves barely literate and striving to educate a recently baptized people, looked to the see of Rome, not only for religious leadership and cultural norms, but also for the shoring up of imperial claims.[7] In 754 Pepin and his sons had been

---

3. At the time of Nicaea II (787). *LP* presents Hadrian's letter as the occasion of the great council (Davis, *Lives of Eighth Century Popes*, 97.88; Mansi 12:1056–72). The Franks, both emperor and bishops, took a very different view on the matter of images and orthodoxy; see Ann Freeman, "Carolingian Orthodoxy and the Fate of the Libri Carolini," *Viator* 16 (1985): 65–108.

4. Peter Hatlie, "Theodore of Stoudios, St.," *EM* 2:1252–53. Paschal's contribution to the defense of icons both in the West and in papal relations in the East is treated by Erik Thunø, *Image and Relic: Mediating the Sacred in Early Medieval Rome* (Analecta Romana Instituti Danici, Suppl. 32; Rome: "L'Erma" di Bretschneider, 2002), 132–41 and passim.

5. For relations between the East and the papacy, see Francis Dvornik, *Les Slaves, Byzance et Rome au IXe siècle* (Paris: H. Champion, 1926), 123–24 and Dvornik, *Byzantium and the Roman Primacy*. The Greek monasteries in Rome are treated by Dvornik, *Les légendes de Constantin et de Méthode vues de Byzance* (2nd ed.; Hattiesburg, MS: Academic International, 1969), 286–300. For letters to Paschal I, see Theodore of Stoudios (the Stoudite), *Theodori Studitai Epistulae*, ed. Georgios Fatouros (Berlin: Walter de Gruyter, [1991] 1992,), 399–403.

6. On the persecution of Eastern monks, whose piety was especially linked to the veneration of images, see Paul J. Alexander, "Religious Persecution and Resistance in the Byzantine Empire of the Eighth and Ninth Centuries: Methods and Justifications," *Speculum* 52 (1997): 238–64.

7. Krautheimer, "Carolingian Revival of Early Christian Architecture," 1–38, reprinted in Krautheimer, *Studies*, 203–56. On manuscripts, see Robert G. Calkins, *Illuminated Books of the Middle Ages* (Ithaca, NY: Cornell University Press, 1983), 93–94; Florentine Mütherich, "Die Buchmalerei am Hofe Karls des Grossen," in *Karl der Grosse: Lebenswerk und Nachleben*, vol. 3: *Karolingische Kunst* (Düsseldorf: Schwann, 1965), 9–53.

anointed kings of the Franks by Pope Stephen II in the abbey church of St. Denis outside Paris.[8] A challenge to the Eastern Roman empire was posed when, on Christmas Day 800, Pope Leo III (795–816) crowned Charles the Great emperor of the Romans in St. Peter's. One author refers to the "complex series of geopolitical negotiations between Rome, Aachen, and Constantinople" during the papacy of Leo III.[9] Especially with respect to old and early Christian Rome, artistic negotiations went hand-in-hand with political manoeuvres.

Completed within the first years of a seven-year pontificate, the decorative programs for S. Prassede's presbyterium (the area reserved for the ministerial action of the eucharistic liturgy) and the Byzantine-style Zeno Chapel are intimately related in theme. Art historians have tended to interpret the two mosaic programs as if they were somewhat separate artistic endeavours. This chapter will analyze the iconography and its sources for both the church's liturgical focus—the triumphal arch and presbyterium at S. Prassede's north end—and the mausoleum-chapel. Reexamination of the biblical and liturgical witnesses will suggest some refinements to iconographic identifications and theories proposed so far by art historians. But my main purpose is to explicate iconology: the interpretation of subject-matter to discover a monument's deep meaning, in this case the foundation myth underlying Paschal's commission and his relation to it.[10] This myth gave birth to presbyterium and chapel programs together. The liturgy celebrated in the main body of the church recalled the death and resurrection of Jesus Christ, foundational faith-events for Christian believers, and animated the assembly's proleptic experience of their own hoped-for future: communion with God through Christ. Analogously, the figural decoration in the main body of the church imaged the expected future toward which its community of believers journeyed together. The mausoleum-shrine linked a revered family member's mortal remains with saintly relics so that, assisted by the saints' intercession, the anticipated salvation of soul and body might be realized after the pattern of Jesus Christ. Both mosaic programs reached

---

8. For capsule reviews of the political situation during each papacy, see Davis, *Lives of Eighth- Century Popes*, passim; on Pepin's crowning, ibid., 94.27 and n. 64.

9. Peter Hatlie, "Theodore of Stoudios, Pope Leo III and the Joseph Affair (808–812): New Light on an Obscure Negotiation," *OCP* 61 (1995): 413.

10. Wisskirchen (*Das Mosaikprogramm von S. Prassede in Rom*) treats iconology in part 3, but the results of her inquiry are partial. By "myth" I mean the story that explains the origins of the church of S. Prassede and its sister-church, S. Pudenziana, through the lives of their donors and leaders.

before and beyond the moment of immediate visual appreciation. Corporate liturgical and personal devotional dimensions were allotted their own space. Interpretation took place in the ambience peculiar to Latin theologians and the Roman church: realized and future eschatology.

Nearly a century's hiatus in mosaic art followed the Greek Pope John VII (705–707).[11] Leo III's no-longer-extant mosaic commission at S. Susanna (795–799), the Lateran triclinium (798–799), the restorations at S. Maria Maggiore (ca. 809), and the apse and arch of SS. Nereo ed Achilleo (ca. 814) near the Caracalla baths marked a renewal of work in mosaic.[12] To Paschal can be ascribed the maturation of this revived art in the city. His ambitious programs, well preserved at S. Prassede and its Zeno Chapel and S. Maria in Domnica, and relatively so at S. Cecilia in Trastevere, were inspired by Roman and Ravennate models of the Constantinian period and later. The pictorial sources are chosen with assurance, originality showing itself in the triumphal arch narrative, individuation of facial features, and iconography that will become characteristic of the Greek East. In Krautheimer's judgment the mosaic technique marks a return to early Christian Roman use of glass tesserae.[13] The renascence taking place under Paschal's direction was not the first to occur during the Carolingian period, but now the initiative had shifted from emperor to pope. Artistic momentum was maintained into the second half of the ninth century with improved construction techniques, and dozens of buildings and mosaics were its result.[14]

---

11. Walter Oakeshott, *The Mosaics of Rome from the Third to the Fourteenth centuries* (London: Thames and Hudson, 1967), 143–94, esp.155–59.

12. Oakeshott, *Mosaics of Rome*, 200–2; Krautheimer, *Rome*, 115–17. An apsidal arch wall decorated with the 24 elders and, lower down, youths waving palm branches were once part of the Lateran triclinium. See Mauck, "Mosaic of Triumphal Arch of S. Prassede," 813–28 and n. 16, citing Caecilia Davis-Weyer, "Die Mosaiken Leos III und die Anfänge der karolingischen Renaissance in Rom," *Zeitschrift für Kunstgeschichte* 39 (1966): 128, fig. 26. The triclinium was probably the proximate model for the lower sections of S. Prassede's apsidal and triumphal arch walls, although the façade of Old St. Peter's (perhaps under Pope Leo I), and the apsidal arch wall of SS. Cosma e Damiano showed the 24 elders. The latter church (526–530), now with a truncated triumphal arch, was the iconographic source for S. Prassede's apse and apsidal wall compositions. On restorations, see Susan Spain-Alexander, "Carolingian Restorations of S. Maria Maggiore in Rome," *Gesta* 16 (1997): 13–21; Krautheimer, *CBCR* 3 (1967): 58; Agnese Guerrieri, *La Chiesa dei SS. Nereo ed Achilleo* (Vatican City: PIAC, 1951), fig. 33.

13. Mackie ("Zeno Chapel," 196–98) summarizes the researches of Per Jonas Nordhagen and Richard Krautheimer and points out that Paschal's mosaics as well as his buildings were constructed of materials recycled from Roman and early Christian antiquity.

14. Krautheimer (*Rome*, 109–42) reviews this latter period.

S. Prassede's figural program represents a creative exercise in ecclesial memory passed on from generation to generation by local hagiographic and liturgical traditions and benefits as well from the infusion of foreign influences. The iconographically unique features point, throughout the process of design and execution, to the active participation of an artistically sensitive patron whose commission was surely intended as a statement to counteract the iconoclasm newly revived (813) in Byzantium. They express in visual symbols what popes Hadrian I, Leo III, and Paschal had upheld as the doctrine concerning images. A letter written by Paschal about 818 to the iconoclast emperor Leo V (813–820) asks, "If God detests images, why do we consider it our highest prerogative to be made after the image of God?"[15]

The second-last grouping of epistles in the Christian Testament—the Pastoral Letters and the brief letter to Philemon—inspired the framework for the story of the Pudens clan. The textual sources for the mosaic programs are the eschatologically freighted Scriptures that conclude the New Testament (Hebrews and especially *apocalypsis beati Joannis apostoli*).[16] The letter to the Hebrews and the book of Revelation play the central role in the *Formgestalt* or structural shape of the liturgy of Catholic churches, while the four-square Zeno Chapel likewise has its biblical sources attuned to the liturgy.

1. Revelation and Hebrews, Presbyterium and Transept Mosaics, and Their Theological Construct

The remarkable program at S. Prassede's north end (mosaics high up in the apse and apsidal arch of the presbyterium, marble revetment closer to the floor, and triumphal arch embellished with mosaic demarcating nave from transept) provides an interpretive frame and a kind of proscenium arch for the eucharistic liturgy (Fig. 2.1). In churches of both East and West the deep structure, depth-dimension or "mystery-content"

---

15. Mackie, "Zeno Chapel," 196, citing Giovanni Mercati, *Note di Letteratura Biblica e Cristiana Antica* (Rome: Tipografia vaticana, 1901), 227–35.

16. Hebrews is characterized in the Vulgate as *Epistola beati Pauli apostoli ad Hebraeos*. For the popularity of the book of Revelation (Apocalypse) from the later 8th to the mid-11th century, see C. Heitz, "Retentissement de l'Apocalypse dans l'art de l'époque carolingienne," in *Roma e l'età carolingia: Atti delle giornate di studio, 3–8 maggio 1976*, ed. Istituto di storia dell'arte dell'Università di Roma (Rome: Multigrafica editrice, 1976), 217–43. For an accessible guide to the book of Revelation, see Frederick J. Murphy, *Fallen is Babylon: The Revelation to John* (Harrisburg, PA: Trinity Press International, 1998).

FIGURE 2.1 Rome, S. Prassede. North (presbytery) end with triumphal and apsidal arches and apse. Scala/Art Resource, NY.

of Christian liturgy has been explained by reference to Hebrews with its doctrine of Christ's priesthood, and to Revelation, with special emphasis on the book's great visions.[17] Christian liturgical-sacramental theology understands that there are always two levels operating in the church's liturgy: the human ritual action and the act of divine bestowal. The church prays that its human social action, a ritualized expression of the community's faith, will be transparent for God's salvific act in Jesus Christ. The Holy Spirit enlivens the faith of the church, which is constituted of the personal faith-acts of believers over time as well as across space, in such a way that the two levels of human and divine action interact to initiate and deepen the divine-human encounter. Through the ritualized choreography of the ministers, the action at ambo and altar, the chants and responses of the choir, and the participatory presence of an assembly that responds

---

17. Terms are drawn respectively from linguistics, Tillichian theology, and the liturgical theology of the Benedictine Odo Casel (d. 1948) to indicate God's action in worship.

with hymn and acclamation, the liturgical-ecclesial event engages the participant in a multifaceted communal symbol.[18]

Over time, activated by the actual experience of liturgical worship, its choreography and texts, Hebrews and Revelation provided the biblical sources for a Christian theology of worship that was expressed in symbolic imagery long before it was given systematic articulation.[19] "Descending christology/ecclesiology" (derived from Revelation) and "ascending christology/ecclesiology" (derived from Hebrews) typify the twofold theological movement of the S. Prassede's christology and ecclesiology as expressed in artistic form. Apse, apsidal arch wall, and the heavenly city's descent on the triumphal arch express the construct "descending christology." "Ascending christology" lies behind the texts of the early Roman canon of the mass, parts of which may predate even the declaration of the Holy Spirit's equality with Father and Son made at the Council of Constantinople (381).[20]

---

18. In visualizing this compound symbol one must start, not with the experience of half-empty titular churches whose pews or chairs isolate members of the assembly, but with the papal stational liturgy on a major feastday. The Ash Wednesday liturgy, held annually at S. Sabina on the Aventine hill, was preceded in the 8th century by a formal *collecta* or gathering at S. Anastasia on the plain below, then a procession with pope and ministers up the steep hill. In S. Sabina there was barely room to stand or to breathe. Only the fenced-off presbytery provided some measure of space for the ministers. The communion of the people was a mêlée. In such circumstances "presence" takes on very concrete dimensions.

19. Hans-Joachim Schulz, *The Byzantine Liturgy: Symbolic Structure and Faith Expression* (New York: Pueblo, 1986); Edward J. Kilmartin, *Christian Liturgy: Theology and Practice*, part 1: *Systematic Theology of Liturgy* (Kansas City, MO: Sheed & Ward, 1988). For examples, see Mary M. Schaefer, "Heavenly and Earthly Liturgies: Patristic Prototypes, Medieval Perspectives and a Contemporary Application," *Worship* 70 (1996): 482–505.

20. "Descending christology" is technical terminology for the perspective that the divine Word took on human flesh in Jesus, whose person, while fully human, is determined by his divinity. I coin the term "descending ecclesiology" to convey the perspective that God's plan is realized when the heavenly Church descends to the earthly sphere. "Ascending" or "Spirit-christology" emphasizes the Spirit's role in anointing the humanity of Jesus as Son of God. It views Jesus from the side of his humanity and thus of his priesthood. My coined term "ascending ecclesiology" expresses the idea that the earthly, fallible church is drawn toward its future, which will only be fully realized when the Lord returns in power. In this way eschatology (that which comes from the future) determines the earthly, present age. The gospel accounts of Jesus' baptism in the Jordan depict the Spirit descending to rest on him as beloved Son (Mark 1:9–11; Matt 3:13–17; Luke 3:21–22; John 1:32–34). Key texts for ascending christology are found in Heb 4:15, 5:7–10, according to which Christ the high priest was subject to human weakness, even temptation, before achieving perfection. See Mary M. Schaefer, "Presence of the Trinity: Relationship or Idea?," *Liturgical Ministry* 19 (2010): 145–56.

Edward J. Kilmartin reviews current official ecclesiastical and scholarly thought on the modes of Christ's presence in the liturgy:

> New Testament sources locate the risen Lord at the right hand of God. A solemn confession of this aspect of the implications of the glorification of Jesus is found in Revelation and the Epistle to the Hebrews. The former source describes the heavenly liturgy already in progress; the latter speaks of Jesus' investiture as High Priest of the new covenant, associated with his entrance into the heavenly sanctuary.

"God's right hand," Kilmartin continues, expresses "the idea that the risen Lord rules all history, that he is present to the world in power (Acts 2:33–36; Col 1:15–20)."[21] Christ's cosmic presence is complemented by another mode: the risen Lord's personal presence to believers as they express the community's faith by word and deed. Revelation and Hebrews contain a Spirit-christology that acknowledges Christ's active presence through the Spirit in and to the community.[22] Using Revelation symbols, Roman apsidal programs express the unity of the liturgy taking place in heaven with the sacrifice of praise offered *per Christum dominum nostrum* by the Christian assembly at its earthly altar. Ursula Nilgen ably develops the symbolic content of the mass.[23] Somewhat less visibly than Revelation, the letter to the Hebrews also stands behind S. Prassede's liturgical-decorative schemes. In the triumphal arch mosaic the heavenward movement of the letter to the Hebrews—theological inspiration for the christology that informs Roman liturgy—is conjoined iconographically with Revelation's theme of New Jerusalem coming down to earth.

---

21. Kilmartin, *Christian Liturgy*, 303–4.

22. Irenaeus of Lyons' famous phrase, "by the hands of the Father, that is, through the Son and the Spirit" (*Against Heresies* 6.1, in Irenaeus (Irénée), Bishop of Lyons, *Contre les hérésies*, ed., trans., and annotated by A. Rousseau and L. Doutreleau, V, 2. [Paris: Editions du Cerf, 1969], 72–73) captures graphically the theological notion that the risen Christ and the Holy Spirit act conjointly. The notion of God's active presence in the biblical word is conveyed by Hebrews' famous text on the word of God as "something alive and active" (Heb 4:12–13; cf. Isa 49:2). On Christ's *Aktualpräsenz*, his living and active presence, see Heb 2:2 (cf. Ps 22:2), 2:10, 4:14, 12:2, 13:20 and Rev 1:1, 1:5, 1:13–20, 3:20–21, 7:17, 8:1, 17:14, 19:11–13, 22:13. On the Spirit's activity, see Heb 3:7–8, 6:4, 9:8, 10:15 and Rev 2:7, 2:11, 17, 3:13, 3:22, 15:3–4, 22:17. The letter of Jude 20–21 exhorts his community to "pray in the Holy Spirit; keep yourselves in the love of God; look forward to the mercy of our Lord Jesus Christ that leads to eternal life."

23. Nilgen, "Bilder über dem Altar," 75–90.

A. Apse: The Risen Christ's Return in Glory

The book of "[t]he revelation of Jesus Christ" (Rev 1:1) is best known for its visions of God and the Lamb receiving the adoration of the hosts of heaven and earth, and of the conflict between the powers of good and evil. The visions are the focus of the S. Prassede program. In Revelation's first chapter, the seer John says of Christ, the one who loves his people, that he has liberated them from sin and made them to be a kingdom and priests serving God (Rev 1:6): "Look! He is coming with the clouds; every eye will see him, even those who pierced him..." (Rev 1:7). In the midst of seven golden lampstands stood "one like the Son of Man, clothed with a long robe and with a golden sash across his chest...In his right hand he held seven stars, and from his mouth came a sharp, two-edged sword...." The Pierced One said to the seer, "Do not be afraid; I am the first and the last, and the living one. I was dead, and see, I am alive forever and ever" (Rev 1:12–13, 16, 17–18). Through the seer John, Christ the faithful witness dictated messages to the seven churches.

At S. Prassede the Christ who is coming soon (Rev 22:12, 20) is not absent from the world he has redeemed. He is already "actively present" by his word and through those who believe in and follow him, who have been baptized in the river Jordan that flows at the feet of the seven monumental figures in the apse: Paschal, Praxedes, Paul, Christ, Peter, Pudentiana, and a saintly deacon (Fig. 2.2).[24] The book of Revelation offers to the reader a liberating figure who is at once "the first-born from the dead and the ruler of the kings of earth" (Rev 1:5). This "one like the Son of Man" (Rev 1:13), that is, a human being, combines in his person a variety of qualities: he is both giver of "authority over the nations" (Rev 2:26) and sacrificed living Lamb (Rev 5:6).

Only after Constantine allied the Roman imperium with the institutional church was Christ represented as emperor and heaven as a kingdom.[25] This imperial theme forms the second category in Christa Belting-Ihm's iconographic study of the programs of Christian apses. The originating subject, Christ giving the scroll of the law to Peter on his left and extending his right hand toward Paul, called *Traditio legis* or *Dominus legem dat*, was a favorite Constantinian scheme found in

---

24. The mutual active presence of Jesus Christ depends on believers' sharing their faith in Christ. It is distinguished from Christ's cosmic presence as sovereign of the universe, his habitual presence in believers by faith, and his somatic real presence in the consecrated bread and wine of the eucharist. See Kilmartin, *Christian Liturgy*, 327–51.

25. Christa Belting-Ihm, *Die Programme der christlichen Apsismalerei vom vierten Jahrhundert bis zur Mitte des achten Jahrhunderts* (Wiesbaden: Steiner, 1960) 11.

FIGURE 2.2 Rome, S. Prassede. Apse: Paschal I, Praxedes, Paul, Christ, Peter, Pudentiana, deacon. Scala/Art Resource, NY.

large and small dimensions in various media: a burial slab from the Priscilla catacomb (Anagni, Museo Civico); gold glass (Vatican, Museo Sacro); a niche mosaic in S. Costanza, Rome, after 354; sarcophagi after 370 (e.g., Milan, San Ambrogio); ivories (the lid of the Pola Casket in the Museo Archeologico, Venice, ca. 440–450).[26] Its popularity suggests the existence of an important monumental archetype, the figural mosaic that replaced the original gold-foil apse decoration of Silvester I (314–335) at Old St. Peter's. Raising his right hand, palm outward in the gesture of a sun-god, Christ stands on a *monticulus* from which four rivers flow into the paradisal landscape (Gen 2:10–14; Rev 22:1–2, 17). Date palms symbolizing imperial triumph fill out the composition, a theophany of the risen Christ in and to his church represented by the two apostolic princes. Making a gesture of acclamation, Paul stands on Christ's right.[27] On Christ's left, holding a cross, Peter receives the

---

26. Either *Traditio legis* or *Dominus legem dat* appears on a scroll in some of the mosaics. Hellemo (*Adventus Domini*, 65–89, pls. 23–26, 47) summarizes the long-standing debate about the meaning of *Traditio legis*.

27. However, on some 4th-century gold glasses where Christ is symbolized by a christogram Peter is depicted on the right. In later large-scale works Paul is on Christ's right hand. For examples, see the exhibition catalogue *Pietro e Paolo: La storia, il culto, la memoria nei primi secoli*, ed. Angela Donati (Milan: Electa, 2000).

opened scroll of the law.[28] Belting-Ihm identifies the apse of SS. Cosma e Damiano (ca. 526–530) on the Forum, which displays the strongly modeled, monumental figures of classical illusionism, as representing the sub-theme: "The princes of the apostles lead martyrs and donor to the standing Christ." The sixth-century Forum mosaic had been transformed from an acclamatory to a presentation scene. The S. Prassede and S. Cecilia apses are ninth-century versions of that powerful sixth-century work.[29]

The S. Prassede Christ, on whose head the hand of God bestows a laurel wreath, is an imposing imperial figure coming from the east on the rosy clouds of dawn. He holds the scroll of the law but does not confer it on the figures who stand at either side: Paschal, Praxedes, and Paul on Christ's right, and Peter, Pudentiana, and a deacon on Christ's left. The frontal figures hover above the prominently titled Jordan river that flows through a paradisal landscape. As the place of Christ's baptism, the Jordan symbolizes the baptismal immersion of Christians into, or "clothing" in, Christ, with Easter and Pentecost the feasts preferred at Rome. Flowing water, moreover, is a symbol of the Holy Spirit, source of spiritual fruitfulness and the personal, divine bond that joins believers to Christ and, in Christ, to God and one another.[30] Two date palms and a phoenix, sign of the resurrection, complete the typical iconography.[31] This imperial Christ is the Alpha and the Omega, the Almighty (Rev 1:8).[32] According to Revelation 20:6, the One coming on the clouds inaugurates the thousand years' co-reign with those

---

28. Hellemo (*Adventus Domini*, 83–88) urges that the giving of the scrolls to Peter symbolizes not the bestowal of a legal document or mandate of power but the promise of transformed life to all who follow the Lord. A composition that gives parity to Paul and Peter could only originate between the mid-4th century and Pope Gregory I (540–604) when popular piety gave them equal honor. *MR* canonized that devotion when it commemorated them together on June 29th.

29. Belting-Ihm, *Programme der christlichen Apsismalerei*, 39–40, II.B.4. The apsidal arch wall of the church on the Forum probably provided the immediate model for S. Prassede's angels and symbols of the evangelists—the Lamb and 24 elders (Rev. 5:6). For the source of SS. Cosma e Damiano, Krautheimer (*Rome*, 93–94) proposes the six figures flanking Christ in the Lateran apse, while St. Paul's Outside the Walls inspired the revelation symbols on the apsidal arch.

30. The Jordan river frequently forms the base of the main register in Roman apse mosaics.

31. Wisskirchen (*Mosaikprogramm*, 44–46) provides sources and bibliographic references.

32. The Christ of the slightly later S. Marco (ca. 829–830 under Gregory IV; Oakeshott, *Mosaics of Rome*, pl. XXIII) stands on a platform emblazoned with the A (Alpha) and the ω (omega).

who have shed their blood for the Lamb. Even now this reign is being realized in the church. The righteous dead, the martyrs, and others rule with the Christ already enthroned in majesty.[33] Medieval commentaries on the Apocalypse present the co-reign of Christ and the church in terms of realized eschatology.[34] The presence of the living pope in conjunction with the theophany on the apse supports this interpretation of conjoined divine-ecclesial sovereignty.

On the central axis of the register below, a Lamb stands on Mount Zion (Rev 14:1), from which pour the four rivers of paradise (Gen 2:10). In his magisterial study of the typologies of the *maiestas Domini*, Frederik van der Meer calls the Lamb on the mountain the first of the Johannine theophanies in art.[35] From two walled towns (over time these came to be identified as Jerusalem and Bethlehem) proceed twelve lambs, six on a side, toward the Lamb. The symbolic meaning of the lamb frieze, a usual feature of the old *Traditio legis* composition, is the least secure. When the Council of Trullo III (692) forbade the representation of Christ in symbolic form as *agnus Dei* (John 1:36), replication of the Lamb in the midst of a lamb frieze, following the ancient iconography, did not cease on Roman apses.[36] Do these other lambs symbolize the Twelve, or the people of God, or those newly baptised, the 144,000 virgins with the name of Christ emblazoned on their foreheads?[37] Symbols are multivalent; we do not need to choose among these various meanings.

---

33. "Iam tamen eorum animae regnant cum Christo, dum isti mille anni decurrunt...Sed a parte (martyres) totum etiam ceteros mortuos intelligimus pertinentes ad ecclesiam, quod est regnum Christi" (Augustine, *De civitate Dei*, 20.9 [*CCSL* 48, 717, 718]).

34. Yves Christe, "Les représentations médiévales d'Ap. IV (-V) en visions de la seconde parousie: origines, textes et context," *CA* 23 (1974): 61–72.

35. Van der Meer, *Maiestas Domini*, 43–54. The lamb frieze, whose archetype was probably found in Old St. Peter's apse, provides an allegorical parallel accompanying a major figural scene.

36. Cf. the unique fresco "Crucifixion with adoring angels and blessed of all nations" above the apse in S. Maria Antiqua, Rome. Following the 82nd canon of the Quinisext Council, the crucified Christ supplants the Lamb (Nordhagen, *Frescoes of John VII*, 43–54).

37. Hellemo (*Adventus Domini*, 117–21, figs. 24, 25, and 47) discusses the allegorical use of the lamb, which became popular in the second half of the 4th century. The 4th-century city-gate sarcophagus in S. Ambrogio, Milan, shows a double composition: Christ teaching the Twelve exactly corresponds, in the lower register, to the Lamb approached by twelve lambs exiting two city gates. Wisskirchen (*Mosaikprogramm*, pl. 7, figs. 18 and 19) indicates that the twelve lambs symbolize the twelve apostles (see Mt 10:16; 48, n. 200), but later (*Mosaiken der Kirche S. Prassede* [Mainz am Rhein: Phillip von Zabern, 1992], 22–24) proposes that the twelve represent the 144,000 redeemed virgins (Rev 14:1). Hellemo (Rev 14:1; *Adventus Domini*, 88) disagrees with the eschatological reading of F. Nikolash, who sees in the lambs an unambiguous reference to the 144,000. For Belting-Ihm (*Christlichen Apsismalerei*, 14) the twelve lambs symbolize the newly baptized.

The lowest register in the mosaic field, slightly narrower than the lamb frieze, is filled with an epigram. Golden *capitalis quadrata* letters on a blue ground carry the epigram:

> The hall (*aula*), ornamented with variegated metals, gleams forth in honor of holy Praxedes, pleasing to the Lord above the heavens, by the zeal of Paschal, supreme pontiff, alumnus of the apostolic See, who, burying bodies from here and there, placed very many saints under these walls, confident that by these deeds he would merit to approach the threshold of the heavens.[38]

Unfortunately,, the oversized altar canopy dedicated by Cardinal Pico della Mirandola (1728–1731) obscures the relationship between the registers.

B. Apsidal Arch Wall: The Heavenly Liturgy

"As for the mystery of the seven stars that you saw in my right hand, and the seven golden lampstands: the seven stars are the angels of the seven churches, and the seven lampstands are the seven churches" (Rev 1:20). As with prior examples, S. Prassede's apsidal arch does not attempt to depict all possible features but uses the formula and vocabulary entrenched in the decorative tradition.[39] On the central axis the enthroned Lamb with a golden cross rising from a bolster, with a scroll on the footstool, is flanked by three and four flaming lampstands respectively. But for the color of the bolster, the Lamb enthroned at the center of the arch copies the reclining Lamb backed by a golden cross and sealed scroll at SS. Cosma e Damiano. This is a more developed image than that of the empty throne with Lamb standing in front known from the Pola Casket, which doubtless reflects images

---

38. "Emicat aula piae variis decorata metallis/Praxedis d[omi]no super aethra placentis honore/Pontificis summi studio Paschalis alumni/Sedis apostolicae passim qui corpora condens/Plurima s[anct]orum subter haec moenia ponit/fretus ut his limen mereatur adire polorum." *Aula*, *aeth[e]ra* and *polus* are terms chosen from classical usage as part of the intentional Carolingian *renovatio* of late antiquity.

39. While individual motifs are widespread, S. Prassede's choice of symbols is richer than what is known of the façades of Old St. Peter's and the Basilica Euphrasiana, Poreč, or the triumphal arch of St. Paul's Outside the Walls (Wisskirchen, *Mosaikprogramm*, pl. 13, fig. 35; pl.15, fig. 42; pl. 17, fig. 49). It is certainly inspired by SS. Cosma e Damiano's arch wall, which most scholars date to the late 7th century (Wisskirchen, *Mosaikprogramm*, 51, n. 2). Only two evangelist symbols, the winged man and the eagle, and parts of two elders survive from alterations made under Urban VIII (1623–1644).

in monumental art.⁴⁰ The reclining, rather than standing, Lamb echoes the posture of the One seated on the throne and shows the Lamb's divinity. For the early church, the enthroned One is not the transcendent, incomprehensible, and imageless *Theos*-Father of the Lord Jesus Christ, but rather the eternal divine Word (*Logos*) manifested in the incarnate sovereign Christ. The Lamb, then, is symbol of the humanity assumed by the Word.⁴¹

Farther along the arch are the four angels of the four winds (Rev 7:1) paired, with the four living creatures (Rev 4:6–8) paired in the outer corners.⁴² Below them, and inspired by the façade of St. Peter's, the apsidal arch of SS. Cosma e Damiano and Leo III's Lateran Triclinium, the twenty-four elders, twelve and twelve, hold out their crowns as if to cast them, those on the top row with arms stretched beyond natural proportions to fill the spandrels (Rev 4:9–11). The apsidal arch unites symbols from the serene visions of Revelation that had first appeared in monumental art in Rome during the second quarter of the fifth century. By this period, the Sanctus

---

40. This is not the antique empty throne, or one carrying imperial symbols that have been enriched by Christian ones (Tilman Buddensieg, "Le coffret en invoire de Pola, Saint-Pierre et le Latran," *CA* 10 [1959]: 157–95, and fig. 30, reconstructing the Lateran apse, or the triumphal arch roundel at S. Maria Maggiore, which includes a wreath at the base of the enthroned cross and is without the Lamb, ibid., figs. 41–42), but a throne occupied by the Lamb with attendant symbols from Revelation (Van der Meer, *Maiestas Domini*, 231–54; Hellemo, *Adventus Domini*, 96, 102–8, 117–21 and fig. 40). The front of the Pola Casket intermingles the two registers of the Lateran apse, bringing the Lamb symbol standing on the four rivers into the cavity of the throne. From there it is a relatively short step to enthronement of the Lamb at SS. Cosma e Damiano.

41. Christ is at once the Son of Man and the Alpha and Omega (Rev 1:8, 21:6; Van der Meer, *Maiestas Domini*, 220–22).

42. 1 Enoch provides much imagery to the book of Revelation, equating the angels (I, 36:4) with the "four winds which bear the earth as well as the firmament" (I, 18:2), later naming these four angels Michael, Raphael, Gabriel, Phanuel (I, 40:9). See *The Old Testament Pseudepigrapha*, vol. 1: *Apocalyptic Literature and Testaments*, ed. James H. Charlesworth (Garden City, NY: Doubleday, 1983), 22, 29, 32. Hellemo (*Adventus Domini*, 56–62) introduces the four "animals" as symbolizing the cosmic kingship of Christ. At S. Prassede the order is lion, human, eagle, ox, thus replicating the SS. Cosma e Damiano mosaic. R. H. Charles (*A Critical and Exegetical Commentary on The Revelation of St. John* [Edinburgh: T & T Clark, 1920], 1:124) observed the differences between Rev 4:6 (the first animal like a lion, the second a calf, the third with a human face, the fourth a flying eagle) (*Biblia Sacra juxta Vulgatam Clementinam* [Rome: Desclée, (1927) 1956], 274) and Ezek 1:10, where the order, typically found in the illuminated manuscript tradition, is man, lion, ox, eagle, with symbolic appropriation of these living creatures to the evangelists. For Jerome (ca. 341–420) the man represented Matthew, the lion Mark, the ox Luke, the eagle John. This is the order of the creatures in the S. Pudenziana apse; lacking books, they cannot be symbols of the evangelists. Augustine inverts the lion and man (Van der Meer, *Maiestas Domini*, 223–38). The varying order suggests a debate over the canonical order of the gospels in the manuscript tradition.

("Holy, holy, holy, Lord God of hosts! Heaven and earth are filled with thy glory. Hosanna in the highest!") had entered the canon of the mass, drawing believers' minds and hearts to the liturgy being celebrated in heaven, prototype of the earthly liturgy carried out around the church's altar. Two prefaces attributed to Leo the Great (440–461) conclude with the Sanctus.[43]

C. Triumphal Arch: Descent of the Heavenly City Jerusalem

The book of Revelation and the letter to the Hebrews provide the interpreting environment for reading this mosaic. Revelation refers scathingly to imperial Rome with its seven hills as Babylon.[44] Especially since Augustine wrote his *City of God* in the aftermath of the disillusionment brought on by Alaric's sack of the city in 410, Christian Rome understood itself to be the earthly representative of the new Jerusalem descending from on high.[45] But there are two "Jerusalems" described in Revelation chapters 21 and 22. J. M. Ford observes that Revelation contains unambiguous references to the heavenly or eternal Jerusalem, especially in the great visions from chapters 4 through 22. Verses in the book's penultimate section (e.g. Rev 21:1–4, 5a; 22:3–5) also refer to the new heaven and new earth, the renewal of all creation. In contrast, the millennial or messianic Jerusalem is described only in Revelation 21:8–27 and 22:1–2.[46] It is the "beloved" or "holy city"

---

43. Pierre-Marie Gy, "Le sanctus romain et les anaphores orientales," in *Mélanges liturgiques offerts au R.P. Bernard Botte* (Louvain: Abbaye de Mont César, 1972), 167–74; Bryan D. Spinks, *The Sanctus in the Eucharistic Prayer* (Cambridge: Cambridge University Press, 1991), 93–96. On the other hand, Robert Taft ("The Interpolation of the Sanctus into the Anaphora: When and Where? A Review of the Dossier. Part I," *OCP* 57 [1991]: 306) believes that the Sanctus "had entered the Roman eucharist as early as the fourth century." Early on, Taft shows, the Sanctus had a special connection with Easter prefaces.

44. Rev 14:8; 17:6, 9; 18:2, 24; cf. 1 Pet 5:13. For the identification of Rome with Babylon, see Brown and Meier, *Antioch and Rome*, 160. St. Paulinus of Nola (353–431) wrote rhetorically, "Rome, you would not need to fear those earnest threats in the Apocalypse...!" See Paulinus of Nola, "Letter 13: To Pammachius," in *Letters of St. Paulinus of Nola*, trans. P. G. Walsh (2 vols.; Westminster, MD: Newman, 1966), 1: 131.

45. This was only the first of several pillages during the 5th and 6th centuries. On the sack of Rome and the resultant program of the 5th-century popes to assert Rome's leadership of the world through the see of Peter, see Krautheimer, *Rome*, 45–46. For sermons that develop a Rome-Babylon typology in response to the sack of Rome, see Augustine's *Enarrationes in Psalmos*, dated 411-412, in *Sancti Aurelii Augustini Enarrationes in Psalmos*, ed. Eligius Dekkers and Johannes Fraipont (3 vols.; Turnhout: Brepolis, 1956).

46. For this complex discussion, see Josephine Massyngberde Ford, *Revelation* (Garden City, NY: Doubleday, 1975), 331–46, 360–70.

(Rev 21:10), prepared for by the description of the millennial kingdom (Rev 20:4–6). The features of the millennial city—the church on earth, bride or wife of the Lamb, in whom God's reign is being realized—are described in architectural terms with references to walls and their measurements, foundations, gates, and construction materials, using precious stones of every kind and hue. The twelve foundation stones of the city wall are emblazoned with the "twelve names of the twelve apostles of the Lamb" (Rev 21:14). Perfect earthly proportions predominate, since the city lies foursquare, the number four being associated with the created order (Rev 21:16). This city has no need of a temple nor of sun or moon because already God and the Lamb dwell here. The Gentiles will enter, but the defiled are excluded. Paradisal elements—trees of life with fruit and curative leaves—are present with God, the Lamb and the river of life, namely, the Spirit.

The processions of saints hastening toward the golden-walled city tell us that the Jerusalem above, not the earthly Jerusalem, is the triumphal arch's subject: "Here we have no lasting city, but we are looking for the city that is to come" (Heb 13:14). Who are these figures hastening across paradisal fields from either edge of the triumphal arch to converge on the heavenly city coming down out of heaven? Identifications can be hazarded for those in the foreground. Heading the crowd coming from the left side, the two sisters with a third, doubtless the martyr Agnes, robed in golden garments and bedecked with jewels, carry their crowns. These gorgeously dressed virgins are embodiments (Rev 19:7–8) of holy city Jerusalem, bride of the Lamb (Rev 21:2, 9–10).[47] After them come their companions (Rev 19:9), lay and cleric, Pudens, Pius I and Pastor distinguished by their garb, those blessed ones who are invited to the marriage feast of the Lamb. All the figures in the foreground bear crowns (*coronae vitae*, Rev 2:10) in veiled hands. From the right process three figures with crowns: a layman (Novatus?), a pope and a presbyter (Simmetrius?).[48] Behind them must be the twenty-two who, with Simmetrius, had been martyred in Praxedes' *titulus*. The great pilgrimages of nations portrayed in Isaiah 2 and Micah 2 are replaced by that of the saints, representatives of the people of God (Heb 12:22–29).

---

47. Ancient cities were always personified as feminine. See Mark E. Biddle, "The Figure of Lady Jerusalem: Identification, Deification and Personification of Cities in the Ancient Near East," in *The Biblical Canon in Comparative Perspective: Scripture in Context IV*, ed. K. Lawson Younger, Jr., William W. Hallo, and Bernard F. Batto (Lewiston, NY: Mellen, 1991), 173–94.

48. Texts from Hebrews frequently used for the commons of popes, martyrs, and other saints include Heb 5:1–6, 7:23, 10:32–38, 11:33, 11:36–39a, 13:9.

The heavenly Jerusalem descends to earth in the center of the triumphal arch's upper register. Novel on this scale and in such detail, the monumental mosaic gives visual form to a "descending ecclesiology" that pictures "the holy city, new Jerusalem, coming down out of heaven from God, prepared as a bride adorned for her husband" (Rev 21:2). All things will be made new, for the seer "heard a loud voice from the throne saying, 'See, the home of God is among mortals. He will dwell with them; they will be his people, and God himself will be with them; he will wipe every tear from their eyes. Death will be no more'" (Rev 21:3–4).[49] This message bears a specific import for the church community for which the image was created. It is a message welcomed by that beleaguered millennial Jerusalem, namely Christian Rome, awaiting the triumphant coming of the Jerusalem from on high. Faced with the Sinai theophany, Moses had said, "I am afraid," and trembled with fright (Heb 12:21). The former covenant provoked awe, the new one peace. Those "seeking a homeland" (Heb 11:14),

> have come to Mount Zion and to the city of the living God, the heavenly Jerusalem, and to innumerable angels in festal gathering, and to the assembly of the first-born who are enrolled in heaven, and to a judge who is God of all, and to the spirits of just persons made perfect, and to Jesus, the mediator of a new covenant.... (Heb 12:22–24)

This very text, in conjunction with Revelation 21, inspires the scene that spans the length of the triumphal arch's upper register. Two moments of the salvation story and two liturgical movements are pictured, the katabatic (descending) and anabatic (ascending) movements, representing respectively God's initiating action and human response to it. In the center, New Jerusalem descends, Mary and Praxedes mediating as intercessors, while saints yet to be haloed carry their crowns (the "crown of life," Rev 2:10) on their pilgrim way.[50] The proposal by Joseph Dyer, that Old Roman antiphons sung during the procession of relics dedicating a

---

49. Cf. Rev 3:12, Pss 86(87):3 and 121(122). Wisskirchen (*Mosaikprogramm*, pls. 22–26) has collected examples of walled cities that could serve as iconographic source.

50. Joyce Rilett Wood has directed my attention to Jer 4:19–26, a text in which the woman Jerusalem is portrayed as mediator for her people. After Jeremiah admonishes Jerusalem for her wickedness (4:14, 18), she laments her imminent demise (4:19–21), then intercedes on behalf of her citizens and the whole earth to prevent total destruction (4:22–26).

new church inspire the subject matter of the triumphal arch, enriches the interpretation given above.[51]

Within the city, whose golden and bejeweled walls show it to be the heavenly homeland, Christ, standing full-figure between two angelic guards depicted frontally (cf. Rev 19:17, 20:1), wears a golden "robe dipped in blood" (delineated in red, Rev 19:13). Holding a scroll, the King of Kings and Lord of Lords (Rev 17:14, 19:16) is the light of this city. On the foreground plane the Twelve appear in three-quarter pose, Paul filling out the post-resurrection number of Eleven before Matthias' election (Acts 1:15–26). Standing to the left of the interceding Theotokos, John the Baptist holds an *agnus Dei*.[52] Paired with the Virgin, the interceding Praxedes uniquely heads the crown-carrying apostles coming from the right.

On either side, within the walls of gold and precious stones, a prophetic figure stands above and behind the last apostle. On the left, a young, beardless man displays a tablet inscribed *Lege*; on the right, a white-bearded elder holds up covered hands, while a majestic angel gestures toward Christ. Who are they? Majority opinion indicates Moses and Elijah of the transfiguration pericope.[53] In reverse position, these whiteclad "prophets" are iconographic relatives of the Elijah and Moses who flank

---

51. Noting that none of the antiphons refers to the angels who are so conspicuous in the mosaic, Joseph Dyer ("Prolegomena to History of Music and Liturgy at Rome," 94–99) singles out two in particular: nos. 6 ("Ambulate sancti dei, ingredimini in civitatem domini; hedificatum est enim vobis ecclesiam novam; tibi populus adorare debeat maiestatem dei)" and 5 ("Ambulate sancti dei ad locum destinatum quod vobis preparatum est ab origine mundi") from Vat. ms. lat. 5319, f. 135–36. Dyer overlooks antiphons 2 and 8, which were almost universally used in the liturgy of dedication. Mauck ("Mosaic of Triumphal Arch of S. Prassede," 813–28) had earlier proposed the funeral liturgy's *In paradisum* antiphon as source. R. Wisskirchen (*Mosaikprogramm*, 98) drew on eschatological texts of the Old (Isa 60; 62) and New Testaments for a global explanation. On the whole scriptural notion, see Joseph Comblin, "La liturgie de la nouvelle Jérusalem (Apoc. XXI, 1–XXII,5)," *Ephemerides theologiae lovanienses* 29 (1953): 5–40.

52. Byzantine artistic convention distinguishes between the theandric Lord and angelic or human beings by showing them in full versus three-quarter-figure poses. Christ between attendant angels and the Virgin and St. John the Forerunner (the Baptist) petitioning Christ on Judgment Day exemplify Byzantine iconography. The Byzantine formula appears in the Zeno Chapel. However, on the arch the Roman Praxedes has claimed John's privileged place at Christ's left hand.

53. Matt 17:1–8; Luke 9:28–36. Jerome gives this commentary on Ezek 13:43: "Moyses et Helias videntur in monte cum Domino, id est lex et prophetae, qui annuntiabant ei quae in Hierosolymis passurus esset." Jerome, *Sancti Hieronymi presbyteri opera*, pt. 1: *Opera exegetica*, vol. 4, *Commentarii in Hiezechielem libri XVI*, ed. F. Glorie (Turnhout: Brepols, 1964), 1:4, 641; 2:1061–63. Noting that Moses is frequently youthful and beardless in early Christian catacomb painting and sarcophagi, Wisskirchen (*Mosaikprogramm*, 87–93) adduces classical

Christ in the transfiguration lunette on the east wall of the Zeno Chapel.[54] The transfiguration episode where Moses and Elijah appear together with Jesus as witnesses to his impending death and future glory is the model for the two prophetic witnesses in Revelation 11 (Rev 11:3; Mark 9:2–9; Matt 17:1–9; Luke 9:28–36).[55] Further, the book's twofold referent in medieval biblical exegesis explains our two prophets. Indeed, Moses and Elijah appear frequently in the readings of the early Roman lectionary outside the Easter cycle (and Moses at the Easter vigil).[56]

---

transfiguration scenes such as at SS. Nereo ed Achilleo where their positions are reversed, and the isolated figures on the apse wall of S. Maria in Domnica. She concludes unsatisfactorily that the Prassede triumphal arch shows an "untypical" representation of the transfiguration (93). Oakeshott (*Mosaics of Rome*, 207) with G. B. de Rossi favors identifying the two men with John the author of Revelation and the Baptist already depicted in the top register, an identification that, in reverse order, better suits the two figures in the arch spandrels at S. Maria in Domnica.

54. The triumphal arch follows the Matthean-Lukan order, placing Moses on the viewer's left (Matt 17:3–4; Luke 9:30, 33). The small Zeno Chapel Transfiguration was doubtless inspired by the same subject at SS. Nereo ed Achilleo commissioned by Leo III ca. 814 (Krautheimer, *CBCR* 3 [1967], fig. 130). Both follow Mark 9:4, which names Elijah first, placing him on the left ("And there appeared to them Elijah and Moses"). From the spectator's viewpoint the youthful, beardless Moses is at the right of the central figure of Christ, his transfigured state shown by enclosure within an aureole, while saints yet to be haloed carry their crowns (the "crown of life," Rev 2:10) on their pilgrim way. On the principle of reversal in scripture to mark a quotation, or to indicate commentary or change of meaning, see, e.g. Pancratius C. Beentjes, "'Inverted Quotations in the Bible': A Neglected Stylistic Pattern," *Biblica* 63 (1982): 506–23.

55. Identifications of the two witnesses ranging from Zerubbabel and Joshua or Enoch and Elijah to Peter and Paul are given in Ford, *Revelation*, 170–81. Daniel William O'Connor (*Peter in Rome: The Literary, Liturgical, and Archeological Evidence* [New York: Columbia University Press, 1969], 65–68) interprets the two witnesses of Rev 11:1–12 as Peter and Paul. On the S. Prassede arch, however, Paul and Peter respectively lead the file of apostles coming from left and right within the city walls; they stand immediately behind the Baptist and the interceding Theotokos on the left and Praxedes interceding on the right, appearing again outside the walls to form a triad with an angel carrying a gold measuring rod (Rev 21:15). Rev 11:4 likens the two prophetic witnesses to two olive trees and two lampstands, originally symbolic language used by Zechariah to describe "two anointed ones," Joshua and Zerubbabel (Zech 3–4; 4:14), but reapplied by John to Elijah and Moses as "my two witnesses," who "will prophesy" (Rev 11:3–4), identifying Luke's "two men who stood with [Jesus]" (Luke 9:32) as the two witnesses who "stand before the Lord of the earth" (Rev 11:4). The witnesses in Rev 11 are identified by way of quotation and allusion to the mighty deeds of Elijah (LXX 3 Kgs 17:1; 4 Kgs 1:10 = MT 1 Kgs 17:1; 2 Kgs 1:10) and Moses (Exod 7:17–20) respectively, the last and first of the prophets. In light of what is said about Elijah and Moses in the biblical tradition (MT Deut 18:15, 18; 2 Kgs 2:11; Ezek 37:5, 10; Mal 3:23), John announces the death of the prophetic witnesses, their resuscitation or return before the end of the world, and the ascent of both Elijah and Moses into heaven (Rev 11:7–8, 11–12). See M. Black, "'The Two Witnesses' of Rev. 11:3f.," *Donum Gentilicium: New Testament Studies in Honour of David Daube*, ed. E. Bammel, C. K. Barrett, and W. D. Davies (Oxford: Clarendon, 1978), 227–37.

56. The commentary on Revelation of Victorinus (d. 303?) is partial to Elijah (Rev 7:2; 11:5; 12:7–9; 14:6 in *Ante-Nicene Christian Library*, ed. Alexander Roberts and James Donaldson [Edinburgh: T & T Clark, 1880], vol. 18:413, 419, 423–24, 427). Moses is a type of Christ

And who is the angel in the red robe with *tablion* standing beside Elijah and carrying a rod?[57] In Augustine's *De civitate Dei* Book 20, when compiling teachings about the Last Judgment, for which he cites Ecclesiastes (Eccl 2:13–14; 8:14 in 20.3), Matthew (Matt 11:22, 24; 12:27, 41–42; 19:28 in 20.5), and Revelation (Rev 20:9–10 in 20.8), Moses and Elijah are linked with the angel of Malachi 3:1.[58] Elijah heralds the great and glorious day of the Lord (Mal 3:1–4:5). *City of God* 20.16 deals with the new heaven and earth: 2 Peter's doctrine of the resurrection of the dead is discussed in 20.18, Pauline doctrine in chapters 19 and 20. The prophecies of Isaiah, Daniel, and David regarding the world's end and the judgment are discussed in 20.21, 23, and 24, followed in 20.25 by that of Malachi 4:4–5, whose two witnesses are Moses and Elijah (20.28–29; cf. Mal. 3:22–23 in Hebrew).[59] Moses is the prototype, Elijah the messianic representative of the law and the prophets. Ten times in Book 20 Augustine draws on the oracle of Malachi as he delineates the role of the two prophets Moses and Elijah in preparing for the Last Judgment (20.25, 27–29).[60] What is to be made of all the angels,

---

(Heb 3). His awe in the presence of God introduces Heb 12:22–24, a thumbnail description of the triumphal arch. Like Abraham Moses was known for faith. Moses kept the Passover and sprinkled the blood (Heb 11:28). Given the imperative singular *Lege* on the tablet, the youth might otherwise be God's witness and servant John: "Beatus qui legit et audit verba prophetiae hujus" (Rev 1:3). For the type of youthful beardless John, see the left-hand medallion above the half-figure of St. Peter (Mt. Sinai, St. Catherine's Monastery) of the late 6th or first half of the 7th century in Kurt Weitzmann, *The Monastery of Saint Catherine at Mount Sinai: The Icons*, vol. 1: *From the Sixth to the Tenth Century* (Princeton, NJ: Princeton University Press, 1976), 24 and pls. VIII and Xb. Weitzmann points out that there was a youthful type of Moses in early Christian art.

57. The angelology of medieval exegesis is complex. Cf. the angel with a golden censer of Rev 8:3 and "another mighty angel" of Rev 10:1, understood to be Christ. The literal Vulgate reading of Rev 11:1, "A reed like a rod was given me saying..." has a variant, "And the angel stood there saying..." (*JB*, Rev 11:1, text note a). Another angel with "a measuring rod of gold to measure the city and its gates and walls" (Rev 21:15) stands outside the walls on the right, between Peter and Paul. A medieval exegete would have no difficulties with the striking parallels between this passage in Revelation and Zechariah's visions of the "man with a measuring line" about to measure Jerusalem, the two angels, the Lord dwelling in the city's midst as Jerusalem's glory (Zech 2; cf. Ps 16:5–6), and other resonances: the vision of lampstand, bowl, seven lamps, and two olive trees (Zech 4), the peoples and nations seeking the Lord in Jerusalem (Zech 8), mourning for the pierced one (Zech 12:10, 14, cf. Rev 1:7), the cleansing fountain (Zech 13), the living waters (Zech 14:8), and the annual return of all worshipers on the feast of Tabernacles (Zech 14:16–21).

58. The Vulgate reads, "Ecce ego mitto angelum meum...." Modern commentators identify the *angelus* (messenger) with Elijah, named in Mal 4:5 (Mal 3:23 in Hebrew).

59. Mal 4:4–5 (Vulgate) reads, "Mementote legis Moysi, servi mei...Ecce ego mittam vobis Eliam prophetam."

60. Augustine, *De civitate Dei* (CCSL 48), Books 11–22: 747–48, 751–53.

messengers to earth, in this upper register of the triumphal arch? There are exactly seven angels and, although some play double roles in this pictorial interpretation of the Apocalypse, at the first level of meaning they certainly represent the angels of the seven churches (Rev 1:20, 8:2). The blue ground visually links the triumphal arch to the apse mosaic. In both, humans are divinized and nature attains its supernatural destiny.

The letter to the Hebrews, possibly written to the Jewish-Christian community at Rome, provides a biblical foundation for the depiction of the pilgrim band approaching its heavenly home, the new Jerusalem whose gates never shut (Rev 21:25). This feature of the millennial Jerusalem suggests that the exegete who advised the image-makers did not distinguish between the two Jerusalems. Both texts are rich in angelologies. But Hebrews is the converse of Revelation; it embodies at the narrative level what systematic theology would define as ascending christology of the Spirit and its corollary, "ascending ecclesiology," with the saintly sisters together with their family, members of their house-church, and ecclesiastical friends journeying to their heavenly homeland.

The spandrels of the triumphal arch accommodate two crowds of white-robed youths, some waving palm branches and some carrying crowns, symbolizing the "great multitude" of the 144,000 sealed (Rev 7:4, 9; 14:1) who stand with the Lamb on Mount Zion.[61] They "sing a new song before the throne, and before the four living creatures and before the elders" (Rev 14:3a). Thanks to the successive planes of triumphal and apsidal arch, they do so literally. These virgin-youths who "follow the Lamb wherever he goes" (Rev 14:4b) acclaim Christ who returns in the time of the church, which is represented in the apse by the apostolic princes, the two sisters as house-church leaders, and the reigning pontiff. But the youths, emulating the acclamation offered by the elders in the realm of supernatural beings represented on the apsidal arch wall, inhabit the foreground plane of the triumphal arch; this is predominantly the human sphere. By

---

61. Youths waving palm branches appear in an Adoration of the Lamb miniature in the Trier Apocalypse (Trier, Staatsbibliothek, cod. 31, f. 23v), dated ca. 800 (Wisskirchen, *Mosaikprogramm*, fig. 54). This manuscript is said to present "the most faithful reflection of an archetype which, most likely, was created in Rome" (Florentine Mütherich and Joachim E. Gaehde, *Carolingian Painting* [New York: George Braziller, 1976], 22). Youths waving palm branches evoke the episode of Christ's triumphal entry into Jerusalem. In Rome, Matt 21:1–9 was read on the First Sunday of Advent with just one verse, Matt 21:9, used as an antiphon on the Sunday *in palmis/ad palmas*. John 12:12–19, read on Holy Monday, gives the fourth evangelist's account of the triumphal entry.

relating visually first to the youths and then to the elders, worshipers at the earthly liturgy are drawn into participation in the heavenly liturgy.[62]

The three components of the mosaics of the presbytery at the north end form a single composition. Governed by a symbolic rather than a literal mode of thought, the whole embraces heaven and earth, beings divine and human. The design unfolds as the worshiper approaches: the human world occupies the arch nearest the assembly, the realm of supernatural beings the wall of the apsidal arch, while the theandric King of Kings and Lord of Lords, reflecting the glory of God and bearing the very stamp of God's nature (Heb 1:3), dominates the apse. Thanks to his prerogative as patron, a living pope shares the company of this heavenly world that the saints mediate.[63] Observers must participate in the world of religious symbols that each beholds, become a hearer of the word and a worshiper in order to enter into Paschal's conceptual world. The goal of participation in the earthly liturgy centered around the church's altar is spelled out visually by the mosaic program that unfolds above and beyond the assembly. Salvific promises of the visions in Revelation 19 and 20—the marriage of the Lamb and the bride-church made ready, the invitation to the marriage supper, encounter with the judge called Faithful and True and Word of God, fellowship with the martyrs "who shall be priests of God and of Christ" (Rev 20:6)—are actualized by participation in the eucharist, celebrated on the altar under a canopy (ciborium) signifying the firmament. Like Matthew's wise householder, Pope Paschal has assembled from the treasury of Roman themes and iconography "the new and the old" (Matt 13:52).

2. *Revelation and Hebrews in the Roman Epistolary*

Revelation's visions provided subject-matter or subtext for the decorative schemes of many of Rome's major basilicas, for instance the façade of Old St. Peter's, and lesser churches in and around the city. The S. Prassede program goes beyond the formulae, expanding and applying the themes in both public liturgical and private devotional space. The intricacies of both the presbyterium and Zeno Chapel programs invite further probing

---

62. Cf. Zech 14:16. The striking parallel is found in Victorinus, who, when he sees the elders casting down their crowns before the throne (Rev 4:10), recalls the children of the Hebrews casting palms before Christ (CSEL XXXIX, 46, 13; 48, 1, 58,8; English translation in *Ante-Nicene Christian Library*, 18:408). The believer attuned to patristic exegesis marveled at multiple identifications and levels of meaning.

63. Mauck ("Mosaic of Triumphal Arch S. Prassede," 828) comments: "the apse inscription...attests to Paschal's desire to be among the number of those saints marching in grand procession through the heavenly gates."

of a possible liturgical source: the epistolary used at Rome on Sundays and in high seasons of the church year and the sanctoral or calendar of saints' feasts, with an eye also to the liturgy of the hours.

We begin with the book of Revelation, assumed to have been authored by John the apostle. As pointed out by Mackie, the figure labelled John on the upper walls of the Zeno Chapel, who holds a jeweled, gilt-covered codex (surely Revelation), faces the throne of judgment on the inside entrance wall instead of the altar niche to the east. Which Revelation pericopes were chosen for liturgical use, and with what frequency were they read at communal worship during the fourth through twelfth centuries when the iconography explored above was in vogue in Rome? In the Roman Office, the daily prayer of clergy and monastics, Revelation was the final book to be read in Eastertide.[64] With one or two exceptions (*Pascha annotina*; the vigil of the transfiguration in one tenth-century book), Revelation is reserved in the Roman mass lectionary for saints' feasts (martyrs, evangelists, All Saints), for the archangel Michael, and for the dedication of churches.[65]

After nearly a century of study, the consensus on the genesis and development of the Roman lectionary can be summarized.[66] The epistolary,

---

64. Following, in the early weeks of Eastertide, lessons from Acts and the seven catholic (Eastern terminology) or canonical (Western) epistles (1–3 John, 1–2 Pet, Jas and Jude). *Ordo* XIV (Vatican, Pal. lat. 277), dated 650–700, prescribes office readings for the monasteries serving St. Peter's: "In diebus autem paschae epistulae apostolorum et actus apostolorum atque apocalypsin usque pentecosten." *Ordo* XIIIA of the Lateran (700–750) sets out the readings for the night office: "In Pascha ponunt actuum apostolorum. Secuntur septem epistolae canonicae. Deinde sequitur apocalypsis usque in octabas pentecosten" (Michel Andrieu, *OR* 3:40, no. 4; 2:483–84, no. 6 with ascription of the Apocalypse to the evangelist John, 486–87). Ordo XIIIB, second recension, gives the option of the seven canonical epistles or the Apocalypse (ibid., 2: 500, no. 7). On the monastic office in Rome, see Robert Taft, *The Liturgy of the Hours in East and West* (2nd ed. rev; Collegeville, MN: Liturgical, 1993), 131–40.

65. N. B. Stonehouse (*The Apocalypse in the Ancient Church: A Study in the History of the New Testament Canon* [Goes: Oosterbaan & Le Cointre, 1929]) studied Revelation's canonicity. Eastern churches except Egypt's situated Revelation outside the Scripture canon. Most Western churches were enamored of it. The Mozarabic church read the Apocalpyse from Holy Saturday through the Sunday after Easter, and then on Sundays until Pentecost; priests who failed to follow the lectionary were threatened with excommunication. Elaborately illustrated commentaries are the legacy of Spanish liturgical usage (Van der Meer, *Maiestas Domini*, 467–79). Revelation provided the ferial readings for Easter week in the Gallican lectionary of Luxeuil. The Bobbio Missal required Revelation readings for Easter, Ascension, Pentecost, the Holy Martyrs, and St. Michael. In Rome, however, from Easter Monday to the Saturday after Pentecost, of the 27 readings for mass, 14 were from Acts and 13 from the canonical epistles (Antoine Chavasse, "L'épistolier romain du Codex de Wurtzbourg," *RB* 91 [1981]: 295–96).

66. Each hand-written liturgical manuscript contains clues to its place of origin, date, and intended usage because it was designed for a particular community in a given year. Variants

consisting of Old and New Testament lections other than the gospel, is older than the evangeliary and its readings are unconnected with the latter.[67] The earliest extant epistle list (W) is available in one manuscript in Würzburg (Universitätsbibliothek, cod. M.p.th.f.62), written circa 700 but representing a "pure Roman" list of circa 600–625.[68] A later epistolary is found in the *comes* of "Alcuin" (A); extant manuscript witnesses date from the early to mid-ninth century but represent in the main a prototype shortly after W, 626–627 or 670–680.[69] "Alcuin's" Supplement was probably by Alcuin of York (d. 804).

About 700 both W and A were drawn on by a third type whose epistolary, evangeliary, and antiphonary were systematically retouched to provide links among the Scripture passages appointed for the day. This type is known in two versions.[70] These manuscripts illustrate a

---

allowing localization are characteristic of medieval Roman liturgical books (A. G. Martimort, *Les lectures liturgiques et leurs livres* [Turnhout: Brepols, 1992], 44). For the *status quaestionis*, see Cyrille Vogel, *Medieval Liturgy: An Introduction to the Sources*, rev. and trans. by William G. Storey and Niels Krogh Rasmussen (Washington, DC: Pastoral Press, 1986), 339–55; Martimort, *Lectures liturgiques et leurs livres*; Eric Palazzo, *A History of Liturgical Books from the Beginning to the Thirteenth Century* (Collegeville, MN: Liturgical, 1998).

67. The evangeliary appears to have been composed following a kind of diatessaron or gospel harmony (Antoine Chavasse, "Les plus anciens types du lectionnaire et de l'antiphonaire romains de la messe," *RB* 62 [1952]: 93). For detailed comparative tables covering the whole early development, see Antoine Chavasse, *Les lectionnaires romains de la messe au VIIe et au VIIIe siècle: sources et dérives* (2 vols.; Fribourg: Éditions Universitaires, 1993).

68. Germain Morin, "Les plus ancien *comes* ou lectionnaire de l'église romaine," *RB* 27 (1910): 41–74; Antoine Chavasse, "Épistolier romain"; "Évangéliaire, épistolier, antiphonaire et sacramentaire. Les livres romans de la messe, au VIIe et au VIIIe siècle," *EO* 6 (1989): 177–255, repr., *La liturgie de la ville de Rome du Ve au VIIIe siècle* (Rome: S. Anselmo, 1993), 160–64. On the Roman calendar, see Chavasse, "Plus anciens types," 3–94; Chavasse, "Le calendrier dominical romain au sixième siècle," *RSR* 41 (1953): 96–122; and Chavasse, *Lectionnaires romains*.

69. André Wilmart, "Le lectionnaire d'Alcuin," *EL* 51 (1937): 136–97, containing 242 and 65 items respectively. The introduction to the Supplement (first quarter of the 9th century with Alcuin's minor changes) is usually attributed to Helisachar, Louis the Pious' chancellor (d. 836). The original is usually dated 626/627 (Honorius I) but cf. Palazzo (*History of Liturgical Books*, 98–99), 670/680. I place "Alcuin" between quotation marks to indicate that the original lectionary was not authored by Alcuin of York.

70. Family A represents primitive Roman usage. Its extant witnesses (none from outside central Italy and none earlier than the 10th century) point to a period circa 731. Vatican, Archivio di S. Pietro, F. 1 is an epistolary written in the late 13th century that Chavasse situates in Family A.2 (constituted of mss. that number the Sundays following Pentecost continuously), in the local Roman liturgy group. Family B is a revision of A still under Roman inspiration made before 740; all the manuscripts in this latter family come from Northern Italy, Switzerland or Gaul; its chief witnesses are Corbie (C), Verona (V), and Murbach (M). See A. Chavasse, "Plus anciens types," 21; Vogel, *Medieval Liturgy*, 349–55. For the Corbie lectionary (Leningrad, Publ. Bibl. Q.V.I, no. 16; ca. 772–780), see Walter Howard Frere, *Studies*

recurring characteristic of Roman liturgy. Conservative rather than innovative, the "pure Roman" text is inculturated, when exported, to make it usable in its new context. When the inculturated version (in this case the Franco-Roman) returns to the Eternal City, it is embraced to the enrichment of Roman liturgical usage.[71] Readings from Revelation appear in a variety of contexts: for a so-called "Sunday of the birthday of the saints"; in the sanctoral cycle and its late addition, the feast of All Saints; for *Pascha annotina*; and in the dedication of a church and of an oratory. In addition, at a relatively late stage in the epistolary's formation, readings from Revelation and Hebrews were inserted into the weekday temporal cycle of Wednesdays and Fridays. Each of these occurrences will be investigated as a possible inspiration for the S. Prassede mosaic programs.

No extant manuscript can be identified as one in liturgical use at S. Prassede during the pontificate of Paschal I. However, the sources noted above witness to Roman lectionary usage in the time leading up to the rebuilding of S. Prassede. A manuscript of Vallombrosan use written in the early thirteenth century (Vatican Library, ms. lat. 8701, *Epistolarium Ordinis Vallombrosani*) known as the S. Prassede Epistolary is indebted to the Murbach *comes*. Vatican ms. lat. 8701 can be compared usefully with others of its class for it appears to have been shaped by its S. Prassede provenance.[72] Copies made at a late date that incorporate changes of their own generation enshrine earlier usages. In the section that follows, the Roman lectionary's use of texts from Revelation and Hebrews is analyzed for clues to the epistle readings that could have inspired Paschal's decorative commission at S. Prassede or, in a few instances, been so inspired.

---

in *Early Roman Liturgy*, vol. 3: *The Roman Epistle-Lectionary* (London: Oxford University Press, 1935), 13. The script of the luxury "Verona Lectionary" (Paris, Bibl. Nat. ms. lat. 9451, ca. 800) of Roman use with both epistles and gospels suggests a North Italian provenance; see Robert Amiet, "Un '*Comes*' carolingien inédit de la Haute-Italie," *EL* 73 (1959): 334–67 at 352. On Murbach (8th century; Besançon, ms. 184), see André Wilmart, "Le *Comes* de Murbach," *RB* 30 (1913): 25–69. The Murbach *comes* was to provide the framework for the *Missale Romanum* of 1570. Vogel defines a *comes* as a collection of pericopes copied out in full and a *capitulare* as a list of these pericopes, but usage differs.

71. Theodor Klauser, *A Short History of the Roman Liturgy*, trans. John Halliburton (London: Oxford University Press, 1969), 77–84.

72. Chavasse, "Plus anciens types," 8–11 lists the families of Roman lectionaries. See also Pierre Salmon, *Les manuscrits liturgiques latins de la Bibliothèque Vaticane*, vol. 2: *Sacramentaires, épistoliers, evangéliaires, graduels, missels* (Vatican City: BAV, 1969), 69, no. 145; *Ora et Labora: Testimonianze Benedettine nella Biblioteca Apostolica Vaticana: XV centenario della nascita di S. Benedetto, 480–1980* (Vatican City: BAV, 1980), 15, no. 22.

Circa 600–625 in Rome, with one notable exception—the first Sunday after Pentecost—Revelation readings at mass were reserved to Holy Innocents, the archangel Michael (29 September), and the dedication of a church. As the sanctoral developed, Revelation lections were gradually added. Around 800 a feast of All Saints with vigil using Revelation readings appeared in some local churches north of the Alps, and by 835 this feast was well established in Rome. We will take these occurrences in turn, considering as well the lections from Hebrews heard during Paschaltide and in proximity to the season of Advent with its theme of the return of Christ at the end of the ages.

A. A "Sunday on the Birthday of the Saints"?

In the fifth century, Pentecost day had concluded Eastertide. The "fast of the fourth month," really a return to the weekly fast following the festive period of Easter, was located in the week following Pentecost.[73] The lengthy Ember Saturday vigil was concluded with a papal mass; newly ordained priests returned to their *tituli* to take up their Sunday responsibilities. No papal stational mass was indicated for the Sunday, and no lessons were provided in the pontifical lectionary for it was *dominica vacat*, an "empty Sunday." However, outside the pontifical liturgy such a vacuum could not last; formularies and readings were required. The Würzburg epistolary of circa 600, with readings from Acts, gives stations to the ferial days following Pentecost Sunday and titles the vacant first Sunday after Pentecost *Dominica in natale sanctorum*.[74] Two Revelation readings were assigned: no. 114, DOMI IN NAT SCORUM Rev 4:1, 7:9–12; and no. 115, ITEM UNDE SUPRA Rev 7:13–17.[75]

---

73. Chavasse, "Plus anciens types," 75–81. As Easter week originally concluded with the Saturday *in albis* when the neophytes took off their white Easter wear, so Pentecost week, which from at least the mid-5th century had mirrored Easter as a time for baptisms in Rome, ended with the Saturday.

74. Morin, "Le plus ancien *comes*," 58, note to CXIIII, and 73. The text reads, "Domi in nat scorum lec lib apocalipsis iohan apo. In diebus illis vidi ostium apertum in caelo..." (Rev 7:9–12). The calendar that prefaces the epistle list includes this DOMINICA IN NAT SCORUM; see W. G. Rusch, "A Possible Explanation of the Calendar in the Würzburg Lectionary," *JTS* 21 (1970): 105–11, at 110. In W the Ember days fall in the following week.

75. W's gospel book shows the "Gregorian" arrangement, i.e., ember days in Pentecost week (Germain Morin, "Liturgie et basiliques de Rome au milieu du VIIe siècle," *RB* 28 [1911]: 307, n. 2). The more advanced epistolary shows a full Pentecost octave terminating in a presumed "Sunday on the birthday of the saints" with the ember days falling in the following week (Morin, "Le plus ancien *comes*," 58–59).

Dom Germain Morin took the enigmatic title of W 114 to refer to a Roman proto-All Saints' feast in the spirit of Eastern traditions. In fourth century Edessa, a feast of all the martyrs was observed on 13 May, the same date that the Pantheon was dedicated as S. Maria ad Martyres in 609.[76] In the late fourth century, St. John Chrysostom refers to a martyrs' feast at Antioch on the Sunday following Pentecost. Before 411, the East Syrian church observed a feast of all the martyrs on Friday of Easter week. These three dates each coincide respectively with the usage of a great Eastern church: Edessa, Antioch-Constantinople, and the Chaldean church.[77] The Eastern influence can be explained by the fact that between the pontificates of Theodore I (642–649) and Zacharias (741–752), "Greek" and Syrian popes and Greek-speaking theologians predominated in Rome.

"Alcuin" (A), the seventh-century Roman epistolary, does not recognize a Sunday *in natale sanctorum*, although a common of martyrs (CLVI) uses the precise verses of W's no. 114.[78] In 1952 Antoine Chavasse developed a complex argument to propose a simpler explanation of the enigmatic *dominica in natale sanctorum* than the attractive case for a Roman proto–All Saints' feast proposed by Dom Morin in 1911 and followed more recently by T. Talley and P. Jounel.[79] Textual comparison suggests that once the ember days were moved to the following week and a "filler" was

---

76. 13 May is the date given by Praxedes' *vita* for the dedication of her baptistery.

77. Morin, "Les plus ancien *comes*," note to no. 114, 73 and Morin, "Liturgie et basiliques," 327–28. For a resumé of the Byzantine feast dedicated to all the martyrs of the world, see John Baldovin, "Saints in the Byzantine Tradition," *Liturgy* 5/2 (1985): 72–74.

78. Wilmart, "Lectionnaire d'Alcuin," 159. Following the Würzburg gospel book, "Alcuin" titles the non-stational Sunday *dominica oct(a)b(arum) pentecosten* (CXXVI), calling for 1 Cor 12:2–11 on the gifts of the Spirit (ibid., 158).

79. Thomas J. Talley ("The Evolution of a Feast," *Liturgy* 5 [1985]: 43–48) proposes that, after the dedication of the Pantheon on 13 May 609 to St. Mary and All Martyrs, this Roman building served as stational church for their commemoration on the Friday after Easter and remained so through 800. Roman devotion to all the saints was enhanced when in 732 Pope Gregory III dedicated a chapel in St. Peter's with a second mass in honor of all the saints to be celebrated every day of the year, enlarging the commemoration to include "the Redeemer, His holy Mother, all the Apostles, Martyrs, Confessors, and all the just and perfect who are at rest throughout the whole world" (Talley, "Evolution," 46; Chavasse, "Le regroupement des formulaires annuels pour la messe dans les livres romains du VIIe et du VIIIe siècle," in *Liturgie de la ville de Rome*, 327). Pierre Jounel ("Le culte collectif des saints à Rome du VIIe au IXe siècle," *EO* 6 [1989]: 287, 289) argues differently, crediting Rome with celebrating during the 6th century, like the Byzantine church, a *dominica in natale sanctorum* until it was abolished by Gregory the Great, with this as the first instance of veneration apart from the place where the saints' corpses rested.

needed for what had been a vacant Sunday in the pontifical liturgy, a contiguous common of saints' reading was displaced to that Sunday.[80] The first of the W readings (the composite Rev 4:1, 7:9–12) is "Alcuin's" CLVI (the first "common" in *natale sanctorum*) after the feast of St. Lawrence (10 August). The second W reading (Rev 7:13–17) is exactly that given for SS. Marcellinus and Peter, which in "Alcuin" follows immediately on the Sunday of the Pentecost octave.[81] In other words, the *dominica in natale sanctorum* results from the proximity of an available lection when the ember week with its Saturday ordinations and Mass moves to the following week and the vacated Sunday requires a lesson.[82] That this Sunday is unique can be seen from the stations in the Würzburg *comes*; unlike the octave of Easter, *dominica in natale sanctorum* (CXIV) is listed without a station.

Family B lectionaries, originating in northern Italy or north of the Alps, abandon Revelation's seventh chapter in favor of chapter four (the first vision of the heavenly liturgy), which had provided Würzburg with its opening verse for the composite lesson (Table 2.1). The Murbach lectionary (XCVII) signals both choices, labeling the Sunday as the octave but keeping Revelation 4:1. A "Sunday on the birthday of the saints" was celebrated at Rome circa 600, displaced by a true octave day in the "Alcuin" *comes* of 626–627 or 670–680. Family B manuscripts maintain a reading from Revelation (ch. 4:1). These lectionaries' readings are enough to explain the content of S. Prassede's apsidal arch. Given the baptismal connotations of Revelation 7 and the Roman tradition of reading Revelation during the night office at the close of the Easter season, it can be seen that either Revelation 4 or 7 would provide an apt lesson to close the fifty days (*pentecostes*).

---

80. Chavasse ("Plus anciens types," 69–72) shows that these occur in doublets.

81. CXXVII (Wilmart, "Lectionnaire d'Alcuin," 158).

82. W's Rev 7:9–12 and 13–17 pericopes are striking for their references to the multitudes dressed in white robes. Since from the mid-5th to the 12th centuries Pentecost was also a baptismal day, when read on the Sunday following, these texts would resonate with the accommodated image of the white-robed neophytes alluded to in "Alcuin's" title for the Saturday of the Easter octave, *sabbato ad Lateranis in albis* (see 1 Pet 2:1–10). Caecilia Davis-Weyer ("Die ältesten Darstellungen der Hadesfahrt Christi, des Evangelium Nikodemi und ein Mosaik der Zeno-Kapelle," in *Roma e l'età carolingia*, 186) cites commentaries of Jerome and Bede that explain the martyrs' "stolas albas" as baptismal garments.

Table 2.1 A "Sunday on the Birthday of the Saints"

Vat. Reg. lat. 74[a]	Rev 4:4–11
Corbie (C): *Dominica Octavas Pentecosten*[b]	Rev 4:1–9
Murbach (M): *Dom octb. pentec. in tl. sanctorum*[c]	Rev 4:1
Verona (V): *Domi in Octa Pent.*[d]	Rev 4:1–10

[a] A. Dold, "Ein ausgeschriebenes Perikopenbuch des 8. Jahrhunderts," *EL* 54 (1940): 12–37. Vogel (*Medieval Liturgy*, 345) designates it a "pure Roman" type, written in north Italy or Gaul in the late 8th century. Close to Murbach, it has several lacunae.

[b] Epistolary of Corbie or *Comes* of Leningrad (C = Leningrad, Publichnaja Biblioteka, cod. Q.V.I, no. 16). Text in W. H. Frere, *Studies in Early Roman Liturgy*, vol. 3: *Roman Epistle-Lectionary*, 1–24. Vogel (*Medieval Liturgy*, 340) dates it around 772–780.

[c] Murbach reads: "Dom. octb. pentec. *[I]n tl. sanctorum*"; see Wilmart, "*Comes* de Murbach," 25–69, here no. XCVII, 44. S. Pietro ad Vincula was the *titulus sanctorum*. "[T]itulo" is undoubtedly a scribal error for "natale," which occurs in purer Roman lists. Vogel (*Medieval Liturgy*, 347), dates it to the late 8th century.

[d] Verona Lectionary/Lectionary of Monza, Paris, Bibl. Nat. lat. 9451 (Amiet, "*Comes* carolingien," 335–67). Vogel (*Medieval Liturgy*, 344) dates it to the late 8th/9th century.

B. The Sanctoral Cycle of the Lectionaries

The development of the Roman sanctoral cycle has been mapped out by Pierre Jounel. Until the end of the Valerian persecution, only Roman pontiffs were commemorated. Afterward martyred clerics were honored with a memorial but only at the place of burial on the date of their *natale*.[83] The best exemplars of the connection of martyr's tomb and memorial are the *Natale S. Petri* (in the Gregorian sacramentary, 29 June, celebrated at

---

83. The majority of Roman martyr cults date from Diocletian's persecution; see Hertling and Kirschbaum, *Roman Catacombs*, 59–60; Pierre Jounel, "Le Sanctoral romain du 8e au 12e siècles," *LMD* 52 (1957): 59–182; Jounel, "The Veneration of the Saints," in *The Church at Prayer*, vol. 4: *The Liturgy and Time*, ed. A. G. Martimort (Collegeville, MN: Liturgical Press, 1986), 108–29. In the later 4th century, some tombs of Roman bishops were systematized in Damasus' crypt of the popes in the Callistus catacomb. Agnes, virgin and martyr, whose deposition is known ca. 304, had an attested cult on the Via Nomentana already in 336. First a covered cemetery was built for the graves clustered near her resting place. In the 7th century an eastern-style galleried basilica with apse mosaic showing the martyr larger than life clad in imperial vestments, the patron Pope Honorius I (625–638) standing by, was sunk into the hill.

the Vatican) with its own vigil, extended by the *Natale S. Pauli* (30 June, on the Ostian Way), which also enjoyed a two-day celebration.[84] Revelation readings had been assigned, by those epistolaries that made provision for sanctoral lessons, to a few of the martyrs' commemorations as well as to Michael the holy angel (Revelation's angelology is notable). That the readings for the propers of martyrs, evangelists, and Michael the archangel were selected with an eye to the subject is apparent from examination of Table 2.2.

As shown below, at various times of the year the Roman lectionary found appropriate readings in the book of Revelation for propers and commons of martyrs, evangelists, and the archangel Michael.[85] In its turn, the letter to the Hebrews provided suitable readings for both the propers and commons of popes' and martyrs' commemorations.

(i) Feasts of Pudentiana, Praxedes, and the Virgin in the sanctoral
A note regarding the introduction of women's feasts into the sanctoral is apposite here. The sixth century marked a new stage in the commemoration of the saints, for until this period bishops and martyrs but not virgins had been included. The transformation of *tituli* bearing the names of their original owners into churches, identified by dedication to homonymous "saints," occurs in the sixth century.[86] Hagiographical stories and legends extended the commemorations. Together these two sources would have

---

84. The Gregorian calendar shows an initial distinct status for feasts of Peter and Paul with synaxes at their respective basilicas (Jounel, "Sanctoral romain," 67). Antoine Chavasse (*Le sacramentaire gélasien* [*Vaticanus Reginensis* 316]: *sacramentaire presbytéral en usage dans les titres romains au VIIe siècle* [Paris: Desclée, 1958], 311–16) has analyzed the two liturgical strata and two stages of development. The weeks following the Pentecost octave are counted past the vigil and feast of John the Baptist (24 June) to the separate vigils and feasts of Peter and Paul. In the 9th century their celebration is combined on 29 June. The octave of Rome's apostles again forms a temporal milestone, after which more Sundays are counted to the feast of the Roman favorite Lawrence (10 August); then, with the September ember days, more Sundays follow the feast of the Archangel Michael (29 September), or rarely Cyprian (16 September) to Advent. An apotropaic function can be inferred from this festal sequence honoring saints whose churches stand at the city walls. For the calendrical divisions, see Chavasse, "Plus anciens types," 7.

85. Rome, Bibl. Vallicellianan, ms. cod. X, a 10th-century epistolary belonging to Roman family A, selects for the vigil of the transfiguration and the beheading of John the Baptist (29 August) Rev 1:13–18 and Rev 20 respectively (Walter Howard Frere, *Studies in Early Roman Liturgy*, vol. 2: *The Roman Gospel-Lectionary*. [London: Oxford University Press, 1934], 69).

86. In the 5th century the *titulus* of Prisca on the Aventine observed a *natale* that was celebrated as the feast of St. Prisca in the 6th century. Chavasse ("Épistolier romain du codex de Wurtzbourg: Son organisation," 330) surmises that the very limited saints' commemorations in W, the earliest epistle list, derive from the dedication feasts of churches.

Table 2.2 Sanctoral Cycle: Martyrs, Evangelists, Archangel Michael

Holy Innocents[a]	Rev 14:1–5	W A C V M	8701	
Marcellinus & Peter[b]	Rev 4:1	M		
Marcus & Marcellianus [c]	Rev 4:1	M		
Luke, evangelist	Rev 4:1	M		
In festivitate sci Michahelis[d]	Rev 12:7–12		8701 (179v)	SP F.1[e]
In natale angeli[f]	Rev 1:1–5		8701 (188v)	

"Alcuin's" commons of saints and evangelists draw on Revelation pericopes

In natale sanctorum[g]	Rev 4:1, 7:9–12	A M		SP F.1
In natale evangelistarum[h]	Rev 4:1–10a	A		

Later lectionaries add a common of martyrs with apposite readings

In natale martyrum[i]	Rev 7:13–17		8701	SP F.1

[a] Feast 28 December. The pericope refers to the 144,000 (male) martyrs sealed who have died virgins.

[b] Marcellinus and Peter were commemorated on 2 June at the "Inter duas Lauros" cemetery; see Amore, *Martiri*, 110–12; Umberto M. Fasola, "Lavori nella catacomba 'Ad duas Lauros,'" *RAC* 62 (1986): 7–37. Peter the exorcist healed Paulina, daughter of Arthemius, who was converted together with his wife Candida and baptized by the presbyter Marcellinus. On the tale of their martyrdom told by Pope Damasus's epigram, see Hertling and Kirschbaum, *Roman Catacombs*, 57–58. Some scraps of the relics of Marcellinus and Peter were obtained by Einhard for his abbey of Seligenstadt. The martyred family triad is named on the S. Prassede nave pier.

[c] Marcellianus and Marcus were commemorated on 18 June at the Basileus Cemetery on the Via Ardeatina. Paschal translated their relics to S. Prassede (Amore, *Martiri*, 199; Davis, *Lives of Eighth-Century Popes*, 92.13), where they are named in reverse order on the pier.

[d] Michael figures in Rev 12:7 and in Dan 10:13, 21 and 12:1; also Jude 9.

[e] Vatican Library, Archivio di San Pietro, cod. F.1 is a 13th-century Family A epistolary of St. Peter's of Roman usage, ca. 700, with some additions before 740 (Vogel, *Medieval Liturgy*, 354).

[f] Listed immediately after the autumn Ember Saturday readings, this feast celebrates the dedication of churches or chapels to the archangel Michael on 29 September. The *natale basilicae Angeli in Salaria* was an old and popular festival in Rome. A chapel at the city walls or north of the Alps, the upper room of a gatehouse or *Westwerk*, might be dedicated to Michael as protector.

[g] A reading appropriate to all saints and not necessarily martyrs. The palm branches signify victory.

[h] By this time the four living creatures of Rev 4:6b–9 had long been codified as symbols of the evangelists, accounting for this lection choice.

[i] The pericope about the "great ordeal" and the white robes "washed in the blood of the Lamb" is martyr-specific.

accounted for Potentiana and Praxedes being accorded the honors of the altar. With their introduction into the Würzburg gospel list (ca. 645), the commemorations of Pudentiana (19 May) and Praxedes (21 July) were celebrated liturgically.[87] Roman liturgical commemoration did not early favor the virgin mother of God. However, by the late seventh century, doubtless thanks to popes of Eastern origin, four feasts of the Virgin celebrated in Eastern churches were observed and their stational liturgies ceremonially enhanced by a *collecta* or procession with sung litanies, introduced by the Syrian Pope Sergius I (681–701).[88]

C. Dedication of a Church and of an Oratory

To the possible Revelation sources for S. Prassede's apsidal and triumphal arch iconography, found especially in the epistle lections for the propers (Rev 4:1) and commons of saints (Rev 7:9–12) and of martyrs (Rev 7:13–17), must be added the readings appointed for the dedication of a church (Rev 21:2–5) and of an oratory (Rev 21:9–27), as shown in Table 2.3.

These pericopes shed light on the unique iconography of the S. Prassede triumphal arch where appears the "holy city, new Jerusalem, coming down out of heaven from God" (Rev 21:2, cf. 3:12). In "Alcuin" the epistle for the dedication of a church (Rev 21:2–5) is invariable, and the mass for the dedication of an oratory uses, but for three verses, the remainder of the chapter (Rev 21:9–27).[89] The Roman rite of dedication of a church, a "ceremonial description of the deposition of relics," is simpler

---

87. Morin, "Liturgie et basiliques," 306 and n. 2, 311 and n. 1, 313 and n. 1, and 322–23; anomalies in placement show their novelty. On gospel lists, see Vogel, *Medieval Liturgy*, 342–44. The 13th-century St. Peter's local Roman epistolary (Vatican Library, Archivio di San Pietro, cod. F. 1) includes the feasts of SS. Pudentiana (74v) and Praxedes (100r), the latter surrounded by the Baptist (97r), Peter and Paul (98r–99r), James (101r), Pastor (101v), and the Assumption vigil and feast (103r–104r).

88. The Purification earlier known as Hypapante or St. Simeon (2 February), Annunciation of the Lord (25 March), Assumption or *natale sanctae Mariae* (15 August), and Nativity of Mary (8 September). The thesis of B. Botte ("La première fête mariale de la liturgie romaine," *EL* 47 [1933]: 425–30) that the first feast of the Virgin to be celebrated by the church of Rome was the *natale S. Mariae* on 1 January (octave of Christmas), with St. Martina sometimes mentioned, has been challenged by Jacques-Marie Guilmard, "Une antique fête mariale au 1er janvier dans la ville de Rome?," *EO* 11 (1994): 25–67. In Hadrian I's time, 1 January began to show an entry for Martina, sometimes written Maria (Frere, *Roman-Gospel Lectionary*, 89–90).

89. The dedication of an oratory is found in Würzburg (CLVI), Corbie (CLX), Paris 9451 (497), and in the Alcuinian Supplement (LXI).

Table 2.3 Dedication of a Church and of an Oratory

	Dedication of a church	Dedication of an oratory
Würzburg	Rev 21:2–5	Rev 21:9–27
Alcuin	Rev 21:2–5a	Rev 21:9b–27
Corbie	Rev 21:2–5 [+ alt.]	Rev 21:9–27
Verona = Paris 9451	3 Kgs [=1 Kgs] 8:14–53	Rev 21:9–27 + Rev 21:2–5
Vat. ms. lat. 8701	Rev 21:2[a]	

[a] In Vat. ms. lat. 8701, the lesson for the dedication of a church, located near the end of the manuscript (185r), is indicated only by an *incipit* since S. Prassede had no need of the lesson.

than that used in Byzantium or Gaul and focuses on the preparation and fitting out of the crypt. In such a ritual, the readings for the mass that achieves the consecration of the altar and church play a correspondingly important role. The dedication rite will be studied in chapter six when investigating the treasury of relics.

D. The Feast of All Saints (1 November) in the Sanctoral Cycle

Our review of possible sources of inspiration available in the liturgical readings looks for those influences that would shape the sensibilities of a liturgically learned patron intent on elaborating the eschatological imagery already in possession for apse and apsidal arch decoration in Rome. When all is considered, the possibility exists that the All Saints' festival already celebrated on 1 November in some locales north of the Alps received its impetus for extension to the universal church at S. Prassede during the pontificate of Paschal I.[90]

There are two views of the Western development of the feast of All Saints on 1 November. The extant evidence, headed by Alcuin of York's collection of masses composed circa 800, indicates that the All Saints feast on 1 November originated north of the Alps.[91] According to one view,

---

90. Jounel ("Culte collectif," 285–300) summarizes the history of the All Saints' feast, which originated north of the Alps and to which Alcuin was "devoted." Jounel (300) considers the triumphal arch to be a pictorial illustration of Rev 7 and 21 but not proof that the All Saints feast had made its way to Rome by 817.

91. André Wilmart, "Un témoin anglo-saxon du calendrier métrique d'York," *RB* 46 (1934): 51–56; J. Deshusses, "Les messes d'Alcuin," *Archiv für Liturgiewissenschaft* 14 (1972): 7–41; Deshusses, "Les anciens sacramentaires de Tours," *RB* 89 (1979): 291–94; Jounel, "Culte collectif," 290. A pupil of Alcuin, Archbishop Arno of Salzburg, attests to a local celebration in his diocese on 1 November 798 (Deshusses, "Anciens sacramentaires," 293–94; Jounel, "Culte collectif," 289).

Alcuin inserted All Saints into the Roman *comes* of 626–627 that otherwise is hardly changed.[92] Very quickly the feast was exported in all directions.[93] However, ninth-century martyrologies, beginning with Florus of Lyon and developed most fully by Ado of Vienne, presented another explanation: that at the request of Gregory IV and with the assent of the bishops, Emperor Louis the Pious (813–840) extended to the whole empire the solemnity of All Saints, already "celebrated generally" in the city of Rome.[94] The epistles for the All Saints' vigil and feast are standard in our two Roman epistolaries written in the thirteenth century (Table 2.4):[95]

The Revelation lections are clearly textual equivalents for the mosaic program of S. Prassede's liturgical center. The vigil highlights the vision of the slaughtered Lamb standing and taking the scroll as the four living creatures, the twenty-four elders and myriads of angels sing the Song of the Lamb. The feast day shows the sealing of the 144,000 servants of God and white-robed multitudes of the redeemed bearing palm branches acclaiming God and the Lamb, while countless angels sing a doxology. Between these two chapters is found the scriptural text "under the altar the souls of those who had been slaughtered for the word of God and for the testimony they had given" (Rev 6:9), which served as warrant for Paschal's relic-horde.[96] Revelation 6 treats the opening of six seals by the only one worthy to do so, the standing Lamb, theological linchpin at the center of

---

92. See Wilmart ("Lectionnaire d'Alcuin," 161, nos. 189, 190 and 176–77), whose view is that the vigil and feast of All Saints is one of the very few emendations made to the Roman epistle list of ca. 626/627 by Alcuin during his abbacy in Tours (796–804). All Saints is located near the end of the sanctoral cycle with the lections respectively Rev 5:6–12 and Rev 7:2–12. Vogel (*Medieval Liturgy*, 340–42), who concurs with Wilmart's date for the original work, thinks that the preface to the Supplement is by Helisachar (d. 836), chancellor of Louis the Pious, with the Supplement's contents drawn from a *comes* like that of Murbach, and that Alcuin introduced the vigil and feast of All Saints and the vigil of St. Martin.

93. All Saints coexisted with the local Roman *Natale S. Mariae ad Martyres* (13 May) into the 12th century. Sometime during the second quarter of the 9th century under Gregory IV (827–844), Rome claims the 1 November feast. However, manuscript evidence is lacking; the earliest extant liturgical manuscript copied in a Roman scriptorium dates from the 10th century (Jounel, "Culte collectif," 293).

94. Jounel, "Culte collectif," 291. The supposed decree, of which there is no extant trace, is dated 835 by Sigebert of Gembloux (ca. 1030–1112).

95. Vat. ms. lat. 8701 lists only *incipits* for most of the sanctoral cycle (fols. 172–188v), but the All Saints pericopes (188v–191v) are given in full.

96. This text had already inspired relic-altars in the catacombs and Gregory I's fixed altar at the west end of Old St. Peter's.

Table 2.4 Feast of All Saints, 1 November

| Vigil | Rev 5:6–12 | A | 8701 (f. 189v) | Archivio di S. Pietro, F.1[a] |
| Day | Rev 7:2–12 | A | 8701 (f. 190v) | Archivio di S. Pietro, F.1 |

[a] Family A.2, group local Roman; Antoine Chavasse, "Plus anciens types du lectionnaire et l'antiphonaire," *RB* 62 (1952): 8.

the apse's middle register, symbolizing the humanity of Christ as Priest and Intercessor for the earthly sphere (ascending christology). Above, in the heavenly sphere of the apsidal arch, the enthroned Lamb receives homage in his divinity (descending christology). Thus, the human and divine spheres are united in the person of the Incarnate Word. His theophany in majestic human form is found twice: pictured on the triumphal arch in the midst of the heavenly Jerusalem coming down from on high and, in oversize with imperial bearing in the center of the apse, in the midst of the patrons Paul and Peter representing the Roman city-church and Praxedes and Pudentiana as leaders of their *tituli*. The harps and bowls full of incense mentioned in Revelation 5:8 are replaced by the golden crowns that the elders had been wearing in the presence of the "seven torches which are the seven Spirits of God" (Rev 4:4–5). To acknowledge the Lord's hegemony, they "cast their crowns before the throne" (Rev 4:10).

Read in the light of Revelation lections for saints' feasts, S. Prassede's mosaic program provides material evidence of the liturgical relations with Rome hankered after by some members of the Carolingian court and church north of the Alps.[97] Is S. Prassede's presbyterium not the visual connecting link between, on the one hand, the developing "idea" of saints (not just martyrs) of all genres, times, and climes, named and anonymous, embodied in the mass lections and prayers Alcuin composed in their honor, and, on the other hand, the ninth-century Lyonnaise martyrologies that catalogued and created the universal calendar of saints? Of course, Louis the Pious would be loathe to acknowledge any connection with Paschal, who by this time had fallen definitively from that monarch's good graces. S. Prassede is a mute yet eloquent witness to the devotion expanded to include "all" the saints, not just bishops or martyrs of the city

---

97. Yitzhak Hen (*The Royal Patronage of Liturgy in Frankish Gaul to the Death of Charles the Bald 877* [London: Boydell Press, 2001]) revises widely accepted theories regarding Carolingian interest in Roman liturgical usages. As in other periods and places, the reality may lie somewhere between adoption and adaptation (or rejection) of Roman liturgical practice.

of Rome. This rapidly growing devotion, which Rome itself was characteristically slow to embrace fully, would shortly be codified by the martyrologists of Lyons and Vienne.

E. *Pascha annotina*

Pascha annotina was the commemorative anniversary of the previous year's baptisms and was therefore a movable feast.[98] It appears in the Würzburg gospel list but has no epistle appointed for it; the majority of early manuscripts show only a gospel reading. *Pascha annotina* was celebrated in Rome from at least circa 700, date of the extant W manuscript, and probably from the mid-seventh century.[99] Unusually, the S. Prassede epistolary (Vat. ms. lat. 8701) transcribes in full Revelation 5:1–10 (fols. 104r–105r, with 104v very rubbed, suggesting that the verso had to be held open during liturgical use). In this manuscript the commemoration is located after the Wednesday (Heb 13:17–21, 102v) and Friday (Rev 1:12–18a, 103) following the octave of Easter (*Dominica oct. pasce*).[100] Infant baptism worked against the annual observance, but Charles Borromeo, S. Prassede's titular cardinal living in Rome 1560–1566, restored the custom together with renewal of baptismal vows. To him may be attributed the worn folio.[101]

F. Developments in the Weekday Temporal Cycle

The Apocalypse's threats were thought to be directed at pagan Rome, its promises claimed by Christian Roman successors. The letter to the Hebrews, some believed, also was peculiarly Roman, written by none other than Paul to the Jewish-Christian community at Rome.[102] Along with

---

98. See Balthasar Fischer, "Formes de la commémoration du baptême en Occident," *LMD* 58 (1959): 111–34; Balthasar Fischer and Johannes Wagner, eds., *Paschatis Sollemnia: Studien zu Osterfeier und Osterfrömmigkeit* (Basel: Herder, 1959), 37–44.

99. Morin, "Liturgie et basiliques," 305. The gospel is John 3:1–15.

100. The so-called Verona Lectionary (Paris: Bibl. Nat. lat. 9451, North Italy?, late 8th century) gives only the standard gospel lesson (John 3:1–16) at no. 220 but lists the epistle lesson (Rev 4:11–5:13, which begins and ends with acclamatory hymns) among the votive masses (Amiet, "*Comes* carolingien inédit de la Haute-Italie," no. 532 at 365).

101. See Alois Stenzel, "Gedenken zur Tauffrömmigkeit," in Fischer and Wagner, *Paschatis Sollemnia*, 38.

102. Jerome, as copied by Ado, did not subscribe to this theory (Dubois, *Ado*, 3). For the author and addressee of Hebrews, see Brown and Meier, *Antioch and Rome*, 139–58.

Revelation, it formed the scriptural foundation to theological explanations of Christian liturgy and, above all, the mass. If, as we have proposed, the upper side panels of S. Prassede's triumphal arch show homeward-bound "saints," both identifiable and anonymous, hastening to the heavenly Jerusalem (Heb 12:21b–23a), we might hope to find an associated witness to support our reading. The Santa Prassede epistolary (Vat. ms. lat. 8701) adds Hebrews' vision of the heavenly Jerusalem to the strata of Hebrews' readings found in earlier *comes*. These had been inserted into certain vacant Wednesdays and Fridays immediately preceding or following the most important sections of the liturgical year.

P. Jounel sketches the history of the Wednesday (feria IV) and Friday (feria VI) weekdays. At the end of the first century they were days of fasting everywhere in the church. In the second century they became "stational" days of fasting and penitential prayer. According to the third century *Didascalia apostolorum*, Wednesday was the day of the Lord's arrest and Friday the day of his crucifixion. Leo the Great seems to witness to these days as non-eucharistic. In the sixth century, Rome had imported from Jerusalem and Cappadocia, or perhaps North Africa, the practice of eucharist on Wednesdays and Fridays. In due time the *comes* would show epistles and gospels for these days. The "Alcuin" lectionary does not show any Wednesdays outside the ember days. Representing the state of the lectionary before 740, Murbach lists gospels for Wednesdays and Fridays throughout the year but includes epistle readings only for Wednesdays.[103]

The readings from Hebrews selected for certain Wednesdays and Fridays appear as separate strata inserted after the blocks that characterize the Easter and Pentecost weeks (their octaves) had been established.[104] Wednesdays adjacent to the octaves of Easter and Pentecost were then filled out, with selected Hebrews readings introduced into the Eastertide lectionary. The "Alcuin" lectionary places the last of the traditional Sunday selections—from Hebrews 13:17–21 ("Obey your leaders...")—on the Wednesday following Sunday I after the octave of Easter, as do Murbach

---

103. On the treatment of Wednesdays and Fridays in Murbach, see Wilmart, "*Comes* de Murbach," 55–63.

104. In epistolaries, nonsequential readings from Acts take up most of the ferias in Easter week. Acts is brought back for Ascension, and again provides a block of readings in Pentecost week. Three of the Catholic epistles—1 Pet, Jas, and 1 John—are read, not in order, beginning with the Friday of Easter week, on the remaining Sundays of Paschaltide (and in W through the "eighth Sunday after the Octave of Easter"), and on the two intervening Wednesdays.

and Vatican ms. lat. 8701 (102v). The pericope from Hebrews 2:9b–3:1, apparently new with Murbach (Wednesday following Sunday I after the Ascension), is a key passage explicating the depth-dimension of Christian worship. Jesus is described as "apostle and high priest" of the worshiping assembly, and quoting Psalm 22:23 (MT Ps 22:23; LXX Ps 21:22; VG Ps 21:23), Hebrews portrays Jesus as a brother to the members of the congregation in suffering for them. In "Alcuin" and Vatican ms. lat. 8701 (114r–115r) this text is found on the Friday following Sunday I after Ascension, maintaining the narrative expression for the ancient patristic understanding of Christ's active presence in the liturgy, which would be recovered by Carolingian monastic theologians during the early ninth century.

Sometime between the eighth and early thirteenth centuries additional lessons were introduced into the weekdays.[105] Prescinding from the already established Lenten, Easter octave and Pentecost weeks, the Friday epistles found in the S. Prassede epistolary are such additions. Revelation 1:12–18a vividly describes the Son of Man appearing in the midst of seven golden lampstands: "I am the first and the last, and the living one" (fol. 103).[106] A unique reading on the Friday following the Easter octave, it appears to have entered this "local" lectionary, under the influence of the presbytery mosaics, on the first available vacant Friday within Eastertide (Table 2.5).

Besides the two pericopes treated above—Wednesday of Week I following the Easter octave (VIIII, Heb 13:17–21) and the Friday of the week following Ascension (XV, Heb 2:9b–3:1)—the Alcuinian Supplement provides lessons from Hebrews in a list of readings for weekdays following the Pentecost octave: Hebrews 12:28b–13:8 (XX); 4:12–16 (XXXII); 10:19–31 (XL); 12:11–14 (XLVIII); 3:12–14 (XLVIIII). Würzburg had ended its list of Pauline pericopes assigned to Sundays (nos. 214–255) with six from Hebrews.[107] A comparison with the table above shows that only some are replicated, and in the lectionaries they appear scattered. At another juncture in the development of the calendar, Murbach and Vatican ms. lat.

---

105. The pericopes from the letter to the Hebrews, appointed for certain Wednesdays and Fridays in Paschaltide and again on Wednesday and Friday of the 24th week and Friday of Trinity week, appear as separate strata, "dropped in" out of sequence. In the late 8th century, Murbach's nonsequential Hebrews readings for the Wednesdays (12:3–9) of Sexagesima (the prefatory week to Lent adopted at the time of Gregory I) and Septuagesima (4:11–16, mid-7th century) appear inserted.

106. If we can judge from the three witnesses cited by Frere, *Roman Epistle-Lectionary*, 58–61.

107. CCL–CCLV from Heb 1:13–2:3; 10:32–38; 4:11–16; 12:3–9; 12:12–23; 13:17–21.

Table 2.5 Revelation and Hebrews: Additions to the Weekday Lectionary

	Wednesday, feria IV		Friday, feria VI	
Wk I post Easter Octave	Heb 13:17–21	A, M, 8701	*Rev 1:12–18a*	*8701*
Wk II post Easter Octave	*Heb 9:24–28*	*8701*		
Wk I post Ascension	Heb 2:9b–3:1	M	Heb 2:9b–3:1	A, 8701
7th Wk post Pentecost	Heb 12:28b–13:8/7	M	Heb 12:28b–13:8/7	8701
Ember Sat[a] in Sept	Heb 9:2–12	W, etc.	Heb 9:2–12	8701
24th Wk post Pentecost	*Heb 3:12–4:3a*	*8701*	*Heb 10:19–27*	*8701*
TrinitySun (25th/last)			*Heb 12:12–23*	*8701*

W = Würzburg

A = "Alcuin"

M = Murbach (provides NO Friday epistles)

8701 = Vat. ms. lat. 8701, 13th-cent. S. Prassede lectionary. Texts unique to 8701 are italicized.

[a] Ember Saturday of September, 6th reading (Vat. ms. lat. 8701, fols. 158–159). Heb 9:2–12 is already present in W (CLI) and is the constant reading for this ordination day.

8701 selected Hebrews 12:28b–13:8/13:7 as an isolated epistle reading for the Wednesday of the seventh week after Pentecost.

The affinity between Murbach's Wednesday epistle selections and Vatican ms. lat. 8701 in Paschaltide is apparent. At the end of the liturgical year, however, there is no such correspondence. Vatican ms. lat. 8701 provides Wednesday and Friday of the twenty-fourth week with apt readings from Hebrews 3:12–4:3a and 10:19–27. The lengthy Hebrews 12:12–23 pericope about approaching the heavenly Jerusalem, in second-last place in the Würzburg epistolary for Sunday (CCLIIII) and not utilized elsewhere, appears in the S. Prassede epistolary on the Friday of Holy Trinity week, that is, the Friday after the twenty-fifth and final Sunday of the liturgical year.

Having explored passages from Revelation and Hebrews in the Roman lectionary, it is not necessary to choose one or other of the above themes (in exclusion to all others) as Paschal's inspiration for the mosaic program of the presbytery. The multiple sources spelled out above would combine to provide weight and depth to the pope's ruminations as he kept vigil in the dilapidated *titulus*.[108]

---

108. Davis, *Lives of Ninth-Century Popes*, 100.8.

3. Ascending Christology, Resurrection Scenes, and Paschal's Small-Scale Art Commissions

Ascending christology, with its theme of Christ's priesthood is as central to the letter to the Hebrews as it is to the Roman canon, where Christ's mediation of liturgical prayer is repeatedly expressed in the phrase *per Christum Dominum nostrum* concluding each section of the presidential prayer. The epistle for the Wednesday following the first Sunday after Ascension in the Murbach *comes*, which the S. Prassede Epistolary (Vat. ms. lat. 8701) uses for the Friday of that same week (Heb 2:9b-3:1), illustrates ascending christology:

> [We see Jesus] crowned with glory and honor...He who sanctifies and those who are sanctified have all one origin...He is not ashamed to call them brothers saying, "I will proclaim your name to my brothers, in the midst of the congregation I will praise you." [He is]...a merciful high priest in the service of God, to make expiation for the sins of the people...Therefore holy brothers, who share in a heavenly call, consider Jesus the apostle and high priest of our confession.

In Hebrews 2:12–13, especially appropriate to the post-Ascension period, the exalted Christ addresses God, his words taken from Psalm 21:23 in the Vulgate (MT Ps 22:23; LXX Ps 21:22), at the transition point where the individual lament becomes a song of praise. The Vulgate of Hebrews 2:12 reads as a verbatim translation of the Hebrew and Greek texts, *Nuntiabo nomen tuum fratribus meis; in medio ecclesiae laudabo te*, "I will proclaim your name to my brothers in the midst of the congregation," the phrase "to my brothers," in synonymous parallelism with "in the midst of the congregation," thus leading medievals to understand the inclusion of the "sisters" with the brothers.[109] Hebrews 2:9b–3:1 throws light on the interpretation of the central panel of a reliquary cross, one of only three of Pope Paschal's small-scale commissions to survive. Now on display in the Museo Sacro of the Vatican Library, its provenance is the Sancta Sanctorum, the old papal chapel and treasury of the Lateran Palace.[110] The top and sides of the silver-gilt cross, which once

---

109. In some manuscripts of the mass ordinary from the Carolingian period onward, "fratres" is expanded to read "et sorores." See Joseph A. Jungmann, *The Mass of the Roman Rite: Its Origins and Development (Missarum Sollemnia)*, trans. Francis A. Brunner (2 vols.; New York: Benziger, 1955), 2:85–86.

110. Achille Petrignani, *Il santuario della Scala Santa* (Vatican City: PIAC, 1941); Wolfgang Fritz Volbach, *Il tesoro della Cappella Sancta Sanctorum* (Vatican: BAV, 1941); Thunø, *Image and Relic*, 17–23. For plates and description of these reliquaries, see Leonard von Matt, *Art*

must have held a relic of the true cross, are decorated with seventeen scenes executed in low relief, all having Marian, paschal, or eucharistic content.[111]

Although for the Carolingian era *Liber Pontificalis* (hereafter *LP*) cites many papal commissions with resurrection themes in metalwork and textiles, no others of Roman provenance appear to have survived.[112] However, at least two ivories, associated with the Court School at Aachen, are extant. A pair of ivory panels for a book cover (Aachen, Schatzkammer), three scenes to a side, share the elongated proportions of consular diptychs.[113] Their style is more sophisticated and sculptural—indeed, a better evocation of the classical world—than the metalwork commissioned by Paschal. The scenes are not readily identifiable.[114] A second ivory book cover of similar proportions, in the Cathedral Treasury of Milan, is arranged four scenes per side, one above the other, divided by ground lines or architectural segments rather than frames.[115] This diptych also contains

---

Treasures of the Vatican Library, text by G. Daltrop and A. Prandi (New York: Abrams: 1970), figs. 70–81, cat. nos. 70–81, pp. 171–73; see Metropolitan Museum exhibition catalogue, *The Vatican Collections: The Papacy and Art* (New York: Metropolitan Museum of Art, H. N. Abrams, 1982), nos. 37–38, 100–102.

111. The inscription reads: PASCHALIS EPISCOPUS PLEBI DEI FIERI IUSSIT. The scenes on the top of the cross-reliquary may be identified as follows: center, Christ presiding at the earthly liturgy (cf. Heb 2:9b–3:1); from the top counter-clockwise: Christ among the Doctors (Luke 2:46–50); Cana (John 2:1–12); Christ appears in the upper room ("Peace be with you," John 20:19–23); the discourse on the true vine (John 15:1–17). The twelve scenes on the sides do not read consecutively but rather are arranged from the spectator's viewpoint. Margaret B. Freeman (*Vatican Collections*, 101) proposes that the cycle begins with "an unusual scene that may depict Christ conducting Adam from Hades, as related in the Apocryphal Gospels," namely, the Anastasis as favored in Byzantine iconography of the resurrection (1 Pet 3:18). The disciples in the upper room and Thomas (John 20:19–29) are paralleled at the base of the cross by the two Marys, Mary of Magdala and another Mary not the Virgin (Matt 28:1–10). Emmaus (Luke 24:15–35) and Jesus appearing to the apostles (Luke 38–43) are completed by the single episode of Peter and John running to the tomb (John 20:3–9). For iconography and complete illustrations of the casket, see Thunø, *Image and Relic*, 79–117 and figs. 65–79.

112. During the Carolingian period resurrection cycles were favored in the West. Of 53 *vestes cum storiis* (historiated altar hangings) bestowed by Leo III on churches, 23 have resurrection themes; see L. Edward Philipps, "A Note on the Gifts of Leo III to the Churches of Rome: 'Vestes cum storiis,'" *EL* 102 (1988): 72–78; Davis, *Lives of Eighth-Century Popes*, 98:99, 101–4, 111.

113. Peter Lasko, *Ars Sacra, 800–1200* (Baltimore, MD: Penguin, 1972), 31.

114. Illustrated in John Beckwith, *The Andrews Diptych* (London: H.M.S.O., 1958), illus. 4. The right panel should be read first. See also Thunø, *Image and Relic*, for these and other comparative materials.

115. K. Wessel, "Das Mailänder Passionsdiptychon, ein Werk der karolingischen Renaissance," *Zeitschrift für Kunstwissenschaft* 5 (1951): 125–38.

rare scenes, with the passion (lacking the crucifixion) and burial on one side and, on the other, two women encountering an angel at the empty tomb and two women encountering Christ (Matt 28), Christ appearing to the Eleven in the upper room, and Christ inviting Thomas to inspect the wound in his side (John 20).

Possible textual sources for Paschal's cross-reliquary and the book covers of the Carolingian court discussed here as well as no longer extant papal objects d'art include the eighth-century fully developed evangeliary (Murbach) and the gospel lessons for Easter Week, as known in their Old Roman version from the homilies of Gregory I (590–593) and his reorganization of these readings in 595–597.[116] However, the sequence of episodes depicted on Paschal's cross reliquary corresponds to none of these but forms an independent pictorial cycle.[117] The provenance, iconography, and sources of this cross reliquary have been treated exhaustively by Erik Thunø.[118]

In the central field on the reliquary's top a beardless Christ as priest of the church's eucharist presides at an altar of Byzantine type equipped with liturgical vessels (Fig. 2.3).[119] Not precisely the Communion of the Apostles so favored in the East both before and after the iconoclastic controversy,[120]

---

116. Chavasse, "Plus anciens types," 73–74.

117. A shorter but similar pictorial cycle in fresco is found on the west wall of the presbytery of S. Maria Antiqua, Rome, in the frescoes attributed to John VII (Nordhagen, *Frescoes of John VII*, 31–38 and pls. XXXIII–XXXVIIIa).

118. Thunø, *Image and Relic*, 79–117.

119. Patristic iconography and theology common to East and West depicted Christ, visually and in euchology and theology, as primary agent of the word and sacraments. Narrative symbols—the figure of the Shepherd, the Cana miracle where water is transformed into wine, presidency of the Church's eucharist, or Christ enthroned as king (later Byzantine)—represent this doctrinal position. Postdating Paschal's reliquary by a few years, the first treatise on the eucharist written in the West, by the abbot of Corbie Paschasius Radbertus (d. 851 or 860; first edition 831–833), capitalizes on the patristic notion of Christ as priest (Paschasius Radbertus, *De corpore et sanguine Domini*, ed. Beda Paulus. [CCCM 16; Turnhout: Brepols, 1969]). Benedictine monastic theology maintained for the Latin church the theme of Christ's active presence in the liturgy (Schaefer, "Heavenly and Earthly Liturgies," 494–503). Paschal's commission anticipates the extant monastic textual witnesses.

120. In Middle Byzantine apse programs the monumental figure of *Maria orans* may be placed above the frieze depicting Christ giving communion to the apostles. William Loerke, "The Monumental Miniature," in Kurt Weitzmann et al., *The Place of Book Illumination in Byzantine Art* (Princeton, NJ: Art Museum, Princeton University Press, 1975), esp. 78–97, gives Byzantine ms. examples; also see Gertrud Schiller, *Iconography of Christian Art*, vol. 2: *The Passion of Jesus Christ*, trans. Janet Seligman (Greenwich, CT: New York Graphic Society, 1972), 28–30 and figs. 56–66.

94   WOMEN IN PASTORAL OFFICE

FIGURE 2.3 Vatican, Biblioteca Apostolica Vaticana: Silver-gilt reliquary cross of Paschal I. Detail: Christ presiding at eucharist. By permission of Biblioteca Apostolica Vaticana, with all rights reserved.

the scene betrays, in style and iconography, a Western hand.[121] Striking, and unique to this subject in East or West, is the placement of the interceding Theotokos at her priestly son's right hand, with Peter at Christ's left and the male disciples crowding behind.[122] All of the vignettes on the cover show Christ holding a rotulus in his left hand, with his mother or one of the women resurrection-witnesses (wearing coif with cross on the

---

121. See Victor H. Elbern, *Die Goldschmiedekunst im frühen Mittelalter* (Darmstadt: Wissenschaftliche Buchgesellschaft, 1988), 56 and pl. 52. Elbern cannot name a parallel pictorial series but discerns an early Christian compositional scheme of ca. 400. Two angels in the upper sections of the scene are reminiscent of deacon-angels holding *rhipidia* (liturgical fans) in post-iconoclastic Byzantine examples, indicating a pivotal place for Paschal's cross-reliquary in iconographical development. Christ standing at the altar and holding a *rotulus* (cf. *Traditio legis* iconography or Heb 10:7) is found in the liturgical scroll of the Jerusalem patriarchate, late 11th century, where it illustrates the Great Entrance; see André Grabar, "Un rouleau liturgique constantinopolitain et ses peintures," *Dumbarton Oaks Papers* 8 (1954): 174 and fig. 10.

122. The only other examples of Christ with his mother and the apostolic band known to the author are those listed among the altar hangings bestowed by Pope Leo III on the basilicas of St. Peter's (the faces of Christ, Mary, and the Twelve; see Davis, *Lives of Eighth-Century Popes*, 98.33), and St. Paul's (Christ, Mary, and the Twelve; ibid., 98.60). Neither of these hangings has survived.

forehead) standing prominently at his right.[123] The importance to Paschal of the mother-son relationship is demonstrated here in small scale. Returning to the eastern side aisle at the church's longitudinal mid-point, and reminiscent of the Archiepiscopal Chapel in Ravenna, a mosaic wall grandly signals the entrance to the Zeno Chapel.

4. The Zeno Chapel and Its Themes

Demanding attention, the white marble doorway giving entry to the Zeno Chapel is framed by two black granite columns bearing Ionic capitals whose impost blocks carry a broad antique cornice (Fig. 2.4).[124] A third-century strigillated marble cinerary urn atop the lintel signals the chapel's funerary function. The urn is framed by a round-headed window, its deep embrasure ornamented with a decorative design in mosaic. Above the lintel-cornice and its flanking expanse of bare wall rises a mosaic wall, intact but for two rectangles of relatively recent manufacture displaying modern busts of two pontiffs at the base of the outside arc. Within the whole rectangular field pierced by the window are three sections consisting of spandrels with two busts (of prophets?) and two roughly concentric arcs. Within each arc, roundels (*clipei*) contain "portrait" busts. A large bust of Christ blessing is placed at the apex of the outer, broader arc. He is flanked by Paul and Peter, with five additional busts of apostles on each side. Two tonsured males flank the inner set of eleven roundels, arranged in a horseshoe shape, with the Virgin and Child at its apex. Eight *clipei*, four to a side, contain women wearing crowns, earrings, and golden

---

123. Of the cover of the cross-reliquary Margaret B. Freeman (*Vatican Collections*, 101) observes, "The events depicted on the lid of this casket seem to have been chosen to honour the Virgin Mary. She played a prominent role in the Gospel accounts of Christ among the Doctors and the Marriage at Cana...She is, however, seldom, if ever, shown at the Communion or Mission of the Apostles." Freeman connects the uninscribed silver-gilt reliquary casket from the *Sancta Sanctorum* (*Vatican Collections*, no. 38, 101–2; *Art Treasures of the Vatican Library*, figs. 78–81, cat. 78–81; Thunø's "rectangular casket" with eschatological imagery on top and front, 53–63) with the apse mosaic of S. Prassede and Pope Paschal's cross-reliquary referred to above; it contained the gold and cloisonné enamel cross (ibid., nos. 75–77, figs. 75–78) with scenes of Christ's childhood (Annunciation to Baptism), indebted to 5th-century iconography, on the back.

124. The Zeno Chapel has been studied by Beat Brenk, "Zum Bildprogramm der Zenokapelle in Rom," *Archivio Español de Arqueologia* 45–47 (1973–1974): 213–21; Klass, "Chapel of S. Zeno"; Marianne W. Asmussen, "The Chapel of S. Zeno in S. Prassede in Rome," *Analecta Romana Instituti Danici* 15 (1986): 67–87; Gillian Mackie, "The Iconographic Programme of the Zeno Chapel at Santa Prassede, Rome" (M.A. thesis, University of Victoria, Canada, 1984) and Mackie, "Zeno Chapel"; Rotraut Wisskirchen, "Zur Zenokapelle in S. Prassede/Rom," *Frühmittelalterliche Studien* 25 (1991): 96–108.

96   WOMEN IN PASTORAL OFFICE

FIGURE 2.4 Rome, S. Prassede, Zeno Chapel. Façade. Scala/Art Resource, NY.

outfits. The juxtaposition of male and female busts in *clipei* brings to mind the arches of the low vault of the Archiepiscopal Chapel, Ravenna (ca. 494–519).[125] Alternation of gold, dark blue, and green grounds for the sections and within the *clipei* provides visual unity in this unique composition on the Zeno Chapel's portal.[126]

Christ and the Twelve are readily identifiable in the larger arc. While there is no clue to the identity of the two busts in the spandrels, Mackie's proposal of Enoch and Elijah, prophets who were transported bodily into

---

125. Where are depicted, but on separate arches, the twelve apostles, including Paul, with Christ in the center; six female saints (Felicitas, Perpetua, Daria, Eufemia, Eugenia, and Cecilia); and six male saints (Chrysanthus, Chrysogonus, Cassian, Polycarp, Cosmas, and Damian), all identified by name.

126. Mosaic busts in roundels are well known in areas of Byzantine influence (the 6th-century apse mosaic at Mt. Sinai, St. Catherine's monastery; at Ravenna, in the St. Vitale presbytery and the Archiepiscopal Chapel; at the Euphrasiana, Parenzo). Mackie ("Zeno Chapel," 189) proposes a model close to home, the 5th-century triumphal arch at S. Sabina.

heaven (Gen 5:24, 2 Kgs 2:11), is intriguing.[127] Of the two male figures who flank Mary and the Child at the apex of the inner horseshoe, the tonsured elder on the right can probably be identified as Zeno the presbyter.[128] The youthful tonsured figure on the left, wearing a yellow dalmatic, might then be a deacon. Thus a deacon and a priest accompany Mary who is *episcopa* by virtue of being mother of the Son. The parallel with Theodora and Paschal is nicely hinted at. Who then are the remaining eight women, companions of Mary and her Child? In other settings they might be the titular saints together with female martyrs named in the Roman canon of the mass.[129] In parallelism with the twelve apostles in the outer arc, it is more likely that these are the eight women disciples who followed Jesus, comparable in the gospels to the twelve male disciples.[130] With this reading of the chapel's façade the interior will now be considered.

---

127. Suggested by the literary source of the Anastasis tympanum in the interior as well as the chapel's general eschatological theme (Mackie, "Zeno Chapel," 190). The Gospel of Nicodemus/Acts of Pilate and Christ's Descent into Hell, 9 (25) reads, "The holy fathers asked [two old men]: 'Who are you, who have not seen death nor gone down into Hades, but dwell in paradise with your bodies and souls?' One of them answered, 'I am Enoch, who pleased God and was removed here by him. And this is Elijah the Tishbite. We shall live until the end of the world. But then we shall be sent by God to withstand Antichrist and to be killed by him. And after three days we shall rise again and be caught up in clouds to meet the Lord." See *New Testament Apocrypha*, vol. 1: *Gospels and Related Writings*, 475.

128. Mackie's ("Zeno Chapel," 189) comparison with the elderly figure on Christ's right in the interior south tympanum is convincing. "Paschal's mosaicists created recognisable facial features which were used wherever a certain individual was portrayed, allowing comparison of unnamed figures with the named figures in the chapel" (ibid., 184). Unfortunately Zeno is nowhere identified by name.

129. So Marguerite Gautier-van Berchem and Etienne Clouzot, *Mosaïques chrétiennes du IVme au Xme siècle* (Rome: Bretschneider, 1965), 238. But which ones? There are seven martyrs named in the *Nobis quoque peccatoribus*: the martyred mothers Felicitas (probably of Rome since she precedes Perpetua) and Perpetua (Africa), and the virgin-martyrs Agatha and Lucy (Sicily), Agnes and Cecilia (Rome) and Anastasia (Orient or Rome). Subtracting the revered martyr of Carthage, Perpetua, and counting Felicity as Roman, five serve as patrons of Roman titular churches (Agatha, Lucia, Agnes, Cecilia, and Anastasia). Adding Praxedes and Pudentiana would yield eight Roman women. All are dressed as brides awaiting Christ, their eschatological husband. The Basilica Euphrasiana apse, Parenzo, displays *clipei* of twelve named female saints, a local variant of those named in the ancient Ambrosian canon; see V. L. Kennedy, *The Saints of the Canon of the Mass* (Vatican City: PIAC, 1963), 40, 71–72, 168–93; Otto von Simson, *Sacred Fortress* (Princeton, NJ: Princeton University Press, 1987), 83–87. Mackie ("Zeno Chapel," 190) favors the Roman canon of the mass theory, noting that "all those named were seen as being present at every eucharistic rite".

130. Joan Morris, *The Lady Was a Bishop: The Hidden History of Women with Clerical Ordination and the Jurisdiction of Bishops* (New York: Macmillan, 1973), 114. The evidence for female disciples comparable to the twelve has been compiled by Carla Ricci, *Mary Magdalene and Many Others: Women Who Followed Jesus* (Minneapolis: Fortress, 1994), 175.

The Zeno Chapel forms an irregular Greek cross in plan.[131] The chapel's squarish center bay (3.5 x 3.6 m) is covered by a groin vault carried on four granite columns resting on ninth-century bases. Typically the three barrel-vaulted arms (*exedrae*) were designed to accommodate sarcophagi. Plan and elevation imitate late antique and early Christian memorial chapels and mausolea.[132]

Since S. Prassede is oriented in a northerly direction, the Zeno Chapel on its east flank receives the rays of the rising sun through a window placed high up on the wall (Fig. 2.5).[133] The youthful Christ pantocrator (all-ruler), encircled by a laurel wreath, is supported overhead on the groin vault by four caryatid angels.[134] A huge porphyry disc in the floor echoes the vault tondo. A proto-Byzantine *deesis* (figures of the Theotokos and John the Baptist) flanks the east window.[135] SCA MARIA and SCS IOHANNIS,

---

131. The cross-in-square (quincunx) was the typical Byzantine church-plan developed during the late 6th through late 9th centuries. See Vincenzo Ruggieri, *Byzantine Religious Architecture (582–867): Its History and Structural Elements* (Rome: PIO, 1991); Richard Krautheimer, *Early Christian and Byzantine Architecture* (Harmondsworth: Penguin, 1965), 362; and Krautheimer, *Rome*, 128–34.

132. Such a tomb chapel dedicated to the martyr Tiburtius was attached to the north flank of the *basilica maior* (large covered cemetery) built by Constantine above the catacomb of saints Marcellinus and Peter on the grounds of his mother's estate (Krautheimer, *Rome*, 130). The mausoleum attached to the east portico and porphyry sarcophagus probably intended for an emperor (Vatican, Museo Pio-Clementino) were ceded to his mother Helena (d. 336). Galla Placidia (d. 450), daughter of Theodosius and *augusta* of the Western Roman Empire from 421 to her death in Rome, built in Ravenna ca. 425 a cruciform domed chapel of brick 15 m by 13 m dedicated to St. Lawrence and attached to the portico of the cruciform church of Santa Croce. Known as Galla Placidia's mausoleum, its arms hold three family sarcophagi. See Giuseppe Bovini, *Il cosidetto Mausoleo di Galla Placidia in Ravenna* (Vatican City: Società Amici Catacombe presso PIAC, 1950); Wolfgang Fritz Volbach, *Early Christian Art* (New York: Abrams, 1962), pls. 144–47 and catalogue, pp. 339–40). Barrel vaults, lunettes, and dome are covered with figural and ornamental mosaic above marble revetments.

133. Wisskirchen ("Zur Zenokapelle," 106–8) discusses the question of "light-symbolism" raised by Asmussen ("Chapel of S. Zeno," 67–86), who had proposed that the light streaming through the east window represented Christ, essential to a *deesis* composition (the Theotokos and John the Forerunner petitioning Christ). But the bust of Christ appears on the vault. The orientation of Mary and the Baptist toward Christ is the solution Mackie ("Zeno Chapel," 175–77) offers to the *deesis* problem.

134. The design, inspired by the Chapel of the Holy Cross in the Lateran (where the medallion contained a cross), is extant in the Archiepiscopal Chapel, Ravenna (with a Chi-Rho within the medallion) and is also seen in the presbyterium vault at S. Vitale, Ravenna (with the Lamb). Mackie ("Zeno Chapel," 173–75) explains the shift from symbol to human figure.

135. Poses, garments, and colors conform to the Byzantine symbolic code. *Maria orans* is caught in the contrapposto pose common to all the women. She is dressed in heavenly blue: a tunic with embroidered wristlets and a gold-edged palla, and gold-bordered *maphorion*. The Baptist wears a yellow tunic with red *clavi* and cloak of penitential purple. In his

Iconography and Sources 99

FIGURE 2.5 Rome, S. Prassede. Zeno Chapel, interior. East wall with *Deesis* and window. Lunette below: Transfiguration. Photograph by Mary M. Schaefer.

as do all the saintly figures who offer acclamations, crowns, or attributes, face the image of the cosmic Christ.[136]

Based on the Cassiano dal Pozzo drawings of 1630–1640, Mackie convincingly reconstructs the left (north) niche of the Zeno Chapel as the location of Theodora's sarcophagus. In fact, the design is inspired by the

---

left hand he carries a cross-staff with an *Agnus Dei* medallion, with the right gesturing with thumb and fourth finger held together. As do all the male figures, he strides forward.

136. Mackie ("Zeno Chapel," 179) interprets all the standing figures on the upper walls as intercessors participating in liturgical prayers for the dead Theodora whose mausoleum this is. Other "liturgical" readings have been proposed. Klass ("Chapel of S. Zeno," 122) claims that the whole is "a Byzantine sanctuary in miniature that answered the liturgical needs of the resident monks. Essential architectural features of a Byzantine church are present: a centrally planned space, a holy table beneath a dome of heaven, a niche which functions as a prothesis, and an iconostasis which separates the clergy from lay participants." The screen demarcating the sanctuary (what centuries later becomes an iconostasis) is presumably the entry portal with its mosaic wall. Wisskirchen (*Mosaiken der Kirche S. Prassede*, 57, 61) locates a (hypothetical) altar *versus populum*, calls the gestures of the six saints on the north and south walls acclamatory, and notes that all the figures are "personally involved" in the offerings of crowns or acclamations to the cosmic Christ overhead, as would be a presider standing at a free-standing altar. These last theories are not convincing; besides, the space is inadequate. The mosaic of Madonna and Child in the niche above the small altar against the east end may date from the 11th century.

arcosolia of catacombs.[137] The dedication of the right (south) niche, with an altar formerly holding a casket containing the relics of Zeno, signals the oratory's double function as mausoleum-martyrium.[138] As with Galla Placidia's mausoleum in Ravenna, the dedication is to a martyr, and the function is funerary. Since burials of popes and ordinary Christians clustered around the place made sacred by the bones of Peter in the Vatican hill, this double function became characteristic of Christian devotion. The shimmering glass mosaics that cover the upper walls and vaults convert the antique design into a Christian symbol of the eschatological garden of paradise. The epistle for the dedication of an oratory (Rev 21:9-27) in W, C, V, and the Alcuinian Supplement is the obvious textual source for the squarish ground plan. A longitudinal basilica did not lend itself to imaging the foursquare plan of New Jerusalem (Rev 21:16; cf. Ezek 41:4) but a small chapel did.

The Zeno Chapel's mosaics have been typified as "the earliest surviving example of a classical Middle-Byzantine decorative programme," related spiritually to Nicaea II (787) and reflecting those Constantinopolitan buildings that did not survive the iconoclastic controversies or could not be built during them.[139] A sober judgment, which acknowledges both the chapel's proto-Byzantine features and the importance of Roman and Ravennate models, might conclude that this unique chapel is a nearly intact production of the first millennium church whose bitter political and theological disputes did not prevent the creative appropriation and salvaging of devotional and artistic resources. The chapel's proto-Byzantine pictorial program was born within a revival of Roman Christian antiquity.

---

137. Tombs were placed within arched niches (arcosolia), reviving Roman catacomb practice during the Carolingian period. See Robert Melzak, "Antiquarianism in the Time of Louis the Pious and its Influence on the Art of Metz," in *Charlemagne's Heir: New Perspectives on the Reign of Louis the Pious (814-840)*, ed. Peter Godman and Roger Collins (Oxford: Clarendon, 1990), 630 and n. 9. For restoration drawings of arcosolia for Sts. Peter and Marcellinus in their catacomb on the via Labicana, and for St. Januarius at Praetextatus, see Nicolai, Bisconti and Mazzoleni, *Catacombes chrétiennes de Rome*, figs. 56, 57.

138. Amore, *Martiri*, 183. Nothing secure is known of Zeno, but sharing the *natale* of 14 February probably accounts for Valentine, another sketchy character, documented as honored here from the 13th century.

139. Mackie, "Zeno Chapel," 172, following Brenk, "Zum Bildprogramm der Zenokapelle," 213-21; Krautheimer, *Rome*, 128-37. Byzantinizing features include the hierarchical design; the earliest version of the human Christ in what is later termed the "Pantocrator" (All-Ruler) type (instead of Lamb, cross, or Chi Rho) at the center of a vault, while utilizing Roman iconographical sources (Mackie, "Zeno Chapel," 173-75); and the Virgin and St. John the Forerunner petitioning the half-figure youthful Christ overhead.

The *Liber Pontificalis* explains the motivation for Paschal's commission:

> ...in his anxiety to gain aid before the Lord almighty by the prayers of those whose holy bodies are buried therein,...he constructed in that place from its foundations a monastery...; he gathered a holy community of Greeks, which he placed therein to carry out carefully by day and night praises to almighty God and his saints resting therein, chanting the psalms in the Greek manner...Also in that church he built an oratory of Christ's martyr St. Zeno....[140]

Both Mackie and Davis take this monastery dedicated to St. Praxedes to have been incorporated into the existing monastery of St. Agnes ad Dua(s) Furna(s), whose oratory was dedicated to the Roman martyr Agnes.[141] Mackie infers that the Zeno Chapel was one of the oratories of the Greek monastery established by Paschal.[142] The chapel is too small to house the daily round of monastic liturgical prayer of even a small community. Nor does it have the earmarks of a Byzantine or Ravennate-Byzantine chapel; rather, in design it is a Roman mausoleum. However, it might have served as a secondary oratory.[143]

While Hebrews and Revelation inspired the presbytery mosaics, the Zeno Chapel's decorative program was inspired by other textual sources: the *epistola catholica* (the letter of James, the two letters of Peter, the three letters of John, and the brief letter of Jude). On the inside wall over the door, slender figures of SCS PETRUS and SCS PAULUS, floating against a gold ground above a flowery lawn symbolic of paradise, acclaim

---

140. Davis, *Lives of Ninth-Century Popes*, 100.9–10.

141. The new monastery was "known later as 'SS. Praxedes et Agnes qui appellatur Duas Furnas'" (Davis, *Lives of Ninth-Century Popes*, 100.9 and n. 27). Theodore Studite (ca. 759–826), who introduced an urban cenobitic reformation into Byzantium, corresponded with Paschal I. However, we have no evidence regarding the origin, associations, or type of monastic organization of those Greek monks Paschal welcomed to Rome, nor of the character of the buildings established for them.

142. Mackie, "Zeno Chapel," 179.

143. Such chapels were found in the *koinobion*, the "monastery as a Christian village" (Ruggieri, *Byzantine Religious Architecture*, 174–75). Eastern monasteries were typically located in a rural area away from the city, but that of St. John Stoudion in Constantinople (f. 463), inhabited by the Stoudite confederation only in 799, is the exception. S. Prassede was located on the edge of the inhabited area of Rome, in an area of vineyards and fields on the Esquiline hill extending to the Lateran, with other monasteries in the neighborhood.

the *etimasia*, the symbolic throne readied for judgment.[144] Peter clutches his key in bare hand; Paul grasps a rotulus. On the south wall are scs IOHANNIS, supposed to have died in Ephesus; scs ANDREAS, proto-apostle of the East who introduced his brother Simon Peter to Jesus; and scs IACOBUS, either the brother of John or more likely the brother of the Lord, first bishop of Jerusalem, and putative author of the letter of James (Fig. 2.6).[145] Facing the heavenly throne of judgment, John cradles the gemmed book of Revelation in draped hands.[146] Andrew and James, carrying scrolls in hands likewise reverently draped, process toward the east. All participate in the heavenly liturgy. "Peter and Paul, Andrew, James, John..." are the first five names recited in the *Communicantes* of the Roman canon. Is there any document that, keeping the same ordering as the Roman canon, can clarify the troublesome identification of the James in the Zeno mosaic? The *Notitia de locis ss. apostolorum* prefacing the Hieronymian Martyrology combines the two Jameses: "VI Kl. Ian., nat. apostolorum s. Iacobi fratris Domini et Iohannis evang."[147]

---

144. The Zeno Chapel's throne, with bolster on which rests a cross, and footstool, is a reduced version of the christological symbol in the Constantinian apse of S. John Lateran (Wisskirchen, *Mosaiken*, 52–55 and fig. 33). Mackie ("Zeno Chapel," 178–79), noting that the empty throne in early Christian art represents Christ's glorious presence, while in post-iconoclastic art it is the throne prepared for Christ's second coming, prefers this latter eschatological reading. For an overview of the iconography, see Van der Meer, *Maiestas Domini*, 229–50.

145. The apostle John "the beloved," whose ministry bore fruit in Asia Minor, was identified as the author of Revelation; cf. Vulgate; St. Gall, cod. 454, 30–31; and Vat. ms. lat. 8701, fol. 104 referring to "Apocalypsis beati Joannis Apostoli." On Andrew as missionary-founder of the see of Byzantium and his death by crucifixion, see St. Gall, cod. 454, 29–30 and Francis Dvornik, *The Idea of Apostolicity in Byzantium and the Legend of the Apostle Andrew* (Cambridge, MA: Harvard University Press, 1958). James could be either James son of Zebedee, first apostolic martyr (Acts 12:2) who was brother of John (St. Gall, cod. 454, 30 and Raymond Brown, *Churches the Apostles Left Behind*, 14–15) or James the Less, brother of the Lord and martyr-bishop of Jerusalem to whom the letter of James was ascribed (St. Gall, cod. 454, 32–33). Mackie ("Zeno Chapel," 177–78) does not distinguish the two Jameses. For recent discussion, see Donald A. Hagner, "James," in *Anchor Bible Dictionary* (New York: Doubleday, 1992), 3:616–18, and Florence Morgan Gillman, "James, Brother of Jesus," *Anchor Bible Dictionary*, 3:620–21.

146. Mackie, "Zeno Chapel," 178.

147. The Pseudo-Jerome list is exceptional in citing James, brother of the Lord (James the Less) before James, brother of John (James the Greater). It is James the Less who, with Philip, was honored at Rome with a basilica, SS. Apostoli, constructed ca. 560 under Pelagius I and John III (Kennedy, *Saints of the Canon of the Mass*, 115–19). At Parenzo the restored (1890–1897) mosaic frieze decorating the 6th-century apsidal wall above the arch shows James, Andrew, and Peter on the enthroned Christ's right, with Paul and John on his left. These are the male saints found on the upper south and west walls of the Zeno Chapel.

FIGURE 2.6 Rome, S. Prassede. Zeno Chapel, interior. South wall with Sts. John, Andrew, and James. Lunette below: Christ flanked by two male saints. Photograph by Mary M. Schaefer.

If the James on the south wall is "the Less," brother of the Lord and bishop of Jerusalem, then these three figures represent three great churches of the East: John, Ephesus; Andrew, apostle of the East, Constantinople; and James the Less, Jerusalem. With the exception of Andrew, the figures on the south and west walls are either authors of, or figure prominently in, the epistle lections read during Easter week (featuring sermons in Acts and 1 Peter), on the octave of Easter (1 John), and in a series selected from the Catholic or "canonical" epistles on the subsequent Sundays until Ascension.[148]

The Würzburg *comes*, the early Roman lectionary of Gregory the Great's time, had established the framework for future Roman usage, selecting without regard to sequence, readings from Acts and the Catholic epistles

---

148. Acts, the Catholic epistles, and Revelation, as noted earlier, constituted the cycle of biblical readings for the office between Easter and the Pentecost octave (Ordo 13A, Lateran, 700–750). In a later period there is a correspondence between the lectionary for mass and the office.

for nine Sundays following the Easter octave. For the weekdays from Easter Monday to the Saturday after Pentecost, Würzburg gives a total of twenty-seven epistle readings, fourteen from Acts and thirteen from the Catholic epistles. A similar choice can be seen in the seventh-century "Alcuin" *comes* and the eighth-century Murbach lectionary. The use during Paschaltide of Acts and the Catholic epistles was therefore well established, although the latter (with the exception of 1 Pet 3:18 and 1 Pet 2:1 for the Friday and Saturday of Easter week) had not been chosen for their Easter and initiatory content.

Scenes under or on the barrel vaults also suit the paschal theme.[149] The lunette under the eastern barrel vault is filled by a transfiguration, its lower half cropped. Peter, John, and a remnant of his brother James round out this event revelatory of Jesus' "departure" soon to take place in Jerusalem.[150] At the eastern springing of the vault on the northern cross-arm, adjacent to the likely location of Theodora's sarcophagus, an *Anastasis* mosaic, iconographically related to early Byzantine psalters, shows Christ accompanied by an angel (Michael?) descending to the dead to release Adam and Eve. Behind the Lord's mandorla, David and Solomon peer out from a common sarcophagus.[151] The Roman sanctoral also favors the two kings: after the Pauline writings had been scavenged for readings suitable for burgeoning saints' feasts, the liturgist resorted to the Wisdom books.[152]

---

149. Mackie makes a particularly strong case for the eschatological theme of the Zeno Chapel, its primary symbol the throne on the inside west wall. My proposal reads this eschatology through the lens of the paschal season.

150. On the other side of the composition, opposite Peter, Giovanni Battista de Rossi, with Enrico Stevenson, and Giuseppi Gatti (*Musaici cristiani e saggi dei pavimenti delle chiese di Roma anteriori al secolo XV* [Rome: Libreria Spithöver di G. Haass, 1899], 102v), thought he observed "una figura di tipo assai giovane, il cui capo sembra quasi terminare in acconciatura femminile, e con gesto storpiato piega ed alza il braccio sinistro." Joseph Wilpert also noted the "feminine hairdo" of one of the apostolic figures.

151. For David's connection to Christ's resurrection and descent into Hades, see Acts 2:24–36 and Davis-Weyer, "Die ältesten Darstellungen der Hadesfahrt Christi," 183–94. Klass ("Chapel of S. Zeno," 95) likewise uses the Gospel of Nicodemus, identifying the angel as Michael. A number of the features named above appear to have been present at S. Maria Antiqua (Nordhagen, *Frescoes of John VII*, 81–86 and pl. C b). On early church thought, see Martin F. Connell, "*Descensus Christi ad Inferos*: Christ's Descent to the Dead," *TS* 62 (2001): 262–71.

152. The compiler of the Roman lectionary created the sanctoral epistolary cycle first of all from the Pauline epistles including Hebrews, then selected from *Liber sapientiae Salomonis*, namely Ecclesiasticus (Sirach), Wisdom, and Proverbs (Chavasse, "Epistolier romain," 302).

Situated high on the north wall at ninety degrees to Peter and Paul and wearing the golden-yellow finery of spouses of the heavenly bridegroom, SCA AGNES, SCA PUDENTIANA, and SCA PRAXEDIS hover (Fig. 2.7). Praxedes stands alone and closest to the east wall. About to participate in the heavenly liturgy's procession, they face frontally, winsome and slender, their contrapposto stances suggesting movement. Jeweled circlets grace their heads. They carry their virgins' crowns in hands covered by an ample white cloth. Red embroidery on the cloth matches that on the white *loros*, a scapular that emerges below the golden diagonal dalmatic each wears over her gold tunic.[153] To express movement, the other end of the *loros* flutters behind each figure.

Three male apostles of the East, Andrew, James, and John, face three female saints of Rome. The virginal John wears an outer cloak of deep yellow that relates him to the ascetic Baptist and the three virgin women directly opposite. Following liturgical tradition, the men take their places on the south, the women on the north wall. There is gender equality in the garden of paradise, for *in resurrectione enim neque nubent, neque nubentur; sed erunt sicut angeli Dei in caelo* (Matt 22:20 and parallels). Parity extends even to the animal kingdom. Lower on the north wall, the top register of the lunette enclosed by the barrel vault shows two pairs of stags and does drinking from the four rivers of paradise (Gen 2:10–14).[154] The rivers gush forth from a *monticulus* (cf. the fountain of the water of life, Rev 21:6) on which stands the cross-nimbed Lamb.[155] Opposite, on the lunette in the south barrel-vaulted arm directly below John, Andrew, and James, a half-figure Christ with gospel book is flanked by a tonsured cleric (Zeno?) holding a gemmed book, and an elderly gentleman identifiable as lay by the *tablion* on his garment.[156]

---

153. François Boucher and Yvonne Deslandres, *A History of Costume in the West* (new ed.; London: Thames and Hudson, 1987), 150, 168, 449–50, pls. 243, 246.

154. Ps 41(42):1 reads in the Vulgate, "Quemadmodum desiderat cervus ad fontes aquarum..." The Greek text has "doe," the Hebrew "hart"; the verb is feminine (JB, Ps 42, note b). Was Paschal visually exegeting a textual difficulty? Ps 41 was sung by the *competentes* in Bishop Zeno's Verona (360s) as they entered the baptismal chamber. Zeno exhorts, "Come on, brothers, parched by the longed-for craving of blessed thirst, hasten with desire and the speed of deer to the water of the life-giving font. Drink deeply..." (Zeno, *The Day Has Come! Easter and Baptism in Zeno of Verona*, comp. and ed. Gordon P. Jeanes [Collegeville, MN: Liturgical, 1995], II.14, 90).

155. This established formula probably was present in the Lateran (429–430) and Old St. Peter's (440–461?) apses and occurs widely.

156. The identifications are uncertain. Zeno was a Roman martyr from the Praetextatus catacomb whose feast day is 14 February. *De locis sanctis martyrum* (ca. 635–645) makes Zeno the brother of Valentine. By the 8th century in the Gelasian Sacramentary of St. Gall, Zeno,

106 WOMEN IN PASTORAL OFFICE

FIGURE 2.7 Rome, S. Prassede. Zeno Chapel interior. Pantocrator (vault). North wall: Sts. Agnes, Pudentiana, and Praxedes (upper wall); lunette. Photograph by Mary M. Schaefer.

These last three male figures have counterparts. Facing them in the lower register of the north lunette are four women who gaze out as if from the gallery of a palace chapel (Fig. 2.8). On the left, at the place commonly assigned to the patron, the head of a veiled woman is set off by a rectangular blue nimbus bordered by white, similar to that which distinguishes the

---

Valentine, Vitalis, and Felicola are all commemorated on the same day (Klass, "Chapel of S. Zeno," 18). The pier inscription designates Zeno a presbyter. The relics of Valentine are not known to have been in the Zeno Chapel earlier than the 13th century (Mackie, "Zeno Chapel," 188). The layman's identity can only be pure conjecture, e.g., St. Vitalis (Klass, "Chapel of S. Zeno," 22). Mackie's theory ("Zeno Chapel," 188) that it "portrays Pudens, the virgin saints' forebear, in the court dress of a senator" is most attractive. As throughout the Zeno Chapel, the lowest portion of the mosaic has been destroyed by renovations or neglect.

FIGURE 2.8 Detail of 2.7: Lamb on mount, two stags, two does (upper register); Theodora episcopa, Praxedes, the Virgin Mary, Pudentiana (lower register). Photograph by Mary M. Schaefer.

living pope in the apse. An inscription in small capitals in the gold ground at left and top identifies her as THEODO[RA] EPISCOPA.[157] To the right are three figures: a crowned and haloed woman; the haloed Virgin Mary wearing blue *maphorion* (woman's enveloping veil); and a third haloed woman, wearing a circlet and arrayed as in the apse mosaic (the upper part of her garment is original). These are the two sisters Praxedes and Pudentiana, individually recognizable when compared to the named saints on the upper wall. Even from photographs the restoration and resetting of the mosaic at the levels of chin or neck is evident, showing the garments of all but the last saint to be conjectural restorations.[158]

---

157. The two-part pier inscription also titles Paschal's most kind (*benignissimae*) mother as Theodora *episcopa*. As with the other niches in the Zeno Chapel, the lowest section of the "women's gallery" has been damaged or destroyed; but unlike the others it has been restored. In most photographs, the larger tesserae of the restoration are readily distinguishable: here, the letters -RA of Theodora, areas around the necks, and most of the clothing. The right-hand figure has remained largely intact. To be questioned are the cross pendants of Theodora and the first saint (See Wisskirchen, *Mosaiken der Kirche S. Prassede*, fig. 57 for a diagram).

158. Wisskirchen (*Mosaikprogamme*, Anhang 4–8; *Mosaiken der Kirche S. Prassede*, figs. 46, 47, 51, 53, 56, esp. 57, 60, 61 after G. Matthiae's drawings) shows the mosaic restorations.

Mackie astutely uses the drawings from the Cassiano dal Pozzo album that show the walls beneath the present truncated tympanum. Originally, she suggests, the figures of Theodora and the two sisters were full-length, the two sisters flanking the enthroned Madonna with Child. The composition would then echo the full-length, standing, square-nimbed figures in the Theodotus Chapel at S. Maria Antiqua.[159] Sometime after 1630–1640, a door was inserted into the niche wall where Theodora's sarcophagus had rested. Mackie theorizes that the door cut into the head of the Child in the Madonna's lap; therefore the whole of the Christ Child had to be eliminated.[160] However, there is no evidence of a Child. If, however, Paschal's intent was to evoke a catacomb cubiculum—which I believe the visual and archeological evidence favors—then half-figures in an arcosolium with the sarcophagus placed below in the niche parallel to the wall, corresponding to the three male busts above the Zeno relic-altar opposite, is the more probable reconstruction.

In the lunette above, a Lamb stands on a *monticulus* from which gush the four rivers of paradise. The text from Revelation 7:17, which this short-hand image represents, forms a promise, first for the martyrs to whom it refers, then appropriated for the saints depicted, then finally for the pope's mother Theodora:

> [T]hey are before the throne of God,
> and worship him day and night within his temple,...
> the Lamb at the center of the throne will be their shepherd,
> and he will guide them to the springs of the water of life,
> and God will wipe away every tear from their eyes.

The four women of the arcosolium project an unusual presence. The matrons, the white-veiled Theodora and the blue-veiled Mary, alternate with Mary's gaudily costumed saint-attendants. The north niche with

---

159. Mackie, "Zeno Chapel," 185 and pl. XXXVIb, from Stephan Waetzoldt, *Die Kopien des 17. Jahrhunderts nach Mosaiken und Wandmalereien in Rom* (Munich: Schroll, 1964), fig. 502. See the 8th-century paintings in S. Maria Antiqua in. Nordhagen, *Frescoes of John VII*; J. D. Breckenridge, "Evidence for the Nature of Relations between Pope John VII and the Byzantine Emperor Justinian II," *BZ* 65 (1972): 364–74; Boucher and Deslandres, *History of Costume in the West*, figs. 279–80.

160. A striking if ill-preserved comparison with a Madonna and Child in a 7th- or 8th-century painting from the catacomb of S. Valentino can be adduced. See Danilo Mazzoleni, "La mariologia nell'epigrafia cristiana antica," *VetChr* 26 (1989): 59–68; John Osborne, "Early Medieval Wall-Paintings in the Catacomb of S. Valentino, Rome," in *PBSR* 49 (1981): 82–90.

its three registers formed a striking composition: the Lamb of God with stags and does drinking from the rivers of paradise; lower, the four bust-length figures; then a tendril-decorated background for the arcosolium that framed Theodora's sarcophagus and was flanked by the raising of Lazarus (?) and the Anastasis.[161] Reading this "restored" wall in its entirety from the bottom up is even more illuminating. The north elevation, a "women's wall," moves from the sarcophagus with its mortal remains to the four frontal female busts, mothers alternating with virgins, to the deer, symbols of thirsty souls, drinking from the living stream that is Christ, and, highest up in the heavenly eschatological realm, to the three female patronesses processing eastward with dancing movement. Together the mosaics of the north wall express hope for Theodora's life after death and bodily resurrection from the sarcophagus where her corpse rests.

The female-male subject matter on the Zeno Chapel's north and south walls recalls the female-male saints in procession on the sixth-century mosaic friezes (556–569) above the nave arcade at S. Apollinare Nuovo in Ravenna. Near the east end, enthroned Mother and Child and enthroned Christ, both with angel attendants, receive them. However, at S. Prassede all notions of hierarchy are absent. True, Mary is slightly taller than the others and her red-bordered halo slightly larger. Nevertheless, a sense of equality appropriate to women disciples of the Lord binds Mary with her virginal companions, and the matron Theodora with Mary the mother. In the Zeno Chapel the mother-son relationship is demonstrated on an intimate scale.

Prescinding from Theodora's title in mosaic—its lettering different in style and scale from elsewhere in the chapel—we know nothing beyond what her portrait and the nearby pier inscription tell us. The latter states that Theodora's corpse rests in the chapel along with that of Zeno the presbyter and two others.[162] Her name is Greek. Theodora's blue nimbus,

---

161. Klass, "Chapel of S. Zeno," 101. Only the roof of an aedicula remains (Wisskirchen, *Mosaiken der Kirche S. Prassede*, 57).

162. The pier inscription refers to her as deceased: "...on the right upon entering the basilica itself where rests the body of his most kindly mother, that is the lady Theodora *episcopa*." The last 4 letters of the mosaic inscription (DORA) were copied in 1630–1640 (De Rossi, *Musaici cristiani e saggi* [1899], 103r–v). G. Ciampini failed to note the inscription (*Vetera Monimenta* [Rome, Komarek, 1690–1699], 2:143). The shamelessly partial Dom Davanzati does not refer to the portrait in his publication of 1725; see Benigno Davanzati, *Notizie al pellegrino della Basilica di S. Prassede* (Rome, Antonio de' Rossi, 1725). Might entirely incomprehensible data be dealt with by being ignored? Was the dim lighting, eyesight, or limited understanding of iconography to blame? Theodora's name and title do not appear in all historical copies and usually are not commented upon until the modern period. Ursula Nilgen ("Die grosse Reliquieninschrift von Santa Prassede: Eine quellenkritische

a convention used for important living personages and to distinguish notable contemporary persons from saints, is unique for a woman in the medieval West, as apparently is the title *episcopa* for the mother of a bishop.[163] Paschal's revered mother may have acquired her title in the course of overseeing the papal household at the Lateran Palace. Her full white veil suggests an ecclesial but not necessarily abbatial status. Conceptually she stands within the tradition of "holy mothers," which survives in the apse of the Basilica Euphrasiana in Poreč (Parenzo, Istria) across the Adriatic from Ravenna, stronghold of Byzantine influence in Italy.

Conclusion

What we have learned from investigating Paschal's artistic commissions in light of the Roman lectionary is the centrality to this pope's design concept of communal and personal salvation and even more of Christ's resurrection and its liturgical celebration at Eastertide. Paschal's baptismal name spelled out in full but in monogram style appears prominently overhead in the center of the intrados (soffit) of both apsidal and triumphal arches. Easter associations with the sisters' *vita* are palpable: the ninety-six baptisms at Easter in the new font built by Pius I at Pudens' *titulus* and the building of yet another font at Praxedes' new *titulus* on top of the Esquiline hill. Paschal has associated himself with Roman liturgical practice dating from the late second century and with the second-century bishop Pius I who, according to *LP*, was given the commission by an angel to celebrate the Easter feast on Sunday. Through his patronage of St. Praxedes' church and commissioned works of art, Paschal has embedded himself in the

---

Untersuchung zur Zeno-Kapelle," in *Römische Quartalschrift für christliche Altertumskunde und für Kirchengeschichte* 69 [1974]: 21, 26–27 and nn. 62, 63) discusses the "incomprehensible" title *episcopa* and its uncertain history in the mosaic (21). Given the uniqueness of image, mosaic title, and epigraphic inscription, the burden lies on those who would disprove the complementary reports. Unexpected testimony can be a criterion of authenticity.

163. Cf. Weitzmann, *Monastery of Saint Catherine*, B14, 37 and pl. XVI, where the square nimbus is green outlined in white. The immediate source is surely the 8th-century frescoes in S. Maria Antiqua at the Forum and especially its Chapel of Theodotus. See Gerhart B. Ladner, "The So-Called Square Nimbus," *MS* 3 (1941): 15–45, published prior to knowledge of Mount Sinai examples, repr. idem, *Images and Ideas in the Middle Ages: Selected Studies in History and Art* (Rome: Edizioni di Storia e Letteratura, 1983), 1:115–70 and 2:1012–20, Addenda; Ernst Kitzinger, "Some Reflections on Portraiture in Byzantine Art," in *The Art of Byzantium and the Medieval West: Selected Studies* (Bloomington: Indiana University Press, 1976), 256–69, fig. 3.

Lord's theophany and the sisters' story, and secured, as much as might be hoped, a place for himself and his mother in the heavenly realm.

Theodora's portrait and title invite taking up a discussion last engaged in during the eighteenth century: the ministerial status of our heroines Pudentiana and Praxedes. Even those theologians who argue against the admission of women to any ecclesiastical office admit the probable existence of an ordered diaconal ministry for women in the Roman city-church during the eighth through eleventh centuries. Did the popularity of the Potentiana and Praxedes story about female householders who headed second-century house-churches correlate with real women engaged in ecclesial ministry? Did it perhaps help to provide models for them that overstepped the restrictions of housebound virgin, enclosed nun, or subordinate wife and mother?

3
Women's Pastoral Offices in Churches Outside Rome

THE FINAL DECADES of the twentieth century saw an outpouring of popular reflection and critical scholarship on women as disciples of Jesus and as sharers in the early Christian mission.[1] The Hebrew and Christian Scriptures were mined for what they tell of women, interpretations growing in sophistication as women's locations within particular cultural and social milieus were delineated. Feminist scholarship identified androcentrism in hallowed texts and their exegesis, and the hermeneutic of suspicion led to fruitful areas of exploration and interpretation.[2] Within the pages of the New Testament there is a telling example of women's participation.

---

1. Susanne Heine, *Women and Early Christianity* (London: SCM, 1987) critically reviews questions that have engaged feminist biblical scholarship. The literature is vast: Ben Witherington III, *Women in the Earliest Churches* (Cambridge: Cambridge University Press, 1988); *The Women's Bible Commentary*, ed. Carol A. Newsom and Sharon H. Ringe (Louisville, KY: Westminster John Knox Press,1992 and expanded edition with Apocrypha,1998); Elisabeth Schüssler Fiorenza, ed., *Searching the Scriptures* (2 vols.; New York: Crossroad, 1993–1994).

2. Elisabeth Schüssler Fiorenza, *In Memory of Her: A Feminist Theological Reconstuction of Christian Origins* (New York: Crossroad, 1983); Bernadette J. Brooten, "Early Christian Women and their Cultural Context: Issues of Method in Historical Reconstruction," in Adela Yarbro Collins (ed.), *Feminist Perspectives on Biblical Scholarship* (Chico, CA: Scholars, 1985), 65–91; Elisabeth Schüssler Fiorenza, "Missionaries, Apostles, Coworkers: Romans 16 and the Reconstruction of Women's Early Christian History," *Word & World* 6 (1986): 420–33; Luise Schottroff, *Lydia's Impatient Sisters: A Feminist Social History of Early Christianity*, trans. Barbara and Martin Rumscheidt (Louisville, KY: Westminster John Knox, 1995); Ivoni Richter Reimer, *Women in the Acts of the Apostles: A Feminist Liberation Perspective*, trans. Linda M. Maloney (Minneapolis, MN: Fortress, 1995). The figure of Mary mother of Jesus is explored by Elizabeth A. Johnson, *Truly Our Sister: A Theology of Mary in the Communion of Saints* (New York: Continuum, 2003). A summary of the turns in feminist interpretation of Marian material is given by Chris Maunder, "Origins of the Cult of the Virgin Mary in the New Testament," in Chris Maunder, ed., *The Origins of the Cult of the Virgin Mary* (London: Burns and Oates, 2008), 24–26.

The author of Matthew's gospel refers to the presence of women and children at the multiplication of the loaves story that, with doublets and redactions, figures eight times in the four gospels.[3] Describing the crowd at the first feeding miracle, Matthew says, "And those who ate were about five thousand men, besides women and children" (Matt 14:21; par. Matt 15:38). But for that chance comment, the participation of women and children in this favored sign of the messianic banquet would have gone unrecorded. Retrieving women's presence and participation in church structures and teasing out information about women's official ecclesial ministry from texts and material evidence differs little from the efforts necessary to discover women's hidden history in other areas of life.

The task of uncovering women's roles is especially difficult within the church of Rome. To establish the context for investigation of women's ministerial roles in the Roman church, this chapter looks at the larger picture of women's ministry in the early Christian world. First to be considered are those New Testament texts that restrict women's active ecclesial ministry. Then pre-Pauline, Pauline and post-Pauline evidence for ecclesially functioning women during the period of formation of the New Testament is summarized.

1. New Testament Texts That Limit or Deny Active Ministerial Offices to Women

The influence exercised for nearly two thousand years by a handful of texts—not more than a dozen verses in all—that give directives regarding women's persons and behavior in the early Christian communities is out of all proportion to their theological content and general applicability. The texts treated below have been addressed in innumerable exegetical, historical, and theological studies and are now judged by the majority of commentators to be products of androcentric culture and misogynist thinking.[4] Their exceptional, embarrassing, and even contradictory character when compared to theological perspectives enunciated elsewhere in the same letters has hindered resolution of the difficult issues of originating episode and intended audience. Characterizing women's persons and activity

---

3. Matt 14:13–21; 15:32–39; Mark 6:31–44; 8:1–10, recalled in Mark 8:14–21; Luke 9:10–17; John 6:1–15.

4. Brooten ("Early Christian Women," 85–86) summarizes texts and context.

as less than normatively human, or presenting good Christian women as submissive and passive instead of as equal sharers in the mission of the early churches, reveals the unredeemed "shadow" side of the gospel. These attitudes stand worlds away from the experience of those women who were protagonists with Jesus and recipients of Jesus' friendship and compassion.

Two texts—1 Corinthians 14:33b–36 and 1 Timothy 2:9–15—have been repeatedly used to prohibit or restrict women's active participation in ecclesiastical affairs. The first is clearly intended as an admonition to wives; the First Timothy text originates in the familial context. Later usage would apply these texts to all women. Because 1 Corinthians 14:33b–36 represents an exceptional perspective in the Corinthian correspondence, the New Revised Standard Version prints it as an interpolation:

> (As in all the churches of the saints, women should be silent in the churches. For they are not permitted to speak, but should be subordinate, as the law also says. If there is anything they desire to know, let them ask their husbands at home. For it is shameful for a woman to speak in church. Or did the word of God originate with you? Or are you the only ones it has reached?)

Not only do these three and a half verses represent a break in thought from the subject of prophecy addressed in the verses immediately preceding and following, but also they contradict 1 Corinthians 11:5 in which, notwithstanding the hierarchical relationship of husband to wife, Paul allows properly veiled, and therefore married women, to pray aloud and prophesy in the assembly. Does 1 Corinthians 14 signal a clash of cultures at communal worship between Jewish custom (referred to as "the law," v. 34b) and typical Christian practice, on the one hand, and what was allowable in the liberated Greek city of Corinth (the full participation of women in worship)?[5] Raymond F. Collins argues that verses 33b–36 "represent a conservative argument that Paul rebuts by means of the double rhetorical question in verse 36. To demand the silence of women in the Christian

---

5. Witherington (*Women in Earliest Churches*, 90–104) argues that 1 Cor 14:33b–36 is not an interpolation but rather Paul's solution to a specific problem in the Corinthian assembly. Certain wives with the gift of prophetic discernment are causing a commotion in the worship assembly by publicly passing judgment on their husbands' or other men's utterances. To end the disorder the apostle prohibits their speaking in the assembly. According to Witherington, this passage does not contradict 1 Cor 11:5 or "any other passage which suggests that women can teach, preach, pray, or prophesy in or outside the churches" (ibid.).

assembly is to claim for oneself a monopoly on the word of God. Such a monopoly no one can claim."[6]

First Timothy 2:9–15, following immediately on advice to men (*andras*) to pray peaceably, commences on a counter-cultural note: the author advises women to refrain from the stylish hairdos and expensive clothing fashionable for young women and matrons in Roman society. "[I desire] also that the women should dress themselves modestly and decently in suitable clothing, not with their hair braided, or with gold, pearls, or expensive clothes, but with good works, as is proper for women who profess reverence for God."[7] The injunction in Timothy 2:11–12 that a woman must learn in silence with submissiveness and without a teaching role or authority over men echoes and expands the conservative argument found in 1 Corinthians 14:34.[8] Although a distinction between clergy and laity would be made only in the third century, Alexandre Faivre observes that a status differentiating women from the *laos* was already signaled when, in Timothy's church, all women were forbidden to speak or teach or have authority over men.[9] Historically, verse 12 has been the most oppressive to women in the church: "I permit no woman to teach or to have authority over a man; she is to keep silent."[10] It is the most frequently quoted or paraphrased verse in

---

6. Raymond F. Collins, *First Corinthians* (Collegeville, MN: Liturgical, 1999), 517. On the issues concerning women, see Jouette M. Bassler, "1 Corinthinans," in *Women's Bible Commentary*, exp. ed., 411–19.

7. The concern expressed in 1 Pet 3:3–6 is equivalent to 1 Tim 2:9: "[Wives,] [d]o not adorn yourselves outwardly by braiding your hair, and by wearing gold ornaments or fine clothing; rather, let your adornment be the inner self with the lasting beauty of a gentle and quiet spirit, which is very precious in God's sight. It was in this way long ago that the holy women who hoped in God used to adorn themselves by accepting the authority of their husbands. Thus Sarah obeyed Abraham and called him lord. You have become her daughters as long as you do what is good and never let fears alarm you."

8. 1 Cor 14:33b–35 is directed only to wives; when in the company of the husbands Paul speaks only to the latter. The Pastoral Letters in general, and this passage in particular, presume a family environment (see v. 15); nevertheless, 1 Tim 2:9–15 enlarges the scope of male domination of females beyond that of the family. For a discussion that presumes genuine Pauline authorship, see Johnson, *First and Second Letters to Timothy*, 198–211.

9. Faivre, *Emergence of Laity*, 43. The anachronism of the traditional restrictions on women in the Pastorals, located in the context of polemic against heretics (2 Tim 3:1–9), is summarized by Ute Eisen, *Women Officeholders in Early Christianity: Epigraphical and Literary Studies* (trans. Linda M. Maloney; Collegeville, MN: Liturgical Press, 2000), 100–103.

10. A Roman parallel is found in 1 Clement 21:7, which calls on women to "reveal the gentleness of their tongues by silence" (Lampe, *From Paul to Valentinus*, 147).

ancient church orders and by church fathers and theologians until very recent times to explain why women cannot be ordained or exercise public leadership functions within the church. Finally, 1 Timothy 2:13–14 places responsibility for the Fall on Eve alone rather than on the first parents together: "For Adam was formed first, then Eve; and Adam was not deceived, but the woman was deceived and became a transgressor."[11] A cultural (not theological) note that flies in the face of Christian faith concludes this section: "Yet she will be saved through childbearing, providing they [women] continue in faith and love and holiness, with modesty" (v. 15). Taken together or separately, these five verses made 1 Timothy 2:9–15 the Christian Scriptures' most "dangerous" text for women.[12]

Titus 2:3–5 treats wives' behavior in a somewhat gentler mode while counseling submission of wives to husbands. The post-Pauline household codes (*Haustafeln*) of Colossians and Ephesians are not immediately applicable to comportment within the church assembly. The admonitions take surprisingly little space in either Colossians or Ephesians: "Wives, be subject to your husbands, as is fitting in the Lord" (Col 3:18). Ephesians 5:22–24 expands the exhortation: "Wives, be subject to your husbands as you are to the Lord. For the husband is the head of the wife just as Christ is the head of the church, the body of which he is the Savior. Just as the church is subject to Christ, so also wives ought to be, in everything, to their husbands." The household codes are too sophisticated to reduce the ills of humankind to Eve's supposed deception by the serpent and burden her with responsibility for the Fall. Although the household codes reflect a growing concern of the Early Church to ensure mutually responsible relationships between Christians, thereby strengthening kinship values

---

11. That women are easily deceived and prone to sin is mentioned in 2 Tim 3:6, which refers to "silly women, overwhelmed by their sins and swayed by all kinds of desires." See also 2 Cor 11:3a, "as the serpent deceived Eve by his cunning." The verses before this line will form a favorite reading in the commons of virgins. Joanna Dewey assesses the interpretation of women's texts in the Pastorals: see "1 Timothy," "2 Timothy," and "Titus," in *Women's Bible Commentary*, exp. ed., 444–52.

12. John H. Wright, "Patristic Testimony on Women's Ordination in *Inter Insigniores*," *TS* 58 (1997): 516–26; George H. Tavard, "The Scholastic Doctrine," in *Women Priests: A Catholic Commentary on the Vatican Declaration*, Leonard Swidler and Arlene Swidler, eds. (New York: Paulist, 1977), 99–106; Jeremy Miller, "A Note On Aquinas and Ordination Of Women," *New Blackfriars* 61 (1980): 185–90 at 187–89; John Hilary Martin, "The Ordination of Women and the Theologians in the Middle Ages," in Bernard Cooke and Gary Macy, eds., *A History of Women and Ordination*, vol. 1: *The Ordination of Women in Medieval Context* (Lanham, MD: Scarecrow, 2002), 31–160. Luise Schottroff (*Lydia's Impatient Sisters*, 69–78) juxtaposes these verses with parallel teachings from contemporary pagan sources.

and obligations, and opening up more liberating attitudes, the theological arguments of the codes are based on cultural practices of hierarchical order within the household.

2. Women's Ministries in the Early Churches

Despite the restrictions placed by the institutional "catholic" churches throughout Christian history on women's participation in its official life, very few biblical texts actually call for women's submission. The good news of women's full personhood predominates in the Christian Scriptures and especially the gospels even if absent in subsequent history and interpretation. Galatians 3:27–28 enunciates the theological principle and initiatory praxis that integrated female persons into the people of God in their own right: "As many of you as were baptized into Christ have clothed yourselves with Christ. There is no longer Jew or Greek, there is no longer slave or free, there is no longer male and female; for all of you are one in Christ Jesus."[13] A quick review of the more readily forgotten Pauline "good news" texts will contextualize our investigation of women's roles in the life of the Roman church, since any such development looks back to the Scriptures, both Hebrew and Christian, for foundational paradigms.

A. Prophets

Prophets are persons oriented to God who proclaim God's ways of working in the world. The widowed prophetess Anna in Luke's story of Mary's purification and Jesus' presentation in the temple is the ideal type of the ecclesial widow (Luke 2:22–28). She prophesies when the infant Jesus as first-born

---

13. In Galatians, Paul fights against insistence on the practice of male circumcision for converts from paganism as sign of entry into the chosen people (2:3; 5:2–6). Acts shows Paul bowing to Jewish custom and having Timothy, a Christian whose mother was a Jew, circumcised (16:3) before taking him as his "constant companion" on his evangelizing mission (JB, notes to Acts 16:1–3). In Judaism, females were members of the chosen people by virtue of their relationship to a circumcised male, even though Jewish identity was established by having a Jewish mother. The household codes of Col 3:22–4:1 and Eph 6:5–9, 1 Tim 6:1–2 and Titus 2:9–10, and 1 Pet 2:18–20 make clear that slavery as an institution was not eliminated by this liberating perspective. For an assessment of the codes within the ambient culture, see Witherington, *Women in Earliest Churches*, 42–61. "Male and female" echoes the egalitarianism of the first creation story (Gen 1:27). Until recently, many exegetes distinguished between equality of the sexes to be achieved in the eschaton and the social inequities appropriate in the church in this (incompletely redeemed!) world. In the first century CE context, however, this axiom was revolutionary: differentiation (not just differentiated roles) is of no moment. In some mss., Col 3:11 also includes the reference to both sexes.

son is brought to the Temple to be offered to God. Exercising a charismatic ministry of prophecy, prayer, and fasting, Anna had spent more than a half century after the death of her husband praying and fasting day and night in the temple (Luke 2:36-38). As with prophets everywhere, lifestyle not office set her apart. In Luke's visitation episode Elizabeth and her young cousin Mary had been presented as prophets (Luke 1:41-45). The four virgin daughters of Philip were prophets (Acts 4:29).[14] In 1 Corinthians 11:2-16, where Paul is concerned to maintain the tradition of male headship, we learn that prophecy is an everyday occurrence in the worship-life of Corinth. As well as men, women prophesy so long as they are properly veiled. On the other hand, for a man to wear a veil on his head (apparently the equivalent of wearing one's hair long) is to supplant Christ by acting the part of the leader of a pagan cult, although this is not the reason the rabbinically trained Paul gives for decrying that comportment (1 Cor 11:4, 7).[15] Some women were anti-prophets, for example Jezebel at Thyatira (Rev 2:18-29).[16] Raymond E. Brown notes,

> Some have suggested that the prophets regularly presided at the Eucharist (Acts 13:1-2 has prophets "liturgizing," and *Didache* 10:7 would permit prophets to give thanks [*eucharistein*]; the "ministry [*leitourgia*] of prophets" in *Didache* 15:1 is related to celebrating the Eucharist on the Lord's Day in 14:1).[17]

There is no reason to discount the possibility that women also exercised this prophetic table ministry.[18]

---

14. Eisen, *Women Officeholders*, 63-87 at 69.

15. According to Andrew D. Clarke, *Serve the Community of the Church: Christians as Leaders and Ministers* (Grand Rapids, MI: Eerdmans, 2000), 184. The cultural origin of Paul's diatribe on head coverings is illustrated by 1 Cor 11 in which Paul—*contra* depictions of Christ in later iconographic traditions—calls long hair degrading when worn by a man.

16. Eisen (*Women Officeholders*, 69-70), who then treats the occurrence of women prophets in the 2nd and 3rd centuries. Invectives against Gnostic and Montanist prophets make these latter women stand out above their orthodox sisters (ibid., 70-73). An intricate discussion of the prophets in the New Prophecy (Montanism) is undertaken by Anne Jensen, *God's Self-Confident Daughters* (Louisville, KY: Westminster John Knox, 1996), 125-88. There is also the case of the Cappadocian prophetess who, in a period of upheaval ca. 235, "for a long time" baptized many and presided at eucharist using the rites of the Catholic Church (ibid., 182-86).

17. Raymond E. Brown, *Priest and Bishop: Biblical Reflections* (London: Geoffrey Chapman, [1970] 1971), 41-42.

18. Teresa Berger (*Gender Differences and the Making of Liturgical History: Lifting a Veil on Liturgy's Past* [Farnham, Surrey: Ashgate, 2011], 131, n. 12) supports the argument that the ministry of presiding at the eucharist was open to women prophets during the first two centuries.

B. Leaders of House-churches, Evangelists, Coworkers, and Eminent Apostles

Ben Witherington suggests that chapter 16 of Paul's letter to the Romans can be titled an "ancient greeting card" or letter of commendation from Paul carried by "our sister" Phoebe, διάκονος (deacon or servant) and προστάτις (presiding officer? patron? protector? benefactor? helper?) of the church at Cenchreae (Rom 16:1-2).[19] It is, first of all, a commendation of Paul himself by way of reference to people whom he knows.[20] Romans 16:1-16 reads like a roll-call of leaders of house-churches, evangelists, persons whom the apostle to the Gentiles unequivocally terms coworkers and prominent apostles.[21] In succeeding verses the names of coworkers (συνεργός) in the early Christian mission are intermingled with Paul's beloved Christian faithful and relatives (Rom 16:3, 21-23). Some of the individuals the apostle commends were converted before Paul. Like the married

---

See Reinhard Messner, "Grundlinien der Entwicklung des eucharistischen Gebets in der frühen Kirche," in Albert Gernards et al., eds., *Prex Eucharistica* 3/1 (Fribourg: Academic Press, 2005), 3-40 at 36.

19. "Sister" and "brother" as titles designating membership in the family of faith were peculiar to early Christianity. The generic address *adelphoi* (m.) often masks female presence and participation. Witherington (*Women in Earliest Churches*, 104-14) discusses Phoebe's titles, representing a diffuse range of leadership possibilities. See also Heine, *Women and Early Christianity*, 89. On *collegia* (voluntary associations) and patronage, see Caroline F. Whelan, "*Amica Pauli*: The Role of Phoebe in the Early Church," *JSNT* 49 (1993): 67-85; on women's status, Wendy Cotter, "Women's Authority Roles in Paul's Churches: Countercultural or Conventional," *Novum Testamentum* 36 (1994): 350-72. Bernadette J. Brooten (*Women Leaders in the Ancient Synagogue: Inscriptional Evidence and Background Issues* [Chico, CA: Scholars Press, 1982]) discusses *prostatēs* (m.) and *prostatis* (f.) besides other titles. Peter Richardson ("From Apostles to Virgins: Romans 16 and the Roles of Women in the Early Church," *TJT* 2 [1986]: 232-61, n. 19) notes that 1 Clement 36:1, 61:3 and 64:1 use this term of Jesus, guardian of all Christians; see also Elisabeth Schüssler Fiorenza ("Missionaries, Apostles, Coworkers," 420-33). In a classic article, Peter Brown ("The Rise and Function of the Holy Man in Late Antiquity," *Journal of Roman Studies* 61 [1971]: 80-101, repr. in Brown, *Society and the Holy in Late Antiquity* [Berkeley: University of California Press, 1989], 103-52, at 115-20) describes the function of the rural patron or *prostatēs*.

20. Whether Chapter 16 of Paul's letter to the Romans (written from Corinth 56 or 57 CE) is original or an appendix and addressed to Rome or destined for Ephesus is still disputed. Joan Cecelia Campbell (*Phoebe: Patron and Emissary* [Collegeville, MN: Liturgical, 2009], 13-17) lists reasons for believing it to be intended for the church in Ephesus. Peter Lampe (*From Paul to Valentinus*, 153-83) presents cogent textual arguments to buttress his case that Rom 16 is an integral part of Romans. Stephen Spence (*The Parting of the Ways: The Roman Church as a Case Study* [Leuven: Peeters, 2004], 245-324) endorses this view. Whichever the case, the Roman church of which we speak took chapter 16 as addressed to itself.

21. Schüssler Fiorenza, "Missionaries, Apostles, Coworkers," 420-33.

couple Prisca and Aquila, they may have evangelized before his arrival. Prisca and Aquila are acknowledged by the apostle to the Gentiles as outstanding coworkers who risked their lives for him (vv. 3–5); they are leaders of a house-church in Rome as well as in Ephesus (1 Cor 16:19). Another friend, Mary, "has worked very hard among you" (v. 6). Andronicus and Junia, Paul's relatives, Christians before Paul and imprisoned with him, are preeminent among the apostles (v. 7).[22] Urbanus is a coworker in Christ (v. 9). Tryphaena and Tryphosa, probably blood-sisters, are "workers in the Lord," along with "beloved Persis" (v. 12). The list includes married couples and single persons. The single women, virgins or widowed, minister in their own right; they are not designated according to relationship or non-relationship to a man.[23] Peter Lampe shows how Paul has singled out Junia, Prisca, Mary, Tryphaena, Tryphosa, and Persis, with possibly Rufus' mother, as women particularly active in the Christian community; these are named over against the men Aquila, Andronicus, and Urbanus, perhaps adding Apelles and Rufus.[24]

The artisan-couple Prisc[ill]a and Aquila appear as Paul's friends six times in the letters and Acts.[25] They had probably left Rome because of the expulsion of Jews and Jewish-Christians by edict of Claudius in the year 49 CE. No doubt they were already Christian when they established themselves in Corinth in the tent-making trade (end of 49 to 51 CE). Paul

---

22. The "apostle" Junia[s] is almost certainly a woman. Heine reviews the textual tradition (*Women and Early Christianity*, 42) as analyzed by Bernadette Brooten, "Junia...Outstanding among the Apostles (Romans 16:7)," in Leonard Swidler and Arlene Swidler, eds., *Women Priests: A Catholic Commentary on the Vatican Declaration* (New York: Paulist, 1977), 141–44. Only Luke restricts the term apostle to the twelve. Eisen (*Women Officeholders*, 47–49) summarizes the textual history. St. John Chrysostom praised Junia as preeminent among the apostles. For a speculative reconstruction identifying Junia with "Joanna the apostle" (Luke 8:3, 24:10), see Richard Bauckham, *Gospel Women: Studies of the Named Women in the Gospels* (Grand Rapids, MI: Eerdmans, 2002), 109–202.

23. Witherington, *Women in Earliest Churches*, 152. On the fact that here women are generally not designated by gender-role, see Elisabeth Schüssler Fiorenza, "Women in the Pre-Pauline and Pauline Churches," *Union Seminary Quarterly Review* 33 (1978): 153–66 at 161.

24. Lampe, *From Paul to Valentinus*, 165–67.

25. Priscilla, used by Luke in Acts, is the diminutive form of Prisca. In Acts 18:2–3, Paul joins them in their tent-making business; in vv. 18–19 they sail with Paul, who is headed for Syria; he leaves them at Ephesus; in vv. 26–27 they instruct Apollos. 1 Cor 16:19 is written ca. 54/55, perhaps from Ephesus, where they have a house-church. Prisca and Aquila reappear in Rom 16:3 (are they in Ephesus with their house-church, or have they returned to Rome and opened a house-church there?). In 2 Tim 4:19 Paul greets them in almost the same breath as Pudens, v. 21. See Reimer, *Women in the Acts of the Apostles*, 195–219; Mary Ann Getty-Sullivan, *Women in the New Testament* (Collegeville, MN: Liturgical Press, 2001), 154–61.

was welcomed by them and worked with them, in tent-making as in evangelization.[26] Prisca is named ahead of her husband in four out of six instances, indicating either that she was of higher birth or that she played the leading role in the Christian mission.[27] Prisca was the chief instructor of the eloquent preacher Apollos and corrected his understanding of the Way of God (Acts 18:2–3, 26). Gaining Paul's praise, Prisca and Aquila's ministry of evangelization was carried out on their own initiative. Of the nine women named in the body of the chapter (17 men are also named), Stephen Spence notes that there are

> seven women singled out for special honour in Paul's list of greetings and only five men. These women occupy prime positions in Paul's list... it indicates an active and an honoured role for women in the Roman church. This is especially true of Mary,...[indicating] that her [hard-working] ministry was exercised among all the Christians of Rome. The same is true of Junia, who is acknowledged as an apostle of some eminence.... Prisca, who is named before her husband, is also a significant leader among the Roman Christians.[28]

Women and men share in functional roles; the model is collaborative teamwork.

A few scholars have proposed one exception, the letter to the Hebrews, to the presumed all-male authorship of the corpus of twenty-seven New Testament Scriptures. Initially this theological treatise bore no author's name. Its affinities with Pauline thought earned it attribution to Paul, yet it has greater literary polish than those works agreed to be authentically his. Keenly aware of the discrepancies between those Pauline letters accepted as genuine and Hebrews, Adolf von Harnack, in 1900, cast about for a possible author whose name, he supposed, must figure somewhere in the Christian

---

26. Reimer, *Women in the Acts of the Apostles*, 113–30.

27. At least in the best witnesses. The Western tradition has inverted their names, inserted Aquila's, or left out Prisca's altogether. Heine details the changes in the text (*Women and Early Christianity*, 43–44) as does Reimer (*Women in the Acts of the Apostles*, 197–98); see also Witherington, *Women in Earliest Churches*, 153–54. Schüssler Fiorenza ("Missionaries, Apostles, Coworkers," 429) notes that Prisca may have been a freedwoman of the *gens* Acilia.

28. Spence, *Parting of the Ways* (272 and n. 108, 273): "The women are identified as fellow-worker, hard-worker, apostle, fellow-countrymen, fellow-prisoners, and the beloved."

Scriptures. First proposing Barnabas, Harnack then stumbled upon a likelier candidate: the authoritative teacher-missionary Prisca with her husband Aquila, close friends, fellow tent-makers and trusted coworkers with Paul in evangelization in Corinth, Ephesus, and Rome. Von Harnack's fascinating theory, in which he ascribed to the couple higher social status than is implied by their arduous craft, has gained sporadic support from exegetes.[29]

We saw that Prisca and Aquila led a house-church in Ephesus (1 Cor 16:19) and also in Rome (Rom 16:5). Philemon, Apphia (whom Paul greets as "our sister"), and Archippus provide the house for the church that meets at Colossae (Phm 1–2); they may be siblings, husband, wife, and son, or three unrelated members of the house-church.[30] Besides married couples, single women (including widows) appear to have hosted the house-churches referred to in Acts. In Jerusalem, Mary the mother of John Mark was probably widowed (Acts 12:12). In Philippi, the merchant Lydia of Thyatira was the central figure in a women's prayer meeting. When "she and her household were baptized," she invited the troupe of evangelists to her home; Paul willingly participated in the founding of a "women's church" (Acts 16:11–15, 40). Nympha of Laodicea hosted a "church in her house" (Col 4:15).[31] A case that the Elect Lady of 2 John may have headed a community of men and women has been made by J. C. O'Neill.[32] The status of the leaders of these house-churches and their function in building up the early church parallel

---

29. Adolf von Harnack, *The Mission and Expansion of Christianity in the First Three Centuries*, trans. and ed. James Moffatt (2nd ed.; 2 vols.; London; New York: G. P. Putnam,1908; repr. Harper Torchbooks, 1961), 1:52, n. 1, and 79. This theory was first offered by von Harnack, "Probabilia über die Adresse und den Verfasser des Hebräerbriefes," *ZNW* 1 (1900): 16–41. His theory, as developed by Ruth Hoppin in 1969, is challenged by Mary Rose D'Angelo, ("Hebrews," in *Women's Bible Commentary* [1992], 364–67) on grounds that the author of the epistle identifies as male by using the masculine form of the Greek participle (Heb. 11:32). Von Harnack's theory has since been elaborated by Ruth Hoppin, *Priscilla's Letter*.

30. Carolyn Osiek, *Philippians, Philemon* (Nashville, TN: Abingdon, 2000), 134.

31. On the whole subject, see Carolyn Osiek, "Women in House Churches," in Julian V. Hills, Richard B. Gardner, et al., *Common Life in the Early Church: Essays Honoring Graydon F. Snyder* (Harrisburg, PA: Trinity Press International, 1998), 300–15; Schüssler Fiorenza, "Women in Pre-Pauline, Pauline Churches," 156. The ms. tradition turned Nympha into the masculine Nymphas (Heine, *Women and Early Christianity*, 88). The environment of the early Christian house is evoked in an exhibition of furnishings at the Krannert Art Museum, University of Illinois at Urbana-Champaign: see Eunice D. Maguire, Henry P. Maguire, and Maggie J. Duncan-Flowers, *Art and Holy Powers in the Early Christian House* (Urbana: University of Illinois Press, 1989).

32. J. C. O'Neill, "New Testament Monasteries," in Hills, *Common Life in the Early Church*, 126–32.

features found in the *vita* of Potentiana and Praxedes. Teresa Berger outlines the case for women as well as men presiding over liturgies in early house-churches.[33]

C. Virgins

Acts 21:8–9 tells us that, in Caesarea, Philip's four prophet daughters are unmarried, suggesting that virginity and publicly exercised charismata may be associated.[34] In 1 Corinthians 7, Paul may be correcting extremist tendencies toward sexual asceticism in libertarian Corinth when he engages in a lengthy discourse on the virtues and deficiencies of marriage and the single life of celibacy. He attempts to balance the two but prefers chaste celibacy, sign of the coming reign of God: "I wish that all were as I myself am. But each has a particular gift from God, one having one kind and another a different kind. To the unmarried and the widows I say that it is well for them to remain unmarried as I am" (vv. 7–8).[35] Displaying the interest in female behavior that not infrequently characterizes celibate leaders, Paul distinguishes the unmarried woman (γυνή ἄγαμος) from the virgin (παρθένος, 7:34). In the First Epistle of Clement to the Corinthians (38.2), probably written in the nineties CE, Clement of Rome warns against boasting by those who are continent, "recognizing that it is someone else" (namely, God) who grants the gift of self-control.[36]

---

33. Berger, *Gender Differences*, 138–40. See also Elaine Mary Wainwright, "Gospel of Matthew," in Schüssler Fiorenza, *Searching the Scriptures*, 2: 659–64; Wainwright, *Towards a Feminist Critical Reading of the Gospel according to Matthew* (Berlin: de Gruyter, 1991), 339–52; Osiek, "Women in House Churches," 300–15.

34. Reimer, *Women in the Acts of the Apostles*, 248–49. Eusebius (*Hist. Eccles.* 3:30) says that Philip would "give his daughters in marriage to husbands"; see Eusebius Pamphilus of Caesarea, *The Ecclesiastical History of Eusebius Pamphilus*, trans. Christian F. Cruse (Grand Rapids, MI: Baker Books, 1955), 115.

35. See Margaret Y. MacDonald, *Early Christian Women and Pagan Opinion: The Power of the Hysterical Woman* (Cambridge: Cambridge University Press, 1996), 133. Some Gnostic sects would embrace sexual asceticism. For a fascinating review of early Christian exegesis of 1 Cor 7, see Elizabeth A. Clark, *Reading Renunciation: Asceticism and Scripture in Early Christianity* (Princeton, NJ: Princeton University Press, 1999), 259–329. Pre-Christian attitudes to the virginal life are explored by Dale Launderville, *Celibacy in the Ancient World: Its Ideal and Practice in Pre-Hellenistic Israel, Mesopotamia, and Greece* (Collegeville, MN: Liturgical, 2010), 230–99.

36. *The Apostolic Fathers: Greek Texts and English Translations*, ed. and rev. Michael W. Holmes (Grand Rapids, MI: Baker Books, 1999), 71.

Chaste celibacy was a choice hardly open to a woman's own decision before the Christian era and not always after (1 Cor 7:36-38). Embedded in an exhortation to wives and husbands to remain true to their spouses, Ignatius of Antioch (d. ca. 117) advises, "If anyone is able to remain continent to the honor of the Lord's flesh, let him remain (so) without boasting; if he boasts, he is lost; and if it is known beyond the bishop, he is destroyed."[37] W. R. Schoedel suggests that Ignatius may evince caution toward the celibate life because most church leaders were married and an ascetic elite could form a challenge to this leadership: "Ignatius does not reject the ascetic way of life but adds considerations that qualify its value."[38] However, Ignatius the bishop on his way to martyrdom was more likely moved by pastoral realism with respect to his flock: not all devout Christians had the gift of continence (1 Cor 7:7). Polycarp the martyred bishop of Smyrna (d. 155) does not mince words when he counsels younger men to "be blameless in all things, caring above all for purity" while "virgins must walk with a blameless and pure conscience."[39]

In the first three Christian centuries, the possibility that families as well as individuals might be required to confess their faith before hostile authorities satisfied the ardor of many believers. However, martyrdom was not always a proximate danger for the fiercely faithful Christian.[40]

---

37. Letter to Polycarp, 5.1–2. For a translation using the androcentric inclusive term, see *Ignatius of Antioch: A Commentary on the Letters of Ignatius of Antioch*, by William R. Schoedel, ed. Helmut Koester (Philadelphia, PA: Fortress, 1985), 272. Carolyn Osiek and David L. Balch (*Families in the New Testament World: Households and House Churches* [Louisville, KY: Westminster John Knox, 1997], 269, n. 222) observe that clerical celibacy developed "more slowly and along different lines."

38. Schoedel (*Ignatius of Antioch*, 272–73) explains that the theological reason for celibacy ("to remain continent, to remain in purity") in Smyrna was given in terms of showing honor to "the flesh of the Lord," possibly referring to "imitation of the Lord's own celibacy" (see Tertullian, *De monogamia*, 5, 6; *Tertulliani Opera*, pars 2: *Opera montanistica*, ed. E. Dekkers and E. Kroyman [Turnhout: Brepols, 1954], 1235). If this is the meaning, then Ignatius is the first to link the choice of continence to imitation of the life of Jesus. However, Schoedel claims (n. 2) that "Christ's flesh" refers to the church, and speculates on "psychologically more complex factors, including the idea that physical union adulterates the purity of the relation with Christ (cf. 1 Cor 6:12–20) or that the virgin is wedded to Christ" (cf. Tertullian, *De virginibus velandis*, 16, 4, ibid., 1225). See also MacDonald, *Early Christian Women and Pagan Opinion*, 187–88.

39. Epistle of Polycarp to the Philippians 5, 3, in *Apostolic Fathers*, 1:289–90.

40. Recent converts, in the height of their enthusiasm, made up a disproportionate number of believers who actually gave blood-witness for the faith. Texts from the book of Revelation suggest the coincidence of martyrdom and virginity. "[T]he souls of those who had been slaughtered for the word of God and for the testimony they had given" under the altar (Rev 6:9) concurs with what becomes the martyr's symbol, the palm branch (Rev 7:9) and the

The choice of a life of continence was already gaining ground against marriage. During the age of the martyrs, steadfast continence might be, especially for women, the presenting reason for martyrdom. From the fourth century, continence would be equated with lifelong martyrdom and even be counted as of greater worth.[41] In the face of the misogynism articulated by some Fathers of the church, much remains to be discovered about the early history of virginity as a Christian state of life.[42] Feminist writers have pointed to its liberating aspects, especially for women. Were women choosing the single life to find freedom from male dominance?[43] Certain pagan philosophical circles encouraged celibacy, while the restrictions placed on women by Roman marriage law and custom might well lead them to see its advantages.[44] Whatever the motivations adduced by modern authors, pursuit of holiness through renunciation of material goods and earthly goals is the expressed if not always realized motive. Celibate virginity gained favor during the course of the second century.

144,000 male virgins "redeemed from the earth," "not defiled" with women, who "follow the Lamb wherever he goes" (Rev 14:3–5). These last, a group not individuals, had not been "seduced away from their loyalty to Christ"; see Peter Brown, *The Body and Society: Men, Women and Sexual Renunciation in Early Christianity* (New York: Columbia University Press, 1988), 72; or they constitute the "Lamb's army," whose temporary chastity prepares them for holy war; see Sophie Laws, *In the Light of the Lamb: Imagery, Parody, and Theology in the Apocalypse of John* (Wilmington, DE: Glazier, 1988), 52–68.

41. Elizabeth Castelli, "Virginity and Its Meaning for Women's Sexuality in Early Christianity," *JFSR* 2 (1986): 61–88 at 67.

42. Jo Ann McNamara, "Sexual Equality and the Cult of Virginity in Early Christian Thought," *Feminist Studies* 3 (1976): 145–58; Margaret Y. MacDonald, *The Pauline Churches: A Socio-Historical Study of Institutionalization in the Pauline and Deutero-Pauline Writings* (Cambridge; New York: Cambridge University Press, 1988), 184–92; Witherington, *Women in Earliest Churches*, 184–92. For a fine summary, see Osiek and Balch, *Families*, 143–55; Elizabeth A. Clark, "Devil's Gateway and Bride of Christ: Women in the Early Christian World," in Clark, *Ascetic Piety and Women's Faith: Essays on Late Ancient Christianity* (Lewiston, NY: Edwin Mellen, 1986), 23–60.

43. Heine, *Women and Early Christianity*, 62–70, 101–105; MacDonald, *Early Christian Women and Pagan Opinion*, 127–82; MacDonald, "Women Holy in Body and Spirit: The Social Setting of 1 Corinthians 7," *NTS* 36 (1990): 164–79; Jo Ann McNamara, *A New Song: Celibate Women in the First Three Christian Centuries* (New York: Harrington Park Press, 1983; repr., New York: Haworth Press 1985), 35–50; Castelli, "Virginity and Its Meaning"; Virginia Burrus, *Chastity as Autonomy*.

44. Rosemary Rader, *Breaking Boundaries: Male/Female Friendship in Early Christian Communities* (New York: Paulist, 1983), 9–17. In a parallel stream, Peter Brown (*Body and Society*, 33–57) provides a picture of the groups and individuals who practiced sexual renunciation in Palestine prior to and stemming from the prophetic ministry of Jesus.

Justin Martyr witnesses to persons of both sexes remaining in chaste celibacy for their lifetimes. After citing Matthew 5:28, 29, 32, and 19:12, Justin says, "And many, both men and women who have been Christ's disciples from childhood, have preserved their purity at the age of sixty or seventy years; and I am proud that I could produce such from every race of men and women."[45] In veiled imagery, Hermas' *Shepherd* refers to groups of virgins, and Margaret MacDonald suggests that the second century knew communities of unmarried Christian women among whom widows found refuge.[46] The ambivalence of male leadership toward unattached females, which is illustrated in the contradictory advice on remarriage given by Paul in 1 Corinthians 7 and by the author of 1 Timothy 5:11, is found in Tertullian (ca. 160–ca. 230). The latter praises virginity and widowhood rather than remarriage, on the one hand, but in his Montanist period, on the other hand, conservatively objects to a young (unattached) "virgin-widow."[47] The apocryphal *Acts of Paul and Thecla* (mid-second century) and the *Acts of Thomas* (early third-century Syria) exhibit encratite tendencies, exalting celibacy at the expense of marriage.[48] The Christian apologist Minucius Felix (d. ca. 250) speaks of *virginitas perpetua*.[49] A recurring theme in the literature is that of the "manly woman" who overcomes the limitations and weakness of

---

45. See 1 Apology 15; Justin Martyr, *Saint Justin Martyr: The First and Second Apologies*, trans. and ed. Leslie William Barnard (New York: Paulist, 1997), 32; see also 1 Apology 14, 31. Chaste celibacy typifies the existence of Christian virgins already in the first century, as observed by Sandra Schneiders, *Religious Life in a New Millennium*, vol. 2: *Selling All: Commitment, Consecrated Celibacy, and Community in Catholic Religious Life* (New York: Paulist, 2001), 166, 426, n. 35.

46. Sim. IX, 10–11; Carolyn Osiek, *Shepherd of Hermas: A Commentary* (Minneapolis, MN: Fortress, 1999), 226–29; MacDonald, *Early Christian Women and Pagan Opinion*, 177.

47. *De virginibus velandis*, 9.2 (*Tertulliani Opera*, pars 2, 1219). Does virgin-widow refer to a youthful virgin who becomes a member of a group of continent widows? Or does Tertullian mean a youthful widowed woman (*univira*) who is too young to be taken (according to 1 Tim 5:11–15) into an ecclesial order of widows? The ancient world held the once-married in high regard (Eisen, *Women Officeholders*, 154, n. 13).

48. Osiek and Balch, *Families*, 153–54; Brown, *Body and Society*, 154–59. On Thecla, see Dennis R. MacDonald, *The Legend and the Apostle: The Battle for Paul in Story and Canon* (Philadelphia, PA: Westminster, 1983). Luise Schottroff (*Lydia's Impatient Sisters*, 128–30) points out how "Paul's divided consciousness" respecting patriarchal dominative structures and women's place in society is played out in the Thecla legend. In their joint apostolate, Thecla is dealt the harsher punishments and even abandoned by her mentor Paul.

49. "Very many of us preserve (rather than take pride in) the perpetual virginity of our undefiled bodies"; see Octavius 31.5, in *The Octavius of Marcus Minucius Felix*, trans. and annotated G. W. Clarke (New York: Newman, 1974), 110.

her gender by eschewing marriage and maternity and embracing virginity.[50] Bridal and erotic rhetoric betokening virginal betrothal and celestial marriage to Christ, appropriated from 2 Corinthians 11:2 and inspired by the Song of Songs, become standard language in the apocryphal acts of the second century. Such rhetoric is found in the lives of holy women, and then developed, sometimes to grotesqueness, by Fathers East and West: Chrysostom, Ambrose, Jerome, and Augustine.[51]

As with women's motives for choosing the celibate life (when indeed they had a choice), information about their living arrangements is scant or lacking in the formative second century.[52] They might live with their families, as did the virgins Potentiana and Praxedes. In the arrangement known as *syneisaktism*, which was based on the patron-client relationship and new possibilities of Christian friendship between men and women, a celibate man and woman (*syneisaktes*) might share a household.[53] This is evocative of the living arrangement alluded to in the Pudens *titulus* with Praxedes and Pastor. Often the sources talk more about the younger female member (Gr. *gyne* or *parthenos syneisaktos* or *agapeta*, Lat. *virgo subintroducta*) than the man. Rosemary Rader writes about the practice

---

50. Eph 4:13 equates perfection with maturation into "a complete male." See Jo Ann McNamara, *New Song*, 87–105. John Chrysostom applauds the "manly spirit" of the virgin; see Elizabeth A. Clark, *Jerome, Chrysostom, and Friends: Essays and Translations* (New York: Edwin Mellen, 1979), 19 and 54–59. Virgins possess *andreia* (virile souls, 57). Jerome asserts baldly that a woman (symbolizing the human body) who prefers Jesus Christ to her husband and the production of babies "will cease to be a woman and will be called man...." (56); and to a couple in a now-continent marriage he dares to say that the wife was "once a woman but now a man, once an inferior but now an equal" (56). Palladius acclaims Chrysostom's friend and benefactor Olympias by saying that she should be called "*anthropos*, a man in everything but body" (57).

51. Castelli, "Virginity and Its Meaning," 71–73. See also Clark, "Devil's Gateway and Bride of Christ," 50–51; Clark, "John Chrysostom and the *Subintroductae*," *Church History* 46 (1977): 171–85, repr. in Elizabeth A. Clark, *Ascetic Piety and Women's Faith: Essays on Late Ancient Christianity* (Lewiston, NY: Edwin Mellen, 1986), 265–90, esp. 272–74; Clark, "The Uses of the Song of Songs: Origen and the Later Latin Fathers," in *Ascetic Piety and Women's Faith*, 401–5; Anne Ewing Hickey, *Women of the Roman Aristocracy as Christian Monastics* (Ann Arbor, MI: UMI Research Press, 1987), 21–48.

52. In a study of the novel phenomenon of heterosexual friendship in early Christian societies, Rader (*Breaking Boundaries*, 5, n. 1.) makes the telling comment that literary data about friendship become available in the 3rd century, while by the 5th century "the more liberal, egalitarian type of heterosexual relationship was itself becoming institutionalized as Church structures became more rigidly hierarchical"; also Clark, *Jerome, Chrysostom, and Friends*, 35–79.

53. Possibly witnessed to by 1 Cor 7:36–38. See Osiek and Balch, *Families*, 154.

of "spiritual marriage," situating the "angelic" asexual life within the cultural requirement that every woman have a male *patronus* and the belief that restoration of the androgynous life prior to the Fall is an essential aspect of preparation for the second coming of Christ, for the asexual life is "angelic."[54] However, if the relatively independent life of the widow attracted criticism in the Pastorals and thereafter, the cohabitation of a celibate man and woman was open to scandalous interpretation. It was vehemently discouraged by Cyprian, inveighed against by Jerome and John Chrysostom whose imaginations ran to the lurid, and prohibited by church councils.[55] Meanwhile, marriages in which the partners retained their virginity or renounced sexual relationship after a time together were not infrequent. That none of these criticisms is addressed to the church in the house of Pudens following his death may indicate our story's representation of the ideals of the Christian community of the first 150 years. The recensions of the conservative *Apostolic Tradition* (ca. 215+) shows that the relationship of the virgin to the structures of the author's church is an arms-length one: the (female) virgin (παρθένος) chooses her lifestyle: "it is her inner life alone that makes her a virgin" (Arabic text). She is not set apart by laying on of hands; unlike the order of widows, she is not even named in the church.[56]

In the East the eremetic (hermit) or cenobitic community life of the "desert" appealed to those Christians of high ascetic ideals who would willingly have embraced martyrdom. Many people, perhaps more women than men, left the cities for the desert.[57] When circa 270 St. Antony, the

---

54. Rader, *Breaking Boundaries*, 62–71.

55. Geoffrey D. Dunn, "Infected Sheep and Diseased Cattle, or the Pure and Holy Flock: Cyprian's Pastoral Care of Virgins," *JECS* 11 (2003): 1–20; Clark, "John Chrysostom and *Subintroductae*," 171–85; Clark, *Jerome, Chrysostom, and Friends*, 158–248; Clark, "Ascetic Renunciation and Feminine Advancement: A Paradox of Late Ancient Christianity," *ATR* 63 (1981): 240–57; Rader, *Breaking Boundaries*, 62–71. For a similar reading, see Susanna Elm, *"Virgins of God": The Making of Asceticism in Late Antiquity* (Oxford: Clarendon, 1994), 47–51. Hermas in *The Shepherd* is told that his wife must become his "sister" (Osiek and Balch, *Families*, 154–55).

56. Paul F. Bradshaw, Maxwell E. Johnson and L. Edward Phillips, *The Apostolic Tradition: A Commentary* (Minneapolis, MN: Fortress, 2002), no. 12, 76–77.

57. Rosemary Rader, "Early Christian Forms of Communal Spirituality: Women's Communities," in William Skudlarek, ed., *The Continuing Quest for God: Monastic Spirituality in Tradition and Transition* (Collegeville, MN: Liturgical, 1982), 88–99, and a 36-page booklet by Margot H. King, *The Desert Mothers: A Survey of the Feminine Anchoretic Tradition in Western Europe* (Saskatoon, SK: Peregrina Publishing, 1985). Faivre (*Emergence of Laity*, 189–205) gives an overview that treats both men and women.

reputed father of Eastern monasticism, "fled" to the nearby desert he placed his sister in an already-existing women's monastery. Of course the eremetic life was more dangerous for women than the cenobitic. The legends of St. Mary Magdalene living as a hermit in the Maritime Alps of Provence and of St. Mary of Egypt (5th century?) would come to be intermingled so as to challenge the imagination, these two saints serving as icons of unnamed women.[58] After an experimental formative period, the fourth century shows a developed female asceticism that attracted much attention, advice, and written counsel from certain of the Fathers. While Augustine was establishing a community of male canons in Hippo and writing a rule for his sister's monastery, his mentor Ambrose of Milan, in a treatise directed to the latter's sister Marcellina, was praising the virtue of virgins, types of the unsullied church.[59] In the West more women than men embraced the life of virginity in the cities or suburban areas, living in the parental or their own household singly or with a group of like-minded women in what has been called "house" or "familial" monasticism. The lives of consecrated virgins and widows became institutionalized but also achieved a new degree of autonomy when they left the parental home and joined together in a monastery under a common rule.

D. Ecclesiastical Widows

The Hebrew and Christian Scriptures are rich in widows.[60] First Timothy 5:3–8 gives advice on how the church should honor and deal with those who are "really widows." A widow is allowed on the list if she is sixty years of age and married only once, if she has a reputation for hospitality and is "well attested for her good works" (1 Tim 5:9–10). Younger widows are not to be enrolled (1 Tim 5:11).[61] Is this a list for welfare support, or of those

---

58. On Mary of Egypt, see King, *Desert Mothers*, 21, n. 20 and *Medieval Saints: A Reader*, ed. Mary-Ann Stouck (Peterborough, ON: Broadview Press, 1999), 97–114. Joyce E. Salisbury (*Church Fathers, Independent Virgins* [London: Verso, 1991], 68–73) gives a feminist reading. Laura Swan (*The Forgotten Desert Mothers: Sayings, Lives and Stories of Early Christian Women* [New York: Paulist, 2001], 106–26) compiles information on holy women.

59. Ambrose, Bishop of Milan, *De virginitate*. For an English translation, see Ambrose, *On Virginity*, trans. Daniel Callam (Toronto: Peregrina, [1980] 1989); also, Teresa M. Shaw, "*Askesis* and the Appearance of Holiness," *JECS* 6 (1998): 485–99.

60. Gustav Stählin, "χήρα," *TDNT* 9:440–65.

61. The pseudonymous author's advice to require remarriage of younger widows contradicts Paul's to the Corinthians (1 Cor 7:7–8).

exercising the ecclesial order of widowhood? Bonnie Bowman Thurston distinguishes between women who administer, and those who receive, charity. The dating of the Pastorals, anywhere between 60 and 150 CE, affects the understanding of an "order of widows." Thurston observes the "almost exact correspondence" in required qualities between 1 Timothy 5:3–15, which speaks of widows, and 1 Timothy 3:11, which, if we follow John Chrysostom and other ancient authorities, refers to deacons who are women.[62] Ecclesial widows developed out of functions already performed by any "good" widow: hospitality, charitable acts including care for the young, the ill, and the elderly in one's own family and beyond, and of course, prayer.[63] Gustav Stählin proposes that Mary the mother of Mark (Acts 12:12), Tabitha (Acts 9:36–41), Lydia (Acts 16:14–15), Mary (Rom 16:6) and even Phoebe (Rom 16:1–2), Chloe (1 Cor 1:11), and Tryphena, Tryphosa, and Persis (Rom 16:12) were wealthy widows who took special care of the church and its members in their respective towns, while Nympha (Col 4:15) hosted a house-church.[64] The title widow did not necessarily imply widowhood. In his letter to the Smyrnaeans (13.1) Ignatius of Antioch, whose letters are usually dated between 100 and 118 CE, refers to "the virgins who are called widows."[65] It may be that some of those women listed above, like Tabitha whose marital status goes unmentioned, are single women not widows. Even less did the title imply advanced age. In the early stages of the development of celibate (single) lifestyles, "widow" (Χήρα) was a catch-all term for "real" and enrolled widows and virgins of all ages. The ambiguity of the title as well as the incompleteness and contradictory character of the extant evidence on widows have led to varying interpretations.[66] Church Fathers preferred that consecrated virgins keep a low

---

62. Bonnie Bowman Thurston, *The Widows: A Women's Ministry in the Early Church* (Minneapolis, MN: Fortress, 1989), 44–55. As the church's leaders came to be chosen from older men who had been married but once, so enrollment as an ecclesiastical widow was open only to those married once (*univira*), a status favored in the ancient world (Hickey, *Women of Roman Aristocracy*, 57, 71, 91–92, 99).

63. Faivre, *Emergence of Laity*, 11.

64. Stählin, "χήρα," *TDNT* 9:451, n. 107, 457, and 465. He stops short of ascribing to these women a ministry of the word; indeed, access to schooling would play a determinative role. Tabitha is called "disciple," the only occurrence of the feminine μαθήτρια (Acts 9:36) in the New Testament (Gail R. O'Day, "Acts," *Women's Bible Commentary* (1998), 398).

65. *Ignatius of Antioch*, 247, 252; Thurston, *Widows*, 54.

66. Eisen (*Women Officeholders*, 12–14) summarizes the state of the question. See also Witherington, *Women in Earliest Churches*; Thurston, *Widows*; MacDonald, *Pauline Churches*.

public profile within protected living arrangements. Widows, on the other hand, had experience of the world and family and thus a special capacity for doing the charitable work of the church among women.

As the governance and services of the Christian churches developed, the unitary nature of the Christian *laos* in the era of the house-church gave way to the separation of clergy from laity.[67] The enrolled widow, a single woman with ministerial functions that associate her with the clergy, bridges that divide. Carolyn Osiek notes two churches where enrolled or canonical widows "may have been considered clergy." In Carthage, widows were included in the council that deliberated over public penitents and requests for second marriages; and in the Syrian congregation represented by the fifth-century *Testamentum Domini*, the widows called "those who sit in front" (1.19) were seated with the clergy and at the liturgy stood in the sanctuary, immediately behind the presbyters on the left side, on equal footing with the deacons who stood behind the presbyters on the right (1.23).[68] In the East, the third century marked the apogee of the ecclesiastical office of widow.[69] If we follow the reconstructed *Apostolic Tradition* attributed to Hippolytus and its lineage into the fifth century, the office of "instituted" widows existed in many churches, especially in the East and Egypt.[70] In *Apostolic Tradition*'s most stable ranking of ministries (that of the Arabic and Ethiopic texts), widows are listed after (male) deacons and

---

67. Faivre (*Emergence of Laity*, 51, 101–2, 209, 213–15) locates this sea change in the 3rd century. Just as women were not usually counted among the clergy or would hold only an ambiguous place there, they were not included among the laity!

68. Carolyn Osiek ("The Widow as Altar: The Rise and Fall of a Symbol," *Second Century* 3 [1983]: 160) cites Tertullian, *De monog.* 11.1; *De pud.* 13.7; and *Testamentum Domini*; see *The Testamentum Domini: A Text for Students*, ed. Grant Sperry-White (Bramcote: Grove, 1991), 13–14, 47.

69. Faivre (*Emergence of Laity*, 97–102) gives a nuanced analysis of the office of widow as presented in the Syriac church order *Didascalia apostolorum* (ca. 230), suggesting that the office of woman deacon "neutralized" the relative power of widows.

70. Paul F. Bradshaw, *Ordination Rites of the Ancient Churches of East and West* (New York: Pueblo, 1990), 109; Bradshaw, Johnson, and Phillips, *Apostolic Tradition*, 71–73. *AT* may not represent the mainstream Roman tradition, or even be Roman (ibid., 14); for a summary of the divergent theories, see Paul F. Bradshaw, *The Search for the Origins of Christian Worship: Sources and Methods for the Study of Early Liturgy* (2nd ed.; Oxford: Oxford University Press, 2002), 80–83. That *AT* can be understood as the product of two redactors, the first a conservative Roman presbyter-bishop, the second, someone interested in reconciling patron-presbyters with the developing mono-episcopate, on which see Hippolytus, *On the Apostolic Tradition: Hippolytus*, trans., introduction, and commentary by Alistair Stewart-Sykes (Crestwood, NY: St. Vladimir's Seminary, 2001). John F. Baldovin ("Hippolytus and the *Apostolic Tradition*: Recent Research and Commentary," *TS* 64 [2003]: 520–42) offers a critique.

confessors.[71] They are appointed or instituted (καθίσταναι) "by the word only" and not ordained (χειροτονεῖν) by laying on of hands because they lack *leitourgia* but serve the church by their prayer.[72] *Apostolic Tradition* adds that the ministry of prayer "belongs to everyone." In Stewart-Sykes' translation, "But a hand shall not be laid on her because she does not lift up the sacrifice nor does she have a proper liturgy. For the laying on of hands is with the clergy on account of the liturgy, whereas the widow is installed on account of prayer, which is for everybody."[73] Texts treating of women's place in the church circumscribe the widow's ministry. In what seems to be a clear rearrangement, the *Canons of Hippolytus* place the widow last in the list of confessor, reader, virgin, subdeacon, healer, and widow.[74] That there were *viduae ecclesiae* functioning in some churches of the West at the end of the fourth century can be concluded from Ambrosiaster's commentary on 1 Timothy 5:3–16.[75] In the fifth century in Gaul, a special dress distinguished these women.[76] Their life has been pictured as ascetical, their ministry limited to fasting and prayer. Prayer, fasting, and the dedicated life of the *ordo viduarum* became the attribute of virgins as the ascetic

---

71. Bradshaw, Johnson, and Phillips, *Apostolic Tradition*, 15. The Ethiopic text uses the term ordination: "If a widow is ordained, she is not to be sealed but should act by nomination" (ibid., 72). The Ethiopic may well represent the earlier state of things, for the Arabic explains, "Ordination is in the case of the clergy for service, and in the case of the widow for prayer, which is for everyone" (*AT*, 10–11; Bradshaw, 72).

72. The *Canons of Hippolytus* 8 explains boldly that widows "are not to be ordained, but one is to pray over them, because ordination is for men" (Bradshaw, Johnson, and Phillips, *Apostolic Tradition*, 73). *Testamentum Domini* requires the bishop to pray in a low voice so that only the presbyters may hear the prayer of institution for "widows who sit in front" (Bradshaw, *Ordination Rites*, 87–88, 120–21; *Testamentum Domini*, ed. Sperry-White, 43).

73. Stewart-Sykes (*Hippolytus*, 95–96) comments, "Whereas it is possible that 'liturgy' is being used here in the sense of a public role in the assembly, it is also possible that it is used in its broader and more ancient sense of a public duty performed as an act of patronage. As is clear in the discussion at chapter 30 below about giving food to widows, the widows receive patronage, and do not exercise it."

74. Bradshaw, Johnson, and Phillips, *Apostolic Tradition*, 15, 83.

75. See Roger Gryson, *The Ministry of Women in the Early Church*, trans. Jean Laporte and Mary Louise Hall (Collegeville, MN: Liturgical, 1976), 97, who cites the commentary on 1 Tim in CSEL 81–83.279.8.

76. Gryson, *Ministry of Women*, 103–4; cf. the "real widows" of 1 Tim 5:5, 9 (8–10). The Old Gelasian Sacramentary (Rome, Vat. Reg. lat. 316, a 7th-century presbyteral sacramentary of the *tituli*, which was copied in Gaul (ca. 750) with Gallican additions, contains a blessing of widows *(Benedictio viduae quae fuerit castitatem professa)* and an anniversary mass. See Antoine Chavasse, *Le sacramentaire gélasien*, 507–10.

life grew in popularity.[77] From early in the third century the institution of widows, once widespread, begins to disappear. The widow's ministry with its charitable work gives way to the office of diacona, who was more easily subjected to hierarchical governance than the instituted widow.[78]

3. Women Holders of Church Office

Alexandre Faivre's observation about women's ministries in the earliest period of the church is germane: "The services performed by women were sufficiently important for them to be regarded as true ministries, even though they had no precise title or status. These women ministers did not constitute a clergy or a caste, but continued simply to be part of the people.... But as far as the functions fulfilled by women were concerned, we have simply to recognize that they existed in fact, but that the women who performed them had no corresponding title or rank."[79] Phoebe, *diakonos* of the church of the port city of Corinth, proves the exception.

Timelines for development of the threefold ordained ministry (diaconate, presbyterate, and episcopate) exercised by men are obscure. What is certain is that the threefold ministry did not emerge full-grown from the head of Zeus, nor was it established by the historical Jesus. Deconstructions of the foundation and development of the hierarchical structure have been provided by Paul Bradshaw and others.[80] How much more difficult, then, to reconstruct

---

77. In keeping with its Eastern sources, the *Statuta ecclesiae antiqua* (Gaul, ca. 475) allows a limited liturgical activity for celibate women. It declares: "Widows or *sanctimoniales*, who are chosen for the ministry of baptizing women, should be so trained for this office, that they are able openly and with clear word to teach ignorant and rustic women, at the time they are being baptized, how baptizands should respond to the questions and how, having accepted baptism, they should live" (CCSL 148, no. 100 [XII], 184); also, "Widows who are sustained by church stipend ought to be so ceaseless in the work of God (*opus Dei*) that both with merits and prayers they assist the church" (ibid., no. 102 [CIII], 185).

78. Faivre, *Emergence of Laity*, 95–104.

79. Faivre, *Emergence of the Laity*, 12. On the invisibility of women in the early Christian mission, see Schüssler Fiorenza, "Missionaries, Apostles, Coworkers," 420–33. An instance is that of the "women" referred to in 1 Tim 3:11 sandwiched between rules for appointment of deacons. Are these women themselves deacons (John Chrysostom's opinion), or wives of deacons? Evidence mounts of women's public leadership in synagogue (*Women Leaders in the Ancient Synagogue*, 149) and church (Eisen, *Women Officeholders*).

80. Bradshaw (*Search for Origins of Christian Worship*, 192–210) cautions against drawing conclusions about women's ecclesiastical ministries on the basis of sparse evidence. Eric G. Jay ("From Presbyter-Bishops to Bishops and Presbyters," *The Second Century* 1 [1981]: 125–62) sets out questions about male offices. Edward Schillebeeckx ("The Catholic Understanding

the possibilities for the holding of church office by female Christians, whose lives were for the most part modestly "invisible." In the following sections evidence for women's ecclesiastical ministries outside Rome is surveyed.

A. Diaconas

The verb *diakonein*, "to serve," is rooted in the gospel narratives of Jesus' own ministry and frequently applied in the gospels to Jesus and to women. Holly E. Hearon summarizes the question for Matthew's gospel: "'Serve' (διακονέω) occurs five times in Matthew's gospel (Matt 4:11; 8:15; 20:28; 25:44; 27:55) and the noun cognate 'servant' (διάκονος) three times (Matt 20:26, 22:13, 23:11)." Jesus serves, but angels, Peter's mother-in-law, and the women, including those who stood at the cross, "serve" Jesus (Matt 27:55).[81] Martha of Bethany's work of hospitality toward Jesus is *diakonia* (Luke 10:38–42) but in the Lukan story that gives to Mary "the better part," Martha's service is belittled.[82] Among the apostolic writings the term is used most frequently in the Pauline and deutero-Pauline correspondence. Paul calls himself *diakonos* and his apostolate *diakonia* (2 Cor 6:3–4). Does *diakonein* refer to menial service such as waiting tables, or does it act as metaphor for responsible discipleship? John N. Collins has shown that the Greek word commonly translated "ministry" (διακονία) has to do with agency. The *diakonos* is a mandated officer who acts as intermediary on behalf of the one who mandates.[83] In the early Christian churches, this is bishop or presbyter.

Ἐπίσκοποι (overseers) and διάκονοι are introduced anonymously as church officers in Philippians 1:1 (written 56–57 CE).[84] Showing an

---

of Office in the Church," *TS* 30 [1969]: 568–69) explains the perennial permanent office(s) representing the church and Christ as divinely willed and established by the risen Christ, not by the historical Jesus.

81. Holly E. Hearon, *The Mary Magdalene Tradition: Witness and Counter-Witness in Early Christian Communities* (Collegeville, MN: Liturgical, 2004), 114–15.

82. However, in John's gospel Martha not Peter articulates the christological faith of the community (John 11:27).

83. John N. Collins, *Diakonia: Re-interpreting the Ancient Sources* (Oxford: Oxford University Press, 1990); Collins, "Once More on Ministry: Forcing a Turnover in the Linguistic Field," *One in Christ* 27 (1991): 234–45. Clarke (*Serve the Community of the Church*, 233–45) critiques Collins' case as it applies to usage in the Christian Scriptures.

84. "Overseers" and "servants": the terms are ambiguous because the masculine gender serves as the androcentric inclusive term for both sexes. The female deacons Posidonia and Agathe as well as a female canon Panchareia are attested in Philippi, 4th or early 5th century (Eisen, *Women Officeholders*, 179–80).

egalitarian strain in primitive Christianity, in Romans 16:1–2 (written ca. 57–58 from Corinth) Paul refers to Phoebe as his "sister" as well as διάκονος (Lat. *minister*) of Cenchreae, port of Corinth, uniquely calling her as well προστάτις (Gr. patron, protector, benefactor).[85] Her appellations "sister" and διάκονος parallel those given to Tychicus, Paul's "dear brother" and "faithful minister" named in the deutero-Pauline Ephesians 6:21 and Colossians 4:7. Were either of these "ministers" installed publicly in church office, or was their service understood functionally? If at this early date Phoebe's title signifies a function not an office, this judgment should also hold for references to contemporary male deacons. Whatever the case, the masculine or feminine article, not the noun, specifies the gender in Greek. Acts 6:1–6, probably written in the late seventies or early eighties, has been taken to describe the "institution of the diaconate" in Jerusalem by way of election of seven men to wait on tables because the widows of the Hellenists were being ill-served.[86] These seven are not called *diakonoi*. Stephen and Philip are shortly found, not exercising works of charity, but rather a ministry of the word similar to the Lukan apostles. Theodor Klauser observes astutely that we know nothing regarding the place and circumstances of the establishment of the diaconate and are instructed only vaguely regarding its original function.[87] There is no more certainty about the male diaconate in the first century than there is about the diaconate of women. Phoebe is the first individual to be termed *diakonos* in the Christian Scriptures, and, acting as his emissary, by none other than Paul.[88]

---

85. Phoebe received a substantial entry as "Sancta Phoebe Diaconissa" in *AA.SS., Septembris* I (Paris: Victor Palmé, 1868) under her feastday, *Dies tertia Septembris* (597–605), with a lengthy tract on deaconesses by John Pinius (fl. 1740) prefacing this volume (ibid., I–XXVIII). Pinius proposed that she was not Paul's wife and more likely a widow than a virgin, presenting well-known patristic references, church documentation, and ordination rites in East and West (IV–XIV).

86. This episode has often been taken to mark the institution of the diaconate. See Ben Witherington, *The Acts of the Apostles: A Socio-Rhetorical Commentary* (Grand Rapids, MI: Eerdmans, 1998), 250–51. Questions to be raised include: Are these men not commissioned rather than ordained? Were the Hellenists' widows not being admitted to eucharist? Were these widows "losing out on the honorable female role of serving at the communal meals?" See Reta Halteman Finger, *Of Widows and Meals: Communal Meals in the Book of Acts* (Grand Rapids, MI: Eerdmans, 2007), 194–214 and 254–64.

87. Theodor Klauser, "Diakon," in Klauser, ed., *Reallexikon für Antike und Christentum: Sachwörterbuch zur Auseinandersetzung des Christentums mit der antiken Welt* (24 vols.; Stuttgart: A. Hiersemann, 1957), 3: 888–909.

88. Gerhard Lohfink, "Weibliche Diakone im Neuen Testament," in Josef Blank, et al., *Die Frau im Urchristentum*, ed. Gerhard Dautzenberg, et al. (Freiburg im Breisgau: Herder, 1983), 320–38; Dirk Ansorge, "Der Diakonat der Frau: Zum gegenwärtigen Forschungsstand," in Teresa

In 1 Timothy 3:11, the noun *diakonos* appears to refer to an office. Ancient authorities presumed that the phrase "[t]he women likewise" (1 Tim 3:11), which interrupts the discourse on male deacons (1 Tim 3:8–10, 12–13), refers to women deacons, not to their wives.[89]

Very close in time is the "first specific reference to early Christian women by a pagan author," found in a letter of Pliny the Younger, governor of Pontus-Bithynia (111–113 CE), to the Emperor Trajan regarding two women "ministers" reported in Bithynia (Asia Minor).[90] Pliny ordered two female slaves (*ancillae*) called *ministrae* to be tortured but all that was extracted by this means was the indication of "excessive superstition." Gathering early in the morning, their community "sang hymns to Christ as if to a god."[91] The Timothy and Pliny texts originated in Asia Minor, where for several centuries women deacons were numerous. Sources such as Tertullian (d. ca. 220) in North Africa and *Apostolic Tradition* (ca. 215+) do not mention women deacons. Is failure to name women as deacons a function of women's social invisibility in the Greco-Roman world?[92]

The Syriac *Didascalia Apostolorum* (ca. 230) exhorts the bishop to choose a male deacon for countless needs and a woman "for the service of the women." It distinguishes, but with an eye to balance, male and female ministries.[93] So far as can be determined on the basis of the fragmentary

---

Berger and Albert Gerhards, eds., *Liturgie und Frauenfrage: Ein Beitrag zur Frauenforschung aus liturgiewissenschaftlichen Sicht* (St. Ottilien: EOS Verlag Erzabtei, 1990), 34.

89. See Jennifer H. Stiefel, "Women Deacons in 1 Timothy: A Linguistic and Literary Look at 'Women Likewise...' (1 Tim. 3:11)," *NTS* 41 (1995): 442–57. Johnson (*First and Second Letters to Timothy*, 228–29) takes 1 Timothy as written to Ephesus in Asia Minor at the end of Paul's life.

90. Pliny the Younger, *Ep.* X, 96.8, dated ca. 112 CE, commentary in *The Letters of Pliny: A Historical and Social Commentary*, by A. N. Sherwin-White (Oxford: Clarendon Press, [1966] 1985), 710; Eisen, *Women Officeholders*, 35, 173, 193. The observation cited is by MacDonald, *Early Christian Women and Pagan Opinion*, 51.

91. *Minister* may be the Latin translation of *diakonos*, suggesting a parallel with Phoebe some 55 years later. Eisen (*Women Officeholders*, 173) reminds us that, in Justin Martyr's reference to deacons administering the eucharist in Rome (Apol. I. 65, 5), there is no reason to exclude women. In opposition to giving *minister* a strong sense, see Kevin Madigan and Carolyn Osiek (ed. and trans.), *Ordained Women in the Early Church: A Documentary History* (Baltimore, MD: Johns Hopkins University Press, 2005), 96, n. 3.

92. These questions are explored by Carolyn Osiek and Margaret MacDonald with Janet Tulloch, *A Woman's Place: House Churches in Earliest Christianity* (Minneapolis, MN: Fortress, 2006).

93. III.12.1–4. *Didascalia et Constitutiones apostolorum*, ed. Franz Xaver Funk (2 vols.; Paderborn: Schoeningh, 1905), 1:208–11 (repr. ed., 2 vol. in 1; Torino: Bottega d'Erasmo, 1964);

Greek original, later Syriac and Latin versions, and the sections repeated in *Apostolic Constitutions* (ca. 380), the generic *diakonos* is preceded by the feminine article or by "woman." The *Didascalia* expands on Ignatius' typology in Magnesians 6, 1 to present a more inclusive image:

> ...the bishop sits among you as a type (εἰς τύπον, *in typum*) of God. The deacon, however, is present as a type of Christ; and is therefore to be loved by you. And the deaconess (ἡ διάκονος) is to be honoured by you as a type of the Holy Spirit. The presbyters are also to be reckoned by you as a type of the apostles, and the widows and orphans are to be considered by you as a type of the altar.[94]

Including the Holy Spirit in a typology in the mid-third century does not imply acknowledgment of equality with Father and Son, to be promulgated by the First Council of Constantinople in 381, but may suit the subordinate situation of the woman deacon demonstrated elsewhere in this church order (ch. XVI). However, early Syriac sources also know the Spirit as mother of Jesus. The feminine gender of "spirit" in Semitic languages underlies this unique typology.[95] Aimé Georges Martimort observes that, in the small church of the *Didascalia*, the deacon, type of Christ, seems to play a higher role than the presbyters, types of the apostles.[96]

Didascalia Apostolorum: The Syriac Version Translated and Accompanied by the Verona Latin Fragments, with introduction and notes by R. Hugh Connolly (Oxford: Clarendon Press, 1929; repr. 1969), 146–47; *The Liturgical Portions of the Didascalia*, ed. Sebastian Brock and Michael Vasey (Bramcote, Nott.: Grove, 1982), 22–23; *The Didascalia apostolorum: an English Version*, ed. Alistair Stewart-Sykes (Turnhout: Brepols, 2009), 192–94. For a discussion including textual issues, see Gryson, *Ministry of Women in the Early Church*, 35–43; Alexandre Faivre, *Naissance d'une hiérarchie: Les premières étapes du cursus clérical* (Paris: Éditions Beauchesne, 1977), 86–87, 131–39 and Faivre, *Emergence of Laity*, 100–102.

94. *Didascalia apostolorum*, II, 26.4–8 (Funk, *Didascalia*, I, II.26; 104–5, 4–8). The translation followed here is that of Stewart-Sykes, *Didascalia Apostolorum: English Version*, 151. See also Connolly, *Didascalia*, 86, 88; Brock and Vasey, *Didascalia*, ch. 9, p. 11. Pseudo-Ignatius, a text reflecting the church order of *Apostolic Constitutions*, says after listing the minor male orders, "Greet the guardians of the holy gates, the [female] deacons in Christ. Greet the Christ-imbued virgins....Greet the distinguished widows....Greet the people of the Lord...and all my sisters in the Lord" (To the Antiochenes, 12); Madigan and Osiek, *Ordained Women*, 65–66.

95. Robert Murray, *Symbols of Church and Kingdom: A Study in Early Syriac Tradition* (rev. ed.; Piscataway, NJ: Gorgias Press, 2004), 143–44, 312–20.

96. Aimé Georges Martimort, *Les diaconesses: essai historique* (Rome: C.L.V. Edizioni Liturgiche, 1982), 33. However, comparison with similar typologies in the Ignatian corpus reveals that deacons are included only three or four times, only once compared with Jesus

Like the enrolled widow, the female deacon of the third and subsequent centuries is only to be accepted as a mature woman.[97] However, epigraphic evidence and special cases such as John Chrysostom's patron Olympias show that younger women were also installed in the office. Only after the First Council of Nicaea (325) is the diminutive διακόνισσα (deaconess) widespread in the East; it seems to have been used interchangeably with διάκονος preceded by the feminine article.[98] Since inscriptions incised in stone are frequently abbreviated, it is usually not possible to determine from gravestones whether the title was *diacona*, the exact feminine equivalent of *diaconus*, or *diaconissa*. But did ordination follow marriage or widowhood? Some inscriptions refer to husband or children, others mention both. Even when these are mentioned it is not necessarily clear that the husband was alive or the diacona widowed. What is clear is that married and virgin women deacons abound in Asia Minor, celibate women deacons are relatively plentiful in Palestine, and in Greece and Macedonia both virgins and married women are identified as deacons.[99] While both married and celibate women exercised the office in at least some of the early churches, lifelong celibacy was to become a requirement for women in both East and West.[100]

Christ (Tr. 2.1; Schoedel [*Ignatius Antioch*, 46, 113]). Vaguer expressions are the rule (Mag. 6.1; Tr. 2.3; Sm. 8.1). Ignatius stresses the bond between bishops and presbyters.

97. The age of 40, according to Canon 15 of the Council of Chalcedon, AD 451. See Peter L'Huillier, *The Church of the Ancient Councils: The Disciplinary Work of the First Four Ecumenical Councils* (Crestwood, NY: St. Vladimir's Seminary Press, 1996), 82–83, 243–47. The tradition in the West is given in Gratian, *Corpus iuris canonici* (decretales), ed. Emil Friedberg (2 vols.; Leipzig: Tauchnitz, 1879–1881; repr., Graz: Akademische Druck-und Verlagsanstalt, 1959), 1: col. 1055: "No woman shall be consecrated as deaconess before she is 40 years old, and then only after careful examination. But if, after receiving this consecration and fulfilling her office for a period of time, she should marry, thus disdaining the grace of God, let her be anathema along with him who entered marriage with her." This exact wording is found in the appendix to the works of St. Leo the Great (*PL* 56, 544A), canon 15.

98. For usage, see William F. Arndt and F. Wilbur Gingrich, *A Greek-English Lexicon of the New Testament and Other Early Christian Literature* (4th rev. ed.; Chicago: University of Chicago Press, 1957), 183–84. On the use of *diaconissa*, see Faivre, *Emergence of Laity*, 100.

99. Inscriptions in Eisen, *Women Officeholders*, 158–98. Since a number of Eastern church orders insist—in a striking imbalance to male marital status—that women ecclesiastical officers be celibate, this apparent indifference to women deacons' marital state is striking.

100. Karl-Heinrich Schäfer, "Kanonissen und Diakonissen: Ergänzungen und Erläuterungen," *RQ* 24 (1910): 49–90; Adolf Kalsbach, *Die altkirchliche Einrichtung der Diakonissen bis zur ihrem Erlöschen*, in *RQ* 22, Supplementsheft (Freiburg in Breisgau: Herder, 1926). By the later 4th century, ordained clergy in the West were supposed to be living continently with their wives. In the East, where presbyters and deacons maintained marriage rights, the insistence on the woman deacon's celibacy suggests a heightened concern for female "purity," or perhaps for freedom from subordination to a husband.

Evidence from *Apostolic Tradition* recensions shows which ancient churches had an active women's diaconate. The *Canones ecclesiasticae apostolorum* (Egypt, ca. 300) mention a widowed *eudiakonos*. The *Canones Hippolyti* (Alexandria, ca. 340) do not refer to women deacons. In the preceding century, however, Clement of Alexandria (d. before 215) and Origen (d. 253) mention women several times. If women deacons are disappearing in Egypt during the fourth century, by that century's end they are certainly attested in Constantinople, Antioch, Caesarea in Palestine, and Cappadocia.[101] *Apostolic Constitutions* (ca. 380, compiled in Antioch or Constantinople) uses the terms ἡ διάκονος and διακόνισσα for a clearly defined ecclesiastical office that is limited to women who will not marry. It provides a rite with laying on of hands for both men and women deacons (see my chapter five). Diaconal ordination rites for women in the Syriac and Byzantine churches paralleled those for men. Instead of refusing the office of the diaconate to women as came to be the practice in Gaul in the sixth century, women's functions were restricted according to the varying cultural norms of the different Eastern churches. Comparisons of the early church orders bear this out. A number of prominent women deacons figured in the early history of Constantinople. Olympias (d. 410), patron and close friend of the bishop John Chrysostom, established a monastery close by the old Hagia Sophia: "Then by the divine will she was ordained deaconess of this holy cathedral of God and she built a monastery at an angle south of it."[102] Other deaconesses were heads of monasteries in or outside the capital city of Byzantium.[103] In 451 the Council of Chalcedon legislated the age of women to be ordained deacons as not younger than 40.[104] Emperor Justinian's third *Novella* (ca. 535) witnesses to their presence

---

101. Swan (*Forgotten Desert Mothers*, 106–26) has compiled biographical data on women deacons.

102. See Clark, *Jerome, Chrysostom, and Friends*, 107–57 for the life of Olympias, who may have been ordained when she was not yet 30; here no. 6, 131. "[B]y the divine will" introduces the Byzantine ordination rite.

103. For a list of women deacons, see Evangelos Theodorou, "Das Amt der Diakoninnen in der kirchlichen Tradition: Ein orthodoxer Beitrag zum Problem der Frauenordination," *Una Sancta* 33 (1978): 162–72 at 171. He names as characteristic activities "the works of love," including the preparation of women's bodies for burial; Theodorou, "Der Diakonat der Frau in der Griechisch-Orthodoxen Kirche,"*Diaconia Christi* 21, 2–3 (July 1986): 29–33. He lists liturgical, missionary, catechetical, and educational activities as typical diaconal work (33).

104. Canon 15; see Charles-Joseph Hefele, *Histoire des conciles d'après les documents originaux* (2nd ed.; Paris: Letouzey et Ané, 1908), vol. 2, pt. 2, 803; Gryson, *Ministry of Women in the Early Church*, 63–64; Eisen, *Women Officeholders*, 161–62; Madigan and Osiek, *Ordained Women*, 121–22.

and numbers at the Great Church (Hagia Sophia) in Constantinople: for its service there were 60 priests, 100 male deacons, 40 female deacons, 90 subdeacons, 110 lectors, 25 singers, and 100 doorkeepers.[105] In fifth-century East Syrian and Persian churches, women deacons assisted with baptism but were prohibited from altar ministry. Among the Syrian Monophysites, however, diaconal abbesses, the highest rank, were allowed to read the epistle and gospel in a non-eucharistic context and, in the absence of a male cleric, to distribute communion to their nuns and to children. In certain Oriental churches, women deacons were appointed to make announcements. Their chief ministries must have been those common to women receiving little public acknowledgment: acts of mercy to the sick, the needy, and the young. Might the female deacon in a parish exercise some male roles in cases of necessity? A broader latitude for women ministers existed in many monastic situations and does so even today.[106] The male deacon, on the other hand, seems always to have been ordained *propter altarem*, although a major responsibility was care and distribution of the church's material goods in the name of the bishop as well as mediation between bishop and people. Baptism of children rather than adults conspired to deprive the female diaconate in the East of an obvious raison d'être, and it finally disappeared or "went underground" in the tenth and eleventh centuries.[107]

There is less evidence for women deacons in the Latin West than in the Eastern churches. In Gaul as elsewhere, the *ordo viduarum* (order

---

105. Justinian, *Justinian Novellae*, in *Corpus Iuris Civilis*, ed. R. Schoell and W. Kroll (5th ed.; 3 vols.; Berlin: Weidman, 1928), III, 1, cited in Rowland J. Mainstone, *Hagia Sophia: Architecture, Structure and Liturgy of Justinian's Great Church* (London: Thames and Hudson, 1988), 229.

106. I observed the same when I visited Varatec in northern Romania in June, 1991. Its monastery has hundreds of nuns and three churches. Since its foundation in 1781, Varatec nuns have played an active role in its vernacular liturgy. In the main church the sister-acolytes exercise several diaconal functions at the eucharist, processing in the Great Entrance and assisting the priest behind the iconostasis. The nun-lector appointed to chant the epistle (a subdiaconal role in the medieval West) does so solemnly from the middle of the nave, facing the priest who has emerged from the Royal Door. In what parallels a presbyteral function, the abbess chants the Lord's Prayer at the beginning of the communion rite.

107. Baptisms of children take place in female monasteries in Greece. The question of women deacons in the Orthodox churches is not only a lively area of discussion, particularly in monastic environments, but some women are now again being ordained. See Kyriaki Karidoyanes FitzGerald, *Women Deacons in the Orthodox Church: Called to Holiness and Ministry* (Brookline, MA: Holy Cross Orthodox Press, 1998). An inter-orthodox dialogue, "The Role of Orthodox Women in the Church and Society," held at Agapia Monastery, northern Romania, 11–17 September 1976, endorsed the ordination of women deacons.

of widows) had evolved over time into the office of deacon.[108] As long as adults were initiated through baptism and confirmation the need for female ministers was evident. From the late fourth to the sixth centuries, local councils of the Gallican church set out to proscribe deaconesses, but this negative trend shows that the institution was alive and perhaps even flourishing in that vast region. What might have occasioned the prohibition of women deacons? Roger Gryson, Suzanne Fonay Wemple, and Donald Hochstetler have proposed that the asceticism and egalitarianism of a movement attractive to women led by the lay evangelist Priscillian, which arose in Spain and Aquitaine around 370, occasioned the backlash.[109] Using the technical word *diacona* taken from the Greek, several Gallican councils prohibited women's exercise of that ministry. Canon 2 of the Second Council of Nimes (394/396 CE) states:

> It has been reported by certain ones that, contrary to apostolic discipline and unknown until today, women seem to have been, one knows not where, admitted to the Levitical ministry. Since it is improper, the ecclesiastical rule does not permit this innovation. Made contrary to reason, an ordination of this type must be annulled, and care must be taken that no one in future shows a similar audacity.[110]

From this canon it is evident that women were functioning as "levites" (deacons) in liturgical activity. The Council of Orange (441 CE) decrees that

---

108. Matthew Brendan Smyth ("Widows, Consecrated Virgins and Deaconesses in Ancient Gaul," *Magistra* 8 [2002]: 53–84) cites the *Statuta ecclesiae antiqua* (Provence, late 5th century) that widows and nuns be well prepared to instruct women for baptism (*Concilia Galliae*, A. 314–A. 506, ed. C. Munier [Turnhout: Brepols, 1963], 100), an important task of women deacons in Eastern churches. Martimort (*Diaconesses*, 187–200) weighs evidence for Gaul. Marie-Josèphe Aubert (*Il diaconato alle donne?: un nuovo camino per la chiesa* [Milan: Paoline, 1989], 129–40) gives a more positive reading, as does Eisen, *Women Officeholders*, 184–85, noting their wide distribution. Madigan and Osiek (*Ordained Women*, 141–49) are more restrained.

109. Gryson, *Ministry of Women*, 100–101; Suzanne Fonay Wemple, *Women in Frankish Society: Marriage and the Cloister, 500 to 900* (Philadelphia: University of Pennsylvania Press, 1981), 137–39; Donald Hochstetler, *A Conflict of Traditions: Women in Religion in the Early Middle Ages, 500–840* (Lanham, MD: University Press of America, 1992), 77–79.

110. Nimes, canon 2 (*Concilia Galliae A. 314–A. 506*, 50); Gryson, *Ministry of Women*, 101. Some church order may have claimed apostolic authorship and thus "apostolic tradition." Cf. Synod of Epaon (517), canon 21 (*Concilia Galliae a. 511–a. 695*, ed. Carlo de Clercq [Turnhout: Brepols, 1963], 29) and Orléans (533), canon 17 (Gryson, 101).

in "no case are women deacons to be ordained: if there are any, let them submit their heads to the blessing which is given the people"; any ordained women are to be treated as though they had not been ordained.[111] The proscription of women deacons by local councils on the basis of "apostolic discipline" (but what of Phoebe?) and impropriety speaks to the existence of the office.[112] The *Statuta ecclesiae antiqua*, attributed to Gennadius of Marseilles (d. ca. 500), is best known for what it proscribes: "37. A woman, though she be learned and holy, ought not presume to teach in a gathering of men.... 41. A woman ought not presume to baptize."[113] This collection, gathered from African and Eastern sources including especially *Apostolic Constitutions*, may have been a reaction to local practices. Madigan and Osiek comment: "The specificity of Canon 37, in particular the prohibition against teaching in a gathering of men, seems to suggest that teaching by women was occurring in precisely such contexts. Otherwise, why forbid it? Similarly, that women were in fact baptizing seems suggested by the prohibition against it."[114]

While Gennadius was compiling his *Statuta*, in the town of Saint-Maximin La-Sainte-Baume in Provence, not far from Marseilles, incised stone panels suggest another reality. Although Gallican conciliar documents would rather not acknowledge women as holding ecclesiastical office, an earlier ideal is represented in the crypt under the basilica of Sainte-Marie-Madeleine at St.-Maximin. This crypt had been a fourth-century Christian mausoleum. Four fine sculptured sarcophagi

---

111. Canon 25 (26), 84.

112. The Council of Epaon (517), canon 21, repealed the "consecration of widows, who are called diaconas" (*Concilia Galliae* a. 511 -a. 695, 29, cited by the Council of Tours [567], 187). As is the nature of canon law, much conciliar legislation regarding the ministry of males was similarly negative and restrictive.

113. *Concilia Galliae* a. 511 -a. 695, 100. Cyrille Vogel ("Statuta Ecclesiae Antiqua," NCE 13 (1967): 682; CCSL 148A, 162–88) gives the probable date of the *Statuta* as between 476 and 485. Canons 1 to 89 are "disciplinary, following the plan of Apostolic Constitutions." Then follows a "succinct but very precise ritual of ordinations and of benedictions of persons following Western non-Roman and so-called Gallican style—bishop, priest, deacon, subdeacon, acolyte, exorcist, lector, porter, psalmist, virgins, widows, spouses." Vogel calls it a "major document for canon law and liturgy of the 5th century in the Gallo-Roman church. It is a work of reform: ascetical, presbyteral and antidiaconal addressed to the episcopate and clergy of Provence." The prohibition against baptism by women may have arisen from their baptizing in cases of clinical necessity.

114. Madigan and Osiek, *Ordained Women*, 190–91.

of the fourth century illustrate gender balance.[115] In the fifth century a paleo-Christian basilica and in the sixth a baptistry were erected on the southwest adjacent to the present Sainte-Marie-Madeleine. A set of four damaged marble slabs now housed in the mausoleum-crypt were probably brought from the paleo-Christian basilica, their primitive, incised linear drawings doubtless once filled with minium. All the subjects, two male and two female, are presented in frontal pose. Early Christian themes—Abraham's sacrifice of Isaac and Daniel in the lion's den—favored in catacomb painting and on sarcophagi, adorn the two smaller, nearly square slabs. Each of the two larger slabs features an even more favored catacomb subject, a female orante. These depictions of orantes in St. Maximin are unique. The more complete (120.65 cm in height and 73.66 cm wide) depicts a young woman orante clothed in a dalmatic with unveiled long hair flowing freely. Above her head three lines in rustic capitals spell *Maria virgo minester de tempulo Gerosale* (Mary the virgin minister of the Jerusalem temple) (Fig. 3.1).[116]

The second more damaged slab shows a mature female orante intact up to the shoulders; she stands on a *suppedaneum* framed by drawn curtains (Fig. 3.2).[117] The location depicted is an architecturally formal one, presumably the presbyterium of a church and its columned templon.

---

115. These fine, homogeneous sarcophagi may have been imported from Rome; the Via Aurelia terminated in Arles. Two sarcophagi carry programs that advance the prerogatives of Peter and Paul and hence of the Roman see presided over at this time by popes Damasus and Siricius. Two have themes relating to the salvation of the deceased. That called "of Saint Sidoine" (the man born blind, John 9), is large enough for a double burial. Showing an unusual interest in gender balance, females figure in four subjects: the raising of Jairus' daughter (Matt 9:23); the woman with the hemorrhage (Matt 9:18); and on the sides two large reliefs showing the raising of Tabitha (Acts 9:36) and a woman in the *pietas* pose with a cylindrical coffer for *rotuli*. See Michel Fixot, *La crypte de Saint-Maximin La-Sainte-Baume: Basilique Sainte-Marie-Madeleine* (Aix-en-Provence: Édisud, 2001). On the crypt type itself, see John Crook, *The Architectural Setting of the Cult of Saints in the Early Christian West c. 300–1200* (Oxford: Clarendon Press, 2000), 31 and 53–54 with figs. 9–10.

116. Henri Leclercq, "Apocryphes," in *DACL* 1/2 (1907), 2555–79 at 2558–59, figs. 831–32; "Marie, mère de Dieu," *DACL* 10/2 (1932), 1982–2043 at 1986–87, figs. 7697–98; and "Maximin (Saint-)," *DACL* 10/2 (1932), 2798–820 at 2816–20. "Information" about the child Mary's service in the temple from the age of three had been provided by the popular apocryphal 2nd-century gospel *Birth of Mary* (the *Protoevangelium of James*). See "The Birth of Mary (The History of James)," in *New Testament Apocrypha*, 7–8, 429; J. K. Elliott, "Mary in the Apocryphal New Testament," in Chris Maunder, *Origins of Cult of Virgin Mary*, 57–70; Brown, *Body and Society*, 273–74. See also Mazzoleni, "Mariologia nell'epigrafia cristiana antica," 67.

117. Henri Leclercq, "Maximin (Saint-)," *DACL* 10/2 (1932), 2816–20 and fig. 7850. The dimensions of the mutilated tablet are 78.74 cm in height on its left, 82.55 cm on the right.

FIGURE 3.1 St.-Maximin La-Sainte-Baume. Limestone slab: *Maria virgo minester de tempulo Gerosale* (ca. 500). *DACL* 10/2 (1932), fig. 7697.

The headless woman's wide-sleeved dalmatic is elaborately decorated, with a tasseled tie at the waist and two circular ornaments at the end of the fringed "sari" or stola wound about her shoulders.[118] Her setting,

---

The width is 63.5 cm across the top and 62.23 cm across the bottom. I am indebted to the Reverend Sue Walters for checking measurements and data, and to Anna Boley of the Office Municipal du Tourisme, Saint-Maximin La-Sainte-Baume for facilitating the obtaining of this information.

118. On the distinctive costume for widow-deaconesses in Gaul, see Martimort, *Diaconesses*, 199, n. 7, who notes that the Councils of Orléans (549, canon 19), II Tours (567, canon 21), and Paris (556/573, canon 5) speak of *mutare vestem* for monastics, widows, and virgins in the world (texts in CCSL 148A, 155, 185–86, 207–208). Gryson (*Ministry of Women*, 103) notes that "a special dress distinguished widows. Although there was already some evidence for this distinctive dress in St. Jerome, it is not absolutely conclusive.... In canon 26 of the First Council of Orange, it is clear that there is a question of a 'uniform': 'The profession

FIGURE 3.2 St.-Maximin La-Sainte-Baume. Limestone slab with *female orante*. DACL 10/2 (1932), fig. 7850.

stance, and ceremonial garb give her a dignified formality even though the missing head and inscription preclude positive identification.[119] Comparison with works of similar naive style indicates a sixth-century date.[120] The original function of these slabs is an enigma. In three articles of the *Dictionnaire d'archéologie chrétienne et de liturgie*, Henri

---

(*professionem*) to persevere in widowhood, made before the bishop in the secretarium, will be marked by the clothing of the widow imposed by the bishop.'"

119. Apart from association with the differently sized Daniel slab there is nothing to support the suggestion that the headless woman is Susanna (Daniel 13) as made by L. Rostan, *Notice sur l'église de Saint-Maximin* (Brignoles: de Brunet-Chabert, 1886) and cited by Fixot, *Crypte de Saint-Maximin*, 30. The figure represents the *Maria orans* type.

120. Fixot, *Crypte de Saint-Maximin*, 32.

Leclercq referred to the *Maria virgo* slab.[121] Leclercq's suggestion that the slabs formed part of a chancel or sanctuary barrier is provocative. But his earlier article on chancels provides no examples embellished with figures. Although chancels may run waist-high (about 1 meter in height), they are decorated with nonfigural designs or, at most, monograms.[122] These slabs could have served as decorative revetment in the nearby fifth-century basilica or its spacious sixth-century baptistry.[123] Whatever the original function of these slabs, they witness to an ideal of women's liturgical ministry.

Women's ecclesiastical ministries were rejected by local Gallican councils. However, by the sixth century, legends about Mary Magdalen's arrival in Provence and her gospel ministry flourished.[124] Mary Magdalen was conflated with Mary of Bethany, the woman who prophetically anointed Christ's body for burial (John 12:1–8). She had followed the risen Lord's command to proclaim the resurrection to the brothers [and sisters] ("the brothers," *adelphoi*, John 20:17).[125] This ministry, at least for churches of the East who lauded her as *apostola apostolorum*, offered ideological support to women's ecclesial ministries. Her legendary preaching to the people of Marseilles responded to the dominical command. Similarly, the

---

121. In the "Marie" article (*DACL* 10/2 [1932], 1987), Leclercq had judged that the slab formed part of a sanctuary railing (chancel). Revising that hypothesis, the "Maximin" article proposed that the four slabs formed the vertical walls of an altar chamber 1 m long, 0.80 m wide, and 1.20 m high, not counting the missing altar mensa. The edges of the slabs would have been embedded in four corner colonnettes.

122. Henri Leclercq, "Chancel," *DACL* 2/2 (1910), 1821–31. Stone barriers demarcated the space in which clergy stood and from which laity, especially women, were excluded. However, a balustrade with inscription from a church in Africa used by Christian virgins is preserved in the Louvre, Paris (*DACL* 2/1 [1910], 1–2 at fig. 1159).

123. Fixot, *Crypte de Saint-Maximin*, 33.

124. The saints of Bethany, Martha, and Mary, were said to have died in Provence (Victor Saxer, *Le culte de Marie Madeleine en occident: des origines à la fin du moyen âge* [Paris: Clavreuil, 1959], 37; Jane Schaberg, *The Resurrection of Mary Magdalene: Legends, Apocrypha, and the Christian Testament* [New York: Continuum, 2002], 82–93).

125. Newer translations of the Christian Scriptures frequently render the noun *adelphoi* as "brothers and sisters" (disciples). Why not here? Although newer translations of John 20:17 retain the exclusive translation "brothers" for *adelphoi* (e.g., NRSV), commentators argue that the noun would have included women. Thus *adelphoi* in John 20:17–18 means "brothers and sisters," a reference to all the disciples who follow Jesus. See, e.g., Gail R. O'Day, "John," *Women's Bible Commentary* (1992), 293–305; Stanley E. Porter, ed. *Dictionary of Biblical Criticism and Interpretation* (New York: Routledge, 2007), 365. On the textual issues, see Arndt and Gingrich, *Greek-English Lexicon of New Testament*, 15–16.

picture depicting the girl Mary as temple *ministra* (*diacona*), both terms figuring in conciliar canons, would have strengthened women's claim to such ministries.

Meanwhile in central and northern Gaul during the sixth century women were exercising liturgical ministry. In 511 three bishops of central Gaul (Tours, Rennes, and Angers) wrote to two Breton priests to object that the latter, in the company of *conhospitae* (perhaps women like the *subintroductae* reprehended by Cyprian, Chrysostom, and others), traveled with portable altars from place to place to celebrate the eucharist in homes, the *conhospitae* assisting by administration of the chalice. Although the bishops suspected a tinge of Montanism, the influence may rather have been that of the Celtic church.[126] In the Irish church the seventh-century Book of Armagh refers to married women who "served" the church, and an Irish deaconess (Gaelic *bandechuin*) is noted in a gloss in the eighth-century manuscript of the Würzburg epistolary (Würzburg, Universitätsbibl. M. th. 12).[127] Elsewhere in Gaul St. Remigius, bishop of Reims (d. 533), calls his daughter Hilary a diacona.[128] Venantius Fortunatus, bishop of Poitiers, writes that Bishop Medard of Noyon, giving way to her pleas, consecrated Queen Radegonde (d. 587) a deaconess by laying on of hand.[129]

Optatus, bishop of Milevi in North Africa writing around 385–390 against the Donatists, refers in passing to virgins with bonnets; Gregory Dix calls them "mitred deaconesses."[130] There are sixth-century examples,

---

126. Smyth, "Widows, Consecrated Virgins, Deaconesses," 80–81; Madigan and Osiek, *Ordained Women*, 188–89.127. Smyth, "Widows, Consecrated Virgins, Deaconesses," 75–76; see also L. Gougaud, "Celtiques (Liturgies)," in *DACL* 2/2 (Paris: Letouzey et Ané, 1910), 2969–3032 at 2998.

128. Remi of Reims, *Testamentum S. Remigii episcopi*, in Heinricus M. Rochais, ed., *Defensoris locogiacensis monachi Liber scintillarum*, (Turnhout: Brepols, 1957), 477, ll. 95–98.

129. Venantius Fortunatus, *De vitae sanctae Radegundis*, 1, 12 in MGH SRM 2; Dick Harrison, *The Age of Abbesses and Queens: Gender and Political Culture in Early Medieval Europe* (Lund, Sweden: Nordic Academic Press, 1998), 283; Anne Röhl-Burgsmüller, "Diakonin Radegundis (520–587)—Demütige Dienerin und mutige Predigeren," in *Diakonia, diaconiae, diaconato: semantica e storia nei Padri della Chiesa: XXXVIII Incontro di studiosi dell'antichità cristiana, Roma, 7–9 maggio 2009* (Roma: Institutum Patristicum Augustinianum, 2010), 667–76. Martimort (*Diaconesses*, 200) cites the text, *manu superposita consecravit diaconam*, explaining Radegonde's consecration as a Gallican anomaly made possible by her high-born status.

130. V.3.4.7 and VI. 4.5 (SC 413; Paris: Cerf, 1996), 2, 174–80. Gregory Dix, *The Shape of the Liturgy* (2nd ed.; New York: Seabury, 1982), 405; see Optat, Bishop of Milève, *Traité contre les donatistes*, ed., intro., trans. Mireille Labrousse (2 vols.; Paris: Cerf, 1995), 1, 280, which speaks about the sacrilegious acts of the Donatists.

attested by epigraphy, of Anna in Rome, a woman deacon from Dalmatia, and another from Gaul.[131] Euphemia, wife of Sergius, archbishop of Ravenna (744–769?), was consecrated deaconess by her husband when from his lay state he was elevated directly to the episcopate.[132] In earlier times Euphemia would have been termed *episcopa* or *episcopissa*. In this period she "enters into the class of ecclesiastical deaconesses properly so-called," Andrieu asserts, "continuing the lineage of primitive deaconesses, auxiliaries and feminine rivals of the deacons."[133] Suzanne Fonay Wemple points out that the office of deaconess reappeared in Germany when the Council of Worms in 868 reissued canon 15 of Chalcedon (canon 73) allowing women over 40 to be ordained.[134] Thus the office of diacona reappeared in the Rhine Valley nearly a century before a ritual for abbesses and others in women's communities was formulated in the Romano-Germanic Pontifical of the Tenth Century and then taken to Rome.

Outside the cloisters, the decline of female diaconal ministry accompanied the gradual diminishment in importance of the "permanent" male diaconate. The latter continued in monasteries where abbots were deacons and in Rome where deacons held high administrative posts. The diaconal office was especially compatible with that of abbesses, whose consecration rite was often exactly the same as that of abbots. Martimort documents how in later periods aspects of the female diaconate were drawn into the monastic cloister. He admits that, especially between the eighth and eleventh centuries in the West, abbesses were sometimes ordained or consecrated using the rites for women deacons.[135]

---

131. Eisen, *Women Officeholders*, 182–85; A. E. Felle, "'Diaconi' e 'diaconissae' tra oriente e occidente: L'apporto della documentazione epigrafica," *Diakonia, diaconiae, diaconato*, 489–537.

132. PL 106, 725B. Agnellus of Ravenna says, "[Sergius] was a layman and had a wife. After he took up the rule of the church, he consecrated his wife Euphemia as a deaconess, and she remained in that condition" (*Liber pontificalis ecclesiae Ravennatis* in English translation, *The Book of Pontiffs of the Church of Ravenna* [by] Agnellus of Ravenna, trans. with introduction and notes by Deborah Mauskopf Deliyannis. [Washington, DC: Catholic University of America Press, 2004], no. 154, 278; no. 157, 281).

133. Michel Andrieu, *OR*, 4:145.

134. Wemple, *Women in Frankish Society*, 146 and n. 111. See J. D. Mansi, *Sacrorum conciliorum nova et amplissima collectio* (Paris: H. Welter, 1901–1927; repr. in Graz: Akademische Druck- u. Verlagsanstalt, 1960–1961), 15:882: "Diaconissam non ordinandam ante annum quadragesimum, & hoc cum summo libramine."

135. Martimort, *Diaconesses*, 205–21, 231–43.

(i) Canonesses

Over the course of the Merovingian and Carolingian reform periods, the bishops had worked to extirpate the ecclesiastical office of diacona in favor of women's monastic communities. The Benedictine Rule and ascetic monastic way of life were imposed wherever possible on communities of women by individual bishops and then by the reforming abbot St. Benedict of Aniane (ca. 750–821).[136] Nevertheless, the term *sanctimoniales* was applied by the Council of Chalons-sur-Saône (817) to women who lived a common religious life, both regular *moniales* and canonesses. The early history of the canonical life as a "nonmonastic form of female consecration" in Gaul and the attempts of episcopal synods to control such forms by religious rule and legislation during the Carolingian era have been set out by Karl-Heinrich Schäfer, Suzanne Fonay Wemple, and especially by Donald Hochstetler.[137] Schäfer proposed that canonesses were seen as diaconas for Merovingian Gaul and the Carolingian realm. Wemple, who finds the term canoness first used in the eighth and ninth centuries, does not agree.[138] Nevertheless, canonesses were in some ways successors of the diaconal office.

During the Ottonian period the prominence of women as secular rulers and spiritual leaders of religious communities is evidenced by an increasing number of women's portraits, the magnificence of gospel and liturgical manuscripts commissioned by royalty and abbesses with presentation scenes, greater frequency of illustrated Scripture episodes featuring women, and the foundations, both monastic and canonical, established to enable women to pursue the devout life.[139] This material evidence stands

---

136. On life in women's monastic communities during the Merovingian period, see Gisela Muschiol, *Famula Dei: Zur Liturgie in merowingischen Frauenklöstern* (Münster: Aschendorff, 1994). Muschiol finds no sure evidence for diaconas in Gallican cloisters (295–300).

137. K. Heinrich Schäfer, *Die Kanonissenstifter im deutschen Mittelalter: ihre Entwicklung und innere Einrichtung im Zusammenhang mit dem altchristlichen Sanktimonialentum* (Stuttgart: Ferdinand Enke, 1907); Schäfer, *Kanonissen und Diakonissen*, 49–90; Wemple, *Women in Frankish Society*; Hochstetler, *Conflict of Traditions*.

138. Wemple, *Women in Frankish Society*, 142 and n. 84; also Muschiol, *Famula Dei*, 295–300. Hochstetler (*Conflict of Traditions*, 81–116) follows the less fine distinctions of Schäfer.

139. Rosamund McKitterick, "Women in the Ottonian Church: An Iconographic Perspective," in W. J. Sheils and Diana Wood, eds., in *Women in the Church: Papers Read at the 1989 Summer Meeting and the 1990 Winter Meeting of the Ecclesiastical History Society* (Cambridge, MA: Blackwell, 1990), 79–100.

in stark contrast to religious women's less visible, more subordinate status during the preceding Carolingian period.[140]

In response to social and ecclesial needs, institutes of canonesses—secular (not guided by a rule shared with other such institutes) or regular (governed by a common *regula*)—were established and flourished especially during the tenth and eleventh centuries, their golden age. Canoness institutes gained their greatest prominence and stability in German-speaking lands, especially in the Franco-Saxon region around Cologne and the Low Countries; they were also found in parts of Switzerland, Austria, and England.[141] The Council of Rome (Lateran, 1059) moved against secular canonesses, while the wave of new orders founded over the course of the twelfth century brought the more ascetic monastic life back into favor.[142]

Non-monastic and not-enclosed canonesses did not adopt the ascetic life laid out by the rules of Benedict, Caesarius of Arles, Columban, and others. There were two basic types of canonical life for women. Secular canonesses (*virgines non velatae*), "women living a devout life who call themselves canonesses," were often of noble rank. Retaining their property and servants, these women might occupy their own houses near the church or cathedral. They received a prebend (salary, usually in food and drink) and also supported themselves out of their own means. The

---

140. During the Carolingian period marriage was considered an *ordo* in which women could seek holiness and participate in the spread of the gospel: see Marie Anne Mayeski, "Women in Medieval Society and Scholastic Theology," in Joseph Martos and Pierre Hégy, eds., *Equal at the Creation: Sexism, Society and Christian Thought* (Toronto: University of Toronto Press, 1998), 70–95 at 74, 76. Mayeski adds that written lives of influential nuns are "virtually non-existent." On abbesses, however, see Mary S. Skinner, "French Abbesses in Action: Structuring Carolingian and Cluniac Communities," *Magistra* 6 (2000): 37–60.

141. Canonesses flourished especially in German-speaking lands. The social and cultural context that gave rise to a preponderance of women's monasteries and canonical institutions housing *ancillae Dei* in the Saxon region has been treated in two chapters by Karl J. Leyser, *Rule and Conflict in Early Medieval Society: Ottonian Saxony* (Bloomington: Indiana University Press, 1979), 49–73. The founding of a religious house by a widow "protected herself and her daughters from family greed"; it also provided a safe-haven for women for whom no suitable marriage was available. Leyser notes that women inherited property, that religious foundations could be given protection and immunity, and that noblewomen were, by their lives of prayer and asceticism, working for the good of menfolk whose secular "vocation" was often rampage and worse. He does not take much account of the liberating opportunities for women so inclined for a higher education and for living the devout life.

142. For a compendium of rules, see online J. Frank Henderson, "Rules, Constitutions and Statutes of Medieval Religious Communities of Women (except Benedictines) and of Related Communities of Men: Bibliography" (September 2002) and "Feminine Versions of the Rule of St. Benedict: Bibliography" (updated June 1999), at www.fhenders@compusmart.ab.ca. Statutes for canonesses tend to be for individual houses and are difficult to obtain.

less wealthy might share an apartment with a few others. Anna Ulrich describes their life. Unless their community was forced to adopt monastic customs, they could carry on business with tenants and townspeople and receive guests. Canonesses were free to leave the canonry for substantial periods of time. Except for the abbess, typically they did not take vows and might leave to marry, though few did. Their apostolic work might include education of girls and boys, study and writing, and the traditional diaconal ministries of caring for the sick and poor and housing pilgrims.[143] In Germany their schools were famous. A special cloak or veil was worn in choir during the *opus Dei* (divine office), which they prayed regularly in church or chapel.[144] As distinguished from secular canonesses, regular canonesses lived and ate in community and wore distinctive garb. On the basis of frescoes at Schwarzrheindorf bei Bonn, Schäfer describes the dress of Abbess Hadewig: a white tunic with a red cloak over the shoulders recalling the dalmatic of deacons, or a *superpellicium* (a linen surplice with sleeves, worn by clergy during the twelfth century and especially by canons regular).[145] The Augustinian Rule, which some have thought was written originally for women by St. Augustine, was found to be particularly appropriate for regular canonesses.[146]

B. Presbyteras

In the early churches the presbyteral function was that typical of an elder in tribal societies: the wise and responsible leader who as member of a council advised the bishop. At first glance references in the Pastorals to an

---

143. Anna Ulrich, "Die Kanonissen: Ein vergangener und vergessener Stand der Kirche," in Berger and Gerhards, *Liturgie und Frauenfrage*, 181–94 at 182, and the works by K. Heinrich Schäfer. On secular canonesses, see Michel Parisse, "Les chanoinesses dans l'empire germanique (IX–XIe siècles)," *Francia* 6 (1978): 107–27. For a critical reading of modern scholarship, see Irene Crusius, "*Sanctimoniales quae se canonicas vocant*: Das Kanonissenstift als Forschungsproblem," in Irene Crusius, ed., *Studien zum Kanonissenstift* (Göttingen: Vandenhoeck und Ruprecht, 2001), 9–38.

144. Crusius ("*Sanctimoniales quae se canonicas vocant*") treats details of their life including their clothing (31–37).

145. Schäfer, "Kanonissen und Diakonissen," 59.

146. Kevin L. Hughes, "Augustinian Rule," in *EM* 1 (2000), 106–7. A remarkably detailed account of the lives of regular canonesses in northwestern Europe during the late Middle Ages is provided by Wybren Scheepsma, *Medieval Religious Women in The Low Countries: The 'Modern Devotion,' the Canonesses of Windesheim and Their Writings*, trans. David F. Johnson (Woodbridge, Suffolk: Boydell, 2004).

"older" or "senior" or "elder" woman (πρεσβυτέρα, 1 Tim 5:2, πρεσβῦτις, Titus 2:3) seem to do simply with venerable age. But it is possible that "woman elder" (*presbytis*) of the Pastorals is a title of honor that also designates an ecclesiastical function, since later on female elders (*presbytides*) leading liturgical services are known for Asia Minor.[147] Tomb inscriptions indicate that female elders (*presbyterae*) were found in several regions of the Christian world. Eisen's collection of datable inscriptions in which the presbyteral title is used for women shows them in Egypt (2nd–3rd centuries), Asia Minor (3rd), and Greece (2nd–4th centuries).[148] Slightly later epigraphic witnesses to *presbyterae* have been found in Sicily (4th–5th centuries, the presbyter Kale) and, from the same period, on the Italian mainland in Bruttium, Calabria (Leta the *presbitera*), and Salona in Dalmatia (*prb* Flavia Vitalia, 435 CE).[149] The question of the meaning of the title and functions of *presbyterae* and *sacerdotae* was broached by Giorgio Otranto.[150] The office existed in the fourth century when several local councils banned further installations or ordinations of women to church office. Phrygia is the region in which canon 11 of the often-cited but obscure "council of Laodicea" originated, whose date (perhaps sometime between 341 and 381) is uncertain and whose contents are known only in summary form.[151] In the text that has come down to us, canon 11 reads, "Concerning those who are called *presbytides* or female presiders (*prokathēmenai*), it is not

---

147. Eisen (*Women Officeholders*, 116–23) discusses the possible meaning of the designation in the Great Church as well as in schismatic groups.

148. Eisen, *Women Officeholders*, 123–28.

149. Palermo, Museo Archeologico Antonino Salinas, epitaph from Centuripae on exhibit; for a clear drawing, see Dorothy Irvin, *Calendar 2005* (July–August); Eisen, *Women Officeholders*, 128–29. On Leta, see *CIL* 10, no. 8079; and Eisen, *Women Officeholders*, 129–31; Irvin, *Calendar 2005*. On Flavia Vitalia, see H. Leclercq, "Presbyter," in *DACL* 14/2 (1948): 1717–21 at 1721 and Eisen, *Women Officeholders*, 131–32.

150. Giorgio Otranto, "Note sul sacerdozio femminile nell'antichità in margine a una testimonianza di Gelasio I," *VetChr* 19 (1982): 341–60; his article was translated by Mary Ann Rossi as "Priesthood, Precedent, and Prejudice: On Recovering the Women Priests of Early Christianity," *JFSR* 7 (1991): 73–94. Rossi provides a translation from the Italian of Otranto's "Notes on the Female Priesthood in Antiquity." Eisen (*Women Officeholders*, 128–34) catalogues the epigraphic evidence and discusses each example.

151. Hamilton Hess (*The Early Developments of Canon Law and the Council of Serdica* [Oxford: Oxford University Press, 2002], 48) notes that the "so-called 'council of Laodicea'" may not have been a council at all. If it did take place the first 19 canons may have a greater claim to authenticity than the rest. On "Laodicean" canons 20–59, which controlled the lower orders, see Faivre, *Naissance d'une hiérarchie*, 228–32.

permitted to appoint (*kathistasthai*) them in the Church."¹⁵² The translation by the canonist and monk Dionysius Exiguus (end of the fifth and first half of the sixth century) is somewhat more suggestive of ordination: "That those who are called *presbyterae* or *praesidentes* in the Churches ought not to be ordained."¹⁵³ Despite the one-sided explanation given it by the heterodox-turned-orthodox bishop Epiphanius as well as by some modern scholars, the Laodicean text makes clear reference to women as directors or leaders.¹⁵⁴ Eisen presents the case for the technical meaning of *presbytides* as ordained "presidents" or eucharistic "presiders" of Christian assemblies and so belonging to the higher clergy, noting that *kathistasthai* in later canons denotes establishment in higher clerical office.¹⁵⁵ Ilaria Ramelli urges that Theosebia, sister of Gregory of Nyssa (d. ca. 395) was a woman presbyter around the time of Laodicea's council.¹⁵⁶ Laodicea's canon 44 (45), "That women ought not to approach the altar," was the most devastating regulation promulgated. The consolidation of the hierarchical order of the church over the course of the fourth century had the effect of excluding women from the sanctuary and from participation in liturgical ministries.¹⁵⁷ Were the

---

152. "Non oportere eos, quae dicuntur presbyterae et praesidentes, in ecclesiis constitui." See Mansi, *Sacrorum conciliorum* 2:563–74 at cols. 565, 566, translation from Madigan and Osiek, *Ordained Women*, 164. Hefele (*Histoire des conciles*, vol. 1, pt. 2, 989–1028 at 1003–5) provided a number of possible interpretations that, taking their lead from Epiphanius, dismiss the presbyteral office for women but range from an office of chief deaconess to that of aged woman. Eisen (*Women Officeholders*, 121–23) proposes that the terms refer to women as worship leaders of communities and makes the point that the verb προκαθῆσθαι is used in Ignatius' letters "in connection with the bishop, the presbyters, and the deacons" always in an "official and hierarchical sense." Since Epiphanius could cite instances of female leadership in groups divided from the Great Church, the existence of such leadership in orthodox circles must be considered a possibility.

153. Mansi, *Sacrorum conciliorum* 2:578.

154. Eisen (*Women Officeholders*, 118–21) discusses Epiphanius' position. Carolyn Osiek ("The Social Function of Female Imagery in Second Century Prophecy," *VetChr* 29 [1992]: 55–74 at 56) typifies Epiphanius as "a career monk, devoted to his own narrow idea of orthodoxy, traumatized as a youth by a sexual encounter with a libertine gnostic sect (*Panarion* 26, 17, 4–9, in *The Panarion of Epiphanius of Salamis: Book 1 (Sects 1–46)*, trans. Frank Williams [2 vols.; Leiden: Brill], 1987), 1: xi), and conditioned by cultural assumptions about intellectual inferiority and seductive danger of women."

155. Canons 12, 13, and 57 (Eisen, *Women Officeholders*, 122).

156. Ilaria Ramelli, "Theosebia: A Presbyter of the Catholic Church," *JFSR* 26 (2010): 79–102.

157. Laodicea came to govern Roman Catholic women's later exclusion from every kind of active ministerial participation during liturgical worship until the final quarter of the 20th century. Following much debate, in 1975 women were permitted to proclaim the Scriptures—excluding the gospel—in Roman Catholic liturgies so long as their place for

presbytides referred to in the Laodicean council recast into "the widows who sit in front" known from *Testamentum Domini*, the fourth- or fifth-century church order probably originating in Asia Minor or Syria?[158] Two negative statutes of Laodicea are cited in the abbreviated canons of Ferrandus, deacon of Carthage (d. 546/547).[159] They read, *Ut mulieres quae apud Graecos presbyterae appellantur, apud nos autem viduae, seniores, univirae et matriculae, in ecclesia [tamquam ordinatas] constitui non liceat* (tit. 11, no. 221) and *Ut mulieres ad altare non ingrediantur* (tit. 43, no. 222). A negative law suggests the existence of an opposite custom. The church of North Africa paralleled Roman practice in its silence about women who were appointed or ordained to ecclesial leadership. However, a grave mosaic in St. Augustine's basilica in Hippo witnesses to a Giulia Runa *presbyterissa*.[160] Madigan and Osiek point out that there is more evidence for presbyteras in the West (Greece, Dalmatia, Sicily, and southern Italy) than in the East.[161]

Comparable to the obscure Laodicean strictures against the ordination of women to hierarchical office during the later fourth century is the letter written by Pope Gelasius I (492–496) to the bishops of Sicily and southern Italy. Using terminology that can be understood of presbyteras, Gelasius inveighs

---

reading was outside the sanctuary rail. During the presentation of the revised Code of Canon Law on 2 January 1983 the statement was made: "From now onward women have a right to all the functions fulfilled by the laity." Women continued to be excluded from the offices of lector and acolyte (Pope Paul VI *Ministeria quaedam* [972]). This manner of thinking originated in the 3rd century when women "were situated apart from both the clergy and the laity" (Faivre, *Emergence of Laity*, 104; cf. also 97, 213).

158. In the church of the *Testamentum Domini*, bishop, presbyter, deacon, subdeacon and these widows who sit in front are all "ordained" (Syr. *mettasthānuta*; *Testamentum Domini*, I.41; *Testamentum Domini*, ed. Sperry-White, 43–44) although the prayer is described as one of "institution." We know of deaconesses from I.23 (pp. 13, 14, 19), I.35 (20), I.19 (47) and II.20 (50) but are not given the text of their ordination or institution. One of the petitions of the diaconal *ektene* (litany) refers to female presbyters: "For the female presbyters let us beseech, that the Lord hear their supplications and in the grace of the Spirit perfectly keep their hearts [and] support their labour" (I.35). Are they wives of presbyters? But such a prayer offered on behalf of a male would be judged to involve ecclesiastical office, the more so as the prayer is situated between biddings for bishop, presbyterate, and deacons and those for subdeacons, readers, and deaconesses. In each case the female office-holders are listed after the male grouping of related offices.

159. *Concilia Africae a. 345–a. 525*, ed. C. Munier (Turnhout: Brepols, 1974), 305.

160. Modern Annaba, Algeria. Giulia died at age 50. See Erwan Marec, *Monuments chrétiens d'Hippone* (Paris: Arts et métiers graphiques [1958]) 59–60 and fig. 57a. For an illustration, see Dorothy Irvin, *Calendar 2003* "The Archaeology of Women's Traditional Ministries in the Church 100 to 820 A.D." (July–August); also Madigan and Osiek, *Ordained Women*, 197–98.

161. Madigan and Osiek, *Ordained Women*, 9 and ch. 8.

against rumors of women's ministering at the altar, in a milieu where the office of presbytera, not diacona, is known.[162] Gelasius is later quoted by popes and bishops to justify their exclusion of women from nuns' traditional liturgical ministries. Pope Zacharias' (741–752) Letter 5, "Against Nuns' Proclamation or Singing" (5 January 747), addressed to Pippin and Frankish ecclesiastical authorities, explicitly invokes the late fifth-century Gelasian letter. Zacharias interprets *sacris altaribus ministrare* to mean "to serve at the divine altars."[163] By this he means less than does Gelasius as he spells out the offenses: publicly reading the Scriptures during mass, singing at mass, or offering an Alleluia or an antiphonal song.[164] Apparently it never occurred to Zachary that *ministrare* might mean to officiate as a presbyter. A later *relatio* from Frankish bishops to Emperor Louis the Pious, also invoking the decree of Gelasius, interprets "to minister" as entering the sanctuary, holding the consecrated vessels, handing the sacerdotal vestments to priests, and administering the consecrated elements to the congregation.[165]

However, not quite eighty years later, the public roles of women assisting at liturgies in many parts of the Carolingian empire seem not to have been affected. The Council of Paris (829) found that in several provinces women "have of their own accord forced themselves up to the sacred

---

162. Eisen, *Women Officeholders*, 129; Otranto, "Note sul sacerdozio femminile," 341–60. Gelasius' decree will be discussed in chapter four.

163. Letter 8, *PL* 89, 933. See Eisen, *Women Officeholders*, 133–4; Madigan and Osiek, *Ordained Women*, 187. Conversely, the Anglo-Saxon Penitential of Theodore (Theodore of Tarsus, archbishop of Canterbury 668–690) reads in the majority of versions, "VII. Of the Rite of the Women, or Their Ministry in the Church. 1. It is permissible for the women, that is, the handmaidens of Christ, to read the lections and to perform the ministries which appertain to the confession of the sacred altar, except those which are the special functions of priests and deacons." A minority of mss. give this canon as "Woman shall not cover the altar with the corporal nor place on the altar the offerings, nor the cup, nor stand among ordained men in the church, nor sit at a feast among priests." See *Medieval Handbooks of Penance: A Translation of the Principal Libri Poenitentiales and Selections from Related Documents*, trans. John T. McNeill and Helena M. Gamer (New York: Octagon Books, [1938] 1965), 205.

164. Zacharias' letter of 747 to the Carolingian leader and bishops of that realm calling for the liturgical invisibility of nuns at public liturgies was still the canonical order of the day when Vatican Council II was convoked; it had been codified in the Code of Canon Law of 1917.

165. Eisen (*Women Officeholders*, 134), giving the text in translation. See also H. Van der Meer, *Priestertum der Frau?:Eine theologiegeschichtliche Untersuchung* (118), trans. in English, *Women Priests in the Catholic Church? A Theological-Historical Investigation*, trans. Arlene and Leonard Swidler (Philadelphia, PA: Temple University Press, 1973), 95; Hochstetler, *Conflict of Traditions*, 99–104.

altars and have impudently touched the sacred vessels and have assisted the priests with their vestments, and, what is even more indecent and more tasteless than all that, they have offered the body and blood of the Lord to the people and done other such things which are shameful even to mention...."[166] What is of greatest interest is not the actions of the women, described in hyperbolic terms and without mentioning the most "shameful" things, but the continuing existence of these practices "in several provinces."[167] In spite of letters and decrees citing the authority of Pope Gelasius that banned the presence of women at the altar, practices persisted in outlying reaches of the Christian world. Custom must have been longstanding or the need great, gaining continuing acceptance by bishops, presbyters and people in those locales.

(i) Canoness-sacerdotes

The liturgical functions of members of canoness communities argue for discussion of this way of life under the category of presbytera as well as diacona. Canonesses shared canons' titles: *praeposita* (prioress), *decana* (dean) or *decumana* (head of ten *sacerdotes*), *custos* (custodian of the church), or *sacerdota* (priest).[168] Joan Morris cites a reference by Widukind, Benedictine of Corvey, who in the tenth-century Saxon Chronicle refers to *utriusque sexus sacerdotes* ("priests of both sexes"). Examples of the title *sacerdotes* for canonesses have been found especially in Germany but also in Monza (Italy). In her 1973 book Morris provided wide-ranging documentation for this golden age of women's ecclesial pastoral ministry, which demands further research and critique.[169] Secular in character like canons

---

166. Eisen, *Women Officeholders*, 134; Gary Macy, "The Ordination of Women in the Early Middle Ages," *TS* 61 (2000): 494–95, repr., in Cooke and Macy, *History of Women and Ordination*, vol. 1: *Ordination of Women in Medieval Context*, 1–39.

167. See Hochstetler (*Conflict of Traditions*, 99–100), who elsewhere describes the successful efforts of bishops to found cloisters in Gaul for women who before had been in active ministry.168. The 16th-century German Lutheran historian George Fabricius lists many such *sacerdotes* (Morris, *Lady Was a Bishop*, 131–35). During the period when canonesses flourished (10th to 12th centuries) the term *sacerdos* might be applied to the simple male presbyter (priest) as well as to his bishop. On their male counterparts, the Canons Regular, see Philip E. McWilliams, "Canons Regular, Origins of," in *EM* 1 (2000), 236–37.

169. Morris, *Lady Was a Bishop*, passim. See also K.-H. Schäfer, *Kanonissenstifter im deutschen Mittelalter*; Schäfer, "Kanonissen und Diakonissen. Ergänzungen und Erläuterungen," 49–90; Heinri Leclercq, "Chanoinesses," *DACL* 3/1 (1913): 248–56; Michael H. Schmid, "Kanonissen," *LThK* 5 (1960), 1288–89; N. Backmund, "Canonesses," *NCE* 3 (1967): 53–54; Gary Macy, "Ordination of Women in the Early Middle Ages," in Cooke and Macy, *History of Women and Ordination*, vol. 1: *Ordination of Women in Medieval Context*, 9–10.

and parish clergy, canonesses were the female counterparts of male canons responsible for the "cure of souls" and were sometimes called their "sisters" (*consorores*). Characteristically canonesses shared the important ecclesiastical duty of praying the cathedral or parish offices "in the name of the church" (*in nomine ecclesiae*) with the canons. For example, the canonesses of S. Maria in Kapitol, Cologne, belonged to the cathedral chapter.[170] In some foundations, intricately choreographed liturgical observances and processions participated in with canons and laity were central to their community life.[171] At Pfalzel bei Trier on the Mosel River, canons and canonesses, with lay participation, followed the *canones* of the Fathers, celebrating mass daily and singing the hours. In the school, girls learned Latin and singing, scripture and church history, and read Latin classical and ecclesiastical authors.[172] While some of the students returned home to marry, others joined the institute. Canoness history—in school, hospital, pilgrim hostel—contains many unexplored areas of pastoral function. As members of the church exercising a devout lifestyle different from that of monastics, canonesses contributed visibly and significantly to the church's work, both liturgical-sacerdotal and diaconal.

C. Episcopas and *Episcope* (Oversight), Monastic and Canonical Abbesses

Paul's letter to the Philippians 1:2 referred in the plural to overseers (later to be called bishops) and helpers (or deacons), titles that indicated functions rather than established offices. Ignatius of Antioch, an early example of a "monarchical" bishop, cites the episcopal function and its relationship to the community's ministerial offices in his letters to the churches written while on the way to martyrdom, insisting that the Catholic church is that community that gathers about its bishop with the presbyters. No one is to do

---

170. Ulrich, "Kanonissen," 181. Into the 19th century they were counted as ranking with the higher clergy.

171. Dramatic as well as liturgical rituals incorporating the golden reliquary known as the Essen Madonna (dated ca. 1000)—the *Palmesel* on the Sunday of Palms; foot or hand washing; an *agape* on Holy Thursday, and the procession to the sepulchre on Good Friday—took place at Essen (Ulrich, "Kanonissen," 186). At least one liturgical witness survives, Essen's 14th-century *Liber Ordinarius* (*Der Liber Ordinarius der Essener Stiftskirche und seine Bedeutung*, ed. Franz Arens. Beiträge zur Geschichte von Stadt und Stift Essen, 21 [1901], 1–156), not available to this author.

172. Ulrich, "Kanonissen," 183.

anything without the bishop's approval. If the bishop is unable to preside at eucharist then the one he appoints does so. Ignatius makes no provision that this person must be a presbyter.[173] The *episcopus* at least as represented in the ordination ritual of *Apostolic Tradition*, perhaps Antiochene in origin, is the sacerdotal leader who exercises the high priesthood on behalf of his flock. Meanwhile in Rome, the presbyteral role is one of patronage and collegial governance of the community, not presidential sacramental function, while the monarchical episcopate was still to be adopted.[174]

A fragmentary inscription of the fifth or sixth century in Salona (Dalmatia) points to a *sacerdota* who at that period would, if the word were in the masculine gender, be considered bishop rather than priest (*sacerdos* in the early centuries referred to the bishop.)[175] Dating from circa 500 a damaged epigraph said to be from Interamna (now Terni) in Umbria reads "...venerabilis femina episcopa Q...."[176] Many scholars have assumed

---

173. See Ignatius' *Letter to the Smyrnaeans* VIII.1, in *The Apostolic Fathers*, ed. and rev. Michael W. Holmes, 189; *Ignatius of Antioch*, ed. Schoedel, 238, 243. Texts that legislate against the abuse of deacons' presidency of eucharistic celebrations indicate that deacons sometimes presided. In Ignatius' Antioch it is possible that presidency either by a deacon or another person appointed by the bishop may have been considered an appropriate response to a need.

174. Alistair Stewart-Sykes (*Apostolic Tradition: Hippolytus*, 49–50) argues for the Roman origin of *AT* even though this church order influenced the East not Rome; its first extensive textual witness is the Latin palimpsest Veronese LV (53) in the Verona Cathedral Library. Stewart-Sykes (55–56) proposes that the presbyteral function was initially that of patronage. Hermas, author of *Shepherd*, is a good test-case; see Stewart-Sykes, "Hermas the Prophet and Hippolytus the Preacher: The Roman Homily and its Social Context," in Mary B. Cunningham and Pauline Allen, eds., *Preacher and Audience: Studies in Early Christian and Byzantine Homiletics* (Leiden: Brill, 1998), 33–63.

175. Eisen, *Women Officeholders*, 132–34; Pierre-Marie Gy, "Notes on the Early Terminology of Christian Priesthood," in *The Sacrament of Holy Orders: Some Papers and Discussions Concerning Holy Orders at a Session of the Centre de Pastorale Liturgique* (Collegeville, MN: Liturgical, 1962), 98–115. From a later period Joan Morris (*Lady Was a Bishop*, 135) cites numerous examples of the title *sacerdota maxima*, in England and especially in Germany. St. Agnes of Bohemia (ca. 1200–ca. 1281/2), a Poor Clare abbess, was called *sacerdos* of Prague.

176. Giorgio Otranto gives her name as Addirittura, dating the epitaph at 491 or 526; see Oranto, "The Problem of the Ordination of Women in the Early Christian Priesthood," lecture at www.womenpriests.org/traditio/otran_2.asp. Eisen (*Women Officeholders*, 199–200) identifies her as *femina episcopa*; Madigan and Osiek (*Ordained Women*, 193) identify her as *episcopa Q* with epitaph at St. Paul's Outside the Walls. Attention has been drawn to a *Maria Venerabelis*, dated 552 from Lyons, France, and a *Chrodoara Venerabelis* from Amay, Belgium, dated ca. 590: see Dorothy Irvin, "The Archaeology of Women's Traditional Ministries in the Church, 60–1500 AD," *Calendar 2005*, map on inside front cover. The question must be asked whether there are additional features besides the adjectival "venerabilis" that show that this person exercised *episcope*. On its varied use, see Eisen, *Women Officeholders*, 200 and n. 5.

Churches Outside Rome 159

that the title *episcopa* must always refer to the deposed wife of a bishop, for instance James Burtchaell citing Brian Brennan with respect to the church in Gaul.[177] In his *History of the Franks* Gregory of Tours (539–594) writes, generally disparagingly, about a number of bishops' wives; but his term for the wife is *coniunx* not *episcopa*. Venantius Fortunatus' epitaph memorializing Euphrasia, widow of Bishop Namatius (d. 559) of Vienne and consecrated religious, calls her *coniunx*.[178] Canon 14 (13) of the Council of Tours (567) reads, Episcopum episcopiam non habentem nulla sequatur turba mulierum; *videlicet salvatur vir per mulierem fidelem, sicut et mulier per virum fidelem*.[179] This canon has been read as referring to the situation where a bishop has a wife.[180] Ute Eisen notes that there is "no other instance in Latin literature of a bishop's wife being titled episcop(i)a" and interprets the canon to mean that a male bishop "who has no (female) bishop (*episcopia*) may have no women in his entourage."[181] Canon 14 (13) of Tours affords a glimpse of gender relationships in the sixth century.

---

177. James Tunstead Burtchaell (*From Synagogue to Church: Public Services and Offices in the Earliest Christian Communities* [Cambridge: Cambridge University Press, 1992]) presents a conservative picture of all the ministries. Brian Brennan ("'Episcopae': Bishops' Wives Viewed in Sixth-Century Gaul," *Church History* 54 [1985]: 311–23) sketches the development of the requirement of continence for clergy in major orders. He does not assess the titles *episcopa* and *presbytera*, applying the canonical references to bishops' deposed wives who, once widowed, were expected to model "the perfect Christian widow" (cf. 1 Tim 5:10) and not remarry (p. 321). Andrieu (*Ordines romani* 4:141, n. 3) gives the discipline for Gaul: "Non licet relicta presbyteri nec relicta diaconi nec subdiaconi post eius mortem maritum accipere" (*Concilium Autissiodorum* [Auxerre], ca. 573–603). *Relicta*, "left behind or abandoned," is an eloquent term for a widow who by church law is not allowed to remarry.

178. Brennan, "'Episcopae,'" passim; *Carmina*, bk. 4, no. 27; see Henri Leclercq, "Vienne en Dauphiné," *DACL*, 15/2 (1953), 3081.

179. *Concilia Galliae, a. 511–a. 695*, ed. Carlo de Clercq, 181. The italicized clause, affirming the interdependence of men and women, is a loose paraphrase of 1 Cor 11:11–12: "Nevertheless, in the Lord woman is not independent of man or man independent of woman. For just as woman came from man, so man comes through woman; but all things come from God." Taken as a whole this canon suggests that gender relationships and collaboration in the church were still under debate.

180. Charles Du Fresne Du Cange (1610–1688), *Glossarium mediae et infimae latinitatis* (10 vol. in 5; Graz: Akademische Druck- u. Verlagsanstalt, 1954), 2:275–76. Carlo de Clercq *Concilia Galliae a. 511 -a. 695* (see n. 193) defines the unique *episcopia* as *uxor episcopi*.

181. Eisen, *Women Officeholders*, 200. Literally the main clause reads "No crowd of women may follow a (male) bishop who does not have a (female) bishop." *Episcopium* refers to the residence of an archbishop, the diocese, or to the ensemble of episcopal lands and rights (Albert Blaise, ed., *Lexicon Latinitatis Medii Aevi = Dictionnaire latin-française des auteurs du Moyen-Age* [Turnhout: Brepols, 1975], 343). The argument is a delicate one turning on an added vowel and change of gender. On the demand of this same synod that higher clergy (bishop through subdeacon) live with their wives in continence, see Madigan and Osiek, *Ordained Women*, 171–72.

The exercise of *episcope* (oversight) was a complex reality in the newly Christianized lands of western Europe. What do we make of those instances where women had spiritual as well as administrative oversight of faith communities? "Mary of the Gaels," Brigid of Kildare (d. ca. 525), enjoyed not only the rank but the oversight characteristic of a bishop. According to Irish hagiography on "The Life of Brigit," "[o]nly this virgin in the whole of Ireland will hold the episcopal ordination," declared Mel the bishop.[182] In the Celtic world abbots and abbesses were held in high regard. During the medieval period a number of double religious communities of men and women were governed by the abbess, who was seen to take the place of the Virgin Mother.[183]

Titles bestowed on noble abbesses (*Reichsfürstinnen*) in Saxon abbeys of the ninth and tenth centuries, founded or maintained by royalty, conveyed realities of power that were secular as well as religious. For instance, the abbess might regularly have a seat in the Imperial Diet and have her own men-at-arms for visitations of her territories. Either a monastic or canonical abbess might be titled *metropolitana*.[184] Canons and other clergy subject to her took oaths of fidelity, perhaps with a feudal gesture of submission such as throwing themselves on their knees or genuflecting before her. Joan Morris' research of a generation ago unearthed a rich fund of documentation on women exercising *episcope* that requires further analysis. Its very quantity indicates that abbesses with quasi-episcopal jurisdiction and canoness-archdeaconesses must be considered seriously.[185] Where quasi-episcopal abbesses were often

---

182. *Celtic Spirituality*, trans. Oliver Davies (New York: Paulist, 1999), 145; Edward C. Sellner, *Wisdom of the Celtic Saints* (Notre Dame, IN: Ave Maria, 1993), 71–72; Leslie Hardinge, *The Celtic Church in Britain* (London: SPCK, 1972), 189–90. In the *Vita Brigidae* Cogitosus presents a folksy picture of Brigit's maternal and down-to-earth concerns for the extended flock over which she ruled as abbess; see *Saint Patrick's World: The Christian Culture of Ireland's Apostolic Age*, trans. Liam De Paor (Notre Dame, IN: University of Notre Dame Press, 1993).

183. Hilda of Whitby and a number of English foundations (Barbara Mitchell, "Anglo-Saxon Double Monasteries," *History Today* 45 [1995]: 1–7); Jouarre and Chelles, the order of Fontevraud; Penelope D. Johnson, "Double Houses, Western Christian," in *EM* 1 (2000), 416–19. Double monasteries of the Basilian order are studied by Daniel F. Stramara Jr., "Double Monasticism in the Greek East, Fourth through Eighth Centuries," *JECS* 6 (1998): 269–312.

184. Suzanne Fonay Wemple, "Women from the Fifth to the Tenth Century," in Christiane Klapisch-Zuber, ed., *History of Women in West*, vol. 2: *Silences of the Middle Ages* (Cambridge, MA: Belknap Press of Harvard University, 1992), 169–201 at 193. See also Leyser, *Rule and Conflict*, 4–73.

185. *The Lady Was a Bishop* was the publisher's title. *The Hidden History of Women with Clerical Ordination and the Jurisdiction of Bishops* represents Morris' own assessment. Many of the references in this section are drawn from her book.

enough dependent for their secular power on their monasteries' foundation by royal charter and continuing support by the crown, for spiritual jurisdiction such abbesses were directly dependent on the pope. They could, and did, appeal to him successfully against the wishes and decisions of the local bishop.[186] The quasi-episcopal abbess exercised spiritual jurisdiction, appointing everyone within her domain, with the local bishop ordaining her appointees.

(i) Canoness-abbesses

The role of abbess or prioress was an essential one for canonesses. In the institution's heyday the canoness-abbess was the female auxiliary of the local bishop whose institute served the pastoral needs of the local church. The superior of a community of canonesses provided a "secular" version of the quasi-episcopal abbess found in distinguished Benedictine, Cistercian, and related monastic foundations. Like a monastic abbess, the presiding canoness took vows. Depending on the importance of her institute the canonical abbess might be called *sacerdos maxima* or simply *sacerdos*. Although not identified as such, the erudite Abbess Uota of Niedermünster outside Regensburg had her portrait included in the remarkable Uta Codex (Munich, Bayerische Staatsbibliothek, Clm 13601, fol. 4r). She is seated with her hands akimbo as if preaching or teaching. Around her neck and showing from underneath her veil is a short stole, sign of sacerdotal or diaconal status.[187] The canoness-abbess might serve as archdeaconess and act as representative of the bishop, or even as his auxiliary. Though not possessing quasi-episcopal jurisdiction, which would have made her independent of the local bishop and directly under Rome, she might nevertheless have jurisdiction over territories large or small, including towns, parishes, hospitals, and schools belonging to or served

---

186. Pope Gregory the Great (590–604) had declared Benedictine monasteries exempt from episcopal jurisdiction and subject only to the pope. Other religious families also gained such exemption, especially if founded by royalty. Examples of exempt monasteries were found throughout Europe: the royal abbeys of Notre-Dame de Jouarre, founded in the 7th century, and Fontevraud, founded ca. 1100 in western France; Ely and others in England; the Benedictine monastery founded ca. 714 and since then continuously in existence on the Nonnberg above Salzburg, Austria; the Benedictine monastery at Brindisi and the Cistercian at Conversano in Apulia, Italy. Privileges of exemption from episcopal authority were repeatedly confirmed when a monastery and its holdings came under threat from the local bishop. For information on many foundations, see www.monasticmatrix.org/monasticon.

187. McKitterick, "Women in the Ottonian Church," 97, pl. 7.

by the canonical institute. In other words, her ecclesiastical role was much more than consultative. She presided over her own chapter of canons, the laity of the town, and the institution's sometimes extensive property. Some abbesses of canonical institutes were termed *ordinaria* and held both secular and spiritual jurisdiction.[188] The abbess of Herford in Westphalia oversaw extensive holdings and visited them accompanied by a large retinue that included men-at-arms. Well-known canoness institutes were found at Clerkenwell, England; Sainte-Croix, Poitiers; Sainte-Waudru at Mons, Belgium; St. Maria in Kapitol, Cologne; Essen, St. Mary's Überwasser near Münster; Quedlinburg, Gernrode; and Gerresheim; all in Germany.[189] The abbess of the canonical institute at Lucca was termed *episcopa* and *metropolitana* because of her jurisdiction.[190] Another reference, to a Swiss *episcopina*, may derive from a canonical environment.[191] Despite Rome's disapproval and without special federations, canonesses belonged to a religious institution that filled both spiritual and social needs.[192] Today there exist remnants of regular canonesses, for instance, the Congregation of the Lateran, whose history roots them in the lineage of their medieval ancestors.

---

188. On restriction of the traditional rights of abbesses by 13th-century canonists, see Ida Raming, *The Exclusion of Women from the Priesthood: Divine Law or Sex Discrimination?*, trans. Norman R. Adams (Metuchen, NJ: Scarecrow Press, 1976), 73-86, 90-93; repr., in Bernard Cooke and Gary Macy, ed. and trans., *A History of Women and Ordination*, vol. 2: *The Priestly Office of Women: God's Gift to a Renewed Church* (2nd ed.; Lanham, MD: Oxford Scarecrow Press, 2004). *Exclusion of Women from Priesthood*, 73-86, 90-93.

189. E.g. Charlotte Warnke, "Das Kanonissenstift St. Cyriakus zu Gernrode im Spannungsfeld zwischen Hochadel, Kaiser, Bischof und Papst von der Gründung 961 bis zum Ende des Investiturstreits 1122," in Crusius, *Studien zum Kanonissenstift*, 201-74.

190. Van der Meer, *Women Priests in Catholic Church?*, 118-19.

191. Josef Siegwart (*Die Chorherren- und Chorfrauengemeinschaften in der deutschsprachigen Schweiz vom 6. Jahrhundert bis 1160: mit einem Überblick über die deutsche Kanonikerreform des 10. und 11. Jh.* [Freiburg Schweiz: Universitätsverlag, 1962], 49-52) suspects that there is in a Swiss *episcopina* tale a relationship to the *episcopa* portrait in the Zeno Chapel built by Pope Paschal I. However, the original text, "Victor founded Kazis for his mother, who was a nun (or canoness) and was named *episcopa*," and its Swiss context points to an institution of canonesses founded by Bishop Victor II at the beginning of the 8th century and to a personage who was also reverentially titled *sancta*.

192. Over time the collaboration between canons and canonesses diminished. Late in their history canonesses would more frequently pray the divine office within their own church or chapel in their institute now removed from the center of town. A few canoness institutes survived up to the 18th and early 19th centuries.

4. The Question of Women "Doing" Liturgy

The primary difficulty in writing women's history of any period is the fact that very little of it has been recorded. Most liturgical customs in women's monasteries and canonries are lost to history. Our information must come from external indicators. Not surprisingly the data available about the liturgical prerogatives of abbesses relate mostly to their visible exercise of jurisdiction. The quasi-episcopal abbess enjoyed much of the same liturgical regalia as was worn and used by her male counterparts with the status of abbot, diocesan, or titular bishop: pectoral cross, episcopal ring, pastoral staff, miter, and throne or faldstool (bishop's folding seat).[193] Study of liturgical and dramatic ceremonial in the houses of monastics and institutions of canonesses, where retrievable as at Hildegard's Bingen or Hrotsvitha's Gandersheim, might add to our scant information about specific liturgical activities undertaken by women over and beyond that of the divine office prayed "in the name of the church" day and night.

Early in their history both men and women monastic leaders were laity, not ordained presbyters or deacons. Monastic communities attended Sunday mass at the parish church. The devotional custom developed of celebrating a communion service in the monastery during the week; this was observed in some monasteries for many centuries. At St. Sophia's, Benevento, in the eleventh–twelfth centuries a communion service for female use was copied from a communion liturgy used by male monastics at Monte Cassino.[194] Jean Leclercq typifies such ensembles of prayers (titled *orationes ad accipiendam eucharistiam*) as essentially constituting "a long eucharistic prayer."[195] Gary Macy comments briefly on the practices

---

193. Johannes Neumann ("Bischof I," "*Das katholische Bischofsamt*," TRE 6 [1980]: 653–697 at 667–69) lists the pontificalia for men. The Benedictine abbey on the Nonnberg (Salzburg), continuously in existence since the early 700s, has in its possession the folding liturgical seat, crozier, crown, gloves, and ring of their abbess. Macy ("Ordination of Women," 11) summarizes the clerical functions of many abbesses.

194. Gary Macy, *The Hidden History of Women's Ordination: Female Clergy in the Medieval West* (Oxford: Oxford University Press, 2008), 63 and n. 71.

195. Jean Leclercq, "Prières médiévales pour recevoir l'eucharistie pour saluer et pour bénir la croix," *EL* 97 (1965): 327–31; Leclercq, "Eucharistic Celebrations Without Priests in the Middle Ages," *Worship* 55 (1981): 160–68, repr., R. Kevin Seasoltz, ed., *Living Bread, Saving Cup: Readings on the Eucharist* (Collegeville, MN: Liturgical, 1987), 222–30. In analyzing 10th- and 11th-century *ordines*, one of which belonged to a female monastery (Vatican ms. lat. 4928, pp. 89–100, provenance Benevento, Abbey of St. Sophia) and another in France (Auxerre, Bibliothèque ms. 25) in which the prayers are in the feminine gender, Leclercq

of lay confession and preaching, studies in themselves.[196] If an abbess had been ordained as a deacon, she was of course no longer lay and would have carried out diaconal functions. In a number of instances, the rule required the abbess to hear the confessions of her subjects, which could include the laity in her territory.[197] Confession to deacons and holy laity continued in some places into the mid-thirteenth century. Only when the number of sacraments was fixed at seven in the later twelfth century and Lateran Council IV (1215) required confession to one's own parish priest during Eastertide did this ancient ascetical practice begin to fall out of use.

Women had formed and entered communities to praise God and to worship eucharistically. Occasionally history informs us of female monasteries whose members were placed under interdict or excommunicated (literally "deprived of communion") for a time by the local bishop.[198] By the later twelfth and thirteenth centuries not only was the eucharistic cup withheld from laity and religious but women in most religious communities received communion less than a dozen times a year. As with Orthodox nuns today, religious women would much more often attend mass than communicate at it.[199] Eucharistic exclusion coexisted with

---

draws on an article by André Wilmart, "Prières pour la communion en deux psautiers du Mont-Cassin," *EL* 43 (1929): 320–27. Besides including, sometimes, extensive penitential elements, these liturgical rituals share a eucharistic and even trinitarian tone. That they were a monastic invention is suggested by the frequent use of the first person singular rather than the "liturgical plural." A 16th-century Beneventan example is given by Virginia Brown, "Latin and Italian Prayers in a Sixteenth-Century Beneventan Manuscript from Naples," in *Ritual, Text and Law: Studies in Medieval Canon Law and Liturgy Presented to Roger E. Reynolds*, ed. Kathleen G. Cushing and Richard F. Gyug (Aldershot, Hants: Ashgate, 2004), 95–122 with text 116–19. On these prayer texts, see also Gary Macy, *Treasures from the Storeroom: Medieval Religion and the Eucharist* (Collegeville, MN: Liturgical, 1999), 174 and nn. 11, 12; Macy, *Hidden History of Women's Ordination*, 63.

196. Macy, *Treasures from Storeroom*, 173–74. The *Penitential of Theodore* (Theodore, archbishop of Canterbury 668–690) may be attempting to control the medieval practice of confession to saintly monks, nuns, and holy persons when it decrees in chap. VII, "Of the Rite of the Women, or Their Ministry in the Church," that "according to the canons it is the function of the bishops and priests to prescribe penance" (no. 2). See *Medieval Handbooks of Penance*, 205.

197. Muschiol, *Familia Dei*, "Confessio," 222–63.

198. Near the end of her life (d. 1179) St. Hildegard of Bingen's community at Rupertsberg on the Rhine was placed under interdict by the ecclesiastical authorities at Mainz. The community was prohibited from singing the divine office, hearing mass, or receiving communion; see Anne H. King-Lenzmeier, *Hildegard of Bingen: An Integrated Vision* (Collegeville, MN: Liturgical, 2001), 166–69.

199. At Varatec Monastery in northern Romania the nuns communicate every three weeks on Saturday except for the elders, who receive communion weekly. Even this would have been considered frequent for most religious women, e.g., the Poor Clares, in the later Middle Ages.

concerted efforts by women mystics to be admitted to frequent, even daily communion. Although generally speaking during the late Middle Ages there was radically decreased eucharistic participation by non-clergy, the duty of praying the divine office remained a constant in the lives of now-cloistered nuns.

Throughout the church's life there have been countless instances of clinical baptisms performed by women—midwives, relatives, diaconas—which gave rise to conciliar decrees against baptism by women. A matter about which we know even less, and always of primary concern to women whether lay or religious, has been the care of the infirm, the aged, and the dying. What provisions were made for liturgical prayer, communicating the sick, and administering viaticum to the dying? Was communion ministry a privilege commonly accorded an abbess or prioress? What might have been the practice in women's circles when theology insistent on the reception of the eucharist as necessary for salvation was a factor?[200]

Conclusion

This chapter has sketched on a broad canvas, over 1,200 years of Christian history, a wide variety of attempts by women determined to devote their lives to the church and participate in its ministry. These ranged from leadership and patronage of early Christian house-churches, the charitable work of widows ministering to women and children, and prayer in the name of the church by consecrated virgins, to the ordered ministry of diaconas, presbyteras or *sacerdotes*, episcopas, and powerful women abbesses. Although women's public ministries encountered many roadblocks, taken overall there exists a significant body of evidence testifying to the welcomed participation of women in the public ministries of the Christian churches East and West through the twelfth century. The scholasticism that developed theological and canonical "answers" to hypothetical as well as real issues during the second half of the twelfth and thirteenth centuries abetted the radical diminishment of women's public service in the church.[201]

---

200. Gary Macy, *The Theologies of the Eucharist in the Early Scholastic Period: A Study of the Salvific Function of the Sacrament according to the Theologians c. 1080–c. 1220* (Oxford: Clarendon, 1984).

201. For an overview and bibliography, see Gary Macy, "Impasse passé: Conjugating a tense past" in CTSA, *Proceedings of the Sixty-fourth Annual Convention, Halifax, Nova Scotia, June 4–7, 2009*, 10–17.

While the cult of the Virgin and the secular ideal of the highborn lady gained eminence during the thirteenth century, a distinctively negative turn for ecclesial women—canonesses, monastics, other *sanctimoniales*, and laywomen whose spiritual calling was to serve the church—manifested itself in ecclesiastical culture. The anti-feminine shift in biological, philosophical, and theological speculation arising in the new universities bereft of women was foreshadowed by an objection raised by the canonist, liturgist, and curialist Pope Innocent III (1198–1216). In a letter of 11 December 1210 to the bishops of Placencia and Burgos (Spain) and the Cistercian abbot of Morimund he wrote:

> Certain novelties, about which we wonder not a little, have recently come to our ears: apparently abbesses in the dioceses of Burgos and Placencia bless their own nuns, and in matters dealing with misdeeds hear their nuns' confessions, and when they read the gospel they presume to proclaim publicly. Since this is equally unseemly and can in no case be permitted by us, we commend to your discretion, by apostolic writing, to see to it that this does not happen any further, to prohibit it firmly by reason of apostolic authority, for although the most blessed virgin Mary stood above and was also more excellent than all the apostles together, the Lord still did not confide to her but to them the keys of the kingdom of heaven.[202]

Innocent's appeal to the local bishops and the Cistercian abbot of Morimond to stop the abbesses' practice of blessing their nuns, preaching, and hearing the nuns' confessions at the Cistercian royal abbey of Las Huelgas (Burgos) did not affect their quasi-episcopal jurisdiction.[203] After all, recognition of

---

202. PL 216, 356 A–B; *Corpus Iuris Canonici, Decretales* 1.5, t. 38, c. 10, ed. E. Friedberg (Graz: Akademische Druck, 1959), 2:886–87, trans. in Van der Meer, *Women Priests*, 125–26. On the situation in Spain, see Morris, *Lady Was a Bishop*, 83–99.

203. Van der Meer (*Women Priests*, 126) indicates that the phrase *moniales benedicere* referred not to a simple blessing but rather to the abbess's reception of her nuns' vow of virginity. Influenced by Eastern practice (cf. V. Ruggieri, *Byzantine Religious Architecture* [582–867], 178), the Columban Rule for nuns provided for regular confession to the abbess. Confessions of devotion to holy lay persons were a common practice into the 14th century (Cooke and Macy, *History of Women and Ordination*, vol. 1: *Ordination of Women in Medieval Context*, 11 and n. 65). The hearing of subjects' confessions by abbesses bespeaks both their jurisdictional authority and nuns' experience of superiors as acting for them "in the person of Christ." Abbesses were responsible for the excommunication and reconciliation of their subjects to the community. Not until 1255 were deacons prohibited from hearing confessions at Poitiers (Morris, *Lady Was a Bishop*, 141). Developments in scholastic theology would make the hearing of private confessions and consequent giving of absolution (a juridical

episcope by women had been enshrined in papal bulls and long-standing custom. Despite the revocation of her diaconal rights the abbess of Las Huelgas continued until 1874 to exercise quasi-episcopal jurisdiction not only over her female religious but also over villages, chaplains, and landholdings. The prohibition of these abbesses' customary blessing of their nuns, hearing of their nuns' confessions, and preaching the gospel was a specific command to male superiors of abbesses in these two dioceses and did not abrogate customs elsewhere. The breadth of the spiritual and secular *episcope* exercised by the Cistercian abbess of Las Huelgas is demonstrated by the following account of her powers and authority:

> Lady, superior, prelate, legitimate administrator of the spiritual and temporal matters of the said royal monastery... as well as the convents, churches, hermitages affiliated with it, and the villages and places of its jurisdiction, manors and vassalages, in virtue of the apostolic bull and concessions with a jurisdiction that is plenary, privative, quasi-episcopal, *nullius diocesis* and with royal privileges: a double jurisdiction which we exercise in peaceful possession, as is publicly well known.... The power to act judicially, just as the lord bishops, in criminal, civil and beneficial cases, to grant dimissorial letters for ordination, faculties to preach, confess, exercise the care of souls, enter into religion, the power to confirm abbesses, to issue censures... and finally to convoke a synod.[204]

It is an irony of ecclesiastical history that Jose María Escrivá, founder of Opus Dei, painstakingly collected the texts of bulls and letters granting prerogatives for Las Huelgas together with many references to other quasi-episcopal foundations and the relevant commentary of theologians to make the case for non-territorial prelature (*nullius diocesis*) benefitting his religious institution.[205]

---

judgment) an exclusively presbyteral or episcopal function (James Dallen, "Reconciliation, Sacrament of," in *NDSW* (1990), 1052–64).

204. *España sagrada*, by H. Floroz des Augustiniens (Madrid: 1772), 27, col. 578, 581, excerpted from the entry "Abbesses," in *Dictionnaire de Théologie catholique* (1930), 1:20–21, commented upon by van der Meer, *Women Priests?*, 119. Gary Macy (*Hidden History of Women's Ordination*, 102–4) discusses how Innocent III's action against Las Huelgas was broadened by scholastic theologians.

205. Jose María Escrivá, *La Abadessa de Las Huelgas* (1944; available online at www.escrivaobras.org/book/abadessa).

The codification of church law and custom during the latter part of the twelfth century and the scholastic spirit of thirteenth-century theology, with its absorption of Aristotelian biology, worked against the recognition of full personhood and the legitimacy of ecclesial functions carried out by women that had developed over the preceding centuries. In the following chapter we will revisit the period from early Christianity through the high Middle Ages in Rome, symbol of past empire and seat of the Roman bishops who "succeeded" Peter as shepherds of Christ's church. Gradual claimant to the position of leadership of all the Christian churches, the church of Rome grew in the shadow of the old Roman Empire, which had hardly been friendly to womankind. One of the assumptions of the Roman church is that it has not known the ordained ministry of women. In this unlikeliest of contexts we will seek for evidence of women in ecclesial offices.

4
Women's Pastoral Offices in the Church of Rome

SAINTS' LIVES STILL copied in the late Middle Ages and read during the night office as meditative texts or recalled at mass on their feastday handed on the stories of the Pudens family to pious generations. Renaissance humanism renewed the curiosity of ecclesiastics about the history of the ancient churches. The rebirth of scriptural exegesis and ecclesiastical scholarship in the sixteenth and seventeenth centuries introduced women of the early church, or at least their names, into the new scholarly environment.[1] In 1655 the Oratorian Jean Morin (Ioannes Morinus, 1591–1659) published an oversized study on ordination rites.[2] That same year the Roman priest-scholar and prolific writer on Roman architecture and art Fioravante Martinelli (1599–1667) stated in print that circa 144/145

---

1. Over two decades (1588–1607) Cardinal Baronius (Cesare Baronio Sorano) published the twelve-volume *Annales ecclesiastici* (Rome: Ex Typographia Vaticana, 1588–1607), a massive, widely cited church history that later writers did not hesitate to correct. Baronius popularized the Pudens clan's importance for early Christian life in Rome and explained that diaconissas, presbyteras, and episcopas were clergy wives now living celibate lives (1:233). Commenting on Paul's epistles, Benedetto Giustiniani, SJ (1551–1622) discussed deaconesses at length when treating Rom 16:1. Cornelius à Lapide, SJ (1567–1637), whose exegetical commentaries contained their share of misogynistic comments, cited the Pudens family and the synaxes held in their house when commenting on 2 Tim 4:21. The archeologist Antonio Bosio (1575–1629) visited over thirty catacombs, leaving his name prominently displayed; he commented on the figures in the cubiculum of the *Velatio* in the Priscilla cemetery. Bosio's two-volume *Roma sotterranea* (Rome: G. Facciotti, 1632) would be known to S. Prassede's prior Dom Benigno Davanzati. A handful of scholars published ordination rites from churches of East and West including those for diaconas and abbesses.

2. Jean Morin, *Commentarius de sacris ecclesiae ordinationibus, secundum antiquos et recentiores, latinos, graecos, syros, et babylonios, in tres partes distinctus* (1st ed., Paris: Gaspari Meturas, 1655; 2nd ed., Antwerp: Barent van Lier; Amsterdam: H. Desbordes, 1695; repr. Farnborough: Gregg, 1969).

CE St. Praxedes had been made presbytera by Pius I, friend of the senatorial Pudens clan. Martinelli's book, *Primo trofeo della Sma Croce eretto in Roma nella Via Lata da S. Pietro Apostolo*, was dedicated to Pope Alexander VII.[3] Martinelli asserted that Pudentiana and Praxedes were baptized by St. Paul about 69 CE, that the younger sister Praxedes lived until the end of Pius I's pontificate (144/145), and that she was created presbytera of the *titulus* in the thermae of Timothy and Novatianus by Pius.[4] Martinelli gave as the historical antecedents for this office the ecclesiastical ministry of Phoebe and the ordination to the diaconate of women at least forty years of age. He then drew on Bishop Atto of Vercelli's (d. 961/964) explanation of the suitability of Christian women engaging in the conversion of women from pagan rites and of their preparing these women for baptism. Finally, to explain women's absence from official church office in later centuries, Martinelli quoted Canon 11 of the fourth century council of Laodicea, which objected to the further ordination of women called *presbyterae* or presidents for the churches.[5]

Coming like a bolt out of the blue, Martinelli's entirely unexpected claim seems not to have been adverted to by ecclesiastics for seventy years. Then in 1725 Prior Benigno Davanzati (1670–1746) published a

---

3. Fioravante Martinelli, *Primo trofeo della santissima Croce eretto in Roma nella via Lata da S. Pietro apostolo* (Rome: Nicolangelo Tinassi, 1655).

4. The longevity of family members led Martinelli to hypothesize that the story involved three generations rather than two (*Primo trofeo*, fol. 41), and that Paul baptized Savinella and her two children (ibid., fol. 55). Novatus is confused with the heretic Novatian, a rigorist presbyter who condemned Pope Cornelius during the Decian persecution of 251. The 11th-century copy of *LP* in Martinelli's keeping (Vat. ms. lat. 3764, fol. 11) reads "thermas novati."

5. "Per tanto concludiamo, che essendo stati più Pudenti, dobiam credere, che le due Vergini Pudentiana e Prassede nascessero dal Pudente, battezzato da S. Paolo nel 69. di Cristo; e che S. Prassede vivesse una lunga età fin al Pontificato di Pio Primo, che secondo la cronologia di Eusebio fù nell'anno 144. in 145. Massimè che dal medesimo Pontefice fu creata Presbitera del Titolo, eretto nelle Therme Timotine, e Novatiane, per aiuto del ministerio ecclesiastico, non altrimente di Feba, della quale parla S. Paolo, 'commendo vobis Febam sororem meam quae est in ministerio Ecclesiae, quae est Cenchris'; Poiche questa carica nella primitiva chiesa non si soleva dare se non à vecchie, considerandosi, che le Diacone loro adiutrici non potevano ordinarsi avanti l'anno quadragesimo secondo il Concilio Calcedonense: anzi bisognava, Cap. 15 che fossero dotte, e ben istrutte nelli riti della Religione nostra, servendo anch'esse per facilitare la conversione dell' donne assuefatte alli rite del paganesimo, & istrutte de dogmi filosofici; il che fù poi proibito dal Concilio Laodicense con il canone, 'Quod Can 11 non oporteat eas, quae dicuntur Presbyterae, vel Presidentes is Ecclesijs ordinari' " (Martinelli, *Primo trofeo*, n. 15, fol. 55).

bulging guide to S. Prassede, where he had been prior for sixteen years. His panegyric of 544 pages about the old church and its patron disputed Martinelli's claims for S. Maria in Via Lata as the inn where St. Peter established his apostolic seat, instead setting out the equally unprovable case for the priority of S. Prassede as the site where the apostle Peter had begun his Roman ministry and as the home of the Pudens named in 2 Timothy 4:21.[6] Here Senator Punicus Pudens had hosted, and along with his wife Priscilla been baptized by, St. Peter on the latter's arrival in Rome in 44 CE. Here Peter had undertaken "his sacred functions" and "established his cathedra."[7] Davanzati speculated that Paul, martyred in 69 CE, arrived in Rome twenty-five years after Peter. Paul baptized Pudens Junior's wife Sabina (Savinella) and their daughters Pudentiana and Praxedes; following the Roman Martyrology, he added Timothy and Novatus as their brothers. After the death of their father, presbyter Pastor became the daughters' guardian. Both sisters died natural deaths; Praxedes was *presbytidis*, very old. If born around 66/67 CE, Praxedes would have been between eighty-two and eighty-four years old when she died during the pontificate of Pius.[8] An ancient lectionary preserved at the Vallombrosan monastery, thought to have come from S. Prassede, gave her year of death as 156.[9] Thus ran the story of a Christian family whose three generations spanned a hundred years. As retold by Davanzati, some of the ambiguous details were made more precise to serve his cause.

Davanzati's guide provides details that do not differ from those of Martinelli seventy years previously: "... by Pope Pius I S. Prassede... was created Presbiteressa of the *Titulus* erected in the Therme of Timothy

---

6. Davanzati, *Notizie al pellegrino*, 21–27. Davanzati claimed to draw on documents found in the monastery of S. Prassede, which had been given into the keeping of the Vallombrosan Benedictines by Innocent III (ibid., 125).

7. Davanzati (*Notizie al pellegrino*, 72) claimed that S. Prassede, built by the apostle Peter in 44/45 CE to establish the Christian cult in Rome, was the *titulo Pudentis*, asserting S. Prassede's priority in the history of Roman Christianity's places of worship and overriding Martinelli's claim for S. Maria in Via Lata. He terms S. Pudenziana the *titolo Pastoris* and notes that a thermae had been converted into the church a century later by St. Pius I at the request of Praxedes in honor of her sister. Davanzati's claims for the Praxedis *titulus* run counter to archeological data and literary reconstructions. Of the two authors, Martinelli is the scholar.

8. Davanzati, *Notizie al pellegrino*, 74–113. His argument is scattered throughout these pages.

9. "[I]o trovo in uno de' Lezzionarj antichi, che si conservano nel Monastero di Vallombrosa, e che si credono cavati di Monastero di S. Prassede di Roma...." (Davanzati, *Notizie al pellegrino*, 124).

and Novatian, to help with ecclesiastical ministry, not differently from Phoebe...."[10] By 1725 scholars and churchmen had greater familiarity with evidence regarding diaconas, presbyteras, and episcopas.[11] Attuned to this growing sophistication, Davanzati sets out to explain the presbyteral title. He begins with the fact that the two sisters were virgins, noting the ancient custom of deputing "some Virgins to ecclesiastical ministry, and to the Custody of the Temple, and these they called *Presbiteresse, o Diaconesse.*" There are two ways, he continues, of understanding the terms *episcopa, presbiteressa,* and *diaconessa.* The first is as title for the deposed wife of bishop, presbyter, or deacon. But Pudentiana and Praxedes cannot be clergy wives because they have only one *Sposo,* Christ. From *Apostolic Constitutions* attributed to the apostle Bartholomew for the ordination of women deacons, Davanzati has learned that true *diaconesse* and *presbiteresse* were ordained through laying on of hands by the bishop. The prior distinguishes deposed wives who carried the titles of their newly ordained husbands of the church of Rome (*episcopae, presbyterae, diaconissae*) from "other Deaconesses or Presbyteressas" who were virgin women, *di senno o prudenza mature,* at least forty years of age, who in a certain way were *ordinate e consagrate da' Vescovi coll'imposizione della mano.* Schooled in scholastic theology, Davanzati concludes that these "ordained" persons could not receive the sacramental character because as women they were *incapace.*[12] We are

---

10. "...dobbiamo credere che le due sorelle Vergini Pudentiana, e Prassede, nascessero dal Pudente battezzato da S. Paolo nel 69 di Cristo, e che S. Prassede vivesse una lunga età sin' al Pontificato di Pio Primo, massime, che dal medesimo Pontefice fu creata Presbiteressa del Titolo, eretto nelle Therme Timotine, e Novatiane, per aiuto del ministerio ecclesiastico, non altrimente di Feba, della quale parla S. Paolo; officio, che non si dava, che alle Matrone di età, e di senno mature" (Davanzati, *Notizie al pellegrino,* 73–74). Davanzati diverges from Martinelli in designating Praxedes by *presbiteressa,* reserving the Italian diminutive form -essa for ecclesiastical offices. On the other hand, *episcopae* are the deposed wives of bishops.

11. Besides Jean Morin, later writers who took note of women's ministries prepared the way for Davanzati's speculations, among them Caspar Ziegler, *De diaconis et diaconissis veteris ecclesiae liber commentarius* (4 vols.; Wittenberg, 1678); J. C. Suicer, *Thesaurus ecclesiasticus e patribus graecis* (Amsterdam, 1682; 2nd ed., 1728); Charles Du Fresne Du Cange, *Glossarium ad scriptores mediae et infimae latinitatis* (2 vols.; Lyons: Anisson & Rigaud, 1688; repr., 6 vols., Paris: O. C. Osmont, 1733–1736); Johann Philipp Odelem, *Dissertatio de diaconissis primitivae ecclesiae* (Leipzig: Fleischer, 1700); Louis Thomassin, *Vetus et nova ecclesiae disciplina circa beneficia et beneficiarios* (3 vols.; Lyons: Anisson & Posuel, 1705–1706); Joseph Bingham, *Origines sive antiquitates ecclesiasticae* (2 vols.; Halle: Orphanotrophei, 1724–1725), in English, *The Antiquities of the Christian Church* (10 vols.; London: Robert Knaplock, 1710–1722).

12. Davanzati, *Notizie al pellegrino,* 116–22, esp. 121. Davanzati discusses the office of presbiteressas and diaconessas (ibid., 122–24) following *Apostolic Constitutions* VIII.19.1–20.2.

left with questions: Why would Fioravante Martinelli state with such assurance in 1655 that Pius I created Praxedes *Presbitera del Titolo* erected in the baths of Timothy and "Novatian"? And why would a respected prior of an old and distinguished Roman *titulus*, newly elected abbot of his Vallombrosan Benedictine order, concur with Martinelli's assertion? When noting the work of Pius in relation to the S. Prassede community—frequent visits to administer the sacraments, celebrate holy mass, make spiritual congresses, and confer with the saint—he adds, "created Presbiteressa by him, as alluded to in her Vita."[13]

Relying on archeological, epigraphical, historiographical, artistic, and textual evidence, this chapter investigates roles and ministerial offices available to women in the Roman church. From the age of the martyrs onward the ecclesiastical office of widow and status of virgin are well attested for Christian women. Whether or not these ranked as "ecclesiastical offices" probably varied according to responsibilities and pastoral setting. Offices of teacher and presbytera, however, have not been recognized by the majority of scholars. Peter Lampe summarizes the evidence for women's ministry in the city of Rome in the early centuries by saying that for Roman Christian women "only a few observations are possible."[14] This chapter provides evidence to counter Lampe's comment. After Constantine, all ecclesiastical offices became more institutionalized, more circumscribed, and more "official." A time of great consolidation in church offices is epitomized by Pope Gelasius I (492–496), whose objections to women in ecclesiastical ministries carried much weight among misogynist clerics in later centuries. By the late seventh century, during the period when Rome was governed by a preponderance of popes from the East and the Greek south of Italy, the office of diacona was given an official place in the papal pontifical. Questions regarding the title *episcopa* and oversight (*episcope*) close out this chapter.

See Ida Raming, *Exclusion of Women from Priesthood*, republished in Bernard Cooke and Gary Macy, eds., *A History of Women and Ordination*, vol. 2: *The Priestly Office of Women: God's Gift to a Renewed Church* (2nd ed.; Lanham, MD: Scarecrow Press, 2004), which presents scholastic and theological reasoning for denying that women are capable of receiving the sacramental character conferred by ordination.

13. Davanzati, *Notizie al pellegrino*, 502.

14. Lampe, *From Paul to Valentinus*, 146–50 at 146.

1. *Women's Offices and Ministries in Rome, Second through Fifth Centuries*

In the first three centuries of the Roman church evidence for the official entrusting of persons with public offices is extant although meager. Identifying by name even major officeholders such as bishops is difficult.[15]

A. Enrolled Widows in Rome

If *Apostolic Tradition* represents the traditional praxis of a conservative sect during the late second and early third centuries, it is clear that enrolled widows were numbered among its instituted nonordained ministries.[16] However, we do not have a third-century text for *Apostolic Tradition*'s chapters on ordained and instituted ministries.[17] Setting aside *Apostolic Tradition* as providing no sure evidence concerning third-century praxis in Rome and the Great Church, other sources attest to widows. Eusebius cites a letter from Pope Cornelius (251–252/3) to Bishop Fabian of Antioch that gives figures: one bishop; forty-six presbyters; seven deacons; seven subdeacons; forty-two acolytes; fifty-two exorcists, readers and doorkeepers; and more than fifteen hundred widows and persons in distress.[18] Are these latter all "poor" widows? Or are some of these widows self-supporting or supported by the church while at the same time participating in the church's ministry? Widows' names appear on tomb inscriptions. To be determined in

---

15. Johannes Neumann, "Bischoff I," 667–69.

16. *Apostolic Tradition* 10: "When a widow is appointed, she is not ordained, but is chosen by name.... A widow shall be appointed by word only, and shall join the rest. But hands shall not be laid on her, because she does not offer the offering, nor has she a liturgical duty. Ordination is for the clergy, on account of their liturgical duties; but a widow is appointed for prayer, which belongs to all." Neither is a reader (*AT* 11) nor a subdeacon (*AT* 13) counted as a member of the clergy; each is named but hands are not laid on them (Bradshaw, *Ordination Rites*, 109).

17. A. F. Walls ("The Latin Version of Hippolytus' Apostolic Tradition," *SP* 3 [1961]: 155–62) has proposed that the Latin text for the ordination rites was translated from a Greek text compiled in North Italy between 380 and 430. Paul Bradshaw suggests that *AT* may be composed of layers from diverse communities and regions. Even if its provenance were Rome, many diverse ethnic groups with their own ecclesial traditions coexisted at this crossroads of the empire.

18. Eusebius, *Hist. Eccles.* 6.43.11, in Eusebius Pamphilus of Caesarea, *The Ecclesiastical History of Eusebius Pamphilus*, 265. The category of widow could include a married woman deposed by her husband on the latter's ordination.

each case is whether the inscription refers to a poor or "real" widow or to an ecclesiastical order of widows: a woman who, on the death of her husband, has chosen a life of continence and been enrolled in an ecclesiastical grade.[19] And might any of these "widows" be virgins who, in preference to marriage, joined the ecclesiastical order of widows for mutual support and opportunities for ecclesial ministry? Eisen cites several inscriptions, including a rare second-century reference in the Priscilla cemetery to one Flavia Arcas Χήρα that she takes to refer to "ecclesiastical widowhood." This is the oldest inscription naming any member of the Roman clergy.[20] Other third- and fourth-century inscriptions name widows who "sat," that is, who had seating provided because of their ecclesiastical office.[21] J. P. Kirsch recognized some inscriptions in Roman catacombs as referring to enrolled widows and deaconesses. Regina's daughter attests that, for sixty years in the fourth/fifth century, Regina "sat" as a widow, serving the church "without burdening the Christian community."[22] The provenance of an epitaph bearing the name of Octavia *vidua dei* (widow of God) is the basilica of S. Sabina, built 422–432. Benedict XIV ordered its transfer to the Lateran collection in 1757; recently the epitaph was mounted on the entrance wall of the Bibliotheca Vaticana. Attesting to the mainstream character of the office of widow, Jerome, Augustine, and later Caesarius of

---

19. The very existence of a tombstone with inscription indicates that the person memorialized was not a "poor" widow but had sufficient means, or was surrounded by a support system with sufficient means, to pay for it.

20. Eisen, *Women Officeholders*, 143–45.

21. Eisen, *Women Officeholders*, 145–48. Churches made no provisions for seating of the common folk. Cf. the widows who "sit in front" and their prayer of institution in the *Testamentum Domini* 1.40 (Bradshaw, *Ordination Rites*, 120–21). During the eucharistic offering they stand on the left side of the presbytery behind the presbyters, opposite the deacons on the right; they receive communion after the deacons but before the subdeacons and readers (ibid., 87; Eisen, *Women Officeholders*, 149). Assigned seating or a place to stand among the ministers symbolized authority; found from the 2nd century, it designated rank. E.g., ca. 220 enthronement marked episcopal ordination in Transjordan; see Edward J. Kilmartin," Ministry and Ordination in Early Christianity against a Jewish Background," *SL* 13 (1979): 42–69; repr.; Kilmartin, in Wiebe Vos and Geoffrey Wainwright, eds., *Ordination Rites: Papers Read at the 1979 Congress of Societas Liturgica* (Rotterdam: Liturgical Ecumenical Center Trust, 1980), 42–69.

22. Johann Peter Kirsch, *Die Frauen des kirchlichen Altertums* (Paderborn: Schöningh, 1912), 21–22. James Spencer Northcote (*Epitaphs of the Catacombs or Christian Inscriptions in Rome during the First Four Centuries* [London: Longmans, Green, 1878], 124–25) had already cited Octavia, Daphne, and Regina, asking whether the appellation "sat" indicated ecclesiastical office.

Arles (470–542) speculated as to the "fruits" earned in each state of life; widows were said to earn sixty-fold.[23]

B. Virgins

Virgins were the most popular category of women who devoted their lives to Christ and the church and the least challenging to the establishment. The prerogative of bishops to consecrate virgins appears to have been jealously guarded; a presbyter could be present at a widow's dedication, which she undertook herself, but only a bishop could preside at the consecration of a virgin. In their *vita* the sisters Praxedes and Pudentiana are typified as virgins, but no reference is made to a ceremony of consecration. They are *virgines non velatae* living in the paternal household. Clearly this category does not do complete justice to their story.

Roman civil religion had its vestal virgins, young women selected from senatorial families who did not themselves choose the role of tending the sacred fire of the goddess Vesta but were dedicated to it from girlhood by their families. The office conferred sacred status and heavy responsibility: they were required, under pain of a slow death, to maintain their virginity intact for the duration of their service of thirty years.[24] Christian virginity was distinguished from the enforced chastity of the vestals by being freely chosen by the individual.[25] Justin Martyr has already been

---

23. See Antoine Chavasse, *Le Sacramentaire gélasien*, 507–10. Gel III, lv gives a blessing for "widows who will have professed chastity."

24. C. Koch, "Vesta," *Paulys Real-Encyclopädie der klassischen Altertumswissenschaft* 2.8 (16), ed. G. Wissowa (Stuttgart: J.B. Metzler, 1958), 1717–76, esp. 1730–34; *Encyclopedia of Women and World Religion*, ed. Serinity Young (2 vols.; New York: Macmillan Reference USA, 1999), 1:407; 2:1002; M. R. P. McGuire, "Vestal Virgins," *NCE* 14 (1967): 632–33.

25. René Metz, *La consécration des vierges dans l'Église romaine: Étude d'histoire de la liturgie* (Paris: Presses Universitaires de France, 1954); Metz, "Les vierges chrétiennes en Gaule au IV siècle," in *Saint Martin et son temps: Mémorial du XVIe centenaire des débuts du monachisme en Gaule, 361–1961* (Rome: Herder, 1961), 109–32. The liturgical development, as witnessed by the manuscript tradition, is traced by Nichola Emsley, "The Rite of Consecration of Virgins," in Anscar J. Chupungco, ed., *Handbook for Liturgical Studies*, vol. 4: *Sacraments and Sacramentals* (Collegeville, MN: Liturgical, 1999), 331–44 at 332–33, with additional bibliography in Eisen, *Women Officeholders*, 194–95; and Gabriele Konetzny, "Die Jungfrauenweihe," in Berger and Gerhards, *Liturgie und Frauenfrage*, 475–92. For a feminist reading, see Ross S. Kraemer, "The Conversion of Women to Ascetic Forms of Christianity," *Signs* 6 (1980): 298–307. The title *ancilla Dei* or *ancilla Christi* on early grave inscriptions was initially bestowed on children. Later this title refers to women living a devout life with or without a vow, and later still to canonesses (H. Leclercq, "Ancilla Dei," *DACL* 1/2 [1907], 1973–93).

Church of Rome 177

cited for his witness that both men and women were living lives of virginity from the first Christian century and that the virginal life was flourishing in the second. From its early years the church viewed consecrated virginity as mystical marriage to Christ, which elevated the role of virgins to one of symbolizing Christ's relationship to the earthly church. The telling comparison made by Sandra Schneiders between male and female approaches to virginity—between self-development and interpersonal relationship—is apt for understanding the phenomenon in early Christian Rome. For men, continence constituted a sexual asceticism that made possible their pursuit of holiness, the highest wisdom. By the late fourth century male continence, frequently following a marriage that had produced progeny, allowed entrance into careers as members of the higher clergy. In keeping with cultural stereotypes and supported by the earliest sources, consecrated virginity for women was experienced and explained as "marriage to Christ." Sexual abstinence was women's "outward expression of spousal fidelity" and "self-donation to the person of Christ," corresponding to the ideal of spousal fidelity proposed for the Roman *matrona* classical or Christian.[26] This held true even if the women were widows not virgins. From living a dedicated life in their parents' or their own home, the next phase in the development of the virginal lifestyle was the sharing of religious life and accommodations. The first monastery of virgins in Rome may have been established 339–350 near the catacomb of the martyr Agnes by Constantina, daughter of the emperor Constantine.[27]

Henri Leclercq accepted the ceremony of *velatio virginum* as probable identification of the left-hand grouping of three figures in the well-known fresco in the cubiculum of the *Velatio* (Rome, Priscilla Catacomb) (see Fig. 4.1).[28] Prior to the fifth century the evidence for a Roman ritual for

---

26. On sexual abstinence, see Schneiders, *Religious Life in a New Millennium*, 166. On spousal infidelity, see Cooper, *Virgin and the Bride*, 92–115. Rome's vestal virgins wore a sacred bridal dress; McGuire, "Vestal Virgins," 632–33.

27. An inscription found in the catacomb gallery is datable to 349; see Augusto Bacci, "Relazione degli scavi eseguiti in S. Agnese," *RQ* 16 (1902): 51–58; Ph. Schmitz, "La Première communauté de vierges à Rome," *RB* 38 (1926): 189–95. Serena, the earliest known abbess for Rome (d. 514), was buried behind the altar of S. Agnese.

28. Henri Leclercq, "Priscille (Cimetière de)," *DACL* 14/2 (1948), 1832 and fig. 10541. But Leclercq ("Viérge, Virginité," in *DACL* 15/2 [1953], 3094–3108 at 3105) recants, proposing a familial theme for the whole lunette. He still considers the young woman to be holding the formula of her virginal profession. Claude Dagens ("A Propos du Cubiculum de la 'Velatio,'" *RAC* 47 [1971]: 119–29) proposes that the fresco, now dated ca. 280, depicts three

FIGURE 4.1 Rome, Priscilla Cemetery. *Velatio* (ca. 280). Scala/Art Resource, NY.

the making of virgins, essentially a prayer of blessing and conferring of the veil, is slim.[29] The first account of such a ceremony, a papal privilege, is found in the veiling of Ambrose's sister Marcellina by Pope Liberius in Saint Peter's, Rome, in 352/353. Ambrose had already named Easter as an appropriate feast. Pope Siricius (384–399) added Epiphany to the Easter masses as appropriate for a virgin's *velatio* as *sponsa Christi*. To these highest of liturgical festivals Pope Gelasius (492–496) would add

---

different states-in-life of the same person: imposition of the *flammeum* (red, orange, or yellow veil with highlights) on the young Christian bride who holds the marriage contract; the deceased in heavenly beatitude; and the young mother and child.

29. Metz, *Consécration des vierges*, 124–38. See Ambrose, *De virginibus* 3.1–4 (*PL* 16, 231–33, with 345–48 for the oldest prayer of blessing). Cesare Alzati (*Ambrosianum Mysterium: The Church of Milan and Its Liturgical Tradition*, trans. George Guiver [2 vols.; Cambridge: Grove Books, 1999], 1:30–31) compiles references scattered through the Ambrosian literature. Jerome refers to the red veil imposed by the bishop (*Ep.* 130.2 [*PL* 22, 1108]). See esp., René Metz, "Benedictio sive consecratio virginum," *EL* 80 (1966): 265–93; Adrien Nocent, "The Consecration of Virgins," in Martimort, ed., et al., *The Church at Prayer*: vol. 3: *The Sacraments* (Collegeville, MN: Liturgical Press, 1988), 209–20; Ignazio M. Calabuig, in collaboration with Rosella Barbieri, "Consécration des vierges," in *Dictionnaire encyclopédique de la liturgie*, ed. Domenico Sartore and Achille M. Triacca (Turnhout: Brepols, 1992), 1:220.

the anniversaries of the apostles Peter and Paul as dates when bishops might bestow the sacred veil (*sacrum velamen imponant*).[30]

The spousal imagery of the bride-Church was appropriated early on for those who remained virgins for the sake of the kingdom. The preeminent symbol of the Roman marriage ceremony, the imposition of the veil, would shape the rite found in the Old Gelasian Sacramentary (Vat. Reg. lat. 316).[31] The episcopal ritual raised the symbol of the consecrated virgin to an exercise in self-reflection on the church's own nature.

C. Presbyteras and *Presbyterissae*

References of Eastern councils to presbyteras and *presbytides* (senior women) as well as epitaphs posed a conundrum for scholastic and humanist scholars.[32] It had been assumed by many that the terms *presbytera*, *presbiteria*, and the diminutive *presbyterissa* always referred to wives of those married men who, upon election to major church office, adopted a life of continence and were ordained presbyters.[33] With the Synod of Elvira in Spain sometime in the first decade of the fourth century, the drive for celibacy of higher clergy had picked up momentum. In Rome from the

---

30. "Venit Paschae dies, in toto orbe baptismi sacramenta celebrantur, velantur sacrae virgines" (Ambrose, *Exhortatio virginitatis*, PL 16, 364A). "Easter" included Easter Monday (Calabuig and Barbieri, "Consécration des vierges," 220). The imposition of the veil (*velatio*) sealing the vow of virginity is attested for Rome by Jerome, *Ep. 130 ad Demetriadem* (Metz, *Consécration des vierges*, 132, n. 29). The *flammeum* (yellow with red highlights) is not different from that worn by wives. On Pope Siricius, see PL 13:1182; Nocent, "Consecration of Virgins," 211, 212.

31. The Verona ("Leonine") Sacramentary gives us the "first liturgical formulary" (Nocent, "Consecration of Virgins," 212). The Gregorian (papal) Sacramentary contains these and additional prayers (Deshusses, *Sacr. grég.* 3:222–29). The consecration of virgins was added to Vat. Reg. lat. 316 when the presider's book for the Roman *tituli* was transcribed at Chelles (providing the only extant copy) at the end of the 7th or beginning of the 8th century (Chavasse, *Sacramentaire gélasien*, 28–35; Calabuig and Barbieri, "Consécration des vierges," 219–33).

32. Henri Leclercq ("Inscriptions latines chrétiennes," *DACL* 7/1 [1926], 694–850 at 768) gives examples.

33. The usage is unmistakable in Canon 20 (19) of the Council of Tours, AD 567: "Nam si inventus fuerit presbiter cum sua presbiteria aut diaconus cum sua diaconissa aut subdiaconus cum sua subdiaconissa, annum integrum excommunis habeatur et depositus ab omni officio clericali inter laicos se observare cognoscat...." See *Concilia Galliae a. 511–a. 695*, ed. Carlo de Clercq, 184; and Canon 21 of the diocesan synod of Auxerre, AD 561–605: "Non licet presbytero post accepta benedictione in uno lecto cum presbytera dormire nec in peccato carnali miscere" (ibid., 268).

time of Popes Damasus (366–384) and Siricius (384–399), the ordained husband and his wife were expected, following his ordination, to live as brother and sister or under separate roofs.[34] An undefined ecclesiastical status accrued to the wife in such "dead" marriages, since several councils stipulate that on the death of the husband the widow was not allowed to remarry.[35] Passing references in letters written by Pope Gregory the Great (590–604) represent a midpoint in the gradually developing requirement for separate domicile for such married couples.[36] On this tendentious issue examined only from the male perspective, Gregory remains the diplomat. But not every reference to a presbytera refers to such couples, either cohabitating or separated. Martimort notes a letter of Gregory the Great in which an abbess asserts her right to wear the dress of a presbytera rather than the monastic habit.[37]

---

34. Samuel Laeuchli, *Power and Sexuality: The Emergence of Canon Law at the Synod of Elvira* (Philadelphia: Temple University Press, 1972). See also Siricius, *Ad episcopos Africae epistola*, V.3 (*PL* 13:1160–61) and *Ad episcopos Galliae* X.2.5 (*PL* 13:1184). On Elvira, see Daniel Callam, "Clerical Continence in the Fourth Century: Three Papal Decretals," *TS* 41 (1980): 3–50 at 3, n. 2, and on the incorrect attribution to Damasus of the letter to the bishops of Gaul, see ibid., 36. See also Faivre, *Naissance d'une hiérarchie*, 313–18; Daniel Callam, "The Frequency of Mass in the Latin Church ca. 400," *TS* 45 (1984): 613–50 at 634–36. The effort to impose celibacy on the higher clergy was made unsuccessfully in the East at this time, where occasionally the general rule prohibiting marriage following ordination to the higher clergy was abrogated even for bishops.

35. A man must have married a virgin if he aspired to be ordained to the higher orders. Before his ordination the husband must have proved his ability to remain continent, e.g., for a year. Once the husband was ordained, a life of continence for the wife without hope of future marriage, even if widowed, was required.

36. Letter I.50 refers to wives of presbyters on the island of Corsica: "We wish furthermore that the priests who are staying in Corsica should be prohibited from living with women, except of course a mother, sister or wife (*uxor*), whose chastity should be preserved" (*The Letters of Gregory the Great*, trans. John R. C. Martyn [Toronto: Pontifical Institute of Mediaeval Studies, 2004], 1:175). Letter IX.111 addresses the issue with respect to bishops of Sicily: "And it has reached our ears that some of the bishops, under the specious pretext of a consolation, are living together with women in the same house.... And if any of the bishops enclosed by the borders of the patrimonies entrusted to you are living with women, you must stop this completely, and in no way allow those women to cohabit with them in future. The exceptions are those women permitted to do so by the judgment of the holy canons, namely a mother, an aunt, a sister and others of that sort, who could not arouse any improper suspicion.... But they do better if they restrain themselves from cohabiting even with women of his sister.... And indeed, we bind no one to this against his will.... Just add the fact that these bishops, as canonical authority has decreed, should not leave their wives, but should be chaste in controlling them" (ibid., 2:609–10). For the Latin, see *S. Gregorii Magni Registrum Epistularum*, ed. Dag Ludvig Norberg (2 vols.; CCSL, 140–140A; Turnhout: Brepols, 1982), 1:50, p. 64 (CCSL 140) and 9:111, pp. 663–64 (CCSL 140A).

37. Martimort, *Diaconesses*, 201, n. 18; Andrieu, *OR* 4:140. We do not know whether Syrica, abbess of the monastery of SS. Gavinus and Luxurius at Caralis (Cagliari), Sardinia, was continuing a tradition of women presbyters in that region or was a "deposed" (and widowed?) wife of a presbyter.

The possibility of a class of presbyteras in the formative periods of the Roman and Roman-influenced churches predating the establishment of the clerical cursus and official administrative machinery is worthy of consideration, since an elderly woman (ἡ πρεσβυτέρα, Shepherd of Hermas, e.g., Vision 2.1.3) figures large in the first part of the pietistic and popular Roman moral treatise *Shepherd*.[38] Reviewing key features established in chapter one, from internal evidence the book dates from the era of the presbyter-bishop Clement (ca. 96 CE) and again from the time of Pius I (ca. 140–150 CE).[39] This apocalypse has been attributed to Hermas, in the earliest texts identified with "Pastor," and one who exercised ineffectively the pastoral oversight of a house-church.[40] Origen wishfully identified its author with the Hermas referred to in Romans 16:14.[41] More popular in the East than the West, some ranked *Shepherd* among the Scriptures although it was not for public reading in church. Besides providing moral teaching, the work recommends penitence and presents the allegory of the Church as a tower in process of being built. Its revelations are made to Hermas, possibly a freed slave, failed businessman, and somewhat disenchanted husband, by Grapte, instructor of widows and orphans. This "senior lady" is a central figure in the first through fourth visions. She sits on a white chair (*cathedra*) and holds a book in her hand or reads out of it. Symbol of the Church, "created the first of all things" (Vision 2.4.1), Grapte counsels penance. Hermas is to teach the presbyters, Grapte the widows

---

38. The first four visions were probably written in Rome in the early second century; see Carolyn Osiek, *Rich and Poor in the Shepherd of Hermas: An Exegetical-Social Investigation* (Washington, DC: Catholic Biblical Association of America, 1983), 7. In the fifth vision an angel of penitence disguised as a shepherd appears. Forming the second and third sections of the work, commands and parables (similitudes) form a tapestry that displays the whole gamut of sinners and saints of the early church of Rome. See Quasten, *Patrology*, 1:92–105. On Hermas, see *Le Pasteur: Hermas; introduction, texte critique, traduction et notes par Robert Joly* (SC 53; Paris: Édition du Cerf, 1958); Osiek, *Shepherd of Hermas*. On specific questions, see Osiek, "Social Function of Female Imagery," 55–74. On the occurrences of *presbytera*, see Alastair Kirkland, "The Literary History of The Shepherd of Hermas Visions I to IV," *Second Century* 9 (1992): 87–102.

39. *Shepherd*'s dating in the formative period is indicated by the binitarian (two-person) theology, which includes the Father and the Spirit, the latter inhabiting the humanity of Christ; thus adopted, Christ is drawn into the trinitarian company.

40. Young, "Being a Man," 237–55.

41. The Muratorian Fragment (end of second or early third century) designated Hermas as the brother of Pius I: "And very recently in our own times, in the city of Rome, Hermas wrote *Shepherd*, when his brother Pius, the bishop, sat upon the chair of the city of Rome."

and orphans. Might she be the head of a house church for that group? As Hermas follows the presbytera's instructions she becomes progressively younger and by the fourth vision is youthful. It has been suggested that Grapte is an episcopa. If so, she would have been one of a college of presbyter-bishops since, until the later second century, the Roman church did not know the monarchical episcopacy.[42] The literary imagery of Grapte is most easily explained in terms of an office of presbytera-bishop.

(a) The Priscilla cemetery

The Priscilla cemetery enjoyed a high reputation among burial places found along the Via Salaria Antica and the Via Salaria Nova at the second mile north of the Roman gate, its name extended to several neighboring cemeteries until Giovanni Battista de Rossi (1822–1894) defined its limits.[43] As far back as Baronius, the Priscilla cemetery had been thought of as the locale for St. Peter's ministry in Rome. Nineteenth-century archeologists and writers dated catacombs as burial places for the Christian community and their frescoes a century or so earlier than what is accepted today. As recently as 1901 Priscilla was favored by Louis Duchesne and Orazio Marucchi as the apostolic center of early Christian Rome.[44] Three

---

42. Eisen (*Women Officeholders*, 208) cites Martin Leutsch's suggestion that Grapte was a Roman bishop. She goes on to make the case that, despite Rome's lack of a monarchical episcopate in this period, Grapte is bishop rather than deacon of the Roman church, both of which offices in *Shepherd* are "given primary responsibility for care of the widows." (There is no evidence for the office of diacona at this period in Rome.) Alone among the seven churches to whom he wrote, Ignatius of Antioch did not address the bishop of Rome, suggesting to Spence (*Parting of Ways*, 345) that this church had a "collegiate form of leadership." See also LP and the *Liberian Catalogue*, where the "pontificates" of Hyginus, Pius, and Anicetus overlap as though co-episcopates.

43. Leclercq, "Priscille (Cimetière de)," 1799–1874. The adjacent cemetery of the Giordani (Jordani) had been discovered and visited in 1578. Priscilla was entered in 1590 by Michele Lonigo. Graffiti in a number of cemeteries show that Giulio Pomponio Leto and members of the Roman Academy had already visited Callistus, Praetextatus, Priscilla, and Peter and Marcellinus in the 1460s (Osborne, "Roman Catacombs," 278).

44. The claim was made by Baronius in *Annales ecclesiastici* 1:460. Alfonso Chacon (1540–1599) "corrected" Baronius, asserting that the "Ostrianum, coemeterium majus ad nymphas S. Petri" on the Nomentana with its stone cathedrae was the "sedes sancti Petri" where the apostle baptized and preached. See Henri Leclercq, "Ostrien (Cimetière)," *DACL* 13/1 (1937), 112–30. From this point forward claims and counter-claims were made for apostolic use of various cemeteries, dwellings and churches. Orazio Marucchi (*The Evidence of the Catacombs for the Doctrine and Organisation of the Primitive Church* [London: Sheed & Ward, 1929], 91–92) gives an excessively apologetic, sacrament-centered interpretation. Marrucchi was a disciple of G. B. de Rossi, who had opted for the Ostrian cemetery as central to Peter's ministry.

hypogea (underground burial chambers) formed the nucleus of the later Christian cemetery, one at least associated with the senatorial Acili *gens* to which a certain Priscilla belonged.[45] One hypogeum was frescoed in the first half of the third century, two Greek inscriptions earning it the title "Greek Chapel" or "Cappella Greca." In the third and fourth centuries a lower level was dug out for Christian burials. Priscilla's galleries, cubicula, and Greek Chapel display an unusual number of female subjects of third-century date.[46] Two frescoes of high artistic quality continue to puzzle scholars.

(1) FRACTIO PANIS

The famous *Fractio panis* fresco spread across the major arch of the Greek Chapel in the Priscilla cemetery was discovered in 1893 and named by the priest-archeologist Joseph Wilpert (1857–1944), who, at first thinking the subject was the breakfast spread by Christ for seven of his disciples beside the sea of Tiberias (John 21) or the Samaritan woman at the well (John 4), then proposed its eucharistic character (Fig. 4.2).[47] Seven figures

---

45. Leclercq, "Glabrion (Manius Acilius)," 1259–74; Vincenzo Fiocchi Nicolai, "L'origine et le développement des catacombes Romaines," in Fiocchi Nicolai et al., *Catacombes chrétiennes*, [8]–69 at 22–23 and fig. 8B.

46. What has been thought to be the earliest depiction of Mary with the Christ-child and Balaam the prophet (but see Geri Parlby, "The Origins of Marian Art in the Catacombs and the Problems of Identification," in Maunder, *Origins of Cult of Virgin Mary*, 41–56); the Annunciation; three subjects featuring women (or the same woman) in the cubiculum of the *Velatio*; in the Greek Chapel the adoration of the Magi, the story of Susanna in three episodes, the raising of Lazarus with his sisters Martha and Mary, and the women in the *Fractio panis* on the major arch.

47. Josef Wilpert, *Fractio panis: Die älteste Darstellung des eucharistischen Opfers in der "Cappella Greca"* (Freiburg im Breisgau: Herder, 1895); French translation (Paris, 1896). The chapel's name derives from two inscriptions in Greek found during Wilpert's uncovering of the paintings on the walls. The chapel, known at least by the 1850s and dated from the 1st through 4th centuries, is now dated around 230–260 CE or the later third century (Bisconti in Fiocchi Nicolai et al., *Catacombes chrétiennes*, 126 and figs. 97, 110, 141). See Henri Leclercq's articles in *DACL*: "Agape," 1/1 (1907), 775–848, esp., the engraving made from a photograph (pl. 172, 799–800); "Cappella Greca," 2/2 (1910), 2084–2106; "Glabrion (Manius Acilius)," 1259–1274; "Ostrien (Cimetière)," 112–130; "Priscille (Cimetière de)," 1799–1874). Questions have been raised over the years about Wilpert's interpretation of catacomb evidence. The Greek Chapel is now so "restored" that conclusions about its original state can hardly be drawn. See the comments by Janet Tulloch, "Women Leaders in Family Funerary Banquets," in Osiek, MacDonald, and Tulloch, *A Woman's Place*, 164–93. On the "bearded" figure, see Dorothy Irvin, "The Ministry of Women in the Early Church: The Archaeological Evidence," *Duke Divinity School Review* 45/2 (Spring 1980), 76–86 at 83. Irvin's conclusions are contested by Kevin W. Irwin, "Archaeology Does Not Support Women's Ordination: A Response to Dorothy Irvin," *Journal of Women and Religion* 3/1 (1984): 32–42.

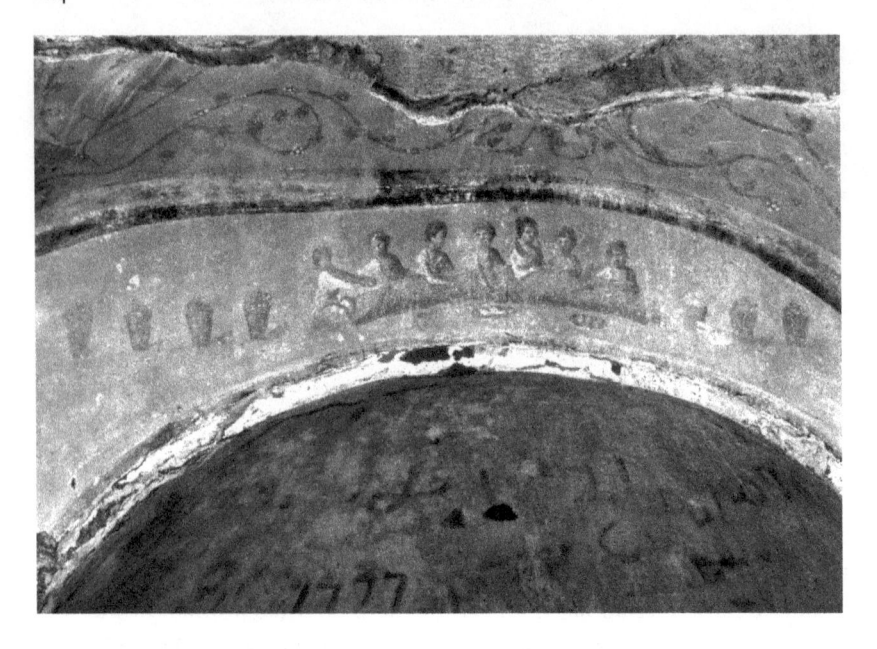

FIGURE 4.2 Rome, Priscilla Cemetery. *Fractio panis* (ca. 230–260). Scala/Art Resource, NY.

FIGURE 4.3 Rome, Priscilla Cemetery. Engraving after photograph of *Fractio panis*. *DACL* 1/1 (1907), pl. 172.

are gathered about a *stibadium* (*sigma*-shaped surface) or "picnic" cloth.[48] The seated figure on the far left extends both arms toward a goblet or cup located in front of the second and third figures. The other six figures are shown behind a rolled cushion, some extending an arm toward the center on which are placed two platters. Wilpert was most enthusiastic about the presence of a "bearded" figure at the far left "who presides" at the eucharistic meal. Wilpert noted only that the beard singled out this figure from the other six; he did not refer to the beardless figures and their hairdos, mentioning only the veiled figure third from the right, which has led some commentators to identify the subject as an agape meal. Henri Leclercq's article "Agape" is illustrated by an engraving made after a photograph of this very fresco (Fig. 4.3). Presuming an early date, Leclercq believes that "around the time that the fresco was made, the celebration of the eucharist was joined to the agape, and both were figured by the miracle of the multiplication, whose symbolism alone permits us to recognize here an agape followed by the eucharist in place of a simple funeral banquet." However, it is unlikely that in the third century the eucharist was still linked to the agape meal.[49] Two platters grace the center and right of the cloth, one holding one or two large fish, the second perhaps five loaves. On the arch to left and right of the main picture are baskets filled with loaves, respectively four and three baskets. The fresco has most frequently been identified as a funeral banquet (*refrigerium*) or agape meal (love feast).[50] In an important contribution that focuses on the late third- and fourth-century depictions of family funerary banquets in the Roman catacomb of SS. Marcellino e Pietro, Janet Tulloch adduces a number of points important

---

48. Seven was considered the ideal number to be seated at a sigma-table; see Andrew Brian McGowan, *Ascetic Eucharists: Food and Drink in Early Christian Ritual Meals* (Oxford: Clarendon, 1999), 132, and seven symbolizes temporal completion. Elisabeth Jastrzebowska analyzes the typology: "Les Scènes de banquet dans les peintures et sculptures chrétiennes des IIIe et IVe siècles," *Recherches Augustiniennes* 14 (1979): 3–90. The first type she catalogues is categorized as "I—Banquet scenes with 7 persons" (14–19). Jastrzebowska does not sufficiently distinguish between these sacred meals of the church and those showing the deceased at the banquet in paradise.

49. Henri Leclercq, "Agape," *DACL* 1/1 (1907), pl. 172, 799–801; see Frank C. Senn, "Agape," *NDSW*, 39–40.

50. The refrigerium or agape interpretation is preferred by C. Bernas, "Agape," in *NCE* 1 (2003), 169–71 at 170–71. On refrigeria and their social-cultural background, see McGowan, *Ascetic Eucharists*, 132–37. Fabrizio Bisconti ("Le décor des catacombes Romaines," in Fiocchi Nicolai et al., *Les Catacombes chrétiennes*, [70]–145 at 126) judges *Fractio panis* to be a simple funerary banquet. But the eucharistic symbolism of the loaves and fish must be accounted for within the typology of this scene.

for understanding the *Fractio panis* fresco. But she fails to note the specifically eucharistic elements that distinguish it from a non-eucharistic refrigerium.[51]

The typology—seven figures seated about a cloth with vessels in front of them, holding food and sometimes drink, but none of the figures raising cups and with no inscriptions—is well known from the simpler example in the Callistus Catacomb's "Chapel of the Sacraments," where all the participants are undoubtedly male.[52] Banquet scenes that are not placed in a specifically paradisal setting and do not contain overt eucharistic symbolism can be identified as "family funerary banquets"; typically but not necessarily, these contain both male and female figures. Depictions of the deceased ushered into the celebratory kingdom banquet are easily enough differentiated and may include both males and females.[53] Tulloch goes into some detail about the seating arrangements at Roman banquets. While there is still disagreement among scholars, by the third century the middle figure seated at the stibadium is most likely the guest of honor. In a refrigerium scene, this would be the deceased person. The person at the viewer's far left would then be the host.[54] Also of moment in the family refrigerium would be the person(s) holding a cup for a toast.[55] Is the meal depicted in the Greek Chapel a family funerary banquet or agape? Is it a symbolic depiction of the Lord's Supper in terms of a pagan custom "baptized" by Christians memorializing the deceased in a Christian eucharistic refrigerium? In fact the Greek Chapel with its elaborately stuccoed and painted walls includes as part of its architectural design a bench for refrigerium participants.

---

51. See Tulloch, in Osiek and MacDonald, *Woman's Place*, 164–93.

52. In Callistus the iconographical references are not only to the feeding of the multitude but also flanking scenes: on the left a man imposing hands on bread on a tripod table with an *orante* standing by; on the right the sacrifice of Isaac showing Isaac, Abraham, the ram, and the bundle of firewood, provide unmistakable corroboration for the reading of the central scene. For illustrations, see Fiocchi Nicolai et al., *Catacombes chrétiennes*, figs. 127, 132, 133.

53. A well-known pagan example, the induction and banquet scene of Vibia, is found in the hypogaeum of Vibia in Rome. See Tulloch in Osiek and MacDonald, *Woman's Place*, 180, fig. 8.6.

54. Ibid., 181.

55. Ibid., 181–83. Tulloch fails to distinguish between the artistic conventions that indicate a eucharist and those of a simple *refrigerium*. For examples of the cups, their inscriptions, and relationship to the banquet scenes, see ibid., 186–91.

In the Cappella Greca rendering, who are the seven figures? As opposed to the others who are shown reclining, the figure on the far left, seated *in cornu dextro*, is regularly designated as presider. Wilpert described the action as "breaking the bread"; some others have anachronistically used the term "consecrating." The figure is likely engaged in a prayer of thanksgiving over the contents of the large cup. Is this seated figure Christ? Is it Peter, prince of the apostles, who gives thanks? Is the figure bearded, or even male?[56] Third from the right, a veiled woman extends her right arm over the picnic cloth.[57] Is she a prophet (Wilpert, Irvin), or even the patron Priscilla, putative owner of the property on which burial sites and eventually this catacomb were constructed? Can she be considered the host? With respect to all the figures Irvin makes the case,

> The slope of the shoulders, feminine postures and jawlines, earlobes, breasts, and upswept hair-dos with forehead curls attest to the femininity of all those seated around the table, as do the long skirt and shadow of the breast below the outstretched arm of the woman on the far left. The woman third from right has sometimes been identified as a prophetess on the basis of her veil....The woman at the far left and the woman in the center have both arms outstretched toward the cup and plate in what is still familiar to

---

56. Cf. the "bishop" in the *cubiculum* of the *Velatio*, much more a "Peter-type." The engraving of "Fractio panis" made after a photograph used to illustrate H. Leclercq's article ("Agape," 799–800, pl. 172) shows no sign of a beard. On the issue of gender, Irvin ("Ministry of Women in Early Church," 81–84) develops her argument from hairdos (a point on which students of late antiquity often base dating) and skirts. The figure on the far left is a feminine type, Irvin says, and wears a full-length skirt (the skirt worn by male laborers was just above the knee, by male officials just below). The "halo" seems to be an addition and there is no apparent beard. Irvin notes that this precious fresco has been "restored" on a number of occasions and is now covered with plexiglas. See also Tulloch, in Osiek and MacDonald, *Woman's Place*, 295, n. 67. For more on the imaginative work of copyists and the difficulties inherent in illustrating material from the catacombs, see Henri Leclercq, "Copies des peintures des catacombes," *DACL* 3/2 (1914): 2801–19.

57. The *sigma/stibadium* dining arrangement originated with a set of cushions placed around a picnic cloth at banquets held out-of-doors (Katherine M. D. Dunbabin, "Triclinium and Stibadium," in *Dining in a Classical Context*, ed. William J. Slater [Ann Arbor: University of Michigan Press, 1991], 121–48). On seating arrangements in the Roman world of late antiquity, see Tulloch, in Osiek and MacDonald, *Woman's Place*, 181 and 294, n. 63. The veiled prophet or patron is not singled out in an other-worldly setting, as would be the case if showing her entrance into paradise (Tulloch, in Osiek and MacDonald, *Woman's Place*, 169, 181–82, and 294, n. 63). In the late second or early third centuries the arrangement was formalized for indoor meals, yielding a typology especially appropriate for depicting the feeding of the multitude.

us today as the gesture of consecration during the liturgy of the Eucharist.[58]

Irvin terms this "not a community Mass but an overnight eucharistic vigil held near the tomb on the anniversary of a Christian's death, her heavenly birthday," noting that other catacomb frescoes "show eucharistic groups of seven males, but no mixed groups for these vigils."[59] Her observations are germane, the most unacceptable aspect of Irvin's analysis being her dating of the fresco to shortly after 100 CE.[60] Other "eucharistic groups" of seven men, whether in a catacomb setting or on sarcophagi, are far simpler in iconography and less polished in style, lacking the individuation of the *Fractio panis* fresco.

To left and right of the Priscilla refrigerium meal, each of seven freestanding, see-through, wicker baskets contains round loaves of bread, clear references to Jesus' feeding of the multitude beside the Sea of Galilee. This feeding miracle, favorite of all gospel miracle stories, appears in all four gospels, with doublets in two and additional redactional references.[61] In each of its four primary versions the event takes on ever more eucharistic features. The *Fractio panis* in the Cappella Greca is laden with the

---

58. Quotations are taken from Dorothy Irvin, *Calendar 2003: The Archaeology of Women's Traditional Ministries in the Church 100 to 820 A.D*, January–February (St. Paul, MN: privately published). See also Irvin, "Ministry of Women," 81–84. Before Irvin, Joan Morris (*Lady Was a Bishop*, 8) identified the figures in this fresco on the basis of dress as "a group of women conducting a Eucharistic banquet" for a burial service. She thought that "in special circumstances, such as burial services, women were permitted to consecrate the Eucharist."

59. Dorothy Irvin ("Women Bishops and Priests in the Early Church: The Archaeological Documentation," a lecture at Women's Ordination Worldwide International Conference held in Ottawa, Canada, July 22–24, 2005) espied in front of the figures a cup and two plates holding bread (some others have seen a large fish on the second plate). Her identification of the gender of all the participants including the presider as female, based on hairdos and skirt length, is relatively convincing given the poor state of the fresco. For a discussion on gender-inclusive and yet gendered Christian table practice, see Teresa Berger, *Women's Ways of Worship: Gender Analysis and Liturgical History* (Collegeville, MN: Liturgical, 1999), 34–35.

60. Irvin's dating, common in popular books on the catacombs of the early twentieth century, is based on depictions of emperors' wives on coins. Epitaphs found in early hypogea on the Priscilla site and the "Pompeian red" background typical of the First Pompeian style of wall-painting were taken by scholars at the turn of the 19th–20th centuries as indicators of an early date.

61. Mark 6:30–44 and Mark 8:1–10; Matt 14:13–21 and Matt 15:32–39; Luke 9:10–17; John 6:1–15, with redactional forms in Mark 8:14–21 and Matt 16:5–12. The first or primary version (Mark and Matt) takes place shortly after the beheading of the Baptist. Five thousand are fed in the hills above the Sea of Galilee, with Matthew adding to his two accounts the telling

eucharistic symbolism that made Jesus' feeding of the multitude beside the Sea of Galilee, often referred to as the multiplication of the loaves and fish, the most frequently told miracle story in the gospels. Depicted is the second episode of Mark's and Matthew's telling (Mark 8:14–21 and Matt 16:5–12) in which the leftover fragments fill seven baskets.

Thanks to Justin Martyr's attempt to explain to Emperor Antoninus Pius the harmless character of the Christian sacramental ritual, we have the outline of a Sunday gathering 150/160 CE in a Roman house-church setting. Justin tells us that there is a presider but does not note any requisite gender. *Diakonoi* carry the sacramental food to those who cannot be present. There is no reason to read back into the second or third centuries the forms and functions of the Roman presbyteral office as it came to be systematized in the late fifth century. And when faced with a possible "women's eucharistic funerary meal" in the Priscilla cemetery's Greek Chapel, there is no reason to assume that the activities of a heterodox group are depicted. In the early period funeral rites were carried out at home and at the place of burial; not until the seventh century do we have texts for a Roman Christian funeral ritual.[62] The likeliest reading of the evidence identifies the *Fractio panis* fresco as a third-century Christian eucharistic funerary banquet celebrated by seven women.

(11) CUBICULUM OF THE *VELATIO*

The second fresco, in the cubiculum of the *Velatio*, now dated around 280–290 CE, is found in Priscilla's highest level (see above, Fig. 4.1).[63] The rich decoration of the entire room includes the three young men in the fiery furnace; the sacrifice of Isaac; a good shepherd in the vault; and peacocks as symbols of immortality. The identity of the subjects in the lunette under the arcosolium arch facing the entrance—on the left a group of three

---

aside, "besides women and children," a detail missing from all the other accounts. The picnic is repeated (Mark 8; Matt 15) with seven loaves and a few small fish for 4000 men, plus the women and children. The numbers fed and loaves left over in both episodes are repeated in the redaction of Mark 8:19–20 and in Matt 16:9–11. Luke has five loaves and two fish feeding 5000, with twelve baskets of leftovers; while John has 5000 men fed with five barley loaves and two fish, twelve baskets remaining. Bread and fish figure in the Johannine post-resurrection episode at the Sea of Tiberias (John 21:1–14).

62. Julia Upton, "Burial, Christian," in *NDSW*, 140–42.

63. See Tolotti, *Il cimitero di Priscilla*, 196–98, with a discussion of dating female figures—and thus the fresco—by hairdo. For an extended discussion of dating by hairdo in the Cappella Greca, see ibid., 266–74.

comprising two men and one woman; in the center a single female orant; and on the right a seated mother nursing her baby—remains disputed. Antonio Bosio (1575–1629) identified the figures in the *Velatio* lunette as members of the Pudens family.[64] Bosio proposed that the *orante* in the center was S. Priscilla Matrona, founder of the cemetery. Bosio saw in the puzzling triad on the left the virginal consecration of Praxedes or Pudentiana when she takes the sacred veil, *quando se le dava il sacro velo*. The woman wears a dull ochre overgarment and holds in her hand a flexible whitish object, not the yellow veil with red highlights that would be expected of bride or virgin.[65] The seated episcopal figure might be Peter, whose ministry in Rome, including that of baptizing and preaching, was popularly associated with cemeteries in this area and Priscilla's "baptismal" well; the head conforms to Petran typology. But if a Pudens daughter is depicted, the bishop would be Pius I and the standing male figure the presbyter Pastor. What would be his role here? The group on the right, Bosio believed, was the most holy Virgin with the Christ child in her arms (When Bosio wrote, the frescoes of the Greek Chapel were still centuries from being uncovered.)

Henri Leclercq had initially proposed that the left-hand picture depicts the veiling of a virgin by a bishop. In his 1948 article "Vièrge, virginité," Leclercq recanted, proposing a familial theme for the whole lunette. Nevertheless, Leclercq once again considered the young woman to be holding a roll containing the formula of her virginal profession.[66] Claude Dagens, who dated the *Velatio* lunette to the late third century, proposed that the frescoes depict three different states-in-life of the same person: imposition of the *flammeum* on the young Christian bride who

---

64. The clavi on the females' garments might support this identification. Antonio Bosio, "Columbus of the catacombs," left his name prominently displayed in many of the thirty catacombs he visited. The "literary history" of the Priscilla cemetery had re-commenced in 1590 with Bosio's explorations, published posthumously in two volumes: see Antonio Bosio, *Roma Sotterranea* (Roma: Guglielmo Facciotti, 1632). On the *Velatio*, see Pt. III, LXI, 549. By chance, he says, "this cubiculum was drawn by us on 16 January when the Santa Chiesa celebrates the *natale* of Santa Priscilla." (This was the martyr St. Prisca.)

65. Sandro Carletti (*Guide to the Catacombs of Priscilla*, trans. Alice Mulhern [Vatican City: Pontifical Commission for Sacred Archaeology, 1982], 17–18) describes the scene on the left as the bishop blessing the marriage of a young woman who holds a partially opened scroll, the Roman document outlining marriage duties; and the *flammeum* edged in red held by the young man.

66. Henri Leclercq, "Priscille (Cimetière de)," *DACL* 14/2 (1948): 1832 and fig. 10541; idem, "Vièrge, Virginité," *DACL* 15/2 (1953), 3105.

holds the marriage contract; the deceased in heavenly beatitude; and the young mother and child.[67] A *velatio virginis* would predate the first evidence of episcopal veiling and consecration of a virgin by nearly a hundred years, while the proposal regarding marriage presumes an ecclesial ceremony with episcopal involvement long before there is evidence of such.[68] In either case, marriage or virginal consecration, the *flammeum* (flame-colored veil) would be imposed.

Giving a strikingly different interpretation, Dorothy Irvin proposes that the lunette figures represent ecclesiastically ordered women.[69] The depiction on the left in which two men flank the central female figure wearing a "chasuble" over an alb and carrying what may be a "gospel scroll," the bishop's hand on her shoulder, would represent her sending forth.[70] The bishop is sending her forth (the *missio canonica* in Irvin's reading). A bishop (Petrine typology) is seated on a cathedra at the left, a grown male figure (an "acolyte" or deacon in Irvin's interpretation) stands close behind her. On this ritual *Apostolic Tradition* offers no information.[71]

---

67. Dagens, "A Propos du Cubiculum de la 'Velatio,'" 119–29. In another vein, Tolotti (*Cimitero di Priscilla*, 196) describes the scene as one of teacher and (female) pupil.

68. On marriage between Christians, J. Evenou ("Marriage," in Martimort et al., *Church at Prayer*, vol. 3: *Sacraments*, 185–91 at 187) states: "Until the Peace of Constantine, the only celebration of marriage that Christians experienced were these rites performed within the family." These included the imposition of the *flammeum*, a yellow veil with red highlights that was the mark of married women, and the reading of the marriage contract. Evenou observes: "[T]here is no evidence before the 4th century of the existence of a liturgical blessing or any participation of a priest in the marriage rites" (188).

69. Dorothy Irvin, *Calendar 2003* (March–April); Irvin, *Calendar 2005* (cover and May–June); and a public lecture "Women Bishops and Priests in the Early Church: The Archaeological Documentation," Women's Ordination Worldwide International Conference, 23 July 2005. It is unclear why Irvin dates this fresco 350+ CE. Scholars now agree on the 3rd century for those subjects presented in an impressionistic, painterly style. The overhead vault carrying one of the finest of all catacomb representations of the Shepherd ("pastor") is proposed by Irvin as an overt reference to ordination (*Calendar 2004* [May–June]). However, its primary meaning is salvation through Christ since the peacock, symbol of immortality, is found here with the prophet Jonah, the three young men in the fiery furnace, and Isaac whose sacrifice has been aborted, all subjects saved out of the jaws of death.

70. Around 280 CE sacred vestments were as yet unknown in Christian liturgy. Much later *Ordo* XXXIV (Rome around 700) lists the chasuble (*planeta*, a liturgical garment common to clerics) with stole as the garment in which an acolyte is vested. A subdeacon also wears the *planeta*. A deacon is vested in dalmatic over white tunic; if he is to be consecrated a presbyter, the dalmatic is removed and replaced by a chasuble (Bradshaw, *Ordination Rites*, 218–20, translated from Andrieu, *OR* 3:603–13).

71. However, the earliest ordination ritual we have, that in *AT*, may not be Roman. It did not know liturgical ministries for women. Written in Greek, the language of the Roman

The central figure in the lunette is best known: a short, powerful female *orante* surges upward, a Jewish prayer shawl *(talikh)* draped over her head. The dark-colored dalmatic with clavi identifies her, according to Irvin, as a woman deacon.[72] On the far right, balancing the enthroned bishop on the far left, is another enigmatic figure, a woman suckling a child; she is dressed like the bishop and enthroned on a cathedra.[73] Does she represent the maternal period of the entombed individual's life-cycle or is she the mother of Jesus? Irvin goes a step further than Antonio Bosio, identifying the woman as the enthroned Mary *episcopa*. Before dismissing Irvin's proposal for this lunette as representing a feminist agenda, it must be admitted that her explanation of any so far offered makes the most sense of one of the highest-quality painted catacomb frescoes of the pre-Constantinian period.

(b) The S. Pudenziana apse: presbyterae?

Christian Rome's oldest extant monumental mosaic fills the apse of the church of S. Pudenziana, down the hill from St. Mary Major's. The church was renovated from a Roman commercial building that had been built over ruins of domestic buildings dated by bricks 123–139 CE. The first textual references to the Pudentiana church date from 384. Sometime before 417 the shimmering apse mosaic of S. Pudenziana was created, perhaps as a thank-offering for its preservation during the assault on Rome by the Huns in 410. An imperial Christ in Majesty sits enthroned among the seated Twelve garbed as senators. Two untitled female figures wearing simple tunics and flowing golden *palla*, one end of which serves as a head-covering over a white frilled bonnet, take an active role in the midst of the apostolic college headed respectively by Paul and Peter (see chap. 1, Fig. 1.2).[74] The two women bestow crowns on the seated apostolic

---

Christian community in the 3rd century, its ordination prayers are first known in a 4th–5th century Latin text. The powerful female central figure is more likely an orante than a diacona.

72. Irvin, *Calendar 2004* (March–April).

73. Irvin, *Calendar 2005* (May–June). Fiocchi Nicolai, ("L'origine et le développement des catacombes romaines," in Fiocchi Nicolai et al., *Catacombes chrétiennes*, 44–45 and figs. 31, 44–45), notes that cathedrae found in several catacombs were part of the furniture used in connection with refrigeria in the post-Constantinian period. They may have served to symbolize the "invisible presence" of the deceased.

74. Only the figure on the left is mostly original; that on the right has been restored. As well the extremities of the mosaic were reduced and some apostles lost. Drawings show the

princes.[75] The question, "Who are these ministering women?" might evoke the response, "Of course they are consecrated virgins." The absence of the flammeum that St. Jerome (ca. 341–420) tells us was worn by consecrated Roman virgins argues against this as a primary identification. Their powerful and enigmatic presence and strategic positioning puzzles scholars. Summarizing scholarly theories, Frederic Schlatter discounts the hypothesis that the two women are Pudentiana and Praxedes, or that their *vita* was inspired by these two female portraits.[76] Identification as Pudens' two daughters had been favored by students of Roman mosaics prior to 1874, with the hypothesis taken up again by the priest-archeologist Joseph Wilpert in 1924.[77] Most modern commentators read back into these two female

---

mosaic's state in 1588; see Stephan Waetzoldt, *Kopien des 17. Jahrhunderts*, no. 1000, fig. 506, from Windsor, Inv. 9196). Walter Oakeshott (*Mosaics of Rome*, 65–67) discusses the original mosaic and the portions that have survived intact. In search of a prototype for these two figures and their meaning, a small, no longer extant mosaic that included two white-albed women (probably Constantina and her sister Helena) in the imperial mausoleum of S. Costanza (ca. 350) has been mentioned. Other unidentified women, singly or in pairs, are found especially in catacomb art, on sarcophagi, in the small-scale art of ivory-carving, and in little-known frescoes. Single female figures are often read as personifying the church. Fredric W. Schlatter ("Two Women," 8–9) discusses the female orant as an allegorical representation vs. Theodor Klauser's view that the *orante* represents the soul of the deceased praising God or "the actual likeness of the deceased" (ibid., n. 25). For the broad picture, see Giorgio Otranto, "Tra letteratura e iconografia: note sul Buon Pastore e sull'Orante nell'arte cristiana antica (II-III secolo)," *VetChr* 26 (1989), 69–87; repr. in *Annali di storia dell'esegesi* 6 (1989), 15–30. A recent study supports the ecclesial symbolism (Daniela Goffredo, "Le personificazioni delle ecclesiae: tipologia e significati dei mosaici di S. Pudenziana e S. Sabina," in Federico Guidobaldi and Alessandra Guiglia Guidobaldi, eds., *Ecclesiae urbis: Atti del Congresso internazionale di studi sulle Chiese di Roma (IV–X secolo), Roma, 4–10 settembre 2000* [3 vols.; Vatican City: PIAC, 2002], 3:1949–62). Goffredo points to the pagan models of *pietas* and *philanthropia* with their special affinity to the "new condensed figures of *orante* and *buon pastore*" as well as to the S. Sabina door panel showing Peter and Paul acclaiming a female figure (Mary? the Church?) by holding a wreath over her head.

75. *Aurum coronarium*, the "golden crown," was a gift given on a special occasion by the populace to a general, senators, or the emperor. The gifts of the magi to the infant Christ and the golden crowns which the 24 elders of Revelation offer to the enthroned Lord are the two best-known Christian examples (Theodor Klauser, "Aurum coronarium," in Klauser, ed., *Reallexikon für Antike und Christentum: Sachwörterbuch zur Auseinandersetzung des Christentums mit der antiken Welt* [29 vols., Stuttgart: A. Hiersemann, 1950–1978], 1:1010–20). The two women do so under the authority of Christ seated in majesty (Fredric Schlatter, "Two Women," 23 and n. 69).

76. Schlatter ("Two Women," 3) cites Giuseppe Bovini ("I mosaici della chiesa di S. Pudenziana à Roma," *CARB* 18 [1971]: 95–113 at 104) for some of the more unlikely interpretations. If following F. Guidobaldi's dating, the *vita* could have inspired the two female figures.

77. Schlatter, "Two Women," 7 and n. 1.

figures the typology of the two standing figures at S. Sabina a scant decade or two later, whose titles "Church from the Circumcision" and "Church from the Gentiles" identify them as personifications of the Jewish and Gentile churches or assemblies of first-century Christianity (Gal 2:1–9). But are the two women of the Pudenziana mosaic really iconographical ancestors of the two S. Sabina matrons?

If we follow the hypothesis preferred by antiquarians, Praxedes is the female figure on the viewer's left, Pudentiana on the right.[78] In S. Pudenziana the typology is unmistakable. As almost everywhere in Rome, Paul is at Christ's right hand.[79] In the story Punicus Pudens is Peter's patron. In the mosaic Peter and Pudentiana the older sister are located on the viewer's right, close to the title DOMINUS CONSERVATOR ECCLESIAE PUDENTIANAE, "The Lord protector of the faith-assembly of Pudens," written in *capitalis quadrata* script on the pages of the book opened on Christ's lap. At the head of the apostles on Christ's right hand is Paul; it follows that the female figure in proximity to him is the younger sister Praxedes. Paul and Praxedes are close by the majestic Lord whose right hand, with index and third finger held together, is raised in the characteristic teaching gesture.

Schlatter proposes, in a complex argument inspired by Jerome's commentary on Ezekiel written 410–414, that the "pair of women...are the worthy partners of priests," and that the virgin "in her person embodies the newly revealed riches of that sapiential wisdom described in Proverbs and Wisdom."[80] Telling against Schlatter's theory is the fact that the Twelve

---

78. Earlier opinions are summarized by Henri Leclercq, "Pudentienne (Basilique de Sainte-)," *DACL* 14/2 (1948), 1967–73 at 1971–72. In his detailed review of the literature, Schlatter ("Two Women," 7, n. 18) notes that in 1924 Josef Wilpert (*Die römischen Mosaiken und Malereien der kirchlichen Bauten vom IV. bis XIII. Jahrhundert* [4 vols.; Freiburg im Breisgau: Herder, 1924], 4:312) returned to the Pudentiana and Praxedes hypothesis. Walter N. Schumacher's revision and republication of Wilpert's work under the title *Die Römischen Mosaiken der kirchlichen Bauten vom IV–XIII Jahrhundert* (Freiburg im Breisgau: Herder, 1976) takes the S. Costanza figures as depicting the two Constantinian princesses buried there, while accepting the Praxedes-Pudentiana identification for the S. Pudenziana mosaic.

79. Gold glasses dated to the 4th century in the Biblioteca Apostolica Vaticana collection show Peter on the viewer's left and Paul on the right, usually without bust or figure of Christ (von Matt, *Art Treasures of the Vatican Library*, figs. 45, 47, 48; catalogue of the exhibition held in Rome during the millennial jubilee *Pietro e Paulo: La storia, il culto, la memoria nei primi secoli*, ed. Angela Donati [Milan: Electa, 2000], cat. nos. 85, 86, 87, 89, 91, 93, 94; exceptions with Christ or christogram nos. 90, 92). At S. Costanza (ca. 350) the *Traditio legis* in the eastern niche has Peter on Christ's left, Paul at Christ's right, allowing Christ to hand the Law to Peter.

80. Schlatter, "Two Women," 21.

sit, not as priests of the Old or New Testaments or even of the church as New Jerusalem, but as senators. The mosaic represents the eschatological period when Christ reigns in glory and the Twelve sit as judges of the twelve tribes of Israel (Matt 19:28, Luke 22:30).[81] To describe, as Schlatter does, the women as priestly consorts of either the two princes of the apostles or of this whole company involves an extreme symbolic and speculative leap. The garb of the women is drawn from life—note the ruffled bonnet worn by the woman on the left.[82] The golden cloak whose end forms her veil shares the color of glory of Christ's vesture.[83] The gesture of offering crowns may provide the key to the figures' meaning. Like those elders of the apocalypse who, in later apse and façade mosaics, will offer their crowns to the victorious Christ returning in majesty at the end of time, these women too are "senior women," *presbyterae* or *presbytides* connected to the church in whose apse they are depicted. They are the first Christian elders of either sex to be depicted on a monumental scale. Fittingly, they are members of the senatorial Pudens clan whose second-century house lay below the church floor and whose aristocratic status was shared with the apostolic council.

(c) "Crispina" and sarcophagi with typology of female teachers and philosophers

A number of fourth-century sarcophagi, held in the Lateran collection and now housed in the Vatican's Museo Pio-Cristiano, display traditional female types of teachers and philosophers. The type of the teacher features a frontally sculpted female as the central figure with two fingers pointing at a book or with a *capsa* containing scrolls at her feet. The

---

81. The iconography is well established in catacomb art, e.g., Christ enthroned between Sts. Paul and Peter (in Sts. Marcellinus and Peter; see Fabrizio Bisconti, "Les décor des catacombes romaines," 131, no. 144 in Fiocchi Nicolai et al., *Catacombes chrétiennes*), or the apostolic college in the millers/bakers' (*pistores*) cubiculum, Domitilla (ibid., 87, fig. 95).

82. In the well-known arcosolium fresco in the Domitilla catacomb (after 356), the figure labelled Veneranda (Fig. 4.8) wears a similar ruffled bonnet (*mitella*). See Fabrizio Bisconti, "Les décor des catacombes romaines," 130, fig. 143; Umberto Maria Fasola, *The Catacombs of Domitilla and the Basilica of the Martyrs Nereus and Achilleus*, ed. Philippo Pergola; trans. C. S. Houston and F. Barbarito (3rd ed.; Vatican City: PCAS, 2002), 42, fig. 9; also Irvin, *Calendar 2004* (September–October).

83. The *palla* is the feminine version of the classical pallium, originally a rectangular piece of white linen, its length three times its width. See Marguerite Gautier-van Berchem and Etienne Clouzot, *Mosaïques chrétiennes*, xlix.

FIGURE 4.4 Vatican, Museo Pio-Cristiano. Crispina. Detail, sarcophagus cover (4th century). Photo Vatican Museums.

teacher can be distinguished from the philosopher-type, who, with hands raised waist-high in a limited *orans* pose, exemplifies the Roman virtue of *pietas*. Imaginative use of the basic typology of the teacher in favor of a specific individual is found in a section from the cover of a sarcophagus now housed in the controlled section of the Vatican's Museo Pio-Cristiano (Fig. 4.4).[84] A bowed, elderly female figure in a life-like three-quarter pose holds a gospel book inscribed with the Chi Rho. Most unusually, her name "Crispina" is carved in the lower right field within the arcade. Evidently this is a made-to-order sarcophagus lid for a woman of considerable repute who holds church office. On stylistic grounds she can be dated to the fourth century. We do not know of diaconas in Rome at this period; is Crispina with her age and attribute not a presbytera?[85]

---

84. For possible sources of the typology, see Goffredo, "Personificazioni delle Ecclesiae," 1949–62, although I propose another conclusion than hers regarding women as personifications of the church.

85. Profs. Cettina Militello and Crispino Valenziano, who alerted me to Crispina's existence, judge that she was a presbytera. This is the likeliest office if one accepts my argumentation for women's offices existing in Rome in the first five centuries.

(d) The Pola casket

Carvings on an ivory reliquary casket dated circa 440/450, its provenance surely Roman, show what I believe to be women presbyteras not in the obscurity of baptistery alcove, funereal commemoration, or the women's world of conventual life, but rather in full view within Roman patriarchal basilicas. The Pola casket, discovered in the village of Samagher outside the old city of Pola (Pula, Istria), is now in the Museo Archeologico, Venice (Fig. 4.5).[86] This remarkably detailed carving has been accepted by architectural historians as an authentic depiction of the early fifth-century state of the Petrine *memoria* and its architectural elaboration in the transept at the west end of Old St. Peter's, begun under Constantine circa 333.[87] The cover features the *Traditio legis*. The front panel shows six apostles acclaiming the Lamb; then clockwise a probable baptism; the offering of a golden cross at Peter's shrine by a man and a woman; and the presentation of a boy-oblate to the church. Three of the five scenes show paired men and women flanking central baptismal and *oblatio* scenes. I consider both men and women to be clergy because, with the exception of the women's veils, their location, garments, and poses are alike.

FIGURE 4.5 Venice, Museo Archeologico. Samagher Casket, rear panel, Old St. Peter's (ca. 430–440). Scala/Art Resource, NY.

The rear panel shows six figures standing in the interstices between the famed spiral columns, which are carved in alternating segmented patterns

---

86. Tillmann Buddensieg ("Coffret en ivoire de Pola," 157–95) argues for the casket's Roman manufacture ca. 440.

87. See Toynbee and Ward-Perkins, *Shrine of St. Peter*, fig. 17; Krautheimer, *Early Christian and Byzantine Architecture*, pl. 8a; *Pietro e Paolo*, ed. Donati, cat. 95 and color plate p. 170.

of strigil or vine scroll. Arranged as an open barrier in a rectangle around the Petrine aedicula and as a link to the apse walls, the spiral columns carry a classical entablature. Accentuating the importance of the shrine that rises through the floor, a corona hangs from arches that spring diagonally from the corner columns surrounding the memoria. In the center of the relief, framed by the arch of the apsidal wall, two small cloaked figures are evidently intended to appear at a greater distance from the viewer than the four who stand on steps at the head of the aisles.[88] Anna Angiolini has summarized scholarly identifications of the two central figures, ranging from Peter and Paul to a marriage ritual, adoration of the cross, or a woman holding aloft a *brandea* as spouses visit the shrine of Peter.[89] Close inspection reveals that a man and woman gesture toward or support a cross. Not a eucharistic liturgy is depicted, but rather a couple's solemn offering. Do we not see Constantine and his mother Helena placing at Peter's *memoria* their gift of one of the golden crosses bestowed by them on the shrines of Peter and Paul?[90]

The four figures flanking the Constantinian shrine have not elicited much scholarly comment. They are two men and two women. Not noting their genders, W. Eugene Kleinbauer identified them as four priests.[91] The

---

88. Old St. Peter's was a westward-oriented five-aisled basilica with western transept terminated by a shallow apse on the major axis. An inscription in St. Peter's makes it "clear that the left was the men's side of the church" (Thomas F. Mathews, "An Early Roman Chancel Arrangement," *RAC* 38 [1962], 73–95); de Blaauw, *Cultus et Decor*, 2:504 and n. 71. The Constantinian shrine to St. Peter rose on the chord of the apse. This shrine, which determined the orientation of the martyrial basilica, was lost to sight when Gregory I (590–604) raised the floor level and placed a fixed altar directly over it. The remnant of the Petrine shrine is still buried under the present high altar.

89. Anna Angiolini, *La capsella eburnea di Pola* (Studia di antichità; Bologna: Riccardo Pàtron, 1970), 12–30.

90. "Then the emperor Constantine built <at bishop Silvester's request> a basilica to St. Peter the Apostle, at the temple of Apollo, where he buried the tomb with St. Peter's body in this way: the actual tomb he sealed on all sides with copper to make it immovable, 5 ft. each at the head, the feet, the right and left sides, the bottom and the top; thus he enclosed St. Peter's body and buried it. Above he decorated it with porphyry columns and other vine-scroll columns which he brought from Greece. He also built the basilica's apse-vault shining with gold-foil; and over St. Peter's body, above the bronze in which he had sealed it, he provided a cross of finest gold weighing 150 lb., made to measure; on the cross itself is written in <fine> nielloed letters: CONSTANTINE AUGUSTUS AND HELENA AUGUSTA. HE SURROUNDS THIS HOUSE WITH A ROYAL HALL GLEAMING WITH EQUAL SPLENDOUR (biography of St. Silvester, from Davis, *Book of Pontiffs*, 16). In ch. 18 we are told that, among the many furnishings of precious metals donated by the emperor, a gold crown (chandelier) "with 50 dolphins, weighing 35 lb." hangs "in front of the body." On the St. Paul's cross, see Davis, *Book of Pontiffs*, 21.

91. W. Eugene Kleinbauer, "The Orants in the Mosaic Decoration of the Rotunda at Thessaloniki: Martyr Saints or Donors?" *CA* 30 (1982): 25–45 at 36, 38. Angiolini (*Capsella*

two orant women stand before the curtains (*vestes*) suspended from two of the spiral columns to face the women assembled in the north aisles. Their arms are extended in the same gesture of public prayer and the locale corresponding to the two similarly garbed men who face the men gathered in the south aisles. Whereas the section on the left side of the Petrine *aedicula* is missing and hence the men's *paenula* from the hip to the relief's bottom edge, the figures of the two women are preserved intact. They wear a short flowing *palla* over a tight-sleeved *tunica talare* (ankle-length tunic). The *palla*, like a short chasuble, is wrapped about the shoulders to fall just below the waist.[92] The men are bareheaded, the women veiled, wearing what A. Angiolini has described as the *credemnon*.[93] They "stand in front" of the women's (north) side, the *matroneum*, of the westward-oriented St. Peter's to lead prayer while men, their mirror-images, stand at the head of the opposite aisles, the *senatorium*. Each figure appears to be actively directing with *orans* gesture the prayer of the populace gathered in the corresponding aisle. The analogy that comes to mind is that of the deacon in the Byzantine Divine Liturgy, who emerges from behind the iconostasis, where he has been assisting the priest, to lead the people in liturgical acclamations. But we have four clergy, not one, all shown in a pose that invites to prayer. The event, it would seem, is not a formally liturgical one but may represent a liturgy of the word incorporating a solemn offering.

The casket's damaged cover displays the *Traditio legis* and the front shows an early etimasia (throne) type with six apostles in front of date

---

eburnea di Pola, 12–14) carefully describes the four figures, noting that those on the rear of the casket stand frontally rather than acting as observers and supporters of the central action. She summarizes previous commentators. A. Gnirs ("La basilica ed il reliquario d'avorio di Samagher presso Pola," *Atti e memorie della Società istriana di archeologia e storia patria* 24/2 [1908]: 36) thought that the four figures ("believers") flanking the shrine alluded symbolically to the Church. J. Wilpert (*Atti e memorie della Società istriana*, 149) proposed that the two *paenulati* and the two women represent respectively the "clergy" and the "devoted female sex," that is, virgins and holy widows; Theodor Klauser (*Die römische Petrustradition im Lichte der neuen Ausgrabungen under der Petruskirche* [Cologne and Opladen: Westdeutscher Verlag, 1956], 111) describes briefly the doublets of males and females and makes them companions in prayer with those active in the center of the relief.

92. Patrizia Angiolini Martinelli, "Il costume femminile nei mosaici ravennati," in *CARB* 16 (1969): 7–64 at 43, cited by Angiolini, *Capsella eburnea di Pola*, 12, n. 16.

93. According to Angiolini (*Capsella eburnea di Pola*, 12), these women wear the veil over the *credemnon*, a head scarf "which covered the face up to the eyes, and fell over the neck and back in folds" (Caroline M. Galt, "Veiled Ladies," *AJA* 35 [1931]: 373–93 at 379). Liddell & Scott's *Greek-English Lexicon* (1968) describes the *credemnon* more generically as a woman's head-dress or veil, a kind of mantilla, which was a separate head cloth not formed by the end of the garment which covered the shoulders.

palms, acclaiming the cross enthroned and the Lamb. Both subjects are connected with Old St. Peter's. On the sides and rear of this well-preserved casket twinned doublets of similarly dressed men and women are found. On the left side, perfectly preserved, are two men and two women dressed as already described. With expressive gestures of the hand they flank and support the central scene in which a cleric opens a grilled and curtained doorway to admit a young child-oblate brought by his mother to be educated for the service of the church. The mother holds in her left hand a rotulus documenting the oblation.[94] On the casket's right side a badly damaged panel shows a polygonal roof richly decorated with scrolls and palmettes, carried on a carved entablature supported by columns. Male and female ministers stand on either side to witness to and affirm the event taking place in the central panel, where only the female figure on the right has survived. Is this setting not intended to represent the Lateran Baptistery built by Constantine? Where the cover and front of the casket exhibit well-known official iconography from St. Peter's, the panels on left, rear, and right contain familial references and show gender parity among clergy.

Is this casket a wealthy family's souvenir of sacred places in the Eternal City and the baptism and dedication of a child to the service of the church? It might well have held *brandea*, linen cloths lowered down the grave-shaft to touch the bones of blessed Peter. The Pola reliquary casket affords a glimpse of ministry in Roman ecclesial contexts toward the mid-fifth century, a period when evidence for women deacons is lacking except for an archdeaconess in question at St. Paul's. These three panels reinforce data from other sources indicating that the presbyteral office in the early fifth century rendered collaborative assistance to the bishop in the patriarchal and titular churches, help which included the leading of prayer.

D. Teachers of Scripture and Theology

Since rabbi ("teacher") was the title most often applied to Jesus during his earthly ministry, it is no surprise that the function of teaching was one of the most important ministries in the fledgling Christian communities. Of the eight lists of charismatic services found in the Christian

---

94. The Lateran palace was the seat of the Roman pontiff and a likely place for clerical education; Popes Gregory II, Leo III, and Paschal I would be educated there.

Scriptures, 1 Corinthians 12:8 opens with a word ministry ("word of wisdom," "word of understanding"), and three other lists name the office of teacher. First Corinthians 12:28–29 puts the office of teacher in third place after apostle and prophet. Romans 12:6–8 likewise lists the teacher third, after prophet and minister. Rome's two imposing extant mosaics of the first third of the fifth century that feature pairs of women—the apse of S. Pudenziana and the interior rear wall of S. Sabina—invite the question whether there existed at this formative period Roman ecclesiastical offices of widow or teacher or presbytera, all potential teaching offices, possibly indicated by distinctive garb.[95]

(a) S. Agnese on the Nomentana
The office of teacher held by a woman is known from the complex on the Via Nomentana, two kilometers northeast of the Porta Pia gate, which memorializes the innocent young Agnes (d. ca. 303) martyred under Diocletian. The site of the revered Agnes' burial had been marked by a great covered cemetery, the largest ambulatory basilica known, to which was attached the mausoleum-chapel of Constantine's daughter Constantina.[96] On its north side the atrium of the cemetery basilica is connected to a wide stairway that led down to the catacomb tomb containing the relics of the martyred innocents Agnes and her foster-sister Emerentiana. On the walls of this wide stairway have been placed slabs, fragments, and even an altar from the early shrine, catacomb, and cemeterial monuments.[97]

---

95. For a discussion of how the "two Roman matrons" can represent the converted churches of the Jews and Gentiles, as well as other questions, see Olaf Steen, "The Apse Mosaic of S. Pudenziana and Its Relation to the Fifth Century Mosaics of S. Sabina and S. Maria Maggiore," in Guidobaldi, *Ecclesiae urbis* 3:1939–48.

96. The ambulatory basilica was built by Constantina probably between 337 and 351. The extant round mausoleum known as S. Costanza's was built as a tomb ca. 355 for Constantina and her sister Helena and was attached to the south wall of the huge basilica, whose dirt floor was stacked with graves of the devout. See Krautheimer, *Early Christian and Byzantine Architecture*, 41–43; Hugo Brandenburg, *The Basilica of S. Agnese and the Mausoleum of Constantina Augusta (S. Costanza)*, offprint from Brandenburg, *Ancient Churches of Rome from the Fourth to the Seventh Century: The Dawn of Christian Architecture in the West*, trans. Andreas Kropp (Regensburg: Schnell und Steiner, 2006).

97. Augusto Bacci, "Ulteriori osservazioni sulla basilica nomentana," *Nuovo Bullettino di archeologia cristiana* 12 (1906): 77–87; J. P. Kirsch, "Anzeiger für christliche Archäologie," *RQ* 16 (1902): 78–80. For an engaging interpretation of the "idea" of the S. Agnese complex, see Margaret Visser, *The Geometry of Love: Space, Time, Mystery, and Meaning in an Ordinary Church* (Toronto: HarperCollins, 2000).

Dated 382, a laudatory epitaph for Magistra Theodora was commissioned by her husband Evacrius.[98] Theodora is epitomized in her tomb-poem as "best keeper of the law" and "best keeper of the faith." Each attribute complements the other, the former indicating that she interpreted Scripture according to its exhortations, the latter pointing to her role as catechist.[99] This same stairway would become the entrance to the splendid galleried basilica, built by Pope Honorius I (625–638), whose presbytery was located over the saint's tomb.

(b) S. Sabina on the Aventine

By the later fourth century, as Elizabeth Castelli notes, widowed "women of the Roman aristocracy pursued the genteel form of home asceticism without renouncing their wealth, though diverting it from the standard route of inheritance."[100] With the help of servants they could emulate the well-known philosophical circle by hosting a salon for the laudable purpose of discussion of scriptural and theological matters. Social status and wealth, even when renounced, undergird their monastic foundations and leadership when a number of these women go into voluntary exile in the Holy Land.[101]

The epigraphically attested title of teacher for a Roman woman of the late fourth century, and the possible personalization of the two female

---

98. Eisen (*Women Officeholders*, 93–96) cites the tomb epitaph that is affixed to the wall beside the stairs descending to the church of S. Agnese.

99. Eisen (*Women Officeholders*, 93–95 with general commentary 100–103) cites *Inscriptiones christianae urbis Romae* (*ICUR* 1:317 [*Supplementum* 1703]) and *Inscriptiones Latinae Christianae Veteres* (*ILCV*) 1:316 (Vol. 5: *Nuove Correzioni alla Silloge del Diehl Inscriptiones Latinae Christianae Veteres*, ed. A. Ferrua [SSAC 7; Vatican City: PIAC, 1981], 12); Madigan and Osiek, *Ordained Women*, 100, n. 71.

100. Castelli, "Virginity and its Meaning," 83. For detailed studies, see Anne Yarbrough, "Christianization in the Fourth Century: The Example of Roman Women," *Church History* 45 (1976): 149–65; Elizabeth A. Clark, "Theory and Practice in Late Ancient Asceticism: Jerome, Chrysostom and Augustine," *JFSR* 5 (1989): 25–46. As for widows who are recognized as constituting an *ordo* or "order" in the church, in the 7th century one of the solemn orations for Good Friday prays for "...confessors, virgins, widows and for the entire holy people of God."

101. Clark, "Authority and Humility: A Conflict of Values in Fourth-Century Female Monasticism," in *Byzantinische Forschungen* 9 (1985) 17–33; repr. in Clark, *Ascetic Piety and Women's Faith*, 209–28. Those aristocratic men who embraced the ascetic life, perhaps following marriage and a worldly career, tended to do so with a studied leisure different from that chosen by women ascetics.

![S. Sabina mosaic inscription]

FIGURE 4.6 Rome, S. Sabina. Interior rear wall: *Ecclesia ex circumcisione, Ecclesia ex gentibus* (ca. 422–432). The Bridgeman Art Library.

figures in the S. Pudenziana apse from the first two decades of the fifth, suggest the usefulness of revisiting the two female figures in the wall mosaic on the interior façade of the church of S. Sabina, built and decorated 422–432 on the Aventine hill (Fig. 4.6). S. Sabina is a well-preserved and carefully restored product of the Sistine renaissance. The extant portion of what was a much larger mosaic on the inside west wall above the door shows two imposing matrons dressed as widows standing on either side of the donor's dedicatory *capitalis quadrata* inscription.[102] Ciampini's late seventeenth-century sketch shows the higher portion that is now missing. Two male figures, apparently Peter and Paul, each with hand raised in a teaching gesture, were turned toward the center, which already was empty when Ciampini sketched it.[103] In the highest register on the far left, the hand of God held a book, while in the spandrels of an arcade design forming the top border, the symbols of the heavenly creatures, the winged ox, lion, eagle and man, all without books, appeared.[104] The two senior matrons,

---

102. Walter Oakeshott, *Mosaics of Rome*, 89–90 and pl. 74. Are they iconographic relatives of the two ecclesial women presenting crowns in the slightly earlier S. Pudenziana apse mosaic? This assumption is discussed and dismissed by Schlatter, "Two Women," 1–10.

103. Schlatter, "Two Women," fig. 2.

104. Giovanni Giustino Ciampini, *Vetera monimenta in quibus praecipuè musiva opera sacrarum, profanarumque, aedium structura, ac nonnulli antiquiritus, dissertationisbus, iconibusque illustrantur* (2 vols.; Rome: Komarek, 1690), 1, tabula 48, reproduced in Schlatter, "Two Women," fig. 1. It has been asked whether the upper part of the wall mosaic dates from a later period, but the archaic character of the then-extant figures, sketched by Ciampini, argues for 5th-century dating. The single standing figures of Peter (on the left) and Paul (right) correspond with the matrons' titles "Church from the Circumcision" and "Church from the Gentiles." We do not know whether the figure of Christ was part of the composition.

formally titled in *capitalis quadrata* script "Church from the Circumcision" and "Church from the Gentiles," are related to the apostolic princes and, given their titles, personify the "churches" founded by Peter and Paul.[105] But there is more. Monumental size, prominent location, and distinctive vesture designate these women as holders of ecclesial office. They stand in a restful pose with a slight contrapposto, bringing to mind the door-keeping role ascribed to deaconesses in *Apostolic Constitutions*. This diaconal duty noted in Eastern church orders does not license us to import lists of official duties from abroad without evidence that they apply in the new cultural milieu.[106] Within the century, Roman lectionaries will select Solomon's ode to a capable (better, "strong") wife (Prov 31:10–31) for the common of feasts of holy women including Sabina. The closing line, "Let her works praise her in the city gates," is resonant of these women's placement above the fifth-century basilica's inner doors.[107]

Each matron wears a dark violet-brown tunic (the dress of widows) with broad black *clavi* (senatorial insignia) and a *palla* draped around the shoulders so that one of the ends serves as a veil to cover the white-coifed head.[108] A white under-tunic shows as a collar at the neck.

---

105. In conjunction with his theory regarding the source and identification of the two female figures in the apse mosaic of Santa Pudenziana, Schlatter ("Two Women," 1–24 at 4–5 and fig. 2) discusses them briefly.

106. Deaconesses in some Eastern churches were the Christian equivalent of "the women who served at the entrance to the tent of meeting" (Exod 38:8). *Didascalia Apostolorum* did not include door-tending among the duties of female deacons (see *Liturgical Portions of Didascalia*, ed. Brock and Vasey, ch. 16, 22–23) but stationed a male deacon at the door (ibid., ch. 12, 16). However, *Testamentum Domini* I.19 (Asia Minor or Syria, before 381?) located the deaconesses "near the door of the Lord's house" (Sperry-White, *Testamentum Domini*, 47). *Apostolic Constitutions* VIII.2.11 (Antioch, late 4th century?) situated the subdeacons by the men's doors and the female deacons by the women's doors; see *The Liturgical Portions of the Apostolic Constitutions: A Text for Students*, ed. and trans. W. Jardine Grisbrooke (Bramcote, Notts.: Grove Books, 1990), 30–31.

107. The "strong woman" lection for the feast of S. Sabina (a shadowy figure) is found as a late addition in the earliest Roman epistle list (Würzburg cod. M.p.th. f. 62, CXCIIII, early 7th century). *In natale scae Sabinae* follows immediately the last of five entries *in natale sanctorum* (Morin, "Plus ancient *comes* ou lectionnaire," 41–74 at 66–67; A. Chavasse, "Épistolier romain du codex de Wurtzbourg," 280–331 at 331); all draw on "Solomon" for the first reading. The imposing presence of the matrons dressed in widows' weeds may have had something to do with the Roman choice of epistle for Sabina's feast.

108. Patrizia Angiolini Martinelli, "Il costume femminile," 15. Daniela Calcagnini ("Le Figure femminili nei mosaici paleocristiani degli edifici di culto romani," in Guidobaldi, *Ecclesiae urbis* 3:1919–38 at 1924) calls the bonnet a "cuffia."

FIGURE 4.7 Rome, S. Sabina. Detail of Figure 4.6: *Ecclesia ex gentibus*. The Bridgeman Art Library.

The woman on the right, whose visage seems especially Roman, holds a white napkin or *mappula* in her left hand along with an end of the long *palla*, like the end of a sari, decorated with oval golden ornament(s).[109] Each balances an open codex on her left arm, each pointing to the text with the right hand in the authoritative gesture of teaching, index and third finger joined as in the Christ in Majesty of S. Pudenziana. The text in the book on the left has the *Formgestalt* of Hebrew lettering, while that on the right approximates Roman cursive (Fig. 4.7).[110] The vesture with its insignia as well as the gesture suggest

---

109. Oakeshott, *Mosaics of Rome*, 89–90 and pl. 74; Brandenburg, *Ancient Churches of Rome from Fourth to Seventh Century*, 174. Compare the *palla* with oval medallion(s) marked with a cross and the two circular decorations ornamenting the end with the very similar ornamented *palla* over a dalmatic worn by the female *orante* at Saint-Maximin in Gaul (Fig. 3.2).

110. Calcagnini, "Figure femminili," 1925, with patristic references.

the office of *magistra* or theological teacher.[111] The locale of these mosaic figures, the Aventine hill, evokes the theological circles comprising wealthy widows and virgins who lived and gathered there and on the nearby Coelius.

Several of these circles, virtual family-monasteries, were animated by Jerome's women friends. He had constituted himself their director and teacher while he was resident in Rome between 383 and 385. A few of these wealthy women, daughters in tow, would follow him to the Holy Land as pilgrims visiting the holy places, then found and support monasteries having exacting regimens of prayer and Scripture study.[112] Among the aristocratic women who might be the inspiration for the S. Sabina matrons, we need look no further than two. The scholarly Marcella (325/35–410/11), widowed ascetic who never left Rome and whose theological circle predated Jerome's arrival, won his approbation as a Scripture exegete and received the compliment of serious correspondence. Marcella lived in a hermitage in the garden of S. Sabina.[113] After Jerome's forced departure from Rome, Marcella's salon continued to be the resort of priests seeking deeper understanding of philosophical and biblical texts. Marcella, Jerome tells us disarmingly, was careful to impute her answers to male authorities so as not to embarrass the male sex or contravene 1 Timothy 2:12.[114] Jerome's favorite, Paula (347–404), with her daughter Eustochium (ca.

---

111. Eisen's (*Women Officeholders*, 89–95) epigraphical sources include the office of διδάσκαλος (teacher of theology) known from Egypt as a lay office in the Alexandrian church and among the ascetics of the desert. The office included not only the teaching of catechumens but also the interpretation of Scripture during non-eucharistic worship. Without drawing the conclusions proposed here with respect to the S. Sabina mosaic depictions, Eisen completes her discussion of the teacher attested to at S. Agnese with cogent data about the famous Roman teachers Marcella, Melania the Elder, Paula, Melania the Younger (the latter three also monastic founders), and the poet Faltonia Betitia Proba whose *Cento* was written in 370 (ibid., 95–97).

112. Yarbrough, "Christianization in Fourth Century," 149–65; Clark, *Jerome, Chrysostom, and Friends*, 35–79; Clark, "Ascetic Renunciation and Feminine Advancement," 240–57; Clark, "Authority and Humility," *Byzantinische Forschungen* 9 (1985): 17–33, repr. in Clark, *Ascetic Piety and Women's Faith*, 209–28; Clark, "Theory and Practice in Late Ancient Asceticism," 25–46; Jane Simpson, "Women and Asceticism in the Fourth Century: A Question of Interpretation," *Journal of Religious History* 15 (1988): 38–60 at 51–53, repr. in *Acts of Piety in the Early Church*, ed. Everett Ferguson (New York; London: Garland, 1993), 296–318 at 309–11.

113. Near the church's entrance the remains of a dwelling, possibly the 4th-century *domus* of the matron Sabina, can be glimpsed through a floor grate. See *ROMArcheologica.: Guida alle antichità della città eterna*, vol. 6: *Il Celio, L'Aventino e dintorni* (Rome: Elio de Rosa editore, 2000), 49–51 and figs. 52–54.

114. Henri Leclercq, "Marcella," in *DACL* 10/2 (1932), 1760–1762; for discussion of Marcella's relationship with Jerome, see Eisen, *Women Officeholders*, 95–97. Jerome dedicated to Marcella his commentaries on Daniel and Galatians (ibid., 96).

368–418/19), followed Jerome to the Holy Land to found a double monastery in Bethlehem.[115] Paula knew the Scriptures by heart and, without the trace of an accent, recited the psalms in Hebrew.[116] On Paula's death, Eustochium inherited the burden of leadership as well as her mother's debts, while Jerome continued to head the male monastery, now short of funds. Both Marcella and Paula were well-known Roman Christian leaders and teachers. Paula's accomplishments in mastering Hebrew and relocating in Bethlehem suited a personification of the "Church from the Circumcision," while Marcella's lifelong residence in Rome qualified her to represent the "Church from the Gentiles." Both had died a sufficient time before the creation of the S. Sabina mosaic to qualify them as historical archetypes.[117] If our hypothesis identifying these mosaic portraits with women widely known as actual teachers in the church of Rome and Bethlehem can be entertained, then the identification of the two women of the S. Pudenziana apse as particular individuals also becomes more tenable. Modest Christian women might be allowed a grander presence if they also served as allegorical personifications. It is noteworthy that S. Pudenziana's Christ in Majesty shares the iconography of book display and teaching gesture with the S. Sabina matrons.

2. Pope Gelasius I and Women's Liturgical Leadership

By the end of the fifth century the wind had shifted. What had been considered appropriate ecclesiastical participation by women in several churches, including the Roman church itself, would be objected to by

---

115. Andrew Cain, "Jerome's *Epitaphium Paulae*: Hagiography, Pilgrimage, and the Cult of Saint Paula," *JECS* 18 (2010): 105–39.

116. *NCE* has entries for Marcella, Paula, Eustochium, and Jerome. See also Hickey, *Women of Roman Aristocracy as Christian Monastics*, passim.

117. The objection that early Christian art did not depict individual women is countered by the opinion of H. Leclercq ("Orant, orante," *DACL* 12/2 [1936], 2291–2324 at 2299) that the female *orantes* who populate catacomb art were intended to represent, not the Church or the praying soul in general, but the individual buried in the cubiculum who yearns for the salvation promised to the baptized. Not as numerous, male orants, chiefly representing biblical characters, do not show the same individuality of features. André Grabar ("Le portrait en iconographie paleochrétienne," *Revue des sciences religieuses* 36 [1962]: 87–109) notes that the evolution toward portraiture in early Christian art, which comes of age over the course of the 4th century, begins with the deceased including those shown as *orantes*. Portrait sculpture also developed in the 4th century.

the Roman pontiff Gelasius I (492–496).[118] The brief pontificate of this canonist pope marked the end of equivalence in men's and women's roles in the Roman city-church. Giorgio Otranto has pointed to evidence of women exercising roles of liturgical leadership in Salona (Dalmatia) circa 425; in Poitiers; probably in local churches in Provence; in Brittany, the northwestern peninsula of Gaul; and in the "vast area of southern Italy."[119] The bishops of this last region, where epigraphical texts are extant, were the recipients of a letter from Pope Gelasius. Otranto judges that the pope's condemnation specifically concerned bishops' installation of women as presbyters. Gelasius does not proffer scriptural or theological reasons but pleads the law: the Christian *regula* (rule), "ecclesiastical rules," and canons.[120] In other regions some bishops' condemnations of women's ministry may have been inspired by concerns about "Montanism." It is worth asking whether the objections of Gelasius and some later bishops are examples of the insensitivity of urban bishops to the exigencies of apostolic work "in the missions" and to actual pastoral needs and women's charisms for responding to them, as well as to sentiments of male entitlement.

---

118. The brilliant Latinist and married man of North Africa, Tertullian (d. ca. 220), had long before asserted (ca. 207, his Montanist period), "A woman is not permitted to speak in church (*Non permittitur mulieri in ecclesia loqui*). Neither may she teach (*docere*), baptize, offer (*offerre*), nor claim for herself (*sibi vindicare*) any function proper to a man (*nec ullius virilis muneris*), especially the sacerdotal office (*nedum sacerdotalis officii*)." See Tertullian, *De virginibus velandis* 9.1, in *Tertulliani Opera*, ed. E. Dekkers (Turnhout: Brepols, 1954), 1218–19. Madigan and Osiek (*Ordained Women*, 178) judge that *offerre* refers to presiding at eucharist. Tertullian's opinion represents a subordinationist strain, based in culture not the gospel, that is traceable through patristic literature. It dips to outright misogyny when Everywoman is equated with Eve and held responsible for sin in the world.

119. Giorgio Otranto, "Note sul sacerdozio femminile," 341–60, trans. Rossi, "Priesthood, Precedent and Prejudice," 73–93. For evidence from several regions, see Italian, 354–56, English, 87–89. The case for female presbyters is argued further by Otranto, "Il sacerdozio della donna nell'Italia meridionale," in *Italia meridionale e Puglia paleocristiane* (Bari: Edipuglia, 1991), 94–121. The practice of women *conhospitae* (companions) assisting men in what appears to have been diaconal ministry was condemned by the bishops of Tours, Rennes, and Angers in 511. These bishops seem not to have known the view of Clement of Alexandria (d. ca. 215) who said that the apostles, "in accordance with their ministry, devoted themselves to preaching without any distraction, and took women with them, not as wives, but as sisters, that they might be their co-ministers in dealing with women in their homes;" see Gary Macy, William T. Ditewig and Phyllis Zagano, *Women Deacons: Past, Present, Future* (New York: Paulist, 2011), 25. A medieval tradition interpreted the Lord's sending out of the 70 (72) in pairs (Luke 10:1) as including husbands and wives.

120. Otranto ("Note sul sacerdozio femminile," 348; Rossi, "Priesthood," 83) names the probable conciliar canons: Nicaea 19, Laodicea 11 and 44, Nimes 2, I Orange 25.

Otranto has argued that the south of Italy, a region influenced by customs of the Greek church, affords examples of married and unmarried *presbyterae* who exercised church office in their own right. The strenuous objection made by Pope Gelasius I against ecclesial ministry exercised by women in the south of Italy and Sicily attests to this presbyteral activity. Gelasius wrote impatiently to the bishops (*sacerdotes*),

> Nevertheless we have heard to our annoyance that divine affairs have come to such a low state that women are encouraged to serve (*feminae sacris altaribus ministrare*) at the sacred altars, and to take part in all things delegated to the service of the male sex (*cunctaque non nisi virorum famulatui deputata sexum*), for which they are not competent (*cui non competunt, exhibere*).[121]

Gelasius expressed annoyance at the officiating or serving of women at the altars (*feminae sacris altaribus ministrare*) in the churches of southern Italy, a region nominally subject to him. The church of Rome over which the popes ruled was constituted not only by the diocese of Rome but also by its suburbicarian dioceses along with the papal states and papal possessions as far south as Sicily.[122] Liturgical ministry exercised

---

121. Gelasius, Ep. 14, 26 in *Epistolae Romanorum pontificum genuinae et quae ad eos scriptae sunt A.S. Hilaro usque ad Pelagium II*, vol. 1: *A. S. Hilaro usque ad S. Hormisdam ann. 461–523*, ed. Andreas Thiel (Braunsberg: Eduardi Peter, 1868; repr.; Hildesheim: Olms, 1974), 376-77 (my translation from the Latin; see also Eisen, *Women Officeholders*, 129); Gryson, *Ministry of Women*, 105 and nn. 33, 34; Otranto, "Note sul sacerdozio femminile." In public lectures at six universities in the United States in 1991, Otranto proposed additional archeological evidence for ministerial roles. Eisen's text translates "ministrare" as "officiate." The idiom "to serve the liturgy" is used today in the Byzantine world to refer to presiding at eucharist. "Assisting" (*adsisto, adsistere*, Christian Latin) means to stand at the altar as "celebrant," *adsto, adstare* to serve or to officiate (Blaise, *Lexicon Latinitatis Medii Aevii*). Madigan and Osiek (*Ordained Women*, 186–88) critique some previous interpretations but argue that overall the texts point to women in the presbyteral role. In a private communication in the early '90s, Edward J. Kilmartin concurred with a positive reading of the evidence.

122. Lucania (Basilicata), Bruttium (Calabria), and Sicilia. The legislation is found in Gelasius' Ep. 14, 2, 3; 15, 1, 16 (Gelasius I, *Epistolae Romanorum Pontificum genuinae*, 1:376–78). For a later time, Louis Duchesne (*Beginnings of Temporal Sovereignty of Popes*, 125–26) lists the territories over which the pope had sovereignty, as found in the terms of the pact entered into by Paschal I and Louis the Pious confirming the rights of the Roman Church over its Italian domain: "the city of Rome, Roman Tuschia as defined before 787, the district of Perugia, ancient Campania, Tibur, the whole of the Exarchy, Pentapolis, including Ancona, Umana, and Osimo, the territory of Sabina, Lombard Tuscia...and, finally, the territories beyond the Liris and the ecclesiastical estates in Southern Italy, i.e., domains over which the Pope had theoretical rather than practical rights." Although not the first, this pact is the earliest such document preserved (Vogel, *Medieval Liturgy*, 297–98).

by women extended beyond the boundaries of the canons and went against the administrative order that Gelasius was putting in place in the church of Rome. What a pope judged to be an abuse elsewhere was unlikely to be tolerated in the papal city whatever the degree of its earlier acceptance.[123]

The "Gelasian renaissance," the period inclusive of Popes Gelasius I at the turn from the late fifth century to Hormisdas (514–523), brought about the standardization of ecclesiastical bureaucracy and even a new understanding of it. Gelasius, Alexandre Faivre explains, was in immediate need of clergy; therefore he reduced the time of apprenticeship in a given ministry. From then on a person deemed suitable for clerical advancement spent a set period in each ministry before installation into the next "higher" one. In general, having passed the interview whose conditions included reaching a requisite age laid down by Gelasius, the candidate needed to spend only three months in each function: lector, acolyte, subdeacon, (deacon), presbyter. Seniority rather than charism or competence was stressed, so that each ministry came to be viewed as a stage in a clerical career. Specifying the particulars of the *cursus honorum* resulted in the definitive clericalization and masculinization of official ecclesiastical ministry.[124]

The brief pontificate of Gelasius extends to the threshold of the sixth century, while the story of Praxedes and Pudentiana may have been written down in the early fifth. Was their *vita*, like the romantic apocryphal acts of the apostles originating in the ascetic milieus of Syria and Asia Minor in the second and third centuries, inspired by memories of a better, golden age when women ministers functioned as public persons representing the church? Can our *vita*'s later popularity be accounted for in part because it was seen as a form of protest literature against the "Gelasian renaissance,"

---

123. Roger Gryson, *Ministry of Women in Early Church*, 105. Yet disparities in liturgical practice in the 21st century as well as the cosmopolitan character of the Eternal City should warn us against hard-and-fast judgments about Roman practice outside the patriarchal basilicas. Martin F. Connell, translator of Innocent I, *Church and Worship in Fifth-Century Rome: The Letter of Innocent I to Decentius of Gubbio* ([Cambridge: Grove Books, 2002], 11) notes that "extant evidence about Roman worship in the first four centuries is scant" with Innocent I's Letter 25 "among the earliest witnesses to the rites of the Church of Rome."

124. Faivre, *Naissance d'une hiérarchie*, 337–40. Laymen might still be elevated directly to the office of bishop or pope, and deacons—in Rome holding weighty administrative posts over the seven ecclesiastical districts—were still promoted directly to the papacy. For a detailed study, see John St. H. Gibaut, *The Cursus Honorum: A Study of the Origins and Evolution of Sequential Ordination* (New York: Peter Lang, 2000).

which, having systematized the clerical bureaucracy, excluded women from ministerial service of the church?[125]

The Roman pontiff Zacharias (741–752), when dealing with disciplinary matters north of the Alps, used Gelasius' pronouncement apodictically. Zacharias responded to Pepin's loaded question, which concerned a certain "offense" of female monastics, also addressing his answer to bishops, abbots, and nobles of the Franks. Was it licit for them to read in public the lessons at solemn mass or on Holy Saturday, and at mass to chant either the alleluia or the *responsorium*? Zacharias had only to quote at length chapter 26 of the decree of "blessed pope Gelasius."[126] Where carried out, this decree would have marked a notable diminution in liturgical practice for female monastics.[127]

3. Bishop Atto of Vercelli, Counter-voice to Pope Gelasius

An explanation of the identity and role of those called *presbyterae* or *presbytides* in early conciliar texts offered by Atto of Vercelli (d. 961 or 964), a learned tenth-century bishop of a town west of Milan, interprets the historical data in a way contrary to the strenuous objections to women's ministry made by Pope Gelasius at the end of the fifth century.[128] Canonist, Scripture exegete,

---

125. This theory about Eastern apocryphal acts is put forward by Dennis R. MacDonald (*Legend and the Apostle*), who does not treat our story, and by Stevan L. Davies, *The Revolt of the Widows: The Social World of the Apocryphal Acts* [Carbondale, IL: Southern Illinois University Press, c1980], whose theory involves a "rebellion against both social order and church hierarchy." See Peter Richardson, "From Apostles to Virgins," 249–51.

126. "Zachariae papae ad Pipinum majorem domus...", canon V of Pope Zacharius' decree *De monachis ancillis Dei, de quibus flagitatum* in which blessed Pope Gelasius' decree 26 ("Quod nefas sit feminas sacris altaribus ministrare, vel aliquid ex his quae virorum sunt efficiis deputata praesumere") justifies Zacharias' refusal to allow nuns to read the lessons in public at solemn mass or on Holy Saturday, and to chant at mass either the alleluia or the *responsorium* (Zacharias, *Epistola* VIII.5, PL 89, 933B–C). Most of the topics addressed had to do with inappropriate behaviours by clergy. Zacharias was of Greek background, but the Eastern church origins of the majority of Roman pontiffs in this period did not always mean that they brought with them "Eastern" viewpoints. This was especially so if they had been refugees from theological disagreements bearing political repercussions.

127. Later still the Council of Paris (829) decried women's ministerial participation in liturgies, touching the sacred altars, assisting priests with their vestments, or offering "the body and blood of the Lord to the people." See Hochstetler, *Conflict of Traditions*, 99–100.

128. Edward Synan, "Atto of Vercelli," in *Dictionary of the Middle Ages*, ed. Joseph R. Strayer (New York: Scribner, 1982–1989), 1:641; Augustin Fliche, *La réforme grégorienne*, vol. 1: *La formation des idées grégoriennes* (Louvain: SSL, 1966), 61–74; Suzanne Fonay Wemple, *Atto of*

and theologian, Atto combs and combines Provençal, African, and Roman disciplinary practice with elements from canons of church councils and synods of the Christian East respecting what might promote good relationships among men and women on the way to the Christian goal of achieving perfect *caritas*. His exegesis of Romans 16 and knowledge of collections of canonical literature form the context for his explanation, made in response to the query of an otherwise unknown Milanese presbyter named Ambrose.[129] The latter's curiosity had been piqued by chapter 3 of a decree attributed to Pope Zacharias forbidding anyone from taking in matrimony a *presbytera, diacona*, or *commater spiritalis* (godmother).[130] Ambrose understands the last, *commater spiritalis*, to refer to the daughter of a spiritual father, namely, a goddaughter (not a godmother).[131] But what can be meant by the decree's reference to *presbytera* or *diacona*?[132]

Atto's reply to Ambrose warrants serious study.[133] This learned and pastorally sensitive bishop considered ecclesial leadership by women presbyters a fact of ancient church history. Warming to his theme, the bishop gives a positive reading of conciliar texts. A radical feature of Atto's exegesis is his assertion that women once exercised public ministry of the

---

Vercelli: Church, State and Christian Society in Tenth Century Italy (Rome: Edizioni di Storia e Letteratura, 1979), 41 and n. 96. Atto based his "long discussion on the subject of 'priestesses and deaconesses'... entirely upon the *Hadriana aucta*" (see her Appendix IV, 217). Atto's view that "the primary mission of priests was the fulfillment of the 'officium charitatis' " in love of neighbor was opposed to some Frankish bishops' insistence on "priestly sacramental powers and legal authority" (ibid., 65). This theological openness admitted the activity of women presbyters in the Great Church in ancient times. Yet Atto was far from allowing laity to criticize priests (*In epist. I ad Cor.*, 337B, noted by Wemple, *Atto*, 13), linking his defense of clerical authority to the subjection of married women to their husbands: "And if they ought to be subject to men so much the more to priests" (*PL* 134, 394D–395A).

129. Letter VII is from Ambrose a presbyter of Milan to Atto bishop of Vercelli (*PL* 134, 112D–113B). Letter VIII (*PL* 134, 113C–115D) is Atto's response to Ambrose the priest's question about what should be understood by the terms *presbytera* and *diacona* in the canons.

130. Mansi, *Sacrorum conciliorum* 12:383, ch. 5.

131. Ambrose cites the papal decree, "That no one may marry presbytera or diacona, or spiritual godmother" and gives his understanding, "Whence it is understood that a godfather may not choose to take a daughter of this kind in marriage" (*PL* 134, 113B). *Commater* in Christian Latin means baptismal godmother or sponsor; the word also has other, less spiritual meanings (Blaise, *Lexicon Latinitatis Medii Aevi*, 204).

132. Ambrose asks Atto, "[D]isclose to us what we ought to understand, which chapter calls the aforesaid [persons] presbytera and diacona, because it is entirely unknown to us" (Ep. VII, *PL* 134, 113B).

133. Letter VIII (*PL* 134, 113C–115D). My translation differs in several respects from that of Madigan and Osiek (*Ordained Women*, 192).

word and governance in the Christian assembly.[134] The bishop first speaks of presbyteras and diaconas who were ordained.[135] They exercised their ecclesial office by publicly performing the same functions as their male counterparts.

> Because your prudence has moved you to inquire how we should understand female presbyter (*presbyteram*) or female deacon (*diaconam*) in the canons: it seems to us that in the primitive church, according to the word of the Lord, *messis multa, operarii pauci* ("The harvest is great, the workers few," Matt 9:37-38; Luke 10:2); to help men (*ad adjumentum virorum*) religious women (*religiosae mulieres*) also used to be ordained as worship leaders (*cultrices*) in the holy church.[136] Which blessed Paul in the epistle to the Romans shows when he says, "I commend to you my sister Phoebe, who is in the ministry of the church which is at Cenchreae" (Rom 16:1). Where it is understood that in those times not only men but also women presided in the churches (*feminae praeerant ecclesiis*), evidently because of great usefulness.[137] For women, long accustomed to the rites of the

---

134. In the ecclesiology of the primitive church, presidency of eucharist and the other sacraments was the outcome of witness given to Christ by preaching the word and leading the community. See Hervé-Marie Legrand, "The Presidency of the Eucharist according to the Ancient Tradition," *Worship* 53 (1979): 413–38. This perspective is represented also in the work of Edward Schillebeeckx and Edward J. Kilmartin among others.

135. Since Atto is writing in the 10th century, canonists have yet to limit the sacraments to seven or specify that females may receive only six of them. Unlike Davanzati in the 18th century, Atto need not draw negative conclusions regarding the validity of the sacramental character, opinions which 13th-century scholastics will argue in their theological *summae*.

136. Not "caretakers" as Madigan and Osiek (*Ordained Women*, 192) typify these *praesidentes*. In classical Latin *cultus* carries as its first meaning an agrarian one ("tilling, cultivation, tending"), and second, education and culture. *Cultor* is a husbandman; its feminine form is *cultrix*, she who tends or takes care of. In the transferred sense *cultor* may indicate a worshiper. But in medieval Latin *cultrix* is the one who occupies herself with cult objects (Blaise, *Lexicon Latinitatis Medii Aevi*, 268, citing Atto's *Ep.* 8). Cult and its derivatives are on the way to the modern meaning, "a system of religious worship, especially as expressed in religious ceremonies" (*The Concise Oxford Dictionary*, 7th ed., ed. J. B. Sykes [Oxford: Clarendon Press, (1982) 1986]).

137. Cf. Atto's commentary on Rom 16, where he twice uses the phrase "feminae praeerant Ecclesias" in relation to Phoebe and Maria, in *Attonis Vercellensis Episcopi Expositio Epistolarum S. Pauli* (PL 134, 125–288). Verses 1 and 2 devoted to the ministry of Phoebe (the Latin Vulgate read "in ministerio") show that "then not only men, but also women presided in the Churches" (281A). Prisca and Aquila, greeted with their "domestic church," are Paul's "cooperators in the preaching of Jesus Christ" (281B-C). Maria "who has worked very hard among you" (v. 6) converted "many of the Romans to faith" (281D), showing that women

pagans, instructed also in philosophical doctrines, were, through these teachings, converted more deeply and led more freely to religious worship. This the eleventh canon of the Council of Laodicea prohibits when it says that it is not proper for those women who are called female presbyters or *praesidentes* to be ordained in the churches.[138] Truly we believe female deacons to have been ministers of such things. For we name the minister (*ministrum*) deacon (*diaconum*), from which we understand *diaconam* (female deacon) to have been derived.[139] Finally we read in the fifteenth canon of the Council of Chalcedon that a female deacon is not to be ordained before her fortieth year—and this with the highest deliberation. We believe also that women were attached to the service of baptizing so that the bodies of other women might be handled by them without any deeply felt sense of shame. For in the Eastern statutes it is written

---

presided in house-churches. Atto understands Andronicus and Julia (sic) to be husband and wife. Collaborators in preaching and imprisoned with Paul, they are among the 72 sent out by Jesus (Luke 10:1; 282A), their apostolic credentials gained in their leaving their own country to preach. The litany of names in v. 14 includes Hermes and Hermas. "Because they don't preach," Atto says, the apostle greets them plainly. Then Atto attributes *Shepherd* to Hermes (sic; 283B) "who wrote the book which is titled 'Shepherd'." Against Paul's exemplary picture of Christian leaders in the early Roman church must be balanced the household codes found in the later Pastoral Letters. These disharmonies Atto does not engage; yet he can discover the gospel message among the thorns. In *Epistola II ad Timotheum* (2 Tim 4.19, 21) he cites Prisca and Aquila as hospitable, and Pudens, Linus, Claudia, and the others as *fratres*, "brothers and sisters" (*PL* 134, 700A–B).

138. Canon 11, translation by Dionysius Exiguus: "That those who are called presbyteras or presidents ought not to be ordained in the churches" ("Quod non oporteat eas quae dicuntur presbyterae vel praesidentes, in Ecclesiis ordinari"). Eisen (*Women Officeholders*, 123 and 137, n. 39) notes the differing translations given by Isidore (360/70–435) "as if ordained" and Dionysius Exiguus (497–545) "to be ordained in the Churches." The *Breviatio Canonum* of Ferrandus, deacon of Carthage (523–546), no. 21, transcribes Laodicea c. 11: "Ut mulieres quae apud Graecos presbyterae appellantur, apud nos autem viduae, seniores, univirae et matriculae, in ecclesia [tamquam ordinatas] constitue non liceat," "That it is not permitted to install in office in the church [as ordained] women who are called presbyteras among the Greeks, among us however are called widows, elders, once-married and 'matriculae'" (*PL* 88, 830). Canon 11 was included as an interpolated translation in the pseudo-Isidorian False Decretals of the 9th century (Wemple, Atto, passim; Gary Macy, "Ordination of Women in Early Middle Ages," 491–92). Macy cites the False Decretals and 12th-century sources which use respectively "matricularia" or "matricuria" (Gratian; see Raming, *Exclusion of Women from Priesthood*, 22). Blaise (*Lexicon Latinitatis Medii Aevi*, 573) understands "matricularia" as a kind of deaconess charged with maintenance of a church and "matricuria" as church warden or deaconess. Scholastic transcriptions use variations of the word "matriculus" (cathedral canon or clergy). "Matricula" is the feminine form of "matriculus."

139. But Phoebe is the first scripturally attested *diakonos*. Showing a fine sense of ministerial functions, Atto does not equate the work of the *diacona* with community leadership.

(Council of Carthage IV, c. 12): "Widows or nuns (*sanctimoniales*) who are chosen for the ministry of baptizing women: let them be instructed for the office so that they may with apt and correct word teach ignorant and rustic women at the time when they are baptized, how they should respond to the questions, and how, having accepted baptism, they should live:" for just as those who were called *presbyterae* took up the office of preaching, ordering (*iubendi*) or teaching, so female deacons had correctly taken up the office of ministry and of baptizing, which just now is not expedient.[140]

Atto sees the prohibition against women's baptizing as a question of ecclesiastical discipline. Since infants, not voluptuous women, are the ones now being baptized, present circumstances do not require a woman for that office. He interprets Canon 11 of the Laodicean synod as witnessing to an earlier office of presidency by women presbyters.

Having exegeted the ancient canonical texts that refer to presbyteras, Atto turns to the office of abbess, which, he finds, is not equivalent to that of diacona. Basing his opinion on an elementary philology, he notes that an abbot is called "father;" hence *abbatissa* should carry the same meaning: "Which appellation (viz., *Pater*) expresses the quality of power, awe and equally love, reverence and affection."[141] His comment was most likely occasioned by his experience of abbesses' actual roles. Atto continues,

We understand *diacona* to mean nothing other than minister. Now if the name of this office also in some way perdures in those things that seem to be administered by women now, we would consider

---

140. "[H]ae quae presbyterae dicebantur, praedicandi, iubendi, vel edocendi, ita sane diaconae ministrandi vel baptizandi officium sumpserant: quod nunc jam minime expedit" (*Epistola* 8, PL 134, 114). Giorgio Otranto ("Note sul sacerdozio femminile," 357–60) analyzes this text carefully. In Christian Latin the first meaning of *sermo* is homily.

141. PL 134, 114D. Atto's exegesis of scripture is in some respects very cautious, becoming less so when drawing from theological insights. Atto lights on the phrase "[V]iriliter agite" ("Act in a manly way," 1 Cor 16:13) to note that sacred Scripture characterizes males as perfect, women as imperfect; therefore the text reads *viriliter*, not weak or soft in the way of women (PL 134, 411A). Then Atto takes the opposite tack when exegeting Titus 2:14 ("He it is who gave himself for us..."). He paraphrases Gal 3:28 and Col 3:11 as found in some ancient witnesses: "For there is no difference of free, and slave, Greek, and barbarian, circumcised, and having the foreskin; of woman, and man, but we are all one in Christ" (711D). Three centuries after Atto, Thomas Aquinas (*Summa Theologiae* 3, q. 67 a. 4) will enunciate the sacramental principle that "It is Christ who is the principal baptizer. Besides Col 3 says that in Christ there is not male nor female. And therefore just as a layman is able to baptize, as minister of Christ, so also a female."

those women deacons who, overtaken by old age, serving religious life with chastity, faithfully preparing the *offerenda* for the priests, are watchful at the threshold of the churches (*ad ecclesiarum limina exubant*) and sweep the pavement (*pavimenta detergunt*).[142]

Atto describes the work of the sacristan as a probable parallel to aspects of the early diaconate of women. After all, the power and respect that accrued to the contemporary office of abbess far exceeded the prerogatives of women deacons as set out in Eastern church orders.[143] Although he likely knew it, Atto does not cite Canon 5 of Pope Zacharius' decree *De monachis ancillis Dei, de quibus flagitatum* regarding Pope Gelasius' decree 26, which justifies Zacharias' refusal to allow nuns their customary liturgical ministries.[144]

Then, the bishop continues, there are the wives of men ordained following marriage. These women had been joined in matrimony to presbyters or deacons before ordination. The terms presbytera and diacona may refer to them. At this point Atto indulges in a creative melding of Eastern and Western disciplines. After a husband's ordination, husband and wife are to live together in continence.[145] He is not to use the pretence of religion to get rid of her (*abjiciat*) and is threatened with excommunication if she is disdained (*rejecerit*). If he continues this course, he is to be cast out (*dejiciatur*).[146] Atto cites a canon from the early Eastern church, since

---

142. The "offerenda" are the bread and wine to be offered by priests (Blaise, *Lexicon Latinitatis Medii Aevi*, 632). Perhaps these religious women baked it (*PL* 134, 114D–115A).

143. Atto's observations present an unusual balancing act with respect to women's roles in the church. He cites Scripture passages or "authorities" (e.g., Ambrosiaster) on women's inferiority and subordination, but places difficult texts within an extenuating exegetical horizon. For instance, Eph 5 begins with the Pauline admonition to be subject to one another. "These things bishops, presbyters and others hear, that they may be subjected to their subjects, just as Christ was, washing the feet of the apostles" (cf. John 13:5). He continues, "[J]ust as the Church is subject to Christ, so also should the woman be to the man. As it is written concerning Sara calling Abraham my Lord" (Gen 28:1, in *In Epist. ad Ephes.* [*PL* 134, 580A]) "... as Christ died for the church, so men should be prepared to face danger for the benefit of holy wedlock" (580B). After all, Eve is "bone of my bones" (581A).

144. *PL* 89, 933B–C.

145. Atto quotes canon six (*sic*) of *The Canons of the Holy Apostles*: "Let not a bishop, presbyter, or deacon put away his wife under pretence of religion; but if he put her away, let him be excommunicated; and if he persists, let him be deposed." See *Ancient Epitome of the Sacred Canons of the Eastern Orthodox Church*, ed. George Mastrantonis (St. Louis, MO: Ologos [ca. 1960], listed as canon five [20]). This set of canons dates from before 550.

146. Demetrios Constantelos ("Marriage and Celibacy of the Clergy in the Orthodox Church," in *Celibacy in the Church*, ed. William Bassett and Peter Huizing. Concilium, 78

by the pontificate of Siricius in Rome husband and wife were required to live apart in order to ensure that continence be maintained.[147] Atto closes his discussion of this controverted topic with the observation that the outcome of the bishop or priest's not sending away the wife, yet possessing her as if not possessing her, will be "spiritual marriage," whence from fleshly may come spiritual union.[148]

In summary, Atto's commentary witnesses to three different classes of women whose titles may not adequately differentiate ecclesiastical status. In the ancient church *presbyterae* were presidents of assemblies and worship leaders (*cultrices*) and diaconas the female counterparts of male deacons. Second, there are the abbesses whom some equate with diaconas.

[New York: Herder & Herder, 1972], 33) presents this text as "protecting married bishops"; it also protects their wives. The varied prefixes for *iacio* echo the language of many of the Greek disciplinary canons. In the case of clerics, excommunication (which is reversible) is a lesser punishment than deposition from the order, the last resort of authority. Canons 17–19 of *Ancient Epitome* list the categories of women to whom marriage rules out ordination for the husband (21). Canon 26 allows marriage for clerics who are readers and singers, a provision that is stated more clearly in the Sixth Ecumenical Synod (Constantinople, 680), Canon 6 which reads, "If any ordained person contracts matrimony, let him be deposed. If he wishes to be married he should become so before his ordination" (13). Gregory the Great had clearly articulated the opposite Roman discipline to the bishops of Corsica in as strong terms.

147. *PL* 13, 1131–47; 1155–62; 1181–94. For the Latin discipline Atto might have appealed to the Regional Synod of Carthage (419 CE), Canon 3: "Let a bishop, a presbyter, and a deacon be chaste and continent" (*Ancient Epitome*, 35); and for the Greek Canon 12 of the Sixth Ecumenical Synod (Constantinople, 680): "Although it has been decreed that wives are not to be cast forth, nevertheless that we may counsel for the better, we give command that no one ordained a bishop shall any longer live with his wife" (ibid., 13). The way around this contradiction was to ordain as bishops only monks. Canon 3 of Constantinople (680) deals with priests who have contracted second marriages or who after ordination have contracted marriage (ibid., 13). The friction between East and West is apparent in Canon 13 of that same synod: "Although the Romans wish that everyone ordained deacon or presbyter should put away his wife, we wish the marriages of deacons and presbyters to continue valid and firm" (ibid., 13). Since in Rome it would be normal for a deacon to be ordained directly to the episcopate and subdeacons to the presbyterate, Latins could presume that the wife had already been put away.

148. Atto cites a decree of Pope Leo that *PL* incorrectly identifies as ch. 17 (*PL* 134, 115A–B). The passage is found in Pope Leo I's Letter 167 to Bishop Rusticus of Narbonne in a response to the latter's question, "Concerning those who minister at the altar and have wives, whether it is licit for them to have marital relations (*misceantur*)?" Leo replies that the law of continence binds those who are bishops and presbyters, but those who are laity or lectors may licitly marry and procreate. "But when they arrive at the aforesaid grades, what was licit for them is not licit. Whence, so that from the carnal may come spiritual marriage, it is necessary that they not send away wives, so as to possess them as if they do not have them, by which both the charity of spouses will be preserved, and the works of marriage may cease" (*PL* 54, 1204).

Of all medieval commentators Atto distinguishes most finely the offices of presbytera, diacona, and abbess. Finally, those wives married to men who put away their wives in order to be ordained were given the title of the office to which their husbands were first ordained. Even-handed, Atto does not cite contemporary Roman practice, which requires men promoted to major orders to put aside their wives, and instead cites the ancient Eastern canon that presents the issue *from the wives' perspective*—their husbands are not free to renounce them out of piety—combining that with the Leonine advice requiring married couples to abstain from marital relations. The carnal will give way to charity.

4. Diaconas

Paul's patron Phoebe, διάκονος and προστάτις of the church at Cenchreae (Rom 16:1–2), has already been discussed in chapter three. If Phoebe carried to Rome a letter of commendation from none other than the apostle to the Gentiles, considerable motivation for maintaining an office so apostolic and explicitly scriptural should have existed in the Eternal City. But compared to the wealth of literary references, texts, and inscriptions in the Eastern churches and a number of Gallican conciliar texts, the documentary silence in the early Roman church is deafening.[149] A century ago J. P. Kirsch assigned the office of deaconess to Grapte, the visionary figure in *Shepherd* who was responsible for widows and orphans. Kirsch appears to equate the office of deaconess with that of widow, noting Octavia as a "widow of God," that is, a widow dedicated to God. There was also Regina, a widow who lived for eighty years, five months and twenty-six days and served the church for sixty years, according to her grave inscription never burdening the Christian community. The ecclesial status of a widow named Dafne who never burdened the Christian community is unclear.[150] The official view in modern times has been that Rome did not know a true ecclesial diaconate for women. Martimort argues that a quasi-diaconate (widows or virgins; wives of deacons) accounts for the sporadic epigraphic witnesses prior to the seventh century, when a "true" but non-sacramental

---

149. Epigraphic witnesses are more numerous in Asia Minor. Antonio Enrico Felle ("'Diaconi' e 'diaconissae' tra oriente e occidente," 489–528 at 489, n. 5) notes that Eisen (*Women Officeholders*, 158–98) has provided relatively few examples: two from Palestine, six from Asia Minor, three from Greece, five from Macedonia, three from the West.

150. Kirsch, *Frauen des kirchlichen Altertums*, 22.

diaconate for abbesses exists for a brief time. Martimort concedes that the prohibitions originating from local councils in Gaul witness to a contested existence for women's ministries but correctly observes that these minor Gallican councils have little or no relevance for Roman practice.[151]

A. Dometius and Anna DIAC at St. Paul's Outside the Walls

Clear evidence for a Roman diaconate of women in the sixth century has been found.[152] Known to scholars since 1699, an epigraphic text on a lintel at St. Paul's Outside the Walls documents a *votum* made to the apostle Paul by brother and sister deacons: "By the gifts of God and the blessed apostle Paul, Dometius, the deacon and manager of the treasury of the holy, apostolic, and papal chair, together with Anna, the deacon, his sister in the body, has presented this *votum* to the blessed Paul."[153] In Christian

---

151. Martimort (*Diaconesses*, 187–217). It is instructive to note that, despite the universalist ecclesiology dominating the Roman magisterium since the 1980s, wide variation in the acceptance of women's ministries is observable between parishes of the same diocese and among dioceses today. In the Middle Ages the absence or suppression of a ministry by a local council cannot be extended to include other dioceses.

152. See the text, comprehensive list and bibliography by Felle, "'Diaconi' e 'diaconissae' tra oriente e occidente," 489–528 at 499, 521, 523. A fragmentary notice may point to an archdeaconess at St. Paul's Outside the Walls in the first half of the 5th century (*ICUR* 2:4839); Felle, "'Diaconi' e 'diaconissae,'" 499, 521. This reading is disputed by Antonio Ferrua, "Le antiche iscrizioni cristianae di S. Paolo f.l.m.," *Rendiconti della Pontificia Accademia Romana di Archeologia* 62 (1989–1990): 185–209 at 192.

153. Martimort gives a somewhat faulty version of the Latin text, citing Raffaele Fabretti, *Inscriptionum antiquarum quae in aedibus paternis asservantur explicatio* (Rome: Ex Officina Dominici Antonii Herculis, 1699), 758, n. 639. Eisen (*Women Officeholders*, 182–83) gives the text: DE DONIS D[E] ET BEATI PAVLI APOSTOLI DOMETIVS DIAC ET ARCARIUS SCAE SED APOSTOL ADQVE PP. VNA CVM ANNA DIAC EIVS GERMANA HOC VOTVM BEATO PAVLO OPTVLERU[N]T, citing Carl Maria Kaufmann, *Handbuch der altchristlichen Epigraphik* (Freiburg im Breisgau: Herder, 1917), 294, and *Inscriptiones christianae urbis Romae* (*ICUR*), ed. Giovanni Battista de Rossi, 1861–1888, completed by Angelus Silvagni, Antonius Ferrua, and Giuseppi Gatti (3 vols.; new series; Rome: Ex Officina Libraria Doct. Befani, 1922–1985), n.s. 2:4788. The epigraph was dated by de Rossi to the 6th century. Silvagni says the 6th century is certain, but gives no location. Kaufmann judged it to postdate that of a diaconissa Theodora who died at Ticini in St. Trinitatis (Pavia) 22 July 539 (Eisen, *Women Officeholders*, 184). Madigan and Osiek (*Ordained Women*, 144) add no further information, referring to Eisen's entry and the "unilluminating discussion in Martimort, *Deaconesses*, 202." Andrieu (*OR* 4:143, n. 2) drops APOSTOL from the votive inscription but locates it "sur le linteau d'une porte," citing Giovanni B. De Rossi, *La Roma sotterranea cristiana* (4 vols.; Rome: Cromo-litografia pontificia, 1877), 3:521, and Duchesne, *LP* 1:355, n. 9. Although brother and sister are both labelled with the abbreviated title DIAC, Andrieu (*OR* 4:143) proposes without evidence that, paralleling the Matrona named below, Anna obtained her title as widow of another deacon.

Latin *votum* may mean prayer. Originally it indicated a solemn vow with the transferred meaning of a votive offering to the gods, which is the likely meaning here. The inscription is of special interest because a brother and sister by blood are both identified by the abbreviated title DIAC (deacon), the brother holding the position of papal treasurer. This well-attested inscription is again confirmed in a recent publication of the Latin inscriptions at St. Paul's.[154]

B. Textual Evidence for Diaconas, Seventh to Eleventh Centuries

Although there appears to be no Roman epigraphic evidence for diaconas dating from the seventh century, the *Tridentinum* recension of the Gregorian (papal) sacramentary of circa 683 contains the first prayer for "making" a diacona. Role models were needed for actual diaconas. Did the first saintly model appear before the Gregorian prayer? Unknown until the seventh century, the presumed martyr and diacona Martina is usually cited in connection with Pope Honorius and the dedication to her of the Roman Forum's *Secretarium Senatus in tribus Fatis*. Her *passio*, a remaking of the life of the Greek martyr Tatiana, appears in the eighth century, when her feast was celebrated on 1 January. In the ninth century an oratory to Martina was found at Mile X on the Via Ostiense.[155]

Michel Andrieu weighs the Roman textual evidence for diaconas that is found from the eighth century onward. In the first instance are wives who receive a special blessing and are consecrated in view of the new life of continence *more romanae ecclesiae* entered into on the day of their husbands' ordination to a major order. Such deaconesses and presbyteras share their husbands' titles.[156] Yet, since we know nothing more about them, their

---

154. *Iscrizioni latine della raccolta de San Paolo fuori le Mura edite in ICVR: indice dei vocaboli*, ed. Rosanna Barbera, with Antonio Magi Spinetti (Vatican City: Musei Vaticana, 2009), 39, 67, 223.

155. *AA.SS., Januarius* I.II (Brussels: Alphonsus Greuse, 1863), 11–18, where she is said to be *per donum Dei Diacona*. See also Agostino Amore, "Martina," in *Bibliotheca Sanctorum* 8:1220–21; Amore, *Martiri di Roma*, 300–301. Jacques-Marie Guilmard ("Antique fête mariale," 34) follows W. F. Frere (*Studies in Roman Liturgy*, vol. 2: *The Roman Gospel-Lectionary*, 89) in attributing the Roman cult of St. Martina to Pope Donus (676–678), who set up a mosaic (*PL* 75, 473) with Martina between Honorius I and himself.

156. The titles *presbytera/presbyterissa* and *episcopa/episcopissa* became archaic as (1) celibacy was required of a man raised to the diaconate in Rome (when husbands were ordained, the

status—celebrated by a blessing, a recognizable outfit, and a place in church processions—concerns more what they cannot do than what they can. Once their husbands are ordained, the women are bound to celibacy. These wives are shown to be established in church office by the negative outcome, excommunication, if they remarry even after death has claimed their spouse. Roman conciliar texts of 721 and 743 appear to refer to these persons. In another example, one Matrona, a *religiosa diaconissa* who had a son and a nephew, received a lease from Gregory II (715–731). Matrona could have been the widow of a layman (and therefore a deaconess in her own right).[157]

In contrast, Andrieu places in a second category those who, constituting "a sort of feminine equivalent of the deacon," exercise a true ecclesiastical role and are ordained.[158] The *LP* describes the return of Pope Leo III (795–816) to Rome thus:

> In great joy the Romans welcomed their pastor. On the eve of Saint Andrew the apostle, all of them as a whole—the leading members of the clergy and all the clergy, the chief men, the senate, the whole militia and the entire Roman people, with the nuns (*sanctimonialibus*) and deaconesses (*diaconissis*) and the most noble matrons and all the women, and at the same time all the *scholae* of foreigners...all united together at the Milvian Bridge—they welcomed him with standards and banners and spiritual chants. They brought him to the church of St. Peter the apostle where he celebrated solemn mass. Faithfully all shared together in common the body and blood of our Lord Jesus Christ.[159]

---

wives acquired the title of his first major order, e.g. *diaconissa*) and (2) the clerical grades were arranged in a *cursus* or regular ascent in rank with subdiaconate preliminary to presbyterate and diaconate to episcopate.

157. OR 4:143, citing the commentary of Paul Fabre and Louis Duchesne, *Le Liber censuum de l'église romaine* (3 vols.; Paris: Fontemoing, 1905), 1:352, no. 61.

158. Andrieu, OR 4:142. Some modern authors use the terms *diacona* and *diaconissa* to distinguish between a true ecclesial ordination and a "minor" church order. Ancient usage is not so clear.

159. As the first of the disciples to be called by Christ and St. Peter's brother, St. Andrew's feast was dignified by a vigil. The procession described took place in 799. See PL 128, Latin of Anastasius Bibliothecarius; Bianchini ed. (1718). Davis, *Lives of Eighth-Century Popes* (rev. 2nd ed., 2007, 98.19 [185–86]) gives a slightly variant translation, identifying these "deaconesses" as "the wives of deacons, but no doubt including the wives of other clergy" (n. 47). The Bianchini edition reads "cum sanctimonialibus et diaconissis ac nobilissimis matronis, seu universis feminis...." The context does not require the inference that they are wives. Andrieu argues that, in conjunction with the *sanctimoniales*, these are ordained *diaconas*.

Who are these "deaconesses"? Andrieu notes the difficulty in distinguishing between true women deacons and "deposed" wives of the men who were elevated to the major orders.[160] Where a text parallels the *diacona* with a *virgo velata*, Andrieu presumes that the former holds ecclesiastical office. The description given above of the papal procession may, Andrieu proposes, refer to women deacons, as also the Roman council notice of 826 that warns against illegitimate unions with *velatam, diaconam vel raptam uxorem*.[161] Marie-Josèphe Aubert believes that these notices show the existence in Rome of a true diaconate for women.[162]

References to women deacons in Rome are most numerous from the ninth century into the eleventh, and the popes themselves are implicated. That the listing of deaconesses in Leo III's welcoming procession did not constitute an exception but continued to be an office recognized by the bishop of Rome is shown by a diploma of 1017 or 1018 in which Pope Benedict VIII (1012–1024) confers on the cardinal-bishop of the *ecclesia Portuensis* (Porto, first the port of Ostia, then one of the two ports of Rome) the right to ordain priests, deacons, deaconesses, and subdeacons for the Trastevere quarter.[163] In 1026 a similar privilege is granted by John XIX to Peter, cardinal bishop of Silva Candida, for the Leonine City. It reads, "We concede and confirm to you and to your successors in perpetuity, as it was mentioned before, consecrations of the high altars of the church of Saint Peter and of other monasteries, and also consecrations of churches, high altars, priests, deacons and deaconesses, of the entire Leonine

---

160. As part of the ordination rite ca. 700/750, candidates for the Roman diaconate or presbyterate were asked, "Coniugem habuit? Disposuit de domo sua?" calling for the response, "Disposuit" (*Ordo* XXXIV, in Andrieu, *OR* 3:609). No longer cohabiting, the sexual abstinence of the husbands was more assured. No information is available about the wives' subsequent living arrangements or about their children.

161. Davis, *Lives of Eighth-Century Popes*, 98.19. Martimort (*Diaconesses*, 202–5) also signals for the second half of the 8th and early 9th centuries rare instances of a distinct class of female deacons.

162. Aubert, *Il diaconato alle donne?*, 137.

163. Not Oporto, Portugal, despite the assumption by Madigan and Osiek (*Ordained Women*, 147). See Henri Leclercq, "Porto," in *DACL* 14/2 (1948), 1533–43. The text reads, "Pari modo concedimus et confirmamus vobis vestrisque successoribus in perpetuum omnem ordinationem episcopalem, tam de presbyteris quam diaconibus vel diaconissis seu subdiaconibus, ecclesiis vel altaribus, quae in tota Transtiberi necessaria fuerit" (*PL* 139, 1621B; Andrieu, *OR* 4:139–46 at 144 on *Ordo* XXXVI). The naming of deaconesses before subdeacons shows their place in a clerical *cursus* otherwise filled by males.

city."[164] Pope Leo IX (1049–1054) confirmed this privilege.[165] Other unofficial notices exist. Abbess-deaconesses were found in Rome, although in the tenth century there were only three monasteries for women with some others in the environs. Names of a few religious termed "venerable diacona and abbatissa" are known from the register at S. Maria in Via Lata: Domna Odocia (921 CE); Alvisinda (947); Eufrosina (950); Agathe (978), Sergia (987).[166] Andrieu notes references to a Sabina *diacona* found in a tenth-century martyrology and to Constantia *diacona*, a donor of her goods to the archpriest of the monastery of St. Martin in 1053.[167]

No doubt aided by Eastern influences in Rome during the seventh and eighth centuries—popes from Syria and regions where Greek culture was strong; business with churches of the East—a diaconal ministry exercised by women made its way into Rome following the ancient precedent of Phoebe, *diakonos* of Cenchreae (Rom 16:1) and bearer of Paul's letter to the Romans.[168] An official diaconate for women in Rome was no anomaly in that 110-year period when the majority of popes had Eastern origins, that is, between 642 and 752.[169] The practice was grounded on references to women deacons in the New Testament; on earlier, theoretically more egalitarian church practice for which scattered material evidence remains; and on the institution of the diaconate in Eastern churches, especially the Byzantine church of Constantinople. In other parts of the East the diaconate was already in decline, overwhelmed by the Muslim conquest. All the more reason, then, to expect its establishment in Rome as Easterners arrived in the monastic diaspora and Eastern tastes and styles left their mark

---

164. "Consecrationes vero altarium ecclesiae sancti Petri et aliorum monasteriorum, necnon consecrationes ecclesiarum, altarium, sacerdotum, diaconorum seu diaconissarum totius civitatis Leonianae vobis vestrisque successoribus in perpetuam, sicut praelibatum est, concedimus et confirmamus" (*PL* 141, 1130C–D).

165. *PL* 143, 602C, noted by Madigan and Osiek, *Ordained Women*, 149, n. 17.

166. Adolf Kalsbach, *Die altkirchliche Einrichtung der Diakonissen bis zu ihrem Erlöschen* (RQ 22; Freiburg im Breisgau: Herder, 1926), 79–80.

167. Andrieu, *OR* 4:143 and n. 4 for Sabina. The martyrology is in Vat. ms. Ottob. 38, fol. 12r. For Constantia, see 143 and n. 5 and reference to L. Schiapparelli, "Le carte antiche dell'Archivio capitolare di San Pietro," in *Archivio della Società Romana di storia patria* 24 (1901), 466–67. See also Martimort, *Diaconesses*, 207 and n. 44.

168. Evangelos Theodorou ("Diakonat der Frau in der Griechisch-Orthodoxen Kirche," 29) remarks cogently that since sources for clerical ordinations are lacking in the first three centuries, the absence of reference to women deacons cannot be used as an argument against their existence.

169. Krautheimer, *Rome*, 90.

on Roman architecture and iconography. This authentic sacramental office coexisted with the *ordo* of deposed wives of ordained members of the Roman clergy. Even the strictest interpretation of Roman texts of the eighth to eleventh centuries that refer to presbyteras and two types of diaconas leads to the conclusion that some women were established in an ecclesially recognized office paralleling, but with less public notice, the office of their male counterparts. This perception is reinforced by the Roman papal prayer, called *benedictio* or *consecratio*, which later developed into a full-scale ritual for establishing a "true" diacona in office, sharing features with the ritual for the male deacon.

5. Episcopae *in Rome*

Dorothy Irvin reproduces a drawing of the Roman tombstone of Ale(k)s(an)dra, attributed to the fourth or fifth century, in which a woman *orans* stands between two sheep. The small Chi Rho monogram flanked by the Alpha and Omega above and to the left of her head leaves no doubt that this is the tomb of a Christian. Irvin is inspired by the mosaic showing the first bishop of Ravenna, St. Apollinaris, flanked by sheep in the beautiful sixth-century basilica dedicated to him when she sees in the sheep the symbol of Aleksandra's pastoral role. A Roman parallel can be cited that was close at hand: in a fourth-century mosaic in a chapel in S. Pudenziana destroyed in 1595, two lambs flanked Peter, prince of the apostles.[170]

A. Veneranda in the Domitilla Catacomb

In the well-known figure labelled Veneranda (Domitilla catacomb, Rome, after 356 CE), Irvin has espied a woman official of the church (Fig. 4.8). Both the title Veneranda and the vestment she wears suggest to Irvin an official ecclesiastical role as bishop.[171] Indeed Veneranda is an imposing

---

170. Irvin, *Calendar 2004* (May–June). The S. Pudenziana mosaic is known from a drawing in Vatican ms. 5407, fol. 82 (H. Leclercq, "Chaire épiscopale," in *DACL* 3/1 [1913], 19–75 at 43–44).

171. Dorothy Irvin, *Calendar 2004* (September–October); Irvin, [lecture] "Women Bishops and Priests in the Early Church" a lecture given in Ottawa, Canada, 2005. Many devotees' tombs were inserted in and around this cubiculum requiring reinforcement of the walls. At Veneranda's right a rose bush denotes paradise. Her patron Petronilla points to an open casket (*capsa*) full of papyrus scrolls, while the open book with ribbon markers above symbolizes the divine law promulgated in the Scriptures. Irvin interprets these as evidence of Veneranda's ministry of teaching and preaching. The fresco is described and illustrated in Fasola, *Catacombs of Domitilla*, 41–43 and fig. 9.

FIGURE 4.8 Rome, Domitilla Catacomb. Veneranda and St. Petronilla (after 356). Scala/Art Resource, NY.

figure; she wears a wide-sleeved dalmatic and a ruffled cap (*mitella*) under pillbox headgear, the veil decorated on its edges with purple roundels and a fringe.[172] Her name or title provided by the gerundive "Veneranda" means "she who must be honored" or "she who demands our respect," similar to the title *venerabilis* that H. Leclercq says is used "everywhere" for a bishop, a priest, a religious, a lay person, a woman.[173] Veneranda's fourth-century costume differentiates her from her martyr-patron and Peter's putative daughter "Petronella."[174] Standing beside her in the same

---

172. Praxedes' simple *palla* evokes the Christian apostolic period. Her bonnet (a *mitella* or ruffled cap, with veil) in the *ecclesia pudentiana* mosaic (ca. 410) resembles Veneranda's headdress except for the latter's pillbox hat.

173. Henri Leclercq, "Inscriptions latines chrétiennes," 769.

174. VENERANDA DEP(OSITA) VII IDUS IANUARIAS (ICUR 3:6963). The personage on the right is labelled PETR O NEL LA MART (Leclercq, "Inscriptions latines chrétiennes," fig. 143; Fasola, *Catacombs of Domitilla*, 41–43).

fresco, Petronilla wears a classical tunic with *palla* and *lorum*, the costume of saintly women of the apostolic period.[175] The open book and the large *capsa* with papyrus scrolls at the right side of the lunette are attributes of the two women depicted, signifying respectively New Testament literature and Old Testament writings.

B. Episcopa "Q"

Madigan and Osiek claim for the cemetery of St. Paul's Outside the Walls an "Episcopa Q" that they say is referred to in a "versified inscription" on a marble fragment.[176] "Here lies the venerable woman bishop Q (*venerabilis fem[ina] episcopa* Q),/Buried in peace for five [years]...+ Olybrio." Madigan and Osiek note that this Olybrius might be the Western consul who died in 410. But does the cross before Olybrius' name indicate episcopal status? If it does, the possibility is heightened that "Episcopa Q" was wife of a bishop. Madigan and Osiek propose that Episcopa Q was the mother or wife of Pope Siricius.[177] Other scholars including Ute Eisen have placed this same inscription at Interamna (modern Terni).[178] In connection with

---

175. H. Leclercq, "Domitille (Cimetière de)" in *DACL* 4/2 [1921], 1404–1442 at 1417, notes that following the barbarian devastation of the cemeteries and basilicas outside Rome in 755, Pope Paul I began the translation of saints' relics into the city. Among the first was the translation of Petronilla's sarcophagus and inscription into the mausoleum built for her attached to Old St. Peter's. Her designation on the fresco as "martyr" but not as saint fits with the mid-4th-century date of the painting (ibid., 1424).

176. Madigan and Osiek, *Ordained Women*, 193 and nn. 76, 77, citing *Corpus Inscriptionum Latinarum* 11.4339, *Inscriptiones Latinae Christianae Veteres* 85; *Anthologia Latina, sive, Poesis Latinae Supplementum*, ed. Franciscus Buecheler and Alexander Riese (Leipzig: Teubner, 1894–, repr., Amsterdam: Hakkert, 1964), 2.3, no. 2026, p. 64. The catalogue of epigraphy held at St. Paul's Outside the Walls does not show this inscription, identified by Madigan and Osiek as in the ancient basilica's cemetery. See Giorgi Filippi, ed., *Indice della raccolta epigrafica di San Paolo fuori le Mura* (Vatican City: Musei Vaticani, 1998); Barbera and Spinetti, *Iscrizioni latine della raccolta di San Paolo fuori le Mura*. It has been dated 5th–6th century or earlier.

177. Madigan and Osiek, *Ordained Women*, 193. Siricius promulgated the rule of celibacy for the higher clergy, which seems to have been proposed by the shadowy synod of Elvira (Spain) in the first decade of the fourth century.

178. *Corpus Inscriptionum Latinarum* (*CIL*): *Inscriptiones Aemiliae Etruriae Umbriae Latinae* (Berolini: Apud G. Reimerum, 1862), 11:4339; Henri Leclercq, "Presbyter," in *DACL* 14/2 (1948), 1717–21 at 1721; *Inscriptiones Latinae Christianae Veteres* (*ILCV*), ed. Ernst Diehl (3 vols.; Berlin: Weidmann, 1925–1931, repr., 1961–1967), 1:1121; 2:2512; 3:349. Adolf Kalsbach ("Diakonisse," in Klauser, *RLAC* 3 [1957], 926) cites *ILCV* 1121. Eisen (*Women Officeholders*, 199–200) dates this same inscription ca. 500, citing *CIL* 11:4339 and *ILCV* 1:1121, 2:512. Kalsbach and Eisen place this epitaph at Interamna (modern Terni).

this inscription, Eisen notes the observation of Johannes Neumann, that "[of] the multitude of bishops in the first five centuries we know only relatively few by name. Still smaller is the number of those of whom we know at least some dates."[179]

C. Theodora *Episcopa*

In the ninth century, in the papal district of the Lateran, in the Zeno Chapel of the church built by Paschal I to honor Praxedes, the mosaic bust of a veiled woman with rectangular blue nimbus accompanies the busts of Praxedes, the Virgin, and Pudentiana above the lintel of the door cut into the north wall (see chap. 2, Fig. 2.8). This portrait bears the title *Theodora episcopa*. Until recent decades Theodora was virtually ignored even by those who otherwise commented at length on the Zeno Chapel.[180] Visual inspection or a good-quality colored photograph will show those sections of the extant mosaic that have been repaired.[181] G. B. de Rossi studied the mosaic, seeing no reason to discount name and title.[182]

---

179. *Women Officeholders*, 208, quoting from Neumann, "Bischof," 659.

180. Davanzati made a number of iconographic mistakes, but poor lighting also may have contributed to misreadings or oversights. He copied "episcopa" on the relic plaque without comment but did not note the inscription in the Zeno Chapel. By contrast the title *episcopa* is taken at face value by Karen Jo Torjesen, *When Women Were Priests: Women's Leadership in the Early Church and the Scandal of their Subordination in the Rise of Christianity* (San Francisco: HarperSanFrancisco, 1993), 10, citing Morris, *Lady Was a Bishop*, 4–6 and Irvin, "Ministry of Women in the Early Church," 79–81. As parallel examples, Morris (*Lady*, ch. 2, n. 5) cites Felice Grossi-Gondi, *Trattato di epigrafia cristiana: Latina e Greco del mondo romano occidentale* (Rome: Università Gregoriana, 1920), 153 re: an *episcopa Terni*; and n. 6, G. Marini, *Inscriptiones christianae*, Vat. ms. 9072, part 2, ch. XXII, no. i, 1608 (1904) for an epitaph from the cemetery of the Basilica of Saint Valentiniane reading *(Hono)rabilis femina episcopa*.

181. A drawing in Windsor, inv. no. 8930 from Cassiano del Pozzo's collection ca. 1630–1640, shows bust-length figures of women in mosaic with lower portions lost (Waetzoldt, *Kopien des 17 Jahrhunderts*, fig. 501, cat. no. 990). Below the mosaic an elaborate design (of inlaid marble?) forms a lunette-like backdrop above the place where a sarcophagus might be located. To the right is an empty space; it is unclear whether the void represents a doorway. This drawing incorrectly replicates rather than provides the mirror-image of the opposite wall with its lunette showing busts of Christ blessing, accompanied by two men over an altar with confessio, with empty space to the right under the entablature (ibid., 502, cat. 991).

182. Giovanni Battista de Rossi, Enrico Stevenson, and Giuseppe Gatti, *Musaici cristiani e saggi dei pavimenti delle chiese di Roma anteriori al secolo XV* (Rome: Libreria Spithöver di G. Haass, [1872]–1899), [103]. De Rossi reflects on the absence of the title from Ciacconio's drawing, noting that other names are omitted and Theodora's rectangular nimbus is drawn as a halo. The black cubes used for the inscription are antique. He concludes that the title as it presently appears is an inexact restoration.

Brian Brennan considers Theodora's status. Above her portrait as well as in the lengthy inscription embedded in the nave pier closest to the Zeno Chapel she is titled *episcopa*. Is Theodora the ninth-century maternal counterpart of those wives of Roman bishops who, from the time of Pope Siricius in the later fourth century, were expected to observe continence? Since there is no evidence that Bonosus the father of Paschal was ever a bishop, Brennan notes that the title *episcopa* cannot be explained on the score of marriage.[183] In recent decades much has been claimed for Theodora episcopa. Joan Morris makes the credible suggestion that Pope Paschal's mother Theodora "might well have retired as a widow to head" (oversee, the work of *episcopē*) a community of virgins.[184] For Karen Jo Torjesen attempts were made, "perhaps even in antiquity," to efface the feminine ending of Theodora's title as episcopa. Dorothy Irvin points to the episcopal crosses worn by Theodora and Praxedes.[185] Unfortunately for Irvin's proposal, the crosses are modern fabrications. The final letters of Theodora's name and title are modern restorations; the lower portion of the mosaic bust was lost even before the Cassiano dal Pozzo drawings of 1630–1640. However, the upper part of Theodora's bust-portrait, as with the other women, is intact. Her white coif (close-fitting cap) and veil completely conceal her hair. Her husband Bonoso was not identified as a cleric in the *LP* account; therefore Theodora did not acquire her title through her husband.[186] But is her headdress not appropriate to a *presbyterissa* or *diaconissa*, in other circumstances a woman "deposed" by her husband and living apart from him in continence, perhaps in a community of women? Could this not also be the dress of one who held official church status? Theodora may have been widowed not deposed when she oversaw her son the pope's Lateran household, meriting the archaic title of *episcopa*.

---

183. Brennan, "'*Episcopae*': Bishops' Wives," 322, n. 52. The *LP* life of Paschal does not give his mother's name (Davis, *Ninth-Century Popes*, 100.1). The last Roman bishop known to have been married before accession to major orders is Hadrian II (867–872), whose wife and daughter were murdered by an importunate suitor (L. Duchesne, *Beginnings of Temporal Sovereignty of Popes*, 163–64). Irvin's ("Ministry of Women," 81) statement that Theodora's coif shows her to have been unmarried does not take account of the pier inscription.

184. Morris, *Lady Was a Bishop*, 4–6. Other suggestions are far-flung, including the proposal that the portrait is that of an earlier Theodora, leader of a 5th-century woman's community connected with S. Prassede.

185. Torjesen, *When Women Were Priests*, 10; Irvin, *Calendar 2003* (September–October).

186. Davis, *Lives of Ninth-Century Popes*, 100.1.

Ute Eisen discusses the Zeno Chapel portrait and the pier inscription (mistitled "the reliquary inscription"), citing especially Ursula Nilgen and Rotraut Wisskirchen. Eisen would not exclude altogether the possibility of a woman as a Roman bishop in the tumultuous ninth century.[187] Despite the stories about a Pope Joan in the later ninth century, the claims above are large ones. If Theodora was Greek (the Zeno Chapel inspired by her culture), and the adjacent monastery was established by Paschal to house a community of Greek monks, might they have been more accommodating of a powerful presence than their Roman counterparts? It is not beyond the realm of possibility that Theodora, mother of their patron, had a special relation to the church's monastic community. Given Roman tradition, such a relationship would not necessarily be a popular one.

(a) Lateran Baptistery, Chapel of S. Venantius: Maria archiepiscopa orans

The interpretation of Theodora's title is assisted by the apse mosaic in the Lateran Baptistery's Chapel of St. Venantius built by the Dalmatian Pope John IV (640–642) with, according to Richard Krautheimer, mosaics dedicated by the Greek Pope Theodore (642–649) from Jerusalem.[188] At the time of the Avar invasion in the mid-seventh century, artistic influences as well as relics of the local martyrs of Salona and Istria were brought to Rome directly from the Adriatic coastlands. These local Dalmatian martyrs are the saints depicted in the Lateran Baptistery's St. Venantius apse and apsidal arch.[189]

---

187. Eisen (*Women Officeholders*, 204–5).

188. John IV (640–642), "...born in Dalmatia, son of the *scholasticus* Venantius.... He built a church for the martyrs Saints Venantius, Anastasius, Maurus, and many other martyrs whose relics he had ordered to be brought from the Dalmatias and Histrias; he deposited them in that church close to the Lateran font and the oratory of St. John the Evangelist; he decorated it...." (Davis, *Book of Pontiffs*, 74.1). Theodore I's *LP* biography (642–49) says nothing of donations to the Chapel of St. Venantius, but he figures among the stylistically cohesive mosaics in the apse and on the apsidal arch walls. See also Oakeshott, *Mosaics of Rome*, 150–53 and figs. 95, 97–104, esp. 101. The sources of this *martyrium* and the saints honored are discussed by Gillian Mackie, *Early Christian Chapels*, 212–30. See also Alessandra Themelly, "Immagini di Maria nella pittura e nei mosaici romani dalla crisi monotelità agli inizi della seconda iconoclastia (640–819)," in *Acta ad Archaeologiam et Artium Historiam Pertinentia*, ed. Siri Sande and Lasse Hodne (Rome: Giorgio Bretschneider, 1989), 21:108–10.

189. All the figures are identified by inscription but for the Virgin and the builders; see H. Leclercq, "Latran (Venantius Chapel)", in *DACL* 8/2 (1929): 1529–1887 at 1576–1581, esp. 1579; Frederik van der Meer and Christine Mohrmann, *Atlas of the Early Christian World* ([London]: Nelson, 1958), fig. 495; Mackie, *Early Christian Chapels*, ch. 8. Those in the apse

230   WOMEN IN PASTORAL OFFICE

FIGURE 4.9 Rome, Lateran Baptistery. Venantius Chapel: *Maria archiepiscopa orans* with Sts. Paul, Peter (642–649). Photograph by Kevin Moynihan.

In the center of the apse under a large bust of Christ, evidently inspired by the one in the apse of S. Giovanni in Laterano, the Virgin *orans* stands as liturgist and intercessor (Fig. 4.9). The theme of the Virgin as *archiepiscopa* is well known in regions under Byzantine influence.[190] She wears a narrow pallium with two or three Maltese crosses extending below her *palla*, which is emblazoned with one large Maltese cross. The popes and bishops, two on each outer edge of the semicircular mosaic, wear similarly narrow *pallia* bearing a single cross; the upper part of this archiepiscopal insignia is draped conspicuously across their shoulders.[191]

---

are John IV carrying a model of the chapel and Sts. Venantius, bishop and martyr, John the Evangelist, Paul, the Virgin *orans* and Sts. Peter, John the Baptist, Domnio first bishop of Salona and an unhaloed pope carrying a book (probably Theodore I who completed the chapel). The saints on the apsidal arch are the officers Paulinianus and Felius, the monk Asterius, Anastasius, Maur the martyred bishop of Parenzo, the deacon Septimius, and the officers Antiochianus and Gaianus. Salona (Split), from whence most of these saints hail, is an early Christian locale rich in churches that has also provided epigraphical texts for ordained women (see *sacerdota* and *presbytera* in Eisen, *Officeholders*, 131–33).

190. For pictures and examples, see www.womenpriests.org/mrpriest/gallery1.asp but transpose figs. 1 and 2.

191. At the time of Gregory the Great the pallium could be bestowed by the pope on those bishops he chose; later the insignia was restricted to archbishops.

(b) Basilica Euphrasiana, Parenzo: Mary and Elizabeth as archbishops

Turning northeastward to the Istrian coast and the exceptionally well-preserved sixth-century Basilica Euphrasiana at Poreč (Parenzo), Istria, originating from that Adriatic coastland whence derive the saints depicted in the Venantius apse and their relics, three monumental mosaics are found that explain the provenance and iconography of the Virgin *archiepiscopa orans* of St. Venantius.[192] On the expanse of curved wall on either side of the apse of the St. Euphrasius basilica (rebuilt and decorated during the episcopate of Bishop Euphrasius (543–554), recently restored under

FIGURE 4.10 Poreč, Croatia. Basilica Euphrasiana. Presbytery wall: Annunciation (ca. 540). The Bridgeman Art Library.

---

192. Bruno Molajoli, *La Basilica Eufrasiana di Parenzo* (2nd ed.; Padua: "Le Tre Venezie," 1943); Ann Terry and Ffiona Gilmore Eaves, *Retrieving the Record: A Century of Archaeology at Poreč (1847–1947)*, ed. Mijenko Jurković (2 vols.; Zagreb-Motovun: University of Zagreb, International Research Center for Late Antiquity and the Middle Ages, 2002).

232 WOMEN IN PASTORAL OFFICE

UNESCO sponsorship) are rectangular panels depicting, respectively, the angel Gabriel and the Virgin annunciate (Fig. 4.10) and Elizabeth and Mary of the Visitation. Inspired by the *Protoevangelium of James*, the annunciate Virgin sits in front of a basilica spinning wool; she wears a diaphanous veil that wraps cloak-like around her shoulders. Two golden stripes (*clavi*) adorn her long-sleeved tunic. In the Visitation scene on the right wall both women are shown as expectant (Fig. 4.11). Elizabeth wears a purple tunic with *clavi* and golden cloak as she stands in front of her house to greet the Virgin.[193] Mary's imperial purple tunic is adorned with glowing golden *clavi* between which, showing beneath the hem of the purple cloak (*palla*) with golden segmenta, is the unmistakable archiepiscopal pallium with its Greek cross in black. Again, wearing the archiepiscopal pallium, this time with a black Latin

FIGURE 4.11 Poreč, Croatia. Basilica Euphrasiana. Presbytery wall: Visitation (ca. 540). Photograph by Mary M. Schaefer.

---

193. The outer cloak, forerunner of the chasuble, protected the wearer and garments while travelling (John D. Laurence, "Vestments, liturgical," in *NDSW*, 1308).

FIGURE 4.12 Poreč, Croatia. Basilica Euphrasiana. Apse: Virgin Mother *archiepiscopa* (543–554). The Bridgeman Art Library.

cross, the Virgin Mother archiepiscopa is enthroned as Seat of Wisdom in the center of the apse (Fig. 4.12). Her child, holding a rotulus and with his right hand raised in blessing, sits enthroned frontally on her lap. She the God-bearer is the heavenly prototype as well as historical archetype of the bishop of Parenzo, whose episcopal throne is located directly below.

Especially in this last panel, the Virgin's wearing of the archiepiscopal pallium explicates the lineage of Theodora's episcopal title. In the main apse of S. Prassede, Paschal takes his place honorably beside the saints acclaiming the returning Christ. The pope's rectangular blue nimbus shows him to have been a contemporary personage when this mosaic was created. In the chapel of S. Zeno, Theodora is privileged to take her place in the company of the Virgin and saintly sisters honored there. As the Theotokos is the honored mother of the Son who sits at God's right hand, so Theodora is venerable mother of a son who heads the church of Rome. If the pier epitaph can be trusted—and there is no reason to consider it untrustworthy—this chapel is her place of burial.

(c) Ravenna, Archiepiscopal Chapel: Sancta Maria archiepiscopa orans

Across the Adriatic from Poreč a later example is found in the Italo-Byzantine imperial town of Ravenna whose fifth- and sixth-century churches are encrusted with mosaics. The tradition of the *Virgo episcopa orans* endures in a twelfth-century mosaic panel of fine tesserae now prominently placed on the entrance wall of the Museo Arcivescovile in the Archiepiscopal Palace.[194] The round-headed mosaic panel shows, against a gold ground, s[AN]c[T]A MARIA *orans* standing frontally on a green "landscape" dotted with conventional flowers. Different in scale, and hieratic as opposed to taking her place within a scene, the Ravenna Virgin stands in a roundheaded, gold-tesseraed frame beneath drawn curtains. Her haloed head is framed by two white drapes (the *parapetasma*) with gray shadows or embroidery. The Virgin wears a coif and ample blue veil (*maphorion*) with a gold border which falls around her shoulders to knee-length in back. Two Greek crosses in gold punctuate the shoulder wrap.[195] An archbishop's white, fringed pallium with golden cross is held in place by a narrow red belt, and a long narrow embroidered golden sash reaches almost to the hem of her tight-sleeved blue tunic.

(d) Universal Judgment (Vatican, Pinacoteca): Maria orans

That the Italo-Byzantine theme of *Maria orans* was at home in Rome is shown by the large keyhole-shaped panel painting of the Universal Judgment attributed to Niccolò and Giovanni, painters of the Scuola Romana (Fig. 4.13). It has been dated variously to the eleventh, second half of the twelfth, or thirteenth century.[196] The very rare women's perspective displayed in the panel's program is outlined by Chiara Frugoni.[197] Two scenes appear at the bottom of this graphic pictogram of the Last Judgment whose composition is subdivided into five registers: on the left, saints on either side of the Virgin Intercessor anticipate paradise, and on the right, the lost are deposited into hell fire. The haloed Vatican Virgin *orans* wears

---

194. Originally this mosaic of the Virgin Intercessor graced the apse of Ravenna's Basilica Ursiana, a location typical for this subject in the Greek world. See Christa Belting-Ihm, "*Sub Matris Tutela,*" pl. XVIb. See also www.womenpriests.org/mrpriest/gallery1.asp, no. 5.

195. This hieratic depiction of *Maria orans* bears an uncanny iconographic resemblance to the 6th-century "headless woman" of the St. Maximin crypt discussed in ch. 3.

196. M. De Luca, "La tavola del giudizio universale già in San Gregorio Nazianzeno (Pinacoteca Vaticana) 1061–1071," in *La pittura medievale a Roma, 312–1431: corpus e atlante*, vol. 4: *Riforme e tradizione, 1050–1198*, ed. Serena Romana (5 vols.; Milan: Jaca Book, 2006–), Pt. 1, 45–55.

197. Chiara Frugoni, "The Imagined Woman," in *A History of Women in the West*, vol. 2: *Silences of the Middle Ages*, ed. Christiane Klapisch-Zuber (London; Cambridge, MA: Belknap Press of Harvard University Press, 1992), 336–422 at 354–57.

FIGURE 4.13 Vatican, Pinacoteca. Universal Judgment. Detail: Maria *orans*, Praxedes (?) and Pudentiana (?), with donors Benedicta and Constantia abbess (1061–1071). Photo Vatican Museums.

a coif under a purplish-red maphorion. Her costume with gold trim at wrists and edges of the tunic is similar to that found in the imposing hieratic mosaic of *Sancta Maria orans* at the entrance to Ravenna's Museo Arcivescovile. Her tight-sleeved tunic is blue, with two short golden sashes hanging conspicuously from her golden belt. Do these golden sashes perhaps represent Mary as diacona, a subject known in Italy in this period, or as presbytera? Mary is portrayed as ordered clergy by virtue of her role in salvation history. The Virgin is flanked by two women saints wearing decorated headgear and earrings and fine red robes with golden collars; they proffer crowns in veiled hands. They have been tentatively identified as Praxedes and Pudentiana. Behind them stand two other women, one white-veiled, one not, garbed in deep purple dresses with golden collars and belts. Higher up on the pictorial plane, and therefore according to artistic convention standing behind the female figures, are two groups of men. The personages mentioned above are separated by a jeweled and gilded wall representing Heavenly Jerusalem. In front of this wall, and below them, hover two white-veiled women who hold respectively a large lighted candle and a portico in hands covered by scarves.[198] Both wear red shoes. Small in scale, they are earthly devotees of the heavenly assembly. Their identities, *Do[(m)n] Benedicta ancilla D(e)i* and *Constantia abbatissa*, are given on the red-painted border framing the whole pictogram.[199] Lady Benedicta is garbed in a dull purplish-red garment that suggests her connection to a noble family. *Ancilla Dei sacrata* was the Roman term for a consecrated woman who did not live the cloistered monastic life. The abbess Constantia is dressed in a dull blue, the same color as the Virgin's tunic. Chiara Frugoni identifies the donor as abbess of the Benedictine convent of S. Maria in Campo Marzio, Rome. Is this the same *Constantia diacona* who in 1053 made a donation to the archpriest of the church of St. Martin behind the Basilica of St. Peter's?[200] Then the panel, the oldest in the Vatican Picture Gallery, can be dated ca. 1061–1071.

Conclusion

The external ecclesial activities of religious women in Rome became sharply circumscribed during the first third of the thirteenth century. Judging that the lifestyles of religious women in Rome required remediation, Innocent III (1198–1216) worked to consolidate the monasteries and enhance the ascetic character of women's religious life. Innocent imposed on the diverse groups of religious women in Rome "uniformity of rule, dress, and discipline to counter 'diversity' in religion and serious charges—possibly untrue—of scandal and decadence."[201] Jacques de Vitry (ca. 1160–1240), auxiliary bishop from Liège who moved to Rome,

---

198. In the women's monastery of Varatec, northern Romania, when holding a burning candle the hands are protected by covering with a scarf.

199. Frugoni, "Imagined Woman," 354.

200. Mentioned in the chapter archive of S. Pietro in Vaticano. Andrieu (*OR* 4:143 and n. 5) cites Schiapparelli, "Carte antiche dell'Archivio capitolare di San Pietro," 466–67.

201. Brenda M. Bolton, "Daughters of Rome: All One in Christ Jesus!," in *Women in the Church: Papers Read at the 1989 Summer Meeting and the 1990 Winter Meeting of the Ecclesiastical History Society*, ed. W. J. Sheils and Diana Wood. (Oxford: Basil Blackwell, 1990), 101–15 at 109.

Honorius III (1216–1227), Hugolino Cardinal-Bishop of Ostia (Gregory IX, 1227–1241), Cardinal Nicholas of Tusculum, the papal chamberlain Stephen of Fossanova, and not least the founder of the Friars Preachers St. Dominic Guzman (ca. 1170–1221) were of one mind with Innocent on the question of nuns' enclosure and over time collaborated in Innocent's project to bring together all the nuns and recluses of Rome under one rule and roof, that at San Sisto.[202]

The definition and shape of ordination to major ecclesiastical office as well as suitable rituals for induction were being developed during the formative period, when the public as well as the private history of women was rarely a matter of record. Until now the disparate pieces of evidence from the variety of sources presented in these pages have not been reviewed as part of a coherent picture. In the ninth century within the city of Rome itself Theodora episcopa stands out. During a time of known immigration of Eastern ecclesiastics and monastics into Rome, the title episcopa seems less far-fetched because the Eastern churches had a longer and more substantial history of women's ecclesiastical participation than the West and, then as now, the heads of female monasteries exercised an important and public role. Diaconissas and presbyterissas existed from the time of Pope Siricius in the Roman church as deposed wives of bishops and presbyters. Siricius had tried, somewhat unsuccessfully, to impose the law of celibacy for higher clergy throughout the wider Christian church. Within Rome he was successful, and later popes including Gregory the Great exhorted their highest clergy to follow the discipline. Presbyteras, the female equivalent of presbyters, seem to have been wiped out by Gelasian decree in the late fifth century. At this time the presbyteral office within the city-church changed, with presbyters taking on some of the sacramental functions previously presided only by the bishop. Meanwhile the office of diacona, under threat from local Gallican councils, made its way into Rome by sometime in the fifth or sixth century, supplanting the office of presbytera. By the later seventh century "true" diaconas—that is, those ordained to the office by the pope of Rome himself—existed in the Eternal City. If we can judge from extant rituals, it would be four or five centuries

---

202. The saga is recounted by Brenda M. Bolton, "Daughters," with some naïveté. Not all "religious" women had a vocation to strict enclosure and not all rules and styles of religious life could be integrated. Gregory IX succeeded in enclosing all the religious women of Rome in 1232 and by his bull *Gloriam virginalem* all those of Germany and the Holy Roman Empire in 1233 (112 and n. 84).

before these diaconas would be drawn into cloister or canonry. The rituals and roles of diaconas would continue "out-of-bounds" in cloisters such as those of Benedictine and Carthusian nuns and among Augustinian canonesses. With Carthusian nuns the symbols still endure. Meanwhile in a few Eastern churches, notably the Armenian Apostolic and the Greek Orthodox, nun-diaconas are again being ordained. Chapter five will investigate ordination rituals and prayers of churches of East and West that have been preserved in manuscripts in the Vatican Library and elsewhere. This evidence is striking especially when compared to the official ecclesiastical invisibility of ministerially active women in today's Roman Catholic Church.

5

Ordination Rites, for Men Only? For Women Too!

THE CATHOLIC CHURCHES have read back into the narrative events of Jesus' public life, passion and post-resurrection appearances his manifest will to establish a church and even to "ordain" leaders, appointing or instituting them permanently with prayer. Inspired by one or another theology of public ecclesiastical office, a scriptural "moment" has been selected to serve as a symbolic high point for the constitution of the church's leadership structure, whether at the Last Supper with the Pauline and gospel mandates, "Do this in memory of me" (1 Cor 11:24–25, Luke 22:19); with the dominical commands to preach the gospel to the whole world (Mark 16:15) and "Go, therefore, baptize" at the Lord's ascension (Matt 28:19); or at the Johannine appearance of the risen Christ to his disciples in the upper room (John 20:22–23).

Whichever charter event founds ministerial self-perception, it is a sociologically verifiable fact that human groups require leaders if they are to hold together and continue in existence. In order to retain fidelity to the Lord Jesus and cohesiveness among themselves, post-apostolic communities required leadership by persons exercising various responsibilities. Within a few decades after Jesus' death and resurrection, patterns of leadership were forming in churches of disparate cultures across the known world. At the beginning these roles were functional, including oversight, shared conciliar decision-making, and maintainance of the network of relationships among the members of the *laos*, the whole people of God including its officers. Because of their charisms or Spirit-given gifts for preaching, community leadership, and communal worship, individuals acted in the community and on its behalf.

Over time the itinerant triads of apostles, prophets, and evangelizers known from Paul's letters and other writings of the apostolic period, whose leadership was based on charismatic gifts, would give way to the more stable and settled household models of overseers (*episcopoi*), elders (*presbyteroi*), and helpers/servants (*diakonoi*) or, following John Collins, mediators and emissaries found in the Pastoral epistles.[1] What would become the "major" orders of episcopacy, presbyterate, and diaconate characterized by permanence, stability, and hierarchical order, each carrying certain evangelical, administrative, and liturgical responsibilities, developed gradually from functional roles. These stable apostolic ministries not only symbolized the Christ of faith but also pointed to the Jesus of history.[2]

The Christian Scriptures do not tell us to whom was entrusted presidency of the Lord's Supper.[3] So far as "priesthood" is concerned, Scripture applies the generic term *iereus* (*sacerdos*, priest) to pagan cultic leaders; to Jesus Christ (Letter to the Hebrews); and to the whole body of the holy people of God (1 Pet). First Clement 40.5 compares Christian worship to the work of high priest, priests, and levites, presenting the bishop's cultic role in terms of high priesthood, a concept inspired by the Old Testament.[4]

---

1. Acts 20:17 and 28 elide the role of elders and overseers in Paul's departing speech to the Ephesian elders, providing a scriptural archetype for Rome's "presbyter-bishops." In proposing the mediatorial or ambassadorial function of the diaconal office, John N. Collins (*Diakonia*; Collins, *Deacons and the Church: Making Connections between Old and New* [Harrisburg, PA: Morehouse Publishing, 2002]) offers a fresh starting point for this rejuvenated ministry.

2. In the Middle Ages a moment or action in Jesus' life was cited as charter-event for each ecclesiastical office. These very popular lists have been called "ordinals of Christ." See Roger E. Reynolds, *The Ordinals of Christ from their Origins to the Twelfth Century* (Berlin; New York: Walter de Gruyter, 1978). Old Testament accounts of Temple worship also provided types for liturgical offices and played a stronger role in shaping ecclesiastical office. For a theological perspective on church office as related to Christ, see Edward J. Kilmartin, "Bishop and Presbyter as Representatives of the Church and of Christ," in Leonard Swidler and Arlene Swidler, eds., *Women Priests: A Catholic Commentary on the Vatican Declaration* (New York: Paulist, 1977), 299.

3. We cannot assume that only "the Twelve" presided at eucharist. "Apostles" (not the 12 but those sent out to evangelize), prophets, and those gifted in leading public prayer certainly did so. Householders and patrons who hosted the Christian community would be obvious choices as presiders at the Lord's Supper, including women heads of households. See Hans Bernhard Meyer, *Eucharistie: Geschichte, Theologie, Pastoral*, 79; and for Matthaean house churches, Wainwright, *Towards a Feminist Critical Reading of the Gospel according to Matthew*, 339–52.

4. E.g., Lev 8–9; Sir 45:6–22. See Pierre-Marie Gy, "Ancient Ordination Prayers," in Wiebe Vos and Geoffrey Wainwright, eds., *Ordination Rites: Papers Read at the 1979 Congress of Societas Liturgica* (Rotterdam: Liturgical Ecumenical Center Trust, 1980), 86; Gy, "Notes on Early Terminology of Christian Priesthood," 113.

What we experience today as the presbyteral or sacerdotal role is the product of a long and convoluted history. It is too easily assumed that the ancient presbyteral office involved presiding as sacramental leader in ways that are standard for the Roman Catholic or Orthodox priest today. But functions that now are presided by presbyters or "priests of the second rank"—initiation rites, reconciliation, eucharist—were presided in the early church by the bishop present in each large town or, before that, by itinerant prophets.[5] So what was the role of presbyter, or presbytera, in the early centuries? The office went through various phases. What would members of a "council of elders," singled out for their dedication to the Christian life and wise in its practice, do? In the city of Rome during the later fourth century presbyters were in charge of preparing catechumens for initiation by the bishop. Later, Flavia Vitalia sold burial places in Salona (Dalmatia) just as male presbyters did.[6] This work in the sphere of "real life" did not exclude her from exercising a public role in sacramental celebrations; on the contrary, it qualified her for liturgical ministry, since the latter functioned as symbolic expression of actual service to the faith community.

During the first concerted missionary initiative of the nascent church, the Pauline mission, women had participated as apostles, heads of house-churches, and evangelizers. Curtailment of these roles in succeeding decades and centuries is discernible in Acts of the Apostles, the post-Pauline letters, and the Pastoral epistles, in the somewhat later apocryphal gospels and *acta* attributed to apostles and their disciples, and in surviving church orders.[7] In antiquity there was no denying the fact of

---

5. In the Catholic churches only a bishop or presbyter, whose office includes the capacity for full pastoral and governance responsibilities in a diocesan church or parish respectively, can exercise the ministerial priesthood, presiding in sacramental liturgies of the assembly and absolving sins in the name of the church. Collegiality of ministries marked the sacramental celebrations of the early churches. The collegial *Symbolgestalt* of Eastern liturgies involves a number and variety of ministers (Schulz, *Byzantine Liturgy*). It is still a notable feature—even if overwhelmingly male-specific—of Eastern (Orthodox and Oriental) liturgies. In the post–Vatican II Roman rite a well-prepared Sunday eucharistic celebration presided by the pastor of the parish with competent persons exercising their ministries provides a counterpart.

6. Eisen, *Women Officeholders*, 131–32. Flavia Vitalia's tomb inscription is dated 425. In Rome the deacon Callistus oversaw the Christian cemeterial complex on the Via Appia before his election as Callistus I (217–222).

7. Reimer, *Women in the Acts of the Apostles*; *Women's Bible Commentary*, exp. ed., 394–402 (Acts), 430–32 (Eph), 438–39 (Col), 444–49 (1 Tim), 450 (2 Tim), and 452 (Titus).

woman's subordination, especially to those males who were her relatives. On them she relied for protection, sustenance, life. In old Rome, father or husband had held power over daughter or wife, concubine, servant, or slave to the point of punishment or even death.[8] Depending on a woman's social stratum the legal niceties differed. A judicious weighing of evidence for women's leadership roles in religious groups is impossible without background knowledge of the position of women in these same ancient and medieval secular societies.[9] Christians acknowledged the equality of women with men in the eschatological realm. But the "order of creation" in the second creation story—God creates the man first, then the animals, and the woman last (Gen 2:4b–3:24)—along with the teachings that arose on the text, supported the maintenance of women's subordinate status, tempered only by martyrdom, when "the weaker sex" endured to death interrogations and agonies. Then women were lauded for displaying "male" fortitude and "virtue."

After the Constantinian Peace and the imperial government's departure from Old to New Rome (Constantinople), church administration developed to fill the vacuum. Ecclesiastical bureaucrats replaced imperial civil servants with consequent shouldering of the latter's responsibilities, honors, and "perks." The transferal of power from civil to ecclesiastical officials resulted not only in the church's spurt of growth and bureaucratic institutionalization but also led to the diminishment or removal of women from visibility in the public ecclesiastical sphere. Later on, pacts of mutual assistance or conflicts between the church and national monarchies also shaped ecclesiastical self-understanding. Communion ecclesiology, in which the ministerial gifts of all were exercised for the benefit

---

8. For an overview with texts available on the internet, see John Wijngaards, *The Ordination of Women in the Catholic Church: Unmasking a Cuckoo's Egg Tradition* (New York: Continuum, 2001), 48–55.

9. For women's leadership in Judaism, Bernadette J. Brooten's study *Women Leaders in the Ancient Synagogue* provides insights for similar studies of Christian women. For women in Christianity, see Mary T. Malone, *Women and Christianity* (3 vols.; Ottawa: Novalis, 2000–2003). The literature covering the gamut of women's life is immense. See, e.g., Shulamith Shahar, *The Fourth Estate: A History of Women in the Middle Ages*, trans. Chaya Galai (London; New York: Methuen, 1983); Pauline Schmitt Pantel, ed., *A History of Women in the West*, vol. 1: *From Ancient Goddesses to Christian Saints* (Cambridge, MA: Belknap Press of Harvard University Press, 1992); Christiane Klapisch-Zuber, ed., *A History of Women in the West*, vol. 2: *Silences of the Middle Ages* (1992); Natalie Zemon Davis and Arlette Farge, eds., *A History of Women in the West*, vol. 3: *Renaissance and Enlightenment Paradoxes* (1993).

of the community, was abandoned; the pope's rule resembled in several ways an absolute monarch's. However, where royalty and nobility wielded power vis-à-vis the church, women of the nobility exercised a measure of influence in church affairs.

1. *Official Rites in the Early Churches*

In the Hebrew and Christian Scriptures, laying on of hands with prayer by recognized leaders, or by the whole people gathered, appears as a rite for either temporary or permanent deputation in the East.[10] There are no ordination rituals extant for anybody prior to at least 200 CE.[11] During the first two centuries of church formation, leadership was based on charism, especially in the Pauline churches. Laying on of hands with prayer, cited in Acts and 1–2 Timothy, was a gesture also used in other contexts. Ceremonial seating or enthronement of a head officer may be counted as one way for establishing a person in office. For incontrovertible ritual evidence we must wait for the fourth century.

Granted, *Apostolic Tradition* (which has been dated ca. 215 and traditionally localized in Rome) contains well-formulated rituals as well as guidelines for choice and installation of church officers. Many older Catholic writers presumed that *Apostolic Tradition*'s ordination rites are those of the official Roman church.[12] But this is a questionable assumption. The provenance of

---

10. Acts and the Pastoral epistles give us three patterns of commissioning for ecclesial deputation. Laying on of hands formalized temporary commissioning (Acts 13:1–3), permanent installation/recognition (Acts 1:15–26 and 6:3–6), and ordination to teaching office (1 Tim 4:14; 2 Tim 1:6), varying according to the kind and duration of activity for which a person was deputed.

11. Edward J. Kilmartin ("Ministry and Ordination in Early Christianity against a Jewish Background," in Vos and Wainwright, *Ordination Rites Past and Present*, 42–69 at 48–49) reconstructs a simple ritual from 1–2 Tim. For resumés of the early evidence, see J. Kevin Coyle, "The Laying on of Hands as a Conferral of the Spirit: Some Problems and a Possible Solution," in Elizabeth A. Livingstone, ed., *Studia Patristica 18/2: Critica, Classica, Ascetica, Liturgica: Papers of the 1983 Oxford Patristic Conference* (Kalamazoo, MI: Cistercian Publications, 1989), 339–53; Cyrille Vogel, "Is the Presbyteral Ordination of the Celebrant a Condition for the Celebration of the Eucharist?," in *Roles in the Liturgical Assembly: The Twenty-Third Liturgical Conference Saint Serge*, trans. Matthew J. O'Connell (New York: Pueblo Publishing Co., 1981), 253–54.

12. Majority opinion has held that *AT* gives the ordination rites of the early Roman church, e.g., P.-M. Gy, "Ancient Ordination Prayers," 72; Antonio Santantoni, "Orders and Ministries in the First Four Centuries," in *Handbook for Liturgical Studies*, vol. 4: *Sacraments and Sacramentals*, ed. Anscar J. Chupungco (5 vols.; Collegeville, MN: Liturgical, 2000), 197–201. A readily available text is *Hippolytus: A Text for Students*, trans. Geoffrey J. Cuming, with

Apostolic Tradition has been proposed as Alexandria or Antioch, this church order representing the praxis of a small, rigorist sectarian group located in Rome.[13] The ordination texts appear to have been translated into Latin from a Greek document compiled in North Italy circa 380–430).[14] *Apostolic Tradition* had no clearly discernible influence on Roman eucharistic or ordination rituals; it played an important role in the East as shown in *Apostolic Constitutions* (Syria or Constantinople ca. 380) and related documents.

The earlier evolution of Christian offices in Eastern Mediterranean regions, and of rites for installing them, presents a striking contrast to Rome. This fact explains why, in many Eastern churches, diaconal or presbyteral offices for women are historical realities witnessed by inclusion in church orders, the decrees of local and general councils, and epigraphy. Even when the offices themselves had long since ceased to exist, conciliar canons were cited by clerics and scholars. Some of the Church Fathers, notably bishops concerned with administration as well as spiritual formation, gave appreciative or adversarial comments on these offices without providing the reportage that would allow a sure reconstruction of a given ministry's profile. Others accepted the ministries but failed to define their scope. Sometimes the liturgical rite itself provides data.

2. Ordination in the Eastern Churches: Early History and Terminology

Ordination rites in those Eastern churches for which there is evidence show a structuring of the sacrament that is common to both men's and women's rites.[15] The essence of the Eastern rites is laying on of hands

---

introduction, translation, commentary, and notes (Bramcote, Notts.: Grove Books, 1976). See also Bradshaw, Johnson and Phillips, *Apostolic Tradition*, 6.

13. It has been cogently argued that the eucharistic anaphora, which has made *AT* a model in late 20th-century liturgies, comes from west of Antioch and Palestine or north towards Asia Minor; see Matthieu Smyth with Paul Bradshaw, "The Anaphora of the So-called *Apostolic Tradition* and the Roman Eucharistic Prayer," *Usus Antiquior* 1 (2010): 5–25 at 23, repr. in Maxwell E. Johnson, ed., *Issues in Eucharistic Praying in East and West: Essays in Liturgical and Theological Analysis* (Collegeville, MN: Liturgical, 2010), 71–97.

14. Walls, "Latin Version of Hippolytus' Apostolic Tradition," 155–62; Eric Segelberg, "The Ordination Prayers in Hippolytus," *SP* 13 (1975): 397–408. Georg Kretschmar ("Early Christian Liturgy in the Light of Contemporary Historical Research," *SL* 16 [1986–1987]: 31–53 at 33) judges that *AT*'s ordination rites are "not archaic."

15. The ordination rite can be analyzed by way of its various levels of signification: the ritual action itself at the level of praxis; its human social dimension (functional delegation *for* office),

with prayer led by the presiding bishop. In the early churches an official appointment to church office was linked to the specific place, the "title," where that ministry would be exercised. "Absolute" ordinations, those without a designated pastoral charge, were forbidden.[16] Terminology came to be used more precisely in the East than in the West, but initially meanings were blurred and must be inferred from their context in particular documents.[17] A blessing or *eulogia* was a simple prayer or blessing formula made without extension of the hands. Even with respect to this simple blessing, *Apostolic Constitutions* VIII insists that the bishop and presbyter may bless but not the deacon or deaconess.[18] The Greek words *cheirotonein* and *cheirotonia*, used by Christians for establishing persons in the major ranks of ecclesiastical office, refer to the whole process of appointment to

---

which recognizes and engages a person as a publicly delegated official of the institution with specified duties; and what is ultimately signified, the theological or depth-dimension of the office. This last includes bestowal of the charism *of* office, which will eventually come to be read in Latin scholastic theology as an ontological change (= change of meaning, often interpreted as a change of being) of the person so delegated.

16. Council of Chalcedon (451), can. 6 (Hefele, *Histoire des conciles*, 2, 2, 787–788). Ordination to a specific pastoral charge was a required condition even if not named during the course of the ritual. The transfer of bishops from one local church to another was not considered normal procedure, nor was the election of the pope from among bishops already ordained. See Cyrille Vogel, "*Vacua manus impositio*: L'inconsistance de la chirotonie absolue en Occident," in *Mélanges liturgiques offerts au R. P. dom Bernard Botte* (Louvain: Abbaye du Mont César, 1972), 511–24; Vogel, *Ordinations inconsistantes et caractère inamissable* (Torino: Bottega d'Erasmo, 1978); Vogel, "Titre d'ordination et lien du presbytre à la communauté locale dans l'église ancienne," *LMD* 115 (1973): 70–85.

17. Appointment or establishment in office (*kathistai* in secular Greek) was the purpose of ordination in its human social dimension. Cyrille Vogel has written extensively on ordination in the early church and medieval periods. See "L'imposition des mains dans les rites d'ordination en Orient et en Occident," *LMD* 102 (1970): 57–72; "*Vacua manus impositio*," 511–24; "Chirotonie et Chirothésie: Importance et relativité du geste de l'imposition des mains dans la collation des ordres," *Irénikon* 45 (1972): 7–21; 207–38; "*Laïca communione contentus*: Le retour du presbytre à son rang des laïcs," *RSR* 47 (1973): 56–122; "'*Vulneratum caput*': Position d'Innocent I (402–417) sur la validité de la chirotonie presbytérale conférée par un évêque hérétique," *RAC* 49 (1973): 375–84 = *Miscellanea in onore di L. de Bruyne e A. Ferrua* 2:375–84; XXIII Semaine d'études liturgiques, Paris, June 28–July 1, 1976; "Handauflegung," in *RLAC* 13 (1986): 482–93. The rite for the ordination of a deaconess is found in Paris, Bibl. Nat. syr. ms. 113, fols. 111r–112v.

18. What the male deacon is prohibited from doing distinguishes his office from the sacerdotal. *Apostolic Constitutions* states, "The [male] deacon does not bless; he does not give the blessing, but accepts [it] from the bishop and presbyter; he does not baptize, he does not offer; but when a bishop or priest has offered, he distributes to the people, not as a priest, but as one who ministers to priests." No. 6 gives the duties of the deaconess: she "does not bless (*eulogei*) and does not do anything of that which the presbyters and deacons do, but to her belongs watching the doors and ministering to presbyters in the baptism of women because of decency" (*Didascalia et Constitutiones Apostolorum*, ed. F. X. Funk

office from election through ritual prayer with laying on of hands.[19] In the euchologies, *cheirothesia* (from *epithesis cheiron* or *cheiras*) refers to the specific, central act of stretching out or laying on of hands by the ordaining prelate.[20] Cyrille Vogel sums it up:

> After a rather lengthy period of development, the tradition of the Eastern Churches came to distinguish between *cheirotonia* (imposition of hands for conferring the offices of episcopate, presbyterate and diaconate) and *cheirothesia* (imposition of hand[s] understood as a simple blessing for ministers of lesser rank). However, the various euchologies ignore this verbal distinction: the imposition of hands, whether called *cheirotonia* or *cheirothesia*, is part of the ritual for ordination to all clerical ranks; in this, the Eastern churches differ from Latin practice.[21]

Later canonical and didactic, as opposed to liturgical, sources maintained the distinction between *cheirotonia* (imposition of hands in the rituals

---

[2 vols. in 1; Turin: Bottega d'Erasmo, 1964; reprint of 2-volume 1905 edition], VIII.28.4–6, pp. 530–531 [1st vol.]). The evidence is carefully weighed by Marcel Metzger, "Pages féminines des *Constitutions apostoliques*," in Hans-Jürgen Feulner, Elena Velkovska, Robert F. Taft (eds.), *Crossroad of Cultures: Studies in Liturgy and Patristics in Honor of Gabriele Winkler* (Rome: PIO, 2000), 515–41. The ordination prayers are remarkably similar, both invoking the Holy Spirit, but some liturgical functions of men and women deacons differ. Their common liturgical service is tending the doors to the place of worship and keeping order; there are also parallels in the social and ecclesial services they render. One segment of *Apostolic Constitutions*, the 85 *canones apostolorum*, knows nothing of a female diaconate.

19. Paul Bradshaw (*Ordination Rites of Ancient Churches East and West*, 34). That this may also be designated *cheirothesia* points to the "ambivalence" of the Greek word *cheirotonia*, "the lifting up of hands" as first signifying the act of election. The term was extended to include the entire ordination rite. Then *cheirotonia* was restricted to the kernel of the ritual, laying on of hands accompanied by prayer.

20. C. H. Turner, "χειροτονία, χειροθεσία, ἐπίθεσις χειρῶν (and the Accompanying Verbs)," *JTS* 24 (1923): 496–504. Developing his own technical vocabulary, the compiler of *Apostolic Constitutions* of the later fourth century sharply contrasts the two words so that *cheirothesia* refers to laying on of hands "exclusive of ordination," e.g., the blessing of catechumens, confirmation, reconciliation of penitents or heretics, healing of the sick, and generally any blessing made by laying on hands. Cipriano Vagaggini ("L'ordinazione delle diaconesse nella tradizione greca e bizantina," *Orientalia Christiana Periodica* 40 [1974]: 169) exegetes *Apost. Constit.* VIII, 37.4 and 39.1 (the bishop's blessing of the people) somewhat differently: *cheirothesia* is "an extension of the hand without physical contact with the one he is blessing." In any case this document makes a clear-cut distinction between the two words, one that will be blurred in later documents.

21. Cyrille Vogel, "Is the Presbyteral Ordination of the Celebrant," 255.

establishing bishop, presbyter, and deacon) and *cheirothesia* (a simple blessing for lower clerics and laity).[22] Vogel's next comment is important: "[T]he gesture of imposing hands becomes non-determinative if it is considered solely from a ritual viewpoint and not given its ecclesial context."[23] Words and gestures are not by themselves sufficient to explicate the meaning of the rite and to accomplish it. The ordaining officer, the presence (or absence) of other ministers and the people, whether the ritual is placed within or outside the liturgy, and its location within the church building (presbytery, doorway, or sacristy), depended on the rank of the office being conferred. All these aspects enter into the significance of the liturgical sign and contribute to actualizing the ecclesiastical status of the ordinand.[24]

A. Ordination Rituals for Women in the Ancient and Medieval Syrian and Byzantine Churches

The rituals found in *Apostolic Constitutions* and those for the Greek-speaking churches were known, studied, and published by scholars of church history and liturgy from at least the mid-seventeenth century. Cipriano Vagaggini analyzes the well-known prayer for the ordination of a woman deacon found in *Apostolic Constitutions* VIII, 19.1–20.2 (Syria? ca. 380).[25] The bishop lays his hands on her head "in the presence of the priests,

---

22. Vagaggini, "Ordinazione delle diaconesse," 179, n. 2 citing Vogel, "Chirotonie et chirothésie," 7–12. Vagaggini provides a detailed analysis.

23. Vogel, "Is Presbyteral Ordination of Celebrant a Condition for Celebration of Eucharist?," 255.

24. As pointed out by Gary Macy in *Hidden History*, 7–8, already in 1655 Jean Morin (*Commentarius de sacris ecclesiae ordinationibus*, 143) had noted that the context in which Greek deaconesses were ordained showed the fullness of their ordination: terminology, location (at the altar by the bishop), hand-laying during prayer by the bishop, bestowal of the stole, and, finally, the mode of taking communion: the woman deacon, having been handed the chalice, received communion in both kinds.

25. Vagaggini, "Ordinazione delle diaconesse," 177–85. Scholars have proposed that *Apostolic Constitutions* is the Syrian product of an Arian compiler in the late 4th century but that the status of its community, if there was one, does not materially affect this prayer (*Didascalia et Constitutiones apostolorum*, ed. Funk, VIII.19–20, 1:524–25). For opinions, see Bradshaw, *Ordination Rites of Ancient Churches East and West*, 4, 84–86, 116. Jean Morin (*Commentarius de sacris ecclesiae ordinationibus*, Part 2, 25) reproduced the introduction and prayer of "The Constitution of Bartholomew concerning a diaconissa."

deacons, and deaconesses" while saying the following solemn epicletic prayer, which parallels that used in ordaining male deacons:

> O Eternal God, Father of our Lord Jesus Christ, Creator of man and woman, you filled Miriam, Deborah, Anna, and Huldah with the Spirit. You did not disdain that your only-begotten Son should be born of a woman. You ordained women to be keepers of your holy gates in the tabernacle of the testimony and in the Temple.
>
> Do now look upon this your handmaid, who is to be ordained to the diaconate, and grant her your Holy Spirit, and cleanse her "from every defilement of body and spirit," that she may worthily discharge the work which is entrusted to her, to your glory, and to the praise of your Christ, to whom with you and the Holy Spirit be glory and adoration for ever. Amen.[26]

Commenting on this prayer, Vagaggini notes that the deaconess is established in her office by *cheirotonia*, the bishop's imposition of hands with physical contact. In the case of the male or female deacon, this gesture is reserved to the bishop alone. Whereas subdeacons and lectors are instituted in the *diaconicon* (sacristy), the presence of presbyters, deacons, and deaconesses at this liturgy presupposes that the ordination takes place in public within the presbytery and at the foot of the altar.[27] The public and solemn nature of this fourth-century rite for deacon or diacona is also shown by the fact that the litany is sung.

An illustration in Paris, Bibliothèque Nationale ms. syr. 341, the "oldest surviving example of the full bible with a unified program of

---

26. Sentiments of need for cleansing (see 2 Cor 7:1) are not limited to prayers for women but are found also in prayers for ordinations of male deacon and presbyter. The translation of *Apost. Constit.* VIII, (19.1–20.2) is given in J. N. M. Wijngaards, *No Women in Holy Orders? The Women Deacons of the Early Church* (Norwich: Canterbury, 2002), 175, slightly emended.

27. Paul Bradshaw (*Ordination Rites of Ancient Churches East and West*, 84) refers to the "institution" of deaconesses because in *Apostolic Constitutions* the term ordination is not found in the ministry's title. Two possibilities might be considered. Since the rite for a deaconess follows immediately on that of a deacon, the title might have been abbreviated. Or the author used the term "ordination" in its civil sense, establishment in an *ordo* or "well-defined social body distinct from the people." Since women were not counted as members of the *laos* in either its original or later sense, by definition they could not be "ordained." "The East Syrian rite specifies that the bishop gives a blessing, laying on his hand not in the manner of an ordination. However, the *explicit* refers to the ritual as an ordination of deaconesses" (ibid., 162–63).

illustration" supports the textual evidence of ordination rites for women.[28] This sixth-century Syriac bible contains an unusually complex illumination (fol. 118r) among the series of single author portraits that introduce each biblical book. The painting prefacing Proverbs and the books of Solomon contains three figures standing frontally, at the left a man, and then two women. The women are somewhat taller and more imposing than the author Solomon, despite the fact that he is robed, nimbed as a Byzantine emperor, and carries a large book.[29] The central female figure is the unnimbed Virgin Panaghia who clasps a child, preexistent Sophia (Wisdom, cf. Proverbs 8:22) enthroned within a cosmic mandorla. Mary's blue robe is decorated with golden clavi, two vertical stripes denoting senatorial rank, so prominent as to suggest an orarion (stole). To the right an unnimbed, veiled woman wears a red cloak over a white tunic with prominent golden clavi or orarion and fringed maniple; in her veiled left hand she clasps a jeweled gospel book, and in her right a full-length cross-staff. The image suggests episcopal status. In any case, she is the ecclesial counterpart of the *imperium* symbolized by Solomon. Henri Omont, writing on this miniature in 1909, identified this figure as a personification of pre-existent Ecclesia.[30] It is apparent that this woman is wearing the vesture of an ecclesiastic of some significance. At this period and for this church we have textual evidence only of women's ordained diaconal ministry; otherwise the episcopal parallel pointed out by Ursula Schubert could be

---

28. A brief notice is given in *Age of Spirituality: Late Antique and Early Christian Art, Third to Seventh Century: Catalogue*, ed. Kurt Weitzmann (New York: Metropolitan Museum of Art, in association with Princeton University Press, 1979), no. 437, 485–86. The Proverbs miniature may possibly be a "spontaneous invention"; it has no known precedent. Art historical evidence suggests a date in the later 6th rather than 7th or 8th century, close to the Rabbula Gospels (Florence, Laur. Plut. I.56, 586 CE). See also the fully illustrated monograph by Reiner Sörries, *Die syrische Bibel von Paris: Paris, Bibliothèque Nationale syr. 341. Eine frühchristliche Bilderhandschrift aus dem 6. Jahrhundert* (Wiesbaden: Ludwig Reichert Verlag, 1991).

29. Sörries (*Syrische Bibel von Paris*, 33–36, and fig. 8) points out that other Old Testament figures carry rotuli. He proposes that the codex carried by Solomon and by Jesus Sirach (f. 218) symbolizes preexistent Wisdom and therefore represents the gospels, Christ being present in a special way in the Wisdom literature.

30. J. Meyendorff ("L'iconographie de la sagesse divine dans la tradition byzantine," *CA* 10 [1959]: 259–77) does not endorse a symbolic reading of f. 118, noting that it would be the only symbolic depiction in the entire manuscript. The interpretation of unidentified female figures as personifications was popular among 20th-century scholars but is unverifiable.

entertained.[31] It seems likely that this sixth-century Syriac Bible manuscript provides us with an ancient image of a female ecclesiastic.

An ordination rite for a Syrian deaconess (Paris, Bibliothèque Nationale ms. syr. 113, fols. 111r–112v) has been made available by Ephrem Carr, who judges it to be no earlier than the ninth century.[32] The diacona is ordained while standing outside the doorway of the altar, a veil spread over her so as not to be seen by the people; the verb used is *cheirotonêtheis*. A *proemium* spells out what she may do: sweep the sanctuary and light the sanctuary lamps when no presbyter or deacon is present. Within a monastery she may give communion to women and children when a presbyter or deacon is absent. She may not touch the altar, but she anoints adult women at baptism and ministers to women who are ill. Given the content of the prayer, this preamble is evidently a restrictive addition. At her ordination the bishop prays, "And accept as deaconess and perfect this your servant who is here present and <awaits> your heavenly gift." The archdeacon then proclaims, "The grace of our Lord Jesus Christ...calls forth and offers from the rank (*taxis*) of sisters to the order of deaconesses N., deaconess for the holy altar of the place N., at the peril of those who presented <her>. Let us all pray, therefore, that grace and indwelling of the Holy Spirit descend upon her." Then the bishop bows and prays: "Yes, O Lord, make her worthy for the calling of deaconess so that she may deserve by your philanthropy to render you good service in a way that is fitting to your holy name and to minister in the temple of your holy glory and to find mercy before you. [Raising his voice]: Because you are God merciful and compassionate." As with the formulaic "deaconess of the holy altar of the place N." the next rubric is instructive, suggesting that the deaconess had once played a larger liturgical role at the altar: the bishop goes out the door of the altar because the deaconess does not come in to the altar until

---

31. Ursula Schubert ("Christus, Priester und König: Eine politisch-theologische Darstellungsweise in der frühchristlichen Kunst," *Kairos*, n.f. 15 [1973]: 201–37 at 227) noted the parallel with the bishop in the 6th-century mosaic showing emperor and clergy in the church of San Vitale, Ravenna. The Ascension miniature in the Syriac Rabbula Gospels (Florence, Laur. Plut. I.56, fol. 13v, dated 586 CE) shows in the lower register the orant Virgin flanked by angels; in the upper register Christ in a mandorla ascends into heaven borne by the living creatures of Ezekiel's vision. A full-length purple orarion emerges under Mary's purplish-blue palla (Van der Meer, *Maiestas Domini*, 257).

32. This unpublished paper was given at the Pontifical Institute of San Anselmo, Rome ca. 2000, and also at a symposium in Vienna. At www.womenpriests.org/traditio/deac_syr.asp, John Wijngaards translates ordination rituals for Syriac deacons and diaconas from Vatican cod. Syr. 19.

the completion of the rite. He inserts his right hand under her head-cloth, laying it upon her head, bows and prays silently:

> O God, who save those who call upon you, who give among women your grace to prophesy and to succeed in all good works, who made Miriam, the sister of Moses, worthy before all (other) women to raise a song to you and to minister (*mekahônû*) to you, who gave the grace of prophecy to Deborah, who also in your new covenant chose certain women for your diaconate, now also, our Lord, fill this your servant with blessing so that she may be a new deaconess according to the type (*kanôn*) of Phoebe, whom your apostle established in Cenchreae. Grant her then diligently to reprimand, instruct and direct children, to show herself blameless with bold confidence (*parrêsia*), to receive strangers (or pilgrims), and to abound in your works, to make responses in gentleness and prudence, to make the acquaintance of all, and to speak and act in your name.

He turns to the East and says the doxology in a loud voice. Despite the restricted role put on women's ministry in the Syriac church at this period, the epicletic prayer (the *sedro* or prayer of consecration) with its exalted language and theology spells out the duties of a deaconess while demonstrating strong support for ordaining women.[33]

A modern link with that ancient period is provided by a handwritten Syriac pontifical (the bishop's ritual book) used by Mar Samuel (1907–1995), Metropolitan of the Syrian Orthodox Church of North and South America, during his time in office.[34] It contains ordination rites for both a deaconess and a woman presbyter. In this version the ordination rite for the modern *presbytera* (wife of a presbyter who after menopause is ordained to do the work of a deaconess) differs from the rite of diaconal ordination.[35] Where in several churches celibacy was expected of a woman

---

33. Cf. the rite of blessing of deaconesses in the East Syrian church and the three benedictions provided in the Georgian church in the 9th–10th centuries (Bradshaw, *Ordination Rites*, 162–63, 68–69). In both rituals these prayers are termed blessings, the usual terminology.

34. This modern manuscript prompted the head of the Coptic Catholic Church in Cairo to ask Mar Samuel for the ordination rite in Arabic, since he intended to start ordaining deaconesses in the Coptic Catholic Church (communication of Mar Samuel to the late Edward J. Kilmartin, SJ, between 1978 and 1982).

35. Although the rites for presbytera and diacona differ, in this modern instance the title "presbytera" is determined by marital status, not by differentiation of duties from those of the deaconess. If there is a deaconess in her village or town, the priest's wife might not be ordained.

deacon, such is not the case for this woman presbyter; but the requirement that she be post-menopausal points to the taboo that has militated against the ordination of women over the centuries.[36]

B. Ordination Ritual for Women in the Byzantine Church

The Byzantine church and Greek language reached as far west as Sicily and southern Italy, the exarchate of Ravenna, and the Dalmatian coastlands. Those rites that were used in the medieval Byzantine churches are found in the oldest Byzantine euchologion, Vatican codex Barberini gr. 336 (780 CE) with the related twelfth- or thirteenth-century manuscript Grottaferrata Γβ I.[37] In the medieval Byzantine church admission to all ecclesiastical orders through that of the diaconate was accomplished by laying on of hand(s) by the bishop alone. The location (inside or outside the sanctuary or in the sacristy) depended on the rank of the office being conferred. In the Byzantine church subdeacons, lectors, and cantors were ordained in what amounted to a quasi-private ceremony outside the sanctuary and without the presence of the ministers in the higher grades. The lower grades were prohibited from wearing the orarion (stole). For the grades of presbyterate and episcopate the ordaining bishop was joined by persons equal in rank to the ordinand for the laying on of hands, signifying admission to a college.

Texts and comparisons of the medieval Byzantine ordination rites for male and female deacons are now readily available.[38] The ordination ritual is more developed than the one in *Apostolic Constitutions* VIII discussed

---

36. On taboos involving ritual purity see Berger, *Gender Differences*, 95–126.

37. Vat. cod. Barb. gr. 336, f. 169r–171v; *L'Eucologio Barberini Gr. 336: ff. 1–263*, ed. Stefano Parenti and Elena Velkovska (Rome: C.L.V.-Edizioni Liturgiche, 1995), nos. 163–64 (republished Rome: PIO, 2000), written in Southern Italy following a Constantinopolitan model. See Bradshaw, *Ordination Rites*, 137–39, and Wijngaards, *No Women in Holy Orders?*, 190–205 with commentary on closely related manuscripts.

38. Vagaggini, "L'ordinazione delle diaconesse." This paper is thought to represent a background study done for a Roman congregation. Wijngaards (*No Women in Holy Orders?*) reviews the evidence for women deacons especially in the early church and the Byzantine world. Relevant documents can be accessed on the website maintained by Wijngaards, womenpriests.org. Earlier, the doctoral dissertation by Evangelos Theodorou, "Η χειροτονία ή χειροθεσία τῶν διακονισσῶν," = "The *Cheirotonia* or *Cheirothesia* of Deaconesses," (University of Athens, 1954) treated the East. See also Miguel Arranz, "Le culte divin à Constantinople au seuil de l'an mille. L'Euchologe byzantin. État d'une recherche," paper given in 1991 at Ludwig-Maximilians Universität, Munich.

at the beginning of this section. One of the male deacon's chief privileges was to assist in the distribution of communion during the Divine Liturgy. Therefore, both male and female deacons were ordained at the conclusion of the anaphora (eucharistic prayer) when, the doors of the sanctuary being opened immediately prior to the distribution of communion, the ordinand was led to the bishop in the presbytery.[39] Ordination of the diacona included the imposition of the orarion after the second consecratory prayer. Slight differences between the rites for male and female deacon are explicable by reason of gender and physique: the male candidate prostrated himself before the altar while the female candidate, because of modesty standing within the presbytery rather than prostrating herself, bowed her head. The male deacon wore the orarion over one shoulder and joined at the opposite hip. The female deacon wore hers around the neck, both ends hanging down in front, passing under her outer garment to be visible below its hem.

The ancient invitation to prayer (the invitatory), that of the Greek euchological tradition used for all the major orders including deacon and diacona, is a formula "found, with some variant readings, in all of the oriental rites" going back to the fourth century.[40] It may be phrased as a prayer or a declaration (proclamation): "Divine Grace, which always heals what is weak and supplies for what is defective, promotes N. to deacon. Therefore let us pray for him/her, that the grace of the most Holy Spirit may descend upon him/her."[41] "In both Constantinople and Rome," Père Gy states, the text "was written on a special document which was a kind of

---

39. Wijngaards (*No Women in Holy Orders?*, 60) places the rite "after the sacred *anaphora* (offertory)." This is not the "offertory" but the anaphora or "offering," the eucharistic prayer. Like the deacon, the diacona is ordained immediately before the communion rite, indicating an important liturgical role as minister of communion even if the woman deacon usually exercises her ministry in a private or semi-private situation.

40. Gy ("Ancient Ordination Prayers," 74) comments on the theory put forward by Bernard Botte, "L'ordre d'après les prières d'ordination," *QL* 35 (1954): 166–79, repr. in *Études sur le Sacrement de l'Ordre* (Paris: Editions du Cerf, 1957) and trans. from French as "Holy Orders in the Ordination Prayers," in *The Sacrament of Holy Orders: Some Papers and Discussions Concerning Holy Orders at a Session of the Centre de Pastorale Liturgique, 1955* (Collegeville, MN: Liturgical, 1962), 5–23. Botte thought that the "Divine Grace" was the most important formula of the ordination rite.

41. Botte, "Holy Orders in Ordination Prayers," 13–15. This invitatory, the prayer or declaration of election, was said aloud. Once the other prayers were said quietly, the theory developed that the Divine Grace was the chief ordination prayer. Wijngaards (*No Women in Holy Orders?*, 117) gives this translation: "Divine Grace which always heals what is infirm and makes up for what is lacking, promotes N. to be a deacon in [place]. Let us therefore pray that the grace of the Holy Spirit may descend upon him/her." The naming of the place ("title") where the ministry is to be exercised was a component of the ordination's validity.

official record of the election, read by the bishop himself. In both places such a formula is supposed to make clear that the ordinand has been chosen by regular procedure. The procedure itself may differ a lot."[42] By this invitation the whole assembly was engaged in beseeching God to send the Holy Spirit on the ordinand for his or her ministry.

The election formula is followed by two solemn epicletic prayers, the actual ordination prayers, which call on God to send the Holy Spirit in favor of the ordinand for his or her work. Wijngaards gives the text of the first prayer with its rubric. The archbishop said the prayer aloud while laying his hand on the woman's forehead, signing it three times with the cross:

> Holy and Omnipotent Lord, through the birth of your Only Son our God from a Virgin according to the flesh, you have sanctified the female sex. You grant not only to men, but also to women the grace and coming of the Holy Spirit. Please, Lord, look on this your maidservant and dedicate her to the task of your diaconate, and pour out into her the rich and abundant giving of your Holy Spirit. Preserve her so that she may always perform her ministry [*leitourgia*] with orthodox faith and irreproachable conduct, according to what is pleasing to you. For to you is due all glory and honour.[43]

After the *Amen* a deacon began the litany, which named the ordinand. While the deacon led the litany the ordaining bishop, still laying on hands, said this second prayer quietly:[44]

> Lord, Master, you do not reject women who dedicate themselves to you and who are willing, in a becoming way, to serve your

---

42. Gy, "Ancient Ordination Prayers," 77. Agreeing with Gy, Stefano Parenti ("Ordinations in the East," in Chupungco, *Handbook for Liturgical Studies*, vol. 4: *Sacraments and Sacramentals*, 205–7), summarizes the question.

43. The texts given here follow translations by J. Wijngaards (*No Women in Holy Orders?*, 190–92) with my slight emendation. See also Bradshaw, *Ordination Rites*, 137–39. Wijngaards provides translations of the same text from other *euchologia*: the 10th-century Sinai codex gr. 956; Codex Grottaferrata ΓβI, copied in Constantinople ca. 1020; Coislin codex gr. 213, Constantinopolitan, 1027; Bodleian codex E.5.13 made for a monastery in Messina, Sicily in 1132; the 12th-century Codex Vaticanus gr. 1872, written in Sicily or Calabria; Cairo codex gr. 149–104, 14th century used by the Patriarch of Constantinople; the Xenophon codex gr. 163, 14th century from the Monastery of St. Xenophon, Mount Athos (ibid., 192–205). Jean Morin (J. Morinus) reproduced this prayer in his *Commentarius de sacris ecclesiae ordinationibus* (1655), Part 2, 99–100.

44. Bernard Botte, "Holy Orders in Ordination Prayers," 5–23. As Gy ("Ancient Ordination Prayers," 75) notes, for those who were not privy to the actual ordination texts this quiet recital by the (arch)bishop gave "the divine grace" a special prominence.

Holy House, but admit them to the order of your ministers [*leitourgon*]. Grant the gift of your Holy Spirit also to this your maidservant who wants to dedicate herself to you, and fulfil in her the grace of the diaconate, as you have granted to Phoebe the grace of your diaconate, whom you had called to the work of the ministry [*leitourgias*]. Give her, Lord, that she may persevere without guilt in your Holy Temple, that she may carefully guard her behaviour, especially her modesty and temperance. Moreover, make your maidservant perfect, so that, when she will stand before the judgment seat of your Christ, she may obtain the worthy fruit of her excellent conduct, through the mercy and humanity of your Only Son. Amen.

The archbishop then put the orarion around her neck under her veil, its two ends hanging down at the front.[45]

The communion rite follows immediately. For the newly ordained deacon male or female it expressed their liturgical privilege. The woman deacon was first given communion of the consecrated bread; then the archbishop handed her the chalice from which she received, afterward placing it back on the altar. In this action the diacona was clearly differentiated from subdeacon, lector, and laity. The rubric ensured that she enacted the sacramental sphere of her responsibility.[46] While the diacona did not participate in the giving of communion in the public assembly, she would most likely take Holy Communion to those women who required ministry in private as well as distribute it to women monastics and to children.[47]

---

45. Martimort (*Diaconesses*, 152) interpreted the way the woman deacon wore her stole as indicative of a non-ordained role. Wijngaards (*No Women in Holy Orders?*, 101–3) explains the difference by reference to women's physique and by comparison with the way the Virgin is depicted wearing a stole.

46. Giving communion from the chalice is traditionally a deacon's privilege. What differentiates the deacon from the diacona is that in the public liturgy after drinking from the chalice the diacona places it on the altar, the final action in ministering the chalice.

47. Especially in the earlier centuries the role of the abbess in communicating her nuns, children under her care, and pregnant and sick women stands out across the cultures investigated by Martimort (*Les diaconesses*, passim). In the Nestorian and Monophysite traditions (5th and 6th centuries), *Testamentum Domini*, Severus of Antioch, John of Tella, and James of Edessa report that women deacons distributed communion to women and girls when priests and male deacons were not present. As well, they took communion to women at home (Vagaggini, "Ordinazione delle diaconesse," 185, n. 3). See J. Wijngaards for the text of Severus of Antioch (*No Women in Holy Orders?*, 183–84).

The diacona-elect was named in the ordination litany. Her ministry was called *leitourgia* in the ordination prayers, in which the *diakonos* Phoebe (Rom 16:1) was named as scriptural warrant. The grace of her office was termed the *charis* (grace, gift) of *diaconia*. Both prayers of consecration explicitly invoked the Holy Spirit, source of divine grace (indeed, grace in person) that the one being ordained might fulfill the ministry to which God called and the bishop commissioned her. Besides their ministries of charity and liturgy, deacons and diaconas were ambassadors of the bishop and intermediaries between the bishop and the people. Her public liturgical functions were centered around preparation for and baptism of women and children. Like presbyters, deacons, and subdeacons, the woman deacon might not marry after ordination. Men already married, except for bishops, might continue to live in matrimony. However, the female deacon must live in continence.[48] In this her dedication paralleled that of nuns. Some famous early diaconas were heads of women's monasteries, and well before the eleventh century most Byzantine deaconesses were nuns. Starting with the twelfth century the ordination rite for deaconesses gradually disappeared from the manuscripts.[49] However, Theodore Balsamon (ca. 1105–1195), canonist and deacon of Hagia Sophia in Constantinople, informs us that deaconesses still continued to be ordained in Constantinople.[50]

---

48. Is this because the married woman was subject to her husband? In the Latin as well as in the Eastern churches cantors, lectors and porters could marry after ordination (what we would now term installation) into the "minor" offices. In some of the ancient churches of the East, women deacons may have been living in marriage after their ordination (Eisen, *Women Officeholders*, 164, 169, 173) or living continently with their husbands. Caring for one's own family would normally interfere with the more extended ministerial responsibilities of a woman deacon.

49. Parenti, "Ordinations in the East," 213.

50. Evangelos Theodorou ("Diakonat der Frau in der Griechisch-Orthodoxen Kirche," 30) notes that some deaconesses are ordained in Greek Orthodox monasteries, as they were in modern times by St. Nektarios on the island of Aigina; see also Theodorou ("Η χειροτονία ή χειροθεσία τῶν διακονισσῶν," = The *Cheirotonia* or *Cheirothesia* of Deaconesses, 30) in which he shows that the female deacon received not only a blessing (*cheirothesia*) but also the laying on of hands (*cheirotonia*), as was the case with her male counterpart. Theodorou's 1954 doctoral thesis on the non-essential differences between the ordination of male and female deacons is reviewed and quoted by Anne A. Jensen, "Das Amt der Diakonin in der kirchlichen Tradition der ersten Jahrtausends," in Peter Hünermann, Albert Hiesinger, Marianne Hembach-Steins, Anne Jensen, eds., *Diakonat: Ein Amt für Frauen in der Kirche: Ein frauengerechtes Amt?* (Ostfildern: Schwabenverlag, 1997), 53–77. For a summary of the 1997 Spring Conference Proceedings at Rottenburg-Stuttgart, see Ida Raming, "Diakonate: Ein Amt für

3. Ordination in the Church of Rome

Whether Romans 16 was written to Christians in Rome or Ephesus, Paul's listing of male and female leaders and members of the apostolic church testifies to the collaborative model of evangelization that accounted for rapid spread of the gospel after Jesus' death and resurrection. The second century marked a period of development in methods of evangelization, doctrine, and ministries. Nothing is known about installation in office beyond the four references to laying on of hands in Acts and 1–2 Timothy, all of which are situated in the East (Acts 6:3–6 and 13:1–3; 1 Tim 4:14; 2 Tim 1:6). In the mid-third century when Bishop Cornelius (251–253) names the various recognized ministries and states of life for which the church had responsibility, there is still no data for installation and ordination rites in the mainline Roman church.

It is not agreed when the Roman church ceased to be governed by a council of presbyter-bishops and came to be governed by a single bishop, the monarchical episcopacy.[51] However, by the mid-third century distinct offices of bishop, presbyter, and deacon are found in the Roman church. Alongside these major offices lesser "clerical" ministries relating to liturgical service begin to take shape and are ranked in ascending order: doorkeeper, lector, exorcist, acolyte, subdeacon.[52] Widows and the poor are also

---

Frauen in der Kirche," *Orientierung* 62 (1998): 8–11, trans. Mary Dittrich and republished in www.womenpriests.org. For an historical overview of the Byzantine deaconess with attention to Balsamon, see Rosa Maria Parrinello, "Diaconesse a Bisanzio: Una messa a punto della questione," in *Diakonia, 'Diaconiae,' Diaconato*, 653–65. At present the Armenian Apostolic Church ordains women deacons with a rite that is equal to that of male deacons except respecting admissibility to future priesthood. See Kristin Arat, "Die Weihe der Diakonin in der armenisch-apostolischen Kirche," in Berger and Gerhards, *Liturgie und Frauenfrage*, 67–75.

51. Faivre, *Naissance d'une hiérarchie*, 299–308. The long-lived memory of this collegial model of governance is shown by Jerome's comment that in Rome presbyter and bishop are synonymous.

52. In the various churches the number and lists of ecclesiastical grades varied somewhat among the lower clergy; they might be cited in an "ascending" (lowest to highest) or "descending" order. Roger E. Reynolds (*Ordinals of Christ from Origins to Twelfth Century*; Reynolds, *Clerical Orders in the Early Middle Ages: Duties and Ordination* [Aldershot: Ashgate, 1999]), and Gibaut (*Cursus Honorum*) study in detail these liturgical ministries and their sequence. For mid-8th-century Rome, *Ordo Romanus* XXXIV named acolyte, subdeacon, deacon, presbyter, and bishop (but not porter, lector, or exorcist); those missing from this list were named elsewhere (Gibaut, *Cursus Honorum*, 204–5). By RGP X the five ecclesiastical grades of psalmist, doorkeeper, lector, exorcist, and acolyte were counted below

named.⁵³ The grades became more important from the fourth century when the highest Roman civil officials left Rome to reestablish government in Constantinople and leaders of the now-legal Roman Christian church took on, along with their ecclesiastical roles, many of the honors and prerogatives of civil officials.⁵⁴ Early in its history hierarchy and bureaucracy became synonymous with the Roman church. Rome's genius for organization, governance, and civil law extended to the clericalization of the ordained ministry. *Ordinatio* was the technical term used in secular Roman life for the appointment of officials who had been received into an *ordo* or "well-defined social body distinct from the *plebs*," a status separate from the people.⁵⁵ During the course of the fourth century this secular term was taken into ecclesiastical vocabulary.

The Roman church obtained its personnel in a variety of ways. Young boys were offered by their families to the church as oblates as a means of their obtaining an education as well as a livelihood. First tonsure around age seven was followed by the minor orders conferred by age fourteen. Marriage was an option for men in the lower grades. Whether to marry and to whom, for instance a virgin not a widow, became pressing questions for lower clergy hoping to go higher.⁵⁶ Over time the five grades of clerical

---

subdeacon, deacon, and presbyter (ibid., 219). *Ordo Romanus* XXXV lists lector, acolyte, subdeacon, deacon, presbyter, and bishop. Later the office of bishop is not included within the ordination list.

53. For Tertullian widows belonged to an *ordo*; but as women their status was ambiguous and they were neither clergy nor lay (Faivre, *Emergence of the Laity*, 51, 213). Perhaps the "enrolled" or "canonical" widow was included tacitly among the clergy but her gender would exclude her from listing among males (ibid., 300–301, 309); see *The Ecclesiastical History of Eusebius Pamphilus*, VI, 43, 11, 265.

54. For a reassessment of the power relations between absentee emperors, Roman aristocrats, and the popes of the Roman church, see Mark Humphries, "From Emperor to Pope? Ceremonial, Space, and Authority at Rome from Constantine to Gregory the Great," in Kate Cooper and Julia Hillner, eds., in *Religion, Dynasty, Patronage in Early Christian Rome, 300–900* (Cambridge: Cambridge University Press, 21–58).

55. Tertullian was one of the first to introduce the word *ordinationes* in connection with offices in the church. In the Roman world *ordo* described a social class, especially a higher one. The matter is clearly summarized in David Power, *Ministers of Christ and His Church: The Theology of the Priesthood* (London: Geoffrey Chapman, 1969). See also Pierre Jounel, "Ordinations," in Cabié and Martimort, et al., *The Church at Prayer*, vol. 3: *Sacraments*, 139–84.

56. Innocent I gave the scriptural justification: 1 Tim 3:2 and Lev 21:13–14 (Geoffrey D. Dunn, "Deacons in the Early Fifth Century: Canonical Developments in Rome under Innocent I," in *Diakonia, diaconiae, diaconato*, 331–40 at 339).

service up to the diaconate came to be understood as brief or longer apprenticeships that could lead, with good behavior and demonstration of some degree of competence, to one of the major orders.[57] Sometimes lengthy periods were served in one of the ministries; in other cases, mature men were ordained directly to office and on rare occasions even consecrated bishop from the lay state. Coinciding with the newfound status of ecclesiastical officials had come the demand for the expression of ritual sacredness in the life of these officials. Faivre suggests that the category of "sacral persons" contributed to the papal policy of continence of the higher clergy. Papal decretals and letters issued by Pope Siricius in the 380s required that higher clergy, even if married, live in absolute continence.[58] Because of difficulty in enforcing continence on cohabiting spouses, it became common practice for a "deposed" wife, called *diaconissa, presbyterissa,* or *episcopissa* according to the husband's rank, to retire to a monastery.

A. *Tituli* and the *fermentum*

At some time in the late second or early third century, Roman ecclesiastical leadership had evolved from a "fractionated" city-church governed by presbyter-bishops to a unified model with one bishop for the whole city. What would become the Roman system of twenty-five *tituli* was under development. *Tituli* were not self-standing parishes but "papal pastoral outposts" whose staff carried forward the ministry of the bishop of Rome by providing for the influx of new Christians for whom Christianity was now spiritually or economically attractive.[59]

---

57. In Rome deacons exercised greater administrative power than presbyters since there were only seven deacons for the city, one for each district. As administrators directly under the pope, the Roman pontiff was usually elected from their ranks. Cornelius (251–253) was the first Roman bishop to have been both deacon and presbyter and Lothar of Segni (Innocent III, 1198–1216) the last deacon to be ordained directly to the bishopric of Rome. Originally the presbyterate was a collegial office. Once presbyters were delegated to preside at baptisms and eucharist, this grade was understood to exercise sacramental power individually.

58. The requirement of clerical continence seems to have originated in Spain with the Council of Elvira (ca. 306?). The decretals are Pope Siricius, *Epistola I ad Himerium* (385); *Siricius ad Gallos episcopos*; and Siricius, *Epistola 5 ad episcopos Africae* (386). *Ad Gallos episcopos* has also been attributed to Pope Damasus (366–384). See Faivre, *Naissance*, 313–23; Callam, "Clerical Continence," 3–50.

59. In the 4th and 5th centuries the major basilicas (St. John Lateran, St. Peter's, and St. Paul's, later the Liberian basilica dedicated as St. Mary Major and St. Lawrence's), which served as worship centers when the Christians of Rome gathered around their bishop, augmented the system of *tituli* and were served by presbyters from the various regions.

Presuming that an earlier ritual, liturgy, or ministry had the same shape as its present manifestation remains a pitfall for both worshipper and liturgist. Pope Innocent I's letter 25 to the bishop of Gubbio should warn us against retrojecting into the late fourth century—the period by which S. Pudenziana was established as a place of Christian assembly, the era when the acts of Potentiana and Praxedes were being compiled—the functions of ordained ministries as configured later in Rome.[60] In answer to a query of Bishop Decentius of Gubbio, Innocent counseled that there was no need for him to send the *fermentum* (eucharistic bread consecrated by the bishop) to presbyters within the town of Gubbio because his community was small and compact with one basilica and all would be able to attend the bishop's mass. The city of Rome presented a different case.[61] Reading between the lines, Innocent's advice indicates that at this period presbyters in the Roman *tituli* were not celebrating the eucharist, either for themselves or for their communities constituted of baptized penitents and not-yet-baptized inquirers, catechumens, and "elect." Rather, *tituli* staff were occupied with non-eucharistic ministry to such persons. Eucharistized bread was sent from the bishop's eucharist to the *tituli* presbyters so that they might not be separated from communion but could partake in the body of the Lord and in his blood (the wine consecrated through contact with the consecrated host). Reception of the *fermentum* by these presbyters maintained their communion with the bishop and with the eucharist of the city-church.[62] On the other hand, presbyters who

---

60. *Ep.* 25, 8; Pope Innocent I, *La lettre du pape Innocent Ier à Décentius de Gubbio (19 mars 416)*, trans. and comment. by Robert Cabié (Louvain: Publications Universitaires de Louvain, 1973), 26–29, 50–53; *PL* 20:556–57; also Pope Innocent I, *Church and Worship in Fifth-Century Rome: The Letter of Innocent I to Decentius of Gubbio*, trans. and comment. by Martin F. Connell (Cambridge: Grove Books, 2002), 39–40.

61. Over time the sending of the *fermentum* or portion of the bread consecrated by the bishop to other communities changed its purpose but not its content, consecrated bread exchanged as a sign of unity. Eusebius cites a letter of Victor I (189–199) during the paschal controversy, when the *fermentum* was exchanged by presbyters despite their differing observance of Easter (*Ecclesiastical History of Eusebius Pamphilus*, V, 24).

62. When seeking the origins of the custom *LP* refers to Miltiades (310–314) who "brought it about that consecrated offerings from what the bishop consecrated should be sent around the churches; this is called the *fermentum*" (Davis, *Book of Pontiffs*, 33.2). Siricius (384–399) "decreed that no priest should celebrate Mass every week without receiving the guaranteed consecrated element from the designated bishop of the place—this is called the *fermentum*" (Davis, 40, 2). Its function during the 6th century (a portion of eucharistic bread consecrated by the pope to be placed in the presider's cup to symbolize the unity of the papal with the presbyteral eucharist) was retrojected back into the pontificate of Siricius.

served at the cemeteries outside the walls of old Rome had been given the right (*ius*) and the faculty (*licentia*) of eucharistic presidency because it was inadvisable to carry the consecrated *fermentum* to distant shrines.[63] Therefore, around the year 400 presbyters *intra muros* would not have "possessed the faculties" to celebrate mass.[64] When they could not join with the other clergy and the baptized populace in the one eucharist of the bishop, city presbyters were able to communicate in the bishop's eucharist through reception of the *fermentum*.

A number of liturgical and patristics scholars have endorsed the view that, within the city, the presbyters stationed at the *tituli* were not "mass-saying priests" but rather animators of catechumenal communities offering instruction to enquirers and enlightenment to the elect as they prepared for Easter initiation by the bishop of Rome.[65] With characteristic clarity Robert Taft states, "[T]he Sunday synaxis in the *tituli* was originally only a Liturgy of the Word for the catechumens, and the *fermentum* was communion for the presbyters presiding over these non-eucharistic services, not a particle of the pope's eucharist to be added to theirs, as it will later become."[66] These presbyters with their assistants led gatherings for celebration of the Word and other liturgical and devotional exercises that

---

63. Country-pastors (called *chorbishops* in the East) exercised such faculties and could ordain some minor ministers (P. Joannou, "Chorbishop," *NCE* 3 [2003]: 625–26).

64. When presbyters attended the bishop's mass, if we follow *LP*'s account of celebrations presided by Zephyrinus (198/199–217), glass patens were held by deacons in front of the *sacerdotes* who would, at communion, receive from the hand of the bishop "an already consecrated ring [of communion bread, author's note] to give to the people" (Davis, *Book of Pontiffs*, 16.2).

65. In a recent "reconstruction" of the identity of Ambrosiaster (fl. 370s–380s), a picture is drawn of the life of a presbyter in late 4th-century Rome; see Sophie Lunn-Rockliffe, *Ambrosiaster's Political Theology* (Oxford: Oxford University Press, 2007), 80–86. She proposes that he might have been a presbyter at "one of the important cemetery churches." Ambrosiaster composed homiletic texts; but this function did not equate with presidency of the eucharist especially in titular churches. Lunn-Rockliffe's reference to deacons' usurpation of bishops' right to preside at *convivia* and the *oratio* might better see those terms translated "agape" and "prayer" (84 and 115, n. 33). Other recent scholars also consider the shadowy exegete Ambrosiaster to have been a presbyter, e.g., Ambrosiaster, *Ambrosiaster: Contre les païens et Sur le destin*, ed. Marie-Pierre Bussières (Paris: Les Éditions du Cerf, 2007), 38–40. David G. Hunter ("The Significance of Ambrosiaster," *JECS* 17 [2009]: 1–26 at 16), who judges that Ambrosiaster was a Roman cleric writing in the 380s, distinguishes between presbyters at the great cemetery churches who had the "right to preside, preach, and consecrate the eucharistic elements" and those in the city who did not.

66. Robert F. Taft, (*A History of the Liturgy of St. John Chrysostom*, vol. 5: *The Precommunion Rites* [6 vols.; Rome: Pontificio Instituto Orientale, 2000], 413–16) renews the view of

formed part of an active Christian community's life of prayer and celebration. They oversaw the regimen of public penance that commenced in Lent and culminated in reconciliation with the church presided by the bishop on Holy Thursday. Finally, they sold burial places in cemeteries *extra muros* and attended to the burial of the dead. In Innocent's time (401–417) titular presbyters and, according to the *vita* of Pudentiana and Praxedes, presbyteras were engaged in forming and animating members of communities, as suggested in the Pola Casket reliefs. Initiated Christians in good standing assembled with other members of the city-church and representative members of its clergy at a prearranged basilica or *titulus* to celebrate a stational eucharist with the bishop of Rome.

Liturgical functioning precedes formalization of offices and rites. Since history does not provide us with hard data, we can only speculate that the influx of new Christians required that the one-man initiatory and eucharistic ministry of the bishop of the city, assisted by the variety of ministers of whom we have already heard, give place to shared presidency of the sacraments. When did city-presbyters "receive the faculties" to preside at eucharist? Perhaps this happened episodically as circumstances warranted, once prospective converts had been absorbed into church membership and ministry on behalf of catechumens and penitents no longer wholly engaged *tituli* clergy. What strikes the modern observer as a major development in eucharistic practice has apparently left no clear trace in history. Not much easier to determine is when mass became a daily liturgical practice.[67]

B. Regulations for Ordination

An important step in the development of the church's ministerial structure was the orderly and public admission of clerics into its ranks. When translating, Jerome (d. 420) equated *cheirotonian* with "ordination of clerics,"

G. W. O. Addleshaw, *The Beginnings of the Parochial System* (York: St. Anthony's Press, 1953). Other notable commentators include Pierre Nautin, "Le rite du 'Fermentum' dans les églises urbaines de Rome," *EL* 96 (1982): 510–22 and John F. Baldovin, "The 'Fermentum' at Rome in the Fifth Century: A Reconsideration," *Worship* 79 (2005): 38–53. Nautin's very clear reconstruction of presbyteral roles in the city-church in the fifth century and perhaps even up to the eighth needs only to be corrected for the earliest centuries by the evidence of "fractionization" of worship communities.

67. Callam, "Frequency of Mass in Latin Church," 649, n. 129, regarding aliturgical synaxes under Leo the Great; see Marie-Bernard de Soos, *Le mystère liturgique: d'après Saint Léon le Grand* (Münster Westfalen: Aschendorff, 1958), 43–45, 50, 91, 125.

a meaning that immediately caught on in Rome and referred to establishment in any of the ecclesiastical grades except episcopate (the bishop was blessed or "consecrated").[68] The long-reigning pope Leo I (440–461) established general rules. Leo located episcopal consecrations on a Sunday vigil following a fast by ordainer and ordinand. The gesture of laying on of hand(s) was well known and probably used widely but without a predetermined ritual text to accompany it; the prayer improvised by the ordaining bishop would have followed an established pattern. Actual texts for installation in Roman ecclesiastical office are lacking for the early period and, in an era when presidential prayers were created *ex tempore,* there is no reason to expect to find them. Gelasius I (492–496) may have been among the first to create such prayers. He set out a basic schedule for ordinations, designating Ember Saturdays for ordinations to be concluded by a papal mass ending the vigil. The Sunday was a *dominica vacat* in the schedule of papal stational liturgies. Responding to a clergy shortage, Gelasius telescoped the sometimes-lengthy time required for apprenticeship in each grade, stating conditions for accession to the next rank and determining the bestowal of the power (*potestas*) of each function; the rules were not always followed.[69] Even with the distinction of functions now in place, it is disputed whether one can speak of a "clerical state." This may have come only with the Symmachan Apocrypha, when the hierarchical order was set out with subordination of inferior to superior involving a clerical state embracing all grades.[70] Precedents for the clerical *cursus* in which the

---

68. Jerome, *Commentarius in Isaiam* XV, 58, 10 (*PL* 24, 591) cited in Jounel, "Ordinations," 140, n. 5. *AT* is exceptional: bishop, presbyter, and deacon are "ordained" but not the subdeacon. Its ordination rites known from a fourth century Latin text, *AT* marks the first attempt to distinguish ordained and instituted ministries. It does not represent "the" Roman tradition although it may be a church order of a Greek-speaking community in Italy, perhaps one stemming from Antioch. *AT* has no sure Roman descendants until the Roman Pontifical of Paul VI. See *The Roman Pontifical: Revised by Decree of the Second Vatican Ecumenical Council and Published by Authority of Pope Paul VI* (Washington, DC: International Commission on English in the Liturgy, 1978).

69. Faivre, *Naissance d'une hiérarchie*, 309–28, 337–40. Gibaut (*Cursus Honorum*) gives many instances of exceptions; likewise Andrieu, *OR* 3:565–69. In Rome in the 8th and 9th centuries, popes typically came from among the diaconal ranks without passing through the presbyterate while presbyters did not exercise a prior diaconate.

70. Faivre, *Naissance d'une hiérarchie*, 343–52. According to Raymond Davis (*Book of Pontiffs*, xxiv), these apocryphal writings were "forged ca. 502 to support Symmachus' claim to the papacy against that of Lawrence." The terminology of *auctoritas* and *potestas*, the notion of *gradus* and the clericalization of the ordained ministries (i.e., their clear distinction from the laity) are treated in an illuminating way by David Power, *Ministers of Christ*, 53–88.

various grades would be systematized have been found in the military and civil services, both limited to males. By the pontificate of Pelagius I (555–561) the "simple clerical state" as gateway to ecclesiastical or monastic life or the temporal administration of the church was finally in place, marked by the prayer *Oratio ad clericum faciendum*.

C. Texts, Early Sacramentaries, and Ordination Prayers

Circa 560–580 the *Veronensis* (the so-called "Leonine" sacramentary) gives three prayers (XXVIII, in the month of September), and later adds the *consecratio* for the deacon also found in the Old Gelasian and Gregorian sacramentaries.[71] With prayers sometimes brief and understated, at other times verbose but short on scriptural reference, Roman prayers exhibit a cultural temper that other Western rites will borrow from, improve, and elaborate on according to their genius, and then export back to Rome. The next and more reliable witness to Roman ordination prayers is the Gregorian sacramentary, which gives prayers but not instructions for carrying out the liturgies. Attributed to Pope Gregory the Great (590–604) for whom succeeding generations could imagine or invoke no greater authority, the Gregorian sacramentary probably contained some individual prayers composed by that great pontiff. But the primitive Gregorian was first redacted under Honorius I (625–638).[72] During the course of the seventh century the original papal sacramentary would be added to and copied for presbyteral use, leaving out any ceremonies conducted exclusively by the pope. The rubrics or "stage directions" for the ceremonies are

---

71. *Sacramentarium Veronense* (Cod. Bibl. Capit. Veron. LXXXV [80]), ed. Leo Cunibert Mohlberg with Leo Eizenhöfer and Petrus Siffrin (Rome: Herder, 1956), XXVIII, nos. 942–54, pp. 118–22. Not a liturgical book, *Veronensis* ("Leonine" sacramentary) appears to be a private collection of prayers from *libelli* originating with the popes in the 5th–6th centuries and copied elsewhere than in Rome. A number of authors endorse Francesco Bianchini's attribution in 1735 of the "Verona Sacramentary" to Pope Leo I (440–461). Cyrille Vogel's (*Medieval Liturgy*, 38–43) summary of theories places *Veronensis* with other compilations of the first half of the 6th century, like the *LP*. Some of its prayers may go back to Pope Gelasius I (492–496). Harry Boone Porter (*The Ordination Prayers of the Ancient Western Churches* [London: SPCK 1967, 12–35]) shows variations in titles and wording among the Leonine, Gelasian, *Missale Francorum*, Eighth-Century Gelasian, and Gregorian sacramentaries and in the *ordines romani*; so too does Bradshaw (*Ordination Rites*, 215–18). The *Veronensis* forms the base text for the Gregorian sacramentary prayers.

72. Honorius is depicted as patron in the apse mosaic of the 7th-century basilica of S. Agnese on the Nomentana, built above her tomb.

available only in the next century, collected in *ordo* XXXIV circa 700–750 and the later Frankish *ordines* XXXVI and XXXIX, all known from texts copied outside Rome.

When sent north of the Alps to Charlemagne, the Gregorian became the basis for an expanded sacramentary that would be used here and there throughout the Frankish empire. Charlemagne had sought from Pope Hadrian I a pure (*inmixtum*) sacramentary, one composed by Gregory the Great. Somewhat belatedly between 784 and 791, Hadrian sent along a sacramentary of papal use, hence called the *Hadrianum*, which was already somewhat out-of-date although it included the masses for the Thursdays of Lent.[73] No longer extant, the "only surviving complete, uncorrected copy" of Hadrian's gift book is the Sacramentary of Hildoard, copied in Cambrai in 811–812.[74] The *Hadrianum* was a liturgical book for the exclusive use of the pope at the Lateran and while making the rounds of the *tituli* in the city; it was singularly unsuited for use elsewhere. Received north of the Alps as an *editio typica*, it lacked many items required for parochial use and very quickly was discovered by Carolingian liturgists to be wanting. Unsatisfactory when transplanted to another locale, nevertheless it was considered authoritative because of its origin. The references to Roman stational churches were kept in each new copy, while adjustments to local needs were introduced. Circa 810–815 St. Benedict of Aniane (750–821), the Benedictine reforming abbot in the Carolingian lands, provided the Gregorian sacramentary with a supplement containing masses needed for parishes as well as other missing texts, including the Sundays after Easter and Pentecost.[75] Thanks to the wide network of Benedictine monasteries,

---

73. Gregory II (715–731) added these masses. This augmented but archaic edition of the *Gregorianum* was the edition sent; see *Le sacramentaire grégorien: ses principales formes d'apres les plus ancient manuscrits*, ed. Jean Deshusses (Édition comparative 1–3; Fribourg, Suisse: Éditions Universitaires, 1988–92), 1:50–75. See also Vogel, *Medieval Liturgy*, 79–102.

74. Fortunately the *Hadrianum* was copied at the order of Bishop Hildoard of Cambrai, as noted at the very end of the ms., and is still held in that city (Bibliothèque Municipale, cod. 164, fols. 35v–203r). Eric Palazzo (*History of Liturgical Books*, 51) notes that its contents are very close to the edition of Pope Honorius. A prefatory note, "ex authentico libro bibliothecae cubiculi scriptum," that is, "copied from the authentic exemplar deposited in the palace library," attests that the copies made in the Aachen palace library were from the very book sent from Rome (Vogel, *Medieval Liturgy*, 81–82). Deshusses characterizes the Cambrai copy as "rough, sometimes faulty"; its model was the same, with rough latinisms.

75. Deshusses, *Sacr. grég.*, 1:354–55, 386–407. For the change of opinion regarding attribution of the *Supplementum Anianense* from Alcuin to Benedict of Aniane, see Vogel, *Medieval Liturgy*, 85–86.

this enlarged and improved sacramentary quickly made its way through Europe. The Cambrai copy and its immediate descendants retain papal usages.[76] The brief prayer for "making" women deacons would, a century and a half later north of the Alps, develop into a full ritual.

Jean Deshusses has published the text of the *Hadrianum* known through its copy made in Cambrai for Bishop Hildoard as well as copious material from related manuscripts.[77] Such an exact copy of a liturgical manuscript is a rarity, as a liturgical book was usually upgraded for time and place during the laborious copying process.[78] By comparing other editions of the Gregorian sacramentary, scholars have been able to reconstitute it prior to 735.

To understand the origin of the Roman prayer for a diacona and weigh its importance, some background to this papal book and its editions is necessary. Of the three "lines" or recensions that stem from the primitive Gregorian sacramentary used at the Lateran and redacted under Honorius I, *Tridentinum* and *Paduensis* are retrievable only as "reconstituted" texts (Deshusses' *tronc commun* datable to 670–80).[79] Two lines (the older *Tridentinum* ca. 685 and the newer *Hadrianum* ca. 735) form Type I.[80] Type

---

76. Part 3 contains the dedication of churches, an anniversary mass of a pope and an ordination mass of a presbyter, a marriage mass (H 194–200), miscellaneous prayers (H 201–204 belonging to the "primitive Gregorian"), and a section (H 205–225) characterized as "additions." Immediately following two prayers for making clerics and shaving the beard are two concerning women: H 214, "Prayer for making a diacona" and H 215, "Prayer for veiling virgins of God," followed by the unisex H 216, "Prayer for making an abbot or abbess." Deshusses (*Sacr. grég.*, 1:36) describes these as interesting complements added by diverse, nearly contemporary hands. The final entry, H 226, is an embolism (insert) for the consecratory prayer to ordain a pope. Neither Deshusses, Vogel nor Palazzo speculate on the origin of the "additions." Each entry is here designated H__ while subsections are referred to by their marginal number.

77. See especially the introduction (3rd edition, 1:29–81). The thirty-six 9th-century mss. or fragments utilized by Deshusses in establishing the Gregorian text out of "innumerable" possibilities are listed in *Sacr. grég.*, 1:34–47.

78. Vogel, *Medieval Liturgy*, 62–64.

79. Deshusses, *Sacr. grég.*, 1:50–60.

80. On the extant Sacramentary of Trent (Trent, Castel del Buon Consiglio), see Jean Deshusses, "Le sacramentaire grégorien de Trente," *RB* 78 (1968): 261–82; Deshusses, "Le sacramentaire grégorien préhadrianique," *RB* 80 (1970): 213–37. It was probably copied in the Tyrol ca. 825–30 from a book obtained by Arno bishop of Salzburg from Alcuin. The 9th-century Trent ms. has been updated by reference to the *Hadrianum*, the latter's Supplement provided by Benedict of Aniane, and probably also Alcuin's sacramentary. Comparison of the 7th-century *Paduensis* with the 9th-century Sacramentary of Trent allows retrieval of their common core. Trent's base text reflects the state of the pre-Hadrianic sacramentary (Type I) in use one century before the *Hadrianum* was received in Aachen (Vogel, *Medieval Liturgy*, 97–102).

II, *Paduensis*, the archetype copied for presbyteral use at the shrine-church of Saint Peter's circa 650–689 and the earliest version of the Gregorian sacramentary that has been reconstituted so far, contains neither baptism nor ordination rites (including the prayer for making a diacona).[81] Those rites were celebrated by the pope at the Lateran; therefore initiation and ordination rituals would have been superfluous in a book intended for presbyteral use at St. Peter's.[82] Its *canon missae* was placed toward the end, before the daily office prayers. The older *Tridentinum* puts the ordinary of the mass at the front and the ordination prayers for bishop, presbyter, and deacon in the appendix. Like the *Tridentinum*, *Hadrianum* puts the mass ordinary (*Qualiter missa romana caelebratur*, 1) in the first place. But it moves forward those orations required by the bishop of Rome, the *Benedictio episcoporum* (in the plural, several bishops being ordained at the same ceremony) and ordination prayers for a single presbyter and deacon, to H 2–H 4. An embolism (insertion) for the consecratory prayer used in ordaining a pontiff of the apostolic see (H 226) remains at the very end of the book.

The three elements that the Gregorian provided for the ordination of a deacon include an invitatory (no. 30), a collect *Exaudi domine preces nostras* (no. 31), and the consecratory prayer (nos. 32a, 32b). The collect reads:

> Hear O Lord, our prayers, and send forth the spirit of thy blessing upon this thy servant, that, enriched by this heavenly gift, he may obtain the grace of your majesty and set an example of good living to others. Through.[83]

---

81. Besides Deshusses' introduction in volume 1 of *Sacr. grég.*, see Vogel (*Medieval Liturgy*, 61–106) on the early sacramentaries. Deshusses (*Sacr. grég.*, 3:79–83) hypothesizes that the Type II Gregorian sacramentary was created around or shortly after 663.

82. Deshusses judges that the ordination prayers (H 2–H 4) were added ca. 682–683 (Vogel, *Medieval Liturgy*, 128, n. 240), at the same time as the prayer for making a diacona (H 214) and other prayers found in the appendix (H 194–H 200 and H 205–225).

83. "Exaudi domine preces nostras, et super hunc famulum tuum spiritum tuae benedictionis emitte, ut caelesti munere ditatus et tuae gratiam possit maiestatis adquirere et bene vivendi aliis exemplum praebere. Per." This collect was a new Gregorian creation inspired in part by elements found in two passages from *Veronensis* (the "Leonine sacramentary") for the ordination of deacons (Leonine 121, 25 and 121, 2–3) to which is joined 127, 21 from the same collection (Chavasse, *Sacramentaire gélasien*, 507 and n. 20), and the Old Gelasian sacramentary. This prayer was still found in *The Rite of Ordination according to the Roman Pontifical*, ed. J. S. M. Lynch (4th rev. ed. and enl., ed. Joseph H. McMahon; New York: Cathedral Library Association, [1892] 1912).

The consecratory prayers for bishop, presbyter, and deacon open on a strongly hierarchical note. That for the deacon addresses "Almighty God, giver of honors, distributor of orders, and bestower of offices," in its first section setting out how God acts in the world through the Word and graces the church.[84] The Old Testament's sons of Levi are given as types of deacons. In the second epicletic part the prayer beseeches God, more clearly than in the consecratory prayers for bishop and presbyter, for the Spirit's work in the ministry of the ordained: "Pour on him, Lord, we beseech, the Holy Spirit by which he may be strengthened by the gift of sevenfold grace to follow faithfully to the end in the work of the ministry." Presumably the laying on of hands initiates or accompanies this prayer, but the Gregorian sacramentary contains no rubrics.[85] The prayer ends by naming those virtues that will make the deacon an example to all as he lives out his vocation, including the modest exercise of authority and all the virtues supporting continence.[86] No mention is made of the exercise of the works of charity. The final hope expressed, that the deacon may move from this lower rank to a higher, views this ministry as a step toward a higher career. In the seventh, eighth, and ninth centuries Roman deacons were not normally promoted to the presbyterate but elected to the papacy. All three ordination texts (invitatory, collect, and *consecratio*) are found in only some of the textual witnesses, suggesting these prayers' relatively recent composition or at least compilation in a ritual grouping.[87]

---

84. With but an occasional word change, this is the *Benedictio super diaconos* found in *Sacramentarium Veronensis*, para. 951, pp. 120–21.

85. Laying on of hands came to be done in silence *before* the consecratory prayer. For presbyteral and diaconal rubrics, see *Ordo* XXXIV (Andrieu, *OR* 3, nos. 3–13) and, contaminated by Gallican usages, *OR* 4, XXXVI (nos. 4–28) and XXXIX (nos. 1–31).

86. The *consecratio* for the deacon refers to his service within God's "holy places." After articulating at length caution that God is the true "discerner of hearts," the kernel of the epicletic prayer reads: "Emitte in eum domine quaesumus spiritum sanctum quo in opus ministerii fideliter exequendi septiformis gratiae munere roboretur." Finally the chaste behavior expected of a deacon is detailed, that he "persevere firm and stable in Christ, and from a lower grade by fitting steps may deserve through your grace to take up higher things." Latin text in Deshusses, *Sacr. grég.*, 1, H 4 (32a and b), 96–98; Porter, *Ordination Prayers of Ancient Western Churches*, Latin and English texts, 32–35.

87. The Gregorian prayers made use of phrases and ideas found in *Veronensis* and the Old Gelasian Sacramentary (Vat. Reg. lat. 316) as is shown by Miquel S. Gros, "Les plus anciennes formules romaines de bénédiction des diacres," *EO* 5 (1988): 45–52 at 47. Gros's dating of Veronensis' "benediction of deacons" (nos. 948–951) before the mid-4th century relies on too little evidence. The Old Gelasian Sacramentary (Vatican, Reg. lat. 316), composed between 628 and 715, contains older prayers used by Roman presbyters. It was copied, with

4. Women's Officially Recognized Diaconal Ministry in the City-Church of Rome

We saw that a sixth-century epigraph naming Dometius and Anna DIAC at St. Paul's Outside the Walls is extant.[88] Conditions were ripe for the development of some form of women's diaconal office in the mid-sixth to mid-eighth centuries, when many churches of the East and West were in communion and thirteen of twenty Roman pontiffs came from the eastern and southern regions of the Christian world.[89] However, the first Roman prayer for the "making" of a diacona is not borrowed from Eastern models that, given the origins of popes and theologians in southern Italy and Sicily, Greece, and Syria, were certainly known, but is found in a recently composed collect in the Roman ordination rite for male deacons in the Gregorian sacramentary. Where the ordination rite for diaconas in the Byzantine church is theologically strong and spiritually inspiring, the same cannot be claimed for the ordination collect used for Roman deacons and diaconas. Its importance lies in the fact that, but for change of gender, it is the very same prayer. Later Roman rituals for the ordering of women's ecclesiastical ministry stand in a sterling lineage, Type I of the papal Gregorian sacramentary originating at the Lateran. The *Exaudi preces nostras*, a "prayer for making a diacona" in the *Hadrianum*, reads:

> Hear our prayers, Lord, and over this your [female] servant *illam* [demonstrative pronoun "that one"], send forth the spirit of your benediction, that enriched by heavenly office she may be able to acquire both the grace of your majesty and prove an example of good living to others. Through.[90]

Frankish editing and additions ca. 750, in the nuns' scriptorium of Chelles (Vogel, *Medieval Liturgy*, 64–70). Its composition and use therefore paralleled that of the Gregorian (Palazzo, *History of Liturgical Books*, 42, n. 92).

88. Thanks to its patron and Paul's letter to the Romans 16, the San Paolo basilica (built ca. 380) with its monasteries may have proven especially hospitable to women's ministries.

89. Krautheimer (*Rome*, 89–92) gives an overview. On liturgy, see S. J. P. van Dijk, "The Urban and Papal Rites in Seventh- and Eighth-Century Rome," *Sacris Erudiri* 12 (1961): 411–87; van Dijk, "The Old-Roman Rite," *SP* 5 (1962): 185–205.

90. "Orationem ad diaconam faciendam. Exaudi domine preces nostras, et super hanc famulam tuam *illam*, spiritum tuae benedictionis emitte, ut caelesti munere ditata et tuae gratiam possit maiestatis adquirere, et bene vivendi aliis exemplum prebere. <per>" (Deshusses, *Sacr. grég.*, H 214, no. 994). Deshusses is of the view that these are in another

Except for the change in gender from *hunc famulum*, the prayer for the woman deacon is identical to the *Exaudi* collect used for male deacons designated as *alia* ("another") in *Hadrianum*'s H 4 entitled *Orationes ad ordinandum diaconum*.[91] This prayer became the most widely used of the Roman ordination collects. Betraying the Roman way of thinking implicit in the *Exaudi*, reference is made indirectly to the Holy Spirit, uncreated grace.[92] The *Hadrianum* collect for the diacona first appears in the *Tridentinum* edition of the Gregorian (papal) sacramentary, datable to the pontificate of the Sicilian Pope Leo II (682–683).[93] Its title "the making of" in the *Hadrianum* aligns it with two recently composed prayers for making a cleric and shaving the beard (H 212–H 213), an oration for veiling *ancillae Dei* (H 215, handmaidens of God, perhaps canonesses), and the very brief unisex prayer (H 216) for making an abbot or abbess.[94] These short orations are each single prayers in the *Hadrianum*, most to be expanded in the rituals of the Romano-Germanic Pontifical of the Tenth Century developed two centuries later at Mainz. The prayer insertion for ordaining the

---

hand but contemporaneous with the preceding sections of the manuscript. The *Hadrianum* prayer for the diacona as well as the male deacon reads "ditata" (enriched), but for the diacona the earlier *Tridentinum* reads "dicata" (consecrated, dedicated, devoted, set apart), a stronger theological motif that might be read as "consecrated to heavenly office (ministry)." "Dicata" is found in a minority of mss. for diaconas, and not elsewhere. In a prayer for ordination the key word is "munus." Is "munus" to be translated as "office" (its classical meaning), "ministry," "gift," "favor" (or "bounty," as translated by Porter in *Ordination Prayers of Ancient Western Churches*, 31, n. 3)? Church office involves public service. Porter's "bounty," "gift," or "favor" (medieval meanings) accents the imparting of grace by God without reference to ecclesiastical office. The varied translations are predicated on different theologies. "Ministerium" is in medieval parlance a charge, office, or function. Ecclesiastical office or ministry is the preferred reading given the prayer's 7th-century origin.

91. Deshusses, *Sacr. grég.*, 1, H 4, no. 31; Andrieu, *OR* 4:146.

92. This may be due to the absence of pneumatological controversies in the West. Because Western Trinitarian theology did not develop the notion of the personal missions of Son and Spirit the Roman tendency, even in the Roman Canon, was to overlook the Spirit. On the other hand, the comparable *Exaudi* prayer for a presbyter (no. 28) asks for "benedictionem sancti spiritus," offsetting more limited pneumatological references elsewhere.

93. Whether the "trunk" from which these two editions sprang contained the office of diacona will not likely be known until all the sacramentaries of the Gregorian family are edited. Leo II's stamp on *Tridentinum* is found in a mass for the feast of St. George; Leo built the diaconia of S. Giorgio-in-Velabro near the Tiber.

94. "Grant, we beseech, almighty God, that you attend with the gift of your grace your servant *illum* or *illam* whom we choose for the governance of souls, so that through your bounty, we may please you by our choice." Frequently in these texts "servant" (*famulum*) is modified by *illum vel illam*, not translated here. Deshusses, *Sacr. grég.*, 1, H 216; Macy, *Hidden History*, 146 (D).

bishop of Rome (H 226), the very last addition to *Hadrianum*, is separated from the rites for bishop, presbyter, and deacon and is not far distant from H 214 for the making of women deacons. Found in *Tridentinum*, it is lacking in a number of manuscripts.

A. G. Martimort refers to the handful of texts pointing to the Roman office of diacona at this period and acknowledges that from the second half of the seventh century in Italy, in addition to the wives of deacons, there existed *diaconesses proprement dites*. In his view, this does not mean that these deaconesses were equivalent to male deacons; the diaconal prayer does not point to "an ordination, even minor," but is rather "the recognition of a form of religious state."[95] His judgment is based on *Hadrianum*'s location of the prayer for making the diacona between single clerical and monastic collects near the back of the sacramentary. Martimort fails to take note of the earlier layout of the Gregorian sacramentary when the ordination prayers for bishops, priests, and a deacon, thought by Deshusses to date from the same period as that for making a diacona, were located at the back of *Tridentinum*. If location is significant, why is the *Ad pontificem ordinandum*, an embolism (insertion) for the pontiff's consecration prayer, placed as the final item in *Tridentinum* and *Hadrianum* (H 226)? The fact that the Roman Pontifical of Gregory VII retains the *Missa ad diaconam consecrandam* but without the prayer *Exaudi* and the rubrics suggests to Martimort that by the later eleventh century this ritual was falling into abeyance.[96]

Michel Andrieu's position is opposed to that of Martimort. Andrieu had noted that the *Exaudi* prayer for making women deacons "is identical, but for use of the feminine, to that which follows the invitatory and precedes the *Consecratio* in the ordination of the deacon." He continues, "Ses termes ne conviennent donc parfaitement qu'aux diaconesses proprement dites, dont la vocation spirituelle correspondait à celles des diacres."[97] We do not know the circumstances of its use. It is likely that the oration for making diaconas would be called on when needed within the lengthy Ember Saturday ordination ceremonies. Andrieu does not see in this diaconal prayer a blessing for the wives of deacons, blessed on the day of their

---

95. Martimort, *Diaconesses*, 204.

96. Martimort, *Diaconesses*, 216–17.

97. OR 4:146 and n. 4. Andrieu does not suggest that these diaconas were not ordained.

husband's ordination to major orders; nor do we possess the text of that blessing.[98]

For the diacona neither invitatory nor consecration prayer is given. In another context Andrieu asks, without answering the question, whether "the term *oratio consecrationis* designates only the long prayer *Adesto, quaesumus, omnipotens Deus*, called *consecratio* in the Gelasian and Gregorian, or whether it also includes the prayer *Exaudi, Domine, preces nostras* of the Gregorian?"[99] In other words, does the *Exaudi* prayer function as a kind of "code" for the whole consecratory prayer?[100]

The Pontifical of Egbert, Archbishop of York (732–766) contains the *Exaudi* collect that, using the masculine gender, is here entitled "another blessing of a deacon or deaconess," and an episcopal blessing for a virgin-diacona.[101] Egbert had been educated in Rome and ordained a deacon there. For diaconas Egbert used the Gregorian's ordination prayer for deacons, completing the ritual with the *Benedictio episcopalis in ordinatione Diaconissae*, which is located *between* the blessings for a deacon and a presbyter.[102] The Leofric Missal (Oxford: Bodleian Library, Bodley 579),

---

98. Here I part company with Joseph Ysebaert ("The Deaconesses of Late Antiquity and Their Origin," in G. M. Bartelink, A. Hilhorst and C. H. Kneepkens, eds., *Eulogia: Mélanges offerts à Antoon A. R. Bastiaensen à l'occasion des son soixante-cinquième anniversaire* [Steenbrugge: in Abbatia S. Petri; The Hague: Nijhoff, 1991], 423–36) for not sufficiently distinguishing deposed wives, who gain their husbands' titles, from diaconas "properly called deaconesses" by Andrieu, *OR* 4:146.

99. Andrieu, *OR* 3 (1961), 559. He continues that the succinct description does not even mention the laying on of hands, a traditional part of the rite. It may be added that this omission suggests a relatively late date for the ritual, since *AT*, the *Statuta ecclesiae antiqua*, and Jerome (*PL* 24, 591) all refer to it. In the modern Latin rite prior to 1968, the *Exaudi* collect is found at the end of the ordination, immediately following the handing over of stole, dalmatic, and gospel-book to the man "to be ordained" deacon. The rubric indicates that the ordination was accomplished with its proclamation.

100. The common practice in the laborious and expensive making of manuscript books was not to duplicate but to direct the user to the same text found elsewhere in the book. The Gregorian's collect for the making of a diacona (*Hadrianum*, H 214) changed only the masculine *hunc famulum* (H 4, no. 31) to the feminine *hanc famulam* but was copied in its entirety. A number of liturgical texts invite presiders to change the gender or number of pronouns. Alternatively, the changed gender may be shown in superscript.

101. See *The Pontifical of Egbert, Archbishop of York A.D. 732–766*, ed. William Greenwell (Durham: George Andrews, 1853), 19 and 94; Macy, *Hidden History*, 133A and 133B.

102. "By the intercession of his holy virgins may almighty God, who desired to triumph over the ancient enemy also through women, deign to bless you. Amen. And may he who desired to confer on them hundredfold fruit, the beauty of virginity and the suffering of the martyr, deign to cleanse you of the misery of vices, and obtain for you the brightness of virtues. Amen. To the extent that the lamps of sinners may be thus filled with the oil

a Gregorian sacramentary, pontifical, and ritual written for Plegmund, archbishop of Canterbury (890–923) and updated for Bishop Leofric, Exeter's first bishop (1050–1072), includes the *Exaudi, domine, preces nostras* entitled *Oratio ad diaconissam faciendam* that is separate from the ritual for deacons.[103] Given the freedom with which gender issues are addressed elsewhere in this combination of sacramentary, pontifical, and ritual, it requires no stretch of the imagination to suggest that the consecratory prayer for male deacons could have been utilized for females. Its *Oratio ad abbatem vel abbatissam faciendum* includes the figure of Moses as type of the abbess's as well as abbot's office and includes changes of gender in the text.[104] In the same missal the blessing of virgins is gender-blind: "When she accepts the sacred veil the consecration is said '... that you will be worthy to associate with the 144,000 who have not consorted with women.'"[105]

What is to be made of official recognition of women as officeholders in the papal sacramentary? There had been dedications of churches to the Theotokos, for example Saint Mary Major's and the former Pantheon, S. Maria Rotunda (*ad Martyres*) dedicated to the Virgin and all martyrs in 609, but so far only women martyrs had been included in the Roman sanctoral. About 670, shortly before the appearance of the collect for making a diacona, a swell in Marian piety is discernible.[106] Since in the seventh century the Roman church was finally endorsing the liturgical veneration of Mary, older or homemade texts were added to *Paduensis*, and the slightly later *Tridentinum* acquired its own. Under the Syrian Pope Sergius I (687–706) new feasts, formularies, and processions for the Marian feasts were

---

of virtue, may you now be able to enter the chamber of the heavenly bridegroom. Insofar as this may be possible[?] (Quod ipse). Amen. The blessing." For the Latin text, see Macy, *Hidden History*, 133B.

103. *The Leofric Missal*, ed. F. E. Warren (Oxford: Clarendon Press, 1883); now *The Leofric Missal*, ed. Nicholas Orchard (2 vols.; London: Boydell Press for Henry Bradshaw Society, 2002).

104. See n. 100 above for the Gregorian collect (H 216): "Concede, quaesumus, omnipotens deus." A second prayer begins, "God, justifier of all, who through Moses your servant established priors (*praepositos*) for the governance of churches...." (*Leofric Missal* [1883]: 227–28; *Leofric Missal* [2002]: 2:424, no. 2438).

105. *Leofric Missal* (1883), 227; cf. Rev 14:3–4.

106. Veneration of Mary in the Roman calendar along with liturgical celebrations in her honor had come late to the Roman church. In the Würzburg gospel book (ca. 645) is found the *natale sanctae Mariae* (the Assumption), this last with the choice for gospel of Luke 10:38–42 (the Martha and Mary pericope) or Luke 11:27–28 ("Blessed is the womb").

added.[107] Could not this infusion of Marian devotion represented by the Roman church calendar be related to the inclusion of women ministers within the official ecclesiastical structure?

In summary, neither *Tridentinum, Paduensis*, nor *Hadrianum* is extant, but scholars have been able to reconstitute the seventh century papal (Type I) and presbyteral (Type II) Gregorian sacramentaries and, thanks to an exact copy (Cambrai 164), know its eighth-century Type I (papal) successor, the *Hadrianum*. The single prayer for a diacona found toward the back of *Hadrianum* stands in a sterling lineage. But for one gendered reference, the collect for the diacona is the same as that for a male deacon. The most irrefutable textual evidence for women's official diaconal service in Rome from the later seventh century through the papacy of Gregory VII is provided by the collect for making a diacona in the Gregorian sacramentary and by the developed rite in the very popular Romano-Germanic Pontifical of the Tenth Century.

5. *The* ordines romani *and Early Pontificals*

Roman liturgical books were desired as models of corporate prayer for the new churches north of the Alps and were soon adapted to the new cultural situations.[108] Roman usages had been carried beyond the Alps by individuals: missionaries (Augustine of Canterbury, d. ca. 604), pilgrims, abbots (Benedict Biscop, d. ca. 690), and bishops (Chrodegang of Metz, 742–766, who introduced the Roman mass into Metz shortly after 754 along with

---

107. Found in Rome from the time of Pope Theodore (642–649), *Hypapante* on 2 February (the meeting of the infant Jesus with Simeon in the Temple, also referred to as St. Simeon and celebrated as a feast of the Lord until retitled *Purificatio*) had a procession that formed at St. Hadrian's-in-the-Forum and went to St. Mary Major's for mass; see Martin F. Connell, "'Just as on Easter Sunday': On the Feast of the Presentation," *Studia Liturgica* 33 (2003): 159–74 at 171–73. Under Pope Sergius (687–701) the Marian feasts of *Annunciatio* (25 March); *Natale S. Mariae* or *Assumptio* (15 August); and *Nativitas* (8 September) were celebrated with new texts, "collecta" (gatherings), and processions. On the complicated story of the "oriental" Marian feasts in Rome, see Vogel, *Medieval Liturgy*, 69, 95, and 128, n. 24 and A. Chavasse, *Sacramentaire gélasien*, 375–80. On the supposed *Natale S. Mariae*, considered since Bernard Botte's thesis ("L'ordre d'après les prières d'ordination") to be Rome's first Marian feast (1 January), see Guilmard, "Une antique fête mariale," 25–67.

108. Yitzhak Hen, *Royal Patronage of Liturgy in Frankish Gaul*, revises widely accepted theories regarding Carolingian interest in adopting Roman liturgical usages. As in other liturgical situations the reality may lie somewhere between adoption or adaptation and all-out rejection of Roman practice.

Roman chant).[109] By 760 the Roman mass had supplanted the Gallican rite. Pepin the Short (reigned 751–768) undertook a program of liturgical unification that was continued and intensified by Charlemagne (reigned 768–814).[110] Stating his intention of following the example set by his father Pepin, Charlemagne promulgated the *Admonitio generalis* (23 March 789), extending the Roman liturgy—actually, a hybrid Romano-Frankish liturgy—throughout the realm.[111] Bones from the Roman catacombs together with whatever other relics were available were spirited north of the Alps. And so were Roman books.

Liturgically creative, the churches north of the Alps were eager to adopt and adapt Roman ways, not be limited by them. The combining in one text of directions for carrying out ceremonials and the required prayers in the face of new ecclesial situations culminated in a bishop's ceremonial or "pontifical," which would prove very popular from its inception in the mid-tenth century. The successful Romano-Germanic Pontifical of the Tenth Century was preceded by local efforts to draw up a more usable bishop's book than the *Hadrianum* and its manuscript relatives had provided. The Gregorian sacramentary had not been equipped with rubrics. For instance, no indication was given if or when laying on of hands would take place. For the choreography of the ritual the presider or master of ceremonies looked to *ordines*, documents that gave stage directions for

---

109. Helmut Hucke, "Toward a New View of Gregorian Chant," *Journal of the American Musicological Society* 33 (1980): 437–67; Giulio Cattin, *Music of the Middle Ages*, trans. Steven Botterill (2 vols.; Cambridge: Cambridge University Press, 1984), 1:53–56.

110. Cyrille Vogel, "Les échanges liturgiques entre Rome et les pays francs jusqu'à l'époque de Charlemagne," in *Le chiese nei regni dell'Europa occidentale e i loro rapporti con Roma sino all'800* (Spoleto: Presso la sede del Centro, 1960), 229–46; Vogel, *Medieval Liturgy*, 147–50. Eric Palazzo (*History of Liturgical Books*, 237) sums it up: "Historians have often observed that in the kings' and emperors' search for political stability within their territories, liturgical books had played a fundamental role. First, the Carolingians, with the Gregorian Sacramentary, then the Ottonians, with the Roman-Germanic Pontifical, attempted, with different degrees of success, the liturgical unification of the empire. Each time, the liturgical books were part of an array of administrative 'instruments' (juridical, political, economic) whose purpose was to impose new regulations.... First Pepin's and then Charlemagne's politics were aimed at liturgical unification based on the Roman model, supported by books in use in Rome, the sacramentary in particular.... [T]he authoritative voice in matters of worship could only come from Rome."

111. Cyrille Vogel, "La Réforme liturgique sous Charlemagne," in *Karl der Grosse: Lebenswerk und Nachleben*, vol. 2: *Das geistige Leben*, ed. Bernhard Bischoff (Düsseldorf: L. Schwann, 1965), 217–32 at 218; also vol. 5: *Registerband*, ed. Wolfgang Braunfels (1968): 100.

each ritual (*ordo*).¹¹² Originating as separate booklets, such ritual directories enabled presider and ministers to carry through a liturgical service. From circa 700 onward the individual booklets were gathered into collections of *ordines*; all examples now extant were copied or constructed north of the Alps.

A. *Ordo* XXXIV and the Ordination Prayers of the *Hadrianum*

Ordo XXXIV, written by a Lateran cleric shortly before 750 and therefore of the same vintage as *Hadrianum*, is the first document we have that gives the Roman practice of ordinations of acolyte, subdeacon, deacon, presbyter, and bishop.¹¹³ Entitled *In nomine domini ordo quomodo in sancta romana ecclesia acholitus ordinatur*, the rubrics are written for an individual ordinand rather than for a group. The ceremony is bare-bones, commencing with an acolyte. Assisting clergy vest the cleric in chasuble and orarium. Mass is celebrated. Before the communion the bishop or the *domnus apostolicus* himself (the pope) gives the cleric a small acolyte's sack and says a generic prayer for the Lord's protection by invoking the Virgin and Peter the apostle.¹¹⁴ One to be ordained subdeacon must take an oath that he has not committed the four capital crimes: sodomy, rape of a consecrated virgin, bestiality, adultery.¹¹⁵ He is given a chalice, and the same generic prayer is offered, requesting the intercession of the Virgin and St. Peter. The ministry is defined by the "instrument" bestowed, a borrowing from feudal ceremonial.

The liturgy for making a deacon is more complex. At the introit of the mass the subdeacon, vested in a white tunic and holding orarium in hand, stands at the balustrade of the altar. Instead of the *Kyrie eleison*, the bishop

---

112. Michel Andrieu, *OR*, vol. 1: *Les manuscrits*; vols. 2–5: *Les textes* (*Ordines I–L*). (Louvain: Spicilegium Sacrum Lovaniense, 1931–1961). For abbreviated commentary, see Vogel, *Medieval Liturgy*, 135–224.

113. Andrieu, *OR* 3: XXIV, 601–13; Vogel, *Medieval Liturgy*, 174–75, English translation in Bradshaw, *Ordination Rites of Ancient Churches East and West*, 218–21.

114. "By the intercession of the blessed and glorious only ever-virgin Mary and of blessed Peter the apostle, may the Lord save and keep and protect you. Amen" (Andrieu, *OR* 3: XXXIV, no. 2); Porter, *Ordination Prayers of Ancient Western Churches*, 13.

115. Andrieu (*OR* 3:549–53) discusses why these and not other crimes like homicide are named. Those who had been publicly reconciled to the church were excluded from the clergy.

gives the opening prayer. Paul's admonition to deacons is read (1 Tim 3:8–14), followed by the chanting of the gradual. Then the subdeacon's chasuble is taken off, and the bishop gives the invitatory (bidding), "Let us pray God the Father almighty, dearly beloved, that he may mercifully pour out the blessing of his grace over this his servant, whom he considers worthy to assume sacred order, and grant him the gift of consecration, through which he may lead him to eternal rewards" (no. 7). At this point the choir begins the *Kyrie* litany. The bishop prostrates himself before the altar with the subdeacon behind him. When the litany is finished, the two rise and at once the bishop gives the consecratory prayer.[116] *Ordo* XXXIV does not mention the laying on of hands or the bestowal of the orarium, although the subdeacon holds it in his hand at the introit of the mass. Remarks over some centuries indicate that imposition of hands was practiced. No further reference is made to the stole. When the consecration is done, the new deacon exchanges the kiss of peace with the bishop and priests and, vested in a dalmatic, stands at the bishop's right. The prayers of consecration for the deacon can be found in *Hadrianum* H 4, with the invitatory or bidding above transcribed as no. 30 and "another prayer" (*alia*, no. 31), *Exaudi domine preces nostras*, already discussed in connection with the diacona (H 214), being the true collect. It is not difficult to imagine a diacona's ordination within such a ceremonial context. That it might go undocumented is understandable; the ordination rites of Rome are written for a single diaconal ordinand.

The ordination of a presbyter follows the same pattern; he is led outside the balustrade of the altar by the archdeacon. His deacon's dalmatic is removed, and he is vested with the chasuble (*planeta*), then led to the bishop for the prayer of consecration. Following his ordination, he stands among the order of presbyters. The Alleluia or tract and gospel follow, and the mass of his ordination continues. Again we hear nothing at all of the imposition of hands.[117] Unlike the ordinations of acolyte and subdeacon,

---

116. Porter (*Ordination Prayers of Ancient Western Churches*, 12–35) gives the Latin text with variants in the "Leonine" (Verona) sacramentary, the Gelasian, Missale Francorum, Eighth-Century Gelasian (Angoulême) and the Gregorian, with translations. For prayers originating in the Verona "sacramentary" and translation of *Ordo* XXIV, see Bradshaw, *Ordination Rites of Ancient Churches East and West*, 215–21.

117. The consecration of the presbyter includes an invitatory and "another" prayer (actually the collect): "Hear us, Lord our God, and over this your servant pour the blessing of the Holy Spirit and the strength of sacerdotal grace...." The consecratory prayer itself

no "instrument" is handed over to deacon or presbyter as sign of the office; their vestment itself serves as insignia.

Michel Andrieu has masterfully analyzed the *ordines romani* so as to distinguish the purely Roman texts from those with Frankish additions and changes. In the ninth century, especially north of the Alps, rubrics from *ordines romani* and non-eucharistic prayers excerpted from the sacramentaries (e.g., the *Hadrianum* with its supplement by Benedict of Aniane) were combined to form the book for the use of bishops, the pontifical.[118] Now the bishop had just one book for sacraments and other rites including ordinations and blessings. Vogel summarizes the research so far and gives some examples of the first pontificals, which were experimental and idiosyncratic to the local church that used them.[119]

6. The Romano-Germanic Pontifical of the Tenth Century (RGP X)

Rites tend to develop genetically from an isolated prayer to more complex and fulsome rituals until finally they lose their relevance, are suppressed, or external factors cause their disintegration. The next stage in the development of ordination rites culminated in the well-received Romano-Germanic Pontifical of the Tenth Century.[120] First compiled by gifted liturgists at the Benedictine abbey of St. Alban, Mainz, circa 950–962, each manuscript as it was copied was tailored to suit the requirements of a diocese with all the local peculiarities that entailed. This newly designed pontifical, in its multiple manifestations called the Romano-Germanic Pontifical of the Tenth Century (RGP X), could trace its origin to the papal Gregorian sacramentary.

---

takes into account the various grades of hierarchy and the bishop's self-declared infirmity that requires helpers; the whole is shaped by Old Testament types (Deshusses, *Sacr. grég.*, 1: H 3, nos. 27–29b).

118. Rather than the Frankish Gelasian or Eighth-Century Gelasian sacramentary. The process is discussed by Vogel, *Medieval Liturgy*, 70–78.

119. See Vogel, *Medieval Liturgy*, 225–30, 237–39, on the early development of the pontifical; also Palazzo, *History of Liturgical Books*, esp. 27–61 and 195–212; and Roger E. Reynolds, "Pontifical," *Dictionary of the Middle Ages* 10 (1982): 30–31.

120. *Le Pontifical Romano-Germanique du dixième siècle*, vol. 1: *Le Texte (NN. I–XCVIII)*; vol. 2: *Le Texte (NN. XCIX–CCLVIII)*; vol. 3: *Introduction générale et Tables*, ed. Cyrille Vogel with Reinhard Elze (3 vols.; Vatican City: BAV, 1963–1972).

With Franco-German embellishments it was brought back to Rome—now a liturgically impoverished center—under the aegis of the Holy Roman emperor, Otto I, and validated by its use in papal ordinations in the Eternal City circa 963 to 965. Between 996 and 1002 a poem was interpolated in the pontifical used for these ordinations or in a similar manuscript, either in Mainz or more probably on the occasion of Otto III's visit to Rome on 15 August 999. Whatever the case, two manuscripts that allow a retrieval of RGP X's oldest overall plan and most archaic features, Monte Cassino Abbey Library codex 451 (copied ca. 1022/35) and Vallicelliana D.5 (slightly later), were both transcribed in Beneventan script from a descendant of this Roman manuscript.[121] These two central Italian manuscripts of Benedictine provenance provide early texts of the newly elaborated episcopal rituals for installing women in the ecclesiastical offices of diacona and canonical or monastic abbess.

Fifteen manuscripts out of some forty used to establish the text of RGP X contain rituals for "making" diaconas.[122] Most of these extant RGP X pontificals containing rituals for women date from the eleventh century, suggesting that the period between the Franco-romanization of the liturgy and scholasticism was especially welcoming of a place for them in the

---

121. On careful study, the faults and incompleteness of the *Cassinensis* prove that several manuscripts intervened between the Mainz original and this archaic copy. As with *Tridentinum* and *Hadrianum*, the original or "archetypal" book is not extant.

122. The mss. listed by Andrieu in OR 1 containing rituals for diaconas and canonical and monastic abbesses (in this order) are: Bamberg, Oeffentl. Bibl. cod. Lit. 50 (11th cent.), 43r–45v, 48r–50v and 50v–51v; Bamberg, Oeffentl. Bibl. cod. Lit. 53 (11th cent.), f. 22r–23r, 23v–24v, 24v–25v; Eichstätt, Episcopal Archives, Pontifical of Gondekar II (1057–1075), f. 21r–v, 22v–23r, 23r–v; London, B.M. Add. 17004 (11th cent.), 366–69, 372–75, 375–80; Lucca, Bibl. Cap., cod. 607 (2nd half 10th cent., with neumes), making of a diacona with mass, f. 32r–33v (*fatiendam* revised *ordinandam*), 33v–34v, 34v–36r; Milan, Ambrosiana Bibl. cod. Z.52 Sup. (first half of 11th century), 161r–163r, 155r–157r, 157r–160v; Monte Cassino, Abbey Libr. cod. 451 (1122/35), 14r–15r, 12v–13v, 19v–20r; also Rome, Vall. D. 5 (ca. 1050), 11v–12v, 10r–v, 16r–17r; Pistoia, Chapter Library Pontifical (2nd half of 11th cent.); Vendôme, Bibl. Mun. cod. 14 (first half of 11th century), 13r–14r, 11r–12r, 14r–15v; Paris, Bibl. Nat. cod. Lat. 820 (2nd half of 11th century), 29r, 27r, 29v; Vitry-le-François, Bibl. Mun. cod. 36 (11th–12th cent.), 16v, 14r, 17r; [Vendôme, Paris and Vitry-le-François very close to Monte Cassino and Rome Vallicelliana D. 5]; Vienna, Nationalbibl. cod. lat. 701 (2nd half of 11th century), 94r–95r, 95r–v, 95v–96v; Wölfenbüttel, Landesbibl. lat. 164 (first half of 12th century), f. 77r–v, 79r–v, 79v–80v, probably from the monastery of St. Michele de Lunebourg, diocese of Verden; Wölfenbüttel, Landesbibl. lat. 530 (beginning 12th cent.), 218v–219v, 219v–221v, 221r–222r. In eight of these mss., the ritual for making a diacona precedes that for the canonical, and then monastic, abbess; in seven the canonical abbess appears first. In addition Metz, Bibl. Mun. 334 (11th century) contains rituals for monastic (137v–141v) and canonical (141v–145r) abbesses.

church's official ministry.[123] The provenance of these manuscripts is not limited to a single area; the distribution is wide.

A. The Romano-Germanic Pontifical of the Tenth Century: a Comparison of Rituals

Many, although not all, of the extant manuscript copies witnessing to the diaconal office of women, either by a single prayer or by a ritual, were written outside Italy. Some decades ago in connection with books of the ninth and tenth centuries, Andrieu noted that the prayer for the making of a diacona is found, "alone or incorporated into a true *ordo*, in several liturgical books compiled north of the Alps."[124] Thanks to mid-tenth century transalpine initiatives in developing ritual orders for official ecclesiastical ministries in these more recently evangelized regions, the evidence for recognized offices for women is richer and more diversified than in the old Roman sacramentaries.

Eight manuscripts were used by Vogel and Elze to establish the ritual texts for male deacons, diaconas, and canonical and monastic abbesses.[125] These manuscripts, listed in alphabetical order below, are identified by letters and have been grouped by family. The family CDTV comprises Monte Cassino

---

123. Vogel and Elze (*Pontifical Romano-Germanique*, henceforth *PRG X*) retroject many of these extant copies back to now-lost manuscripts made in the later 10th century. The strong leadership of the Ottonian dynasty with its Byzantine connections enabled the quick spread of this liturgical reform.

124. Andrieu (*OR* 4:146, n. 5) names Cologne, Bibl. Capit. cod. 138, f. 36r, from the first quarter of the 9th century (*OR* 1:106); the Pontifical d'Aurillac of the 9th–10th centuries (Albi, ms. 34, f. 42v); and the Leofric Missal (see *Leofric Missal* [1883], [2002]). Andrieu indicates that there are others.

125. The Vogel-Elze (*PRG X*: 1, 38–48) compilation groups rituals for women together, following masses on the anniversary of diaconate or priesthood for men. The lengthy and verbose consecration of a virgin with mass is followed immediately by the "ordination of a canonical abbess professing a rule" (48–51), the consecration of a virgin who will live privately in her home (51–54), then that for making a diacona (54–59), the consecration of a widow who professes chastity (59–62), the ordination of an abbot [or abbess] (62–69), the mass for an abbot (69–70), the *ordo* for making a monk (70–72), the ordination of a monk (72–74), orations for monks (74–75), orations and prayers for monks at mass (75–76), and finally the ordination of a monastic abbess (76–82). The Roman order for dedicating a church (82–89) and related rituals follows the consecration of persons. For the Latin texts and variants, see Vogel-Elze, *PRG X*: 1. See also Michel Andrieu, *Le Pontifical Romain au Moyen-Âge*, vol. 1: *Le Pontifical Romain du XIIe Siècle* (4 vols.; Vatican City: BAV, 1938), 69, 80, 168–69. Gary Macy (*Hidden History*, 133–56) gives many Latin texts for the ordination of women deacons and abbesses.

451 (C); Rome, Vallicelliana D.5 (D); Vienna 701 (T); and Vendôme 14 (V). The group BGKL is comprised of Bamberg, lit. 53 (B); Eichstätt, Pontifical of Gondekar (G); Pistoia C.141 (K); and Lucca 607 (L). The rituals for diaconas and monastic abbesses show slight variations in order and only slight differences in content. The ritual for canonical abbesses follows a standard order. The liturgical structure of the diacona's *ordo* given here follows CDTV and has similarities with the invariable *ordo* of the canonical abbess.[126] The order for the monastic abbot and abbess will be compared to show their striking similarities.

(a) For male and female deacons

Andrieu observed that in RGP X "several rubrics [for the ordination of diaconas] recall...the ordination of deacons."[127] Few comparative studies have been carried out for these Western rituals. One of the first in connection with the contemporary debate over the ordination of women was published by Josephine Massyngberde Ford, who provides English translations of the Latin rubrics and prayers.[128] Martimort has analyzed the ritual for a diacona with its sources, commenting on its dependence on earlier Frankish rituals for widows professing chastity and *ancillae Dei*, the Roman consecration of virgins, and perhaps even a penitential *ordo*.[129] The resulting pastiche may represent an early effort at developing a ritual for an ecclesiastical office that was being reestablished after a lapse of time. Borrowing of phrases and prayers from various sources had been a time-honored method for constructing Roman rites.

The structure of the rites for a diacona in RGP X parallels that for a male deacon even though the content is changed to suit the gender of the

---

126. CD follow the order presbyter, deacon and subdeacon, consecration of a virgin, ordination of a canonical abbess, consecration of a virgin at home, diacona. In CDV ordination of a monastic abbess immediately precedes that of a bishop. For ease in comparisons we follow the order given in BGL: diacona, [consecration of a widow, BG], canonical abbess, monastic abbess.

127. For the ordination of male deacons see *PRG X*: 1, *Ordinatio diaconorum*, 24–28; on diaconal and presbyteral rites see also Andrieu, *OR* 3:557–61.

128. Josephine Massyngberde Ford, "Order for the Ordination of a Deaconess," *Review for Religious* 33 (1974): 308–14.

129. Martimort, *Diaconesses*, 211–15. Martimort comments that the word *diacona* appears only three times (in the rubrics), and that the bestowal of the orarium and the Alleluia verse are the only allusions to the office in the rite. He overlooks the reference in the *consecratio* to baptismal responsibilities retained from the Frankish consecration of a widow.

ordinand and circumstances of ministry. These parallels include the bishop's bestowal of the orarium and the consecratory prayer said "in the manner of a preface."[130] Mass texts are provided by several manuscripts. The ordination of both male and female deacons takes place following the gradual and before the proclamation of the gospel, since in the church of Rome the chief liturgical ministry of deacons is proclaiming the gospel.[131] In the case of the diacona, the mass texts into which the ritual is inserted are given. This suggests its usual celebration in a female monastery or convent, whereas the mass ritual is not provided for the deacon whose ordination on Ember Saturday in Rome followed that of subdeacons and preceded that of presbyters. The comparison below (Table 5.1) shows the structure and content of the rituals for deacon and diacona.[132]

The rite for ordaining male deacons refers to them in the plural. This is not the rite of old Rome where fewer deacons than presbyters were ordained. It commences with the rubric that specifies laying on of hands by the bishop alone (no. 9), not indicating where in the ritual the gesture occurs. For the seven regionary Roman deacons the dalmatic, bestowed by the bishop of Rome whose vestment it is, is their chief sign of office.[133] Originating in a Germanic culture, RGP X includes "explanatory" rites for ordination derived from feudal culture and developed in the Gallican world. Adding to the solemnity, they will come to be accepted as "essential" rites. Their effect is to individualize the ministerial "power" (*potestas*) in question, understood as a personal possession rather than ecclesial empowerment to act on behalf of the community of faith. For instance,

---

130. Does "in modo praephationis" refer to the liturgical structure of the prayer, to the presider's gesture with arms extended?

131. A rubric found in two codices (BG) of RGP X tells us, "All who are destined for holy orders ought firstly to be consecrated by the bishop before the proclamation of the gospel, because the preaching of the holy gospel by them ought to be spread throughout the world. But virgins and widows ought to be veiled after the gospel reading, because it is fitting that they be instructed through the gospel" (*PRG X*, 1: 38–39). Nevertheless CDTV complete the consecration of virgins before the proclamation of the gospel.

132. Summarized from *PRG X*, 1: 24–28 (for a deacon) and 54–59 (for a diacona). The complete Latin text for deacon and diacona are given in Macy, *Hidden History*, (G) 9–20, 137–40; (F) 1–23, 134–37. The content of the rituals is standard even if the order may differ between recensions.

133. According to Angelo Lameri (*La traditio instrumentorum e delle insegne nei riti di ordinazione: studio storico-liturgico* [Rome: C.L.V.-Edizioni liturgiche, 1998], 159), the orarium is not attested in Roman use before the late 5th–6th centuries. Andrieu (*OR* 4:129–38) reviews the evidence for the the orarium or stole in the West.

Table 5.1 Comparison of the ordination/making of deacons and a diacona

Ordination of [male] deacons	For making a diacona
[rubric: only bishop lays hand on head]	[before entering the church the bishop places orarium on her neck[a]]
Mass for the consecration of a deacon	*Mass for the consecration of a diacona*
–Introit	–*Deus in nomine tuo salvum.* Ps 53:5
–Collect	–Prayer: *Deus castitatis amator*[b]
–Epistle: *Diaconos similiter pudicos, non bilingues*	–Epistle: *Fratres, nescitis quoniam corpora vestra*
(1 Tim 3:8–14)	(1 Cor 6:15–20)
–Gradual psalm	–Gradual psalm
–Invitatory (not found in the diacona's ritual)	–Prostration before altar, with litany (*Kyrie*)
–Prostration before altar, with litany (*Kyrie*)	
Allocution to people: *Commune votum*	
Blessing of stoles (*stolae*): *Deus invictae virtutis triumphator*	
Prefatio diaconorum: *Oremus, dilectissimi, Deum patrem omnipotentem, ut super hos famulos ad officium diaconatus dignatur assumere*	
Collect: *Exaudi, domine, preces nostras et super hunc famulum tuum spiritum tuae benedictionis emitte, ut caelesti munere ditata, et tuae gratiam possit maiestatis acquirere et bene vivendi aliis exemplum praebere. Per.*	Collect: *Exaudi, domine, preces nostras et super hanc famulam tuam spiritum tuae benedictionis emitte, ut caelesti munere ditata, et tuae gratiam possit maiestatis acquirere et bene vivendi aliis exemplum praebere. Per.*
Deacon's consecration "in the manner of a preface": *Omnipotens Deus, honorum dator, ordinum distributor, officiorumque dispositor*	Diacona's consecration "in the manner of a preface": *Deus qui Annam filiam Phanuelis vix per annos septem sortitam iugale coniugium ita annos octoginta*
Traditio: *Accipe stolam tuam, imple ministerium tuum, potens est enim Deus*	The bishop places the orarium around her neck: *Stola iocunditatis induat te dominus*
Alia. *Accipe stolam candidatam de manu domini, ab omnibus vitiorum sordibus*	
	Veiling (by herself); Ant. *Ipsi sum desponsata*

Continued

Table 5.1 Continued

Ordination of [male] deacons	For making a diacona
	Prayer: *Preces famulae tuae...benignus exaudi*
Clothing with stole, *traditio* of the gospel book: *Accipite potestatem legendi evangelium in ecclesia dei tam pro vivis quam pro defunctis in nomine domini. Amen.*	
	Traditio of the ring: *Accipe anulum fidei, signaculum spiritus sancti.*
	Traditio of the wreath: *Accipe signum Christi in capite, ut uxor eius efficiaris.*
	Antiphon
Blessing: *Domine sanctae, spei, fidei*	Prayer: *Famulam tuam, quaesumus, domine, pia devotione iuvante, perducat ad veniam*
Clothing with the dalmatic and exchange of the kiss of peace; the newly ordained deacon stands at the bishop's right [Presbyteral ordination follows, then the remainder of the mass]	
	• Gospel: John 3: 27–30
	• Offering made to bishop "in the order of the veiled"
	• Offertory, Secret
	• Preface
	• *Hanc igitur*
	• Blessing
	• Communion verse
	• Thanksgiving *Bonorum, Deus operum institutor, famulae tuae cor purifica*
	• The newly ordained diacona communicates in the sacred mysteries. After mass the bishop confirms her pastoral jurisdiction.

[a] The bishop places the orarium around her neck. Since it must be adjusted so that its ends hang down under the tunic, propriety would account for its initial bestowal in a location outside the church. BGKL place the diaconal collect common to men and women before Ps 53.

[b] This prayer refers to sixty-fold fruits, indicating that its model is the consecration liturgy for a widow.

the handing over (*traditio*) of the "instrument" of the gospel book (*materia*) of the ministry is accompanied by the bishop's statement (*forma*), an "imperative of will" with respect to the use of that instrument. It concedes the deacon "power" (*potestas*) to proclaim the gospel.[134] The orarium (Greek *orarion*), ancient sign of ecclesial ministry used even by minor clerics in Rome, in later Gallican sources is called *stola*, a term that would eventually be introduced into Roman ordination culture along with other liturgical influences from north of the Alps. The RGP X formula for the deacon, "Receive your stole, fulfill your ministry," expresses it well. This formula or charge accompanying its bestowal may not have been accepted into Roman ordination rites until the twelfth century. The RGP X acknowledges, and perhaps restores, laying on of hands with epicletic prayer to a place of importance in the rite.[135] Over time the highpoint of the ritual will shift from the bishop's laying on of hands with epicletic prayer to the concluding rites immediately preceding the exchange of the peace.

The female deacon is instituted in a ritual that shares the same basic structure as her male counterpart, some adjustments being made because of her gender and less public role.[136] Before entering the church the bishop places the orarium about her neck, giving her an opportunity in private to thread its ends under her tunic. The ritual for making a diacona does not mention laying on of hands, but as we saw with the deacon, this gesture does not stand out as central to the ordination rite. The prayer of consecration is borrowed from Gallican sources for the consecration of a widow, with some few phrases suppressed to suit the new use.[137] The recognition of the infant Christ in the Jerusalem temple by Anna the prophetess,

---

134. The bishop's declaration accompanying the "traditio" or handing over of the gospels in RGP X may not have been received in Rome until the 13th century.

135. See especially the ordination rite for presbyters, PRG X, 1: XVIII.26.

136. Evidence regarding the ministries of diaconas is lacking, no doubt because women's work is so little documented. Within communities of women or of women and children, pastoral and educational works and liturgical-sacramental ministries (communion ministry and communion services, care and anointing of the sick, the divine office) would have offered many opportunities to a woman deacon in parochial, canonical, or monastic settings.

137. *Missale Francorum* (*Cod. Vat. Reg. Lat. 257*), ed. Leo Cunibert Mohlberg, Leo Eizenhöfer, and Petrus Siffrin (Rome: Herder, 1957), 17, no. 55; *Missale Gallicanum vetus* (*Cod. Vat. Palat. Lat. 493*), ed. Leo Eizenhöfer, Petrus Siffrin, and Leo Cunibert Mohlberg (Rome: Herder, 1958), 7–8, no. 16. *Missale Francorum* (Vat Reg. lat. 257) and *Missale Gallicanum vetus* (Vat. Palat. lat. 493) date from ca. 700. In his detailed critique, Martimort (*Diaconesses*, 211–15) notes the prayer's source, concluding, "The ensemble of the ceremony [for the diacona] is therefore only the consecration of a widow, more solemn than the formulary which follows

misconstrued as the circumcision rather than the child's presentation, is followed by recollection of the diacona's ministry in early churches of the East, that of anointing females during the initiation rite. Much of the prayer's concern focuses on the diacona's embrace of continence, presented as particularly difficult for women.[138]

Bestowal and adjustment of the orarium by the bishop take place within the sanctuary. During the section of the ritual that is concerned with diaconal office proper, symbolized by the orarium's bestowal, the bishop prays that the Lord will clothe the new diacona with the "stole of joy."[139] The bestowal of the orarium has marked the making of the new diacona; now the focus shifts to the personal commitment of the woman to Christ. She herself takes the veil from the altar and places it on her head,

---

in the Mainz Pontifical: *Consecratio viduae que fuerit castitatem professa*; this last is not, like the other, reserved to the bishop; it does not allow prayer said 'in modum praefationis,' neither the giving of the ring and the crown, nor the chant of antiphons." Its solemnity, and the textual suppressions relating to widows, argue against Martimort's dismissal of it as an ordained office. It reads, "O God, you preserved Anna daughter of Phanuel, who lived the married bond for seven years, then in holy and pure widowhood to eighty-four years so that, Just Rewarder, you might bring her, who by night and day combined prayer with fasting, even to the grace of prophecy on the occasion of the circumcision of your Anointed One; and then, following on that, through apostolic institution of this ordination of holy women you prescribed that young women and youth of that gender be provided with the bestowal of holy chrism. Almighty God of all things, deign to accept, with the utmost devotion, the demanding and laborious purpose of this your servant, not much differing from perfect virginity. For you, maker of all worldly creatures, know well that it is impossible that worldly attractions can be avoided. Terrible passions or the blandishments of pleasure never disturb souls that have once been given life through you. For those senses into which you deign to be infused, nothing is more desirable than your kingdom, nothing more dreadful than your judgment. Therefore, Lord, to our petition for this your servant, give the thirty-fold fruit of the wedded as well as the sixty-fold of the widow. In her may there be governance with mercy, liberality with humility, honesty with liberty, sobriety with humanity. May she meditate day and night on your work, that in the day of her calling she may obtain such as you have willed for her through the spirit of prophecy. Grant [this] through the Lord." Josephine M. Ford ("Order for Ordination of Deaconess," 310, n. 9) notes difficulties in the translation and refers to the ancient "anointing as part of the baptismal rite before the women candidates were presented to the bishop." Latin text in *PRG X*, 1: 55–56 and Macy, *Hidden History*, (F) 8, 135. The complete RGP X diaconal ritual is translated, with some variations from mine offered here, by John Wijngaards at www.womendeacons.org/minwest/cassino451.shtml.

138. Deacons were as likely to leave their wives because of ecclesial advancement as to lose them in death. Dare one suggest that the sexual content of some of the prayers for women receiving ecclesiastical status represents a transference of male response to sexual abstinence?

139. Cf. the first sentence of the bishop's bestowal of the chasuble on priests: "May the Lord clothe you with the stole of innocence" (*PRG X*, 1: XVI.31).

accompanied by the antiphon, "I am espoused to him."[140] The subsequent objects bestowed on the new diacona, ring and wreath together with their accompanying imperatives of will using the verb *accipe*, parallel the *traditio instrumentorum* of the male deacon, but these signs added to the ritual for a diacona were earlier used and continued to be so used at the consecration of a virgin. The virgin was consecrated because of her personal decision rather than the delegation of the local church.[141] The *traditio* of the ring and the wreath (*torques*) were perhaps intended to parallel the giving of the gospel book to the deacon.[142] As with the virgin's consecration, the ring is said to be "seal of the Holy Spirit, that you may be called spouse of Christ if you serve him faithfully." The wreath is "the sign of Christ on the head, that you may be made his wife...." As with the virgin's ritual, both Christ and the Spirit are central to the diacona's consecration. The rubric at the end of the rite reads, "Indeed the diacona herself may communicate in the sacred mysteries." Does this phrase suggest the more active and full participation symbolizing the traditional diaconal privilege of assisting with the distribution of the cup?[143] The bishop's proclamation of the banns at the end of the ceremony, found in CDTV, indicates that the diacona, like other ministers and consecrated virgins as well, is commissioned to a specific "charge" or "title." The extent and location of the diacona's duties at this period can only be surmised. Except for laying on of hands, from the standpoint of liturgical structure the rite for a female deacon is substantially the same as that for a male deacon.

---

140. This differs from the rite of consecration of virgins, during which the bishop himself veils the woman. The tradition that the bishop veiled only virgins but that widows themselves took the veil blessed by the bishop from the altar or were veiled by a presbyter is found in Gallican canons and was reinforced by papal reminders. The rite for making a diacona is clearly predicated on her widowed state since the temptations supposed to surround her embrace of the state of continence are developed at length.

141. *PRG X*, 1: 45 (*Consecratio sacrae virginis*, XX. 23, 24). Of course, the virgin's choice is ratified by the decision of the bishop acting in the name of the church to consecrate her.

142. It is only later, with those rituals in the lineage of the widely popular 13th-century pontifical of William Durandus, that the diaconissa's power (= empowerment) to read the gospel with homily at the divine office will be the centerpoint of the official rite. With the mid-15th-century pontifical of the bishop of Bergamo her empowerment to read the gospel and homily in the church will more closely parallel the responsibility given to the male deacon.

143. "Diacona vero illa inter misteria sacra communicet" (*PRG X*: 1: XXIV.24); cf. the ritual practice known from Eastern diaconal rituals. Wijngaards locates this rite in the sanctuary.

With respect to the diacona's ordination ritual, the "conundrum of the widow" remains. Why, in the oration early in the ritual and again in the consecratory prayer, is the sixtyfold fruit of continence, traditionally that of the widow, held up for the diacona? In fact, why is the consecratory prayer used for widows in eighth-century Gallican sacramentaries reused for the diacona with very few omissions? Why is Anna the widowed prophetess the scriptural type of the diacona?[144] And why, immediately after the bestowal of the orarium by the bishop, does the diacona take her veil from the altar and veil herself, while singing the antiphon *Ipsi sum desponsata*? The self-veiling echoes that of the earlier order of widows that evolved into the office of diacona.

Traditionally the office of diacona had carried out its ministry in "the world." Perhaps when this ritual was compiled in the tenth century, those women with experience of life outside a monastery were considered more likely candidates for the diaconate than those enclosed within it from an early age. The example of many foundresses of early women's communities must have played a role in relation to the RGP X diaconal consecration prayer that takes its images from widowhood. Many women's religious houses founded in the early Middle Ages were first governed by widows. Well-placed widows had access to lands and funds, but they also could readily assume a maternal role with the virgin *sanctimoniales*.[145] The "handing over of the instruments" of the female diaconal office is taken verbatim from the consecration of virgins. Does this indicate that in the tenth century the office was exercised primarily within the women's world of canonry and monastery and that single, virginal women were now most often its recipients?

Ritual practice changes slowly. We have manuscript witnesses to these rites for roughly two centuries, not too long for rituals to achieve their content and shape. It takes no stretch of the imagination to propose that the consecration rite for a diacona developed in various locales during the early Middle Ages as a response to the ecclesial status of a widow

---

144. Anna is also mentioned in the rite for the consecration of a widow who will profess chastity (*PRG X*, 1: XXV.14). However, the widow's consecration is to take place following the reading of the gospel (XXV.1), while the rites for the diacona, like those for bishop, presbyter, deacon, and virgins, take place prior to the reading of the gospel.

145. A Wölfenbüttel pontifical (Landesbibl. cod. lat. 530, 223v) of the beginning of the 12th century indicates the perspective on the widow: she was released from the "law of the man" (*Vidua...soluta est a lege viri*; *PRG X*, 1: XXV.2).

within canonical institute or monastic house that she herself had founded and, adopting the religious life, served as its first leader. As these houses grew they became populated chiefly by unmarried women. Intended for those who would exercise ecclesiastical duties with some equivalence to those of the male deacon, the ritual also incorporates espousals of the newly ordained person to Christ, represented on the earthly level by his Body-spouse the Church. Thus the ritual incorporates the expectation that the diacona, like the male deacon, maintain continence from the time of her consecration.[146] In what may be our oldest extant manuscript (Lucca, Biblioteca Capitulare cod. 607) containing the making/ordination of a diacona, the ritual (fols. 32r–33v) follows immediately that for the "consecration" of deacons and presbyters, after which the ordinations of a canonical, then a monastic abbess, are given (fols. 33v–36r). No ritual for the consecration of virgins, whether from the old Roman rite or for *ancillae Dei* living at home, is provided. In Lucca, did the ritual for a diacona replace the consecration of virgins while supplying features of that venerable Roman rite?[147]

(b) Ordination rituals for abbesses

As with the rituals for deacons and diaconas discussed above, those that follow are taken from RGP X and found in manuscripts with wide geographical distribution.[148] A number of older ordination rites for abbots and abbesses

---

146. The ritual for the consecration of a widow who professes chastity did not include orarium or symbols of espousal to Christ. It was available to a woman who joined a religious institute or house after death of a spouse or a mutually-agreed-upon separation from her husband (*PRG X*, 1: XXV.1–16).

147. Lucca had a "metropolitan" abbess, hence women's leadership played an important role in that church. On this early ms. see Andrieu, *OR* 1:159–60. The heading for the diaconal ritual reads "Ad diaconam fatiendam," revised to "ordinandam." Single prayers in sacramentaries are often titled "making," and developed rituals for women deacons in RGP X continue to use this title. William Durand's 13th-century pontifical refers to a deaconess' "ordination." Abbots and abbesses are sometimes "made," but are later more often "ordained" as this term comes into vogue.

148. For major RGP X manuscripts containing the ordination rituals for canonical and monastic abbesses, see above, n. 122. Rituals are discussed following the order in Vogel-Elze's ms. group BGKL (*PRG X*, 3: 65–67; Vogel, *Medieval Liturgy*, 230–31). Bamberg 53 (B) and Eichstätt, Gondekar (G) are dated in the 11th century and give the order consecration of a virgin, veiling of *ancillae Dei* (canonesses?), making of a diacona, consecration of a widow professing chastity, ordination of a canonical abbess, and ordination of a monastic abbess. Dating from the second half of the 10th century, Lucca 607 (L) is the oldest of the group. Its order is very simple: the making of a diacona ("fatiendam" revised to "ordinandam") and her consecration mass, ordination of a canonical abbess, ordination of a monastic abbess, ordination of an abbot, and consecration of abbot or abbess within the monastery.

include the episcopal laying on of hands and giving of the staff, showing few or no differences between the sexes.[149] Besides being termed ordinations, the early medieval versions from outside Rome tended to have a strong sacramental sense, with imposition of hand and explicit prayer for the Spirit.[150]

The most obvious features of the RGP X rituals are their continued use of the term "ordination" and their reference to the "sacred order" into which the ordinand is admitted.[151] In this section two rituals are analyzed, one for ordaining the abbess of an institute of canonesses professing a rule, likely that attributed to St. Augustine; and one for ordaining an abbess of a monastic community, most frequently that of St. Benedict. While sharing the same ritual structure in a ceremony that is termed an ordination, the content of each reflects differences of lifestyle. The canonical abbess headed an institution especially favored in Germanic lands and appearing elsewhere in Europe. The ritual for her ordination reflected the content of the prayer of consecration of male deacons; indeed, she often acted as deacon as well as episcopal-abbess. The monastic abbess headed an ecclesial institution for women with even older roots, perhaps going back to the third century.[152] Both abbot and abbess held what had originally been lay offices. Reminiscences of the old, virtually unisex ritual from outside Rome perdured in the simple rite for abbot and abbess, available in

---

149. See the Visigothic *Liber ordinum episcopal* (*Cod. Silos, Arch. Monástico, 4*), ed. José Janini (Santo Domingo de Silos: Abadia de Silos [Burgos], 1991), 101–2; Latin text in Macy, *Hidden History*, 143–44. In the sacristy prior to the ceremony, the abbess is invested with the "religious miter." In the presbytery the *oratio* of consecration referring to the bishop's imposition of hands is said. The bishop exchanges the kiss of peace with her and gives her the rule and staff. The abbot is invested with wool garment and sandals in the sacristy. After the prayer of consecration, he is given the staff and rule, then he exchanges the kiss of peace with the bishop and his brothers. The prayer for the abbot, addressed to Christ, does not refer to the imposition of hands.

150. Cf. the incredibly laconic Gregorian H 216 (Deshusses, *Sacr. grég.*, I, no. 996). Might the Western rituals from outside Rome have been inspired by the stronger theological content of Eastern liturgies? Spain in particular was distant enough from Rome that in general its liturgies were not contaminated until the second millennium.

151. As Gary Macy and others have shown, the terminology of ordination is used more broadly prior to scholastic systematization of orders in the late 12th century. For medieval authorities arguing in favour of the sacramental ordination of abbesses, see Gary Macy, "Heloise, Abelard and the Ordination of Abbesses," *JEH* 57 (2006): 16–32 and *Hidden History*, 93–96. Not the use or lack of the term but the actual components of the installation rite under discussion need to govern any judgment about its "sacramentality" and the sacramental status conferred on the person receiving it.

152. Hugh Feiss, "Monasticism, Definitions of: Christian Perspectives," in *EM* 2:871–73.

the Eighth-Century Frankish-Gelasians and in *Paduensis* (Padua, D 47) in its ninth-century state.[153] The RGP X included these prayers within its more complex rituals of abbatial ordination.[154] The RPG X ritual for the ordination of an abbess of a community professing a monastic rule was an elaborate, self-standing liturgy bearing striking parallels with that for abbots of related men's communities. Perhaps it was used in the ordination of a quasi-episcopal abbess of a venerable and important group of women of an abbey *nullius*, that is, a territory exempt from the rule of the local bishop. We do not know, although careful study of individual manuscripts and their provenance might yield some clues. Following Eastern custom, mass for the solemn ordination of abbots and abbesses was to be said by the bishop, a regulation cited in the Penitential of Theodore as also applicable to the ordination of Roman deacons and presbyters.[155] Late descendants are found, for example, in the fourteenth-century Vatican latin manuscript 6839, where folio 104v gives the blessing for a monastic abbess, and fol 109v the blessing for a canonical abbess.

ORDINATIO ABBATISSAE CANONICAM REGULAM PROFITENTIS: THE
ORDINATION OF AN ABBESS WHO HEADS AN INSTITUTE OF CANONESSES

The following questions might be asked while studying this *ordo*. For whom would the rite be used? Was it only for ordaining abbesses of institutes of "regular" canonesses (i.e., those professing a rule)? What about those canoness institutes headed by deacon-abbesses or metropolitans whose members were not subject to a traditional rule but only to that of the institute? These women also exercised spiritual and secular authority

---

153. The first prayer of the Frankish-Gelasian sacramentary in Berlin, ms. Phillipps 1667 *(Liber Sacramentorum Augustodunensis*, ed. Odilio Heiming [Turnhout: Brepols, 1984], 368, 193–94) is the standard "Cunctorum institutor deus qui per Moysen famulum tuum"; the *benedictio* begins "Omnipotens sempiterne deus affluentem illum spiritum tuae benedictionis super famulum tuum *illum* (famulam tuam *illam*) nobis orantibus propitiatus infunde ut qui per manus nostras hodie inpositione abba (abbatissa) instituetur." The Miriam prayer is also provided as a second blessing for abbesses. The same prayers are found in *Liber Sacramentorum Gellonensis*, ed. André Dumas (Turnhout: Brepols, 1981), 392, 399–400. The text of the first blessing refers to the abbess but neglects to mention the abbot although using the masculine gender. This ms. was probably written 790–800 in the scriptorium of Holy Cross Abbey, Meaux, for Cambrai Cathedral.

154. Cf. *PRG X*, 1: XXVI, 6–7, 14a; XXXII.5, 8 for the consecratory prayers.

155. "Canon of St. Theodore. In the ordination of presbyters or deacons the bishop ought to sing mass; similarly the Greeks do when an abbot or abbess is elected." See McNeill and Gamer, *Medieval Handbooks of Penance*, Penitential of Theodore, III.2, 201.

in conjunction with the local bishop and had a chapter of canons dedicated to their service. An outline of the salient aspects of the ritual structure for ordaining a canonical abbess recalls aspects of the rite for diaconas and also for monastic abbesses. Often it has been said that the canonical abbess was the sole member of the canoness community who vowed chastity. Was she usually a consecrated widow? Had the abbess-elect already been consecrated a virgin? Unlike the diacona's ritual there is no ceremony for either canonical or monastic abbess that specifically represents espousals to Christ. Yet the ritual for veiling "handmaidens of God" who observe chastity in their own homes is suitable for canonesses and appears in close proximity to the ritual for ordaining a canonical abbess in the majority of the manuscripts.

The structures of the rites for diaconas and canonical abbesses are similar; however, the best parallels for the verbal and theological content of the prayers for these deacon-abbesses are found in those for male deacons. The mass commences, omitting the *Kyrie*. After the gradual, accompanied by two or three of her sisters, the abbess-elect prostrates herself before the altar and the litany is intoned.[156] The bishop's *Oremus* invites the assembly to pray. The ordination of a canonical deacon-abbess unfolds as follows:

- *Exaudi, domine, preces nostras*
- [*Omnipotentiam tuam ... ut super hanc famulam tuam quam ad sacrum ordinem assumere dignatus es benedictionis tuae donum dignanter infundas ...*][157]
- Preface dialogue
- Oration *in modum prefationis*
- Giving of the rule
- Oration for abbesses: *Domine Deus omnipotens, qui sororem Moysi Mariam praeeuntem*
- Blessing

---

156. The ordination of the canonical abbess takes place before the gospel. The ritual as enacted indicates that preaching the gospel is an expectation of this sacred office, as it is of bishops, presbyters, and deacons. The ritual for the consecration of virgins who will live in their own homes (which might include canonesses) also takes place before the gospel. The traditional distinction between those who are ordained to proclaim the gospel with their lips (e.g., abbesses) and those who preach the gospel in their lives (e.g., vowed virgins) is not observed.

157. Omitted by CDGKL (of which CD belong to the Montecassino recension).

Ordination Rites 293

- *Te Deum laudamus, Kyrie* by people with closing prayer; or, if consecrated outside the monastery, a procession of the choir of virgins with crosses, blessed water, incense, and gospel book returns to the monastery with the chants and prayer as noted.

The Gregorian collect, *Exaudi, domine, preces nostras* for deacons and diaconas, is proclaimed. In the manuscripts BTV, this collect from the *Tridentinum* recension of the Gregorian sacramentary was followed by the prayer *Omnipotentiam tuam* containing a reference to admission of the ordinand to "sacred order" (*ad sacrum ordinem*): "We humbly beg your omnipotence, Lord, that over this your servant whom you deign to raise to sacred order you may properly pour out the gift of your blessing and grant to her the grace of consecration, that what she receives by your giving, she may keep unsullied by your protection."[158]

The lengthy consecratory prayer *in modum prefationis* for ordaining the canonical abbess incorporates the thought and phrases of the central epicletic text in the consecratory prayer for male deacons, which reads: "Pour on him, Lord, we beseech, the Holy Spirit by which he may be strengthened by the gift of sevenfold grace to follow faithfully to the end in the work of the ministry."[159] The epicletic prayer for the canonical abbess-deaconess, somewhat more elaborate, utilizes the same ideas and even phrases:

> Pour forth, we ask you, Lord, the grace of the Holy Spirit on this your handmaid, whom we faithfully consecrate to divine office (*officium divinum*), that her service may worthily please you at all times, and that you will deign to bless and sanctify and consecrate her with the right hand of your power in the work of ministry very worthy of you, so that she may accomplish faithfully the act of ministry

---

158. "Omnipotentiam tuam, domine, humiliter imploramus, ut super hanc famulam tuam quam ad sacrum ordinem assumere dignatus es benedictionis tuae donum dignanter infundas eique gratiam consecrationem tribuas, ut quod te donante percipit, te protegente inlesum custodiat. Per." PRG X, 1: XXII, 4; Macy, *Hidden History*, (E) 4, 147. The consecratory prayer for male deacons in *Hadrianum* refers to the three grades of ministers exercising a "service of sacred office" (Deshusses, *Sacr. grég.*, 1, H 32).

159. Cf. the parallel text in *Hadrianum* and PRG X's consecratory prayer for deacons: "Emitte in eum domine quaesumus spiritum sanctum quo in opus ministerii fideliter exequendi septiformis gratiae munere roboretur" (Deshusses, *Sacr. grég.*, 1, H 4, no. 32b; PRG X, 1: XVI.14, in the plural; Porter, *Ordination Prayers of Ancient Western Churches*, 35).

entrusted to her, and that she be strengthened by the power of the sevenfold grace of the same Holy Spirit.[160]

For the canonical abbess there is no reference in rubric or prayer text to laying on of hands. However, the epicletic prayer is so strong in its theology and so similar in its content to that for the deacon that the use of this central ritual gesture can be presumed. For both deacon and abbess the consecratory prayers are concluded by naming what are deemed essential virtues of the office. The consecratory prayer for canonical abbesses uses as its scriptural typology the parable of the bridegroom and ten bridesmaids (Matt 25:1–13). The petition for the virtue of chastity, to be cultivated by the new abbess so that she will be ready to receive the heavenly spouse and be among the virgins with lamps ready, closes the consecratory prayer, as does the petition for male deacons for chastity and other virtues required for his office.

After the bishop gives the rule to the new abbess, he prays for her, invoking in the traditional collect for abbesses the prophetess Miriam sister of Moses as archetype of the abbess:

> Lord God almighty, who made Miriam sister of Moses, going in front of death, come to the shore of the sea leading other women between the sea-waves with tympani and dance, we beseech you on behalf of your faithful servant, who today is placed abbess over all in the maternal abbatial dignity, in order that the canonical rule of your whole family be protected, by your help, to eternal glory, that joyful she may enter with all, and there exulting with the angels, singing a new song, she may follow the lamb wherever Christ our Lord will go. Who with you.[161]

As Miriam led the women with tambourines in their dance through the waters of the Red Sea, so may our abbess lead her community of women safely to glory following the Lamb Christ and singing a new song with

---

160. "[E]ffunde, quaesumus, domine, super hanc famulam tuam, quam in officium divinum fideliter dedicamus, gratiam spiritus sancti, ut tibi omnium tempore eius servitus dignanter complaceat, eamque dextra potentiae tuae benedicere et sanctificare sive consecrare digneris in opus ministerii tui condignum, quatinus actum ministrationis sibi creditae fideliter exequatur et *eiusdem sancti spiritus septiformis gratiae virtute corroboretur*" (italics mine; PRG X, 1: XXII.5); Macy, *Hidden History*, (E) 5, 147.

161. "Materna in cathedra," literally "maternal throne." PRG X, 1: XXVI.18a; cf. Padua D. 47, "Oratio quando abbas aut abbatissa ordinatur," Deshusses, *Sacr. grég.*, 3:477, no. 4241; Macy, *Hidden History*, (E) 7, 147.

the angels. The term *ordinatio* is used once again (no. 9). If she has been consecrated somewhere other than in the canonesses' own house (e.g., in the cathedral), the entire choir of virgins goes out to meet her with crosses, holy water, and incense while singing the *Te Deum*. The assembly sings the acclamation *Kyrie eleison* and the procession ends with a prayer in the presbytery of the church. The ordination has ended on a high triumphal note. Although there has been no formal rite signifying espousal to Christ, the content of the consecratory prayer is replete with such reference.

(11) *ORDINATIO ABBATISSAE MONASTICAM REGULAM PROFITENTIS*: ORDINATION OF AN ABBESS PROFESSING A MONASTIC RULE

The ritual for ordaining a monastic abbess corresponds in liturgical structure and high dramatic content to that for the canonical abbess discussed above. Laying on of hands by the bishop is noted explicitly, corresponding to Spanish and Gallican unisex ordination prayers for abbot and abbess.[162] The ritual for an abbot begins with the giving of staff and sandals, the collect, and an *allocutio* (the latter like that for the deacon).[163] Thereafter the ritual for both abbot and abbess, already familiar in several particulars, shares mostly identical components and identical prayers. The bishop presiding, the ordination mass is said up to the gospel. The abbess-elect with two or three companions prostrates herself, the litany is sung, and the *Pater Noster* and psalms are recited.

- Oration *Concede... affectui nostro... ad regimen animarum*
- *Cunctorum bonorum institutor Deus, qui per Moysen famulum tuum ad gubernandas*
- *aecclesias prepositos instituisti...*
- *Exaudi, quaesumus, domine, preces humilitatis nostrae et super hanc famulam tuam N. gratiam tuae benedictionis effunde, quatinus per nostrae manus impositionem*[164]

---

162. Since *Apostolic Tradition*, imposition of hands by the ordainer had been the defining gesture of ordination to major office in Eastern churches. Rome had been reticent in mentioning the laying on of hands for ordination to major office. The Spanish and Gallican traditions of ordination rites for abbots and abbesses explicitly called for the laying on of hands, and RGP X retains this expressive gesture.

163. Following ACDTV.

164. "Hear our humble prayers, we ask, Lord, and over this your [female] servant N.__ pour out the grace of your blessing, since through the imposition of our hand...." This prayer is absent from the ordination liturgy of the abbot.

- Following the sung Preface dialogue, laying on of hand with prayer while a lengthy preface is said: *Omnipotens sempiterne Deus, affluentem spiritum tuae benedictionis... ut qui per manus nostrae hodie impositionem abbas [abbatissa] constituitur*[165]
- the rule is given *ad regendum custodiendumque gregem tibi* [or another text, with prayer]
- *Domine Deus omnipotens qui sororem Moysi Mariam... materna in cathedra*[166]
- *Concede... famulae tuae abbatissae*[167]
- *Omnium... fons bonorum.*[168]

The differences between the solemn rituals for abbot and abbess are few, and are even less noticeable in the liturgy of consecration when an abbot or abbess is ordained in the monastery.[169]

The ritual commences following the same pattern as with the canonical abbess. The first part of the mass having taken place *usque evangelium*, accompanied by two or three of her sisters, the abbess-elect prostrates

---

165. Unlike the ordination prayer for the abbot said "in modum praefationis," that for the abbess is termed "preface." It is considerably longer but not different in essence from the prayer for the abbot. The prayer accompanying imposition of hands is the same for abbot and abbess.

166. "Deus omnium fidelium pastor et rector" is the prayer for the abbot.

167. This prayer for the abbess substitutes for the handing of the staff to the abbot accompanied by "Accipe baculum pastoralitatis [alt. Accipe praelationis virgam, pastoralis custodiae curam significantem]. "Receive the pastoral staff, which you may rightly display to the flock entrusted to you as an example of sternness and rebuke." The case for distinguishing the paternal power of the abbot from the maternal love of the abbess is made by Felice Lifshitz, "Is Mother Superior? Toward a History of Feminine *Amtscharisma*," in John Carmi Parsons and Bonnie Wheeler, eds., *Medieval Mothering* (London: Garland Publishing, 1996), 117–38. From the Miriam prayer we know that the prayer of the abbess is a "maternal" abbatial dignity. Failure to confer the staff may well indicate that the woman is viewed as not capable of receiving full pastoral authority. However, the ordainer's charge that accompanies the giving of the abbot's staff indicates a severity in wielding it that may have been considered inappropriate for his female counterpart.

168. Another oration "Deus cui omnis potestas et dignitas famulatur" is reserved for the abbot.

169. *PRG X*, 1: XXVI.14a. This simpler ceremonial consists of key elements of the liturgy outlined above, including the prayer "Cunctorum operum," imposition of hand on the head with the prayer "Omnipotens sempiterne Deus" said "in the manner of a preface"; the prayer "Deus omnium fidelium pastor et rector"; another oration "Omnium Deus fons bonorum iustorumque" or alternate, followed by the "Te Deum laudamus" and the acclamation "Kyrie eleyson," and concluded by "Deus aeternae lucis inventor." Two manuscripts, K and L, add for the abbess the blessing "Domine... qui sororem Moysi Mariam" (*PRG X*, 1: XXVI.18a).

herself before the altar and the litany is begun.[170] As in the ordination of an abbot, the *Pater Noster* is followed by psalms. The bishop prays an oration for God's servant, whom "we elect *ad regimen animarum,*" for the governance of souls (no. 4). The prayer *Cunctorum bonorum institutor Deus* ("God institutor of all good things," no. 5) presents Moses, shepherd of his father-in-law Jethro's sheep (Exod 3:1), then leader of the Hebrew people to the Promised Land, as type of the abbess leader of her flock.[171] The abbess's leadership role is based on the preeminent one of Moses, and the fruit of her labors is said to be a hundredfold, "Everyone who has left houses, brothers, sisters, father, mother, or land for the sake of my name will be repaid a hundredfold" (Matt 19:29). Interpreting the Scriptures in their application to both men and women, this prayer ends with a citation from the parable of the talents in which the departing landowner entrusts his property to male servants. Using an egalitarian hermeneutic, the servant of the parable is feminized: "Well done, good and faithful handmaiden, because you have been faithful in little things, I will establish you over many, enter into the joy of your Lord" (Matt 25:23). The Scriptures are used with gender-blindness, the gendered text applied equally to women and men.

The bishop, referring to the imposition of hands that is about to take place, prays a version of the *Exaudi* prayer that asks God to pour forth the grace of his benediction on this his handmaiden. Then in a higher voice he intones the preface dialogue. While imposing his hand, he prays the preface, calling on God to send as the Spirit's gifts the "spirit of wisdom and understanding, the spirit of counsel and fortitude, the spirit of knowledge and piety, and to fill her with the spirit of awe." Other virtues deemed necessary to the office are prayed for. Found in the recension connected with Monte Cassino (CDTV) but not in that of Bamberg (BGKL), this lengthy prayer appears to be a new composition. Then follows a second

---

170. The ordination of abbesses prior to the proclamation of the gospel indicates that their ecclesial leadership is considered to parallel that of male clerical leadership.

171. This prayer is standard in unisex rituals for ordinations within a monastery. For the Gregorian "oratio" for ordaining abbot or abbess in their monastery, see Padua, Bibl. Capit. D. 47 (Deshusses, *Sacr. grég.*, 3:477, no. 4239, p. 222, and for the Miriam prayer for abbesses, ibid., 477, no. 4241, p. 222). Its first prayer, "Cunctorum institutor deus qui per moysen famulum tuum ad gubernandas ecclesias," is found in PRG X, 1: XXVI.6 (ACDTV) for the abbot and for the monastic abbess in PRG X, 1: XXXII.5. The consecration, the same for abbot and abbess, names imposition of hand and prays for the necessary virtues (for the abbot, PRG X, 1: XXVI.7; for the abbess, PRG X, 1: XXXII.8); Macy, *Hidden History*, (F) 14a, 148–49.

imposition of hand with a prayer "in the manner of a preface." Referring to the imposition of his hand constituting her as abbess, the bishop implores God to pour out the freely flowing spirit of his blessing on her together with all the virtues needed.[172] St. Stephen the "levite" chosen by the apostles is the type of her ministry, which is to govern and rule as overseer (*speculatrix*) among her colleagues. This is exactly the same text as is prayed for the abbot (*speculator*).[173] To the abbot the bishop gives both rule and staff. In contrast to the Visigothic rite for the ordination of abbot or abbess, a staff is normally not given to her.[174] After the giving of the rule, the prayer naming Miriam sister of Moses as type of the female leader is proclaimed. As with the canonical abbess, if the ordination has taken place within the monastery, the *Te Deum laudamus* is intoned, and the people sing the acclamatory *Kyrie*, followed by a brief prayer concluding the liturgy. If she has been consecrated outside the monastery, the chorus of monastics come out to meet the monastic abbess with crosses, blessed water, incense, and gospel book. The *Te Deum* is intoned, the crowd sings the acclamatory *Kyrie*, and a brief prayer in the presbytery concludes the celebration.

From study of the ordination rites for canonical and monastic abbesses, it can be seen that a thousand years ago the installation of women ecclesial leaders took place within a context of remarkable parallelism with men in language and in rite. Less than two centuries intervened between the scripturally impoverished and theologically circumscribed rites, provided for Charlemagne's clerics by the papal Gregorian sacramentary, and the imaginative and egalitarian—if sometimes linguistically overblown— liturgical efforts of local churches and monasteries north of the Alps. Far outshining the single collect that was its Gregorian root and building on what rites for widow-diaconas existed, the liturgical rituals for women in leadership positions provided by RGP X drew on the Frankish genius for

---

172. Laying on of hands accompanies the oration in the manner of a preface: "ut quae per manus nostrae hodie impositionem abbatissa constituitur, sanctificatione tua digne a te electa permaneat" ("...that the abbess, appropriately chosen by you, who is installed today by the imposition of our hands, by your holiness may endure.") See *PRG X*, 1: XXXII.8; Macy, *Hidden History*, (G) 8, 152.

173. *PRG X*, 1: XXXII.8; for the abbot, 1: XXVI.7.

174. The womanly authority (*cathedra materna*) exercised by the female leader may have led to withholding the crozier, symbol of pastoral authority. Nevertheless this insignia of pastoral office was bestowed on abbesses of the Cistercian order, and by the mid-13th century, with other pontificalia, on Benedictine abbesses at the Nonnberg, Salzburg.

language and drama. The "sobriety" of the Roman rite was replaced by expressive rituals tailored to circumstances and the feudal gesture of the "tradition of the instruments."[175] Laying on of hands played a more prominent role, for example replacing bestowal of the dalmatic as the chief outward sign of the Roman deacon's ordination. The source of that *potestas* that had governed Roman thought since Gelasius I was named: God's Holy Spirit. Indeed, a genuine liturgical *renovatio* of Roman liturgy at the turn of the first to the second Christian millennium can be seen in these ordination rites.

How do these rituals for installing male and female leaders of religious communities compare in sacramental terms? The parallelisms in ritual action and text between ordination of abbots and abbesses and "major orders" (deacon, presbyter and bishop) indicate that installation in abbatial office at the turn of the first millennium was not a "simple sacramental" although consecration of abbots and abbesses is not at present counted as an aspect of the sacrament of orders. The question of the validity and authenticity of sacramental ordination of women must be decided ultimately on liturgical-theological grounds. If, according to liturgical and theological criteria, the rite for an abbess is substantially the same as that for an abbot and includes laying on of hands and invocation of the Holy Spirit, is it possible to claim that the abbot is ordained in a sacramental rite and the abbess is given a "non-sacramental" blessing? The answer is in the negative, since both are baptized Christians.

7. *The Roman Pontifical of the Twelfth Century*

Chapter XIV of the Roman Pontifical of the Twelfth Century contains a *Missa ad diaconam consecrandam*.[176] Two of the three manuscript witnesses have a Roman source.[177] The mass is structured like the RGP X liturgy,

---

175. Lameri, *Traditio instrumentorum*, 171–77.

176. Andrieu, *Pontifical Romain au Moyen-Âge: du XIIe Siècle*.

177. The full text of the mass prayers, together with delivery of ring and crown, is given in Andrieu, *Pontifical Romain au Moyen-Âge: du XIIe Siècle*, 168–69. Three mss. are used to establish the short recension of the text: B = London, British Museum Add. 17005 (fols. 73v–76v, second half of the 12th century, from the Upper Rhine); C = Rome, Vat. Barb. lat. 631 (fols. 150r–152v, second half of the 11th century, Montecassino); O = Vat. Ottob. lat. 270 (65r–67v, 12th century, very rustic hand). Manuscripts O and B are "closely related," from the same Roman exemplar. The long recension available in the Pontifical of Apamea (Lyons, Bibl. Mun., ms. 570) written in Syria omits the diacona ritual altogether.

except that the collect *Exaudi, domine, preces nostras* is not found, its place having been taken by the oration *Preces famulae tuae*, and bestowal of the stole is only alluded to in the second "gradual." The mass for consecrating a diacona in RGP XII is structured as follows:

- Introit: *Deus in nomine tuo salvum me fac*
- Prayer: *Deus castitatis amator*
- Epistle: 1 Corinthians 6:15–20
- Gradual: *De necessitatibus meis*, litany with *Kyrie*
- Oration: *Preces famulae tuae, quaesumus domine, benignus exaudi, ut sumptam castitatis gratiam te auxiliante custodiat. Per.*
- Consecration: *Deus qui annam filiam Phanuelis, que vixit per annos septem*
- Gradual [= Alleluia verse]: *Amavit eam dominus et ornavit eam stola. Vs. Induit eam dominus cyclade*
- Gospel: John 3:27–30
- Offertory: *Miscere michi, domine, secundum magnam misericordiam tuam*
- Secret: *Munera...famulae tuae ill.*
- Preface
- *Hanc igitur*
- Communion: *Servite domino in timore*
- Thanksgiving (Ad complendum): *Bonorum Deus operum institutor, famulae tuae corda purifica, ut nichil in ea quod punire sed quod coronare possis invenias. Per.*[178]

Nos. 14 (giving of the ring) and 15 (bestowal of the wreath), which in the RGP X ritual for diaconas were bestowed prior to the reading of the gospel, are added to this text following the *Ad complendum* with the same formulas as are used for the consecration of virgins in the Roman Pontifical of the Twelfth Century.[179] Andrieu observes that the Roman Pontifical of the

---

178. "Ad complendum" or "Ad completa" is, in the Gregorian sacramentaries, a prayer of thanksgiving to be followed by a blessing prayer. In the Gelasian sacramentaries it is labelled "Post-communionem" (Jungmann, *Mass of Roman Rite*, 2:421).

179. Ibid. But cf. the rubric, "Antequam vero legatur evangelium, dat ei anulum dicens, 'Accipe anulum fidei, signaculum spiritus sancti, ut sponsa Dei voceris, si ei fideliter servieris'" ("Receive the ring of faith, sign of the Holy Spirit, so that you will be called spouse of God if you serve him faithfully"). See Andrieu, *Pontifical Romain au Moyen-Âge: du XIIe Siècle*, XIV.14; and Macy, *Hidden History*, (H) 14, 142, who gives the mass texts. The imperative above parallels that used in bestowing the bishop's ring: "Accipe anulum, fidei scilicet signaculum, quatenus sponsam, Dei sanctam videlicet ecclesiam, intemerata fide ornatus

Twelfth Century retains the RGP X diaconal mass while omitting those rubrics for diaconas that echo the ordination of deacons, keeping the mass formularies, the entirety of the consecratory prayer *in modum praefationis*, and the imposition of "tokens" or signs, that is, ring and crown.[180] Were the rubrics for this liturgy too well known to be written down? Since ordinations of canonical and monastic abbesses are not provided for, does this reduction of the diaconal ritual signal a reduction in the ecclesial participation of women in the Roman church, one which, at least in the city, was not all that strong in the medieval period? The thirteenth-century Pontifical of the Roman Curia would drop the *ordo* altogether.

8. The Pontifical of William Durand

Even after canonists and theologians of the scholastic period developed law and theology inimical to the ecclesial ministry of women and Innocent III decreed the end of monastic traditions respecting the episcopal and diaconal privileges of the abbess of Las Huelgas, contemporary or later pontificals included rituals for establishing women abbesses and diaconas, the latter now more often called deaconesses, in cloister and canonry. Bishop William Durand (d. 1296) of Mende in southern France compiled an enormously popular pontifical (ca. 1291–1295) that formed the basis for Roman ordination rites until the Second Vatican Council reforms.[181] Thirteen witnesses of the Roman Pontifical of William Durand contain chapter XXII, *De ordinatione diaconissae*, the same manuscripts that in chapter XXI give the blessing of an abbess.[182] The rite is brief and is treated as an historical memory. The text reads:

---

illibate custodias" ("Receive the ring, the sign of faith, so that you, adorned with unspotted faith, may protect with undiminished faith the spouse, that is the holy church of God," Andrieu, *Pontifical Romain au Moyen-Âge: du XIIe Siècle*, X.28).

180. Andrieu, *OR* 4:146–47. Vatican ms. Ottobon. 270 is a 12th-century "specifically Roman" pontifical that, following the rite of tonsure (1r) includes ordination rites for porter through presbyter (2v–10v). For the blessing of an abbot or abbess with imposition of hand, nouns and pronouns are given in the masculine gender with the feminine form written above in red ink (52–55v).

181. Michel Andrieu, *Le Pontifical Romain au Moyen-Âge*, vol. 3: *Le Pontifical du Guillaume Durand* (Vatican City: BAV, 1940); Latin text "De ordinatione diaconisse" in Macy, *Hidden History*, (I) XXII, 142. A brief summary of the ordination rites for men as given in Durand's pontifical is found in Lameri, *Traditio instrumentorum*, 95–103.

182. Andrieu, *Pontifical Romain au Moyen-Âge: Pontifical du Guillaume Durand*, 411.

1. In times past a deaconess, not however before the fortieth year, was ordained in this way. For indeed the epistle having been read, having prostrated herself on the ground before the altar, the bishop said over her: "Our help," etc. "Let us pray."
Prayer. "Hear, Lord, our prayers and over this your handmaid," et cetera, as above.[183] Look [require] above, under the blessing of an abbot.

2. Then he gave her the orarium saying: "Let us pray."
Prayer: *Famulam tuam, quaesumus, domine, tue custodia...illarum custodiat. Per Christum* as above.[184]

Durand's pontifical is replete with instructions for adjusting gender references in the blessing of abbot and abbess.[185]

As scholasticism gained headway the participation of religious women in normal church life was under threat probably nowhere more than in Rome. The growing restriction of religious women to convents would have consolidated diaconal tasks about which the documents of the Roman church tell us nothing. The *traditio* of the gospel book (its accompanying formula "received" in Rome in the thirteenth century) with consequent *potestas* for proclaiming the gospel was a defining element in the

---

183. This is the "Exaudi, domine, preces nostras" prayer that first appeared in the 7th-century Gregorian sacramentary for deacons and diaconas.

184. This prayer for the consecration of virgins is found in PRG X, 1: XX.18 and in the document known as Pontifical of the Roman Curia of the Thirteenth Century; see Michel Andrieu, *Le Pontifical Romain au Moyen-Âge*, vol. 2: *Le Pontifical de la Curie romaine au XIIIe siècle* (Vatican City: BAV, 1940), XVIII.11: "Lord, may the protection of your devotion strengthen your handmaiden so that the promise of holy continence, which she received by your inspiration, may keep her inviolate" ("Famulam tuam, domine, tuae custodia muniat pietatis, ut continentiae sanctae propositum quod te inspirante suscepit, te protegente, illesum custodiat. Per").

185. The striking out of a word or writing of the pronoun may indicate an ordinand of the opposite gender. Directions may be given regarding change in gender or number of pronouns. When blessing an abbess (Andrieu, *Pontifical Romain au Moyen-Âge*, vol. 3: *Pontifical du Guillaume Durand*, XXI, 2), the presider is admonished, "And he continues in his blessing through everything just as it is said up to the end in the blessing of an abbot, with words of masculine gender changed into feminine, quite properly in place of the last oration, that is the Exaudi domine, the following prayers are said" (see Michel Andrieu, *Le Pontifical Roman au Moyen-Âge*, vol. 3: *Le Pontifical du Guillaume Durand* [Vatican City: BAV, 1940]). These two prayers are *Concede, omnipotens Deus* and the Miriam prayer. Further on the bishop is directed, when the abbess is being enthroned on the cathedra, to use the prayer in the ordination of abbots (XXI, 7). Then mass is said as for the blessing of virgins, *verbis pluralis*.

ordination of male deacons.[186] The need for diaconas within cloister precincts would have become apparent as regulations were formulated and applied that limited certain liturgical acts to ministers of a specific rank. Noting incongruities in the application of the Benedictine rule to women, Heloise (ca. 1100–1163/4), abbess of the Paraclete near Troyes, objected to the impropriety of having a priest or deacon enter the monastery to begin the night readings.[187] Where liturgical law and custom were followed, the formula, "Receive authority to read the gospel at vigils and to begin the Hours in the Church in the name of the Lord," found in texts for the ordination of deaconesses, must be read as a pastoral response to a perceived danger as well as to a grave inconvenience.

9. Resurgence of the Diaconal Role among Nuns

A lacuna in ordination rites for women is evident in the thirteenth century; none were included in that century's pontifical of the Roman Curia, while reasons for the denial of women's official service of the church were under theological discussion in the schools. William Durand's pontifical reintroduced the possibility of a nun's ordination as deaconess, one that was taken up quite widely judging from extant texts and illustrations. Aimé Georges Martimort discusses manuscript witnesses to this "resurgence" of the diaconal role in women's religious houses from the fourteenth to seventeenth centuries.[188] Such evidence allows us to infer that there existed purposes for that office.[189] Martimort points to an Arles Pontifical (Paris,

---

186. RGP X included for deacons the formula "Accipite potestatem legendi evangelium in ecclesia dei tam pro vivis tam pro defunctis in nomine Domini" ("Receive (pl.) the power of reading the gospel in the church of God for the living and the dead in the name of the Lord.")

187. See Deborah Vess, "Abelard," and "Heloise," in *EM* 1:11–13, 574–75; J. T. Muckle, ed., "The Personal Letters Between Abelard and Heloise," in *MS* 15 (1953): 47–94; Muckle, "The Letter of Heloise on Religious Life and Abelard's First Reply," *MS* 17 (1955): 240–81, esp. 253. See also Linda Georgiana, "Any Corner of Heaven: Heloise's Critique of Monasticism," in *MS* 49 (1987): 221–53; Macy, "Heloise, Abelard and Ordination of Abbesses," 16–32; Macy, *Hidden History*, 93–98.

188. Martimort, *Diaconesses*, 231–43.

189. For instance, how were sick and infirm nuns cared for sacramentally? What was done when the priest-chaplain himself was infirm, or when there were no male servers for mass to assist the priest? References to the office of diaconissa are found in Abelard's rule written for the Paraclete (T. M. McLaughlin, "Abelard's Rule for Religious Women," *MS* 18 [1956]: 241–92 at 259–63).

B.N. lat. 1220, 41v–42r) of the first half of the fourteenth century in which William Durand's *ordo* is phrased in the present tense.[190] Distinguishing the diaconal blessing from the proper office of deacon, Martimort cites three textual witnesses of fifteenth-century Italian "deaconess nuns." Vatican Chigi ms. C V 148 reads for *De ordinatione dyaconisse*:

1. She [the deaconess, sing.] having prostrated herself before the altar after the reading of the Epistle, let the bishop say over her *Adiutorium nostrum in nomine Domini. Dominus vobiscum. Oremus. Exaudi Domine preces nostras...exemplum prebere. Per dominum. Oremus. Familiam tuam...custodiat.* Then let the bishop hand to them (pl.) the book of the gospels and give to them the power of reading the gospel at vigils and of beginning the hours in the church. Let him say to all in common: *Accipite potestatem legendi evangelium ad vigilias et incipiendi horas in ecclesia in nomine Domini.* R. *Amen.* Then let them kiss the hands of the bishop.[191]

It appears from this brief rite that the deaconess is ordained individually using the seventh-century Gregorian collect, while the *traditio evangeliorum* takes place communally with other nuns ordained that day, the same pattern as is found in the ordination of male deacons.

Vatican manuscript latin 1145 is a splendid example of the Pontifical of William Durand made for Giovanni Barozzi (Barocci) shortly after his election as bishop of Bergamo (1445–1469); Barozzi died soon after his

---

190. Martimort, *Diaconesses*, 232. Examples of Martimort's "resurgence" can be found in the Vatican Library. A splendid 14th–15th century *Show* Pontifical of the Hermitesses of St. Augustine (Vat. lat. Ottobon. 502) includes the ordination of a king and the blessing of a queen (80v), and in an added, much-used, section, when the orarium is given to the deaconess (CLXXII) the antiphon is sung, "Dextram meam et collum meum cinxit lapidibus pretiosis" ("He has encircled my right hand and my neck with very precious stones"). Mary Magdalen is prefixed to the Roman women saints invoked in the litany (184v). Other examples of Durand's pontifical in the Vatican Library—Vatican ms. lat. 4744, 20v of the 15th century and Vat. Reg. lat. 1930, 37v—use the title *De Ordinatione dyaconisse*. A rubric in Vatican ms. Ottobon. 1037 of the 15th–16th century indicates the change from masculine to feminine gender in the blessing of an abbess. She is depicted seated on her cathedra (70v) with the mass for the "ordination" of virgins, its plurals changed to singular number. This last ms. also includes Durand's brief rite for the ordination of a deaconess (71v).

191. Martimort, *Diaconesses*, 234. The "imperative of will" formula is typically said in the plural also at the ordinations of males.

election as patriarch of Venice.[192] The pontifical recalls the past ordination of deaconesses but does not transmit Durand's chapter XXII. However, after the lengthy and much-used blessing and consecration of virgins (50r–59v), it adds a reduced and variant text (59v) that reads:

> And if any of them will be made a deaconess, having been given the crown, let him [the bishop] give to her the book of homilies, saying: "Receive the power of reading the gospel with the homily in the church of God, in the name of the Father and of the Son and of the Holy Spirit. Amen."[193]

The text strictly read does not limit this faculty to vigils and the divine office.[194] This glimpse into the female diaconate concludes:

> At this time there are no deaconesses, but commonly in whatever place the hebdomadary reads the gospel, or another one according to the custom of her monastery.[195]

Barozzi's pontifical has extended the "power" of the vanished deaconess—and her successor, the hebdomadary—to include the reading of gospel and homily "in the church of God" in a pastoral charge with some equivalence to that of a male deacon. The blessing of a "regular abbess" follows immediately (59v–62r). If she is Cistercian, the pastoral staff is bestowed; however, the *pontificalia* or *sacerdotalia* proper to bishop or abbot are withheld (61r).

---

192. Andrieu, *Pontifical Romain au Moyen-Âge: Pontifical du Guillaume Durand*, 218, 223. This ms. contains decorated and historiated initials that include kneeling nuns with candles and bishops, and much chant.

193. "Et si aliquam earum fecerit diaconissam, data corona, det ei librum omeliarum, dicens: Accipe potestatem legendi evangelium cum omelia in ecclesia Dei, in nomine pa+tris et fi+lii et spiritus + sancti." Resp.: "Amen."

194. The ordination of the male deacon includes the formula, "Accipite potestatem legendi evangelium in ecclesia dei tam per vivis quam pro mortuis in nomine domini. Amen" (Vat. ms. lat. 1145, 16r). It is unlikely that deacons in this period enjoyed the faculty of preaching.

195. "Hoc tempore non fiunt diaconissae, sed communiter in quocumque loco ebdomadaria legit evangelium, vel alia secundum consuetudinem monasterii sui" (Vat. lat. 1145, f. 59v; see also Andrieu, OR 4:146–47). Andrieu points out that there is no relationship with the corresponding chapter (XXII) in Durand's pontifical (Andrieu, *Pontifical Romain au Moyen-Âge: Pontifical du Guillaume Durand*, 223).

Durand's pontifical continued to enjoy great popularity in French-speaking regions. Together with a succinct discussion of ordination rites, Abbé Victor Leroquais lists manuscripts containing ordinations of deaconesses, describing illustrations where these exist.[196] Earlier rituals of the RGP X are neatly distinguished by the terminology *diacona* from the later ones, which read *diaconissa*.

10. The Carthusian Rite for the Profession of Nuns

While related to the Roman Rite, early Carthusian liturgical rites drew on those of local churches, especially that of Lyons.[197] The austere cloistered monastic life of Carthusian nuns was lived out in solitary "deserts." Their participation in clerical ministries was needed if the divine office was to be celebrated even with the limited solemnity embraced by this order.[198] Johannes Pinius (Jean LePin, fl. 1740) gives the text of the diaconal ordination rite of Carthusian use. This is nothing else than the RGP X ritual with the additional bestowal of maniple and cross, ceremonial insignia of the historical fact that professed nuns had the faculty of reading the gospel during the divine office and abbesses that of proclaiming the gospel during mass.[199] Countering his own argument against the diaconal character

---

196. *Les Pontificaux manuscrits des Bibliothèques Publiques de France* by V. Leroquais, 1–2 (3 vols.; Paris: Macon, Protat, 1937). Besides listing a number from RGP X, he gives from the late Gothic period: Aix-en-Provence, Bibl. Méjanes, ms. 13, 56v (1329–1348); Avignon, B.M. ms. 205, 31–42 with 12 drawings (end of 17th century); Boulogne-sur-Mer, B.M. ms. 85 (93), 70r (1st half of 15th century); Cambrai, B.M. 180 (175), 41v (early 14th century); Carpentras, B.M. 97 with a deaconess in an historiated initial 50v (1st half of 14th century); Metz, B.M. ms. 222, 34v (end of 15th century); Paris, B.N. lat. 968, 155v–158r with blessing of a deaconess and imposition of the stole on 156 (2nd half of 14th century); Paris, B.N. lat. 1220, 41v–42r (1st half of 14th century); Paris, B.N. lat. 9479, 86r–87v (2nd half of 14th century); Paris, Bibl. Ste.-Geneviève ms. 143, 63v with illustration of the blessing of a deaconess (2nd half of 14th century).

197. John B. Wickstrom, "Carthusians," in *EM* 1:244–47; Mary M. Schaefer, "Liturgy: Western Christian," in *EM* 1:786–94 at 791–92. For additional bibliography, see Macy, Ditewig, and Zagano, *Women Deacons*, n. 24.

198. Martimort (*Diaconesses*, 242) himself gives an example. In 1566 the nun's charterhouse in Bruges was unable to chant the divine office for six months because no priests were available to read the 12th lesson of the vigil and to proclaim the concluding gospel.

199. *Ritus antiquus consecrandi Diaconissas apud Latinos; qui ex aliqua parte perseverat in monialibus Ordinis Cartusiani* (AA.SS., September v. I, x–xii) gives the RGP X rite for consecrating a diacona with additional rituals for bestowing the maniple, cross, and black veil. As reported by K. Heinrich Schäfer, until the 19th century the Carthusian abbess sang the gospel at mass on solemn feastdays (Van der Meer, *Women Priests in Catholic Church*, 87).

of the rite, Martimort cites a late fourteenth-century manuscript containing the consecration of virgins of the Charterhouse of St. Barbara, Cologne (Darmstadt, Hessische Landes- und Hochschulbibliothek, cod. 710, 176r). The following rubrics are written in the same hand as the remainder of the ritual: for the delivery of the maniple, "Here is given the power of reading the epistle" and, in the bestowal of the stole, "Here is given the power of reading the gospel in the morning homily."[200] While not called deaconesses, Pinius observes, the Carthusian nuns nevertheless constitute a parallel with deaconesses of the Roman church.[201] To this comment might be added the ministry of the subdeacon, and indeed some Carthusian nuns were so described in their death notices.[202]

Abbé Leroquais describes the twelve miniatures found in a late seventeenth-century Roman pontifical (Avignon, Bibl. Mun. ms. 205, 31–42) that depict high points of the Carthusian ritual.[203] This pontifical dates from that time when the prior of the Grande Chartreuse Dom Innocent le Masson (d. 1703) published the consecration ritual of the nuns as found in several manuscripts and defended its use in Rome.[204] The miniatures retain a living memory of women's ordination within the cloistered Carthusian order. Their consecration as virgins included, as it still does, vesting with stole and maniple (an armcloth used by bishops, presbyters, deacons, and subdeacons) as well as bestowal of a cross and a black veil.[205] Martimort comments that some Carthusian monasteries of women insisted on maintaining traditions from the diaconate and subdiaconate even when bishop, priests, or deacons were present.[206]

---

200. "Hic datur potestas legendi epistolam. Hic datur potestas legendi evangelium in omelia matutinali" (Martimort, *Diaconesses*, 240).

201. Pinius, *Ritus antiquus consecrandi Diaconissas* (Martimort, *Diaconesses*, xi).

202. Martimort, *Diaconesses*, 241.

203. Leroquais, *Pontificaux Manuscrits*, 1, no. 22, 67–68.

204. Although citing a number of mss., Martimort (*Diaconesses*, 237–43) gives a negative assessment.

205. Dom Yves Gourdel ("Chartreux: Les moniales," *Dictionnaire de spiritualité* 2/1, 1953, 705–776 at 722) refers to the "double consecration" of Carthusian nuns: to virginity (of which the insignia are veil, ring, and crown) and to a restricted diaconate (with the insignia of maniple and stole). At the conventual mass a Carthusian nun chants the epistle (but without wearing the maniple). At matins, "if there is no male religious to preside at the office, a consecrated religious chants the gospel" wearing the stole. This is also the case on Holy Thursday for the chanting of the *Mandatum* gospel. Besides wearing the diaconal insignia on the day of their consecration, they are so vested on their fiftieth jubilee and on the day of their funeral.

206. Martimort, *Diaconesses*, 240–41.

11. *The Pontifical of Clement VIII (1595)*

Pope Clement VIII (d. 1605) would reform the Roman Pontifical, promulgating this new edition in 1595/6.[207] The rites given in it were little changed until the reform of the Roman pontifical mandated by Vatican Council II. The office of deaconess, witnessed to by the *Exaudi* collect, was retained from the Pontifical of 1497 as an attachment at the end of the consecration of virgins. The duties of deaconess were restricted, at least officially, to the divine office: *Accipe potestatem legendi officium et incipiendi horas in ecclesia. In nomine Patris et Filii et Spiritus sancti.* Martimort notes that, with "a few variants," this rite was included in the Clementine pontifical.[208]

Conclusion

What are we to make of the variegated history of women's ordination that waxed and waned, was favored in certain cultures and times and suppressed in others? The prayer for the blessing of the Holy Spirit for both male and female deacons expressed in the *Exaudi* was generic, typical of the place of its genesis, Rome. The consecratory ritual for making a diacona in the Romano-Germanic pontificals of the tenth and twelfth centuries was not as theologically strong as that for a male deacon. It is certain that her ministry did not enjoy the same degree of public presence. The consecratory prayer lacks imposition of hands with explicit prayer for the grace of the Holy Spirit, although it can be inferred that in RGP X laying on of hands with consecratory prayer for the deacon no longer carried the sacramental weight it formerly enjoyed. Comparison of rituals for widows and "making" diaconas available in manuscripts such as Lucca, Capitular Library ms. 607 (2nd half of the 10th century) might throw light on the genesis and development of this newly minted liturgy for installing women in church office.

---

207. *Pontificale Romanum: Clementis VIII a.c. Urbani VIII jussu editum et a Benedicto XIV* (Roma: S. Congregationis de Propaganda Fide, 1868).

208. On the pontificals of 1495, 1497, and 1595, see Martimort, *Diaconesses*, 235–37, and on the Clementine pontifical in general, see J. Nabuco and T.C. O'Brien, "Pontifical, Roman," *NCE* 11 (2003): 474. In the 1868 edition of Clement's pontifical the consecration of virgins begins on p. 97. The closing rite replacing the diaconate, which empowers its recipients to begin the canonical hours and read the office in the church, reads in the plural number (p. 108).

What of the female *sacerdotes* who are known especially in Saxony and surrounding areas? In this instance as in the early church, the functions performed rather than a presumed "ontological status" determined the terminology used. Women monastics dedicated their lives to praying the divine office. In a more public manner, canonesses carried out the liturgical work of officially praying in the name of the church, often in concert with canons in shared worship spaces. The modern concept and theology of an "ontological change" effected by sacerdotal ordination of males, the sex that thirteenth-century scholasticism concluded possessed the capacity to receive it, was at variance with the practice and theology of the earlier Middle Ages. Sacerdotal identity was understood to reside in the carrying out of priestly functions in the name of the church; in so doing the one ultimately represented was Christ.

Especially in monastic circles and in the creative liturgical enterprise inaugurated in the tenth century in the region of Mainz, to be quickly dispersed across the Christian world, there existed a surprising lack of interest in gender-determined Scripture applications. In the use of Scripture at this period, especially with regard to the unmarried, the reign of God seems already at hand. The scriptural image utilized at the blessing of the virgin's habit ("uberrimae benedictionis imbre perfunde, sicut perfudisti oram vestimentorum Aaron, benedictione unguenti profluente a capite in barbam") is taken from Psalm 132:2 (Vulgate), which had been associated with bishops since the *Veronensis*.[209] The rituals of canonical and monastic abbesses provide the strongest evidence we have in the Western church for ordination of women to offices that are the female equivalents of the diaconate and episcopate exercised by men.[210] For the periods in

---

209. *Consecratio sacrae virginis* (*PRG X*, 1: XX.8), 40. *Veronensis* alludes to the psalm: "Hoc, domine, copiosae in eorum caput influat, hoc in oris subiecta decurrat, hoc in totius corporis extrema descendat..." (*Sacramentarium Veronense*, ed. Mohlberg, XXVIII, 947). Perhaps the close association of bishops with the consecration of virgins is its explanation! The Vulgate reads: "Sicut unguenteum in capite, quod descendit in barbam, barbam Aaron, quod descendit in oram vestimenti ejus." ("It is like the precious oil on the head, running down upon the beard, on the beard of Aaron, running down over the collar of his robes," Ps 133:2, NRSV).

210. There is no doubt that women's menstrual cycle functioned as a taboo that governed age requirements for widows and diaconas laid down in canon law and eventually would exclude women from service of the altar. Taboos surrounding "ritual impurity" still govern the custom of refraining from communion in some Orthodox women's monasteries. In the West these customs were known well into the 20th century. Such "impurity" is undoubtedly an unspoken component of much objection to the ordination of women to eucharistic presidency.

question—various times and places during the thousand-year period that constitutes the Middle Ages—we can speak of "female equivalency" with offices held by men. Equivalency is not exactly equality. However, equivalency represents an important step toward equality when contrasted with the official Catholic anthropology of female complementarity taught by popes Paul VI, John Paul II, and Benedict XVI.[211]

While we cannot now be transported back to that ecclesiastical world that resonated, at least in some times and places in the West, with opportunities for women's official ecclesial ministries, something of that reality can be found in Orthodox monasteries in Romania, a country that bridges East and West, old Rome and modern orthodoxy. For eight days in the spring of 1991, as Pentecost ended Eastertide and the meatless fast was undertaken in preparation for the feast of Sts. Peter and Paul, I found myself in the midst of the religious life of Varatec Monastery, a women's community in northern Moldavia, which in many respects breathed the life of the undivided church of the tenth century.[212] Located in a broad valley on the slope of Mount Stinişoarei, in layout, patterns of life, daily schedules, and liturgical rhythms it replicated monastic life at the turn of the first millennium. Mother Nazaria Nita Natalia was lifelong abbess of this bustling monastery, which comprised three monastic villages of several hundred black-robed Basilian nuns surrounded by peasant homes, farm fields, pastures, woodlands, and nature sanctuary. In the 1980s and '90s Mother Nazaria still did what eleventh century abbesses in the West, especially canonical abbesses and quasi-episcopal abbesses, did: oversee the spiritual and material life of her nuns living a variety of lifestyles: cenobitic, idiorhythmic, and eremetical.[213] Depending on her as well were the

---

211. See John Paul II, *Christifideles laici* ("The lay members of Christ's faithful people"), 30 December 1988, nos. 49–52, in English translation, *Post-Synodal Apostolic Exhortation Laici Christifides of His Holiness John Paul II on the Vocation and the Mission of the Lay Faithful in the Church and in the World* (Ottawa: Canadian Conference of Catholic Bishops, 1988). See also Ivy A. Helman, *Women and the Vatican: An Exploration of Official Documents* (Maryknoll, NY: Orbis, 2012).

212. I wish to express my gratitude to the Archbishop and External Affairs Department of the Romanian Orthodox Church in Bucharest and to the Pontifical Council for Christian Unity for facilitating this visit.

213. Cenobism gathers monastics in communities of shared life, prayer, and work. The idiorhythmic lifestyle groups together three to five nuns who, living and praying in their small home, parallel the lifestyle of some medieval canonesses in the West. Hermits live as solitaries.

many layfolk with families who cared for the monastery's extensive farmlands and woodlots and ensured its physical survival. Hers were also the worries about paying bills and maintaining properties in the new political situation of a fledgling quasi-democratic government. Three elderly priests staffed the monastery's three churches. Otherwise the works of art and craft, running of the museum and library, gardening and farming, cooking, cleaning, education, welcoming of visitors and retreatants (whether patriarch, scholar, literary figure, traveler, peasant, or child) were carried on by the sisters along with an intense life of asceticism and prayer. Their demanding daily schedule included (and still does) ascetical practices of *proskynesis, gonyklisia,* and the little and great *mătania,* daily choir practice in preparation for praying the divine office, liturgical service as acolytes and "deacons" during the Divine Liturgy (processing in the Great Entrance and entering behind the iconostasis or sacred screen during the anaphora to assist the priest).[214] During the daily Divine Liturgy a nun chanted the epistle in the center of the church's nave, a duty of the subdeacon in the old churches. Mother Nazaria presided in the nave, ensuring that guests were not exhausted by the daily two- to three-hour liturgy. Her official abbatial role was to chant the Lord's Prayer beginning the communion rite. Mother Nazaria's portrait shows her wearing pectoral cross and carrying a crozier. As abbess Mother Nazaria blessed visitors and her nuns, accepted and tonsured novices, and received the sisters' religious professions. She advised archbishops and commissions and consulted with the hierarchy of the national church, traveling globally on its behalf to attend councils whether Orthodox or sponsored by the World Council of Churches. The spiritual energy of Varatec nuns led by their abbess is apparent in their reopening of historic monasteries founded centuries before by male monastics of the Paisian reform. Some of these are attached to the famous "painted churches" of northern Moldavia, architectural and artistic gems enshrining Romanian heritage and awarded UNESCO status.

A few kilometers to the north of Varatec, in a narrow valley cradled by the same Carpathian ridge, is another women's monastery. Agapia was founded in the seventeenth century, higher up the mountain at the

---

214. Mary M. Schaefer, "Romania," in *EM* 2:1079–85. Varatec was founded in the 18th century by the daughter of a village priest and built by hand by the first women to join her. Part of the Paisian reform, from its founding it enjoyed vernacular liturgy and active liturgical ministerial participation by its nuns.

still-flourishing Agapia Vecchia. More than two hundred nuns live, work, and pray at Agapia, which in recent times has been known for Scripture study and the hosting of an international women's congress. At the top of the mountain ridge is the cave of the hermit St. Theodora of Sihla (b. ca. 1650), a favored goal of pilgrimage and now the site of a small men's monastery. On the other side of the mountain, at the head of a secluded valley, is the male monastery and retreat centre of Sihastria. Two large historic walled monasteries along the spreading valley floor, Secul and Neamț, are inhabited by small men's communities. This region of northern Romania has been aptly named "the Romanian Athos" although, unlike their namesake, both female and male Basilian monastics provide a religious presence.

Women's monasticism in the Orthodox world still retains important vestiges of religious life common to the undivided churches of the first millennium. This glimpse enables us to better contextualize women's ecclesial leadership and full participation in the work of the church in the Western Middle Ages, as self-standing canoness institutes with their varied ministries to "seculars," as monastic families living autonomously, or as members of large congregations sharing a common rule.

6

A Second Look at Myth, History, and Monument

WHEN READ IN church on the vigils of their feasts or in the meditative atmosphere of the cloister, the story of Pudentiana and Praxedes transported the devout back to the apostolic and post-apostolic periods. In our reconstitution of their story, chapter one introduced the Pudens clan and their clergy friends Pius and the presbyter Pastor as well as important aspects of second-century church life in Rome. Chapter two investigated the church of S. Prassede, Pope Paschal's most intact architectural project, concentrating on the iconography of its mosaic program and the unusual prominence it gives to women. Chapter three afforded a broad overview of ministerial possibilities for women by looking afield to distant and culturally distinct churches in communion with Rome. Chapters four and five studied the Roman church especially with a view to women's official ministries and deputation for ecclesial office.

This final chapter reassesses the story and the material evidence connected with the churches of S. Prassede and S. Pudenziana. The exceptional place given to family and women in Paschal's choice of church restorations, iconography, and dedicatory inscriptions is considered. Features of the foundation myth of the sisters and their life of Christian charity that might be recoverable history for us nearly two millennia later are identified by revisiting those persons, places, and events known from the *vita* that can be located historically. Placing the *vita*'s characters in the Roman sanctoral had begun with early hagiographers. The process of "actualizing" the story by introducing additional historical references was undertaken in the twelfth century. Later still, scholars and admirers looked to it as an authentic witness of second-century church life. The background to Paschal's "relic recovery project," culminating in the deposit of a horde of relics at S. Prassede on 20 July 819, in preparation for the dedication of the church a day later, entails a brief sketch of the development from *martyria*, martyrs' shrines built to house and memorialize the remains (*reliquiae*) of Christian heroes at their initial place of martyrdom or burial, to "high" altars erected above burials and relic-altars placed in the subterranean chamber (crypt, confessio) underneath.[1] The following questions emerge from this enquiry: When relics are transferred or "translated" from their initial place of rest to another location, what ritual accompanies this translation and dedication of the new resting place? And what was discovered nine hundred years later when Paschal I's altar was brutally dismantled in the relic-hunt undertaken during the nocturnal visit made by Pope Benedict XIII (1724–1730) on 2 January 1729?

Some scholars judge that Potentiana and Praxedes were venerated as saints by the fourth or fifth centuries.[2] Taking the position that the Pudentiana of our story has the greater claim to being a "pure narrative artifice," Claudia Angelelli does not appear to question the authenticity of our hero Praxedes.[3] This is despite the fact that for almost two centuries (between 595 and 783–784) the Praxedes *titulus* was absent from the ecclesiastical record until it gained status as a Lenten station on feria II (Monday) of Holy Week sometime in the eighth century. We remember that a stational church achieved prominence because the pope, his aides, the clergy of the region, and people from the city gathered there on a specific day in the liturgical calendar for the "station," the celebration of mass, this assembly representing the communion of the whole local church united with its bishop. The stational system had become well- established during the course of the fifth century. Pope Hadrian I's restoration of the partly ruined building of S. Prassede *ab integro* may be related to its replacement of Sts. Nereus and Achilleus near the Caracalla baths as a station on

---

1. Richard Krautheimer (*Early Christian and Byzantine Architecture*, 361) defines a martyrium as a "site which bears witness to the Christian faith, either by referring to an event in Christ's life or Passion, or by sheltering the grave of a martyr, a witness by virtue of having shed his blood; the structure over such a site." He defines a *confessio* as "[i]n a church, a subterranean chamber or recess located below or near the altar and sheltering a relic" (ibid., 359). Michel Andrieu (*OR* 4:388) adds that the most ancient texts include reference to doors giving access to a small enclosure communicating with the tomb itself. See also Henri Leclercq, "Confessio," in *DACL* 3/2 (1914), 2503–8.

2. Claudia Angelelli, *Basilica titolare di S. Pudenziana*, 25 and n. 232. Since Praxedes was not martyred, her name is absent from the earliest martyrologies.

3. Angelelli, *Basilica titolare di S. Pudenziana*, 25. Cf. Guidobaldi ("Osservazioni sugli edifici romani," 1040) who develops the case for the attested martyr S. Potentiana as the "real" patron of S. Pudenziana.

Holy Monday. Did Praxedes' "liturgical personality" play some part in the shift of the Holy Monday station?

Caroline Goodson has stated that "[a]t S. Prassede, as in all early medieval buildings, the patron imbued meaning not only in architectural form (plan as well as elevation and decoration) but also through choices of materials, images, and the different activities that the building was designed to house. Paschal built S. Prassede for multiple overlapping systems of worship, some radically new for the city of Rome."[4] Goodson does not enumerate these worship forms. Presumably they would include liturgical services of word and eucharist as well as liturgy of the hours in the Greek monastic rite; celebration of sacraments in favor of individuals; private veneration of relics, in which the Zeno Chapel plays a dual function as martyrium commemorating one or more saints and mausoleum. The chapel of St. Agnes would have been available within the monastery for the lesser monastic hours and private prayer. None of these uses is radically new. Recently, architectural historians have embraced the notion of papal aggrandizement of power and prestige through building programs in general and through the addition and renovation of altars, including Gregory I's high altar and Leo III's embellishments at St. Peter's. Scholars have also noted that political and spiritual power can be expressed through reinforcement of the papal role as mediator of salvation in sacramental life and veneration of saints. When Paschal celebrated the eucharist at S. Prassede he entered into a sacred area accessible only to clergy, offering the church's sacrifice of praise at an altar located over a multitude of saints' bones. What were the influences that shaped Paschal's commission?

1. Motifs of Family and Women in Paschal's Life and Art Commissions

What characterizes Pope Paschal's intended role in his building projects—his architectural commissions and mosaic decoration—are motifs of saintly family and friends and signs of his personal relationship with his mother.[5] Within the circle of the saintly Pudens family and their

---

4. Goodson, "Revival and Reality," 163–92 at 163.

5. At St. Peter's a "familial" commemoration can be seen in the chapels honoring S. Petronilla, St. Peter's putative daughter, and St. Andrew, his brother. The *oratorium Pastoris* was understood as being dedicated to St. Peter, explaining the strong Petrine connections claimed for S. Pudenziana. It also provides a motive for Paschal's interest in the *vita* of a Roman family whose roots extended back to the Roman ministries of Peter and Paul.

friends, all the chief players share the initial letter "P": Peter and Paul, Punicus Pudens and Priscilla, Pudens "Junior," Potentiana and Praxedes, Pastor and Pius. Paschal's appearance in the apse mosaic displays his intention to associate himself with this graced circle.

Paschal was quick to identify himself as faithful servant of God's mother. Humble obeisance was expressed verbally in the dedicatory inscriptions on the reliquaries discussed in chapter two. The pope's attitude is displayed for all to see in the apse mosaic of S. Maria in Domnica where Paschal kneels in humble veneration, daringly cradling in both hands the Queen of Heaven's slippered foot. Under Pope Benedict XIV (1740–1758), renovations in 1747 below the confessio of S. Maria Maggiore's high altar revealed an inscription on a marble reliquary, now conserved within the high altar of the church. It reads:

> Receive, O immaculate Virgin, the prayers of your servant Pope Paschal; protect, O Christ, your servant Pope Paschal; give ear to the prayers, O my king and O my God, of Pope Paschal; listen, O Lord, to the voice of your servant Pope Paschal.[6]

Paschal was cognizant of a number of historical parallels: those between his own mother (and himself as her son) and God the Son's mother Mary, the latter depicted with the Christ-child placed centrally on the façade of the Zeno Chapel. The representation of Mary together with her son in episodes during Christ's public life and in the post-resurrection events on the silver-gilt reliquary cross discussed in chapter two is unique. Another striking mother-son parallel to be considered is that between the empress Helena, "discoverer" of the holy places in Jerusalem and patron of the church established in her Sessorian palace near the Lateran, and her son Constantine. Constantine's commissioning and bankrolling of church building projects were probably inspired by suggestions from his mother, who had preceded him as a Christian by many decades. To what extent did Paschal respond to his mother Theodora's suggestions for patronage and dedications? The reference to her on S. Prassede's relic inscription expresses the attitude of a devoted son: "...where [in the Zeno Chapel]

---

6. The S. Maria in Domnica mosaic of Pope Paschal is placed within its larger historical context by Robert Deshman, "Servants of the Mother of God in Byzantine and Medieval Art," *Word and Image* 5 (1989): 33–70 at 57.

certainly rests the body of his most kind mother, namely Lady Theodora episcopa."[7]

The remnants of frescoes and *tituli* preserved in S. Prassede's west transept arm have been studied by Caroline Goodson.[8] Besides the Pudens family, the martyrs featured were mostly family groups. Goodson summarizes the subject-matter: some of the married couples depicted had lived in continence; others were buriers of martyrs including their own children; and yet others endowed the church. Especially in view of the "segregation" of families by gender on the martyrs' inscription embedded in the church's northeast pier, the familial motif is striking. Centuries later the church of S. Prassede continued to afford an environment favorable to women. Typically, Jewish and Christian iconography knows male angels. However, the nave paintings of graceful female angels bearing instruments of the Passion, commissioned under Cardinal Alessandro de'Medici (titular 1594–1596), were inspired by the Arch of Constantine's pedestal reliefs of Nike, Greek mythology's winged goddess of victory.

Measured against the culture of the Roman church and the Carolingian empire generally, the very presence of women in Paschal's programs is remarkable.[9] According to *LP*, Cecilia had a primary claim on Paschal by virtue of appearing to him as he rebuilt her church, the saint directing his ultimately successful efforts at finding her relics and those of her husband and companions.[10] Among Paschal's projects Praxedes' church was pre-eminent in terms of its planning, size, and coherence of design. Paschal linked the sisters with the girl-martyr Agnes, Rome's favorite, by dedicating a chapel to her in the adjacent monastery and having her depicted on

---

7. "...ubi utique benignissimae suae genetricis scilicet domnae Theodorae episcopae corpus quiescit."

8. Caroline Goodson, "The Relic Translations of Paschal I: Transforming City and Cult," in Andrew Hopkins and Maria Wyke, eds., *Roman Bodies: Antiquity to the Eighteenth Century* (London: British School at Rome, 2005), 123–41 at 131–34.

9. Among patrons of saintly women, 7th-century popes come to mind: Honorius I (625–638) who built the basilica of S. Agnese over her catacomb in proximity to the huge 4th-century covered cemetery on the Via Nomentana; he or Pope Donus (676–678) converted the Curia Senatus into an oratory dedicated to a late-discovered supposed martyr of the Diocletianic persecutions, St. Martina. The Sicilian Pope Leo II (682–683) included the prayer for making a diacona in the Gregorian Sacramentary, while Pope Sergius I (687–701) introduced Rome to elaborated celebrations of feasts of the Virgin.

10. Davis, *Lives of Ninth-Century Popes*, 100.14–17.

the upper north wall of the Zeno Chapel as well as in the group of figures on the left side of the triumphal arch. Of course, devotion to venerated deceased women may substitute for recognition of living women. We can only speculate whether Paschal's personal devotion to local saints, best represented in the S. Cecilia apse by that saint's sisterly hug of the pope standing next to her, and the filial devotion of Paschal for his mother, may have contributed to actual preferential treatment of "real women" outside his family.[11]

2. *Early Church Development and the* vita

Connecting the Christian origins of a Roman aristocratic family with Rome's martyred apostolic princes gave the story of the Pudens clan the highest possible authority.[12] Set within the hundred years between the end of Peter and Paul's Roman ministries and Pius I's episcopate, our *vita* contains features characteristic of various periods of Roman ecclesiastical life.[13] Scholarly views have shifted from near-total acceptance of the story perduring into the first quarter of the twentieth century to a period of almost total disbelief. In the last thirty-five years, perhaps inspired by biblical criticism, scepticism has been replaced by attempts to recognize historical realities "behind" the story. P. A. B. Llewellyn's political reading placed the *vita* in the late fifth century, in the episcopates of Symmachus (498–514) and the antipope Laurentius.[14] The archeologist Federico

---

11. The well-documented example of Paschal's raising the episcopal chair at S. Maria Maggiore so as to distance himself from women crowding near (Davis, *Lives of Ninth-Century Popes*, 100.30) is a case in point.

12. Compilers of apocrypha and early church orders regularly involved one or more of the Twelve or attributed a document pseudonymously. Ann Graham Brock (*Mary Magdalene, the First Apostle: The Struggle for Authority* [Cambridge, MA: Harvard University Press, 2003], 105–22) compares the 2nd-century Acts of Peter and Acts of Paul, pointing to a pattern implied in our story, namely, Peter's affinity for males in leadership and Paul's openness to women in the Christian mission.

13. For a succinct overview, see Charles Pietri, "Liturgy, Culture and Society: The Example of Rome at the End of the Ancient World (Fourth-Fifth Centuries)," in Mary Collins and David Power, eds., *Liturgy: A Creative Tradition* (New York: Seabury, 1983), 38–46. For a review of church architecture, liturgy, organization, and politics in detail during the 4th- to mid-5th centuries, see Charles Pietri, *Roma christiana: recherches sur l'Église de Rome, son organisation, sa politique, son idéologie de Miltiade à Sixte III (311–440)* (2 vols.; Rome: École française de Rome, 1976).

14. Laurentius may have been archpriest of S. Prassede when clergy and senators were at odds and the *titulus* required legitimizing. See Llewellyn, "Roman Church during Laurentian Schism," 417–27.

Guidobaldi, basing his theory on legal concepts and terminology, dates the *vita*'s composition earlier in the fifth century but contextualizes it in the relatively placid fourth century, after the Constantinian peace.[15] Claudia Angelelli dates the establishment of the church centers under discussion to the time of Pope Damasus I (366–384), suggesting that the *acta* may have been composed by a clergyperson of one or other of the *tituli* in the fifth or early part of the sixth century as a foundation-story establishing the legal status of both house-churches.[16] In her view the *vita*, by providing an etiology for two well-known *tituli*, functions as a kind of ownership certificate for church property. In these readings the story was set in the fourth century, written down sometime in the fifth, and edited again in the sixth.

However, additional features of the *vita* need to be taken into account. Decades and even centuries may have been merged in much the same way that *LP* credited early popes with later liturgical or management decisions. Markers in the story may help to situate it in a particular historical period. Persecution is one such marker. Praxedes had ministered for two years as presbytera at her new church complex. When persecution began she hid many Christians, feeding them both with earthly food and the word of God. The on-site martyrdoms of the presbyter Simmetrius with twenty-two others in her *titulus*, and Praxedes' natural death shortly after in her 80s, are set during the episcopate of Pius I and the reign of emperor Hadrian's adopted son Antoninus Pius (138–161). Both are undisputed historical personages. The dating is credible, but there is no evidence of persecutions under Antoninus Pius' beneficent rule. The *Vita sanctae Potentianae virginis* (*BHL* 6991) refers with appreciative respect to *Antoninus piissimus augustus* while the *Vita sanctae Praxedis virginis* (*BHL* 6920) speaks of *Antonio imperatori* and the death of the twenty-three without trial.[17] We can infer that in the latter case Pius' adopted son Marcus Antoninus Aurelius is intended, under whom persecution did take place.[18]

---

15. Guidobaldi, "Osservazioni sugli edifici romani," 1038, 1041. We saw that Guidobaldi accepts the real existence of Potentiana/Pudentiana (ibid., 1040), and the possible authenticity of Pastor, Novatus, Timothy (1041), and members of a Pudens gens in the second century (1063–64).

16. Angelelli, *Basilica titolare di S. Pudenziana*, 18, 29. On early *tituli*, their legends and location, see Lampe, *From Paul to Valentinus*, 19–23.

17. Mombritius, *Sanctuarium* 1:390–91.

18. Justin Martyr addressed Antoninus Pius in *I Apology*, written ca. 150 CE. The acts of Justin Martyr's judicial process, among the very few to survive the destruction of church

On 28 October 312 Constantine (d. 337), protected by a visionary sign, defeated Maxentius at the Milvian bridge. The Edict of Milan (313) changed the course of history by including the Christian faith as one among many to be tolerated, the first such Roman declaration in its favor. Bishops were recognized by the state, confiscated properties were returned to Christians, and cemeteries definitively became church property. Bishop Silvester I (314–335) was recipient of Constantine's largesse as the emperor gave over the Lateran Palace and the area of the razed imperial horse barracks for use by the bishop of Rome. Constantine, if baptized at all then only on his deathbed, may also have commissioned the since-remodeled baptistry building as early as 315. His mother the empress Helena returned from pilgrimage to the Holy Land with relics of the true cross, establishing within her Sessorian Palace to the northwest of the Lateran the church later to be called S. Croce in Gerusalemme. Unable to win over the senatorial aristocracy, in 330 the emperor moved with his court to Constantinople, "New Rome." From this moment the Roman bishop and clergy began to fill the void left by the departure of civil officials, acquiring public properties, taking on civil roles, and appropriating ceremonial of the imperial bureaucracy. As male Christian clergy achieved a recognized place within this hierarchical system, women's opportunities for ecclesial leadership diminished drastically.

A brief, fierce period of persecution of Christians returned under Emperor Julian (361–363). By the later fourth century Pope Damasus I (366–384) had improved access to the Christian cemeteries as places of pilgrimage, and Pope Siricius (384–399) inaugurated the discipline of celibacy for the higher Roman clergy.[19] This brings us to the first attested

---

records during the persecution of Diocletian, inform us that Justin and his companions were executed by beheading ca. 165 under Marcus Aurelius (161–180). Although a philosopher, Marcus Aurelius did nothing to stop sporadic persecution throughout the empire. Eusebius (*Hist. Eccles.* V.1.47) reports that Marcus Aurelius "told the governor of Lyons and Vienne that Christians should be executed if they did not recant." The bloody, tortured martyrdoms of 177 at Lyons reported by Irenaeus belong to that period. Fierce, if short-lived, persecutions were ordered under the emperors Decius (249–251) and Valerian (257–259/60), while the last great persecution prior to the Edict of Milan (313) took place 303–305 under Diocletian (284–305). The archives of the Roman church were destroyed, leading to the later fabrication of the *gesta martyrum* to take their place. Such facts as are known about the latter persecutions do not well fit our *vita*.

19. Ironically, improved accessibility to the catacombs made easier not only devout pilgrims' visits but their raiding by the Lombards for loot and by Christians to provide relics for altars north of the Alps, where a reputed saint's bones were an enduring source of pilgrims' offerings and income for the church or monastery having custody.

date (384) for *ecclesia pudentiana* (Pudens' assembly) in the Viminal, where there is evidence of a faith community already on site. This extant building is connected with Popes Damasus I and Siricius, and its monumental mosaic with Innocent I (401–417). Later fifth-century popes Celestine I (422–432), Leo I (440–461), and Gelasius I (492–496) "built" the structure of the Roman church ecclesiologically, canonically, and architecturally.[20] The sixth century, era of compilations, saw *LP*'s attempt to recapture the Roman church's early history by cataloguing outstanding features of the ministry of each bishop and retrojecting customs whose genesis was lost to history. The *gesta martyrum*, over one hundred fictional martyr accounts written down during the fifth to seventh centuries, attempted to fill the gap caused by the loss of authentic martyr acts during the Diocletianic persecution.[21]

Features of the sisters' story fit with more than one phase of early church life, and it is no easy task to reconstruct these phases. There is a bit of confusion in the storyline when the various recensions are compared. Most scholars have followed the "standard integrated" version of the Bollandists (*BHL* 6988, 6989). Since the sixteenth century scholars have proposed conflicting interpretations of the archeological evidence. "Hard" data for the second and third centuries is in short supply; however, Peter Lampe's book on early Christian life in Rome, first published in 1987, has led to further clarity about that obscure period. In any analysis both Roman civil and ecclesiastical canon law must be considered. In this section I attempt to establish the relative "truthfulness" of the Pudens

---

20. On law and governance in the early Roman church see Faivre, *Naissance d'une hiérarchie*, 299–370. The formation of the canonical collections rather than interpretation of their ecclesiological content has preoccupied most scholars. See Detlev Jasper and Horst Fuhrmann, *Papal Letters in the Early Middle Ages* (Washington, DC: Catholic University of America Press, 2001), 3–87; Hess, *Early Development of Canon Law*; Brian Edwin Ferme, *Introduction to the History of the Sources of Canon Law: The Ancient Law up to the 'Decretum' of Gratian*, trans. William J. King (Montreal: Wilson & Lafleur, 2007).

21. The literary materials available in the *gesta martyrum* and *LP* are weighed for historical authenticity by Cooper, "Martyr, Matrona and Bishop," 297–318. The sisters' *vita* does not fit the *gesta martyrum* profile. Nor does it fit that of the romantic apocryphal acts of Paul, Peter, John, and Andrew composed ca. 160–225 in Greece or Asia Minor. Placing "exceptional emphasis on sexual continence," probably written for "ecclesiastical widows" and perhaps composed by them, women are "favourably contrasted" with a Christian man, including the apostle Paul, who "repeatedly fails" them (Davies, *Revolt of the Widows*); see also MacDonald, *Legend and Apostle*.

clan story, attending to categories of Christian assembly-space while taking into account changes in church governance.

The basic storyline about the ministries of two women in the first and early second centuries breathes the spirit of chapter 16 of Paul's letter to the Romans, when women's agency was at its highest. Women's leadership of a church community is nothing unusual, legitimizing for later generations women's ecclesial ministries in the apostolic and post-apostolic periods. However, the story as we have received it has been adjusted to later church life and drastic reduction of women's agency. In the first century the Christian assembly (*ecclesia*) had gathered in believers' private houses or apartments. The gathering of Christians in the Pudens family home represents the Pauline phase, the "church in the house of...." While Pudens was alive the sisters lived there in seclusion, praying and fasting as befitted women dedicated to chaste life in the privacy of the home, encouraged and educated by their father.

The second and early third centuries gave rise to a "domestic" Christianity centered in house churches (*domus ecclesiae*) overseen by women and men, teachers and presbyter-bishops.[22] The Christian house of Dura Europos in Syria, dated 231 ce, shows renovations to its ground floor to accommodate a congregation's activities: an assembly hall for 50 or 60, a baptistry, and adjacent rooms. Its leader with family occupied the upper floor. House-churches possessed everything necessary for practicing the life of faith without reference to a larger episcopal center. Inquirers became catechumens, the elect were prepared for Christian initiation, baptisms and chrismations carried out on-site; the word was preached and eucharist celebrated. Individuated communities are typical of pre-Constantinian Christianity's organization—what Franz Alto Bauer has called its *frammentazione* and Peter Lampe its "fractionation."[23] Krautheimer has speculated that neighborhood house-churches remained worship centers into the fourth century, when the Christian population of Rome grew too rapidly to be accommodated in the existing churches.[24]

---

22. Peter Lampe (*From Paul to Valentinus*, 363, n. 17) points out that 9 women and 10 men can be named as founders of the 20 pre-Constantininian *tituli*. "Socially distinguished matrons" were singled out by the emperor Valerian as inimical to the good of the state.

23. Franz Alto Bauer, "La frammentazione liturgica nella chiesa romana del primo medioevo," *RAC* 75 (1999): 385–446; Lampe, *From Paul to Valentinus*, 359–408; on governance and the Roman system of presbyter-bishops until Victor (189–199), see Lampe, 397–408.

24. Krautheimer, *Three Christian Capitals*, 102–3. Presbyteral presidency at the Lord's Supper by men or women, householders, prophets, or teachers (Justin Martyr's description

The "house-church phase" is not given much play as the edited story moves very quickly to the establishment of *tituli*.[25]

On the death of Pudens' wife Savinella and of his parents Punicus Pudens and Priscilla, Pudens' house is called *titulus Pudentis*. A new phase is inaugurated when the dying Pudens transfers his house to Pastor, naming it for its clerical administrator.[26] Civil laws regarding guardianship and ecclesiastical laws respecting establishment of a *titulus* are pertinent. The presbyter Pastor functions as the sisters' guardian, a legal requirement for fatherless men and women under the age of twenty-five.[27] The sisters' simplicity of life as well as their youth explain why a member of the clergy takes title to Pudens' property while the sisters continue to live in it.[28] When transferred to Pastor in his name, the house-church becomes a *titulus* properly speaking (ecclesiastical property).[29] Pastor appears to be the sole incumbent in the sisters' second-century house-church, but he is never depicted as presiding at the eucharist or other sacraments. Peter

---

in *I Apology* is not gender-specific) is much more likely when communities were still "fractionated," predating the organization of Christians in Rome into one visibly connected, hierarchically ruled city-church. Felice Lifshitz ("The Martyr, the Tomb, and the Matron: Constructing the [Masculine] 'Past' as a Female Power Base," in *Medieval Concepts of the Past: Ritual, Memory, Historiography*, eds. Gerd Althoff, Johannes Fried, Patrick J. Geary [Washington, DC: German Historical Institute and Cambridge University Press, 2002], 333) remarks that "women's presidency could have evaporated overnight in the fourth century, especially given Roman women's official roles, e.g., as Vestal virgins."

25. This may be where an "upper layer" of the story overlays an earlier. In its original meaning a *titulus* was the identifying name at the doorway of a private individual's property.

26. This name change took place well after the fact as ecclesiastical documents attribute the site to Pastor only in the 6th and 7th centuries, perhaps in connection with the *vita*'s editing.

27. Kristina Sessa, "Domestic Conversions: Households and Bishops in the Late Antique 'Papal Legends,'" in Cooper and Hillner, eds., *Religion, Dynasty, and Patronage in Early Christian Rome*, 79–114 at 92, n. 58.

28. The "purpose of the Roman institution of guardianship was to keep control of family property in the hands of those next entitled to succeed to it.... Women under guardianship could only alienate their property upon authorization of their guardians" (J. A. Crook, "Feminine Inadequacy and the Senatusconsultum Velleianum," in Beryl Rawson, ed., *The Family in Ancient Rome: New Perspectives* [Ithaca, NY: Cornell University Press, 1986], 84). However, senatorial family houses could be transmitted not only to the eldest son but also to a younger son or even to daughters in late antique Rome (Julia Hillner, "*Domus*, Family, and Inheritance: The Senatorial Family House in Late Antique Rome," *Journal of Roman Studies* 93 [2003]: 129–45 at 130).

29. Lampe, *From Paul to Valentinus*, 359–80. *Tituli* were centers of pastoral care connected directly with the pope, expressed liturgically by the *fermentum* delivered on Sundays to the presbyters serving there. They may have developed out of pre-Constantinian house churches or been new foundations (one by a bishop, others by private founders). *LP* claims that the

Lampe observes that second-century house-churches seem to have had one leader. Ingeniously arguing from numbers of clergy as well as archeological evidence, Peter Lampe places the formation of the majority of the Roman *tituli* in the third century, as does John Baldovin.[30]

After the death of their father Pudentiana and Praxedes engage in a more active ministry, leading the faith community gathered in their home, carrying out the works of mercy, and presiding at regular *synaxes* (assemblies of praise and of the word). Potentiana and Praxedes never joined Christians from elsewhere in the city for a eucharistic "liturgy of the city-church" presided by (presbyter)-bishop Pius. Instead of "going to the bishop's place," the bishop came to them for baptisms and the eucharist.[31] Bishop Pius exercised spiritual oversight from outside the household. Was he one of a plurality of bishops, as the earliest lists of Roman bishops suggest?[32] Following the death of Pudens the presbyter Pastor consulted with the sisters and with Pius of the apostolic see regarding a baptistry. Pius designed it himself. That Easter, baptism presided by the bishop was celebrated in *titulus Pastoris*, as would have been the case in a house-church.[33] Pastor has responsibility for family

---

network of 25 *tituli* was organized by Pope Marcellus (305/6–306/7) "as dioceses for the baptism and repentance of many converts from paganism and for the burial of martyrs" (Davis, *Book of Pontiffs*, 31.2). A 4th–5th century date for their foundation is claimed by Alan Thacker, "Martyr Cult within the Walls: Saints and Relics in the Roman Tituli of the Fourth to Seventh Centuries," in *Text, Image, Interpretation: Studies in Anglo-Saxon Literature and its Insular Context in Honour of Éamonn Ó Carragáin*, ed. Alastair Minnis and Jane Roberts (Turnhout: Brepols, 2007), 31–70 at 34. The question of patronage is explored in Cooper and Hillner, *Religion, Dynasty and Patronage*. See also Julia Hillner, "Clerics, Property and Patronage: The Case of the Roman Titular Churches," *Antiquité Tardive* 14 (2006): 59–68.

30. Lampe, *From Paul to Valentinus*, 360–65; Baldovin, *Urban Character of Christian Worship*, 112–14.

31. John Baldovin (*Urban Character of Christian Worship*, 105–66) dates the beginning of stational practice, namely, the Roman bishop visiting different communities to preside at sacraments, from the end of the second or first half of the third century.

32. Lampe, *From Paul to Valentinus*, 397–412.

33. The baptismal celebration described in the sisters' *vita* approximates what might be expected of pre-Constantinian communities in the Great Church. Cf. the church of *AT* where a bishop leads an "alternate" community, one which might not have been "in communion with" the Roman bishop. After the construction of the Lateran Baptistry in 315, Easter initiations were celebrated there until such time as their number overwhelmed the bishop's baptistry. What cannot be ascertained prior to the 4th century is that initiation of adults was confined to Easter and Pentecost, the Roman practice underscored by Pope Siricius ca. 385. The consecration of a baptismal font in the Pudens *titulus* to handle the large number of Easter baptisms represents a historical feature of the late 4th and 5th centuries when St. Peter's and several *tituli* including that of Pudens are given the privilege of fonts.

burials.[34] In their extended household the sisters exercise spiritual oversight and the corporal works of mercy.

Then Pudentiana dies and is buried in Priscilla's cemetery.[35] Praxedes mourns the death of her elder sister. A certain Novatus, brother of the presbyter Timothy who is absent throughout the story, arrives to console Praxedes. Taken ill, on his deathbed Novatus wills "all his substance" to Pastor and Praxedes. Pastor in his role as guardian exercises his legal responsibility by writing a letter to Timothy seeking permission for the disposition of Novatus' inheritance to Praxedes and himself. Timothy concurs, writing to Pastor and Praxedes, "Therefore receive the fullness of control over everything."[36] However, "having received authority" [over property], Praxedes alone determines its disposition.[37] This turn in the story leads to the queries: Do Pastor's responsibilities as administrator and family funeral director reflect those of a *titulus* presbyter around 400 and the papacy of Innocent I? Is Pastor a "straw figure" required by the epistolary genre of pastoral letters and the rules of guardianship?[38] Given her new authority, Praxedes asks Bishop Pius, who has to approve a new church building, to designate Novatus' bath-building a *titulus* with worship-hall.[39] Praxedes' new *titulus* in the baths of Novatus (as stated in

---

34. On house-church leadership, see Peter Lampe (*From Paul to Valentinus*, 400, n. 8) and on types of such communities, here composed of Christian slaves and Christian guests (379).

35. Among the corporal works of mercy overseen at *tituli* was burial of believers. The Pudens clan with associates is fittingly buried in the family cemetery. Cemeteries in the various quarters were cared for by presbyters of the *tituli* of one of the seven ecclesiastical regions of Rome. *Titulus Praxedis* and *titulus Pudentiana* presbyters (region III) were in charge of cemeteries along the Via Tiburtina, where they themselves were usually buried.

36. Pastor brings Timothy up-to-date on the Pudens clan from this midway point in their story. Agreeing to Novatus' last testament, Timothy hands over his rights of inheritance to Pastor and Praxedes jointly. Pastor then retreats, reappearing only in time to bury Praxedes.

37. "Accipite itaque plenarium de omnibus potestatem" (Vat. ms. lat. 1191, 100v), a version of the statement found in *passiones* devoted to Praxedes' story. Praxedes makes her request of Bishop Pius. In the Praxedes' feastday accounts that I have seen, both *titulus* and "ecclesia" are established in her name alone. Read by someone trained in scholastic theology, "potestas" might be understood as denoting sacramental power.

38. Angelelli (*Basilica titolare di S. Pudenziana*, 19–24) makes the opposite case for Pastor's facticity on the basis of his appearance in another story and his *titulus* in six. But the obvious identification of Pastor with Hermas, brother of Pius I according to our earliest sources, is not made. This holds even for Vat. ms. lat. 1191 (100v–101r), where the *LP* notice, about an angel's appearance in the dress of a shepherd who mandates Easter's celebration on Sunday, is copied.

39. Hillner ("Clerics, Property, and Patronage," 66) and others present Pastor as the major or even sole decision-maker on the ecclesiastical use of the property. However, the story gives the agency to Praxedes.

her *passio*, not in the integrated acts, *BHL* 6988 and 6989), includes an *ecclesia* in her name.[40] In her own community center Praxedes is clearly in charge of the spiritual and corporal works of mercy.

After 313, holding title to church properties involved civil legal and ecclesiastical canonical requirements, with ecclesiastical ownership vested in the bishop of the diocese. When did it become a canonical requirement that the church complex be held in the name of bishop or presbyter?[41] Probably retrojecting later practice, *LP* claims that Bishop Dionysius (260–267) gave the "churches to the priests" and organized "the cemeteries and parishes (*parrochiae*) as dioceses" during the period of peace brought in by Emperor Gallienus, while Bishop Felix (268–273) "decreed that mass be celebrated over the memorials of the martyrs."[42] Presbyters with sacramental faculties were installed at cemeterial shrines outside the city by 400.[43] Establishment of church property held in a bishop's or presbyter's name suggests a post-Constantinian layer in the *vita*.[44] The bishop of the diocese establishes (*constituere*) a new church complex,

---

40. On the basis of the integrated *vita*, Guidobaldi has made the case that the *ecclesia Pudentianae* is the assembly-hall within Praxedes' *titulus*. The discrete Praxedes recensions have Pius dedicating the Novatus thermae in the Lateran quarter in Praxedes' name alone; an "ecclesia Pudentiana" is not mentioned (e.g., Mombritius, *Sanctuarium*, 354).

41. The change of name from *titulus Pudenti* to *titulus Pastoris* between the 6th and 8th centuries is explicable if we think in terms of ecclesiastical ownership. Julia Hillner ("Families, Patronage, and the Titular Churches," 225–61; "Clerics, Property and Patronage," 59–68) discusses the legal title of *tituli* during the 5th and 6th centuries. She indicates that *tituli* belong to the "bishop's church," which I take to be synonymous with the diocesan or "local" church, including rural parishes (*parocchiae*).

42. Davis, *Book of Pontiffs*, 26.2; 26.27. The first statement could refer to the assignment of presbyters to a specific geographical charge—*titulus*, cemetery shrine, or rural parish—as an indispensable condition of ordination. The Council of Chalcedon (451) formulated the principle that "absolute ordination," that is, without reference to a specific pastoral charge, was null and void (canon 6). Shortly after 458/459, Leo I (440–461) enunciated the same principle (Letter 167 to Rusticus of Narbonne). See Vogel, "Titre d'ordination," 70–85. Canon 6 was adhered to in the West until the late 12th century and is in the East still today.

43. In the later fifth century, Pope Simplicius (468–483) would make the three suburban basilicas of S. Pietro, S. Paolo, and S. Lorenzo part of the pastoral network of *tituli* by establishing presbyters on a rotating basis for ministry to penitents and for baptisms (Davis, *Book of Pontiffs*, 49.2).

44. Julia Hillner ("Clerics, Property and Patronage," 59–68) endorses Charles Pietri's position that many *tituli* were post-Constantinian. Where Pietri ascribed many of the church foundations to laity, Hillner, using perspectives of Roman civil law, looks for initiatives by wealthy clerics. The source of church building funds arises now as in late antiquity: Is a church foundation ascribed to the pope or bishop instead of to the laity who usually underwrite it?

overseen by a presbyter, in the territorial district for which the bishop has responsibility. The bishop, as only he can, dedicates (*dedicare*) the worship space. "Establishing" the use and "dedicating" it are two distinct episcopal actions, the first juridical and canonical, the second liturgical and spiritual.[45]

Information about installation of clergy in the Great Church is unavailable for the early period. The generic concepts of *ordinatio* (arrangement, setting in order) and *potestas* (power to do something, authority over property) in the Praxedes story are more at home in the third century than the fifth. Sacramental "powers" and faculties to exercise a ministry are dependent upon reception of a pastoral charge and jurisdiction over a specific ecclesial locale.[46] Praxedes' presbyteral office is the outcome of her appointment to ecclesiastical leadership in a newly established church complex.[47] Praxedes moves to the property held in her name, the *titulus Praxedis* provided with worship-hall and baptistry near the top of the Esquiline hill, to be administered by her as the ecclesiastically recognized incumbent. She has entered into a new phase in her life, that of a presbytera heading a pastoral center on behalf of a bishop of Rome.[48] She provides leadership and resources for the spiritual and corporeal works of mercy in her *titulus*. But is she without benefit of resident male clergy? The martyrdom of Simmetrius the presbyter in her *titulus*, along with twenty-two others, raises the question: Did Simmetrius share the presbyteral duties

---

45. In late antique Rome, a cosmopolitan city attracting people and traditions from across the world, emphasis was placed on the bishop's unifying role as presider of the sacraments, each of the other ministers playing their proper role. Presbyters were not allowed to assume the presidential role. The unity thus symbolized countered the earlier "fractionation" of the city-church, both in its worship communities and its leadership. We cannot yet map out when and how these structural changes in governance took place. Further confusing the picture, private churches and chapels were built and maintained by wealthy families and staffed by clergy deputed by the bishop but selected and paid for by patrons.

46. See Martinelli, *Primo trofeo*, f. 55; Davanzati, *Notizie al pellegrino*, 74. The "power" of presbyters and presbyteras in the city-church of Rome to confect eucharist is debatable at the time of Innocent I.

47. Ordination rites may have been as simple as laying on of hands with spontaneous prayer following a basic pattern for installation in office.

48. A ms. from the Carthusian monastery of Sainte-Barbe, Cologne, now in Berlin, Staatsbibliothek Theol. fol. 706, fol. 249v, ca. 1460 (*BHL* 6920g), is the sole example listed by the Bollandists of a truncated epitome that contains phrases from *BHL* 6920 (Mombritius, *Sanctuarium* 1-2, 353–54). Its final clause reads, "quam Pius papa consecrans baptisterium ibidem ordinavit." The relative pronoun probably referred to the new church ("ecclesiam") on the Esquiline that Bishop Pius arranged for ("ordinavit") in response to

in Praxedes' *titulus*? If so, she had lost her pastoral coworker as well as members of her congregation.[49]

Our multilayered story has as its kernel an edifying account reflecting the early church in its exuberant post-pentecostal phase. Its second-century themes lead me to propose post-apostolic roots for the *vita*'s core. An editorial updating incorporated fourth-century civil and ecclesiastical regulations. At the end of the fifth century the story was adjusted to that canonically minded period.[50] Gelasius I's strong antipathy to women's active engagement in liturgical leadership signals that a new era without women in such roles had dawned.[51] This brings us to the sixth century, which is that of the compilers, when *passiones* and *acta* of the martyrs were written and re-edited side by side with *LP*, the official lives of the popes. At the end of this century, Gregory the Great will write his *Dialogues*, possibly in an attempt to correct or even to reverse the orientation of the more fantastic *passiones*.[52] When in the course of the twelfth century women's ecclesial horizons are again reduced, the sisters' *vita* is enriched with historical references and interpolations from the Scriptures and liturgy.[53] In this way

---

Praxedes' request. However, in the scholastic period "ordinavit" would have been been read as "ordained" and might have been taken as referring to the new church's incumbent, Praxedes. Had Martinelli, and Davanzati after him, seen such a text? There is no evidence of this recension in Italy. The contents of the legendary containing this recension (attributed to Praxedes, but pertaining chiefly to Pudentiana) are listed in Baudouin de Gaiffier, "Le martyrologe et le légendier d'Hermann Greven," *Analecta Bollandiana* 54 (1936): 316–58 at 353, no. 235.

49. Noële Maurice-Denis Boulet ("Titres urbains et communauté," 14–32 at 16–17), observes that typically at Roman synods two presbyters signed in for each *titulus* (26, n. 26). Peter Lampe's (*From Paul to Valentinus*, 387–408) deductions about fractionation, monarchical episcopacy, and presbyteral governance include co-responsibility by presbyters dating from the mid-third century (Lampe, 400, n. 8).

50. The decrees of popes and church councils formed the basis of early church law. For the Roman church Siricius (384–389), Celestine I (422–432), Leo I (440–461), and Gelasius I (492–496) were important legislators because of the amount and content of their correspondence with other bishops and churches. Leo I, styling himself vicar of Peter, extended papal power as far away as Sicily.

51. P. A. B. Llewellyn ("Roman Church during the Laurentian Schism," 418 and n. 7) suggested that *BHL* 6991, "Vita auct. Ps.-Pastore presb.," is one of those *gesta martyrum* against which the so-called *Decretum Gelasianum de libris recipiendis et non recipiendis* was directed. Julia Hillner ("Families, Patronage, and Titular Churches," 254–56, n. 118) counters this suggestion, giving text with translation of the so-called Gelasian decree.

52. Conrad Leyser, "The Temptations of Cult: Roman Martyr Piety in the Age of Gregory the Great," *EME* 9 (2000): 289–307 at 291–92.

53. *BHL* 6920c, "Vita Praxedis et Pudentianae."

the popular *vita* of Potentiana and Praxedes keeps alive memories of a golden age of women's ecclesial ministry in the very heart of old Rome.

3. Burials and Relics: The Memorial to St. Peter and the Roman Cult of Relics

Since Richard Krautheimer published "The Carolingian Revival of Early Christian Architecture" in 1942, the church of S. Prassede has been recognized by architectural historians as a medieval "copy" of Constantine's Old St. Peter's.[54] Rome as a pilgrim's destination was inextricably linked to Peter. The first known development of a site to mark the grave of a hero of the faith in the West is the one presumed to be the *memoria* of Peter. By the late second century, a *tropaion* (trophy) or *memoria* (memorial shrine) in the form of a two-storied aedicula, a niche with shelf framed by columns supporting a gable, was inserted in a courtyard within a pagan necropolis that contained mausolea, burial rooms of wealthy families on the Vatican Hill hard by the reputed site of Nero's circus. Prayerful graffiti were scribbled in profusion on a red wall standing at right angles to the wall onto which the tropaion backed. Eusebius cites a reference to the memorials to Peter and Paul by the presbyter Gaius (ca. 200), "But I can show the trophies of the apostles. For if you go to the Vatican, or to the Ostian road, you will find the trophies of those who have laid the foundation of this church."[55] Belief in the existence of Peter's grave is the only way to account for the moving of a million cubic feet of earth to allow for the building circa 333, under the Emperor Constantine's authority, of the westward-oriented basilica of Old St. Peter's on the slope of the Vatican Hill. Excavations undertaken from 1939 show that Old St. Peter's, which uneasily combined transept (a narrow transverse nave constituting the martyrium or martyr's shrine) and apse with a covered cemetery in the nave and aisles, was situated over the late-second-century memoria marking Peter's supposed place of burial, its remnants still under the high altar of the present basilica.

The focus of Constantine's basilica was at the west where the upper part of the memorial aedicula could be seen. Sheathed in marble with a strip of porphyry, it protruded through the floor of the transept on the chord of

---

54. Krautheimer, "Carolingian Revival," 1–38 at 17–20.

55. Eusebius, *Ecclesiastical History*, II, xxv, 80.

the apse. Four beautiful vine-carved spiral columns of Greek provenance dating from about 200, connected by architraves, supported an open ciborium. Two additional columns bearing architraves from which curtains were suspended connected this penetrable screen to the apse walls.[56] Old St. Peter's was martyrium (transept) and funerary hall (nave and aisles) juxtaposed, not a place for regular eucharistic assembly. Functionally it combined a memorial to Peter at the presumed site of his burial, a covered graveyard for the faithful, and a funeral banqueting hall.[57] A eucharistic refrigerium could be celebrated at a portable altar wherever people gathered for obsequies within the building. This funerary and memorial function changed when Pope Symmachus (498–514) briefly took over St. Peter's as his episcopal seat. The first indication of an altar in the western transept is documented at the turn to the sixth century in connection with this pope, who also positioned additional altars in the transept. To the two huge mausolea, which projected from the south side of the church, later popes would add martyrial shrines.

By the late sixth century, pilgrims throunging to venerate Peter's shrine during the eucharistic liturgy had created a traffic problem. Under Pope Pelagius II (579–590) and his successor Pope Gregory I (590–604), an ingenious solution was found. A high platform for the altar at which the pope celebrated mass was raised over the shrine, while a confessio or subterranean crypt controlled access to the relic area and its second-century aedicula. Through an open screen, created by the now-reconfigured colonnade comprising six strigilated vine-columns, the shrine area could be seen from the front, while at the back a distinctive annular crypt corresponding to the apse, its corridor accessed from the sides, was devised to handle the steady stream of pilgrim traffic without disturbance to the presider and clergy at the altar above. Approaching from the rear on the major axis, the pilgrim was stopped short by the "altar of the confessio" or relic-altar, possibly dating from Gregory's time but certainly in place by the eighth century. Thus there were two altars, one on each level, the higher "public" one superimposed over the lower one deep within the corridor. Gregory I's architectural innovation

---

56. The rear panel of the Pola Casket depicts the Petrine shrine's 4th- and 5th-century state. See Toynbee and Perkins, *Shrine of St. Peter and the Vatican Excavations*, esp. 202–4 and figs. 20, 21.

57. S. Agnese on the via Nomentana founded by Constantia, S. Lorenzo in Verano, the Basilica Apostolorum (later S. Sebastiano) on the Appian way, and SS. Marcellino and Pietro were similar constructions.

would be repeated at Honorius I's S. Pancrazio, at S. Crisogono (731–741), at Paschal I's S. Prassede, as well as in numerous churches north of the Alps.[58]

Paschal's relic-altar in his newly built church dedicated to Praxedes would remain until modern times the most extreme example of its type and probably the best-preserved. Initially in Rome those designated as saints were exclusively the martyrs ("witnesses") and confessors who had professed faith in Christ by shedding their blood or undergoing torture in his name. Because of Diocletian's persecution, Rome was the Christian treasure-house of "first-class" relics, namely, saints' bodies. Possession of and proximity to these *relicta*, "remains," was believed to bring blessings through saintly intercession. The pagan Roman practice of honoring the remains by maintaining their integrity and not moving or dividing them was a cultural inheritance that Christians honored and later popes promulgated by persuasion or threat.[59] Following the peace of the church, oratories and large chapels were built with their altars located in proximity to tombs. At first almost all were *extra muros*, the building protecting the interment and providing a place for prayer.[60] Gradually relics made their way inside the city.[61]

Contrary to Eastern practice, Gregory the Great (590–604) refused to disturb the remains of the saints, to transfer them to another resting place, or to dismember them for distribution, considering it a grave sacrilege if bodies were even touched.[62] Refusing to provide emperors and empresses with first-class relics, Gregory devised ingenious arguments,

---

58. John Crook, *Architectural Setting of the Cult of Saints in Early Christian West*.

59. There were exceptions. "Translation" or transfer of remains without public ceremony was already underway in the 3rd to 5th centuries. Pontianus and Hippolytus, Cornelius, and Quirinus had died martyrs' deaths outside Rome, and their relics were returned to the city. Bodies of saints might be discovered in the Roman countryside. Ambrose transferred bodies at Milan, Bologna, and Florence.

60. Pope Damasus (366–384) devoted himself to making the catacombs more accessible. However, these concentrated depositories of saints' relics were under threat, not only from Lombards seeking loot but from pious pilgrims hankering for relics to carry north of the Alps. Relics constituted an enduring income for church or monastery, ensuring mass with its offer of divine grace and stipend for the priest.

61. Thacker, "Martyr Cult within the Walls."

62. "In Romanis...omnino intolerabile est atque sacrilegium, si sanctorum corpora tangere quisquam fortasse voluerit" (Gregory I, *Ep*. IV, 30, in *S. Gregorii Magni, Registrum epistularum*, 1:249). Solemn translations were typical in Byzantium; see the 6th-century ivory in the Trier Domschatz (Kenneth G. Holum and Gary Vikan, "The Trier Ivory, *Adventus* Ceremonial, and the Relics of St. Stephen," *DOP* 33 [1979]: 113–33).

passing on stories of unfortunate events resulting from the disturbance of tombs. He was reluctant to reduce the "treasure" of the Roman church, this powerful presence of the saints to work wonders for believers or invite punishment on skeptics. Gregory sponsored the distribution of secondary "contact" relics (*brandea, palliola, sanctuaria*)—strips of cloth left for some time in proximity to a holy body and enclosed in a pyx or small box, or vials of oil that had burned at a martyr's tomb. During the sixth century the acquiring of secondary relics had become common practice in Rome. Thanks to contact relics, papal policy was able to resist the translation or partition of holy bodies for some fifty years after Gregory's pontificate (d. 604).

A. Relics and Crypt-Altars

Churches with no relic were dedicated simply by the saying of mass. This communal act of prayer by a holy people was understood to dedicate both the church and the altar.[63] As Michel Andrieu notes, Gregory I did not need to indicate where relics should be placed. The book of Revelation provided the answer:

> When [the Lamb] opened the fifth seal I saw under the altar the souls of those who had been slaughtered for the word of God and for the testimony they had given; they cried out with a loud voice, "Sovereign Lord, holy and true, how long will it be before you judge and avenge our blood on the inhabitants of the earth?" They were each given a white robe and told to rest a little longer....[64]

This passage was taken to mean that the grave of a martyr was fittingly located under an altar, symbol of Christ's self-offering and place where the faithful offered the sacrifice of the mass.

When a crypt, a term that initially referred to subterranean areas in cemeteries, was developed above an existing tomb or purpose-built in

---

63. Public celebration of mass was forbidden in an undedicated church. The popes controlled the development of public places of worship. Gelasius, Pelagius I, and Gregory I judged it an abuse to celebrate mass in a church that had been dedicated without receiving papal permission. As late as 865 Nicholas I required that even a bishop should have this permission. If a restored church possessed *sanctuaria*, they should be deposited anew and then the mass celebrated.

64. Rev 6:9–11. *Jerusalem Bible* (annotated edition) identifies this heavenly altar as the altar of holocaust.

a church, it suggested catacomb passages and cubicula.[65] Altars placed in crypts as relic-repositories, whether for bones or objects sanctified by contact, suggested a reduced version of a monumental tomb. Several old crypt-altars present the same general arrangement, showing clearly how relics were placed.[66] Cubic in form, these altars had a hollow interior, the table resting on four marble slabs raised from the ground. On the front façade of this framework was a small bay or niche, the *fenestella*, primitively closed by a grilled door that allowed the hand to be advanced or the devout to peer into the altar's interior. The floor inside was formed by a horizontal slab, the *tabula*. A small square or round cover in the middle of the slab, also with a closure, connected the interior of the altar with a tiny subterranean cavity, the sepulchre containing the relics.

The altar in the crypt of Old St. Peter's, a rectangular block of masonry rather than a hollow boxlike structure, illustrates the next stage of development.[67] When its upper table (*mensa*) was raised, a niche for relics (20 x 30 x 23 cm deep) closed by a marble plaque, summarily sealed with lime, was discovered. The cavity contained only a residue of cinders and indeterminate debris.[68] Another square niche had been hollowed out on the front face of the altar; some cinders and fragments of bone and glass were found there. Architectural historians have pointed out the popularity of such crypt-altars following Gregory's invention of the annular crypt at Old

---

65. Bauer's essay ("Frammentazione liturgica nella chiesa romana," 385–98) is pertinent to this whole area of study.

66. Andrieu, *OR* 4:373–75; Leclercq, "Confessio," 2503–8. Examples are extant from the 5th-century basilica of S. Alexander on the Via Nomentana, the subterranean church of SS. Cosmas and Damiano (probably the primitive basilica), and Holy Apostles (pontificate of John III, 561–574) discovered in 1873.

67. Andrieu, *OR* 4:374–75. Although thought by the excavators to be 8th century because of its rough masonry, this altar may date from Gregory's renovation. See Emerick, "Altars Personified," in Emerick and Deliyannis, *Archaeology in Architecture*, 43–64 at 52 and n. 35. The life of Pope Silvester (314–335, *LP* 34.16) recounts Constantine's supposed donation of a copper cubic altar 5 feet in all dimensions to contain Peter's body, with porphyry and vine-scroll columns brought from Greece placed above it on the transept pavement.

68. Engelbert Kirschbaum (*The Tombs of St Peter and St Paul*, trans. John Murray [London: Secker & Warburg, 1959], 203–5) noted that this relic altar was identified as the *altare ad caput b. Petri* (shrine for Peter's head), which by the 11th century was joined with the head attributed to Paul in the Sancta Sanctorum, now housed in the Lateran altar ciborium; see also Sible de Blaauw, *Cultus et decor*, 2:618 and fig. 24. The head of St. Agnes (or at least one of them!) was brought by Honorius I (625–638) to the Lateran, to be joined later by the reliquary said to contain Praxedes' head now in the Vatican Library; on this last, see Goodson, *Rome of Pope Paschal I*, 243.

St. Peter's. The crypt-altar provided a focus for pilgrims' devotion as they approached the subterranean tomb or repository under the "high" altar overhead. But it also provided security by preventing immediate access to the holy relics; contact had to be mediated by clergy.

How was the Roman church's refusal to translate relics transformed into the opposite papal policy carried forward with such daring by Paschal I? John M. McCulloh addressed this question, seeing it as indicating the change in world-view from late antiquity to the Middle Ages.[69] In any case, aided by the predominance of Easterners in the papal chair, translations of relics became more common during the seventh century.[70] Before Paschal I the practice of bringing in relics of saints for safekeeping from cemeteries that ringed the city had been undertaken modestly by only a few popes, for example, Pope Paul I (757–767) immediately following the Lombard invasion of 756. Caroline Goodson has interpreted Paschal's large-scale transfer of relics from catacombs outside the city as displaying and consolidating his spiritual as well as temporal power.[71] To this insight might be added a "pilgrim demographics" plan by Paschal to redress the imbalance between the popularity of St. Peter's at Rome's northwest edge and the isolation of papal cathedral and palace in the Lateran quarter to the far southeast.[72] Theoretically at least, a "copy" of St. Peter's—S. Prassede with its enormous cache of relics situated within 90 meters of S. Maria Maggiore, a basilica sized for the most important papal celebrations—might provide such a devotional refocus.

---

69. John M. McCulloh, "From Antiquity to the Middle Ages: Continuity and Change in Papal Relic Policy from the 6th to the 8th Century," in Ernst Dassmann and Karl Suso Frank, eds., *Pietas: Festschrift für Bernhard Kötting* (Münster Westfalen: Aschendorff, 1980), 313–24.

70. The Pantheon was converted to a church in 609 and dedicated as S. Maria ad Martyres and a feast "for all the saints" celebrated there, purportedly after cartloads of martyrs' bones had been transported to this "baptized" building. In Rome the first public translation of saintly bones was that of the martyrs Primus and Felicianus (642–649) by Pope Theodore I to Sto. Stefano Rotondo. In these same years relics of foreign martyrs (Venantius, Anastasius, and others from Istria and Salona) were brought to the Venantius Chapel at the Lateran. These saints were depicted as standing figures on either side of *Maria archiepiscopa orans* in the apse and adjacent apsidal walls. See Gillian Mackie, "The San Venanzio Chapel in Rome and the Martyr Shrine Sequence," *Revue de l'art canadienne/Canadian Art Review* 23 (1996): 1–13.

71. Much recent scholarship in various disciplines has explained the building activity of Popes Hadrian I, Leo III, and Paschal I as cementing the papal headship of the Republic of St. Peter, in other words, aggrandizement of power and authority in the secular sphere.

72. Krautheimer, *Three Christian Capitals*, 107–21.

B. The S. Prassede Relic-List

Paschal translated bones from cemeteries on every major road leading out of town to equip his chapels at Old St. Peter's, to provide a relic-hoard at his thoughtfully designed and lavishly equipped new church of S. Prassede, and to re-unite Cecilia and companions in the new church dedicated to her across the Tiber.[73] Caroline Goodson has advanced the discussion of the two-piece marble slab mounted on the north side of the pier between S. Prassede's side entrance and the Zeno Chapel façade. The inscription, observed in its present location by John Capgrave circa 1450 and transcribed in full by many antiquarians, has been studied by several scholars.[74] Its lower part is badly damaged, as might have happened if set into the floor of the presbytery or damaged when moved, then pieced together at some later time. Goodson lists the slab's earliest observers, summarizes the most important theories regarding its dating, and gives a literal translation of the text with annotations respecting the saints.[75] She provides a map showing the roads leading out of the city to the cemeteries from which relics were collected, and notes that these cemeteries form a ring around Rome, with at least one martyr's relic taken from each major road.[76] The hierarchical ranking of the

---

73. Goodson, "Relic Translations of Paschal I," 123–41 and fig. II.1.

74. Krautheimer (*CBCR* 3:235, n. 1) supposed that the plaque, renewed in 1730, was originally carved in the 13th century based on a 9th-century document. Davis conservatively follows Krautheimer, who cites Felice Grossi-Gondi, "La celebre iscrizione agiografica della basilica di S. Prassede in Roma," *Civiltà Cattolica* 67 (1916): 443–56. The saints interred are listed by hierarchical category (bishops, presbyters, deacons, male martyrs, female virgins and martyrs, and widows). The inscription's final line claims 2,300 saints. Davis (*Ninth-Century Popes*, 10, n. 23) counts 2,151. My count is 2,251. The inscription and its dating are discussed by Antonio Ferrua ("Il catalogo dei martiri di S. Prassede," in *Atti della Pontificia accademia romana di archeologia*, Serie 3, Rendiconti 30–31 [1957–59]: 129–40), opting for a 9th-century dating for the whole, and Ursula Nilgen, "Grosse Reliquieninschrift von Santa Prassede," 7–29. Nilgen judges that the first 37 lines are authentically Paschalian, while the remaining 19 are a Quattrocento expansion. In Nilgen's reading, the Theodora inscription was copied from an earlier text of unknown date. Goodson (*Rome of Pope Paschal I*, 228–34) judges the entire inscription to be Carolingian. The provenance of the relics and the martyrs' *dies natalis* is given by Caterina-Giovanna Coda, *Duemilatrecento corpi di martiri: La relazione di Benigno Aloisi (1729) e il ritrovamento delle reliquie nella basilica di Santa Prassede in Roma* (Rome: La Società alla Biblioteca Vallicelliana, 2004), 127–50.

75. Goodson, "Relic Translations," 136–37 and n. 65; Goodson, *Rome of Pope Paschal I*, 166–67, 327–33.

76. Goodson's map can be usefully compared with a recent map of paleo-Christian Rome and its environs (3rd to 6th centuries), which shows all the cemeteries, in Fiocchi Nicolai, Bisconti, and Mazzoleni, *Catacombes chrétiennes de Rome*.

names (popes, bishops, presbyters, deacon, male martyrs, female virgins, and widows including martyrs) on the slab parallels that found in litanies of the saints.[77] Many of the unnamed "saints" would have been St. Paul's rank-and-file Christians, their remains collected from *loculi* in the walls of catacomb galleries or in floor tombs (*formae*) near a martyr's resting place.

Walter Frere's account of martyrs' interments in cemeteries outside the city provides a handy cross-reference for Goodson's discussion.[78] Each cemetery had a chapel or oratory where the martyr's cult required mass on the feast day. The return journey to some of these shrines would have taken an entire day. Of those listed by category on the marble slab where families are separated by gender, we find in a ring close to the city: Cyrinus interred *Ad catacumbas*; Gordian (10 May) at Via Latina; Nicomedes at St. Nicomede on the Via Nomentana; Marcus and Marcellianus (18 June) at the cemetery of Balbina on the Via Ardeatina; Basilla (11 June and 22 September) at Basilla; and Chrysanthus and Daria retrieved from *Thrasonis*.[79] Felix was found on the Via Portuensis. Cyriac and companions (8 August) were seven miles out along the Via Ostiensis; Felicula seven miles out the Via Ardeatina; Marius and Martha with their children Audifax, Habacuk, and Abbacus twelve miles out on the Via Cornelia.[80] Zoticus, Amantius, Irenaeus (Hereneus), and Hyacinth were ten miles out on the Via Labicana; Pontian (13 August) at Callistus; Candida *ad ursum pileatum* (3 October); Castulus (12 or 26 March) and Stratonicus (30 November) at Castulus on the Via Labicana. Preeminent among the relics gathered would have been those of the martyr Potentiana and Praxedes from the Priscilla cemetery on the Via Salaria Nova.[81]

---

77. At least one scholar has suggested that the lengthy two-piece epigraphic inscription may represent the relic-list as written out on a parchment at the time of deposition. To obtain the litany structure, the original list would have needed to be collated, with names placed in hierarchical order rather than cemeterial place of origin.

78. Walter Howard Frere, *Studies in Early Roman Liturgy*, vol. 1: *The Kalendar* (London: Oxford University Press, 1930), 24–29. Frere notes that saints' celebrations initially took place only at the actual places of interment. Once incorporated into the liturgical calendar of the Roman church, they could be celebrated everywhere.

79. This married couple is separated by gender on the slab, Daria being listed with the "virgins and widows." Tellingly, the inscription lacks a "wives" category.

80. Marius is transcribed Marus on the tablet, Abbacus is missing, and Martha is included among the virgins and widows.

81. *Notitia ecclesiarum urbis Romae* (ca. 625–649), no. 10, p. 306, and *De locis sanctis martyrum* (ca. 635–645), in *Itineraria et alia geographica*, no. 24, p. 320. Both texts name S. Prisca; Simmetrius is noted in *De locis sanctis*. From the time of Antonio Bosio's posthumous

C. The Dedication of S. Prassede and Its Date

The *proemium* of the two-piece marble inscription gives as the date for the deposition of the relics under the high altar of S. Prassede 20 July of Indiction X (817). It reads in part:

> ...the pope, bearing those [= the bodies of saints] resting in ruin, extracted from cemeteries or crypts, with the greatest care placed [them] with his own hands, under this most sacred altar, in the month of July, the 20th day, in the 10th indiction.[82]

Decades ago Richard Krautheimer noted the problematic dating of the dedication of S. Prassede a mere six months after Paschal's election.[83] We have no evidence that S. Prassede's building campaign was begun during Stephen IV's brief papacy of less than a year (816–817), or even while Leo III (795–816), a pope demonstrably interested in building and instrumental in advancing Paschal's career, was in office. Could a church as large and lavish as S. Prassede be brought in six months to the point that relics were interred and its high altar dedicated, even by a pope who was elected precipitately one day after the death of his predecessor?

Read with the system of indictions laid out by Herman Geertman, *LP* gives us a more reasonable date than does the marble plaque, for *LP* provides a framework within which Paschal's building program was carried forward.[84] Applying that framework, during Indiction XI (1 September 817–31 August 818) Paschal, realizing the decrepit character of the *ecclesia* that Hadrian had restored forty years previously, shifted the site of his new church "not far away" from S. Prassede's former site:[85]

> ...this venerable pontiff anticipating its ruin and applying care to that church, often being on the watch there, shifted and erected it

---

publication *Roma sotterranea* (1632), the sisters were popularly thought of as once having been buried in the cubiculum of the *Velatio*.

82. Adapted from Goodson's translation (*Rome of Pope Paschal I*, 327 and 330, n.2). As have most scholars, Goodson ("Relic Translations," 126) dates the relic translation to 817.

83. Krautheimer, "Carolingian Revival of Early Christian Architecture," 18, n. 25.

84. The chronological system governing the *LP* biographies from Hadrian I (772–795) through Stephen V (885–891) is that of indictions (Herman Geertman, *More Veterum*, 81). An indiction was a recurring fiscal period of fifteen years, instituted by Constantine in 313 for the assessment of property tax.

85. The west wall of the present atrium as well as remnants of an insula flanking the Via di S. Martino ai Monti might be part of the original titulus and "ecclesia" (Krautheimer, *CBCR* 3: 258).

in another place not far away, an improvement on what it had formerly been. He fittingly decorated this church's apse adorned with mosaic work in different colours. Likewise he embellished the triumphal arch with the same minerals, carrying it out in a marvelous fashion.[86]

The foundations were laid, walls erected, and the crypt, presbyterium, and arches carried forward including their decorative embellishment (Fig. 6.1).This work during Indiction XI led to the next phase, completion of the remainder of the church, which allowed for the translation of relics. Geertman's chronology places S. Prassede's dedication during Indiction XII, September 818–August 819.[87] The ritual for the dedication of an altar and a church was identified by its first and most memorable aspect, the burying of relics under the altar. The title of *Ordo* XLII, which gives the rubrics for the dedication of churches in Rome, is revealing: *In nomine Dei summi ordo quomodo in sancta romana ecclesia reliquiae conduntur.* What we know as Roman usage from the second or third decade of the eighth century had mostly to do with the deposition of relics. The dedication ceremony was complete when mass was said, effecting the church's consecration, on the newly vested altar.[88] The interval between the deposition of relics in crypt or altar and offering of mass was filled in with additional ceremonies inspired by Gallican usage, which in the Romano-Germanic Pontifical of the Tenth Century were very lengthy.[89] As we have it, *Ordo* XLII gives some prayers and may include some additions to the primitive form of the ritual.[90] The

---

86. Davis, *Lives of Ninth-Century Popes*, 100.8.

87. See also Davis, *Lives of Ninth-Century Popes*, 100.9, n. 23. The embellishments outlined in 100.10 and the provision of St. Agnes' oratory in S. Prassede's monastery (100.11) should be included.

88. For the text and rubrics of the pure Roman order XLIIA known in Gaul by 750, see Andrieu, *OR* 4:[359]–394; Vogel, *Medieval Liturgy*, 181. Brian Repsher (*The Rite of Church Dedication in the Early Medieval Era* [Lewiston, NY: Edwin Mellen, 1998]) treats in detail the most popular Carolingian dedication rite but omits the Gregorian *Hadrianum* text.

89. *PRG X*: 1, XXXIII. Repsher (*Rite of Church Dedication*, 139–69, Appendix A) gives a full translation of the *Ordo ad benedicandam ecclesiam.*

90. Andrieu, *OR* 1:22–23; *OR* 4:395–402. For Italian and papal church dedications with augmented ritual at the time of the Gregorian reform, see Louis I. Hamilton, *A Sacred City: Consecrating Churches and Reforming Society in Eleventh-Century Italy* (Manchester: Manchester University Press, 2010) and Repsher, *Rite of Church Dedication.*

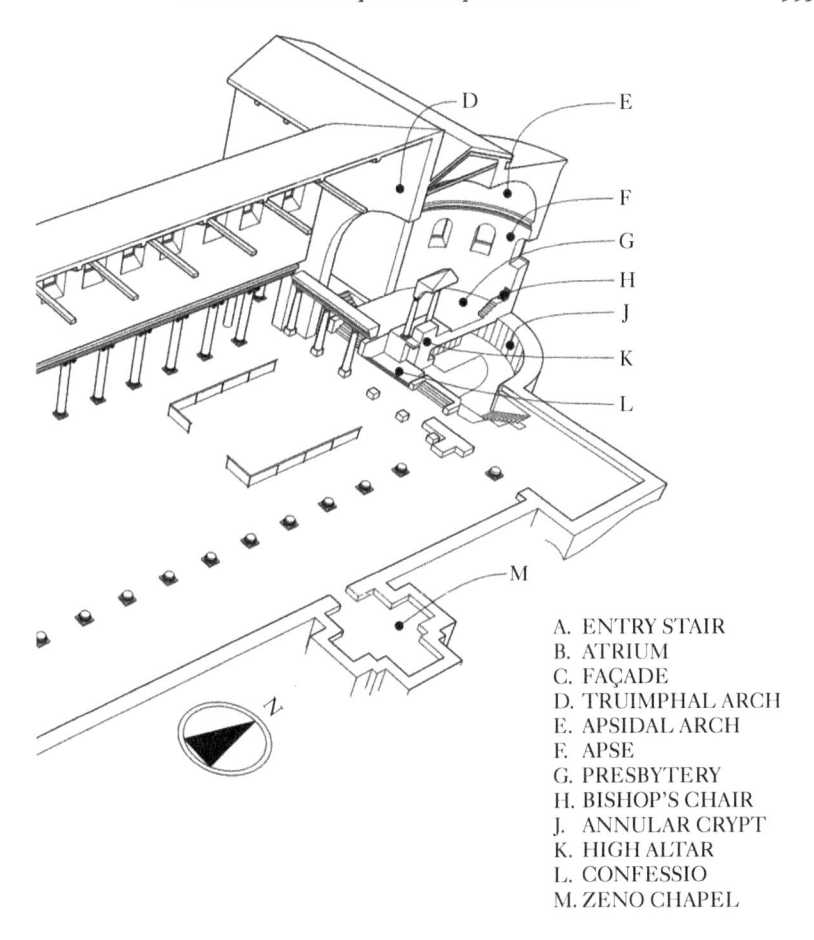

A. ENTRY STAIR
B. ATRIUM
C. FAÇADE
D. TRUIMPHAL ARCH
E. APSIDAL ARCH
F. APSE
G. PRESBYTERY
H. BISHOP'S CHAIR
J. ANNULAR CRYPT
K. HIGH ALTAR
L. CONFESSIO
M. ZENO CHAPEL

FIGURE 6.1 Rome, S. Prassede. Building information model (BIM) for imaging and visualization. Detail of north end. By permission of Gregory J. MacNeil, Roderick J. MacNeil, Jerry MacNeil Architects Limited, Halifax, Nova Scotia.

prayers of the "pure" Roman rite, unaccompanied by rubrics, are found in *Hadrianum*.[91] Since both *Hadrianum* and *Ordo* XLII are Roman from the mid-eighth century, taken together they allow a close approximation of the ritual used by Paschal in the dedication of his churches.

---

91. The *Hadrianum* contains three orations (H 194–196), two of which (*Oratio quando levantur reliquiae*; *Oratio in dedicatione ecclesiae*) pertain to the relic deposition and one (*Oratio post velatum altare*) that follows the vesting of the new altar. H 197 gives the mass texts (Deshusses, *Sacr. grég.*, 1). The three prayers provided in the papal sacramentary rather than the alternates in *Ordo* XLII would almost certainly have been used by Paschal.

The *LP* informs us that during Indiction XII (1 September 818–31 August 819) Paschal "removed and buried [many bodies] in the church of Christ's said martyr St. Praxedes, which he had wonderfully renewed and constructed, with the assistance of all the Romans, bishops, priests, deacons and clerics chanting psalms of praise to God."[92] The chronology of *LP* indicates that the actual deposition and consecration took place in 819.[93] What would have been more appropriate for Praxedes, burier of martyrs, than the burial of relics on the vigil of Praxedes' feastday and dedication of her church? The Roman dedication rite called for the translation of relics from the church or place where they had been temporarily kept to the new church. Paschal's translation of relics was said to have engaged the whole populace as well as the clergy.[94] Had the relics been collected earlier at one place as the rubric for a deposition indicates? Or were they brought from their many locations on every major road outside the city, or from "depots" established at various points of the compass *intra muros*, in order to facilitate the participation of the whole city, laity and clergy alike? We do not know. In any case, the ceremony began at the church where the relics had remained overnight and vigil kept. First, the litany of the saints was chanted. Then the first of the collects (found in both the papal sacramentary and the *Ordo*) was said by the bishop as the relics were removed to be processed to the new church: "Remove our sins from us, we beseech, O Lord, that we may worthily enter with pure minds into the holy of holies. Through our Lord."[95] Since the Roman ritual represents a reburial of saintly bodies, chanting of the seven penitential psalms was called for enroute to the new location.[96] Presbyters

---

92. Davis, *Lives of Ninth-Century Popes*, 100.9. During this period Paschal had begun the building of S. Maria in Domnica, which though grand was a simpler church in every respect. The next year he would begin S. Cecilia's.

93. Without providing his reasoning, Sible de Blaauw (*Cultus et decor*, 1:391) gives the completion dates for S. Prassede and S. Maria in Domnica as 819 and S. Cecilia as 820.

94. The people's participation is in the spirit of Byzantine translations. J. Baldovin (*Urban Character of Christian Worship*, 158–66 and chapters 6 and 7) discusses the phenomenon of public processions. For an 11th-century procession translating relics, see the fresco in the lower church of S. Clemente, Rome, depicting the return of that saint's relics to the church in 868, and the 6th-century ivory relief (Trier, Domschatz) showing a Byzantine procession (Holum and Vikan, "Trier Ivory," 128–32).

95. "Aufer a nobis, domine, quaesumus, iniquitates nostras et ad sancta sanctorum puris mereamur mentibus introire. Per [Christum dominum nostrum]" (H 194, in Deshusses, *Sacr. grég.*, 1:303).

96. Inspired by funeral rites, psalms 6, 32, 38, 51, 102, 130, and 143 were chanted. Antiphons, many of which are known from later manuscripts, "colored" the character of the psalms and established their "mood."

were fitted with a linen cloth tied about the neck, helping them support the relics that they carried on patens while singing the antiphon *Cum iocunditate exibitis*: "With delight you will go forth, and with joy you will be led away; for the mountains and hills are leaping with joy in expectation of you."[97]

The relics were processed to S. Prassede on the vigil of Praxedes' feast. Arriving at the church, *OR* XLII, 3 describes the bishop, with two or three assistants, entering and closing the door prior to blessing water of exorcism to be used in washing out the confessio.[98] The anointing of the repository with chrism and mixing of the mortar to be used later to seal in the relics as well as sponging down ("baptizing") the altar with exorcised water (*OR* XLII, 5, 6) were preparatory rites. Standing outside awaiting the bishop's return, the presbyters continued to hold the relics that they had carried in procession. The *Oratione in dedicatione ecclesiae* was probably said at the church door: "We ask you, Lord, to kindly enter your house and establish an everlasting place for yourself in the hearts of your faithful, so that [this very building] may become a splendid home for whom this structure stands."[99] The relics were then carried in to the accompaniment of a litany. The whole of the relics requisitioned by Paschal could not have been placed on the altar as called for by the ritual, not only because of their quantity but also because the exceptional shaft-depository was built up in distinct layers from the bottom. (By this period the altar did not simply stand over the relic-burial but relics were included within it.) The altar's *mensa* had to be put down last over the entire carefully laid construction,

---

97. *Cum iocunditate* (2015), based on Bar 5:9 and Isa 55:12, is found in most Western rites for the ceremonial translation of relics and may have been composed for that purpose; see Thomas Davies Kozachek, "The Repertory of Chant for Dedicating Churches in the Middle Ages: Music, Liturgy and Ritual" (Ph.D. dissertation, Harvard University, 1995), 178, 239 and n. 7, and 246.

98. The rather long and exorcistic *Deus, qui ad salutem* (*OR* XLII, 4) is not found in *Hadrianum*. In Gregory I's time only pagan temples were lustrated. Lustrations of altar and the whole building as found in *OR* XLII, 6 and 17 appear to be a Gallican "infection." Influence of the Gallican on the Roman rite would produce, mid-10th century, the conflated rite found in RGP X.

99. "Domum tuum quaesumus domine clementer ingredere et in tuorum tibi corda fidelium perpetuam constitue mansionem, ut cuius aedificatione subsistit, huius fiat habitationis praeclara" (H 195, Deshusses, *Sacr. grég.*, 1:303). This prayer does not appear in *OR* XLII but is given in the papal sacramentary, and we can expect it to have been used by Paschal. *OR* XLII, 8 gives a different prayer: "Deus, qui in omni loco tuae dominationis dedicator adsistis, exaudi nos, quaesumus, ut inviolabilis huius loci permaneat consecratio, ut beneficia tui muneris universitas quae supplicat mereatur. Per." Cf. Repsher, *Rite of Church Dedication*, 166, no. 134.

which extended from near the floor of the purpose-built *confessio* to the full height of the altar (see above, Fig. 6.1).

The relics having been brought into the church, the bishop washed the inside of the repository with the exorcised water and marked it in four places with chrism in the form of a cross (OR XLII, 10). Everyone made the sign of the cross while the bishop greeted them: "In the name of the Father and of the Son and of the Holy Spirit. Peace to you," eliciting the response, "And with your spirit." This preparatory ceremony evoked the washing and chrismating of Christian initiation rites. The relics were then laid to rest and sealed in.[100] While the repository was being closed, the antiphon ("You have accepted seats under the altar of the Lord, intercede on our behalf through whom you have merited [your reward]") was sung.[101] A *tabula* or stone cover was put in position and another prayer said (OR XLII, 13–14).[102] The relics now being enclosed, the altar was chrismated and vested (14–16). Both *Hadrianum* and OR XLII provide the epicletic prayer: "We beg, Lord our God, that your Holy Spirit, who may sanctify the gifts of your people and cleanse the hearts of those partaking, may descend over this altar. Through our Lord."[103] Normally mass would then have commenced, achieving the consecration of the altar and completing the dedication of the church.[104]

The deposition took place on the vigil of Praxedes' feast. Transport of the 2,300 relics and their careful arrangement in a crypt, created not in relation to an existing burial but precisely for the purpose of receiving bones brought from elsewhere, would have taken Paschal and his assistants the entire day. The required dedicatory mass could not have been held on that

---

100. OR XLII, 11 is the earliest text to mention the burial of three particles of the sacred host, which may have been intended to supply for lack of relics, and three particles of incense. Particles of the host were certainly not needed in this instance.

101. "Sub altare domini sedes accepistis, intercedite pro nobis per quem meruistis" (D370). This is the other standard antiphon given in OR XLII. Kozachek has culled a large number of dedication antiphons from ms. sources, most of which are later than the 9th century.

102. OR XLII, 13 shows the "Deus qui ex omni coaptatione" being said after the relics are placed and before their sealing in the repository. This prayer appears in third place among the *Hadrianum*'s collects for the dedication mass, H 197.

103. "Descendat quaesumus domine deus noster spiritus sanctus tuus super hoc altare qui et populi tui dona sanctificet et sumentium corda [dignanter] emundet. Per" (H 196; cf. Andrieu, OR 4:16).

104. *Hadrianum* gives a complete mass with three collects, a prayer *super oblata*, a preface, and the post-communion prayer (H 197). The celebration continued with an octave of masses said during the following week (OR 4:19–20).

same day but would have been celebrated on the saint's feastday, 21 July 819, a Thursday.[105] By any standard the unusual two-day dedication ritual would have been memorable. Its success can be measured by the fact that Paschal's stripping of saints' relics from catacombs and their deposition within the city walls in a special repository in a new, gorgeously decorated church kept them secure for 910 years.

D. The S. Prassede Relic Deposit: Material Evidence for the Attribution of Ecclesial Ministry to Praxedes

A clue that official ecclesiastical ministry was attributed to Praxedes in the ninth century—evidence that neither Fioravante Martinelli in 1655 nor Benigno Davanzati in 1725 could have known—is to be found in the crypt under the high altar of S. Prassede. Its annular corridor emulated the design attributed to Gregory the Great at Old St. Peter's. Entered from either side of the presbytery, S. Prassede's corridor allowed the pilgrim to approach from the rear (north) a shallow altar whose shelf was embedded in the relic depository, while from the center of the nave the devout could descend a few steps to a large niche built into the *camera delle reliquie*. During fifteenth-century renovations Paschal's crypt had probably been filled in by Bernardo Rossellino (1409–1464) working under Pope Nicolò V (1449–1455), and then forgotten.[106] This was its state when in the mid-sixteenth century St. Charles Borromeo (titular cardinal 1564–1584) commissioned central stairs giving access to the presbytery through a brass altar rail, a new ciborium over the high altar, and two tabernacles for the display of relics cut into the apsidal arch mosaic.

A decree of the Roman synod of 1725 requiring proof that all altars in the Eternal City had been properly consecrated may have inspired the Vallombrosan monks to think of updating S. Prassede's shabby presbytery. At first Cardinal Pico della Mirandola (titular cardinal 1728–1731) intended only to refurbish the main altar by enlarging it. What today's visitor sees in presbytery and crypt is the renovation work commissioned by

---

105. The noted liturgist and canonist William Durandus (d. 1296), who spent much of his career in Rome, noted old Roman practice: "By law, church consecrations may take place on any day, but nevertheless take place most fittingly on Sundays, or on the feast days of the saints" (*Pontifical of Durandus of Mende*, 2/2.1, cited by Kozachek, "Repertory of Chant," 93).

106. The history of the building is reviewed by Maurizio Caperna, *La Basilica di Santa Prassede: Il significato della vicenda architettonica* (Rome: Monaci Benedettini Vallombrosani, 1999).

Cardinal Pico: the graceful ciborium that partially hides the apse mosaic and the central crypt-corridor entered from the nave and extending under the presbyterium to terminate in a small altar centered in the annular corridor, its frontal clad with mosaic in cosmatesque style.[107] Four sarcophagi, two antique and two carved in the eighteenth century, were stacked in pairs along the major corridor's sides.

A report written in 1729 by Dom Benigno Aloisi, the new prior of S. Prassede, recounts the circumstances of the discovery of the undisturbed relic-chamber and its subsequent demolition along with Paschal's altar and ciborium.[108] Giving an uncommon glimpse into papal and curial idiosyncrasies, Aloisi's report reads like a detective thriller. Concerned that many altars in use in Rome had not been episcopally blessed, Pope Benedict XIII (29 May 1724–21 February 1730), accompanied by an entourage of high clerics, his head stonemason, and some workmen, appeared at the monastery door about 9 o'clock on the evening of 2 January 1729. Born Pietro Francesco Orsini in 1649, Benedict XIII was a man known for his love of pastoral work and his determination to carry out Tridentine directives.[109] Benedict wanted to assure himself that all the basilica's altars had been consecrated. As tension among the clergy mounted in Rome over the status of their churches' altars, the pope determined to make his own inspection of S. Prassede. First, he commended the monks for recent consecrations of altars at side chapels. The high altar, however, consumed the pope's interest, and he carefully examined the *mensa*, admiring its size, beauty, and untouched condition.

---

107. The cosmatesque frontal of the high altar referred to by Aloisi as the Paliotto was reused in the crypt-altar fabricated during the 18th-century renovations (Aloisi, *Relazione*, Quinta Giornata, in Coda, *Duemilatrecento corpi*, 44–45; Emerick, "Focusing on the Celebrant," 143–44).

108. Until the 1970s Aloisi's original ms. could be found in the archives of the Abbey of Vallombrosa near Florence. Abbot Battistoni's copy, made in 1881 and preserved in the monastery attached to S. Prassede, has been published by Coda, *Duemilatrecento corpi*. Two partial copies exist (Ursula Nilgen, *Reliquieninschrift*, 9, n. 11; Goodson, *Rome of Paschal I*, 241 and n. 189). The archeologist G. Baldracco ("La cripta del sec. IX nella chiesa di Santa Prassede a Roma," *RAC* 18 [1941]: 277–96) based his reconstruction of the Carolingian crypt and account of the elaborate arrangement of relics in chambers, chests, and sarcophagi on Abbot Battistoni's ms. copy.

109. In defense of Paschal's high altar, the Vallombrosan Fathers had already provided the authorities to no avail a treatise based on principles of sacramental theology and canon law that supported the dedication of the altars in their church (Coda, *Duemilatrecento corpi*, Secunda Giornata, 21–28). Apparently Benedict XIII did not find adequate the Roman church's longstanding tradition that saying mass on an altar consecrated it.

Traditional Roman unwillingness to disturb the resting places of the deceased had preserved intact the S. Prassede relic treasury until now. Rectangular in shape, Paschal's Carolingian altar with *mensa* measuring 2.01 by 1.53 meters was larger than later antique altars. Over the altar table an open canopy 2.13 by 1.13 meters, which had once been sheathed in silver, was supported by four white marble arches carried on four porphyry columns. These arches may now be seen attached to the stairwell leading up to the atrium from Via di S. Martino di Monti. Until the eighteenth century only the canopy had been restored under Charles Borromeo; its four porphyry columns would be reused by Cardinal Pico to carry the elegant but obtrusive altar-canopy now in place.[110] Almost certainly the six antique columns found during the renovation and now engaged in the side walls of the presbyterium formed an open screen in front of Paschal's altar and crypt. Initially inspired by Gregory the Great's innovative design to control pilgrim traffic at Old St. Peter's and provide a sacred boundary in front of the crypt-altar, Gregory III (731–741) had subsequently doubled Gregory I's six columns in front of the confessio.[111] Leo III (795–816) would clad St. Peter's presbytery yet more lavishly in porphyry. Paschal, whose career had developed during Leo's pontificate, followed his predecessor's lead, differentiating the "holy of holies" or *sancta sanctorum* from the people's space to emphasize the separation of the presiding celebrant from the people.[112]

---

110. A comparison can be made with an altar with canopy (ciborium) carried on four columns in the left aisle of S. Apollinare in Classe, Ravenna. Constantine commissioned canopies over the tombs of Peter in Rome and of Christ at the Holy Sepulchre, Jerusalem; sometimes these martyrial canopies were associated with altars. From the early 6th century in Rome canopies began to be placed over altars in churches without tombs. In the 8th and 9th centuries, relics were translated and interred under the altars of city churches and marked by canopies (Molly Teasdale Smith, "The Development of the Altar Canopy in Rome," *RAC* 50 [1974]: 379–414).

111. The six columns carved with vines, found walled-up along the sides of the presbytery during Cardinal Pico della Mirandola's renovations to S. Prassede's presbytery, are similar to the remarkable set of six strigilated marble columns (ca. 200 from Greece, gift of Constantine) carved with alternating bands of vine-scrolls and spiral fluting, which had formed the open screen at the apostle's memorial shrine in the west end of Old St. Peter's, and are judged to date from the same period. In keeping with S. Prassede's "halving" of design elements, the screen would have been formed of six columns. On the *templon* design defining a clerical zone, see Bauer, "Frammentazione liturgica," 443. The allegorical notion of the pontifex (pope) as "high priest" who alone enters into the holy of holies is enough to account for changes in presbyterium design under Leo III and Paschal I described by Emerick, "Focusing on the Celebrant," 142–51.

112. For a reconstruction of Paschal's screen, see Emerick, "Focusing on the Celebrant," 129–59, esp. 148–51 and figs. 10, 12; Emerick, "Altars Personified," 43–64. This theme has been picked up by Goodson, *Rome of Pope Paschal I*, 156, fig. 29.

Benedict XIII's appreciative inspection of the altar-table late in that evening of January 1729 revealed no relic repository or cavity cut into the surface of the marble *mensa*. Noting the altar's intact beauty, the aged pope did not want Paschal's *mensa* to be disturbed and proposed that the altar be (re-)consecrated very soon. But Cardinal Fini (Finij), just arrived from St. Peter's at the pontiff's invitation and abetted by the desire of the monks for the presbytery's improvement, urged an investigation. During the course of that evening and subsequent explorations and depredations lasting until 5 May 1729, Paschal's altar would be disassembled and the relics, arranged with such care at the church's dedication nine centuries earlier, removed and relocated without ceremony.

First the remarkable marble one-piece *mensa* of the high altar was lifted off. Beneath it a slate slab (the *tabula*) had been plastered in place. This was pried open to reveal a large square cavity (0.88 x 0.88 x 0.80 m) in the masonry. Nearly cubic, its dimensions may have been intended to recall the tomb of copper or bronze reportedly placed by Constantine around Peter's tomb.[113] The cavity contained stores of bones carefully arranged by type, on top of which lay three skulls. A particularly large skull was wrapped turban-like in linen and pitch with aromatic spices in a manner attributable to the first or second century. For some days after its discovery the fragrance of the spices filled the church.[114] Directly beneath the large altar cavity was a small sepulchre (33 x 44 x 7 cm deep) that contained some ashes and a small empty box.

A shallow arch roofed the next lower level. The inner cavity thus formed again measured about 0.88 meter square. On either side, four cypress caskets full of relics were stacked in two tiers at right angles to, and resting on, the long sides of two ancient marble sarcophagi, which in turn rested on blocks of travertine set on the earth. Baldracco referred to the sarcophagi as A and B. Sarcophagus A, holding a large quantity of bones mixed in with cloths, showed reliefs of Jonah reclining (center) and two Good Shepherds (on the corners). The other (B), a strigilated sarcophagus with

---

113. Davis, *Lives of Pontiffs*, 34.16.

114. Potentiana and Praxedes' *vita* refers to this funeral custom: "Completing sixteen years, Potentiana the virgin of the Lord passed to the Lord. With her one sister we wrapped her corpse in spices with all care, and we hid it in the aforesaid *Titulus*" (AA.SS. IV, Maii, 299A). Charles Maitland (*The Church in the Catacombs: A Description of the Primitive Church of Rome, Illustrated by Its Sepulchral Remains* [London: Longman, Brown, Green, and Longmans, 1846], 51) reports that, opening some graves thought to be of the first or second centuries, Canon Boldetti had noted the odor of spices; but the superintendent of cemeteries, who was part of the papal entourage on this occasion, had never encountered the likes of this.

a curved lid, held two boxes of bones separated by a transverse marble slab. These relics the cardinals took to be the remains of the two sisters.[115] From the center of sarcophagus B, presumably that of the sisters, rose a pilaster, 0.88 meter wide, directly toward the high altar. On the horizontal plane, a marble slab extended outward from the top of each sarcophagus. Southward toward the nave, the slab formed the floor for a sort of *fenestella confessionis* (small grilled window) created by the cavity; northward toward the crypt corridor, the second marble slab created a shelf-altar, one end of which was embedded in the relic treasury. Above this shallow "altarino" was a small niche containing a painting of a cross with Potentiana and Praxedes standing on either side; higher yet, a small sepulchre contained three little cypress vases that disintegrated when touched. In the pilaster supporting the diminutive altar was a white strigilated vase containing a sponge stained with blood and some ashes.

On top of sarcophagus A the large niche or "tabernacle" (0.88 m wide and 1.32 m high) referred to above opened toward, and was accessible from, the nave via stairs.[116] On the rear wall of this niche was a painting of three women. According to Aloisi, the fresco was copied by the painter Giovanni Battista Bigetti before being removed in the demolition; it depicted the two sisters, similar to one another both in pose and color, wearing "the stole at the neck with a virgin's crown in hand"; between them, a larger crowned figure, without stole, raised her hand in blessing (Fig. 6.2).[117] This supposedly destroyed painting, damaged but repaired with faces retouched in eighteenth-century style, is in place above the

---

115. S. Pudenziana has no crypt; therefore it was reasonable that Potentiana's bones be reburied with those of her sister retrieved from the Priscilla cemetery. A silver reliquary now in the Vatican Library is said to be the container for the head of St. Praxedes (von Matt, *Art Treasures of Vatican Library*, figs. and cat. nos. 82–88). The provenance of this 11th-century casket, of Byzantine manufacture, is the Sancta Sanctorum, the papal treasury at the Lateran Palace. The *LP* life of Leo IV (847–855) claims that Praxedes' and Cecilia's heads, and relics of Pudentiana and some others named on the S. Prassede relic plaque, were housed in Quattro Coronati (Davis, *Lives of Ninth-Century Popes*, 105.41).

116. Goodson (*Rome of Pope Paschal I*, 242) gives the dimensions as 0.89 x 1.34 m, and compares the annular corridor and confessio to others (ibid., 129–34). Emerick ("Focusing on the Celebrant," 145 and fig. 11) proposes "five easy steps down" to the paved confessio floor from the level of the nave pavement.

117. Aloisi, *Relazione*, Quinta Giornata in Coda, *Relazione*, 45. Those present at the excavation were convinced that the central figure was the sisters' mother "Sabina, o Sabinella." But the iconography of Mary was well known in Rome from 432–440 (triumphal arch of S. Maria Maggiore). See especially Maria Regina *orans* in the destroyed Oratory of John VII,

FIGURE 6.2 Rome, S. Prassede. Restored crypt painting with Praxedes and Pudentiana flanking the Virgin. Photograph by Mary M. Schaefer

cosmatesque altar at the head of the rearranged crypt.[118] The sisters wear a brocaded, diagonally draped dalmatic over their under-tunic, with external sash hanging down in front. A broad, reddish-brown band of cloth covers their shoulders. Aloisi referred to stoles about their necks. Typically the female deacon's stole was visible at the neck, the longest section being covered by the dalmatic with its ends emerging at the hem.[119] What did Aloisi

---

dedicated 706 in St. Peter's (Waetzoldt, *Kopien des 17. Jahrhunderts*, fig. 478; Eileen Rubery, "Pope John VII's Devotion to Mary: Papal Images of Mary from the Fifth to the Early Eighth Centuries," in Maunder, *Origins of the Cult of the Virgin Mary*, 155–99).

118. See Baldracco, "La cripta," 290, and on the painting's removal from the original surface to canvas and subsequent salvage, Caperna, *Basilica di Santa Prassede*, 114. The second painting on the north of the *camera delle reliquie* depicting two women on either side of a bare cross appears to have been destroyed; for a similar composition, see the apse at S. Stefano Rotondo, ca. 650 (Krautheimer, *Rome*, fig. 78).

119. The rubric from the 10th-century diaconal ordination rite reads, "Episcopus cum diaconam benedicit, orarium in collo eius ponit. Quando autem ad ecclesiam procedit, portat illud super collum suum, sic vero ut summitas orarii ex utraque parte sub tunica sit" (*PRG* X, 1: XXIV.1).

mean by stola?[120] Given the history of the word, it seems likely that he used the term in the technical sense of the orarium/stola vestment.

The fresco has been badly damaged at the bottom. At the feet of the figure on the right, Aloisi read the title "Pudentiana." The titles of the other figures were indecipherable. However, close inspection reveals that a broad ochre band of cloth, different from the external sash, emerges from under Praxedes' dalmatic. The closest artistic analogy to this ochre band is found on the earliest known icon of Christ, the sixth-century Byzantine "portrait" discovered in St. Catherine's Monastery, Sinai, where the ochre undercoating retains traces of its original gilding. There the argument can be made that the senatorial clavus (approximating what will become an orarion or stole but not yet distinct from its classical prototype) symbolizes Christ's dignity and priesthood. We have seen these golden clavi signifying the dignity of the pregnant Mary and Elizabeth in the mosaic depictions of the Annunciation and Visitation at Parenzo's sixth-century Euphrasiana basilica.[121] This fresco of Praxedes and Pudentiana dating from Paschal's building campaign has good claim to show the sisters as diaconas or presbyteras, while the image of Mary blessing those who venerated her picture would suggest a qualified episcopal-abbatial status. On the south the sunken confessio, accessed from the nave by a few steps down, its fresco placed within a lunette, replicated the catacomb burial of family members or notable persons. On the north the "altarino" or predella in front of sarcophagus B, thought to contain the relics of the two sisters, identified

---

120. In ancient Rome the stola (not the orarium) was an undertunic with fitted sleeves, the wristlets sometimes embroidered, worn by women of imperial and noble families; see Rubery, "Pope John VII's Devotion to Mary," in Maunder, *Origins of Cult of Virgin Mary*, 199. Also called a stola (orarium) was a narrow face-towel which by the early medieval period had become a liturgical vestment worn exclusively by clergy (Ernst Hofhansl, "Gewänder, liturgische," *TRE* 13 [1984]: 159–67 at 163). In Italy in recent centuries, a cape or scarf worn by matrons and mothers was sometimes called a stola. But this would not be described as "a stole at the neck." Besides, the sisters were virgins.

121. Weitzmann, *Monastery of Saint Catherine: Icons*, 13–15 and pl. B1. At Parenzo the women's tunics are adorned with broad golden clavi, sign of senatorial dignity. While all the male figures including Bishop Euphrasius wear traditional classical garb, white tunics bearing two narrow dark purple bands (the clavi of the equestran order), the enthroned Virgin-mother's fringed pallium hangs between two broad golden bands emerging from under her outer garment. They appear to be attached to the garment, having a width and prominence distinguishing them from the clavi worn by ecclesiastics and martyrs. In the Annunciation scene the Virgin Mary's golden orarium, following the curves of her body, can be seen through her translucent shawl. In the Visitation Elizabeth wears both pallium and broad golden orarium. Mary is depicted with pallium and two single lines of gold tesserae ornamenting the vertical lines of her royal violet garment.

the relic area and gave limited access from the axial corridor. To enhance the mimetic cemeterial impression, inscriptions from various catacombs were built into the annular corridor.

E. The Chancel Barrier

A number of whitish slabs carved with abstract geometric or foliate figures in low relief, some filled with interlace, were discovered when the nave floor was renovated in the early twentieth century; they are presently attached to the walls of the Crucifixion Chapel east of the presbytery.[122] Such slabs, fixed between low piers or colonnettes, formed chancel barriers about one meter high that, at least from the sixth century, separated the space of the presbytery and the demarcated area in front of it, areas used by clergy and monastics respectively, from the people who occupied the unencumbered space of nave and aisles. Its architectural predecessor was the Byzantine solea or walled processional way leading from the chancel to the ambo in the center of the nave.[123] Goodson describes the structure as a barrier creating a zone in front of the presbytery with walls projecting into the nave allowing laity to approach from three sides.[124] The existence of these chancel slabs at S. Prassede led Davanzati to reflect on the ministry of a *diaconissa* or *presbiteressa*, who, in his thinking, would have stood within the enclosure during the liturgy. The references to and speculations about women's ordained ministry in the early churches recurring throughout the prior's guidebook doubtless led the commission

---

122. Goodson, *Rome of Pope Paschal I*, 138–43 and fig. 21.

123. In early churches seating was provided for senior clergy while the populace stood; the assembly was therefore mobile. In Byzantium the solea was a processional way for the ministers that linked the chancel area and its barrier to the ambo standing free within the nave. *LP* attributes the commissioning of cancelli (barrier slabs) to Constantine in Rome, where the solea was transformed into a wider demarcated area in front of the presbytery, which later came to be called the "schola cantorum." In this protected space, liturgical ministry could be exercised without jostling by the assembly. But whose ministry? Scholars now agree that this area served monastics or canons for celebrating the liturgy of the hours. A chancel barrier is displayed in the Romanesque chapel in the Metropolitan Museum of Art, New York, while in the upper (12th-century) church of S. Clemente, Rome, chancel barriers, the choir, and two ambos are still intact. The Roman evidence has been discussed by Mathews, "Early Roman Chancel Arrangement and Liturgical Uses," 73–95 with special reference to S. Sabina, Rome. The evidence for churches of East and West has been reviewed by Stephen G. Xydis, "The Chancel Barrier, Solea, and Ambo of Hagia Sophia," *Art Bulletin* 29 (1947): 1–24.

124. Goodson, *Rome of Pope Paschal I*, 138–43 and figs. 13, 21.

charged with revising the Roman martyrology under Pope Benedict XIV (1740–1758) to declare Praxedes' *vita* a fable.[125]

4. Paschal and the Easter Ceremonies

Recent scholarship has emphasized linkages between the spiritual and political role of the pope as head of the Republic of St. Peter, developments in the martyr-cult, and architectural changes to the high altar. In this section, my aim is to show the centrality of the liturgical commemoration of Holy and Easter weeks to Paschal's project at S. Prassede.

A. *Propitiatorium* and *Sancta Sanctorum*

Relics confer holiness on their place of repose. The opening prayer at the requisition of relics for a church dedication referred to the *sancta sanctorum* (the "Holy of Holies"), the confessio or relic-altar of the church from which the relics were to be collected for translation. In treating of Christ's entrance into the Holy Place with his own blood, Hebrews 9:2–12 describes the Tent-Sanctuary used by the Israelites in the desert. The Holy Place with its appurtenances (seven-branched lampstand and offering-table for the bread of the Presence) was distinguished from the Holy of Holies where the square golden altar of incense, the manna, and Aaron's rod (cf. Exod 25:17–22 for the Tent of Meeting, and 1 Kgs 6 for Solomon's temple) were kept.[126] Its most precious furnishing was the ark of the covenant (referred to as the *kapporeth*, "throne of mercy," "mercy seat," or *propitiatorium*, and thought of as a kind of archive of the law)

---

125. Although Praxedes' feast has been suppressed in the current martyrology, she is invoked as patroness in her church. The discovery of an actual burial with bones attributable to Praxedes and Pudentiana must have caused some discomfiture in the rationalistic Enlightenment.

126. The high priestly connotation is apparent in the lectionary's use of Heb 9:2–12 for Ember Saturday in September (fols. 158–159 in Vat. ms. lat. 8701). By the 9th century, references to Temple priesthood were read as types of the "sacerdotes" (bishops and presbyters) of the Christian dispensation. Once the altar or relic-place was equated with the *sancta sanctorum*, steps were taken to separate it architecturally from the assembly. This was a marked departure from earlier practice in several regions of the Christian world including Rome, North Africa, and Lebanon, where the altar had been located at the head of or near the center of the nave so that the people could gather on three sides. Thus the reference in the old Roman mass canon to the "circumadstantes" (Jungmann, *Mass of the Roman Rite*, 2:166).

covered on all sides with gold, its golden lid overshadowed by two cherubim. The Holy of Holies was entered only by the high priest and only on Yom Kippur, when he smeared the lid or propitiatory with sacrificial blood (Lev 16:14–20).[127] In *LP* the term *propitiatorium* appears seven times in all, but only in connection with two ninth-century popes: six times in Paschal I's life and once in that of Leo IV (847–855).[128] Uncertain of the word's meaning, Richard Krautheimer identified it with the front face of the altar (altar frontal), a panel, or a jewel-encrusted golden crown. Although the scriptural reference to the *propitiatorium* as a "lid" suggests that it could best be equated with the tabula (horizontal slab) that covered and sealed the relics in their subterranean depository, Sybille de Blaauw expressly rejects that possibility.[129] Goodson follows De Blaauw, saying that at S. Maria in Domnica it was "a metal panel that surrounded the opening into the confessio."[130] The *LP* informs us that the propitiatory surrounding the *fenestella confessionis* or small grilled window into the confessio at S. Prassede was sheathed in silver. In conjunction with the propitiatory Paschal provided an image or statue: "And at the virgin's holy body he presented an image with silver sheets in relief, weighing 99 lbs."[131]

Although *LP* uses *propitiatorium* chiefly in connection with Paschal's relic-altars or depositories, the notion of the Holy of Holies seems already

---

127. *Jerome Biblical Commentary* (Englewood Cliffs, N.J.: Prentice Hall, 1968), 711–13 (sect. 76:44–48).

128. Davis, *Lives of Ninth-Century Popes*, 315 (glossary) lists 100.6, 10, 11, 19, 31, 38 (Paschal I) and 105.109 (Leo IV), with opinions by various authors. At S. Prassede Paschal "also wondrously adorned the holy altar's *propitiatorium* with silver sheets. He beautifully embellished and gilded her confessio, with its grills...." (100.10). At S. Cecilia he "finished and marvelously embellished the holy altar's *propitiatorium* and the confessio inside and out, and its grills, with silver sheets...." (100.19).

129. At least when the relics were deposited below the altar and separate from it. De Blaauw (*Cultus et decor*, 537–38) describes it as a metal sheet which covers the altar block and frames the "fenestella confessionis." The term "propitiatorium" was also favoured at Theodulf's oratory at Germigny-des-Prés and in the *Libri Carolini* (ibid.).

130. Goodson, *Rome of Pope Paschal I*, 142.

131. Krautheimer (*CBCR* 3:235) paraphrases "a silver-plated statue or relief." Davis *(Lives of Ninth-Century Popes*, 100.10, n. 34) notes that "'praefiguratis' seems to mean 'in relief.'" Relief was likelier than a free-standing statue. Paschal's other gifts are detailed: a silver canopy over the altar weighed 910 lbs.; a golden crown with gems 5 lbs. 2 1/2 oz.; 300 lbs. of silver for silver sheets for the altar's propitiatorium and for the gilded barriers and grating of the confessio (ibid., 100.10; as later at S. Cecilia (ibid., 100.19; see Goodson, *Rome of Pope Paschal I*, 246–47).

to have been given concrete form by the later eighth century.[132] The *basilica Sancti Laurentii de palatio*, the small private oratory of the popes at the Lateran Palace, is first clearly mentioned by *LP* in the life of Stephen III (768–772) and was called probably from the time of Leo III the *Sancta Sanctorum*.[133] It was located above the *scrinium* or archives of the holy Roman church that contained documents, relics, and papal memorabilia; the chapel is now reached by the stairs called the *Scala Santa*.[134] The procession that formed upon the election of a pope stopped at this chapel on its way from the chapel of St. Silvester to the Lateran Palace.[135] The chapel's incorporation into stational liturgies developed as the person of the pope achieved greater theological and political prominence.[136]

B. The Stations of Holy Week

Official liturgical visits of the popes to most of the *tituli*, the papal pastoral outposts with their own clergy, were scheduled annually.[137] Basing

---

132. Jungmann (*Mass of the Roman Rite*, 2:104) discusses the performance of the eucharistic prayer by the Carolingian period, citing a comment in *Ordo romanus I* (ca. 700): "surgit pontifex solus et intrat in canone." The eucharistic prayer following the Sanctus is the holy of holies reserved for the presider alone and "even the bystanders cannot hear it."

133. Davis, *Lives of Eighth-Century Popes*, 96.4. The papal chapel has been claimed as dating from the end of the 4th to mid-5th centuries when the Roman curia was established (Mario Cempanari and Tito Amodei, *Scala Santa e Sancta Sanctorum* [Rome: Edizioni Quasar, 1999], 63). A wooden cabinet made of cypress enclosed within a gated iron grill and supporting the altar bears an inscription attributing the relic-cabinet to Leo III. The small tablet so inscribed is separate from the cabinet (von Matt, *Art Treasures of Vatican Library*, 74; Cempanari and Amodei, *Scala Santa*, fig. 63); it is now dated to the 13th century and the case made for its replacing a tablet from Leo III's time (Thunø, *Image and Relic*, 160–61).

134. Cempanari and Amodei, *Scala Santa*, 14–18. Later the appurtenances of the Holy of Holies listed in Heb 9 would be claimed as included in the altar in the Savior's basilica. See Sible de Blaauw, "The Solitary Celebration of the Supreme Pontiff: The Lateran Basilica as the New Temple in the Medieval Liturgy of Maundy Thursday," in Charles Caspers and Marc Schneiders, eds., *Omnes circumadstantes: Contributions Towards a History of the Role of the People in the Liturgy: Presented to Herman Wegman on the Occasion of his Retirement from the Chair of History and Theology in the Katholieke Theologische Universiteit Utrecht* (Kampion: J. H. Kok, 1990), 120–43.

135. Von Matt, *Art Treasures of the Vatican Library*, 73.

136. Cempanari and Amodei, *Scala Santa*, 82.

137. Antoine Chavasse, "Les célébrations eucharistiques à Rome, Ve–VIIIe siècle," *EO* 7 (1990), 69–75. At first the Lateran, the Jerusalem church, and St. Mary Major's, St. Stephen's rotunda, the Apostolorum and S. Maria in Trastevere within the city and St. Peter's and St. Paul's Outside the Walls had no clergy of their own. Clerics from the various regions were coopted for papal celebrations. These spacious basilicas were utilized on great feastdays when multitudes participated in liturgical functions.

his comment on the researches of Hartmann Grisar, John Baldovin says, "[T]here is a dialectical relationship between the choice of stations and the readings from Scripture. It is often difficult to tell whether the reading or the *statio* was selected first."[138] With respect to the Holy Week stations, Grisar claimed that the formularies were so governed by Christ's passion that ties between the Scripture of the day and the church's saint or local customs completely vanished.[139] During Holy Week venues appropriate to the day were utilized, including the great basilicas closest to the papal palace that, in an anomaly of history, were located far from the population centers. Crowds could be expected on Palm Sunday and Holy Wednesday, Thursday, and Easter Sunday. The Good Friday service with the pope presiding took place at "Jerusalem," Helena's palace along the Aurelian wall dedicated to the holy cross. Clergy especially would attend there; liturgies that included readings, prayers, veneration of the cross, and a communion service would be celebrated also at the *tituli*. The invariable stations for Holy Week were:[140]

Palm Sunday (*Dominica indulgentia*) at "Our Saviour's," the Lateran[141]
Holy Monday (feria II) at SS. Nereus ed Achilleus near the Caracalla baths[142]

---

138. Baldovin, *Urban Character of Christian Worship*, 154, citing Hartmann Grisar, *Das Missale im Lichte römischer Stadtgeschichte* (Freiburg im Breisgau: Herder, 1925), 19–84.

139. Grisar, *Missale im Lichte römischer Stadtgeschichte*, 50. Others accept his opinion, e.g., Willis, *Further Essays in Early Roman Liturgy*, 84.

140. The list of Holy Week stations given in the Würzburg epistolary (ca. 600) is the same also in "Alcuin" (626/7 or later), Murbach (the ms. is from Alsace, ca. 775 belonging to Family B, ca. 740), Paris, B.N. lat 9451 (Verona, late 8th century), and Type Γ of the Roman *capitulare evangeliorum*.

141. In Jerusalem the Saturday before the Sunday of Palms was known as Lazarus Saturday because the gospel telling of Jesus' resuscitation of Lazarus would foreshadow his own resurrection. Sunday's reading beginning the procession with palms was John 12:12–18. A 4th-century pilgrim's description of the liturgies is given in John Wilkinson, *Egeria's Travels to the Holy Land* (rev. ed.; Jerusalem: Ariel Publishing, 1981), 131–32.

142. Herman Geertman, *More Veterum*, 106. First called the *titulus Fasciolae*, its saints were originally buried in the Domitilla catacomb. The stational liturgy had already been moved to S. Prassede when Leo III rebuilt the church on a new site. Krautheimer (*Rome*, 111) attributes the deaconry to Leo. Stational celebrations were typically situated across the seven regions of the city with Monday stations usually in the fourth region; see Antoine Chavasse, "L'organisation stationale du Carême romain avant le VIIIe siècle: une organisation 'pastorale,'" *RSR* 56 [1982]: 17–32. But SS. Nereus ed Achilleus was in region I and S. Praxedis in region III.

Holy Tuesday (feria III) at S. Prisca on the Aventine
Holy Wednesday (feria IIII) at St. Mary Major's, the "Manger church" on the Esquiline
Holy Thursday at the Lateran
Good Friday at S. Croce in Gerusalemme ("Jerusalem," Helena's Sessorian palace)
Holy Saturday at the Lateran Baptistry and the Lateran, "Our Savior's"
Holy Sunday (Easter) at St. Mary Major's

In all the early lectionary lists, Sts. Nereus and Achilleus with its gospel telling of Mary of Bethany's anointing of Jesus six days before his passion (reading the whole or a part of John's chapter 12) was the feria II (Holy Monday) station. This little church down the hill from the Lateran was turned into a diaconia sometime between 600 and 776/777. Its place among the stations was taken by S. Prassede around the mid-eighth century. The Gregorian *Hadrianum* is the first extant manuscript to designate S. Prassede as the Holy Monday station (H 74).[143] Although a *titulus*, until this point S. Prassede had not been utilized as a stational church at any time during the year.

A "woman's story" set in Bethany forms a memorable component of both the Sunday and Monday gospels inaugurating Holy Week.[144] The story of the woman who anoints Jesus' head from her alabaster jar (Matt 26:6–13) is inserted into machinations against him that introduce the lengthy Passion reading for Palm Sunday (Matt 26:1–27:66). Jesus commends her "folly": "...she has prepared me for burial.... [W]hat she has done will be told in memory of her" (vv. 12, 13). From the time of the earliest lectionaries or lists, Holy Monday had had as its gospel reading a portion of John's chapter 12. The lection might be as short as twelve

---

143. *Hadrianum* contains the very same four prayers (H 74, *feria II ad sanctam praxidem*) that had already appeared in *Paduense* (LXVIIII) for *feria II ad sanctos Nereum et Achillen*. See Deshusses, *Sacr. grég.*, 1:168–69 and 629, where SS. Nereus ed Achilleus was still the Holy Monday station. *Hadrianum* dates from between 735 and before 784–791, by which time it had certainly arrived in Aachen.

144. Mark 14:3–9 and Matt 26:6–13 recount the same episode. Two days before the Passover a woman at a dinner in Simon the leper's house at Bethany brings ointment in an alabaster jar and anoints Jesus' head (Mark 14:3, Matt 26:7). Luke places this or a similar episode earlier in Jesus' ministry (Luke 7:36–50) when a sinner-woman with alabaster jar at Simon the Pharisee's house (v. 37) anoints Jesus' feet and wipes them with her hair. Six days before Passover Mary of Bethany (John 12:1–8) performs the same prophetic gesture. In this instance alone no alabaster vase is mentioned.

verses or as many as thirty-six.[145] The Holy Monday commemoration of the anointing of Jesus at Bethany six days before his death at *titulus Praxedis* approximated the time period before the passion. An alabaster vase mounted prominently above the entrance to the Zeno Chapel proclaims the affinity between the women's actions in proleptically preparing Christ for his burial and Praxedes' ministry of burying the martyred dead. Prisc(ill)a, patron of the Holy Tuesday station, would have been, in the popular mind, readily identified with Paul's helper and with the Priscilla of the well-known cemetery. Besides, Prisca and Aquila are named in 2 Timothy 4:19, Pudens in 2 Timothy 4:21 and, according to the pilgrims' itineraries, all were buried near one another in the Priscilla cemetery. S. Maria Maggiore, with its lengthy reading of Luke's passion account (22:1–23:53), was the Wednesday station. From the seventh century, St. Mary Major's had claimed the relics of the manger at Bethlehem; the association between the wood of the manger and the wood of the cross was easily made in Holy Week. With the transferal of Monday's stational liturgy to S. Prassede, the Monday, Tuesday, and Wednesday of Holy Week as well as Easter Sunday mass were now celebrated at churches dedicated to women. The configuration of Holy Week services, presided by the pope and culminating in the greatest festival of the Christian year, was given increased meaning by S. Prassede's introduction to the stational list. This complex of locales evoked memories of those holy women who mourned for Jesus during his passion and, going to the tomb to anoint his corpse, were surprised by Christ risen.

C. The Paschal Triduum

The annual stational celebrations featuring the pope, his assisting clerics, and his entourage would have shaped Paschal's perception of St. Praxedes and her place within the liturgical-devotional life of the city-church. Holy Thursday, the day for confecting the holy oils of which chrism was preeminent, might not be thought to figure in our exposition. However, the sacramental use of

---

145. Jerusalem's customs inspired Roman ones, where John 12:1–36 was read on Monday of Holy Week. Verses 1–8 recount Mary of Bethany's anointing of Jesus' feet "six days before the Passover" in preparation for his burial; vv. 9–10 tell of the plot to kill Lazarus; vv. 12–19 give John's account of the triumphal entry; vv. 20–32 include Jesus' soliloquy about his coming death. Antoine Chavasse ("Le calendrier dominical romain au sixième siècle," *Recherches de science religieuse* 41 [1953]: 96–122 at 118, n. 56) reviews the use of John 12 as a Lenten reading in the West.

oil is founded on its natural properties of enhancing bodily well-being, healing, and covering over the stench of decay. Jesus' washing of his disciples' feet (John 13:1–16) was the immediate precedent; however, the pope's washing of feet also evoked the ministry of Mary of Bethany who had anointed Jesus' feet with precious ointment and wiped them with her hair.

The paschal Triduum, with its physically taxing services presided by the pope, was celebrated in the vicinity of his palace: at "Our Savior" (also called St. John's in the Lateran from the seventh century); at "Jerusalem," Helena's basilica of Santa Croce up the street; at St. Mary Major's, a decent processional distance away; and also in the pope's private chapel dedicated to St. Lawrence, the Sancta Sanctorum. A ninth-century manuscript of Einsiedeln Abbey gives an account of the ceremonies of the last three days of Holy Week as transcribed by an observant northern pilgrim to Rome, certainly a liturgist, between circa 700 and 750.[146] On Holy Thursday at the seventh hour (early to mid-afternoon), the pope entered the Lateran for the eucharist at which the chrism was blessed; then he repaired to the Sancta Sanctorum for the *mandatum* or foot washing ceremony. The liturgical development of the Holy Thursday eucharist as the one "solitary" celebration of the pope at the Lateran's high altar illustrates the development of the papal person and office as antitype for the liturgical activity of the high priest in the Jerusalem Temple.[147]

On Good Friday at the eighth hour (mid-afternoon), the pope, barefoot, left the Lateran Palace for St. John's; there the procession, chanting the lengthy Psalm 118 (119), *Beati immaculati*, formed for "Hierusalem."[148] The archdeacon held the left hand of the pope, who carried in his right a thurible with incense, with a deacon behind the pope carrying "the wood of the precious cross" in a golden casket (*capsa*), ornamented with gems,

---

146. Einsiedeln Abbey, ms. 326 (Andrieu, OR Ordo XXIII, 3:265–73; Baldovin, *Urban Character of Christian Worship*, 136).

147. See the 7th-century Roman *ordo* "et altare est cavum" (*Ordo* feria V2; Antoine Chavasse, "A Rome, le Jeudi-Saint, au VIIe siècle, d'après un vieil ordo," *Revue d'histoire écclésiastique* 50 [1955]: 21–35); Sible de Blaauw, "Solitary Celebration of Supreme Pontiff," 120–43. Altar and column screen had changed over time at St. Peter's, the most recent renovation copied in Paschal's S. Prassede and at S. Maria Maggiore.

148. Ps 118 (119), "Beati immaculati," was chanted, its antiphon probably "Behold the wood of the Cross on which hung the salvation of the world"; see Patrick Regan, "Veneration of the Cross," *Worship* 52 (1978): 2–13 at 4.

oil confected with balsam providing a sweet odor inside the cavity.[149] Arriving at "Jerusalem," the deacon placed the casket on the altar, and the "apostolic lord" opened it, prostrated and prayed; kissing the cross, he went to his chair. As soon as the pope kissed the cross, the service of readings began.[150]

Holy Saturday recalled Jesus' descent to the realm of the just dead (1 Pet 3:18) to release the "spirits in prison."[151] St. John Lateran figured in the Easter Vigil liturgy. Baptisms were, of course, celebrated at the Lateran baptistry. However, early on Easter morning the pope's liturgy commenced again at the Sancta Sanctorum. The pope adored at his private altar and kissed the feet of the image of the *Acheiropoietos*, the treasured image of Christ "made without hands."[152] Then solemnly he processed to S. Maria Maggiore for the stational mass of this "holy Sunday," the pope announcing the good news of the resurrection to the people.[153]

---

149. The *capsa* probably held the gemmed cross of the 6th or 7th century that disappeared from the Vatican Museum in the last century; see Cempanari and Amodei, *Scala Santa*, fig. 64; Petrignani, *Il santuario della Scala Santa*, fig. 36. The cruciform reliquary casket of Paschal's commissioning bore 17 reliefs, most depicting post-resurrection episodes, and appropriate for a cross-relic. Rings were attached at the upper and lower edges of the central relief of Christ presiding at the eucharist. The reliquary could be hung from these rings or slung from poles for carrying. Later a handle was added. The extant cushion for cradling the cross-relic is saturated with perfumed oils.

150. All the bishops and other ministers venerated the wood of the cross at the altar. It was then put on the *arcellam ad rugas*, a movable balustrade in front of the sanctuary, and the *populus*, that is, the males present, venerated it. Finally, it was carried to another part of the church for veneration by the women. Following the general intercessions (*orationes sollemnes*), the clergy returned to the Lateran in procession again chanting psalm 118 (119). Neither pope nor deacons communicated. Others at the Jerusalem church might receive bread consecrated on Holy Thursday or go to their *tituli* for a liturgy of the presanctified to communicate from the bread consecrated on the previous day and wine consecrated by *immixtio*, the placement of a particle of consecrated bread in an unconsecrated cup. On Good Friday rites, see Louis van Tongeren, "A Sign of Resurrection on Good Friday: The Role of the People in the Good Friday Liturgy until c. 1000 A.D. and the Meaning of the Cross," in Caspers and Schneiders, *Omnes circumadstantes*, 101–19.

151. According to the Johannine chronology, Jesus died on the day of Preparation for the Passover (John 19:14, 31, 42). The sabbath following was "a day of great solemnity."

152. Innocent III (1198–1216) had all but the head of the Acheiropoietos covered with an ornamental metal sheet. Two silver flaps (14th century?) covered the feet; each contained two pictures in low relief. These flaps could be opened so that the feet could be anointed and, on Easter, kissed (Cempanari and Amodei, *Scala Santa*, 95 and pl. XXVII; von Matt, *Art Treasures of the Vatican Library*, 73–74).

153. Cempanari and Amodei, *Scala Santa*, 83–84. During the procession to St. Mary's the pope was informed of the number of persons initiated during the Easter Vigil.

D. Easter Week

The celebration of Easter week did not put rigorous demands on the pope. Papal liturgical celebrations could be situated in the large basilicas and spread expansively across the city and even outside the walls, with lections suited to the venues.[154] The gospels retold the resurrection story. Thursday's and Saturday's readings in Murbach featured Mary Magdalene (John 20:11, John 20:1). The first lections were related to the specific station. Monday of the Easter octave was held at St. Peter's with the reading of Acts 10:36; Tuesday at St. Paul's Outside the Walls, with Acts 13:26.[155] Wednesday was at St. Laurence's (Acts 3:12); Thursday *Ad apostolos*.[156] Friday's station was held *ad sca mariam* (S. Maria ad Martyres).[157] Saturday's station, the first week's anniversary for the newly baptized and that day when the white baptismal robes were laid aside, returned to the Lateran, dedicated to Our Savior and the Baptist. Its epistle (1 Pet 2:1–10) instructed the neophytes about their belonging to a "holy priesthood" that offered spiritual sacrifices. Fittingly too the octave day of Easter was celebrated at the Lateran, when the epistle 1 John 5:4 proclaimed Jesus as God's Son and the Spirit as witness. Its gospel John 20:19–29 described Thomas' encounter with Jesus in the upper room on the Sunday following Easter. Akin to the associations of persons, times, and places in the liturgical memorials of the passion and death of Jesus celebrated during Holy Week, most of the Easter week epistle readings from Acts and 1 Peter, which represented apostolic "sermons," related to their specific venues.

This book has provided numerous instances showing that Paschal's S. Prassede was shaped by his meditation on the lives and ministries of Praxedes and Pudentiana and their colleagues. Did Paschal understand his own name as shaping his destiny? That Easter was central in Paschal's

---

154. The readings for Easter week are already found in the Würzburg lectionary (590/600) and in Murbach, the Franco-Roman lectionary (Family B, from ca. 740), which gives incipits of both epistles and gospels. Acts 10:36 shows Peter preaching Christ's resurrection on the third day (Chavasse, "Plus anciens types du lectionnaire," 3–94 at 73–74).

155. Paul preaches "God raised [Christ] from the dead."

156. "Ad apostolos" was dedicated to Sts. Philip and James. The Acts 8:26 pericope features Philip baptizing the queen of Ethiopia's eunuch on the road to Gaza.

157. 1 Pet 3:18–22 speaks of Christ, while his flesh lay in the tomb on the sabbath, descending "in the spirit" to preach to "the spirits in prison," that is, proclaiming salvation to the souls of the just in Hades. It also refers to Noah's flood, type of baptism whose solemn celebration is concluded the following day.

spiritual consciousness is suggested by the cruciform reliquary he commissioned, most of whose scenes retell resurrection episodes. Rebuilding and embellishing the *titulus Praxedis* allowed Paschal to develop the Easter theme that his papal name trumpeted while publicly establishing his close spiritual relationship with the saintly daughters of the Pudens family whose ministries reached their highpoint in the celebration of Easter baptisms in their house-church.[158] The iconography inspired by the book of Revelation, which typified the decorative programs of the patriarchal basilicas of Peter, Paul and the Lateran, resonates with Easter echoes. Paschal's commission employs these allusions to shape a daring conceit on his name. Alumnus of the Lateran school of the popes, Paschal was "imbued with studies of the divine and life-giving scriptures."[159] His monogram, placed at the apex of both the apsidal and triumphal arches, situates the papal patron within the program's global symbolism and links him to the pontificate of Pius I (142?–155), whom *LP* credited with fixing the Easter celebration on Sunday, the Lord's Day.

5. The "Liturgical Personality" of Saint Praxedes

Praxedes' popularity came into its own under Carolingian popes. The sacramentary known as *Hadrianum*, already archaic when Hadrian I (772–795) sent it to Charlemagne, located the Holy Monday station for the papal liturgy *ad sanctam Praxidem*. Hadrian restored her old *titulus*. The gospel pericope long established for that day, John's chapter 12 with its chronology *ante sex dies paschae*, recounts the anticipatory preparation of Jesus' body for burial by Mary of Bethany, sister of Lazarus. Praxedes could easily be read as Mary of Bethany's Roman antitype.[160] Even before Paschal's ecclesiastical career gave him the opportunity to rebuild the *titulus* Hadrian had restored, St. Praxedes' community center had occupied a prominent place

---

158. The pope's "paschal connection" was reinforced when on Easter Sunday, 5 April 823, he crowned Lothar Emperor and Augustus (Davis, *Lives of Ninth-Century Popes*, 2).

159. Davis, *Lives of Ninth-Century Popes*, 100.1.

160. The long reading for Holy Monday, John 12:1–36, is found in a late 6th-century uncial fragment of a full lectionary containing both epistles and gospels (Munich, Clm. 29155). See K. Gamber, "Das Münchner Fragment eines Lectionarium Plenarium aus dem Ende des 6. Jahrhunderts," *EL* 72 (1958): 268–80 at 269–75, as also in Paris, B.N. lat. 9451 (Amiet, "Un '*Comes*' Carolingien," 348). Either the short or long reading would resonate with the Praxedes story and iconography.

in Roman liturgical celebration. Paschal did not "discover" or "make" Praxedes' reputation. By the mid-eighth century Praxedes possessed a liturgical persona related to the most solemn week of the liturgical year.

Reflection on the dialectical relationship between a given stational church for Holy and Easter weeks and the liturgical memorial celebrated there suggests the usefulness of such an inquiry also for those lections chosen for the feastday celebrations of St. Praxedes and her sister. We saw that women not martyred were slow to acquire lections for festal celebrations. The Würzburg epistle-lectionary (590/600) does not include the sisters' feasts on their *natale* and names few women in its sanctoral. However, the seventh century, perhaps as early as Honorius I, marks women's inclusion as public spiritual figures in the Roman church. St. Praxedes' feast first appeared, slightly out of place, in the Würzburg evangeliary list of circa 645 that contained only gospels. Thereafter the gospel reading for the feast of Praxedes, "The kingdom of heaven is like a treasure hidden in a field...." (*Simile est regnum caelorum thesauro,* Matt 13:44–52), remained constant. The parables regarding the merchant's sale of everything to buy the field or the pearl, and the concluding verse referring to the figure of the householder (οἰκοδεσπότης), "every scribe who has been trained for the kingdom of heaven is like a householder who brings out of his treasure what is new and what is old" (v. 52), well-suited the Praxedes story.[161] Pudentiana's feast was noted in May (*die XVIIII*) but without a gospel. Showing its novelty, the copyist inserted it incorrectly before an entry for the Wednesday preceding Ascension Thursday.[162]

In the seventh-century "Alcuin" epistolary, readings from Ecclesiasticus (Sirach) were frequently chosen for commons of saints. The lections for Praxedes and Pudentiana listed in early Roman epistolaries equated the sisters with Wisdom figures, a parallel later extended to other virgin saints. The Franco-Roman Murbach lectionary gave Ecclesiasticus (Sirach) (Ecclus/Sir 51:1, *Confitebor tibi*; Ecclus/Sir 51:13–17, *Domine Deus meus exaltasti*; Ecclus/Sir 24:1, *Sapientia laudabit*) a prominent role in its choices of lections for commons of virgins (CXIIII). Also listed were the book of Wisdom 7:30b

---

161. Morin, "Liturgie et basiliques," 311 and n. 1. The other gospel pericope early established for virgins' commemorations was the parable of the ten virgins, *Simile est regnum caelorum decim virginibus* (Matt 25:1).

162. Ibid., 306 and n. 2.

(*Sapientia vincit*) and 1 Corinthians 7:25 (*De virginibus autem*), setting the pattern for the Roman lectionary until 1969.[163]

Ecclesiasticus (Sirach) 24, the book's "pivotal chapter," is based on Proverbs 8:22–31.[164] The earliest first reading we have for *natale sanctae praxitis* is Lady Wisdom's eulogy of herself, *Sapientia laudabit* (Ecclus/Sir 24:1), in Murbach.[165] Christian exegesis applied the text to the preexistent Word. The continuous Wisdom reading—if, for instance, read from a Bible or a collection of Wisdom books—might have included the following: "Before the ages, in the beginning, he created me, and for all the ages I shall not cease to be. In the holy tent I ministered before him, and so I was established in Zion."[166] Roland E. Murphy notes that personified Lady Wisdom, who is more than a "personified order of creation" but "somehow identified with the Lord" as God's self-revelation, "leads the liturgical service in the Holy Tent."[167] Murphy invites comparison of the

---

163. Murbach (Family B, ca. 740) gives the incipits for both first reading and gospel but does not provide full texts or indicate endings. We cannot be sure what was the length and exact content of lections read in a particular liturgy. For virgins the gospel is Matt 13:44 or Matt 25:1. Murbach has added numerous saints' feasts as well as commons, but gives no feast of Pudentiana, Marina, or Mary of Magdala. Transcribed in northern Italy or Gaul, Vat. Reg. lat. ms. 74 (late 8th century) is close to the Murbach lectionary, witnessing to the pure Roman epistles and gospels about the time of Paschal's pontificate (Dold, "Ein ausgeschriebenes Perikopenbuch," 12–37). But it yields no information for our enquiry. The late 8th-century purple *comes* from Verona (Paris, Bibl. Nat. lat. 9451, Roman family type B) gives for its common of virgins (nos. 484–88) Ecclus/Sir 24:11–20, 51:1–12, 51:13–17 as well as the two gospels above, dropping Ecclus/Sir 24:1. The 12th-century S. Prassede Epistolary (Vat. ms. lat. 8701) lists for Praxedes' first mass reading "Qui gloriatur in dno" (1 Cor 1:31, 185r); for Pudentiana "Mulierem fortem" (Prov 31:10, 180r).

164. Although formally known in Greek as *The Wisdom of Jesus, Son of Sira* (or *Sirach*), many mss. of the Latin Vulgate call Sirach *Ecclesiasticus*, the "book of the church." See Roland Murphy, *The Tree of Life: An Exploration of Biblical Wisdom Literature* (3rd ed.; Grand Rapids: MI: Eerdmans, 2002), 67.

165. A. Wilmart, "Le *Comes* de Murbach," 46 (*CXIIII/5*), misprinted "Eccli. XIV,1."

166. "Ab initio et ante saecula creata sum, et usque ad futurum saeculum non desinam: et in habitatione sancta coram ipso ministravi" (Ecclus/Sir 24:14 in the Vulgate). The numbering differs, v. 14 = v. 10 in modern editions translated from the Greek Septuagint. There is no Hebrew text for Ecclus/Sir 24. The textual history of this book is very complex; see *The Wisdom of Ben Sira*, by Patrick W. Skehan with introduction and commentary by Alexander A. DiLella (New York: Doubleday, 1987), 51–62, and *Biblia Sacra iuxta Latinam Vulgatam versionem ad codicum fidem*, vol. 12: *Sapientia Salomonis, Liber Hiesu filii Sirach* (Rome: Benedictines of San Girolamo Abbey, 1964). A much later epistolary originating outside Rome, Vatican Palat. lat. 497 (76r) of the 12th century, selects Ecclus/Sir 24: 1–5, 21b–22 of the Vulgate, its final verses comparing the female personification of Wisdom to incense that rises up in the temple. However, this ms. cannot witness to 9th century usages.

167. vv. 10–11. See Murphy, *Tree of Life*, 138–39.

figure of Wisdom and her liturgical work with that of Simon the high priest later in the text (Ecclus/Sir 50:5–21).[168] But there is a more important theological point to be made. A personified female figure, handmaid of the Creator, functions to explain the person of the incarnate Word. Jesus' depiction in the letter to the Hebrews is shaped by Wisdom-christology, expressed in his creative and iconic role in Hebrews 1:2–3 and again in Hebrews 8:2: "[W]e have such a high priest, ... ca minister in the sanctuary and the true tent."[169] Was the lection from the Wisdom of Sirach 24, a poem of great beauty, initially understood as pertaining in a special way to Praxedes and Pudentiana as leaders of a house-church, afterward becoming standard for the Virgin Mary? Did the pope's ceremonial actions as high priest of the church's worship and icon of the eternal Priest's mediatorial role in heaven not resonate with Wisdom's role in leading worship in the Holy Tent and even with that of Praxedes in her house-church? We have already noted that the multiple symbolic associations beloved by medievals were operative on Holy Monday at S. Prassede's stational celebration as well as during the paschal Triduum.[170]

6. A Ninth-Century Fresco and the Mariano Oratory at S. Pudenziana

Earlier in this chapter the damaged fresco in the lunette of S. Prassede's *confessio* was investigated for what it might reveal of early ninth-century beliefs about the ecclesial ministry of the sisters. Additional pictorial clues that Pudentiana and Praxedes enjoyed ecclesiastical standing are found at the sister-church of S. Pudenziana. High up under the ceiling of the now subterranean "house of Pudens," excavated in 1891, is a fresco in byzantinizing style dated to the second half of the ninth century. In the

---

168. Ibid., 263. Mary becomes antitype of Wisdom when Ecclus/Sir 24:11–31 (the verses selected may vary) are read on the vigil of the Assumption and her Nativity. On Assumption day Ecclus/Sir 24:11b–20 may be the lection.

169. Heb 1:3 (JB, note c), and *Jerome Biblical Commentary* 383 (sect. 61:7–8); Heb 8:1–2, 44, JBC 394–395 (sect. 61:44). Cf. LXX Ps 21:23; MT Ps 22:23.

170. Investigation of the manuscript tradition may yield further insights. In general it can be said that mss., especially those of the late Middle Ages, interchange the standard lections for virgins so that they lose their personality and are treated generically. "Alcuin" lists for the Virgin Mary Prov 31:10–31 ("A perfect wife"), Ecclus/Sir 24:23–31 and Wis 7:30b. Prov 31 was also occasionally forced into service for Pudentiana (Vat. ms. lat. 8701), Mary of Magdala, or Sabina.

rectangular niche three figures standing frontally, their heads disproportionately large, are clearly labeled: SCA PRAXEDES, SCS PETRUS, SCA POTENTIANA. The apostle wears a maniple (*mappula*) bearing a large initial "P." The two sisters, larger than Peter, hold the martyr's cross. Each wears an ochre tunic with maroon cloak, and on her left arm a maroon fringed maniple decorated with three horizontal bars.[171] Earlier serving as a functional item of dress for high civic officials and ecclesiastics, by the Carolingian period the maniple is an accoutrement of subdeacons to bishops.

The former convent's "Mariano" oratory behind the apse of S. Pudenziana opens onto Via Cesare Balbo but is inaccessible from the street. In 1915 the art historian C. R. Morey examined extant frescoes there. Over the altar is a painting of the two sisters garbed in dalmatics, offering crowns to the enthroned Madonna and Child. Under Mary's typical costume of blue tunic and reddish-violet palla with red ceremonial half-cape trimmed with a broad gold band, the end of a *loros*, a kind of Greek embroidered stole traditionally worn by members of the imperial family, is visible. The sisters' depiction in this fresco assists their identification in the damaged cycle of four paintings in two registers on the opposite wall. The oratory of Pastor in the body of the church had been restored during the pontificate of Gregory VII (1073–1085), but this cycle is probably somewhat later, in the first twenty years of the twelfth century.[172] The compositions reproduced and commented on by Morey a century ago on the basis of sixteenth- and seventeenth-century drawings allow a fuller reading.[173] In the upper left register Paul preaches to disciples, presumably including

---

171. Waetzoldt, *Kopien des 17. Jahrhunderts*, fig. 509, cat. no. 1001 (without hand cross); Richard Adelbert Lipsius, *Die apokryphen Apostelgeschichten und Apostellegenden: ein Beitrag zur altchristlichen Literaturgeschichte* (2 vols.; Braunschweig: Schwetschke, 1887), 2/1:418; J. Wilpert, *Römischen Mosaiken*, 1084 and pl. 218; Renzo U. Montini, *Santa Pudenziana* (Rome: Edizioni "Roma" [1958?]), 92 and fig. 27; Vanmaele, "Potenziana (Pudenziana) e Prassede," 10: 1063–64. On the maniple, see Andrieu, *OR* 4:135; Hofhansl, "Gewänder, liturgische," 162.

172. *La pittura medievale a Roma, 312–1431: corpus et atlante*, vol. 4: *Riforma e Tradizione, 1050–1198*, ed. Serena Romano (Milan: Jaca Book, 2006–), Pt. 2, 30. For descriptions, see in the same volume Jérôme Croisier, "La decorazione pittorica dell'oratorio mariano di Santa Pudenziana," 199–206 at 202. Four damaged scenes on the northeast wall illustrating high points in the lives of the Pudens siblings are accompanied by titles. Fragments showing personages from Cecilia's *vita* are on the northwest wall.

173. Antonio Eclissi [1588], Morey's Plate IV and fig. 9. On what was visible in the early 20th century see, C. R. Morey, *Lost Mosaics and Frescoes of Rome of the Mediaeval Period* (Princeton, NJ: Princeton University Press, 1915), 40–48.

Second Look at Myth, History, and Monument 365

FIGURE 6.3 Rome, S. Pudenziana. Mariano Chapel fresco. Ordination of Timothy (?), (early 12th century). Photograph by Kevin Moynihan.

Timothy, Novatus, Pudens, and the two sisters in the rear. Claiming the whole family as his disciples, the *titulus* reads: "The preaching of St. Paul to the Pudens family." In the right register Paul baptizes two nude men (Morey thinks they are Timothy and Novatus), while two women, probably Potentiana and Praxedes, one holding the tunic of a baptizand, stand beside the font. Much of the area of the lower register has been lost to a large door. Morey reproduced a 1588 Antonio Eclissi drawing of the badly damaged lower left register (Fig. 6.3]), describing it as Timothy's ordination to priesthood by Paul (cf. 1 Tim 4:14; 2 Tim 1:6). A tonsured and nimbed male bows his head before the apostle. The ordinand's halo suggests the identification, already made by Ado of Vienne in his *Parvum romanum*, of Timothy with Paul's disciple who was claimed as sainted bishop of Ephesus.[174] Morey continues, "The Apostle is attended by a youth and what

---

174. St. Gall, Stiftsbibliothek, cod. 454, 4 and 12. The manner of ordination cannot be determined: Is it laying on of hands? Is Timothy receiving the instruments of office? In the case of a presbyter, in RGP X these "instruments" were paten and chalice.

appears to be a maiden—the dress of the figure is apparently female, but the copyist seems to have indicated a tonsure."[175] The heads of the figures in this fresco, including that of the tonsured woman, are still extant. Is the female figure Praxedes? Dom Benigno Davanzati, who had been rector of S. Pudenziana, may not have known the two lower frescoes, which at some unknown time had been concealed under plaster.[176] The lower right register shows a remnant of what Morey judged to be the baptismal scene of Potentiana and Praxedes, but three grown women are depicted; the most intact figure is costumed like the saintly sisters who flank the enthroned Virgin and Child. Also remaining is a fragment of the halo of a tall personage on the left (St. Paul?). These frescoes show the longevity of the tradition of Paul's relationship with the Pudens family and, as well, the sisters' participation in the ecclesial ministries of the Pudens *titulus*.

7. *Praxedes and Her Neighbours in Vatican Manuscript Latin 1191*

In the folio pages of Vatican ms. lat. 1191, a late twelfth-century Roman sanctoral whose provenance was S. Maria in Trastevere, the feast of Praxedes on 21 July forms the centerpiece for two other women saints whose apostolic and ecclesial roles were held in high regard during the Middle Ages.[177] On the vigils of 20, 21, and 22 July the reader or listener would hear of women's preaching in the person of Marina (Margaret of Antioch); of leadership of house-churches by Praxedes and Pudentiana; and of apostolic preaching and evangelization by Mary of Magdala at the

---

175. Morey, *Lost Mosaics*, 43. Canon 15 of the Fourth Ecumenical Council attests that deaconesses in the East were tonsured; see Constantelos, "Marriage and Celibacy," in Bassett and Huizing, *Celibacy in the Church*, 30–38 at 33. Orthodox nuns are tonsured at their profession.

176. Benigno Davanzati, *S. Pudenziana ed altri santi tre mila martiri sepolti in detta chiesa con notizie della medesima* (Rome, 1713); idem, *Divozione a S. Pudenziana ed altri santi tre mila martiri sepolti in detta chiesa con notizie della medesimi* (Rome, 1713); apparently neither publication is extant.

177. In the 17th century this legendary belonged to S. Maria in Trastevere. Frequently cited by the Bollandists, it was originally bound in two volumes but now forms three, Vat. lat. 1194, 1193 and, by a different hand, 1191 (in this order), to which should be added Vat. lat. 10999 (cycle from 28 August to 30 November). E. B. Garrison (*Studies in the History of Mediaeval Italian Painting* [4 vols.; Florence: L'Impronta, 1953–1962], 4:277–83) judged the mss., designed as a group for a single church in Rome or its environs, to have originated in the same scriptorium in the third quarter of the 12th century; see also Giovanni Battista Borino, *Codices Vaticani latini 10876–11000* (Vatican City: BAV, 1955), 13:309–14.

command of the risen Lord. Later in the codex (182v–183r), the diaconissa Romana of Jerusalem, "spiritual mother" of Pelagia, would serve as a model for those women still being ordained to the diaconal office.[178]

A. Marina (Margaret of Antioch)

The virgin Marina appears in sixth place among the women named on the S. Prassede pier plaque. Her Latin feastday is 20 July.[179] The figured initial "I" commencing Marina's *vita* in our twelfth-century Vatican manuscript (90r–93v) depicts this heroine of a fabulous story wearing an unusual outfit: a headdress with fringed ribbons, a diagonal dalmatic, and a cincture in what may be an artist's rendition of the vestments of a Syrian deaconess. With a long blue choir sleeve covering her left hand and arm, Marina cradles a gospel book; in her right hand she carries a lighted oil lamp of the variety known from early Christian finds in Syro-Palestine (Fig. 6.4).[180] The narrative does not call Marina a deaconess. However, in the same century that Hildegard of Bingen was preaching in the public squares of the Rhineland, Marina was converting many by her preaching.

B. Praxedes and Pudentiana

In the passionals, the *vita* of the sisters was ordinarily given in two parts so that each story could be read on their vigils (18 May and 20 July). But Vatican ms. lat. 1191 includes a unified and expanded *Vita sanctarum*

---

178. A deaconess appears in connection with the tale of Pelagia, repentant prostitute of Antioch (d. ca. 457), whose spiritual mother the *venerabilis diaconissa nomine romana* was given her own *vita* (Vat. ms. lat. 1191, 182v–183r). After baptism assisted by Romana, Pelagia wore male clothing in order to pass as an ascetic eunuch living on the Mount of Olives in Jerusalem. Unlike some other aspects of the story, the ecclesiastical title is credible and attested for the Jerusalem area (Eisen, *Women Officeholders*, 158–60). What might the given name "Romana" be meant to suggest?

179. Farmer, *Oxford Dictionary of Saints*, 281–82; Agnes Smith Lewis, trans., "The Story of the Blessed Mary Who Was Called Marina," *Vox Benedictina* 2 (1985): 305–17; King, *Desert Mothers*, 27, n. 43. Vat. ms. lat. 8701, the 12th-century "S. Prassede Epistolary," assigns "Domine deus meus exaltabit" (Ecclus/Sir 51:13–17) for "Margarita's" first reading.

180. In Vat. ms. lat. 1191 two other saints wear similar garb: the physician Pantaleon (fol. 125r), martyred at Nicomedia, and the virgin-martyr Seraphia (29 July; fol. 135r), the Syrian servant-girl who converted Sabina. Both hold the gospel book on covered arm; the costume may be meant to indicate Syrian origin. The unusual costume can be compared to the vested female figure in a full-page miniature in the most ancient Syrian gospel book extant, Paris, Bibl. Nat. syr. 341. See Reiner Sörries, *Syrische Bible von Paris*, 104 and fig. 8.

FIGURE 6.4 Vatican, Biblioteca Apostolica Vaticana, ms. lat. 1191, fol. 90r: St. Marina of Antioch (late 12th century). By permission of Biblioteca Apostolica Vaticana, with all rights reserved.

virginum Praxedis et Pudentiana, et Pius Papa (f. 96v–101v).[181] Prolix, pious, and historical additions make Pudentiana and Praxedes even more perfect models of the Christian life. Three generations of the Pudens clan are involved. In a lengthy deathbed sermon (98r–v), the sisters' saintly father quotes Paul the apostle and paraphrases fragments of Scripture. Making use of the classical *topos* of the "woes of marriage," the dying *paterfamilias* exhorts his daughters to live the virginal life.[182] However, as with all recensions of the story, negative attitudes toward women are absent. Equality in Christ reigns among the choirs of holy women: virgins, widows, and wives. The virgins are headed by Mary mother of the Lord, the widows by Anna daughter of Phanuel, and the wives by Elizabeth mother of the Baptist (98v).[183] Revelation 14:3–4 and its reference to the new song sung by

---

181. *BHL* 6920c, beginning with the prologue *de inepto et corrupto sermone*.

182. A stock theme in literature regarding the servitude of a married woman to her husband (cf. 1 Cor 7:28b, 7:34 and Gen 3:16). See Elizabeth A. Clark, *Reading Renunciation*, 308 and nn. 270–271, and for Jerome's "mocking elaboration of the 'anxieties' of 1 Cor 7:32–34," see 319–20.

183. In contrast to the speculations of Jerome, Augustine, and Caesarius of Arles, no suggestions are made respecting the differing percentages of "fruits" awarded the various states of life.

144,000 male virgins is appropriated by Pudens (98v) in his sermon to his daughters. On the holy patriarch's death, a multitude of Christians with the bishop Pius converge for the funeral rites celebrated with hymns and canticles, after which Pudens is buried in Priscilla's cemetery. Christians enjoy peace in Rome, and our *vita* includes an excerpt from Justin Martyr's *First Apology* to Emperor Antoninus Pius (99r) explaining the Christian way of life. Yet more "historical" detail, this time concerning Bishop Pius, is provided by a paraphrase from *LP* in which Hermas' *Shepherd* is cited to support the fraternal relationship between Pastor and Pius and to found the Roman church's celebration of Easter on a Sunday (100v–101r).[184] The story continues to unfold along the lines of the Bollandists' integrated version given in *Acta Sanctorum*, but for putting in Praxedes' name both *titulus* and *ecclesia* established in the Novatus thermae in the Lateran quarter (100r).[185] Praxedes, "fervent in the Holy Spirit," hides many Christians to whom she ministers nourishment for body and soul (101r). She dies shortly after burying the twenty-three Christians martyred in her *titulus*. In our enriched version, Praxedes hears the invitation of Christ her spouse to accept her crown: "*Veni de libano sponsa, veni de Libano, veni*" (Song of Songs, 4:8; 101v).[186] She is laid to rest by the presbyter Pastor in the Priscilla cemetery next to her father Pudens and holy sister Pudentiana.

C. Mary of Magdala

Mary of Magdala, the woman who appears prominently in all four gospels as leader of the women disciples of Jesus, went to his tomb on the third day after his death to anoint his body. The theme of anointing led to the Magdalene's conflation with other anointing women. First among these

---

184. "Quo etiam tempore constituit beatus pius eps. ut sanctum pascha die tantum dominico celebraret cum usque ad tempus illud a plerisque aliis celebraret diebus. Eo autem gubernante ecclesiam Hermes librum conscripsit in quo continetur quod angelus domini sibi in habitu pastoris apparuit precipiens quod omnibus divulgaret ut deinceps pascha die tantum dominico celebraret. Post menses autem duos obiit beatus pius et sepultus est in vaticano iuxta corpus beati petri apostoli" (100r–101v).

185. *BHL* 6988–89. See Angelelli, *Basilica titolare di S. Pudenziana*, 16, Tabella 2, for the recensions of the *vita*. *Passiones* of Praxedes and Vat. ms. lat. 1191 locate the baths of Novatus in the Lateran quarter.

186. "Veni, sponsa Christi, accipe coronam, quam tibi Dominus praeparavit in aeternum" is used in the tract for feasts of virgins and holy women during Septuagesima and Lent.

was Mary of Bethany. In a fateful homily preached at S. Clemente on 21 September 591, Gregory the Great (540–604) conferred papal authority on this conflation of the anonymous woman (sinner), Mary of Bethany, and Mary of Magdala.[187] When read apart from their context the Scriptures lent themselves to the conflation.[188]

The Magdalene's *vita* in Vatican ms. lat. 1191 is lengthy (101v–105r, made up from BHL 5439, 5443, and 5446). It quotes Jesus' praise of the anointing woman at the house of Simon the Pharisee in Bethany (Mark 14:9; Matt 26:13), "Amen I say to you, wherever this gospel will be preached in the whole world what she has done will be told in memory of her" (103v), the latter account read in the Palm Sunday Passion gospel. The sinner-woman of Luke 7:36–50 was a more egregious identification. This repentant woman who poured out her heart with her tears was identified as the Magdalen because of Luke's locating the group of women "cured of evil spirits and infirmities" immediately following the pericope recounting this woman's conversion. When Luke, unsympathetic to the Magdalen's priority over Peter in the Johannine tradition, relegated her to secondary status, in part by defining Mary as the one "from whom seven devils had gone out" (Luke 8:2), the groundwork

---

187. Mark 15:40, 16:1, 16:9; Matt 27:56, 28:1, 9–10; Luke 8:2–3, 24:10; John 19:25, 20:1, 11–19. See Ricci, *Mary Magdalene and Many Others*. Schaberg (*Resurrection of Mary Magdalene*, 300–56) expands the fields of reference in order to retrieve Mary as successor to Jesus, thereby counterbalancing the inclination to prioritize Peter. Holly E. Hearon (*Mary Magdalene Tradition*) analyzes the references to Mary Magdalene in Matthew and John for evidence that they circulated first as stories before being introduced into the canonical gospels. For a brilliant discussion of Gospel women whose stories impact on or are recapitulated in that of the Magdalen, see Mary Rose D'Angelo, "Reconstructing 'Real' Women from Gospel Literature: The Case of Mary Magdalene," in Ross Shepard Kraemer and Mary Rose D'Angelo, eds., *Women and Christian Origins* (New York: Oxford University Press, 1999), 105–28. For her title *apostola apostolorum* ("apostle of the apostles"), see Susan Haskins, *Mary Magdalen: Myth and Metaphor* (Old Saybrook, CT: Konecky & Konecky, 1993), 58–97. For a review of the literature and a broad reading of the Magdalen story in its application to ecclesiology, see Mary Ann Hinsdale, "St. Mary of Magdala: Ecclesiological Implications," in *CTSA Proceedings* 66 (2011): 67–90, Presidential Address, presented to the Sixty-Sixth Annual Convention of the CTSA, San Jose, California, June 9–12, 2011. Pseudo-Hippolytus of Rome had conflated the Magdalene with Mary of Bethany. The Magdalene had occasionally been conflated with Jesus' mother.

188. For an exegetical analysis, see Craig S. Keener, *The Gospel of John: A Commentary* (2 vols.; Peabody, MA: Hendrickson Publishers, 2003), 2:859–66. For an analysis of intertexuality and interfigurality in the stories of John 11, 12, 20, see Ingrid R. Kitzberger, "Mary of Bethany and Mary of Magdala—Two Female Characters in the Johannine Passion Narrative," *NTS* 41 (1995): 564–86. Intertexuality explores the relationships—the dialogue and points of contact—in the hearing and reading of given texts. Interfigurality redefines and transforms an earlier tradition (586, n. 62). By contrast, harmonization simply combines information from different sources and smooths out the differences between them.

was laid for her later persona as a penitent prostitute.[189] That the Magdalene was the first disciple commissioned to preach the good news of the Lord's resurrection—"I have seen the Lord" (John 20:18)—was recognized in both Eastern and Western traditions.[190] Alluding to Jesus' command, the text in Vatican ms. lat. 1191 is not without a trace of male condescension. Through the woman death was introduced into the world but "through the feminine sex" (that is, the Magdalene) Christ "wished to announce to men (*viris*) the joys of the resurrection" (104v).[191] The *vita* ends with the apocryphal trip by boat to Marseilles and the Magdalene's ministry of preaching and penance in Provence. Saint-Maximin La-Sainte-Baume, the church with ambo and tomb supposedly built in her memory by bishop St. Maximin, is named (fol. 105r). Mary's apostolic activities of destroying idols, preaching to Jews and pagans, and teaching in Provence, finally dying there as an ascetic, would be elaborated in tale and painting.[192]

Mary of Magdala enjoyed three festal days in Eastern churches: 30 June, 22 July, and 4 August. Bede's martyrology of circa 720 set the date

---

189. Brock, *Mary Magdalene, First Apostle*, 168–69. The several personas of Mary Magdalene have been distinguished by Haskins, *Mary Magdalene*.

190. Acknowledgment of the Magdalene's apostolic status, from which is derived the title *apostola apostolorum*, still current in the Eastern churches, reaches back to a commentary on the Song of Songs once attributed to Hippolytus of Rome.

191. The "Hippolytan" text already knows that motif: "Christ himself came to them so that the women would be apostles of Christ and by their obedience rectify the sin of the ancient Eve.... Christ showed himself to the (male) apostles and said to them:... 'It is I who appeared to these women and I who wanted to send them to you as apostles.'" Katherine Ludwig Jansen (*The Making of the Magdalen: Preaching and Popular Devotion in the Later Middle Ages* [Princeton, NJ: Princeton University Press, 2000], 28) cites *Corpus Scriptorum Christianorum Orientalium* 264 (1965), 43–49, from a commentary which survives only in Georgian.

192. E.g., *De vita Beatae Mariae Magdalenae et sororis ejus Sanctae Marthae*, in English translation, *The Life of Saint Mary Magdalene and of Her Sister Saint Martha: A Medieval Biography*, trans. David Mycoff (Kalamazoo, MI: Cistercian Publications, 1989), improbably attributed to Rabanus Maurus. Judged to have late 12th-century Cistercian authorship, it is deeply influenced by Bernard of Citeaux, incorporating erotic imagery inspired by the Song of Songs. In this text Mary is present through all the episodes of Jesus' passion. Later she is titled "the special friend and first servant of the Saviour" (ll. 1760–1, p. 82). [Christ] "defended Mary.... ; he excused her...; he praised her..., and destined her to be apostle to his apostles.... among the daughters of men, only the Queen of Heaven is equal to and greater than Mary Magdalene" (84–85, ll. 1860–68). "[J]ust as she had been chosen to be the apostle of Christ's resurrection and the prophet of his ascension, so also she became an evangelist for believers throughout the world" (96, ll. 2262–65). The 13th-century panel painting of the Magdalene as hermit in the Accademia, Florence, shows eight vignettes of her eventful life.

of 22 July for her commemoration in the West.[193] Given lections in the ninth century at Tours, the feast did not quickly make its way to Rome.[194] Although Pudentiana and Praxedes are inserts into the Würzburg gospel list of around 645, the feast of the Magdalene appears neither there nor in Murbach (ca. 740/775), and its appearance in later books continues to be occasional.[195] It is found in none of the lectionaries earlier investigated for virgins' feasts until its belated appearance in Vatican ms. lat. 8701, the thirteenth-century Vallombrosan epistolary. Basile Vanmaele's *Bibliotheca Sanctorum* article on the two sisters is illustrated with a fifteenth-century manuscript page by Giovanni de' Maineri entitled *Le ss. Prassede e Maria Maddalena*.[196]

In view of the deliberateness that characterized medieval Rome's nostalgic "imitation" of the holy places of Jerusalem, the proximity of Praxedes and Mary of Magdala would have been considered providential because of their similar ministries on behalf of the dead and their ministry of proclamation. The Magdalene had encountered the risen Christ as she sought

---

193. "Natale sanctae Mariae Magdalenae, de qua, ut evangelium refert, septem daemonia ejecit Dominus: quae etiam inter alia dona insignia, Christum a mortuis resurgentem prima videre meruit" (*PL* 94:982).

194. Vat. ms. lat. 5411 (12th century) contains the lives of Mary Magdalene (215r–v, *BHL* 5454) and of Marina (215v–217, *BHL* 5628) but not of Praxedes or Pudentiana. Vat. Pal. lat. 439 (15th century) places Mary Magdalene (196r–197v) after Praxedes (195r–196r).

195. The variability, even haphazardness, of feasts and readings is shown by the following samples. The 11th-century Breviary-Missal Vatican lat. 7018 (late 11th century) does not list Potentiana. For Praxedes the lection is "De virginibus" (1 Cor 7:25) with no gospel cited and the collect is generic (f. 89r–v); there is no sign of the Magdalene. *Missale Aretinum*, Vat. ms. lat. 6080 (11th century, from Chiusi?, 127v) gives for Praxedes the martyr a collect which recalls the fragility of her sex and the same readings as for Lucy ("Domine deus meus exaltasti," 180r). Mary Magdalene's collect recalls Christ's forgiveness of her sins; the lections are "Sapientia vincit" and the penitent woman (Luke 7:36–50). Vat. lat. 44, a *capitulare evangeliorum* (12th century) gives for Holy Monday the long reading John 12:1–36; for Potentiana, Praxedes, Sabina, and Lucy the gospel pericope is Matt 13:44. There is no trace of the Magdalene. Vat. Pal. lat. 497 (12th century, German?) gives for the Magdalene Song of Songs 3:1. The 13th-century epistolary of the Vallombrosan order (Vat. ms. lat. 8701) has the briefest of notations for sanctoral feasts. The reading for St. Pudentiana (fol. 180) is indicated with great brevity ("Muliere[m] fortem," Prov 31:10–31). Folio 185r shows the trio St. Margaret (Marina) with the reading "Domine Deus me exaltasti" (Ecclus/Sir 51:13); "Qui gloriatur in dno" (2 Cor 10:17) for "paxedis vigis"; and "Sapientia vi[n]cit" (Wis 7:30b) for Mary of Magdala. Vat. Archivio di San Pietro, cod. F.1 (family A, 13th-century epistolary of St. Peter's) gives "Sapientia laudabit" for Pudentiana (74v), "Qui gloriatur" for Praxedes (100r), and for Mary of Magdala "Mulierem fortem" (100r–v).

196. *Messale della Rovere* miniature in Torino, Biblioteca Nazionale. See Vanmaele, "Potenziana (Pudenziana) e Prassede," 1067–68.

his body to anoint it; Praxedes anointed and prepared for burial the bodies of Christ's martyrs. The two share the same iconographical attribute, a vase.[197] On Holy Monday Praxedes is Rome's Mary of Bethany. Praxedes is also Rome's Magdalene. The large alabaster vase centered above the architrave of the Zeno Chapel door powerfully evokes these gospel associations.

---

197. J. E. Fallon ("Mary Magdalene, St.," *NCE* 9 [2003]: 285–88 at 288) mentions ancient resurrection scenes in various media that show Mary as the first witness.

Afterword

EARLY CHRISTIAN AND medieval Rome is full of treasures brought from other Christian centers and guarded under layers of paint or locked away in cabinets and reliquaries to be displayed on high feast days. If readers have been persuaded to view the story of Praxedes and the beautiful church she inspired as one of Rome's mysteries to be solved, then a major objective of this book—to unveil the meaning of Santa Prassede—has been accomplished. Praxedes' *titulus* was influenced by places near and far. The history, liturgy, and hagiography of the Eternal City had nourished the educated piety and creative imagination of a Roman cleric destined for high church career whom providence was to locate at the interface between Byzantine and Carolingian empires. Paschal's church incorporated old and new in its design and iconography in the manner of Matthew's wise householder (Matt 13:44, 52).

A second purpose in writing this book should be evident. Whether historical figure or fictional personage modeled on the women Paul names in chapter 16 of his letter to the Romans, Praxedes is archetype of those ecclesial women who, in every generation, have responded to the call to preach Christ's gospel and collaborate in advancing the reign of God. Easter themes of resurrection and Christ's sovereignty in the time of the church are central to a decorative program centered around an ideal Christian family, gender parity, and church leadership. Today most Protestant churches give competent women their share of responsibility for church governance and publicly deputed leadership. However, a large portion of ministry in Catholic, Orthodox, and Oriental churches is carried out by women working in many, often unnoticed, capacities. Given the history of women's once-recognized leadership, why should their work not be enabled by access to pastoral office for those whom the Spirit calls and the church tests?

Equality of women with men was not realized within the official ranks of the undivided Christian churches, even in those halcyon days along the Rhine and in Saxony during the tenth to twelfth centuries. On its own, historical recounting does not answer the theological question whether women should be ordained to pastoral office. However, history opens our eyes to present and future possibilities by showing what has already been thought and done. In the past, the old churches of the East and the Roman church in its first 1200 years were welcoming of women's participation in official ministry. Why was women's ecclesial leadership visible and validated in more androcentric times? Why is it less visible today, when equality of the sexes is an accepted principle? Where might reflection on renewed ministry that includes women start? Many theologians agree that there is no obstacle to retrieving the office of "permanent deacon" for women, although some would argue that an office held by women could not be considered part of the sacrament of orders.

Latin mass commentaries show that, during the course of the twelfth century in the West, the relationship between priest and people, and the understanding of the priest's relationship to Christ, underwent a sea-change.[1] In many lectures and publications Gary Macy has demonstrated the radical and restrictive changes to the meaning of sacramental ordination during the scholastic period. The presbyterate became ever more sacerdotalized and exclusive, its raison-d'être the power to confect the body and blood of Christ and administer other sacraments. Despite its sacramental responsibilities, the episcopate was treated as a hierarchical privilege. But personal possession of powers vested in hierarchically ordered individuals cannot be the theological criterion for sacramental action. In "Apostolic Office: Sacrament of Christ," the liturgical theologian Edward Kilmartin, SJ, pointed to the necessity of rethinking the reigning scholastic theology of sacraments and presbyteral office before decisions are made about pastoral office for women.[2] Current unwillingness to discuss the topic hinges on the meaning given to the priest's action *in persona Christi*, "in the person of Christ," playing the very role of Christ, even "taking the place of Christ," especially in sacramental celebrations. This meaning has grown out of allegorical interpretation, been applied within

---

1. Mary M. Schaefer, "Latin Mass Commentaries from the Ninth through Twelfth Centuries: Chronology and Theology," in *Fountain of Life: In Memory of Niels K. Rasmussen O.P.*, ed. Gerard Austin (Washington, DC: Pastoral Press, 1991), 35–49.

2. Edward Kilmartin, SJ, "Apostolic Office: Sacrament of Christ," *TS* 36 (June 1975): 243–64.

a scholastic framework, and been carried forward as official teaching. The special relationship of the priest to Christ is secured through sacerdotal ordination and consequent "ontological identification" with Christ. To overcome the deficiencies of this explanation, the need for "iconic maleness" in Christ's representative has recently come to the fore.

In the tradition, the concept *in persona Christi* was accompanied by its correlative: action undertaken *in nomine ecclesiae* ("in the name of the Church") by persons so deputed. In present discussion this complementary notion is too often left out of the model. Failure to theologically relate action *in persona Christi* and *in nomine ecclesiae* results in a skewed understanding of pastoral office. Deprived of an ecclesiological base that is not founded on a sound theology of the church, it fails to account for Christ's Body, the acting community of faith. Indeed, Christ is liturgically absent, his presence secured by the priest acting in ontological identification with the Lord of the Church, the priest making available Christ's substantial presence in the eucharistic species. In modern times, *in persona Christi* has been placed within the horizon of christomonistic ("Christ-only") communion ecclesiology. To use Kilmartin's phraseology, failure to reexamine "the christological and pneumatological-ecclesiological dimensions of pastoral office" has left the Roman Church reeling, unable to address its deepest challenges.

Of two papally endorsed theologies since Pope Pius XII pertaining to Christ and presidency of the church's eucharist, we have sketched the first, the allegorical notion of the priest acting in Christ's person. This officially favored theology of priesthood does not arise out of an ecclesiology inclusive of the faith community *moved by the Holy Spirit*. An adequate theology of church must do justice to Christian belief in the Trinity. There is such an ecclesiology, that of Trinitarian communion; it began to find a place in the final documents of Vatican Council II. Against the scholastic model, current theology of ministry returns to scriptural and patristic sources. It favors the perspective of the church's first 1150 years by locating liturgical-sacramental activity within the *ecclesial context* of all the baptized, with the gathered faith-assembly as active subject of liturgy. In the human social dimension, the ordained office-holder officially represents the faith of both local and universal church, thereby representing Christ. Through its ordained leader, each local community is united with the whole believing church and grows into one heart and mind with its head and Lord, Christ Jesus. An integral component of Trinitarian communion ecclesiology, most easily seen when operative within the church's liturgy, is the active or acting presence of Christ. But this has been presented in official documents within an ecclesiology of christomonistic communion! It too is deficient as long as the Holy Spirit, Energizer of the faith of the whole church and each of its members, the Inspirer who structures the sacramental rites and ecclesial governance, is overlooked or not allowed to flourish.[3] Attending to Trinitarian communion ecclesiology and entrusting decisions to the guidance of the Holy Spirit, who acts with Christ as sharing source of faith and divine Energizer of Christian life, the church in its inclusive life and governance strives to model itself on the life of the Trinity. The surprising Holy Spirit is given room to operate in all the many ways appropriate to the charisms of believers.

In various times and places in the past women's official ministry has been recognized by the churches of East and West, including the Church of Rome. We easily forget that the Latin church was, before the development of universalist ecclesiology, a communion of local churches. Even when the scope of women's ministry was radically restricted in the public sphere, women leaders were liturgically established in office in ways equivalent to their male counterparts.

Paschal's church of Santa Prassede does not necessarily represent a proto-feminist undertaking. Piety and spiritual understanding can coexist alongside autocratic attitudes and a will-to-power. Deceased saintly women may be viewed very differently from women living in the real world. Nonetheless papal openness in the early medieval period resulted in a building that is a work of art and enduring architectural legacy representing women's reality in church life. Paschal was not the only pope so inclined. Pius I of our story, Honorius I of S. Agnese's, perhaps Donus of St. Martina's in the Forum, Leo II with the prayer for making a diacona, Hadrian I, rescuer of the ruined *tituli* of Pudentiana and Praxedes, and, in our own time, John XXIII and John Paul I, come to mind. The church whose heart is Rome can once again recognize that family ties can encourage holiness and parity in gender relationships and can build the faith community, and that giftedness for pastoral office can be found among both women and men. The evidence presented in this book invites us to

---

3. On these ecclesiological models as developed by Edward Kilmartin and their practical implications for governance and liturgy, see Schaefer, "Presence of the Trinity," 145–56. On the active presence of Christ, Schaefer, "In Persona Christi": Cult of the Priest's Person or Active Presence of Christ?," in J. Z. Skira and M. S. Attridge, eds., *In God's Hands: Essays on the Church and Ecumenism in Honour of Michael A. Fahey, S.J.* (Louvain: Peeters, 2006), 177–201.

a renewed way of being church, including the recognition of faith-filled women's capacities for Christian offices of pastoral leadership. Pope Paschal's remarkable achievement at Santa Prassede poses the old but always relevant question: When the Lord comes from the future to renew his church and to bring into being a new heaven and a new earth, will he find it ready and willing?

Bibliography

PRIMARY SOURCES
(A) Manuscripts

Berlin, Libr. ms. theol. lat. fol. 706, 249v.
Rome, Bibl. Vallicelliana cod. D.5.
Rome, Bibl. Vallicelliana, cod. VII.
Rome, Bibl. Vallicelliana, cod. X.
Saint Gall, Stiftsbibliothek, cod. 454.
Saint Gall, Stiftsbibliothek, cod. 577.
Trier, Staatsbibliothek, cod. 31.
Vatican, Archivio di San Pietro, cod. F. 1.
Vatican, Barb. gr. 336.
Vatican, Barb. lat. 586.
Vatican, Barb. lat. 681.
Vatican, Barb. lat. 4423.
Vatican, Burgh. lat. 297.
Vatican, Ottobon. lat. 38.
Vatican, Ottobon. lat. 270.
Vatican, Ottobon. lat. 502.
Vatican, Ottobon. lat. 1037.
Vatican, Pal. lat. 277.
Vatican, Pal. lat. 439.
Vatican, Pal. lat. 477.
Vatican, Pal. lat. 497.
Vatican, Pal. lat. 846.
Vatican, Reg. lat. 316.
Vatican, Reg. lat. 593.

Vatican, Reg. lat. 1930.
Vatican, Rossiani lat. 608.
Vat. Syr. Cod. 19.
Vatican, ms. lat 44.
Vatican, ms. lat. 49.
Vatican, ms. lat. 67.
Vatican, ms. lat. 1145.
Vatican, ms. lat. 1188.
Vatican, ms. lat. 1191, 1192, 1193, 1194.
Vatican, ms. lat. 3764.
Vatican, ms. lat. 4744.
Vatican, ms. lat. 5319.
Vatican, ms. lat. 5407.
Vatican, ms. lat. 5411.
Vatican, ms. lat. 6075.
Vatican, ms. lat. 6080.
Vatican, ms. lat. 6748.
Vatican, ms. lat. 6839.
Vatican, ms. lat. 6933.
Vatican, ms. lat. 7018.
Vatican, ms. lat. 8565.
Vatican, ms. lat. 8701.
Vatican, ms. lat. 8942.
Vatican, ms. lat. 9072.
Vatican, ms. lat. 10999.
Vatican, ms. lat. 14872.

(b) Printed Books

Acta Sanctorum quotquot toto orbe coluntur. 70 vols. Antwerp, 1643. New edition by Johannes Bolland, Jean Baptiste Carnandet, and Godefridus Henschenius. 69 vols. in 70. Paris; Rome: Victor Palmé, [1863]–1940.

Ado, Archbishop of Vienne. *Le martyrologe d'Adon: Ses deux familles, ses trois recensions, texte et commentaire.* Edited by Jacques Dubois and Geneviève Renaud. Sources d'histoire médiévale. Paris: Éditions du Centre national de la recherche scientifique, 1984.

Das älteste Liturgiebuch der lateinischen Kirche. Edited and revised by Alban Dold. Beuron: Hohenzollern, 1936.

Ambrose, Bishop of Milan. *De virginitate: liber unus.* Edited by E. Cazzaniga. Corpus scriptorium latinorum paravianum. Torino: Paravia, 1954. In English,

On Virginity. Translated by Daniel Callam. Peregrina Translation Series 7. Toronto: Peregrina, [1980] 1989.

———. *Opere morali*. 2 vols. in 3. Milan: Biblioteca Ambrosiana, 1977–1989.

Ambrosiaster. *Contre les païens et Sur le destin*. Introduction, texte critique, traducion et notes par Marie-Pierre Bussières. Sources chrétiennes 512. Paris: Éditions du Cerf, 2007.

Ancient Epitome of the Sacred Canons of the Eastern Orthodox Church, ed. George Mastrantonis. St. Louis, MO: Ologos, ca. 1960.

Andrieu, Michel. *Les ordines romani du haut moyen âge*. 5 vols. Études et documents, fasc. 11, 23, 24, 28, 29. Louvain: Spicilegium Sacrum Lovaniense, 1931–1961.

———. *Le Pontifical Romain au Moyen-Âge*. Vol. 1: *Le Pontifical romain du XIIe siècle*. Studi e Testi 86. Vatican City: Biblioteca Apostolica Vaticana, 1938.

———. *Le Pontifical Romain au Moyen-Âge*. Vol. 2: *Le Pontifical de la Curie romaine du XIIIe siècle*. Studi e Testi 87. Vatican City: Biblioteca Apostolica Vaticana, 1940.

———. *Le Pontifical Romain au Moyen-Âge*. Vol. 3: *Le Pontifical du Guillaume Durand*. Studi e Testi 88. Vatican City: Biblioteca Apostolica Vaticana, 1940.

———. *Le Pontifical Romain au Moyen-Âge*. Vol. 4: *Tables alphabétiques* . Studi e Testi 88. Vatican City: Biblioteca Apostolica Vaticana, 1940.

Ante-Nicene Christian Library: Translations of the Writings of the Fathers down to A.D. 325. Edited by Alexander Roberts and James Donaldson. 24 vols. Edinburgh: T & T Clark, 1867–1872.

Anthologia Latina, sive, Poesis Latinae Supplementum. Edited by F. Buecheler and A. Riese. 2nd ed. Bibliotheca scriptorum Graecorum et Romanorum Teubneriana. Lipsiae: Teubner, 1894. Reprint. Amsterdam: A. M. Hakkert, 1964–.

The Apocryphal Jesus: Legends of the Early Church. Edited by J. K. Elliott. Oxford: Oxford University Press, 1996.

The Apocryphal New Testament: A Collection of Apocryphal Christian Literature in an English Translation. Edited by J. K. Eliott. Revised and newly translated edition of *Neutestamentaliche Apokryphen*. Translated by Montague Rhodes James. Oxford; New York: Oxford University Press, [1924] 1993.

The Apostolic Fathers. Translated by Kirsopp Lake. 2 vols. Loeb Classical Library. Cambridge, MA: Harvard University Press, 1912–1917.

The Apostolic Fathers: Greek Texts and English Translations. Updated edition. Edited and revised by Michael W. Holmes after the earlier edition of J. B. Lightfoot and J. R. Harmer. Grand Rapids, MI: Baker Books, 1999.

Atto, Bishop of Vercelli. *Attonis Vercellensis Episcopi Expositio Epistolarum S. Pauli*. PL 134, 125–288. In *Ep. Ad Rom. Epistola II ad Timotheum. Epist. Ad Ephes.*, 545–86.

Augustine (Augustinus Aurelius), Bishop of Hippo. *The City of God (De civitate Dei)*; John Healey's translation; edited by R. V. G. Tasker; introduction by Ernest Barker. Everyman's Library. London: Dent, 1945.

———. *Sancti Aurelii Augustini De civitate Dei*. Edited by Bernhard Dombart and Alphons Kalb. 2 vols. Corpus Christianorum. Series Latina 47, 48. Turnhout: Brepols, 1955.

———. *Sancti Aurelii Augustini Enarrationes in Psalmos*. 3 vols. Edited by Eligius Dekkers and Johannes Fraipont. Corpus Christianorum. Series Latina, 38–40. Turnhout: Brepols, 1956.

Baronius, Cesare Sorano, Cardinal. *Annales ecclesiastici*. 19 vols. Rome: Ex Typographica Vaticana, 1588–.

———. *Martyrologium Romanum*. Venice: Polum, 1609.

The Bible in the Early Church. Edited with introductions by Everett Ferguson. Studies in Early Christianity 3. New York: Garland, 1993.

Biblia Sacra iuxta Latinam Vulgatam versionem ad codicum fidem. Vol. 12: *Sapientia Salomonis, Liber Hiesu filii Sirach*. Rome: Benedictines of San Girolamo Abbey, 1964.

Biblia Sacra juxta Vulgatam Clementinam. Rome: Desclée, [1927] 1956.

Bibliotheca hagiographica latina antiquae et mediae aetatis. Edited by Socii Bollandiani. 2 vols. Subsidia Hagiographica 6. Brussels: Société des Bollandistes, 1898–1901.

Bibliotheca hagiographica latina antiquae et mediae aetatis: Novum supplementum. Edited by Heinricus Fros. Subsidia Hagiographica 70. Brussels: Société des Bollandistes, 1986.

Bingham, Joseph. *Origines sive antiquitates ecclesiasticae*. 2 vols. Halle: Orphanotrophei, 1724–1725. In English, *The Antiquities of the Christian Church*. 10 vols. London Robert Knaplock, 1710–1722.

The Book of Pontiffs (Liber Pontificalis): The Ancient Biographies of the First Ninety Roman Bishops to AD 715. Translated with an introduction and notes by Raymond Davis. Translated Texts for Historians 6. Rev. ed. Liverpool: Liverpool University Press, 2000. 3rd ed. rev., 2010.

The Book of Pontiffs of the Church of Ravenna. Translated with an introduction and notes by Deborah Mauskopf Deliyannis. Medieval Texts in Translation. Washington, DC: Catholic University of America Press, 2004.

Borino, Giovanni Battista. *Codices Vaticani latini 10876–11000*. Vatican City: Biblioteca Apostolica Vaticana, 1955.

Bosio, Antonio. *Roma sotteranea*. 2 vols. Rome: G. Facciotti, 1632.

Breviatio canonum Fulgentii Ferrandi Ecclesiae Carthaginensis Diaconi, a. 523–546. PL 88, 818–30.

Ciampini, Giovanni Giustino. *Vetera monimenta in quibus praecipuè musiva opera sacrarum profanarumque aedium structura: ac nonnulli antiquiritus dissertationisbus iconibusque illustrantur*. 2 vols. Rome: Komarek, 1690–1699.

The Complete Gospels: Annotated Scholars Version. Edited by Robert J. Miller. Sonoma, CA: Polebridge, 1992. Revised and expanded edition, 1994.

Concilia Africae a. 345–a. 525. Edited by C. Munier. Corpus Christianorum. Series Latina 149. Turnhout: Brepols, 1974.

Concilia Galliae a. 314–a. 506. Edited by C. Munier. Corpus Christianorum. Series Latina 148. Turnhout: Brepols, 1963.
Concilia Galliae a. 511–a. 695. Edited by Charles Carlo de Clercq. Corpus Christianorum. Series Latina 148A. Turnhout: Brepols, 1963.
Corpus Iuris Canonici. Decretales. Edited by Emil Friedberg. 2 vols. Leipzig: Bernhard Tauchnitz, 1879–1881. Reprint. Graz: Akademische Druck- und Verlagsanstalt, 1959.
Corpus scriptorum ecclesiasticorum latinorum. 95 vols. Vienna: Tempsky, 1866–.
Davanzati, Benigno. *Notizie al pellegrino della Basilica di S. Prassede.* Rome: Antonio de'Rossi, 1725.
De corpore et sanguine Domini, treatise by Paschasius Radbertus. Edited by Beda Paulis. Corpus Christianorum. Continuatio Mediaevalis 16. Turnhout: Brepols, 1969.
Defensoris locogiacensis monachi Liber Scintillarum. Edited by Heinricus M. Rochais. Corpus Christianorum. Series Latina 117. Turnhout: Brepols, 1957.
The Didascalia apostolorum: An English Version. Edited, introduced and annotated by Alistair Stewart-Sykes. Studia traditionis theologiae. Explorations in Early and Medieval Theology 1. Turnhout: Brepols, 2009.
Didascalia apostolorum: The Syriac Version Translated and Accompanied by the Verona Latin Fragments. Introduction and notes by R. Hugh Connolly. Oxford: Clarendon Press, 1929. Reprint, 1969.
Didascalia et Constitutiones apostolorum. Edited by Franz Xaver Funk. 2 vols. Paderborn: Schoeningh, 1905. Reprint 2 vols. in 1. Torina: Bottega d'Erasmo, 1964.
Early Christian Fathers. Translated and edited by Cyril C. Richardson, with Eugene R. Fairweather, Edward Richie Hardy, and Massey Hamilton Shepherd. Library of Christian Classics 1. New York: Macmillan, 1970.
Eisen, Ute E. *Women Officeholders in Early Christianity: Epigraphical and Literary Studies.* Translated by Linda M. Maloney. Collegeville, MN: Liturgical Press, 2000.
Epiphanius of Salamis. *The Panarion of Epiphanius of Salamis.* Vol. 1: *Book 1 (Sects 1–46).* Translated by Frank Williams. Nag Hammadi and Manichaean Studies. Leiden: Brill, 1987.
L'Eucologio Barberini Gr. 336:ff. 1–263. Edited by Stefano Parenti and Elena Velkovska. Bibliotheca "Ephemerides liturgicae." Subsidia 80. Rome: C.L.V.-Edizioni liturgiche, 1995.
Eusebius Pamphilus of Caesarea. *The Ecclesiastical History of Eusebius Pamphilus.* Translated by C. F. Cruse. London: George Bell, 1876. Reprint. Grand Rapids, MI: Baker Book House, 1955.
Fabretti, Raffaele. *Inscriptionum antiquarum quae in aedibus paternis asservantur explicatio.* Rome: Ex Officina Dominici Antonii Herculis, 1699.
Gelasius I, Pope. *Epistolae Romanorum Pontificum genuinae et quae ad eos scriptae sunt a S. Hilaro usque ad Pelagium.* Edited by Andreas Thiel. 2 vols. Braunsberg: Eduardi Peter, 1868. Reprint. Hildesheim: Olms, 1974.

The Gregorian Sacramentary under Charles the Great. Edited from three manuscripts of the 19th century by H. A. Wilson. Henry Bradshaw Society 49. London: Harrison, 1915.

Gregory I, Pope. *The Letters of Gregory the Great*. Translated with introduction and notes by John R. C. Martyn. 3 vols. Toronto: Pontifical Institute of Mediaeval Studies, 2004.

———. *S. Gregorii Magni Registrum Epistularum*. Edited by Dag Norberg. 2 vols. Corpus Christianorum. Series Latina, 140–140A. Turnhout: Brepols, 1982.

Grossi-Gondi, Felice. *Trattato di epigrafia cristiana: Latina e Greco del mondo romano occidentale*. I Monumenti cristiani dei primi sei secoli. Rome: Università Gregoriana, 1920.

Hefele, Charles-Joseph. *Histoire des conciles d'après les documents originaux*. 11 vols. in 21. Paris: Letouzey et Ané, 1907–1921.

Helman, Ivy A. *Women and the Vatican: An Exploration of Official Documents*. Maryknoll, NY: Orbis, 2012.

Hermas. *Le Pasteur: Hermas; introduction, texte critique, traduction et notes par Robert Joly*. 2nd ed. Sources chrétiennes, 53. Paris: Édition du Cerf, 1958.

Hippolytus. *Hippolytus: A Text for Students*, with introduction, translation, commentary, and notes by Geoffrey J. Cuming. Grove Liturgical Study 8. 2nd ed. Bramcote, Notts.: Grove Books, 1976.

———. *On the Apostolic Tradition: Hippolytus*. An English version with introduction and commentary by Alistair Stewart-Sykes. Crestwood, NY: St. Vladimir's Seminary Press, 2001.

Icon and Logos: Sources in Eighth-Century Iconoclasm; An Annotated Translation of the Sixth Session of the Seventh Ecumenical Council (Nicaea, 787) Containing the Definition of the Council of Constantinople (754) and Its Refutation and the Definition of the Seventh Ecumenical Council. Translated by Daniel J. Sahas. Toronto Medieval Texts and Translations 4. Toronto: University of Toronto Press, 1986.

Ignatius of Antioch: A Commentary on the Letters of Ignatius of Antioch, by William R. Schoedel. Edited by Helmut Koester. Hermeneia. Philadelphia, PA: Fortress Press, 1985.

Innocent I, Pope. *Church and Worship in Fifth-Century Rome: The Letter of Innocent I to Decentius of Gubbio: Text with Introduction, Translation and Notes by Martin F. Connell*. Joint Liturgical Studies 52. Cambridge: Grove Books, 2001.

———. *La lettre du pape Innocent Ier à Decentius de Gubbio 19 mars 416: Texte critique, traduction et commentaire* by Robert Cabié. Bibliothèque de la Revue d'histoire ecclésiastique fasc. 58. Louvain: Publications Universitaires de Louvain, Bureau de la R. H. E., 1973.

Irenaeus (Irénée), Bishop of Lyons. *Contre les hérésies*. Edited, translated, and annotated by A. Rousseau and L. Doutreleau. Vol. 2. Sources chrétiennes. Paris: Éditions du Cerf, 1969.

Itineraria et alia geographica. 2 vols. Corpus Christianorum. Series Latina 175–176. Turnholt: Brepols, 1965.

Jerome. *Sancti Hieronymi presbyteri opera,* pt. 1: *Opera exegetica,* vol. 4, *Commentarii in Hiezechielem libri XIV.* Edited by F. Glorie. *Commentariorum in Hiezechielem Libri XVI,* ed. F. Glorie. Corpus Christianorum. Series Latina 75. Turnhout: Brepols, 1964.

John Paul II, Pope. *Post-Synodal Apostolic Exhortation Christi Fideles Laici of His Holiness John Paul II on the Vocation and the Mission of the Faithful in the Church and in the World.* Ottawa: Canadian Conference of Catholic Bishops, 1988.

Justin Martyr. *Saint Justin Martyr: The First and Second Apologies.* Translated with introduction and notes by Leslie William Barnard. Ancient Christian Writers 56. New York: Paulist Press, 1997.

Justinian. *Novellae of Justinian.* Vol. 3 of *Corpus Iuris civilis.* Edited by R. Schoell and Wilhelm Kroll. Berlin: Weidmann, 1928.

Karl der Grosse: Lebenswerk und Nachleben. Edited by Wolfgang Braunfels, P. E. Schram, and H. Schnitzler. 2nd ed. 5 vols. Düsseldorf: L. Schwann, 1966–1968.

Kaufmann, C. M. *Handbuch der altchristlichen Epigraphik.* Freiberg im Breisgau: Herder, 1917.

Latin Commentaries on Revelation. Commentary on the Apocalypse, by Victorinus of Petovium, Apringius of Beja, Caesarius of Arles, and Bede the Venerable. Edited and translated with introduction and notes by William C. Weinrich. Ancient Christian Texts. Downers Grove, IL: InterVarsity Press Academic, 2011.

The Leofric Missal. Edited by Nicholas Orchard. 2 vols. Henry Bradshaw Society 113–114. London: Boydell Press, 2002.

The Leofric Missal as Used in the Cathedral of Exeter during the Episcopate of Its First Bishop, A.D. 1050–1072. Edited with introduction and notes by F. E. Warren. Oxford: Clarendon Press, 1883.

Le Liber censuum de l'église romaine, publié avec une introduction et un commentaire par Paul Fabre et L. Duchesne. 3 vols. Bibliothèque des écoles françaises d'Athènes et de Rome. 2. ser. 6. Paris: Fontemoing, Thorin, 1889–1952.

Liber ordinum episcopal: (Cod. Silos, Arch. Monástico 4). Edited by José Janini. Studia Silensia 15. Santo Domingo de Silos: Abadia de Silos, 1991.

Le Liber pontificalis: Texte, introduction et commentaire par Louis Duchesne. 2 vols. Bibliothèque des Écoles françaises d'Athènes et de Rome. 2e série 3. Paris: E. Thorin, 1886–1892. Reprint. 2nd ed. 3 vols. Republished by Cyrille Vogel, with a third volume on the history of *LP,* including additions, corrections, and indices since Duchesne's edition. Paris: E. De Boccard, 1955–1957. Reprint of the 1955–1957 edition. Paris: E. de Boccard, 1981.

Liber sacramentorum Augustodunensis. Edited by O. Heiming. Corpus Christianorum. Series Latina 159B. Turnhout: Brepols, 1984.

Liber sacramentorum Gellonensis. Edited by André Dumas. Corpus Christianorum. Series Latina 159, 159A. Turnhout: Brepols, 1981.

The Life of Saint Mary Magdalene and of Her Sister Saint Martha: A Medieval Biography. Translated and annotated by David Mycoff. Kalamazoo, MI: Cistercian Publications, 1989.

The Liturgical Portions of the Apostolic Constitutions: A Text for Students. Translated, edited, annotated, and introduced by W. Jardine Grisbrooke. Grove Liturgical Study 61. Bramcote, Notts.: Grove Books, 1990.

The Liturgical Portions of the Didascalia. Edited by Sebastian Brock and Michael Vasey. Grove Liturgical Study 29. Bramcote, Notts.: Grove Books, 1982.

The Lives of the Eighth-Century Popes (Liber Pontificalis): The Ancient Biographies of Nine Popes from AD 715 to AD 817. Translated with introduction and commentary by Raymond Davis. Translated Texts for Historians 13. Liverpool: Liverpool University Press, 1992. 2nd ed., 2007.

The Lives of the Ninth-Century Popes (Liber Pontificalis): The Ancient Biographies of Ten Popes from AD 817–891. Translated with an introduction and commentary by Raymond Davis. Translated Texts for Historians 20. Liverpool: Liverpool University Press, 1995.

Mansi, J. D. *Sacrorum conciliorum nova et amplissima collectio*. 54 vols. in 58. Florence and Venice, 1758–1798. Reprint. Paris: Hubert Welter, 1901–1927. Reprint. Graz: Akademische Druck- u. Verlagsanstalt, 1960–1961.

Marcus Aurelius and His Times: The Transition from Paganism to Christianity. Introduction by Irwin Edman. New York: Walter J. Black, 1945.

Martinelli, Fioravante. *Primo trofeo della santissima Croce eretta in Roma nella via lata da S. Pietro apostolo*. Rome: Nicolangelo Tinassi, 1655.

Martyrologium Romanum: Gregorii Papae XIII jussu editum Urbani VIII et Clementis X. Edited by Benedict XIV. Rome: Vatican Polyglot Press, 1913. 5th ed. Turin: Marietti, 1949.

Medieval Handbooks of Penance: A Translation of the Principal Libri Poenitentales and Selections from Related Documents. Translated by John T. McNeill and Helena M. Gamer. Records of Civilization, Sources and Studies 29. New York: Octagon Books, [1938] 1965.

Migne, Jacques Paul, ed. *Patrologiae cursus completus, series Latina*. 221 vols. Paris, 1857–1887.

Missale Francorum (Cod. Vat. Reg. Lat. 257). In conjunction with Leo Eizenhöfer and Petrus Siffrin. Edited by Leo Cunibert Mohlberg. Rerum ecclesiasticarum documenta. Series maior, Fontes 2. Rome: Herder, 1957.

Missale Gallicanum vetus (Cod. Vat. Palat. Lat. 493). In conjunction with Leo Eizenhöfer and Petrus Siffrin. Edited by Leo Cunibert Mohlberg. Rerum ecclesiasticarum documenta 3. Rome: Herder, 1958.

Mombritius, Boninus. *Sanctuarium seu Vitae Sanctorum*. 2 vols. Edited by Monks of Solesmes. Paris: Fontemoing, 1910. Reprint. Hildesheim; New York: Georg Olms, 1978.

Morin, Jean (Ioannes Morinus). *Commentarius de sacris ecclesiae ordinationibus, secundum antiquos et recentiores, latinos, graecos, syros, et babylonios, in tres partes distinctus.* Paris: Gaspari Meturas, 1655. 2nd ed. Antwerp: Barent van Lier; Amsterdam, H. Desbordes, 1695. Reprint. Farnborough: Gregg, 1969.

New Testament Apocrypha. Vol. 1: *Gospels and Related Writings.* Translated and edited by R. McL. Wilson. Cambridge: J. Clarke and Co., 1991.

The Octavius of Marcus Minucius Felix. Translated and annotated by G. W. Clarke. Ancient Christian Writers 39. New York: Newman Press, 1974.

Odelem, Johann Philipp. *Dissertatio de diaconissis primitivae ecclesiae.* Leipzig: Fleischer, 1700.

Old Testament Pseudepigrapha. Vol. 1: *Apocalyptic Literature and Testaments.* Edited by James H. Charlesworth. Garden City, NY: Doubleday, 1983.

Optat, Bishop of Milève. *Traité contre les donatistes: introduction, texte critique, traduction et notes par Mireille Labrousse.* 2 vols. Sources chrétiennes 412–413. Paris: Cerf, 1996.

The Other Gospels: Non-Canonical Gospel Texts. Edited by Ron Cameron. Philadelphia, PA: Westminster, 1982.

Paulinus of Nola. *Letters of St. Paulinus of Nola.* Translated and annotated by P. G. Walsh. 2 vols. Ancient Christian Writers 35–36. Westminster, MD: Newman, 1966–1967.

Pliny, the Younger. *The Letters of Pliny the Younger: Literally Translated, with Notes.* English translation by William Melmoth. Revised by W. M. L. Hutchinson. 2 vols. Loeb Classical Library. London: W. Heinemann, 1915.

———. *Letters of Pliny: A Historical and Social Commentary,* by A. N. Sherwin-White. Rev. ed. Oxford: Clarendon Press, [1966] 1985.

The Pontifical of Egbert, Archbishop of York A.D. 732–766. Edited by William Greenwell. Publications of the Surtees Society 27. Durham: George Andrews, 1853.

Le Pontifical romano-germanique du dixième siècle. Edited by Cyrille Vogel and Reinhard Elze. 3 vols. Studi e Testi 226, 227, 269. Vatican City: Biblioteca Apostolica Vaticana, 1963–1972.

Pontificale Romanum: Clementis VIII a.c. Urbani VIII jussu editum et a Benedicto XIV Rome: S. Congregationis de Propaganda Fide, 1868.

Les Pontificaux manuscrits des Bibliothèques Publiques de France, by Abbé Victor Leroquais. 2 vols. Paris: Macon, Protat frères, imprimeurs, 1937.

Rabani Mauri Martyrologium. Edited by John McCulloh. Corpus Christianorum. Continuatio Mediaevalis 44. Turnhout: Brepols, 1979.

The Rite of Ordination according to the Roman Pontifical. Translated by J. S. M. Lynch. 4th ed., rev. and enl. New York: Cathedral Library Association, [1892] 1918.

The Roman Pontifical: Revised by Decree of the Second Vatican Ecumenical Council and Published by Authority of Pope Paul VI. Washington, DC: International Commission on English in the Liturgy, 1978.

Sacramentarium Veronense (Cod. Bibl. Capit. Veron. LXXXV [80]). Edited by Leo Cunibert Mohlberg with Leo Eizenhöfer and Petrus Siffrin. Rerum Ecclesiasticum Documente, Series minor. Subsidia studiorum, 4. Rome: Herder, 1956.

Siricius, Pope. *Epistola 5 ad episcopos Africae epistola.* Vol. 3 (PL 13, cols. 1160–61). *Epistola 10 ad episcopos Galliae* (PL 13. 10.2.5).

Severano, Giovanni. *Memorie sacre della sette chiese di Roma.* Rome: Giacoma Mascardi, 1630.

The Testamentum Domini: A Text for Students. Edited by Grant Sperry-White. Translated from the Syriac text of Ignatius Ephraem II Rahmanis edition. Grove Liturgical Study 66. Bramcote, Notts.: Grove Books, 1991.

Tertullian. *De monogamia. De virginibus velandis.* In *Tertulliani Opera, pars 2: Opera montanistica.* Edited by E. Dekkers, et al. 2 vols. Corpus Christianorum. Series Latina 1–2. Turnhout: Brepols, 1954.

———. *De praescriptione hereticorum.* In *Traité de la prescription contre les hérétiques.* Edited by R. F. Refoulé. Translated by P. de Labriolle. Sources chrétiennes 46. Paris: Cerf, 1957.

Theodore of Stoudios (the Stoudite). *Theodori Studitai Epistulae.* Edited by Georgios Fatouros. 2 vols. Corpus Fontium Historiae Byzantinae 31. Berlin: Walter de Gruyter, [1991] 1992.

Thomassin, Louis. *Vetus et nova ecclesiae disciplina circa beneficia et beneficiarios.* 3 vols. Lyons: Annison and Pasuel, 1705–1706.

The Wisdom of Ben Sira: A New Translation with Notes by Patrick W. Skehan. Introduction and Commentary by Alexander A. Di Lella. Anchor Bible 39. Garden City, NY: Doubleday, 1987.

Zacharias, Pope. *De monachis, id est ancillis Dei, de quibus flagitatum. Epistola* VIII.5, PL 89, 933.

Zeno, Saint, Bishop of Verona. *The Day Has Come! Easter and Baptism in Zeno of Verona.* Compiled and edited by Gordon P. Jeanes. Alcuin Club Collection 73. Collegeville, MN: Liturgical Press, 1995.

Ziegler, Caspar. *De diaconis et diaconissis veteris ecclesiae liber commentarius.* 4 vols. Wittenberg, 1678.

SECONDARY SOURCES

(a) Dictionaries, Encyclopedias, and Lexicons

The Anchor Bible Dictionary. Edited by David Noel Freedman. 6 vols. New York: Doubleday, 1992.

Arndt, William F., and F. Wilbur Gingrich. *A Greek-English Lexicon of the New Testament and Other Early Christian Literature.* 4th ed. rev. Chicago: University of Chicago Press, 1957.

Bibliotheca Sanctorum. 13 vols. Rome: Pontificia Università Lateranense, 1961–1970.

Blaise, Albert, ed. *Lexicon Latinitatis Medii Aevi: praesertim ad res ecclesiasticas investigandas pertinens = Dictionnaire latin-française des auteurs du Moyen-Age.* Corpus Christianorum. Continuatio Medievalis. Turnholt: Brepols, 1975.

The Concise Oxford Dictionary. 7th ed. Edited by J. B. Sykes. Oxford: Clarendon Press [1982] 1986. 10th ed. rev. Edited by Judy Pearsall. Oxford; New York: Oxford University Press, [1995] 1999.

Dictionary of Popes and the Papacy. Edited by Bruno Steimer and Michael G. Parker. Translated by Brian McNeil and Peter Heinigg. New York: Crossroad, 2001.

Dictionnaire d'archéologie chrétienne et de liturgie. Edited by Fernand Cabrol et al. 15 vols. in 30. Paris: Letouzey et Ané, 1907–1953.

Dictionnaire de spiritualité ascetique et mystique, doctrine et histoire. Edited by Marcel Viller et al. 17 vols. Paris: G. Beauchesne, 1937–1995.

Encyclopedia of Monasticism. Edited by William M. Johnston. 2 vols. Chicago: Fitzroy Dearborn, 2000.

Encyclopedia of Women and World Religion. Edited by Serinity Young. 2 vols. New York: Macmillan Reference, 1999.

Klauser, Theodor, ed. *Reallexikon für Antike und Christentum: Sachwörterbuch zur Auseinandersetzung des Christentums mit der antiken Welt.* 24 vols. Edited by Theodor Klauser et al. Stuttgart: A. Hiersemann, 1957–.

New Catholic Encyclopedia. 18 vols. New York: McGraw-Hill, 1967–1997. 2nd ed. 15 vols. Washington, DC: Catholic University of America Press, 2003.

The New Dictionary of Sacramental Worship. Edited by Peter Fink. Collegeville: Liturgical Press, 1990.

The Oxford Dictionary of Popes, by J. N. D. Kelly. Oxford: Oxford University Press, 1986. 2nd ed., revised by Michael J. Walsh, 2010.

The Oxford Dictionary of Saints, by David Hugh Farmer. 2nd ed. Oxford: Oxford University Press, 1987.

The Papacy: An Encyclopedia. Edited by Philippe Levillain. 3 vols. New York: Routledge, 2002.

Paulys Real-Encyclopädie der klassischen Altertumswissenschaft. 24 vols. in 44. Stuttgart: J. B. Metzler Verlagsbuchhandlung, 1894–1963.

Reallexikon für Antike und Christentum: Sachwörterbuch zur Auseinandersetzung des Christentums mit der antiken Welt. Edited by Theodor Klauser et al. 24 vols. Stuttgart: A. Hiersemann, 1950–.

Suicer, J. C. *Thesaurus ecclesiasticus e patribus graecis.* Amsterdam, 1682. 2nd edition, 1728.

Theological Dictionary of the New Testament. Edited by Gerhard Kittel and Gerhard Friedrich. Translated and abridged in one volume by Geoffrey W. Bromiley. Grand Rapids, MI: Eerdmans, 1985.

(B) Modern Books and Articles

Addleshaw, G. W. O. *The Beginnings of the Parochial System*. St. Anthony's Hall publications 3. York: St. Anthony's Press, 1953.

Age of Spirituality: Late Antique and Early Christian Art, Third to Seventh Century: Catalogue of the Exhibition at the Metropolitan Museum of Art, November 19, 1977 through February 12, 1978. Edited by Kurt Weitzmann. New York: Metropolitan Museum of Art in association with Princeton University Press, 1979.

Alexander, Paul J. "Religious Persecution and Resistance in the Byzantine Empire of the Eighth and Ninth Centuries: Methods and Justifications." *Speculum* 52 (1977): 238–64.

Alzati, Cesare. *Ambrosianum Mysterium: The Church of Milan and Its Liturgical Tradition*. Vol. 1. Translated by George Guiver. Cambridge: Grove Books, 1999.

Amiet, Robert. "Un '*Comes*' carolingien inédit de la Haute-Italie." *Ephemerides Liturgicae* 73 (1959): 334–67.

Amore, Agostino. "Martina." In *Bibliotheca Sanctorum* 8:1220–21. Rome: Pontificia Università Lateranese, 1966.

———. *I martiri di Roma*. Spicilegium Pontificii Athenaei Antoniani. Rome: Antonianum, 1975.

Angelelli, Claudia. *La basilica titolare di S. Pudenziana: nuove ricerche*. Monumenti di antichità cristiana 2. Ser., 21. Vatican City: PIAC, 2010.

Angiolini, Anna. *La capsella eburnea de Pola*. Studia di antichità cristiana 7. Bologna: Riccardo Pàtron, 1970.

Ansorge, Dirk. "Der Diakonat der Frau. Zum gegenwärtigen Forschungsstand." In *Liturgie und Frauenfrage: Ein Beitrag zur Frauenforschung aus liturgiewissenschaftlichen Sicht*, edited by Teresa Berger and Albert Gerhards, 31–65. Pietas liturgica 7. St. Ottilien: EOS Verlag Erzabtei, 1990.

Antonelli, F. "I primi monasteri di monaci orientali in Roma." *Rivista di archeologia cristiana* 5 (1928): 105–21.

Arat, Kristin. "Die Weihe der Diakonin in der armenisch-apostolischen Kirche." In *Liturgie und Frauenfrage: Ein Beitrag zur Frauenforschung aus liturgiewissenschaftlichen Sicht*, edited by Teresa Berger and Albert Gerhards, 67–75. Pietas Liturgica 7. St. Ottilien: EOS Verlag Erzabtei, 1990.

Armstrong, Jonathan J. "Victorinus of Pettau as the Author of the Canon Muratori." *Vigiliae Christianae* 62 (2008): 1–34.

Arranz, Miquel. "Le culte divin à Constantinope au seuil de l'an mille. L'Euchologe byzantin. État d'une recherché." Paper given in 1992 at Ludwig-Maximilians Universität, Munich.

Asmussen, Marianne Wirenfeldt. "The Chapel of San Zeno in S. Prassede in Rome: New Aspects on the Iconology." *Analecta Romana Instituti Danici* 15 (1986), 67–87.

Aubert, Marie-Josèphe. *Il diaconato alle donne? Un nuovo cammino per la chiesa.* Milan: Paoline, 1989.

Aune, David. *Revelation 1–5.* Word Biblical Commentary 52A. Dallas: Word Books, 1997.

Bacci, Augusto. "Relazione degli scavi eseguiti in S. Agnese." *Römische Quartalschrift für christliche Altertumskunde und für Kirchengeschichte* 16 (1902): 51–58.

———. "Ulteriori osservazioni sulla basilica nomentana." *Nuovo Bullettino di archeologia cristiana* 12 (1906): 77–87.

Backmund, N. "Canonesses." In *New Catholic Encyclopedia.* Volume 3, 53–54. New York: McGraw Hill, 1967.

Baldovin, John F. "The 'Fermentum' at Rome in the Fifth Century: A Reconsideration." *Worship* 79 (2005): 38–53.

———. "Hippolytus and the Apostolic Tradition: Recent Research and Commentary." *Theological Studies* 64 (2003): 520–42.

———. "Saints in the Byzantine Tradition." *Liturgy* 5/2 (1985): 71–75.

———. *The Urban Character of Christian Worship: The Origins, Development, and Meaning of Stational Liturgy.* Orientalia Christiana Analecta 228. Rome: Pontifical Oriental Institute, 1987.

Baldracco, G. "La cripta del sec. IX nella chiesa di Santa Prassede a Roma." *Rivista di archeologia cristiana* 18 (1941): 277–96.

Barbera, Rosanna. *Iscrizioni latine della raccolta de San Paolo fuori le Mura edite in ICVR: indice dei vocaboli.* Inscriptiones Sanctae Sedis 3.1. Vatican City: Musei Vaticani, 2009.

Bassler, Jouette M. "1 Corinthians." In *Women's Bible Commentary*, exp. ed., edited by Carol Newsom and Sharon H. Ringe, 411–19. Louisville, KY: Westminster/John Knox, 1998.

Bauckham, Richard. *Gospel Women: Studies of the Named Women in the Gospels.* Grand Rapids, MI: Eerdmans, 2002.

Bauer, Franz Alto. "La frammentazione liturgica nella chiesa romana del primo medioevo." *Rivista di archeologia cristiana* 75 (1999): 385–446.

Beckwith, John. *The Andrews Diptych.* Victoria and Albert Museum 12. London: Her Majesty's Stationery Office, 1958.

Beentjes, Pancratius. "'Inverted Quotations in the Bible': A Neglected Stylistic Pattern." *Biblica* 63 (1982): 506–23.

Belting-Ihm, Christa. *Die Programme der christlichen Apsismalerei vom vierten Jahrhundert bis zur Mitte des achten Jahrhunderts.* Forschungen zur Kunstgeschichte und christliche Archäologie 4. Wiesbaden: Steiner, 1960.

———. *"Sub matris tutela": Untersuchungen zur Vorgeschichte der Schutzmantelmadonna.* Abhandlungen der Heidelberger Akademie der Wissenschaften 3. Heidelberg: Carl Winter, 1976.

Berger, Teresa. *Gender Differences and the Making of Liturgical History: Lifting a Veil on Liturgy's Past.* Liturgy, Worship and Society. Farnham, Surrey: Ashgate, 2011.

———. *Women's Ways of Worship: Gender Analysis and Liturgical History*. Collegeville, MN: Liturgical Press, 1999.

———, and Albert Gerhards, eds. *Liturgie und Frauenfrage: Ein Beitrag zur Frauenforschung aus liturgiewissenschaftlichen Sicht*. Pietas liturgia 7. St. Ottilien: EOS verlag Erzabtei, 1990.

Bernas, C. "Agape." In *The New Catholic Encyclopedia*, 2nd ed. Vol. 1, 169–71. Washington, DC: Catholic University of America, 2003.

———. "Eucharist." In *The New Catholic Encyclopedia*. Vol. 5, 594–99. New York: McGraw Hill, 1967.

Biddle, Mark E. "The Figure of Lady Jerusalem: Identification, Deification and Personification of Cities in the Ancient Near East." In *The Biblical Canon in Comparative Perspective: Scripture in Context IV*, edited by Lawson Younger, Jr., William W. Hallo and Bernard F. Batto, 173–94. Ancient Near Eastern Texts and Studies 11. Lewiston, NY: Mellen, 1991.

Blaauw, Sible de. *Cultus et decor: liturgia e architettura nella Roma tardoantica e medievale*. 2 vols. Translated by Maria Beatrice Anniss. Studi e Testi 355–356. Vatican City: Biblioteca Apostolica Vaticana, 1994.

———. "The Solitary Celebration of the Supreme Pontiff: The Lateran Basilica as the New Temple in the Medieval Liturgy of Maundy Thursday." In *Omnes circumadstantes: Contributions towards a History of the Role of the People in the Liturgy: Presented to Herman Wegman on the Occasion of his Retirement from the Chair of History and Theology in the Katholieke Theologische Universiteit Utrecht*, edited by Charles Caspers and Marc Schneiders, 120–43. Kampen: J.H. Kok, 1990.

Black, M. "The 'Two Witnesses' of Rev 11:3f." In *Donum Gentilicium: New Testament Studies in Honour of David Daube*. Edited by E. Bammel, C. K. Barrett and W. D. Davies, 227–37. Oxford: Clarendon Press, 1978.

Bolton, Brenda. "Daughters of Rome: All One in Christ Jesus!" In *Women in the Church: Papers Read at the 1989 Summer Meeting and the 1990 Winter Meeting of the Ecclesiastical History Society*, edited by W. J. Sheils and Diana Wood, 101–15. Studies in Church History 27. Cambridge, MA: Basil Blackwell, 1990.

Borino, Giovanni Battista. *Codices Vaticani latini 10876–11000*. Vatican City: Biblioteca Apostolica Vaticana, 1955.

Botte, Bernard. List of his publications drawn up by F. Petit, in *Mélanges liturgiques offerts au R. P. Dom Bernard Botte*. Louvain: Abbaye du Mont César, 1972.

———. "L'ordre d'après les prières d'ordination." In Études *sur le sacrament de l'ordre*. Paris: Éditions du Cerf, 1957. Translated as "Holy Orders in Ordination Prayers." In *The Sacrament of Holy Orders: Some Papers and Discussions Concerning Holy Orders at a Session of the Centre de Pastorale Liturgique, 1955*, 5–23. Collegeville, MN: Liturgical Press, 1962.

———. "La première fête mariale de la liturgie romaine." *Ephemerides liturgicae* 47 (1933): 425–30.

Boucher, François, and Yvonne Deslandres. *A History of Costume in the West.* New ed. London: Thames and Hudson, 1987.
Boulet, Noële Maurice-Denis. "Titres urbains et communauté dans la Rome chrétienne." *La Maison-Dieu* 36 (1953): 14–32.
Bovini, Giuseppe. *Il cosidetto Mausoleo di Galla Placidia in Ravenna.* Collezione "Amici delle catacombe" 13. Vatican City : Società Amici Catacombe presso PIAC, 1950.
———. "I mosaici della chiesa di s. Pudenziana à Roma." *Corso di cultura sull'arte ravennate e bizantina* 18 (1971): 95–113.
Bowersock, G. W. *Martyrdom and Rome.* Wiles Lectures. Cambridge: Cambridge University Press, 1995.
Bradshaw, Paul F. *Ordination Rites of the Ancient Churches of East and West.* New York: Pueblo, 1990.
———. "The Origins of Easter." In *Passover and Easter: Origin and History to Modern Times*, edited by Paul F. Bradshaw and Lawrence A. Hoffmann, 81–97. Two liturgical traditions. Notre Dame, IN: University of Notre Dame Press, 1999.
———. *The Search for the Origins of Christian Worship: Sources and Methods for the Study of Early Liturgy.* 2nd ed. Oxford: Oxford University Press, 2002.
———, Maxwell E. Johnson, and L. Edward Phillips. *The Apostolic Tradition: A Commentary.* Edited by Harold W. Attridge. Hermeneia. Minneapolis, MN: Fortress Press, 2002.
Brandenburg, Hugo. *The Basilica of S. Agnese and the Mausoleum of Constantina Augusta (S. Costanza).* Regensburg: Verlag Schnell und Steiner, 2006. (Offprint from: Hugo Brandenburg, *Ancient Churches of Rome from the Fourth to the Seventh Century: The Dawn of Christian Architecture in the West.* Translated by Andreas Knopp. Bibliothèque de l' Antiquité tardive 8. Turnhout: Brepols, 2005.)
Branick, Vincent P. *The House Church in the Writings of Paul.* Zacchaeus studies. Wilmington, DE: Glazier, 1989.
Breckenridge, J. D. "Evidence for the Nature of Relations between Pope John VII and the Byzantine Emperor Justinian II." *Byzantinische Zeitschrift* 65 (1972): 364–74.
Brenk, Beat. "Zum Bildprogramm der Zenokapelle in Rom." *Archivio Español de Arqueologia* 45–47 (1972–1974): 213–21.
Brennan, Brian. "'*Episcopae*': Bishops' Wives Viewed in Sixth Century Gaul." *Church History* 54 (1985): 311–23.
Brent, Allen. *Hippolytus and the Roman Church in the Third Century: Communities in Tension before the Emergence of a Monarch-Bishop.* Supplements to Vigiliae Christianae 31. Leiden: E. J. Brill, 1995.
Brock, Ann Graham. *Mary Magdalene, the First Apostle: The Struggle for Authority.* Harvard Theological Studies 51. Cambridge, MA: Harvard University Press, 2003.
Brooten, Bernadette J. "Early Christian Women and their Cultural Context: Issues of Method in Historical Reconstruction." In *Feminist Perspectives on Biblical Scholarship*, edited by Adela Yarbro Collins, 65–91. Chico, CA: Scholars Press, 1985.

———. "Junia...Outstanding among the Apostles (Rom. 16:7)." In *Women Priests: A Catholic Commentary on the Vatican Declaration*, edited by Leonard Swidler and Arlene Swidler, 141–44. New York: Paulist Press, 1977.

———. *Women Leaders in the Ancient Synagogue: Inscriptional Evidence and Background Issues*. Chico, CA: Scholars Press, 1982.

Brown, Peter. *The Body and Society: Men, Women, and Sexual Renunciation in Early Christianity*. Columbia Classics in Religion. New York: Columbia University Press, 1988.

———. *The Cult of the Saints: Its Rise and Function in Latin Christianity*. Chicago: University of Chicago Press, 1981.

———. "The Rise and Function of the Holy Man in Late Antiquity." *Journal of Roman Studies* 61 (1971) 80–101. Reprint. Brown, Peter. *Society and the Holy in Late Antiquity*, 103–52. Berkeley: University of California Press, [1982] 1989.

Brown, Raymond E. *The Churches the Apostles Left Behind*. New York: Paulist Press, 1984.

———. *Priest and Bishop: Biblical Reflections*. London: Geoffrey Chapman, [1970] 1971.

———, and John P. Meier. *Antioch and Rome: New Testament Cradles of Catholic Christianity*. New York: Paulist Press, 1983.

Brown, Virginia. "Latin and Italian Prayers in a Sixteenth-Century Beneventan Manuscript from Naples." In *Ritual, Text and Law: Studies in Medieval Canon Law and Liturgy Presented to Roger E. Reynolds*, edited by Kathleen G. Cushing and Richard F. Gyug, 95–122. Aldershot, Hants: Ashgate, 2004.

Buddensieg, Tilman. "Le coffret en ivoire de Pola, Saint-Pierre et le Latran." *Cahiers archéologiques* 10 (1959): 157–95.

Burrus, Virginia. *Chastity as Autonomy: Women in the Stories of the Apocryphal Acts*. Studies in Women and Religion 23. Lewiston, NY: Mellen, 1987.

Burtchaell, James Tunstead. *From Synagogue to Church: Public Services and Offices in the Earliest Christian Communities*. Cambridge; New York: Cambridge University Press, 1992.

Cain, Andrew. "Jerome's *Epitaphium Paulae*: Hagiography, Pilgrimage, and the Cult of Saint Paula." *Journal of Early Christian Studies* 18 (2010): 105–39.

Calabuig, Ignazio M., and Rosella Barbieri. "Consécration des vierges." In *Dictionnaire encyclopédique de la liturgie*, vol. 1, edited by Domenico Sartore and Achille M. Triacca, 219–33. Turnhout: Brepols, 1992.

Calcagnini, Daniela. "Le figure femminili nei mosaici paleocristiani degli edifici di culto romani." In *Ecclesiae Urbis: Atti del Congresso internazionale di studi sulle Chiese di Roma (IV–X secolo), Roma 4–10 settembre 2000*, vol. 3, edited by Federico Guidobaldi and Alessandra Guiglia Guidobaldi, 1919–38. Studi di antichità cristiana 59. Vatican City: PIAC, 2002.

Calkins, Robert G. *Illuminated Books of the Middle Ages*. Ithaca, NY: Cornell University Press, 1983.

Callam, Daniel. "Clerical Continence in the Fourth Century: Three Papal Decretals." *Theological Studies* 41 (1980): 3–50.

———. "The Frequency of Mass in the Latin Church ca. 400." *Theological Studies* 45 (1984): 613–50.

Campbell, Joan Cecelia. *Phoebe: Patron and Emissary. Paul's Social Network*. Collegeville, MN: Liturgical Press, 2009.

Caperna, Maurizio. *La Basilica di Santa Prassede: Il significato della vicenda architettonica*. Rome: Monaci Benedettini Vallombrosani, 1999.

Carletti, Sandro. *Guide to the Catacombs of Priscilla*. Translated by Alice Mulhern. Vatican City: Pontifical Commission for Sacred Archaeology, 1982.

Castelli, Elizabeth. "Virginity and Its Meaning for Women's Sexuality in Early Christianity." *Journal of Feminist Studies in Religion* 2 (1986): 61–88.

Cattin, Giulio. *Music of the Middle Ages* 1. Translated by Stephen Botterill. Cambridge: Cambridge University Press, 1984.

Celibacy in the Church. Edited by William Bassett and Peter Huizing. Concilium 78. New York: Herder & Herder, 1972.

Celtic Spirituality. Translated by Oliver Davies. Classics of Western Spirituality. New York: Paulist Press, 1999.

Cempanari, Mario, and Tito Amodei. *Scala Santa e Sancta Sanctorum*. Rome: Edizioni Quasar, 1999.

Charles, R. H. *A Critical and Exegetical Commentary on The Revelation of St. John*. International Critical Commentary. Edinburgh: T. & T. Clark, 1920.

Chavasse, Antoine. "A Rome, le Jeudi-Saint, au VIIe siècle, d'après un vieil ordo." *Revue d'histoire écclésiastique* 50 (1955): 21–35.

———. "Le calendrier dominical romain au sixième siècle." *Recherches de science religieuse* 41 (1953): 96–122.

———. "Les célebrations eucharistiques à Rome, Ve–VIIIe siècle." *Ecclesia orans* 7 (1990): 69–75.

———. "L'épistolier romain du codex de Wurtzbourg: son organisation." *Revue bénédictine* 91 (1981): 280–331.

———. "Evangéliare, épistolier, antiphonaire et sacramentaire: Les livres romains de la messe au VIIe et au VIIIe siècle." *Ecclesia orans* 6 (1989): 177–255.

———. *Les lectionnaires romains de la messe au VIIe et au VIIIe siècle: sources et dérives*. 2 vols. Spicilegii Friburgensis subsidia 22. Fribourg, Suisse: Éditions universitaires, 1993.

———. *La liturgie de la ville de Rome du Ve au VIIIe siècle*. Analecta liturgica 18. Rome: S. Anselmo, 1993.

———. "L'organisation stationale du Carême romain, avant le VIIIe siécle: une organisation 'pastorale.'" *Revue des sciences religieuses* 56 (1982): 17–32.

———. "Les plus anciens types du lectionnaire et de l'antiphonaire romains de la messe." *Revue bénédictine* 62 (1952): 3–94.

———. "Le regroupement des formulaires annuels pour la messe dans les livres romains du VIIe et du VIIIe siècle." *Ecclesia orans* 7 (1990): 335–342.

———. *Le sacramentaire gélasien (Vaticanus Reginensis 316): sacramentaire presbytéral en usage dans les titres romains au VIIe siècle.* Paris: Desclée, 1958.

Christe, Yves. "Apocalypse et interprétation iconographique: quelques remarques liminaires sur les images du règne de Dieu et de l'église a l'époque paléo-chrétienne." *Byzantinische Zeitschrift* 67 (1974): 92–100.

———. "Les représentations médiévales d'Ap. IV (-V) en visions de la seconde parousie: origines, textes et contexte." *Cahiers archéologiques* 23 (1974): 61–72.

Chupungco, Anscar J. *Handbook for Liturgical Studies.* Vol. 4: *Sacraments and Sacramentals.* Collegeville, MN: Liturgical Press, 2000.

Clark, Elizabeth A. *Ascetic Piety and Women's Faith: Essays on Late Ancient Christianity.* Studies in Women and Religion 20. Lewiston, NY: Edwin Mellen Press, 1986.

———. "Ascetic Renunciation and Feminine Advancement: A Paradox of Late Ancient Christianity." *Anglican Theological Review* 63 (1981): 240–57.

———. "Authority and Humility: A Conflict of Values in Fourth-Century Female Monasticism." *Byzantinische Zeitschrift* 9 (1985): 17–33.

———. *Jerome, Chrysostom, and Friends: Essays and Translations.* New York: Edwin Mellen Press, 1979.

———. "John Chrysostom and the *Subintroductae.*" *Church History* 46 (1977): 171–85.

———. *Reading Renunciation: Asceticism and Scripture in Early Christianity.* Princeton, NJ: Princeton University Press, 1999.

———. "Theory and Practice in Late Ancient Asceticism." *Journal for the Feminist Study of Religion* 5 (1989): 25–46.

Clarke, Andrew D. *Serve the Community of the Church: Christians as Leaders and Ministers.* First-Century Christians in the Graeco-Roman World. Grand Rapids, MI: Eerdmans, 2000.

Coda, Caterina-Giovanna. *Duemilatrecento corpi di martiri. La relazione di Benigno Aloisi (1729) e il ritrovamento delle reliquie nella basilica di Santa Prassede in Roma.* Miscellanea della Società romana di storia patria 46. Rome: La Società alla Biblioteca Vallicelliana, 2004.

Collins, John N. *Deacons and the Church: Making the Connections between Old and New.* Harrisburg, PA: Morehouse, 2002.

———. *Diakonia: Re-interpreting the Ancient Sources.* New York: Oxford University Press, 1990.

———. "Once More on Ministry: Forcing a Turnover in the Linguistic Field." *One in Christ* 27 (1994): 234–45.

Collins, Raymond F. *First Corinthians.* Edited by Daniel J. Harrington. Collegeville, MN: Liturgical Press, 1999.

Comblin, Joseph. "La liturgie de la nouvelle Jérusalem (Apoc. XXI, 1–XXII, 5)." *Ephemerides theologiae lovanienses* 29 (1953): 5–40.

Connell, Martin F. "*Descensus Christi ad Inferos*: Christ's Descent to the Dead." *Theological Studies* 62 (2001): 262–71.

———. "Just as on Easter Sunday: On the Feast of the Presentation." *Studia Liturgica* 33 (2003): 159–74.

Constantelos, Demetrios. "Marriage and Celibacy of the Clergy in the Orthodox Church." In *Celibacy in the Church*, edited by William Bassett and Peter Huizing, 30–38. Concilium 78. New York: Herder & Herder, 1972.

Cooper, Kate. "The Martyr, the Matrona and the Bishop: The Matron Lucina and the Politics of Martyr Cult in Fifth- and Sixth-Century Rome." *Early Medieval Europe* 8 (1999): 297–318.

———. *The Virgin and the Bride: Idealized Womanhood in Late Antiquity*. Cambridge, MA: Harvard University Press, 1996.

———, and Julia Hillner, eds. *Religion, Dynasty and Patronage in Early Christian Rome, 300–900*. Cambridge; New York: Cambridge University Press, 2007.

Corpus Inscriptionum Latinarum (CIL): Inscriptiones Aemillae, Etruriae, Umbriae Latinae. Vol. 11. Berlin: Apud G. Reimerum, 1862.

Costambeys, Marios, and Conrad Leyser. "To Be the Neighbour of St. Stephen: Patronage, Martyr Cult, and Roman Monasteries, c. 600–c. 900." In *Religion, Dynasty, and Patronage in Early Christian Rome, 300–900*, edited by Kate Cooper and Julia Hillner, 262–87. Cambridge: Cambridge University Press, 2007.

Cotter, Wendy. "Women's Authority Roles in Paul's Churches: Countercultural or Conventional." *Novum Testamentum* 36 (1994): 350–72.

Coyle, J. Kevin. "The Laying on of Hands as a Conferral of the Spirit: Some Problems and a Possible Solution." In *Studia Patristica 18/2: Critica, Classica Ascetica, Liturgica: Papers of the 1983 Oxford Patristic Conference*, edited by E. A. Livingstone, 339–53. Leuven: Peeters Press, 1989.

Croisier, Jérôme. "La decorazione pittorica dell' oratorio mariano di Santa Pudenziana." In *La pittura medievale a Roma, 312–1431: corpus e atlante*. 5 vols. Vol. 4: *Riforme et tradizione, 1050–1198*. Edited by Serena Romano, 199–206. Milan: Jaca Book, 2006–.

Crook, John A. "Feminine Inadequacy and the Senatusconsultum Velleianum." In *The Family in Ancient Rome: New Perspectives*. Edited by Beryl Rawson, 83–92. Ithaca, NY: Cornell University Press, 1986.

Crook, John. *The Architectural Setting of the Cult of Saints in the Early Christian West, c. 300–1200*. Oxford: Clarendon Press, 2000.

Crusius, Irene. "*Sanctimoniales quae se canonicas vocant*: Das Kanonissenstift als Forschungsproblem." In *Studien zum Kanonissenstift*, edited by Irene Crusius, 9–38. Veröffentlichungen des Max-Planck-Instituts für Geschichte 167: Studien zur Germania sacra, 24. Göttingen: Vandenhoeck & Ruprecht, 2001.

Cunningham, Mary B. and Pauline Allen, eds. *Preacher and Audience: Studies in Early Christian and Byzantine Homiletics*. A New History of the Sermon 1. Leiden: Brill 1998.

D'Angelo, Mary Rose. "Hebrews." In *Women's Bible Commentary*, edited by Carol A. Newsom and Sharon H. Ringe, 364–67. Louisville, KY: Westminster John Knox, 1992.

———. "Reconstructing 'Real' Women from Gospel Literature: The Case of Mary Magdalene." In *Women and Christian Origins*, edited by Ross S. Kraemer and Mary Rose D'Angelo, 105–28. New York: Oxford University Press, 1999.

Dagens, Claude. "A Propos du Cubiculum de la 'Velatio.'" *Rivista di archeologia cristiana* 47 (1971): 119–29.

Dallen, James. "Reconciliation, Sacrament of." In *The New Dictionary of Sacramental Worship*, edited by Peter E. Fink, 1052–64. Collegeville, MN: Liturgical Press, 1990.

Davies, Stevan L. *The Revolt of the Widows: The Social World of the Apocryphal Acts*. Carbondale, IL: Southern Illinois University Press, 1980.

Davis, Natalie Zemon, and Arlette Farge, eds. *A History of Women in the West*. Vol. 3: *Renaissance and Enlightenment Paradoxes*. 5 vols. Cambridge, MA: Belknap Press of Harvard University Press, 1993.

Davis, Raymond. *The Lives of the Eighth-Century Popes (Liber Pontificalis): The Ancient Biographies of Nine Popes from AD 715 to AD 817*. Liverpool: Liverpool University Press, 1992.

———. *The Lives of the Ninth-Century Popes (Liber Pontificalis): The Ancient Biographies of Ten Popes from AD 817–891*. Liverpool: Liverpool University Press, 1995.

———. *The Book of Pontiffs (Liber Pontificalis): The Ancient Biographies of the First Ninety Roman Bishops to AD 715*. Revised Edition. Liverpool: Liverpool University Press, 2000.

Davis-Weyer, Caecilia. "Die ältesten Darstellungen der Hadesfahrt Christi, des Evangelium Nikodemi und ein Mosaik der Zeno-Kapelle." In *Roma e l'età carolingia. Atti delle giornate di studio, 3–8 maggio 1976*, edited by Istituto di Storia dell'Arte dell'Università di Roma, 183–94. Rome: Multigrafica editrice, 1976.

———. "Die Mosaiken Leos III. und die Anfänge der karolingischen Renaissance in Rome." *Zeitschrift für Kunstgeschichte* 29 (1966): 111–32.

———. "Das Traditio-Legis Bild und seine Nachfolge." *Münchner Jahrbuch der bildenden Kunst* 12 (1961): 7–45.

De Luca, M. "La tavola del giudizio universale già in San Gregorio Nazianzeno (Pinacoteca Vaticana) 1061–1071." In *La pittura medievale a Roma*. 5 vols. *Corpus*, vol. 4: *Riforma e tradizione, 1050–1198*, edited by Serena Romana, part 1, 45–55. Milan: Jaca Book, 2006–.

Delehaye, Hippolyte. *The Legends of the Saints*. Translated by Donald Attwater. New York: Fordham University Press, 1962. First published as *Les légendes hagiographiques*, Brussels: Société des Bollandistes, 1905.

Deshman, Robert. "Servants of the Mother of God in Byzantine and Medieval Art." *Word and Image* 5 (1989): 33–70.

Deshusses, Jean. "Les anciens sacramentaires *grégorien* de Tours." *Revue bénédictine* 89 (1979): 281–302.

———. "Les messes d'Alcuin." *Archiv für Liturgiewissenschaft* 14 (1972): 7–41.

———. "Le sacramentaire de Trent." *Revue bénédictine* 78 (1968): 261–82.

———. "Le sacramentaire grégorien préhadrianique." *Revue bénédictine* 80 (1970): 213–37.

———, ed. *Le sacramentaire grégorien: ses principales formes d'après les plus ancien manuscrits. Édition comparativ.* 3 vols. Fribourg, Suisse: Éditions Universitaires, 1988–1992.

Dewey, Joanna. "1 Timothy," "2 Timothy," "Titus." In *Women's Bible Commentary.* Exp. ed. Edited by Carol Newsom and Sharon H. Ringe, 444–52. Louisville, KY: Westminster John Knox, 1998.

Diakonia, diaconiae, diaconato: semantica e storia nei padri della chiesa, XXXVIII Incontro di studiosi dell'antichità cristiana, Roma, 7–9 maggio 2009. Studia ephemerides Augustinianum 117. Rome: Istitutum Patristicum Augustinianum, 2010.

Dijk, S. J. P. van. "The Old-Roman Rite." *Studia Patristica* 5 (1962): 185–205.

———. "The Urban and Papal Rites in Seventh- and Eighth-Century Rome." *Sacris Erudiri* 12 (1961): 411–87.

Dix, Gregory. *The Shape of the Liturgy.* 2nd ed. New York: Seabury, 1982.

Dold, Alban. "Ein ausgeschriebenes Perikopenbuch des 8. Jahrhunderts." *Ephemerides liturgicae* 54 (1940): 12–37.

Donum gentilicium: New Testament Studies in Honour of David Daube. Edited by E. Bammel, C. K. Barrett and W. D. Davies. Oxford: Clarendon Press, 1978.

Dubois, Jacques. *Le martyrologe d'Usuard: texte et commentaire.* Subsidia hagiographica 40. Brussels: Société des Bollandistes, 1965.

———. *Les martyrologes du moyen âge latin.* Typologie des sources du Moyen Age occidental, fasc. 26. Turnhout: Brepols, 1978.

———, and Geneviève Renaud. *Édition pratique des martyrologes de Bède, de l'Anonyme lyonnais et de Florus.* Paris: Éditions du Centre national de la recherche scientifique, 1976.

———, and Geneviève Renaud, eds. *Le martyrologe d'Adon: Ses deux familles, ses trois recensions: texte et commentaire.* Source d'histoire médiévale. Paris: Éditions du Centre national de la recherché scientifique, 1984.

Du Cange, Charles Du Fresne. *Glossarium ad scriptores mediae et infimae latinitatis.* 2 vols. Lyons: Anisson & Rigaud, 1688. Reprint. 6 vols. Paris: O. C. Osmont, 1733–1736.

———, et al. *Glossarium mediae et infimae latinitatis.* 7 vols. Paris: Firmin Didot, 1840–1850. 10 vol. Paris: Libraire des sciences et des arts, 1937–1938. Reprint. Graz: Akademische Druck- und Verlagsanstalt, 1954.

Duchesne, Louis Marie Olivier. *The Beginnings of the Temporal Sovereignty of the Popes A.D. 754–1073.* Translated by Arnold Harris Mathew. International Catholic Library 11. London: Kegan Paul, Trench, Trübner, 1908.

---. "Les monastères desservants de Sainte-Marie-Majeur." *Mélanges d'archéologie et d'histoire* 27 (1907): 479–94.
Dufourcq, Albert. *Étude sue les Gesta martyrum romains: Étude sur les Gesta martyrum.* Vol. 1. Paris: Albert Fontemoing, 1900.
Dunbabin, Katherine M. D. "Triclinium and Stibadium." In *Dining in a Classical Context*, edited by William J. Slater, 121–48. Ann Arbor, MI: University of Michigan Press, 1991.
Dunn, Geoffrey D. "Deacons in the Early Fifth Century: Canonical Developments in Rome under Innocent I." In *Diakonia, diaconiae, diaconato: semantica e storia nei padri della Chiesa.* XXXVIII Incontro di studiosi dell'antichità cristiana, Roma, 7–9 maggio 2009, 331–40. Studia ephemeridis Augustinianum 117. Rome: Istitutum Patristicum Augustinianum, 2010.
---. "Infected Sheep and Diseased Cattle, or the Pure and Holy Flock: Cyprian's Pastoral Care of Virgins." *Journal of Early Christian Studies* 11 (2003): 1–20.
Dvornik, Francis. *Byzantium and the Roman Primacy*. Translated by Edwin A. Quain. New York: Fordham University Press, 1966.
---. *The Idea of Apostolicity in Byzantium and the Legend of the Apostle Andrew.* Dumbarton Oaks Studies 4. Cambridge, MA: Harvard University Press, 1958.
---. *Les légendes de Constantin et de Méthode vues de Byzance.* 2nd ed. Byzantinoslavica. Supplementa 1. Hattiesburg, MS: Academic International, 1969.
---. *Les Slaves, Byzance et Rome au IXe siècle.* Travaux publiés par l'Institut d'études slaves 4. Paris: H. Champion, 1926.
Dyer, Joseph. "Prolegomena to a History of Music and Liturgy at Rome in the Middle Ages." In *Essays on Medieval Music in Honour of David G. Hughes*, edited by Graeme M. Boone, 87–116. Isham Library Papers 4. Cambridge, MA: Harvard University Press, 1995.
Ehrensberger, Hugo, ed. *Libri Liturgici Bibliothecae Apostolicae Vaticanae Manuscripti.* Freiburg im Breisgau: Herder, 1897.
Eisen, Ute E. *Women Officeholders in Early Christianity: Epigraphical and Literary Studies.* Translated by Linda M. Maloney. Collegeville, MN: Liturgical Press, 2000.
Elbern, Victor H. *Die Goldschmiedekunst im frühen Mittelalter.* Darmstadt: Wissenschaftliche Buchgesellschaft, 1988.
Elliott, J. K. "Mary in the Apocryphal New Testament." In *Origins of the Cult of the Virgin Mary*, edited by Chris Maunder, 57–70. London: Burns and Oates, 2008.
Elm, Susanna. *"Virgins of God": The Making of Asceticism in Late Antiquity.* Oxford Classical Monographs. Oxford: Clarendon Press, 1994.
Emerick, Judson J. "Altars Personified: The Cult of the Saints and the Chapel System in Pope Paschal I's S. Prassede (817–819)." In *Archaeology in Architecture: Studies in Honor of Cecil L. Striker*, edited by Judson J. Emerick and Deborah M. Deliyannis, 43–63. Mainz: P. von Zabern, 2005.

———. "Focusing on the Celebrant: The Column Display inside Santa Prassede." In *Mededelingen van het Nederlands Instituut te Rome* 59 (2001):129–59.
Emmerson, Nicola, and Bernard McGinn, eds. *The Apocalypse in the Middle Ages*. Ithaca, NY: Cornell University Press 1992.
Emsley, Nichola. "The Rite of Consecration of Virgins." In *Handbook for Liturgical Studies*. Vol. 4: *Sacraments and Sacramentals*. 5 vols., edited by Anscar J. Chupungco, 331–42. Collegeville, MN: Liturgical Press, 2000.
Evenou, Jean. "Marriage." In *The Church at Prayer*. Vol. 3: *The Sacraments*, edited by Aimé Georges Martimort, 185–91. Collegeville, MN: Liturgical Press, 1988.
Faivre, Alexandre. *The Emergence of the Laity in the Early Church*. Translated by David Smith. New York: Paulist Press, 1990.
———. *Naissance d'une hiérarchie: Les premières étapes du cursus clérical*. Théologie historique 40. Paris: Éditions Beauchesne, 1977.
Fallon, J. E. "Mary Magdalene, St." In *New Catholic Encyclopedia*. 2nd ed. Vol. 9, 285–88. Washington, DC: Catholic University of America Press, 2003.
Fasola, Umberto Maria. *The Catacombs of Domitilla and the Basilica of the Martyrs Nereus and Achilleus*. 3rd ed. rev. Edited by Phillipo Pergola. Translated by C. S. Houston and F. Barbarito. Vatican City: Pontificia Commissione di Archeologia Sacra, 2002.
———. "Lavori nella catacomba 'Ad duas Lauros.'" *Rivista de archeologia cristiana* 62 (1986): 7–40.
Feiss, Hugh. "Monasticism, Definitions of: Christian Perspectives." In *Encyclopedia of Monasticism*. Edited by William M. Johnston, vol. 2, 871–73. Chicago: Fitzroy Dearborn, 2000.
Felle, A. E. "'Diaconi' e 'diaconissae' tra oriente e occidente: L'apporto della documentazione epigrafica." In *Diakonia, diaconiae, diaconato: semantica e storia nei padri della chiesa*. XXXVIII Incontro di studiosi dell'antichità cristiana, Roma, 7–9 maggio 2009, 489–537. Studia ephemeridis Augustinianum 117. Rome: Institutum Patristicum Augustinianum, 2010.
Ferme, Brian Edwin. *Introduction to the History of the Sources of Canon Law: The Ancient Law up to the 'Decretum' of Gratian*. Translated by William J. King. Montreal: Wilson & Lafleur, 2007.
Ferrari, Guy. *Early Roman Monasteries: Notes for the History of Monasteries and Convents at Rome from the V through the X Century*. Studi di antichità cristiana 23. Vatican City: PIAC, 1957.
Ferrua, Antonio. "Il catalogo dei martiri di S. Prassede." In *Atti della Pontificia accademia romana di archeologia (Serie 3) Rendiconti* 30–31 (1957–1959): 129–40.
———. "Le antiche iscrizioni cristianae di S. Paolo f.l.m." *Rendiconti della Pontificia academia romana di archeologia* 62 (1989–1990): 184–209.
Filippi, Giorgio. *Indice della raccolta epigrafica di San Paolo fuori le Mura*. Inscriptiones Sanctae Sedis 3. Vatican City: Vatican Museums, 1998.

Finger, Reta Halteman. *Of Widows and Meals: Communal Meals in the Book of Acts.* Grand Rapids, MI: Eerdmans, 2007.

Fiocchi Nicolai, Vincenzo. "'Itinera ad sanctos': Testimonianze monumentali del passaggio dei pellegrini nei santuari del suburbio Romano." In *Atti del XII congresso internazionale di archeologia cristiana, Bonn 22–28 settembre 1991*, 2:763–75. Studi di antichità cristiana 52. Vatican City: Pontifical Institute of Christian Archaeology, 1995.

———, Fabrizio Bisconti, and Danilo Mazzoleni. *Les catacombes chrétiennes de Rome: origine, développement, décor, inscriptions.* Translated by Jean Guyon. Turnhout: Brepols, 2000.

Fischer, Balthasar. "Formes de la commémoration du baptême en Occident." *La Maison-Dieu* 58 (1959): 111–34.

———, and Johannes Wagner, eds. *Paschatis Sollemnia: Studien zu Osterfeier und Osterfrömmigkeit.* Basel: Herder, 1959.

FitzGerald, Kyriaki Karidoyanes. *Women Deacons in the Orthodox Church: Called to Holiness and Ministry.* Brookline, MA: Holy Cross Orthodox Press, 1998.

Fixot, Michel. *La crypte de Saint-Maximin La-Sainte-Baume, Basilique Sainte-Marie-Madeleine.* Aix-en-Provence: Édisud, 2001.

Fliche, Augustin. *La réforme grégorienne.* Vol. 1: *La formation des idées grégoriennes.* Louvain: Spicilegium sacrum Lovaniense bureaux, 1966.

Ford, Josephine Massyngberde. "Order for the Ordination of a Deaconess." *Review for Religious* 33 (1974): 308–14.

———. *Revelation: Introduction, Translation and Commentary.* Anchor Bible 38. Garden City, NY: Doubleday, 1975.

Freeman, Ann. "Carolingian Orthodoxy and the Fate of the Libri Carolini." *Viator* 16 (1985): 65–108.

Frend, W. H. C. *Martyrdom and Persecution in the Early Church: A Study of a Conflict from the Maccabees to Donatus.* Oxford: Blackwell, 1965.

Frere, Walter Howard. *Studies in Early Roman Liturgy.* Vol. 1: *The Kalendar.* Alcuin Club Collections 28. London: Oxford University Press, 1930.

———. *Studies in Early Roman Liturgy.* Vol. 2: *The Roman Gospel-Lectionary.* Alciun Club Collections 30. London: Oxford University Press, 1934.

———. *Studies in Early Roman Liturgy.* Vol. 3: *The Roman Epistle-Lectionary.* Alcuin Club Collections 32. London: Oxford University Press, 1935.

Frugoni, Chiara. "The Imagined Woman." In *A History of Women in the West.* Vol. 2: *Silences of the Middle Ages*, edited by Christiane Klapisch-Zuber, 336–422. Cambridge, MA: Belknap Press of Harvard University Press, 1992.

Frutaz, Amato Pietro. "Titolo di Pudente: denominazione successive, clero e cardinali titolari." *Rivista di archeologia cristiana* 40 (1964): 53–72.

Gaiffier, Baudouin de. "Le martyrologe et le légendier d'Hermann Greven." *Analecta Bollandiana* 54 (1936): 316–58.

———. "Un prologue hagiographique hostile au Décret de Gélase?" *Analecta Bollandiana* 82 (1964): 341–53.

Galt, Caroline M. "Veiled Ladies." *American Journal of Archaeology* 35 (1931): 373–93.

Gamber, Klaus. "Das Münchner Fragment eines Lectionarium plenarium aus dem Ende des 6. Jahrhunderts." *Ephemerides liturgicae* 72 (1958): 268–80.

Garrison, E. B. "Dating the Vatican Last Judgment Panel, Monument vs Document." *La Bibliofilia* 72 (1970): 121–60.

———. *Studies in the History of Mediaeval Italian Painting*. 4 vols. Florence: L'Impronta, 1953–1962.

Gautier-van Berchem, Marguerite, and Etienne Clouzot. *Mosaïques chrétiennes du IVme au Xme siècle*. Rome: "L'Erma" di Bretschneider, 1965.

Geertman, Herman. *More Veterum: il Liber Pontificalis e gli edifici ecclesiastici di Roma nella tarda antichità e nell'alto medioevo*. Archaeologica traiectina 10. Groningen: H. D. Tjeenk Willink, 1975.

Georgiana, Linda. "Any Corner of Heaven: Heloise's Critique of Monasticism." In *Mediaeval Studies* 49 (1987): 221–53.

Getty-Sullivan, Mary Ann. *Women in the New Testament*. Collegeville, MN: Liturgical Press, 2001.

Gibaut, John St. H. *The Cursus Honorum: A Study of the Origins and Evolution of Sequential Ordination*. Patristic Studies 3. New York: Peter Lang, 2000.

Gillman, Florence Morgan. "James, Brother of Jesus." In *Anchor Bible Dictionary*, 3:620–21. New York: Doubleday, 1992.

Gnirs, A. "La basilica e il reliquario d'avorio di Samagher presso Pola." In *Atti e memorie della Società Istriana di Archeologia e Storia Patria* 24 (1908), 4–48.

Godman, Peter, and Roger Collins, eds. *Charlemagne's Heir: New Perspectives on the Reign of Louis the Pious (814–840)*. Oxford; New York: Clarendon Press, 1990.

Goffredo, Daniela. "Le personificazioni delle ecclesiae: tipologia e significati dei mosaici di S. Pudenziana e S. Sabina." In *Ecclesiae urbis: Atti del congresso internazionale di studi sulle Chiese di Roma (IV–X secolo), Roma, 4–10 settembre 2000*, vol. 3, edited by Federico Guidobaldi and Alessandra Guiglia Guidobaldi, 1949–62. Studi di antichità cristiana 59. Vatican City: PIAC, 2002.

Goodson, Caroline J. "The Relic Translations of Paschal I (817–824): Transforming City and Cult." In *Roman Bodies: Antiquity to the Eighteenth Century*, edited by Andrew Hopkins and Maria Wyke, 123–41. London: British School at Rome, 2005.

———. "Revival and Reality: The Carolingian Renaissance in Rome and the Case of S. Prassede." In *Continuatio et Renovatio*, edited by Siri Sande and Lasse Hodne. Acta ad archaeologiam et artium historiam pertinentia 20 (n.s. 6), 163–92. Rome: Bardi Editore, 2006.

———. *The Rome of Pope Paschal I: Papal Power, Urban Renovation, Church Building and Relic Translation 817–824*. Cambridge Studies in Medieval Life and Thought, 4th ser., 77. Cambridge: Cambridge University Press, 2010.

Gougaud, L. "Celtiques (Liturgies)." In *Dictionnaire d'archéologie chrétienne et de liturgie*, vol. 2, pt. 2, cols. 2969–3032. Paris: Letouzey et Ané, 1910.

Gourdel, Yves. "Chartreux." In *Dictionnaire de spiritualité ascétique et mystique: doctrine et histoire* vol. 2, part 1: cols 705–776. Paris: Beauchesne, 1953.

Grabar, André. "Le portrait en iconographie paleochrétienne." *Revue de sciences religieuses* 36 (1962): 87–109.

———. "Un rouleau liturgique constantinopolitain et ses peintures." *Dumbarton Oaks Papers* 8 (1954): 161–99.

Greeley, Andrew. *Confessions of a Parish Priest: An Autobiography*. New York: Simon & Schuster, 1986.

Grisar, Hartmann. *Das Missale im Lichte römischer Stadtgeschichte: Stationen, Perikopen, Gebräuche*. Freiburg im Breisgau: Herder, 1925.

Gros, Miquel S. "Les plus anciennes formules romaines de bénédiction des diacres." *Ecclesia Orans* 5 (1988), 45–52.

Grossi-Gondi, Felice. "La celebre iscrizione agiografica della basilica di S. Prassede in Roma." *Civiltà Cattolica* 67 (1916): 443–56.

Gryson, Roger. *The Ministry of Women in the Early Church*. Translated by Jean Laporte and Mary Louise Hall. Collegeville, MN: Liturgical Press, 1976.

Guerrieri, Agnese. *La Chiesa dei SS.* [Santi] *Nereo ed Achilleo*. Collezione "Amici delle Catacombe" 16. Vatican City: PIAC, 1951.

Guidobaldi, Federico. "L'inserimento delle chiese titolari di Roma nel tessuto urbano preesistente: ossservazioni ed implicazione." In *Quaeritur inventus colitur: miscellanea in onore di Padre Umberto Maria Fasola*, vol. 1, edited by Philippe Pergola, 381–96. Studi di antichità cristiana 40. Vatican City, PIAC, 1989.

———. "Osservazioni sugli edifici romani in cui si insediò l'Ecclesia Pudentiana." In *Ecclesiae urbis: Atti del congresso internazionale di studi sulle chiese di Roma (IV–X secolo), Roma, 4–10 settembre 2000*, vol. 2, edited by Federico F. Guidobaldi and Alessandra Guiglia Guidobaldi, 1033–71. Studi di antichità cristiana 59. Vatican City: PIAC, 2002.

Guilmard, Jacques-Marie. "Une antique fête mariale au 1er janvier dans la ville de Rome?" *Ecclesia orans* 11 (1994): 25–67.

Gy, Pierre-Marie. "Ancient Ordination Prayers." In *Ordination Rites Past and Present: Papers Read at the 1979 Congress of Societas Liturgica*, edited by Wiebe Vos and Geoffrey Wainwright, 70–93. Rotterdam: Liturgical Ecumenical Center Trust, 1980.

———. "Notes on the Early Terminology of Christian Priesthood." In *The Sacrament of Holy Orders. Some Papers and Discussions Concerning Holy Orders at a Session of the Centre de Pastorale Liturgique, 1955*, 98–115. Collegeville, MN: Liturgical Press, 1962.

———. "Le sanctus romain et les anaphores orientales." In *Mélanges liturgiques offerts au R.P. Bernard Botte*, 167–74. Louvain: Abbaye du Mont César, 1972.

Hagner, Donald A. "James." *Anchor Bible Dictionary*, 3:616–18. New York: Doubleday, 1992.

Hamilton, Louis I. *A Sacred City: Consecrating Churches and Reforming Society in Eleventh-Century Italy*. Manchester Medieval Studies. Manchester: Manchester University Press, 2010.

Hardinge, Leslie. *The Celtic Church in Britain*. Church Historical Society 91. London: SPCK, 1972.

Harnack, Adolf von. *The Mission and Expansion of Christianity in the First Three Centuries*. Vol. 1. Translated and edited by James Moffatt. 2nd ed. rev. New York: G. P. Putnam, 1908.

———. "Probabilia über die Adresse und den Verfasser des Hebräerbriefes." *ZNW* 1 (1900): 16–41.

Harrison, Dick. *The Age of Abbesses and Queens: Gender and Political Culture in Early Medieval Europe*. Lund, Sweden: Nordic Academic Press, 1998.

Haskins, Susan. *Mary Magdalen: Myth and Metaphor*. Old Saybrook, CT: Konecky & Konecky, 1993.

Hatlie, Peter. "Theodore of Stoudios, Pope Leo III and the Joseph Affair (808–812): New Light on an Obscure Negotiation." *Orientalia Christiana Periodica* 61 (1995): 407–23.

———. "Theodore of Studios, St." In *The Encyclopedia of Monasticism*, 2:1252–53. Chicago; London: Fitzroy Dearborn, 2000.

Hearon, Holly E. *The Mary Magdalene Tradition: Witness and Counter-Witness in Early Christian Communities*. Collegeville, MN: Liturgical Press, 2004.

Heine, Susanne. *Women and Early Christianity*. London: SCM, 1987.

Heitz, C. "Retentissement de l'Apocalypse dans l'art de l'époque carolingienne." In *Roma e l'età carolingia: Atti delle giornate di studio, 3–8 maggio 1976*. Edited by Istituto di storia dell'arte dell'Università di Roma [Institute of Art History of the University of Rome], 217–43. Rome: Multigrafica editrice, 1976.

Hellemo, Geir. *Adventus Domini: Eschatological Thought in 4th-Century Apses and Catecheses*. Translated by Elinor Ruth Waaler. Supplements to Vigiliae Christianae 5. Leiden: E. J. Brill, 1989.

Hen, Yitzhak. *The Royal Patronage of Liturgy in Frankish Gaul to the Death of Charles the Bald (877)*. Henry Bradshaw Society. Subsidia 3. London: Boydell Press, 2001.

Hertling, Ludwig, and Engelbert Kirschbaum. *The Roman Catacombs and Their Martyrs*. Translated by M. Joseph Costelloe. Milwaukee, WI: Bruce, 1956.

Hess, Hamilton. *The Early Developments of Canon Law and the Council of Serdica*. Oxford Early Christian Studies. Oxford: Oxford University Press, 2002.

Hickey, Anne Ewing. *Women of the Roman Aristocracy as Christian Monastics*. Ann Arbor, MI: UMI Research Press, 1987.

Hillner, Julia. "Clerics, Property and Patronage: The Case of the Roman Titular Churches." *Antiquité Tardive* 14 (2006): 59–68.

———. "*Domus*, Family, and Inheritance: The Senatorial Family House in Late Antique Rome." *Journal of Roman Studies* 93 (2003): 129–45.

———. "Families, Patronage, and the Titular Churches of Rome, c. 300–c.600." In *Religion, Dynasty, and Patronage in Early Christian Rome, 300–900*, edited by Kate Cooper and Julia Hillner, 225–61. Cambridge: Cambridge University Press, 2007.

Hinsdale, Mary Ann. "St. Mary of Magdala: Ecclesiological Implications." In *Proceedings of the Catholic Theological Society of America* 66 (2011): 67–90.

Hochstetler, Donald. *A Conflict of Traditions: Women in Religion in the Early Middle Ages 500–840*. Lanham, MD: University Press of America, 1992.

Hofhansl, E. "Gewänder, liturgische." *Theologische Realenzyclopädie* 13 (1984): 159–67.

Holmes, Michael W., ed. *The Apostolic Fathers: Greek Texts and English Translations.* Updated and revised after the earlier edition of J. B. Lightfoot and J. R. Harmer. Grand Rapids, MI: Baker Books, 1999.

Holum, Kenneth G., and Gary Vikan. "The Trier Ivory, *Adventus* Ceremonial, and the Relics of St. Stephen." *Dumbarton Oaks Papers* 33 (1979): 113–33.

Hoppin, Ruth. *Priscilla's Letter: Finding the Author of the Epistle to the Hebrews*. Fort Bragg, CA: Lost Coast Press, 1997.

Hucke, Helmut. "Toward a New View of Gregorian Chant." *Journal of the American Musicological Society* 33 (1980): 437–67.

Hughes, Kevin L. "Augustinian Rule." In *Encyclopedia of Monasticism*, 1:106–17. Chicago; London: Fitzroy Dearborn, 2000.

Humphries, Mark. "From Emperor to Pope? Ceremonial, Space and Authority at Rome from Constantine to Gregory the Great." In *Religion, Dynasty and Patronage in Early Christian Rome, 300–900*, edited by Kate Cooper and Julia Hillner. Cambridge; New York: Cambridge University Press, 2007.

Hunter, David G. "The Significance of Ambrosiaster." *Journal of Early Christian Studies* 17 (2009): 1–26.

Inscriptiones christianae urbis Romae. Rome: 1857–1888. Edited by Giovanni Battista de Rossi, A. Silvagni, A. Ferrua, and Giuseppi Gatti. New Series. Rome: Ex Officini Libraria Doct. Befani, 1922–1985.

Inscriptiones Latinae Christianae Veteres (ILCV). Edited by Ernst Diehl. 3 vols. Berlin: Weidmann, 1925–1931. Reprint, 1961–1967.

Irvin, Dorothy. *Calendar 2003: The Archaeology of Women's Traditional Ministries in the Church 100–820 AD*. St. Paul, MN: n.p.

———. *Calendar 2004: The Archaeology of Women's Traditional Ministries in the Church, 300–1500 AD*. St. Paul, MN: n.p.

———. *Calendar 2005: The Archaeology of Women's Traditional Ministries in the Church, 60–1500 AD*. St. Paul, MN: n.p.

———. "The Ministry of Women in the Early Church: The Archaeological Evidence." *Duke Divinity School Review* 45 (1980): 76–86.

Irwin, Kevin M. "Archaeology Does Not Support Women's Ordination: A Response to Dorothy Irvin." *Journal of Women and Religion* 3/1 (1984): 32–42.

Jansen, Katherine Ludwig. *The Making of the Magdalen: Preaching and Popular Devotion in the Later Middle Ages.* Princeton, NJ: Princeton University Press, 2000.

Jasper, Detlev, and Horst Fuhrmann. *Papal Letters in the Early Middle Ages.* History of Medieval Canon Law. Washington, DC: Catholic University of America Press, 2001.

Jastrzebowska, Elisabeth. "Les Scènes de banquet dans les peintures et sculptures chrétiennes des IIIe et IVe siècles." *Recherches Augustiniennes* 14 (1979): 3–90.

Jay, Eric G. "From Presbyter-Bishops to Bishops and Presbyters." *Second Century* 1 (1981): 125–62.

Jeanes, Gordon P. *The Day Has Come! Easter and Baptism in Zeno of Verona.* Compiled and edited by Gordon P. Jeanes. Alcuin Club Collection 73. Collegeville, MN: Liturgical Press, 1995.

Jensen, Anne. "Das Amt der Diakonin in der kirchlichen Tradition der ersten Jahrtausends." In *Diakonat: Ein Amt für Frauen in der Kirche: Ein frauengerechtes Amt?* Edited by Peter Hünermann, Albert Hiesinger, Marianne Heimbach-Steins, Anne Jensen, 53–77. Ostfildern: Schwabenverlag, 1997.

———. *God's Self-Confident Daughters: Early Christianity and the Liberation of Women.* Translated by O. C. Dean, Jr. Louisville, KY: Westminster John Knox Press, 1996.

The Jerome Biblical Commentary. Edited by Raymond E. Brown, Joseph A. Fitzmyer, and Roland E. Murphy. 2 vols. in 1. Englewood Cliffs, NJ: Prentice-Hall, 1968.

Joannou, P. "Chorbishop." *New Catholic Encyclopedia,* vol. 3, 625–26. New York: McGraw-Hill, 1967.

Johnson, Elizabeth A. *Truly Our Sister: A Theology of Mary in the Communion of Saints.* New York: Continuum, 2003.

Johnson, Luke Timothy. *The First and Second Letters to Timothy.* Anchor Bible 35A. New York: Doubleday, 2001.

Johnson, Penelope Delafield. "Double Houses, Western Christian." In *Encyclopedia of Monasticism,* 1:416–19. Chicago; London: Fitzroy Dearborn, 2000.

Jounel, Pierre. "Le culte collectif des saints à Rome du VIIe au IXe siècle." *Ecclesia orans* 6 (1989): 285–300.

———. "Ordinations." In *The Church at Prayer.* Vol. 3: *The Sacraments,* edited by Robert Cabié and Aimé Georges Martimort et al., translated by Matthew O' Connell, 139–84. New ed. Collegeville, MN: Liturgical Press, 1988.

———. "Le sanctoral romain du 8e au 12e siècles." *La Maison-Dieu* 52 (1957): 59–88.

———. "The Veneration of the Saints." In *The Church at Prayer.* Vol. 4: *The Liturgy and Time,* edited by Aimé Georges Martimort, translated by Matthew O'Connell, 108–29. New ed. Collegeville, MN: Liturgical Press, 1986.

Jungmann, Joseph A. *The Mass of the Roman Rite: Its Origins and Development (Missarum Sollemnia).* Translated by Francis A. Brunner. 2 vols. New York: Benziger, 1951–1955.

Kalsbach, Adolf. *Die altkirchliche Einrichtung der Diakonissen bis zur ihrem Erlöschen. Römische Quartalschrift für christliche Altertumskunde und für Kirchengeschichte.* Supplement Heft 22. Freiburg im Breisgau: Herder, 1926.

———. "Diakonisse." *Reallexikon für Antike und Christentum* 3 (1957): 917–928.

Keener, Craig S. *The Gospel of John: A Commentary.* 2 vols. Peabody, MA: Hendrickson, 2003.

Keller, Marie Noël. *Priscilla and Aquila: Paul's Coworkers in Christ Jesus.* Collegeville, MN: Liturgical Press, 2010.

Kelly, J. N. D. *Oxford Dictionary of Popes.* Oxford: Oxford University Press, 1986. 2nd ed., revised by Michael J. Walsh, 2010.

Kennedy, V. L. *The Saints of the Canon of the Mass.* Vatican City: PIAC, 1963.

Kessel, Elisja Schulte van. "Virgins and Mothers between Heaven and Earth." In *A History of Women in the West.* Vol. 1: *Renaissance and Enlightenment Paradoxes.* Edited by Natalie Zemon Davis and Arlette Farge, 132–66. Cambridge, MA: Belknap Press of Harvard University Press, 1993.

Kilmartin, Edward J. "Apostolic Office: Sacrament of Christ." *Theological Studies* 36 (1975): 243–64.

———. "Bishop and Presbyter as Representatives of the Church and of Christ." In *Women Priests: A Catholic Commentary on the Vatican Declaration*, edited by Leonard Swidler and Arlene Swidler, 295–302. New York: Paulist Press, 1977.

———. *Christian Liturgy: Theology and Practice.* Part 1: *Systematic Theology of Liturgy.* Kansas City, MO: Sheed & Ward, 1988.

———. "Ministry and Ordination in Early Christianity against a Jewish Background." *Studia Liturgica* 13 (1979–1980): 42–69. Reprint. In *Ordination Rites: Papers Read at the 1979 Congress of Societas Liturgica*, edited by Wiebe Vos and Geoffrey Wainwright, 42–69. Rotterdam: Liturgical Ecumenical Center Trust, 1980.

King, Margot H. *The Desert Mothers: A Survey of the Feminine Anchoretic Tradition.* Saskatoon, SK: Peregrina Publishing, 1985.

King-Lenzmeier, Anne H. *Hildegard of Bingen: An Integrated Vision.* Collegeville, MN: Liturgical Press, 2001.

Kirkland, Alastair. "The Literary History of the Shepherd of Hermas Visions I to IV." *Second Century* 9 (1992): 87–102.

Kirsch, Johann Peter. "Anzeiger für christliche Archäologie." *Römische Quartalschrift für christliche Altertumskunde und für Kirchengeschichte* 16 (1902): 78–80.

———. *Die Frauen des kirchlichen Altertums.* Charakterbilder der katholischen Frauenwelt 1, 2. Paderborn: Schöningh, 1912.

———. *Die römischen Titelkirchen im Altertum.* Studien zur Geschichte und Kultur des Altertums. Paderborn: Schöningh, 1918.

Kirschbaum, Engelbert. *The Tombs of St Peter and St Paul.* Translated by John Murray. London: Secker and Warburg, 1959.

Kitzberger, Ingrid R. "Mary of Bethany and Mary of Magdala—Two Female Characters in the Johannine Passion Narrative." *New Testament Studies* 41 (1995): 564–86.

Kitzinger, Ernst. "The Cult of Images in the Age before Iconoclasm." *Dumbarton Oaks Papers* 8 (1954): 83–150. Reprint in Ernst Kitzinger, *The Art of Byzantium and the Medieval West: Selected Studies*, edited by W. Eugene Kleinbauer, 90–156. Bloomington: Indiana University Press, 1976.

———. "Some Reflections on Portraiture in Byzantine Art." In *The Art of Byzantium and the Medieval West: Selected Studies*, edited by W. Eugene Kleinbauer, 256–69. Bloomington: Indiana University Press, 1976.

Klapisch-Zuber, Christiane, ed. *A History of Women in the West*. Vol. 2: *Silences of the Middle Ages*. 5 vols. Cambridge, MA: Belknap Press of Harvard University Press, 1992.

Klass, Margo Pautler. "The Chapel of S. Zeno in S. Prassede in Rome." Ph.D. thesis, Bryn Maur College, 1972.

Klauser, Theodor. "Diakon." In Klauser, ed. *Reallexicon für Antike und Christentum: Sachwörterbuch zur Auseinandersetzung des Christentums mit der antiken Welt*, 3:888–909. 24 vols. Stuttgart: A. Hiersmann, 1957.

———. *Die römische Petrustradition im Lichte der neuen Ausgrabungen unter der Petruskirche*. Arbeitgemeinschaft für Forschung des Landes Nordrhein-Wesfalen Heft 24. Cologne-Opladen: Westdeutcher Verlag, 1956.

———. *A Short History of the Western Liturgy*. Translated by John Haliburton. London: Oxford University Press, 1969.

———, et al. "Aurum coronarium." In *Reallexikon für Antike und Christentum: Sachwörterbuch zur Auseinander-Setzung des Christentums mit der antiken Welt*, edited by Theodor Klauser, 1:1010–20. Stuttgart: A Hiersemann, 1950.

Kleinbauer, W. Eugene. "The Orants in the Mosaic Decoration of the Rotunda at Thessaloniki: Martyr Saints or Donors?" *Cahiers archéologiques* 30 (1982): 25–45.

Koch, C. "Vesta." In *Paulys Realencyclopädie der klassischer Altertumswissenschaft*. Vol. 2. Edited by G. Wissowa, 8 (16), cols. 1717–76. Stuttgart: J. B. Metzler, 1894–1980.

Konetzny, Gabriele. "Die Jungfrauenweihe." In *Liturgie und Frauenfrage: Ein Beitrag zur Frauenforschung aus liturgiewissenschaftlicher Sicht*, edited by Teresa Berger and Albert Gerhards, 475–92. Pietas Liturgica 7. St. Ottilien: EOS Verlag, 1990.

Kozachek, Thomas Davies. "The Repertory of Chant for Dedicating Churches in the Middle Ages: Music, Liturgy and Ritual." Ph.D. dissertation, Harvard University, 1995.

Kraemer, Ross S. "The Conversion of Women to Ascetic Forms of Christianity." *Signs* 6 (1980): 298–307.

———, and Mary Rose D'Angelo, eds. *Women and Christian Origins: A Reader*. New York: Oxford University Press, 1999.

Krautheimer, Richard. "The Carolingian Revival of Early Christian Architecture." *Art Bulletin* 24 (1942): 1–38. Reprint in Richard Krautheimer, *Studies in Early Christian, Medieval, and Renaissance Art*, 203–56. New York: New York University Press, 1969.

———. *Corpus basilicarum Christianarum Romae: Le basiliche cristiane antiche di Roma* (sec. IV–IX) = *The Early Christian Basilicas of Rome (IV–IX cent)*. Monumenti di antichità Ser. 2, v. 2. 5 vols. Vatican City: PIAC, 1937–1976.

———. *Early Christian and Byzantine Architecture*. Pelican History of Art. Harmondsworth: Penguin, 1965.

———. *Rome: Profile of a City, 312–1308*. Princeton, NJ: Princeton University Press, 1980. Reprint, 2000.

———. *Studies in Early Christian, Medieval, and Renaissance Art*. New York: New York University Press, 1969.

———. *Three Christian Capitals: Topography and Politics*. Berkeley: University of California Press, 1983.

Kretschmar, Georg. "Early Christian Liturgy in the Light of Contemporary Historical Research." *Studia Liturgica* 16 (1986–1987): 31–53.

L'Huillier, Peter. *The Church of the Ancient Councils: The Disciplinary Work of the First Four Ecumenical Councils*. Crestwood, NY: St. Vladimir's Seminary Press, 1996.

La Piana, George. "The Roman Church at the End of the Second Century." *Harvard Theological Review* 18 (1925): 201–77.

Ladner, Gerhart B. "Origin and Significance of the Byzantine Iconoclastic Controversy." *Mediaeval Studies* 2 (1940): 127–49.

———. *Die Papstbildnisse des Altertums und des Mittelalters*. Vol. 1: *Bis zum Ende des Investiturstreits*. Monumenti di antichità cristiana Ser. 2, 4. Vatican City: PIAC, 1941.

———. "The So-Called Square Nimbus." *Mediaeval Studies* 3 (1941): 15–45, reprinted in *Images and Ideas in the Middle Ages: Selected Studies in History and Art*, edited by Gerhart B. Ladner, vol. 1, 115–70; vol. 2, 1012–20. Storia e letteratura 155–156. Rome: Edizioni di Storia e Letteratura, 1983.

Laeuchli, Samuel. *Power and Sexuality: The Emergence of Canon Law at the Synod of Elvira*. Philadelphia: Temple University Press, 1972.

Lameri, Angelo. *La traditio instrumentorum e delle insegne nei riti di ordinazione: studio storico-liturgico*. Bibliotheca "Ephemerides liturgicae." Subsidia 96. Collana Studi di liturgia nuova ser. 35. Rome: C.L.V.-Edizioni liturgiche, 1998.

Lampe, Peter. *From Paul to Valentinus: Christians at Rome in the First Two Centuries*. Translated by Michael Steinhauser. Edited by Marshall D. Johnson. Minneapolis, MN: Fortress Press, 2003.

Lasko, Peter. *Ars Sacra, 800–1200*. Pelican History of Art. Baltimore, MD: Penguin, 1972.

Launderville, Dale. *Celibacy in the Ancient World: Its Ideal and Practice in Pre-Hellenistic Israel, Mesopotamia, and Greece*. Collegeville, MN: Liturgical Press, 2010.

Laurence, John D. "Vestments, Liturgical." In *The New Dictionary of Sacramental Worship*. Edited by Peter E. Fink, 1305–14. Collegeville, MN: Liturgical Press, 1990.

Laws, Sophie. *In the Light of the Lamb: Imagery, Parody, and Theology in the Apocalypse of John*. Good News Studies 31. Wilmington, DE: Glazier, 1988.

Leclercq, Henri. "Agape." In *Dictionnaire d' archéologie chrétienne et de liturgie*, vol. 1, pt. 1, cols. 775–848. Paris: Letouzey et Ané, 1907.

———. "Ancilla Dei." In *Dictionnaire d'archéologie chrétienne et de liturgie*, vol. 1, pt. 2, cols. 1973–1993. Paris: Letouzey et Ané, 1907.

———. "Apocryphes." In *Dictionnaire d'archéologie chrétienne et de liturgie*, vol. 1, pt. 2, cols. 2558–2559, figs. 831–32. Paris: Letouzey et Ané, 1907.

———. "Cappella Greca." In *Dictionnaire d'archéologie chrétienne et de liturgie*, vol. 2, pt. 2, cols. 2084–2106. Paris: Letouzey et Ané, 1910.

———. "Chaire épiscopale." In *Dictionnaire d'archéologie chrétienne et de liturgie*, vol. 3, pt. 1, cols. 19–75. Paris: Letouzey et Ané, 1913.

———. "Chancel." In *Dictionnaire d'archéologie chrétienne et de liturgie*, vol. 2, pt. 2, cols. 1821–1831. Paris: Letouzey et Ané, 1910.

———. "Chanoinesses." In *Dictionnaire d'archéologie chrétienne et de liturgie*, vol. 3, pt. 1, cols. 248–256. Paris: Letouzey et Ané, 1913.

———. "Confessio"; "Copies des peintures des catacombes." In *Dictionnaire d'archéologie chrétienne et de liturgie*, vol. 3, pt. 2, cols. 2503–2508; 2801–2819. Paris: Letouzey et Ané, 1914.

———. "Domitille (Cimetière de)"; "Petronilla." In *Dictionnaire d'archéologie chrétienne et de liturgie*, vol. 4, pt. 2, cols. 1404–1417. Paris: Letouzey et Ané, 1921.

———. "Glabrion (Manius Acilius)." In *Dictionnaire d'archéologie chrétienne et de liturgie*, vol. 6, pt. 1, cols. 1259–1274. Paris: Letouzey et Ané, 1924.

———. "Inscriptions latines chrétiennes." In *Dictionnaire d'archéologie chrétienne et de liturgie*, vol. 7, pt. 1, cols. 694–850. Paris: Letouzey et Ané, 1926.

———. "Latran (Venantius Chapel)." In *Dictionnaire d'archéologie chrétienne et de liturgie*, vol. 8, pt. 2, cols. 1576–1581. Paris: Letouzey et Ané, 1929.

———. "Marcella"; "Marie, mère de Dieu"; and "Maximin (Saint-)." In *Dictionnaire d'archéologie chrétienne et de liturgie*, vol. 10, pt. 2, cols. 1760–1762; 1986–1987, figs. 7697–7698; 2816–2820. Paris: Letouzey et Ané, 1932.

———. "Orant, orante." In *Dictionnaire d'archéologie chrétienne et de liturgie*, vol. 12, pt. 2, cols. 2291–2324. Paris: Letouzey et Ané, 1936.

———. "Ostrien (Cimitière)." In *Dictionnaire d'archéologie chrétienne et de liturgie*, vol. 13, pt. 1, cols. 112–130. Paris: Letouzey et Ané, 1937.

———. "Porto"; "Presbyter"; "Priscille (Cimetière de)"; "Prisque (Sainte)"; and "Pudentienne (Basilique de Saint-)." In *Dictionnaire d'archéologie chrétienne et de liturgie*, vol. 14, pt. 2, cols. 1533–1543; 1721; 1799–1874; 1876–1887; 1967–1973. Paris: Letouzey et Ané, 1948.

———. "Vienne en Dauphiné"; "Viérge, virginité." In *Dictionnaire d'archéologie chrétienne et de liturgie*, vol. 15, pt. 2, cols. 3038–3094; 3094–3108. Paris: Letouzey et Ané, 1953.

Leclercq, Jean. "Eucharistic Celebrations Without Priests in the Middle Ages." *Worship* 55 (1981): 160–68. Reprint in *Living Bread, Saving Cup: Readings on the Eucharist*, edited by R. Kevin Seasoltz, 222–30. Collegeville, MN: Liturgical Press, 1987.

———. "Prières médiévales pour recevoir l'eucharistie pour saluer et pour bénir la croix." *Ephemerides liturgicae* 97 (1965): 327–40.

Legrand, Hervé-Marie. "The Presidency of the Eucharist according to the Ancient Tradition." *Worship* 53 (1979): 413–38.

Lestocquoy, J. "Administration de Rome et diaconies du VIIème au IXème siècles." *Rivista di archeologia cristiana* 7 (1930): 261–95.

Lewis, Agnes Smith, trans. "The Story of the Blessed Mary Who Was Called Marina." *Vox Benedictina* 2 (1985): 305–17.

Leyser, Conrad. "The Temptations of Cult: Roman Martyr Piety in the Age of Gregory the Great." *Early Medieval Europe* 10 (2000): 289–307.

Leyser, Karl J. *Rule and Conflict in Early Medieval Society: Ottonian Saxony.* Bloomington: Indiana University Press, 1979.

Lifshitz, Felice. "Gender and Exemplarity East of the Middle Rhine: Jesus, Mary and the Saints in Manuscript Context." *Early Medieval Europe* 9 (2000): 325–43.

———. "Is Mother Superior? Toward a History of Feminine *Amtscharisma*." In *Medieval Mothering*. Edited by John Carmi Parsons and Bonnie Wheeler, 117–38. New York: Garland Publishing, 1996.

———. "The Martyr, the Tomb, and the Matron: Constructing the (Masculine) 'Past' as a Female Power Base." In *Medieval Concepts of the Past: Ritual, Memory, Historiography*, edited by Gerd Althoff, Johannes Fried, and Patrick J. Geary, 311–41. Washington, DC: German Historical Institute and Cambridge University Press, 2002.

Lipsius, Richard Adelbert. *Die apokryphen Apostelgeschichten und Apostellegenden: ein Beitrag zur altchristlichen Literaturgeschichte.* Vol. 2. Part 1. Braunschweig: Schwetschke, 1887.

Llewellyn, Peter A. B. "The Roman Church during the Laurentian Schism: Priests and Senators." *Church History* 45 (1976): 417–27.

———. *Rome in the Dark Ages.* London: Faber & Faber, 1971.

Loerke, William. "The Monumental Miniature." In Kurt Weitzmann et al., *The Place of Book Illumination in Byzantine Art.* Princeton, NJ: Art Museum, Princeton University Press, 1975.

Lohfink, Gerhard. "Weibliche Diakone im Neuen Testament." In Josef Blank et al., *Die Frau im Urchristentum*, edited by Gerhard Dautzenberg et al., 320–38. Quaestiones disputatae 95. Freiburg im Breisgau: Herder, 1983.

Lunn-Rockliffe, Sophie. *Ambrosiaster's Political Theology.* Oxford Early Christian Studies. Oxford: Oxford University Press, 2007.

MacDonald, Dennis R. *The Legend and the Apostle: The Battle for Paul in Story and Canon.* Philadelphia, PA: Westminster, 1983.

MacDonald, Margaret Y. *Early Christian Women and Pagan Opinion: The Power of the Hysterical Woman.* Cambridge; New York: Cambridge University Press, 1996.

———. *The Pauline Churches: A Socio-Historical Study of Institutionalization in the Pauline and Deutero-Pauline Writings.* Monograph Series, Society for New Testament Studies 60. Cambridge; New York: Cambridge University Press, 1988.

———. "Women Holy in Body and Spirit: The Social Setting of 1 Corinthians 7." *New Testament Studies* 36 (1990): 161–81.

Mackie, Gillian V. *Early Christian Chapels in the West: Decoration, Function, and Patronage.* Toronto: University of Toronto Press, 2003.

———. "The Iconographic Programme of the Zeno Chapel at Santa Prassede, Rome." Master's thesis, University of Victoria, Canada, 1984.

———. "The San Venanzio Chapel in Rome and the Martyr Shrine Sequence." *Revue d'art canadienne = Canadian Art Review* 23 (1996): 1–13.

———. "The Zeno Chapel: A Prayer for Salvation." *Papers of the British School at Rome* 57 (1989): 172–99.

Macy, Gary. "Heloise, Abelard and the Ordination of Abbesses." *Journal of Ecclesiastical History* 57 (2006): 16–32.

———. *The Hidden History of Women's Ordination: Female Clergy in the Medieval West.* Oxford: Oxford University Press, 2008.

———. "Impasse passé: Conjugating a tense past: Plenary Address." In Jonathan Y. Tan, ed., *Catholic Theological Society of America: Proceedings* 64 (June 4–7, 2009, Halifax, Nova Scotia): 2–17.

———. "The Ordination of Women in the Early Middle Ages." *Theological Studies* 61 (2000): 481–507. Reprint in *A History of Women and Ordination.* Vol. 1: *The Ordination of Women in Medieval Context*, edited by Bernard Cooke and Gary Macy, 1–30. Lanham, MD; London: Scarecrow Press, 2002.

———. *The Theologies of the Eucharist in the Early Scholastic Period: A Study of the Salvific Function of the Sacrament according to the Theologians, c. 1080–c. 1220.* Oxford: Clarendon Press, 1984.

———. *Treasures from the Storeroom: Medieval Religion and the Eucharist.* Collegeville, MN: Liturgical Press, 1999.

———, William T. Ditewig, and Phyllis Zagano. *Women Deacons: Past, Present, Future.* New York: Paulist Press, 2011.

Madigan, Kevin, and Carolyn Osiek, eds. and trans. *Ordained Women in the Early Church: A Documentary History.* Baltimore, MD: Johns Hopkins University Press, 2005.

Maguire, Eunice D., Henry P. Maguire, and Maggie J. Duncan-Flowers. *Art and Holy Powers in the Early Christian House.* Illinois Byzantine Studies 2. Krannert Art Museum, University of Illinois at Urbana-Champaign. Urbana: University of Illinois Press, 1989.

Maier, Harry O. *The Social Setting of the Ministry as Reflected in the Writings of Hermas, Clement and Ignatius.* Dissertations SR 1. Waterloo: Wilfrid Laurier University Press, 1991.

Mainstone, Rowland J. *Hagia Sophia: Architecture, Structure and Liturgy of Justinian's Great Church.* [London]: Thames and Hudson, 1988.

Maitland, Charles. *The Church in the Catacombs: A Description of the Primitive Church of Rome, Illustrated by its Sepulchral Remains.* London: Longman, Brown, Green, and Longmans, 1846.

Malina, Bruce J. *Timothy: Paul's Closest Associate.* Paul's Social Network. Collegeville, MN: Liturgical Press, 2008.

Malone, Mary T. *Women and Christianity.* 3 vols. Ottawa: Novalis, 2000–2003.

Mango, Cyril A. *The Art of the Byzantine Empire, 312–1453.* Englewood Cliffs, NJ: Prentice-Hall, 1972.

Marec, Erwan. *Monuments chrétiens d'Hippone.* Paris: Arts et métiers graphiques, 1958.

Marrou, Henri-Irénée. "L'origine orientale des diaconies romaines." In *Mélanges de l'école française de Rome* 57 (1940): 95–142.

Martimort, Aimé Georges. *Les diaconesses: essai historique.* Bibliotheca "Ephemerides liturgicae." Subsidia 24. Rome: C.L.V. Edizioni Liturgiche, 1982.

———. *Les lectures liturgiques et leurs livres.* Typologie des sources du moyen âge occidental, fascicule 64. Turnhout: Brepols, 1992.

Martin, John Hilary. "The Ordination of Women and the Theologians in the Middle Ages." In *A History of Women and Ordination.* Vol. 1: *The Ordination of Women in Medieval Context*, edited by Bernard Cooke and Gary Macy, 31–160. Lanham, MD: Scarecrow Press, 2002.

Martinelli, Patrizia Angiolini. "Il costume femminile nei mosaici ravennati." *Corsi di cultura sull'arte ravennate e bizantina* 16 (1969): 7–64.

Marucchi, Orazio. *The Evidence of the Catacombs: For the Doctrine and Organisation of the Primitive Church.* London: Sheed & Ward, 1929.

———. *Guide des catacombes romaines.* 2nd French ed. Paris: Desclée, Lefebvre & Cie, 1902.

Mathews, Thomas F. *The Clash of Gods: A Reinterpretation of Early Christian Art.* Princeton, NJ: Princeton University Press, 1993.

———. "An Early Roman Chancel Arrangement." *Rivista di archeologia cristiana* 38 (1962): 73–95.

Matt, Leonard von. *Art Treasures of the Vatican Library.* Text by Georg Daltrop and Adriano Prandi. Translated by Robert Allen. New York: H. N. Abrams, 1970.

Mauck, Marchita B. "The Mosaic of the Triumphal Arch of S. Prassede: A Liturgical Interpretation." *Speculum* 62 (1987): 813–28.

Maunder, Chris. "Origins of the Cult of the Virgin Mary in the New Testament." In *The Origins of the Cult of the Virgin Mary*, edited by Chris Maunder, 23–39. London: Burns and Oates, 2008.

Mayeski, Mary Anne. "Women in Medieval Society and Scholastic Theology." In *Equal at the Creation: Sexism, Society and Christian Thought*, edited by Joseph Martos and Pierre Hégy, 70–95. Toronto: University of Toronto Press, 1998.

Mazzoleni, Danilo. "La mariologia nell'epigrafia cristiana antica." *Vetera christianorum* 26 (1989): 59–68.
McCulloh, John M. "From Antiquity to the Middle Ages: Continuity and Change in Papal Relic Policy from the 6th to the 8th Century." In *Pietas: Festschrift für Bernhard Kötting*, edited by Ernst Dassmann and Karl Suso Frank, 313–24. Jahrbuch für Antike und Christentum; Ergänzungsband 8. Münster Westfalen: Aschendorff, 1980.
McGowan, Andrew Brian. *Ascetic Eucharists: Food and Drink in Early Christian Ritual Meals*. Oxford Early Christian Studies. Oxford: Clarendon Press, 1999.
McGuire, M. R. P. "Chronographer of 354." In *New Catholic Encyclopedia*. Vol. 3, 569–70. 2nd ed. Washington, Catholic University of America, 2003.
———. "Vestal Virgins." In *New Catholic Encyclopedia*. Vol. 14, 632–33. New York: McGraw-Hill, 1967.
McKitterick, Rosamund. "Women in the Ottonian Church: An Iconographic Perspective." In *Women in the Church: Papers Read at the 1989 Summer Meeting and the 1990 Winter Meeting of the Ecclesiastical History Society*, edited by W. J. Sheils and Diana Wood, 79–100. Studies in Church History 27. Cambridge, MA: Basil Blackwell, 1990.
McLaughlin, T. P. "Abelard's Rule for Religious Women." *Mediaeval Studies* 18 (1956): 241–92.
McNamara, Jo Ann. *A New Song: Celibate Women in the First Three Christian Centuries*. New York: Harrington Park Press, 1983. Reprint. New York: Haworth Press, 1985.
———. "Sexual Equality and the Cult of Virginity in Early Christian Thought." *Feminist Studies* 3 (1976): 145–58.
McWilliams, Philip E. "Canons Regular, Origins of." In *Encyclopedia of Monasticism*, 1:236–37. London: Fitzroy Dearborn, 2000.
Medieval Saints: A Reader. Edited by Mary-Ann Stouck. Readings in Medieval Civilizations and Cultures 4. Peterborough, ON: Broadview Press, 1999.
Meer, Frederik van der. *Maiestas Domini. Théophanies de l'apocalypse dans l'art chrétien: Étude sur les origines d'une iconographie spéciale du Christ*. Studi di antichità cristiana 13. Vatican City: PIAC, 1938.
———, and Christine Mohrmann. *Atlas of the Early Christian World*. London: Nelson, 1958.
Meer, Haye van der. *Priestertum der Frau?: Eine theologiegeschichtliche Untersuchung*. Quaestiones disputatae 42. Freiburg im Breisgau: Herder, 1969. English translation, *Women Priests in the Catholic Church? A Theological-Historical Investigation*. Translated by Arlene and Leonard Swidler. Philadelphia, PA: Temple University Press, 1973.
Melzak, Robert. "Antiquarianism in the Time of Louis the Pious and its Influence on the Art of Metz." In *Charlemagne's Heir: New Perspectives on the Reign of Louis the Pious (814–840)*, edited by Peter Godman and Roger Collins, 629–40. Oxford: Clarendon Press, 1990.

Messner, Reinhard. "Grundlinien der Entwicklung des eucharistischen Gebets in der frühen Kirche." In *Prex Eucharistica*. Vol. 3: *Studia*. Pars prima: *Ecclesia antiqua et occidentalis*, edited by Albert Gerhards et al., 3–41. Spicilegium Friburgense: Texte zur Geschichte des Kirchenlebens 42. Fribourg:: Academic Press, 2005.

Metz, René. "Benedictio sive consecratio virginum." *Ephemerides liturgicae* 80 (1966): 265–93.

———. *La consécration des vierges dans l'Église romaine: Étude d'histoire de la liturgie.* Paris: Presses Universitaires de France, 1954.

———. "Les vierges chrétiennes en Gaule au IV siècle." In *Saint Martin et son temps: Mémorial du XVIe centenaire des débuts du monachisme en Gaule 361–1961*, 109–32. Studia Anselmiana 46. Rome: Herder, 1961.

Metzger, Marcel. "Pages féminines des *Constitutions apostoliques*." In *Crossroad of Cultures: Studies in Liturgy and Patristics in Honor of Gabriele Winkler*, edited by H.-J. Feulner, E. Velkovska, Robert F. Taft, 515–41. Orientalia Christiana Analecta 260. Rome: Pontifical Oriental Institute, 2000.

Meyendorff, Jean. "L'iconographie de la sagesse divine dans la tradition byzantine." *Cahiers archéologiques* 10 (1959): 259–77.

Meyer, Hans Bernhard. *Eucharistie: Geschichte, Theologie, Pastoral*. Gottesdienst der Kirche: Handbuch der Liturgiewissenschaft 4. Regensburg: Pustet, 1989.

Miller, Jeremy. "A Note on Aquinas and the Ordination of Women." *New Blackfriars* 61 (1980): 185–90.

Mitchell, Barbara. "Anglo-Saxon Double Monasteries." *History Today* 45 (1995): 1–7.

Molajoli, Bruno. *La Basilica Eufrasiana di Parenzo*. 2nd ed. Padua: Le Tre Venezie, 1943.

Montini, Renzo U. *Santa Pudenziana*. Chiese di Roma Illustrate 50. Rome: Edizioni "Roma," [1958?].

Morey, Charles Rufus. *Lost Mosaics and Frescoes of Rome of the Mediaeval Period: A Publication of Drawings Contained in the Collection of Cassiano dal Pozzo, now in the Royal Library Windsor Castle*. Princeton Monographs in Art and Archaeology 4. Princeton, NJ: Princeton University Press, 1915.

Morin, Germain. "Liturgie et basiliques de Rome au milieu du VIIe siècle d'après les listes d'Évangiles de Würzburg." *Révue bénédictine* 28 (1911): 296–330.

———. "Les plus ancien *comes* ou lectionnaire de l'église romaine." *Révue bénédictine* 27 (1910): 41–74.

Morris, Joan. *The Lady Was a Bishop: The Hidden History of Women with Clerical Ordination and the Jurisdiction of Bishops*. New York: Macmillan, 1973.

Muckle, J. T. "The Letter of Heloise on Religious Life and Abelard's First Reply." *Mediaeval Studies* 17 (1955): 240–81.

———, ed. "The Personal Letters Between Abelard and Heloise." *Mediaeval Studies* 15 (1953): 47–94.

Murphy, Frederick J. *Fallen Is Babylon: The Revelation to John.* New Testament in Context. Harrisburg, PA: Trinity Press International, 1998.

Murphy, Roland E. *The Tree of Life: An Exploration of Biblical Wisdom Literature.* 3rd ed. Grand Rapids, MI: Eerdmans, 2002.

Murphy-O'Connor, Jerome. "Prisca and Aquila: Travelling Tentmakers and Church Builders." *Bible Review* 8 (1992): 40–51, 62.

Murray, Robert. *Symbols of Church and Kingdom. A Study in Early Syriac Tradition.* Rev. ed. Piscataway, NJ: Gorgias Press, 2004.

Muschiol, Gisela. *Famula Dei: Zur Liturgie in merowingischen Frauenklöstern.* Beiträge zur Geschichte des alten Mönchtums und des Benediktinertums 41. Münster: Aschendorff, 1994.

Mütherich, Florentine. "Die Buchmalerei am Hofe Karls des Grossen." In *Karl der Grosse. Lebenswerk und Nachleben.* Vol. 3: *Karolingische Kunst*, edited by Wolfgang Braunfels and Percy E. Schramm, 9–53. Düsseldorf: Schwann, 1965.

———, and Joachim E. Gaehde. *Carolingian Painting.* Introduction by Florentine Mütherich; provenances and commentaries by Joachim E. Gaehde. New York: George Braziller, 1976.

Nabuco. J., and T. C. O'Brien. "Pontifical Roman." In *New Catholic Encyclopedia.* Vol. 11, 474. 2nd ed. Washington, DC: Catholic University of America Press, 2003.

Nautin, Pierre. "Le rite du 'Fermentum' dans les églises urbaines de Rome." *Ephemerides liturgicae* 96 (1982): 510–22.

Neumann, Johannes. "Bishof I. Das katholische Bischofsamt." *Theologische Realenzyclopädie* 6 (1980): 653–97.

Newsom, Carol A. and Sharon H. Ringe, eds. *The Women's Bible Commentary.* Louisville, KY: Westminster John Knox Press, 1992. Expanded ed., 1998. 3rd ed., 2012.

Nilgen, Ursula. "Die Bilder über dem Altar: Triumph- und Apsisbogenprogramme in Rom und Mittelitalien und ihr Bezug zur Liturgie." In *Kunst und Liturgie im Mittelalter: Akten des Internationalen Kongresses der Bibliotheca Hertziana und des Nederlands Instituut te Rome, Rom. 28–30. September 1997*, edited by Nicolas Bock, S. de Blaauw, D. I. Frommel, and H. Kessler, 75–90. Munich: Hirmer 2000.

———. "Die grosse Reliquieninschrift von Santa Prassede: Eine quellenkritische Untersuchung zur Zeno-Kapelle." *Römische Quartalschrift für christliche Altertumskunde und für Kirchengeschichte* 69 (1974): 7–29.

Noble, Thomas F. X. *The Republic of St. Peter: The Birth of the Papal State, 680–825.* The Middle Ages. Philadelphia: University of Pennsylvania Press, 1984.

Nocent, Adrien. "The Consecration of Virgins." In *The Church at Prayer.* Vol. 3: *The Sacraments*, edited by Aimé Georges Martimort, 209–20. Collegeville, MN: Liturgical Press, 1988.

Nordhagen, Per Jonas. *The Frescoes of John VII (A.D. 705–707) in S. Maria Antiqua in Rome.* Edited by Hans Peter L'Orange and Hjalmar Torp. Institutum Romanum Norvegiae. Acta ad archaeologiam et artium historiam pertinentia 3. Rome: Bretschneider, 1968.

Northcote, J. Spencer. *Epitaphs of the Catacombs, or Christian Inscriptions in Rome during the First Four Centuries.* London: Longmans, Green, 1878.

Norwich, John Julius. *A Short History of Byzantium.* London: Penguin, 1998.

O'Connor, Daniel William. *Peter in Rome: The Literary, Liturgical, and Archeological Evidence.* New York: Columbia University Press, 1969.

O'Day, Gail R. "Acts." In *The Women's Bible Commentary.* 2nd ed. exp., edited by Carol A. Newsom and Sharon H. Ringe, 394–402. Louisville, KY: Westminster/John Knox Press, 1998.

———. "John." In *The Women's Bible Commentary*, edited by Carol A. Newsom and Sharon H. Ringe, 293–304. Westminster/John Knox Press, 1992.

O'Neill, J. C. "New Testament Monasteries." In *Common Life in the Early Church: Essays Honoring Graydon F. Snyder*, edited by Julian V. Hills et al., 126–32. Harrisburg, PA: Trinity Press International, 1998.

Oakeshott, Walter. *The Mosaics of Rome from the Third to the Fourteenth Centuries.* London: Thames and Hudson, 1967.

Ora et Labora: Testimonianze Benedettine nella Biblioteca Apostolica Vaticana: XV centenario della nascita di S. Benedetto: 480–1980. Vatican City: Biblioteca Apostolica Vaticana, 1980.

Osborne, John. "Early Medieval Wall-Paintings in the Catacomb of San Valentino, Rome." *Papers of the British School at Rome* 49 (1981): 82–90.

———. "The Roman Catacombs in the Middle Ages." *Papers of the British School at Rome* 53 (1985): 278–328.

Osiek, Carolyn. *Philippians, Philemon.* Nashville, TN: Abingdon, 2000.

———. *Rich and Poor in the Shepherd of Hermas: An Exegetical-Social Investigation.* Catholic Biblical Quarterly Monograph Series 15. Washington, DC: Catholic Biblical Association of America, 1983.

———. *Shepherd of Hermas: A Commentary.* Hermeneia. Minneapolis, MN: Fortress, 1999.

———. "The Social Function of Female Imagery in Second Century Prophecy." *Vetera christianorum* 29 (1992): 55–74.

———. "The Widow as Altar: The Rise and Fall of a Symbol." *Second Century* 3 (1983): 159–69.

———. "Women in House Churches." In *Common Life in the Early Church: Essays Honoring Graydon F. Snyder*, edited by Julian V. Hills, Richard B. Gardner et al., 300–15. Harrisburg, PA: Trinity Press International, 1998.

———, and David L. Balch. *Families in the New Testament World: Households and House Churches.* Louisville, KY: Westminster John Knox Press, 1997.

———, and Margaret Y. MacDonald with Janet H. Tulloch. *A Woman's Place: House Churches in Earliest Christianity*. Minneapolis, MN: Fortress, 2006.

Otranto, Giorgio. "Note sul sacerdozio femminile nell'antichità in margine a una testimonianza di Gelasio I." *Vetera christianorum* 19 (1982): 341–60, translated and introduced by Mary Ann Rossi, "Priesthood, Precedent, and Prejudice: On Recovering the Women Priests of Early Christianity." *Journal of Feminist Studies in Religion* 7 (1991): 73–93.

———. "Il sacerdozio della donna nell'Italia meridionale." In *Italia meridionale e Puglia paleocristiane*, 94–121. Bari: Edipuglia, 1991.

———. "Tra letteratura e iconografia: note sul Buon Pastore e sull'Orante nell'arte cristiani antica (II–III secolo)." *Vetera christianorum* 26 (1989): 69–87. Reprint in *Annali di storia dell'esegesi* 6 (1989), 15–30.

Pace, Valentino. "La 'Felix culpa' di Richard Krautheimer: Roma, Santa Prassede e la 'rinascenza carolingia.'" In *Ecclesiae urbis: Atti del congresso internazaionale di studi sulle chiese di Roma (IV–X secolo): Roma, 4–10 settembre 2000*, vol. 1, edited by Federico Guidobaldi and Alessandra Guiglia Guidobaldi, 65–72. Studi di antichità cristiana 59. Vatican City: PIAC, 2002.

Palazzo, Eric. *A History of Liturgical Books from the Beginning to the Thirteenth Century*. Collegeville, MN: Liturgical Press, 1998.

Panofsky, Erwin. *Studies in Iconology: Humanistic Themes in the Art of the Renaissance*. New York: Oxford University Press, 1939.

Parenti, Stefano. "Ordinations in the East." In *Handbook for Liturgical Studies*. Vol. 4: *Sacraments and Sacramentals*, edited by Anscar J. Chupungco, 205–16. Collegeville, MN: Liturgical Press, 1997.

Parisse, Michel. "Les chanoinesses dans l'empire germanique (IX–XIe siècles)." *Francia* 6 (1978): 107–27.

Parker, John Henry. "The House of Pudens in Rome." *Archaeological Journal* 28 (1871): 40–49.

Parlby, Geri. "The Origins of Marian Art in the Catacombs and the Problems of Identification." In *The Origins of the Cult of the Virgin Mary*, edited by Chris Maunder, 41–56. New York: Burns and Oates, 2008.

Parrinello, Rosa Maria. "Diaconesse a Bisanzio: Una messa a punto della questione." In *Diakonia, Diaconiae, Diaconato: semantica e storia nei padri della chiesa*. XXXVIII incontro di studiosi dell'antichità cristiana, Roma, 7–9 maggio 2009, 653–65. Studia ephemeridis Augustinianum 117. Rome: Institutum Patristicum Augustinanum, 2010.

Parry, Kenneth. *Depicting the Word: Byzantine Iconophile Thought of the Eighth and Ninth Centuries*. Medieval Mediterranean 12. Leiden; New York; Cologne: E. J. Brill, 1996.

Parsons, John Carmi, and Bonnie Wheeler, eds. *Medieval Mothering*. Garland Reference Library of Humanities 1979. The New Middle Ages 3. New York: Garland, 1996.

Payton, James R., Jr. "Iconoclasm (Controversy)." In *Encyclopedia of Monasticism,*. 2 vols. Edited by William M. Johnson, vol. 1, 633–34. Chicago: Fitzroy Dearborn, 2000.

Pelikan, Jaroslav. *The Spirit of Eastern Christendom (600–1700)*. The Christian Tradition 2. Chicago: University of Chicago Press, 1974.

Petersen, Joan M. "House Churches in Rome." *Vigiliae christianae* 23 (1969): 264–72.

———. "Some Titular Churches at Rome with Traditional New Testament Connections." *Expository Times* 84 (1993): 277–79.

Petrignani, Achille. *Il santuario della Scala Santa: nelle sue successive trasformazioni*. Collezione "Amici delle catacombe" 7. Vatican City: PIAC, 1941.

Philipps, L. Edward. "A Note on the Gifts of Leo III to the Churches of Rome: 'Vestes cum storiis'." *Ephemerides liturgicae* 102 (1988): 72–78.

Pietri, Charles. "Liturgy, Culture and Society: The Example of Rome at the End of the Ancient World (Fourth-Fifth Centuries)." In *Liturgy: A Creative Tradition*, edited by Mary Collins and David Power, 38–46. Concilium 162. New York: Seabury, 1983.

———. *Roma christiana: recherches sur l'Église de Rome, son organisation, sa politique, son idéologie de Miltiade à Sixte III (311–440)*. 2 vols. Bibliothèque des écoles françaises d'Athènes et de Rome, fasc. 224. Rome: École Française de Rome, Palais Farnèse, 1976.

Pietro e Paolo: La storia, il culto, la memoria nei primi secoli. Edited by Angela Donati. Milan: Electa, 2000.

Pilsworth, Clare. "Dating the *Gesta martyrum*: A Manuscript-Based Approach." *Early Medieval Europe* 9 (2000): 309–24.

La pittura medievale a Roma, 312–1431: corpus e atlante. Edited by Serena Romano and Maria Andalora. Prima edizione italiana, 5 vols. Turnhout: Brepols, 2006–.

La pittura medievale a Roma, 312–1431: corpus e atlante. Vol. 4: *Riforma et tradizione, 1050–1198*. Edited by Serena Romana. Milan: Jaca Book, 2006–.

Poncelet, Albert. *Catalogus Codicum Hagiographicorum Latinorum Bibliotheca Vaticanae*. Subsidia Hagographica 11. Brussels: Société des Bollandistes, 1910.

———, *Catalogus Codicum Hagiographicorum Latinorum Bibliothecarum Romanarum praeter quam Vaticanae*. Brussels: Société des Bollandistes, 1909.

Porter, Harry Boone. *The Ordination Prayers of the Ancient Western Churches*. Alciun Club Collections 49. London: SPCK, 1967.

Porter, Stanley E., ed. *Dictionary of Biblical Criticism and Interpretation*. New York: Routledge, 2007.

Power, David. *Ministers of Christ and His Church: The Theology of the Priesthood*. London: Geoffrey Chapman, 1969.

Quasten, Johannes. *Patrology*. Vol. 1: *The Beginnings of Patristic Literature*. Utrecht-Antwerp: Spectrum, 1966.

Rader, Rosemary. *Breaking Boundaries: Male/Female Friendship in Early Christian Communities*. New York: Paulist Press, 1983.

———. "Early Christian Forms of Communal Spirituality: Women's Communities." In *The Continuing Quest for God: Monastic Spirituality in Tradition and Transition*, edited by William Skudlarek, 88–99. Collegeville, MN: Liturgical Press, 1982.

Ramelli, Ilaria. "Theosebia: A Presbyter of the Catholic Church." *Journal of Feminist Studies in Religion* 26 (2010): 79–102.

Raming, Ida. *The Exclusion of Women from the Priesthood: Divine Law or Sex Discrimination?* Translated by Norman R. Adams. Metuchen, NJ: Scarecrow Press, 1976. Reprint. Raming, Ida. *A History of Women and Ordination*. Vol. 2: *The Priestly Office of Women: God's Gift to a Renewed Church*. Edited by Bernard Cooke and Gary Macy. 2nd ed. Lanham, MD; Oxford: Scarecrow Press, 2004.

———. "Diakonate: Ein Amt für Frauen in der Kirche." *Orientierung* 62 (1998) 8–11.

Regan, Patrick. "Veneration of the Cross." *Worship* 52 (1978): 2–13.

Reimer, Ivoni Richter. *Women in the Acts of the Apostles: A Feminist Liberation Perspective*. Translated by Linda M. Maloney. Minneapolis, MN: Fortress, 1993.

Repsher, Brian. *The Rite of Church Dedication in the Early Medieval Era*. Lewiston, NY: Edwin Mellen Press, 1998.

Reynolds, Roger E. *Clerical Orders in the Early Middle Ages: Duties and Ordination*. Aldershot: Ashgate, 1999.

———. *The Ordinals of Christ from their Origins to the Twelfth Century*. Beiträge zur Geschichte und Quellenkunde des Mittelalters 7. Berlin; New York: Walter de Gruyter, 1978.

———. "Pontifical." *Dictionary of the Middle Ages* 10 (1982): 30–31.

Ricci, Carla. *Mary Magdalene and Many Others: Women who Followed Jesus*. Translated by Paul Burns. Minneapolis, MN: Fortress, 1994.

Richard, M. "La question pascale au IIe siècle." *L'orient syrien* 6 (1961): 179–212.

Richardson, Peter. "From Apostles to Virgins: Romans 16 and the Roles of Women in the Early Church." *Toronto Journal of Theology* 2 (1986): 232–61.

Röhl-Burgsmüller, Anne. "Diakonin Radegundis (520–587)—Demütige Dienerin und mütige Predigeren." In *Diakonia, Diaconiae, Diaconato: semantica et storia nei Padri della Chiesa: XXXVIII Incontro di studiosi dell'antichità cristiana, Roma, 7–9, maggio 2009*, 667–76. Studia ephemeridis Augustinianum 117. Rome: Institutum Patristicum Augustinianum, 2010.

ROMArcheologica: Guida alle antichità della città eterna. Vol. 6: *Il Celio, L'Aventino e dintorni*. Rome: Elio de Rosa editore, 2000.

ROMArcheologica: Guida alle antichità della città eterna. Vols. 16–17: *Le chiese paleocristiane di Roma*. Rome: Elio de Rosa editore, 2003.

Rossi, Giovanni Battista de. *La Rome sotterranea cristiana*. Rome: litografia pontificia, 1877.

———, Enrico Stevenson, and Giuseppi Gatti, *Musaici cristiani e saggi dei pavimenti delle chiese di Roma anteriori al secolo XV*. Rome: Libreria Spithöver di G. Haass, 1899.

Rossi, Mary Ann. "'Priesthood, Precedent, and Prejudice. On Recovering the Women Priests of Early Christianity." Translation from the Italian of Giorgio Otranto, "Notes on the Female Priesthood in Antiquity." *Journal of the Feminist Study of Religion* 7 (1991): 73–93.

Rubery, Eileen. "Pope John VII's Devotion to Mary: Papal Images of Mary from the Fifth to the Eighth Centuries." In *Origins of the Cult of the Virgin Mary*, edited by Chris Maunder, 155–99. London; New York: Burns & Oates, 2008.

Ruggieri, Vincenzo. *Byzantine Religious Architecture (582–867): Its History and Structural Elements*. Orientalia Christiana Analecta 237. Rome: Pontificio Istituto Orientale, 1991.

Rusch, W. G. "A Possible Explanation of the Calendar in the Würzburg Lectionary." *Journal of Theological Studies* 21 (1970): 105–11.

Sahas, Daniel J., trans. *Icon and Logos: Sources in Eighth-Century Iconoclasm; An Annotated Translation of the Sixth Session of the Seventh Ecumenical Council (Nicaea, 787) Containing the Definition of the Council of Constantinople (754) and Its Refutation and the Definition of the Seventh Ecumenical Council.* Toronto Medieval Texts and Translations 4. Toronto: University of Toronto Press, 1986.

Saint Patrick's World: The Christian Culture of Ireland's Apostolic Age. Translations and commentaries by Liam De Paor. Notre Dame, IN: University of Notre Dame Press, 1993.

Salisbury, Joyce E. *Church Fathers, Independent Virgins*. London: Verso, 1991.

Salmon, Pierre. *Les manuscrits liturgiques latins de la Bibliothèque Vaticane*. Vol. 2: *Sacramentaires, épistoliers, évangéliaires, graduels, missels*. Studi e Testi 253. Vatican City: Biblioteca Apostolica Vaticana, 1969.

———. *Les manuscrits liturgiques latins de la Bibliothèque Vaticane*. Vol. 4: *Les livres de lectures de l'office. Les livres de l'office du chapitre, Les livres d'heures*. Studi e Testi 267. Vatican City: Biblioteca Apostolica Vaticana, 1971.

Santantoni, Antonio. "Orders and Ministries in the West," and "Orders and Ministries in the First Four Centuries." In *Handbook for Liturgical Studies*. Vol. 4: *Sacraments and Sacramentals*, edited by Anscar J. Chupungco, 17–52; 197–201 Collegeville, MN: Liturgical Press, 2000.

Saxer, Victor. *Le culte de Marie Madeleine en occident: des origines à la fin du moyen âge*. Auxerre; Paris: Clavreuil, 1959.

Schaberg, Jane. *The Resurrection of Mary Magdalene: Legends, Apocrypha, and the Christian Testament*. New York: Continuum, 2002.

Schaefer, Mary M. "Evidence (5th to 12th Centuries) for Women's Official Ministries in Rome." In *Diakonia, Diaconiae, Diaconato: semantica e storia nei padri della chiesa*. XXXVIII Incontro di studiosi dell'antichità cristiana, Roma, 7–9 maggio 2009, 677–84. Studia Ephemeridis Augustinianum 117. Rome: Istitutum Patristicum Augustinianum, 2010.

———. "Heavenly and Earthly Liturgies: Patristic Prototypes, Medieval Perspectives and a Contemporary Application." *Worship* 70 (1996): 482–505.

———. "*In Persona Christi*: Cult of the Priest's Person or Active Presence of Christ?" In *In God's Hands: Essays on the Church and Ecumenism in Honour of Michael A. Fahey, S.J.*, edited by Jaroslav Z. Skira and Michael S. Attridge, 177–201. Leuven: Leuven University Press, 2006.

———. "Latin Mass Commentaries from the Ninth through Twelfth Centuries: Chronology and Theology." In *Fountain of Life: In Memory of Niels K. Rasmussen O.P.*, edited by Gerard Austin, 35–49. Washington, DC: Pastoral Press, 1991.

———. "Liturgy, Western Christian." In *Encyclopedia of Monasticism*. 2 vols. Edited by William M. Johnston, vol. 1, 786–94.Chicago: Fitzroy Dearborn, 2000.

———. "Presence of the Trinity: Relationship or Idea?" *Liturgical Ministry* 19 (2010): 145–56.

———. "Romania." In *Encyclopedia of Monasticism*. 2 vols. Edited by William M. Johnston, vol. 2, 1079–85. Chicago: Fitzroy Dearborn, 2000.

———. "Twelfth-Century Latin Commentaries on the Mass: Christological and Ecclesiological Dimensions." Ph.D. dissertation. University of Notre Dame, Indiana. Ann Arbor, MI: University Microfilms, 1983.

Schäfer, Karl Heinrich. "Kanonissen und Diakonissen: Ergänzungen und Erläuterungen." *Römische Quartalschrift für christliche Altertumskunde und Kirchengeschichte* 24 (1910): 49–90.

———. *Die Kanonissenstifter im deutschen Mittelalter: ihre Entwicklung und innere Einrichtung im Zusammenhang mit dem altchristlichen Sanktimonialentum.* Kirchenrechtliche Abhandlungen, 43–44. Stuttgart: F. Enke, 1907.

Scheepsma, Wybren. *Medieval Religious Women in the Low Countries: The 'Modern Devotion,' the Canonesses of Windesheim and Their Writings.* Translated by David F. Johnson. Woodbridge, Suffolk: Boydell Press, 2004.

Schiapparelli, L. "Le carte antiche dell'archivio capitolare di San Pietro." In *Archivio della Società Romana di storia patria* 24 (1901): 466–67.

Schillebeeckx, Edward. "The Catholic Understanding of Office in the Church." *Theological Studies* 30 (1969): 567–87.

Schiller, Gertrud. *Iconography of Christian Art*. Vol. 2: *The Passion of Jesus Christ*. Translated by Janet Seligman from 2nd edition of *Ikonographie der christlichen Kunst*. Greenwich, CT: New York Graphic Society, 1972.

Schlatter, Fredric W. "Interpreting the Mosaic of Santa Pudenziana." *Vigiliae Christianae* 46 (1992): 276–95.

———. "A Mosaic Interpretation of Jerome, *In Hiezechielem*." *Vigiliae Christianae* 49 (1995): 64–81.

———. "The Text in the Mosaic of Santa Pudenziana." *Vigiliae Christianae* 43 (1989): 155–65.

———. "The Two Women in the Mosaic of Santa Pudenziana" *Journal of Early Christian Studies* 3 (1995): 1–24.

Schmid, Michael H. "Kanonissen." *Lexikon für Theologie und Kirche*, edited by Josef Höfer and Karl Rahner. Vol. 5, 1288–89. 10 vols. Freiburg: Herder, 1960.

Schmitt Pantel, Pauline, ed. *A History of Women in the West.* Vol. 1: *From Ancient Goddesses to Christian Saints.* 5 vols. Cambridge, MA: Belknap Press of Harvard University Press, 1992.

Schmitz, Ph. "La Première communauté de vierges à Rome." *Revue bénédictine* 38 (1926): 189–95.

Schneiders, Sandra. *Religious Life in a New Millennium.* Vol. 2: *Selling All: Commitment, Consecrated Celibacy, and Community in Catholic Religious Life.* New York: Paulist Press, 2001.

Schottroff, Luise. *Lydia's Impatient Sisters: A Feminist Social History of Early Christianity.* Translated by Barbara and Martin Rumscheidt. Louisville, KY: Westminster John Knox Press, 1995.

Schubert, Ursula. "Christus, Priester und König: Eine politisch-theologische Darstellungsweise in der frühchristlichen Kunst." *Kairos* n.f. 15 (1973): 201–37.

Schulte van Kessel, Elisja. "Virgins and Mothers between Heaven and Earth." In *A History of Women in the West.* Vol. 3: *Renaissance and Enlightenment Paradoxes*, edited by Natalie Zemon Davis and Arlette Farge, 132–66. Cambridge, MA: Belknap Press of Harvard University Press, 1993.

Schulz, Hans-Joachim. *The Byzantine Liturgy: Symbolic Structure and Faith Expression.* Translated by Matthew J. O'Connell; introduced and reviewed by Robert Taft. New York: Pueblo, 1986.

Schumacher, Walter Nikolaus. "Dominus legem dat." *Römische Quartalschrift für christliche Altertumskunde und für Kirchengeschichte* 54 (1959): 1–39.

———. *Die Römischen Mosaiken der kirchlichen Bauten vom IV.–XIII. Jahrhundert.* Based on a 4-vol. work by Josef Wilpert, *Die Römischen Mosaiken und Malereien der kirchlichen Bauten vom IV. bis XIII. Jahrhundert*, 1916. Freiburg im Breisgau: Herder, 1976.

Schüssler Fiorenza, Elisabeth. *In Memory of Her: A Feminist Theological Reconstruction of Christian Origins.* New York: Crossroad, 1983.

———. "Missionaries, Apostles, Coworkers: Romans 16 and the Reconstruction of Women's Early Christian History." *Word & World* 6 (1986): 420–33.

———, ed. *Searching the Scriptures: A Feminist Commentary.* 2 vols. New York: Crossroad, 1993–1994.

———. "Women in the Pre-Pauline and Pauline Churches." *Union Seminary Quarterly Review* 33 (1978): 153–66.

Segelberg, Eric. "The Ordination Prayers in Hippolytus." *Studia Patristica* 13 (1975): 397–408.

Sellner, Edward C. *Wisdom of the Celtic Saints.* Notre Dame, IN: Ave Maria Press, 1993.

Senn, Frank C. "Agape." In *The New Dictionary of Sacramental Worship.* Edited by Peter E. Fink, 39–40. Collegeville, MN: Liturgical Press, 1990.

Sessa, Kristina. "Domestic Conversions: Households and Bishops in the Late Antique 'Papal Legends.'" In *Religion, Dynasty and Patronage in Early Christian Rome, 300–900*, edited by Kate Cooper and Julia Hillner, 79–114. Cambridge: Cambridge University Press, 2007.

Shahar, Shulamith. *The Fourth Estate: A History of Women in the Middle Ages.* Translated by Chaya Galai. New York: Methuen, 1983.

Shaw, Teresa M. "*Askesis* and the Appearance of Holiness." *Journal of Early Christian Studies* 6 (1998): 485–99.

Siegwart, Josef. *Die Chorherren- und Chorfrauengemeinschaften in der deutschsprachigen Schweiz vom 6. Jahrhundert bis 1160: mit einem Überblick über die deutsche Kanononikerreform des 10. und 11. Jh.* Studia Friburgensia, Neue Folge 30. Freiburg Schweiz: Universitätsverlag, 1962.

Simpson, Jane. "Women and Asceticism in the Fourth Century: A Question of Interpretation." *Journal of Religious History* 15 (1988): 38–60, reprinted in *Acts of Piety in the Early Church*, edited by Everett Ferguson, 296–318. Studies in Early Christianity 17. New York; London: Garland, 1993.

Simson, Otto Georg von. *Sacred Fortress: Byzantine Art and Statecraft in Ravenna.* Princeton, NJ: Princeton University Press, 1987.

Skinner, Mary S. "French Abbesses in Action: Structuring Carolingian and Cluniac Commnities." *Magistra* 6 (2000): 37–60.

Slater, William J., ed. *Dining in a Classical Context.* Ann Arbor: University of Michigan Press, 1991.

Smith, Molly Teasdale. "The Development of the Altar Canopy in Rome." *Rivista di archeologia cristiana* 50 (1974): 379–414.

Smyth, Matthew Brendan. "Widows, Consecrated Virgins and Deaconesses in Ancient Gaul." *Magistra* 8 (2002): 53–84.

Smyth, Matthieu, with introduction by Paul Bradshaw, "The Anaphora of the So-Called *Apostolic Tradition* and the Roman Eucharistic Prayer." *Usus Antiquior* 1 (2010): 5–25. Reprint in *Issues in Eucharistic Praying in East and West: Essays in Liturgical and Theological Analysis*, edited by Maxwell E. Johnson, 71–97. Collegeville, MN: Liturgical Press, 2010.

Soos, Maria Bernard de. *Le mystère liturgique: d'après Saint Léon le Grand.* Münster Westfalen: Aschendorff, 1958.

Sörries, Reiner. *Die syrische Bibel von Paris: Paris, Bibliothéque Nationale syr. 341. Eine frühchristliche Bilderhandschrift aus dem 6. Jahrhundert.* Wiesbaden: Reichert Verlag, 1991.

Spain-Alexander, Susan. "Carolingian Restorations of S. Maria Maggiore in Rome." *Gesta* 16 (1977): 13–21.

Spence, Stephen. *The Parting of the Ways: The Roman Church as a Case Study.* Interdisciplinary Studies in Early Culture and Religion 5. Leuven: Peeters, 2004.

Spence-Jones, H. D. M. *The Early Christians in Rome.* London: Methuen, 1910.

Spinks, Bryan D. *The Sanctus in the Eucharistic Prayer.* New York: Cambridge University Press, 1991.
Stählin, Gustav. "χήρα, 'widow.'" In *Theological Dictionary of the New Testament,* vol. 9, edited by Gerhard Friedrich, 440–65. Translated and abridged in one volume by Geoffrey W. Bromiley. Grand Rapids, MI: Eerdmans, 1974.
Steen, Olaf. "The Apse Mosaic of S. Pudenziana and Its Relation to the Fifth Century Mosaics of S. Sabina and S. Maria Maggiore." In *Ecclesiae urbis: Atti del congresso internazionale di studi sulle chiese di Roma (IV–X secolo), Roma, 4–10 settembre 2000.* Vol. 2, edited by Federico Guidobaldi and Alessandra Guiglia Guidobaldi, 1939–48. Vatican City: PIAC, 2002.
Stenzel, Alois. "Gedenken zur Tauffrömmigkeit." In *Paschatis Sollemnia: Studien zu Osterfeier und Osterfrömmigkeit,* edited by Balthasar Fischer and Johannes Wagner, 32–45. Basel: Herder, 1959.
Stewart-Sykes, Alistair. "Hermas the Prophet and Hippolytus the Preacher: The Roman Homily and its Social Context." In *Preacher and Audience: Studies in Early Christian and Byzantine Homiletics,* edited by M. B. Cunningham and P. Allen, 33–63. A New History of the Sermon 1. Leiden: Brill, 1998.
———, trans. *On the Apostolic Tradition: Hippolytus: An English Version with Introduction and Commentary.* Crestwood, NY: St. Vladimir's Seminary Press, 2001.
Stiefel, Jennifer H. "Women Deacons in 1 Timothy: A Linguistic and Literary Look at 'Women likewise...' (1 Tim 3:11)." *New Testament Studies* 41 (1995): 442–57.
Stonehouse, Ned Bernard. *The Apocalypse in the Ancient Church: A Study in the History of the New Testament Canon.* Goes, Holland: Oosterbaan & Le Cointre, 1929.
Stramara, Jr., Daniel F. "Double Monasticism in the Greek East, Fourth through Eighth Centuries." *Journal of Early Christian Studies* 6 (1998): 269–312.
Swan, Laura. *The Forgotten Desert Mothers: Sayings, Lives and Stories of Early Christian Women.* New York: Paulist Press, 2001.
Swidler, Leonard, and Arlene Swidler, eds. *Women Priests: A Catholic Commentary on the Vatican Declaration.* New York: Paulist Press, 1977.
Synan, Edward. "Atto of Vercelli." In *Dictionary of the Middle Ages,* vol. 1, edited by Joseph R. Strayer, 641. New York: Charles Scribners, 1982.
Talley, Thomas J. "The Evolution of a Feast." *Liturgy* 5 (1985): 42–48.
———. *The Origins of the Liturgical Year.* New York: Pueblo, 1986.
Taft, Robert. *A History of the Liturgy of St. John Chrysostom.* Vol. 5: *The Precommunion Rites.* Orientalia Christiana Analecta 261. Rome: Pontifical Oriental Institute, 2000.
———. "The Interpolation of the Sanctus into the Anaphora: When and Where? A Review of the Dossier." Part 1. *Orientalia Christiana Periodica* 57 (1991): 281–308.
———. *The Liturgy of the Hours in East and West.* 2nd ed. rev. Collegeville, MN: Liturgical Press, 1993.

Tavard, George H. "The Scholastic Doctrine." In *Women Priests: A Catholic Commentary on the Vatican Declarations*, edited by Leonard Swidler and Arlene Swidler, 99–106. New York: Paulist Press, 1977.

Terry, Ann, and Ffiona Gilmore Eaves. *Retrieving the Record: A Century of Archaeology at Poreč (1847–1947)*. Edited by Miljenko Jurković. Studies in Early Christian and Medieval Art History and Archaeology. Dissertationes et Monographiae 1. Zagreb-Motovun, University of Zagreb: International Research Center for Late Antiquity and the Middle Ages Motovun, 2002.

Thacker, Alan. "Martyr Cult within the Walls: Saints and Relics in the Roman Tituli of the Fourth to Seventh Centuries." In *Text, Image, Interpretation: Studies in Anglo-Saxon Literature and its Insular Context in Honour of Éamonn Ó Carragáin*. Studies in the Early Middle Ages 18. Edited by Alastair Minnis and Jane Roberts, 31–76. Turnhout: Brepols, 2007.

Themelly, Alessandra. "Immagini di Maria nella pittura e nei mosaici romani dalla erisi monotelità agli inizi della seconda iconoclastia (640–819)." In *Acta ad Archaeologiam et Artium Historiam Pertinentia*, edited by Siri Sande and Lasse Hodne, 21:108–10. N. S. 7. Rome: Giorgio Bretschneider, 1989.

Theodorou, Evangelos. "Η χειροτονία ή χειροθεσία τών διακονισσών" = "The *Cheirotonia* or *Cheirothesia* of Deaconesses." Ph.D. dissertation, University of Athens, 1954.

———. "Das Amt der Diakoninnen in der kirchlichen Tradition. Ein orthodoxer Beitrag zum Problem der Frauenordination." *Una Sancta* 33 (1978): 162–72.

———. "Der Diakonat der Frau in der Griechisch-Orthodoxen Kirche." *Diaconia Christi* 21, 2–3 (July 1986): 29–33.

Thunø, Erik. *Image and Relic: Mediating the Sacred in Early Medieval Rome*. Analecta Romana Instituti Danici. Supplementum 32. Rome: "L'Erma" di Bretschneider, 2002.

Thurston, Bonnie Bowman. *The Widows: A Women's Ministry in the Early Church*. Minneapolis, MN: Fortress, 1989.

Tolotti, Francesco. *Il cimitero di Priscilla: Studio di topografia e architettura*. Collezione "Amici delle catacombe" 26. Vatican City: PIAC, 1970.

Tongeren, Louis van. "A Sign of Resurrection on Good Friday: The Role of the People in the Good Friday Liturgy until c. 1000 A.D. and the Meaning of the Cross." In *Omnes circumadstantes: Contributions towards a History of the Role of the People in the Liturgy Presented to Herman Wegman*, edited by Charles Caspers and Marc Schneiders, 101–19. Kampen: J. H. Kok, 1990.

Torjesen, Karen Jo. *When Women Were Priests: Women's Leadership in the Early Church and the Scandal of their Subordination in the Rise of Christianity*. San Francisco, CA: HarperSanFrancisco, 1993.

Toynbee, Jocelyn M. C. *Death and Burial in the Roman World*. London: Thames & Hudson, 1971.

———— and John Ward Perkins. *The Shrine of St. Peter and the Vatican Excavations.* London: Longmans, Green, 1956.

Turner, C. H. "χειροτονια, χειροθεςία, ἐπίθεςις χειρῶν (and the accompanying verbs)." *Journal of Theologica Studies* 24 (1923): 496–504.

Ulrich, Anna. "Die Kanonissen: Ein vergangener und vergessener Stand der Kirche." In *Liturgie und Frauenfrage: ein Beitrag zur Frauenforschung aus liturgiewissenschaftlicher Sicht*, edited by Teresa Berger and Albert Gerhards, 181–94. Pietas liturgica 7. St. Ottilien: EOS Verlag Erzabtei, 1990.

Upton, Julia. "Burial, Christian." In *The New Dictionary of Sacramental Worship*, edited by Peter E. Fink, 140–42. Collegeville, MN: Liturgical Press, 1990.

Vagaggini, Cipriano. "L'ordinazione delle diaconesse nella tradizione greca e bizantina." *Orientalia Christiana Periodica* 40 (1974): 145–89.

Valenziano, Crispino. "Iconismo e aniconismo occidentale postniceno: dai Libri Carolini al secolo XIII." *Ecclesia orans* 13 (1996): 11–42.

————. "Iconismo e aniconismo occidentale postniceno: il 'caso serio' della croce nel secolo XIII." *Ecclesia orans* 13 (1996): 185–206.

Vanmaele, Basile. *L'église Pudentienne de Rome (Santa Pudenziana): contribution à l'histoire de ce moment insigne de la Rome Chrétienne ancienne IIe au XXe siècle.* Bibliotheca analectorum Praemonstratensium, fasc. 6. Averbode, Belgium: Praemonstratensia, 1965.

————. "Potenziana (Pudenziana) e Prassede, vergini sante, martiri di Roma." *Bibliotheca Sanctorum* 10 (1968):1062–72.

The Vatican Collections: The Papacy and Art. An official catalogue authorized by the Vatican Museums. New York: Metropolitan Museum of Art, H. N. Abrams, 1982.

Verner, David C. *The Household of God: The Social World of the Pastoral Epistles.* Dissertation Series SBL 71. Chico, CA: Scholars Press, 1983.

Vess, Deborah. "Abelard," and "Heloise." In *Encyclopedia of Monasticism.* 2 vols. Edited by William M. Johnston, vol. 1, 11–13, 574–75. Chicago: Fitzroy Dearborn, 2000.

Visser, Margaret. *The Geometry of Love: Space, Time, Mystery, and Meaning in an Ordinary Church.* Toronto: HarperCollins, 2000.

Vogel, Cyrille. "Chirotonie et chirothésie: Importance et relativité du geste de l'imposition des mains dans la collation des orders." *Irénikon* 45 (1972): 7–21, 207–38.

————. "Les échanges liturgiques entre Rome et les pays francs jusqu'à l'époque de Charlemagne." In *Le chiese nei regni dell'Europa occidentale e i loro rapporti con Roma sino all'800*, vol. 1, 185–295. Settimane di studio del Centro italiano di studio sull'alto medioevo 7. Spoleto: Presso la sede del centro, 1960.

————. "Handauflegung." In *Reallexikon für Antike und Christentum: Sachwörterbuch zur Auseinandersetzung des Christentums mit der antiken Welt.* Vol. 13, edited by Theodor Klauser et al., 482–93. Stuttgart: Hiersemann, 1986.

————. "L'imposition des mains dans les rites d'ordination en Orient et en Occident." *La Maison-Dieu* 102 (1970): 57–72.

———. "Is the Presbyteral Ordination of the Celebrant a Condition for the Celebration of the Eucharist?" In *Roles in the Liturgical Assembly: The Twenty-Third Liturgical Conference, Saint Serge, Paris, June 28–July 1, 1976*, translated by Matthew J. O'Connell, 253–64. New York: Pueblo, 1981.

———. "*Laïca communione contentus*: Le retour du presbytre au rang des laïcs." *Revue des sciences religieuses* 47 (1973): 56–122.

———. *Medieval Liturgy: An Introduction to the Sources*. Revised and translated by William G. Storey and Niels Krogh Rasmussen. NPM Studies in Church Music and Liturgy. Washington, DC: Pastoral Press, 1986.

———. *Ordinations inconsistantes et caractère inamissable*. Études d'histoire du culte et des institutions chrétiennes 1. Torino: Bottega d'Erasmo, 1978.

———. "La réforme liturgique sous Charlemagne." In *Karl der Grosse: Lebenswerk und Nachleben*. Vol. 2: *Das geistige Leben*, edited by Bernhard Bischoff, 217–32. Düsseldorf: L. Schwann, 1965.

———. "Statuta Ecclesiae Antiqua." *New Catholic Encyclopedia*. Vol. 13, 682. New York: McGraw-Hill, 1967.

———. "Titre d'ordination et lien du presbytre à la communauté locale dans l'église ancienne." *La Maison-Dieu* 115 (1973): 70–85.

———. "*Vacua manus impositio*: L'inconsistance de la chirotonie absolue en Occident." In *Mélanges liturgiques offerts au R. P. dom Bernard Botte*, 511–24. Louvain: Abbaye du Mont César, 1972.

———. "'*Vulneratum caput*': Position d'Innocent I (402–417) sur la validité de la chirotonie presbytérale conférée par un évêque hérétique." *Rivista di archeologia cristiana* 49 (1973): 375–84 = *Miscellanea in onore di L. de Bruyne e A. Ferrura*, 2:375–84. XXIII Semaine d' études liturgiques. Paris, June 28–July 1, 1976.

———, ed., with Reinhard Elze. *Le Pontifical romano-germanique du dixième siècle*. 3 vols. Studi e Testi, 226, 227, 269. Vatican City: Biblioteca Apostolica Vaticana, 1963–1972.

Volbach, Wolfgang Fritz. *Early Christian Art*. Translated by Christopher Ligota. New York: Abrams, 1962.

———. *Il tesoro della Cappella Sancta Sanctorum*. Guida del Museo Sacro Vaticana 4. Vatican City: BAV, 1941.

Vos, Wiebe, and Geoffrey Wainwright, eds. *Ordination Rites: Papers Read at the 1979 Congress of Societas Liturgica*. Rotterdam: Liturgical Ecumenical Center Trust, 1980.

Waal, A. de. "Titulus Praxedis." *Römische Quartalschrift für christliche Altertumskunde und für Kirchengeschichte* 19 (1905): 169–80.

Waetzoldt, Stephan. *Die Kopien des 17. Jahrhunderts nach Mosaiken und Wandmalereien in Rom*. Römische Forschungen der Bibliotheca Hertziana 18. Munich: Schroll, 1964.

Wainwright, Elaine Mary. "Gospel of Matthew." In *Searching the Scriptures: A Feminist Commentary*. Vol. 2, 339–52. New York: Crossroad, 1994.

———. *Towards a Feminist Critical Reading of the Gospel according to Matthew*. Beihefte zur Zeitschrift für die neutestamentliche Wissenschaft und die Kunde der älteren Kirche 60. Berlin: De Gruyter, 1991.

Walls, A. F. "The Latin Version of Hippolytus' Apostolic Tradition." *Studia Patristica* 3 (1961): 155–62.

Warnke, Charlotte. "Das Kanonissenstift St. Cyriakus zu Gernrode im Spannungsfeld zwischen Hochadel, Kaiser, Bischof und Papst von der Gründung 961 bis zum Ende des Investiturstreits 1122." In *Studien zum Kanonissenstift*, edited by Irene Crusius, 201–74. Veröffentlichungen des Max-Planck-Instituts für Geschichte 167. Studien zur Germania sacra 24. Göttingen: Vandenhoeck & Ruprecht, 2001.

Weitzmann, Kurt. *The Monastery of Saint Catherine at Mount Sinai: The Icons*. Vol. 1: *From the Sixth to the Tenth Century*. Princeton, NJ: Princeton University Press, 1976.

Weltin, E. G. "Anicetus, St. Pope." In *New Catholic Encyclopedia*. 2nd ed. 15 vols. Vol. 1, 455. Washington, DC: Catholic University of America, 2003.

Wemple, Suzanne Fonay. *Atto of Vercelli: Church, State and Christian Society in Tenth Century Italy*. Temi e Testi 27. Rome: Edizioni di Storia e Letteratura, 1979.

———. "Women from the Fifth to the Tenth Century." In *A History of Women in the West*. Vol. 2: *Silences of the Middle Ages*, edited by Christiane Klapisch-Zuber, 169–201. Cambridge, MA: Belknap Press of Harvard University Press, 1992.

———. *Women in Frankish Society: Marriage and the Cloister 500 to 900*. The Middle Ages. Philadelphia: University of Pennsylvania Press, 1981.

Wessel, K. "Das Mailänder Passionsdiptychon, ein Werk der karolingischen Renaissance." *Zeitschrift für Kunstwissenschaft* 5 (1951): 125–38.

Whelan, Caroline F. "*Amica Pauli*: The Role of Phoebe in the Early Church." *Journal for the Study of the New Testament* 49 (1993): 67–85.

Wickstrom, John B. "Carthusians." In *Encyclopedia of Monasticism*. 2 vols. Edited by William M. Johnston, vol. 1, 244–47. Chicago: Fitzroy Dearborn, 2000.

Wijngaards, J. N. M. *No Women in Holy Orders? The Women Deacons of the Early Church*. Norwich: Canterbury Press, 2002.

———. *The Ordination of Women in the Catholic Church: Unmasking a Cuckoo's Egg Tradition*. New York: Continuum, 2001.

Wilkinson, John. *Egeria's Travels to the Holy Land*. rev. ed. Jerusalem: Ariel, 1981.

Willis, G. G. *Further Essays in Early Roman Liturgy*. Alcuin Club Collections 50. London: SPCK, 1968.

Wilmart, André. "Le Comes de Murbach." *Revue bénédictine* 30 (1913): 25–69.

———. "Le lectionnaire d'Alcuin." *Ephemerides liturgicae* 51 (1937): 136–97.

———. "Prières pour la communion dans deux psautiers du Mont-Cassin." *Ephemerides liturgicae* 43 (1929): 320–27.

———. "Un témoin anglo-saxon du calendrier métrique d'York." *Revue bénédictine* 46 (1934): 41–69.

Wilpert, Joseph. *Fractio panis: Die älteste Darstellung des eucharistischen Opfers in der "Cappella greca," entdeckt und erläutert.* Freiburg im Breisgau: Herder, 1895.

Wilpert, Josef. "Eine mittelalterliche Tradition über die Bekehrung des Pudens durch Paulus." *Römische Quartalschrift für christliche Altertumskunde und für Kirchengeschichte* 22 (1908): 172–77.

———. *Die römischen Mosaiken und Malereien der kirchlichen Bauten vom IV. bis XIII. Jahrhundert.* 4 vols. 2nd ed. Freiburg im Breisgau: Herder, 1917. Revised and abridged edition published by Walter N. Schumacher under title: *Die Römischen Mosaiken der kirchlichen Bauten vom IV–XIII Jahrhundert.* Freiburg; Basel; Wien: Herder, 1976.

Wisskirchen, Rotraut. *Die Mosaiken der Kirchen Santa Prassede in Rom.* Mainz am Rhein: Phillip von Zabern, 1992.

———. *Das Mosaikprogramm von S. Prassede in Rom: Ikonographie und Ikonologie.* Jahrbuch für Antike und Christentum, Ergänzungsband 17. Münster Westfalen: Aschendorffsche Verlagsbuchhandlung, 1990.

———. "Zur Zenokapelle in S. Prassede/Rom." In *Frühmittelalterliche Studien, Jahrbuch des Instituts für frühmittelalterforschung der Universität Münster* 25 (1991): 9–108.

Witherington III, Ben. *The Acts of the Apostles: A Socio-Rhetorical Commentary.* Grand Rapids, MI: Eerdmans, 1998.

———. *Women in the Earliest Churches.* Cambridge: Cambridge University Press, 1988.

Wright, John H. "Patristic Testimony on Women's Ordination in *Inter Insigniores.*" *Theological Studies* 58 (1997): 516–26.

Xydis, Stephen G. "The Chancel Barrier, Solea, and Ambo of Hagia Sophia." *Art Bulletin* 29 (1947): 1–24.

Yarbrough, Anne. "Christianization in the Fourth Century: The Example of Roman Women." *Church History* 45 (1976): 149–65.

Young, Steve. "Being a Man: The Pursuit of Manliness in *The Shepherd* of Hermas." *Journal of Early Christian Studies* 2 (1994): 237–55.

Ysebaert, Joseph. "The Deaconesses of Late Antiquity and Their Origin." In *Eulogia. Mélange offerts à Antoon A. R. Bastiaensen à la occasion des son soixante-cinquième anniversaire.* Edited by G. M. Bartelink, A. Hilhorst, and C. H. Kneepkens, 423–36. Steenbruge: Abbatia S. Petri, 1991.

Index of Authors

Aloisi, Benigno, 344, 347–349
Andrieu, Michel, 148, 220–223, 271–272, 278, 332
Angelelli, Claudia, 314, 319
Angiolini, Anna, 198, 199
Aubert, Marie-Josèphe, 222

Baldovin, John, 324, 354
Baldracco, G., 344n108, 346
Balsamon, Theodore, 256
Baronius, Cesare Sorano, 169n1, 182, 182n44
Bauer, Franz Alto, 322
Belting-Ihm, Christa, 60n25, 62
Berger, Teresa, 123
Blauuw, Sybille de, 352
Bosio, Antonio, 189, 192
Bradshaw, Paul, 133
Brennan, Brian, 159, 228
Brent, Allen, 30
Brown, Raymond E., 118
Burtchaell, James, 159

Capgrave, John, 335
Carr, Ephrem, 250
Castelli, Elizabeth, 202
Chavasse, Antoine, 78, 78n79
Ciampini, Giovanni Giustino, 203, 203n104

Collins, John N., 134, 240
Collins, Raymond F., 114
Cooper, Kate, 9

Dagens, Claude, 190
Davanzati, Benigno, xi–xii, 11, 170–172
Davis, Raymond, 38
Delehaye, Hippolyte, 9, 10n26
Deshusses, Jean, 266, 271
Dix, Gregory, 147
Duchesne, Louis, 182
Durand, William, 301–306
Dyer, Joseph, 47, 68, 69n51

Eisen, Ute, xii, 152, 153, 159, 175, 226–227, 229
Elze, Reinhard, 280

Faivre, Alexandre, 115, 133, 210
Ford, Josephine Massyngberde, 66, 281
Fortunatus, Venantius, 147, 159
Frere, Walter, 336
Frugoni, Chiara, 234, 236

Geertman, Herman, 337, 338
Goodson, Caroline, 315, 317, 334, 335, 350, 352
Grisar, Hartmann, 354
Gryson, Roger, 141

Guidobaldi, Federico, 7, 7n19, 19, 19n61, 318–319
Gy, Pierre-Marie, 240n4, 253

Harnack, Adolf von, 121–122, 122n29
Hearon, Holly E., 134
Hochstetler, Donald, 141, 149
Hoppin, Ruth, 25

Irvin, Dorothy, 187–188, 191–192, 224, 228

Jounel, Pierre, 78, 78n79, 80, 88

Kilmartin, Edward J., xii, xiv, 59, 376, 377
Kirsch, J. P., 175, 218
Klauser, Theodore, 135
Kleinbauer, W. Eugene, 198
Krautheimer, Richard, xiii–xiv, 37, 37–38n131, 45, 55, 229, 322, 329, 337, 352

Lampe, Peter, 120, 173, 321–324
Leclercq, Henri, 145–146, 177, 185, 190, 225
Leclercq, Jean, 163
Leroquais, Victor, 306, 307
Llewellyn, Peter A. B., 31–32, 318

MacDonald, Margaret, 126
Mackie, Gillian, 74, 108
Macy, Gary, 163, 376
Madigan, Kevin, 142, 154, 226
Martimort, Aimé Georges, 137, 148, 180, 218–219, 271, 281, 303–304, 307
Martinelli, Fioravante, xi–xii, 169–173, 172n4, 343
Marucchi, Orazio, 25, 25n81, 182
McCulloh, John M., 334
Meer, Frederik van der, 63
Militello, Cettina, 40

Morey, C. R., 364, 365, 366
Morin, Germain, 78
Morin, Jean, 169
Morris, Joan, 156, 160, 228
Murphy, Roland E., 362

Nilgen, Ursula, 59, 229

Omont, Henri, 249
O'Neill, J. C., 122
Osiek, Carolyn, 28, 131, 142, 154, 226
Otranto, Giorgio, 152, 208–209

Panofsky, Erwin, 51
Papebroch, Daniel, 18
Pilsworth, Clare, 9
Pozzo, Cassiano dal, 99, 228

Radar, Rosemary, 127
Ramelli, Ilaria, 153
Rossi, Giovanni Battista de, 13, 14, 14n40, 22, 24, 25n81, 70n53, 182, 227

Samuel, Mar, 251
Schaefer, Mary M. 58n19–20, 93n119, 306n197, 311n214, 376n1, 378n3
Schäfer, Karl-Heinrich, 149, 151
Schlatter, Frederic, 193–195
Schneiders, Sandra, 177
Schoedel, W. R., 124
Schubert, Ursula, 249, 250n31
Spence, Stephen, 121
Spence-Jones, H. D. M., 22–23
Stählin, Gustav, 130
Stewart-Sykes, Alistair, 132, 132n73

Taft, Robert F., xiv, 261
Talley, Thomas J., 78, 78n79
Thunø, Erik, 93
Thurston, Bonnie Bowman, 130
Torjesen, Karen Jo, 228
Tulloch, Janet, 185–186

Ulrich, Anna, 151

Vagaggini, Cipriano, 247–248
Vogel, Cyrille, 246–247, 278, 280

Wemple, Suzanne Fonay, 141, 148, 149

Wijngaards, J., 254
Wilpert, Joseph, 183, 185, 187, 193
Wisskirchen, Rotraut, 229
Witherington, Ben, 119

Young, Steve, 29

Index of Sources

Note: Only specific citations from the text are included. General references to the titles below can be found in the subject index.

Acts of the Apostles
  1:15–26 69
  2:33–36 59
  3:12 359
  4:29 118
  6:1–6 135
  6:3–6 257
  9:36–41 130
  12:12 122, 130
  13:1–3 257
  13:26 359
  16:11–15 122
  16:14–15 130
  16:40 122
  18:2–3 121
  18:26 121
  21:8–9 123
  28:16 13, 20
Alcuin epistles
  VIIII 89
  XV 89
  XX 89
  XXXII 89
  XL 89
  XLVIII 89
  XLVIIII 89
  CXIIII 361
  CXIV 79
  CLVI 78, 79
Apostolic Constitutions
  VIII 245, 252
    19.1–20.2 247
Arles Pontifical (Paris, B. N.)
  lat. 1220, 41v-42r 303–304

Barozzi Pontifical of William Durand
  Vatican ms. lat. 1145
    50r-59v 305
    59v 305
    59v-62r 305
    61r 305
Bibliotheca hagiographica latinae
  5439 370
  5443 370
  5446 370
  6920 319
  6988 321, 326
  6989 321, 326
  6991 319

Carthage, Council of
    IV, canon 12 215
Chalcedon, Council of
    Canon 15 148
City of God. *See De civitate Dei*
    (Augustine)
1 Clement to the Corinthians
    38.2 123
    40.5 240
Colossians
    1:15–20 59
    3:18 116
    4:7 135
    4:15 122, 130
1 Corinthians. *See also* 1 Clement to the
    Corinthians
    1:11 130
    6:15–20 283, 300
    7 123, 126
    7:7 124
    7:7–8 123
    7:25 362
    7:34 123
    7:36–38 124
    11:2–16 118
    11:4 118
    11:5 114
    11:7 118
    11:24–25 229
    12:8 201
    12:28–29 201
    14 114
    14:33b-36 114
    14:34 114
    14:34b 114
    14:36 114
    16:19 120, 122
2 Corinthians
    6:3–4 134
    11:2 127
councils of the Church. *See location of
    council*

De civitate Dei (Augustine)
    20 71
    20:3 71
    20:5 71
    20:8 71
    20:16 71
    20:18 71
    20:21 71
    20:23 71
    20:24 71
    20:25 71
    20:27–29 71
    20:28–29 71
Didascalia Apostolorum
    ch. XVI 137
Ecclesiastes
    2:13–14 71
    8:13–14 71
Ecclesiasticus (Sirach)
    24 362, 363
    24:1 361, 362
    50:5–21 363
    51:1 361
    51:13–17 361
Ephesians
    5:22–24 116
    6:21 135
Exodus
    3:1 297
    25:17–22 351
Ezekiel
    1:5–10 36
    10:8–22 36
    41:4 100

Family A
    A.2, Archivio di S. Pietro,
        F.1 86
Ferrandus, canons of
    tit. 11, no. 221 154
    tit. 43, no. 222 154

Galatians
    2:1–9 194
    3:27–28 117
Pope Gelasius
    decree 26 216
Genesis
    2:4b-3:24 242
    2:8 44
    2:10 63
    2:10–14 61, 105
    5:24 97
Gregorian *Hadrianum*
    H 2-H 4 267
    H 4 270, 277
        no. 30 267, 277
        no. 31 267, 277
        no. 32a 267
        no. 32b 267
    H 74 355
    H 212-H 213 270
    H 214 271, 277
    H 215 270
    H 216 270
    H 226 267, 271

Hadrianum. See Gregorian *Hadrianum*
Hebrews
    1:2–3 363
    1:3 73
    2:9b-3:1 89, 90
    2:12–13 91
    3:12–4:3a 90
    3:12–14 89
    4:12–16 89
    8:2 363
    9:2–12 90
    9:24–28 90
    10:19–27 90
    10:19–31 89
    11:14 68
    12:11–14 89
    12:12–23 90
    12:21 68
    12:21b-23a 88
    12:22–24 68
    12:22–29 67
    12:28b-13:7 90
    12:28b-13:8 89, 90
    13:14 67
    13:17 87
    13:17–21 88, 89, 90
    The Vulgate
        2:12 91

Ignatius of Antioch
    Magnesians
        6.1 137
    Smyrnaeans
        13.1 130
Pope Innocent I
    Letter 25 to bishop of Gubbio 260

John
    1:36 63
    3:27–30 284, 300
    4 183
    12:1–8 146
    13:1–16 357
    20 93
    20:1 359
    20:11 359
    20:17 146
    20:18 371
    20:19–29 359
    20:22–23 229
    21 183
1 John
    5:4 359

3 Kingdoms
    8:14–53 84
1 Kings
    6 351
    8:14–53 84

2 Kings
    2:11 97

Laodicea, Council of
    Canon 11 152, 215
    Canon 44 (45) 153
Laurenziana
    LXVI, 35 18
Leviticus
    16:14–20 352
Liber Pontificalis
    Ch. 1 39
    Ch. 8 41
    Ch. 9 42
Luke
    1:41–45 118
    2:22–28 117
    2:36–38 118
    7:36–50 370
    8:2 370
    9:28–36 70
    10:2 213
    10:38–42 134
    22:1–23:53 356
    22:19 229
    22:30 195

Malachi
    3:1–4:5 71
    3:22–23 71
Mark
    8:14–21 189
    9:2–9 70
    14:9 370
    16:15 229
Matthew
    4:11 134
    5:28 126
    5:29 126
    5:32 126
    8:15 134
    9:37–38 213

11:22 71
11:24 71
12:27 71
12:41–42 71
13:44 375
13:44–52 361
13:52 73, 361, 375
14:21 113
15:38 113
16:5–12 189
16:18–19 32
17:1–9 70
19:12 126
19:28 195
19:29 297
20:26 134
20:28 134
22:13 134
22:20 105
23:11 134
25:1–13 294
25:23 297
25:44 134
26:1–27:66 355
26:6–13 355
26:12 355
26:13 355, 370
27:55 134
28 93
28:19 229
Murbach lectionary
    XCVII 79

Nimes, Second Council of
    Canon 2 141

Ordines Romani
    Ordo XXXIV 265, 276, 277
    Ordo XXXVI 265
    Ordo XXXIX 265
    Ordo XLII 338, 339, 342
        3 341

5 341
6 341
10 342
13–14 342
14–16 342

1 Peter 30
  2:1 104
  2:1–10 359
  3:18 104, 358
Philemon
  1–2 122
Philippians
  1:1 134
  1:2 157
Proverbs
  8:22 249
  8:22–31 29, 362
  31:10–31 201
Psalms
  22:23 89
  53:5 283
  118 (119) 357
  Masoretic Text
    22:23 89, 91
  The Septuagint
    21:22 89, 91
  The Vulgate
    21:23 89, 91
    132:2 309

Revelation
  1:1 60
  1:1–5 82
  1:5 60
  1:6 60
  1:7 60
  1:8 62
  1:12–13 60
  1:12–18a 87, 89, 90
  1:16 60
  1:17–18 60

1:20 64, 72
2:10 67, 68
2:18–29 118
2:26 60
3:12 83
4 48, 79
4:1 77, 79, 80, 82, 83
4:1–9 80
4:1–10 80
4:1–10a 82
4:4–11 80
4:6 36
4:6–8 65
4:9–11 65
5 48
5:1–10 87
5:6 60
5:6–12 86
6 85
6:9 85
6:9–11 332
7 48, 79
7:1 65
7:2–12 86
7:4 72
7:9 72
7:9–12 77, 79, 82, 83
7:13–17 77, 79, 82, 83
7:17 47, 108
8:2 72
11 70
11:3 70
12:7–12 82
14 48
14:1 50, 63, 72
14:1–5 82
14:3–4 368
14:3a 72
14:4b 72
17:14 69
19 48, 73
19:7–8 67

Revelation (*Cont.*)
  19:9 67
  19:13 69
  19:16 69
  19:17 69
  20 73
  20:1 69
  20:4–6 67
  20:6 62, 73
  20:9–10 71
  21:1–4 66
  21:2 67, 83, 84
  21:2–5 83, 84
  21:2–5a 84
  21:3–4 68
  21:5a 66
  21:6 105
  21:8–27 66
  21:9–10 67
  21:9–27 83, 84, 100
  21:9b–27 84
  21:10 67
  21:14 50, 67
  21:16 67, 100
  21:25 72
  22:1–2 61, 66
  22:3–5 66
  22:5 50
  22:12 60
  22:17 61
  22:20 60
Romano-Germanic Pontifical of the
    Tenth Century
  Avignon, Bibl. Mun.
    ms. 205, 31–42 307
  Darmstadt, Hessische Landes- und
    Hochschulbibliothek
    cod. 710, 176r 307
  Lucca, Biblioteca Capitulare cod. 607
    32r-33v 289
    33v-36r 289
  Ordinatio Abbatissae Canonicam
    ordo no. 4 297
    ordo no. 5 297
    ordo no. 9 295
Roman Pontifical of William Durand
  XXI 301
  XXII 301, 305
  Barozzi pontifical - Vatican ms. lat.
    1145
    50r-59v 305
    59v 305
    59v-62r 305
    61r 305
Roman Pontifical of the Twelfth
    Century
  XIV 299
  no. 14 300
  no. 15 300
Romans
  12:6–8 201
  16 20, 119, 212, 257, 375
  16:1 213, 223, 256
  16:1–2 119, 130, 135, 218
  16:3–5 20, 120
  16:5 122
  16:6 120, 130
  16:7 120
  16:9 120
  16:12 120
  16:14 26, 181
  16:21–23 119

The Shepherd (Hermas)
  Holmes edition
    Revelation 25.1–2 29
    Similitude (Parable) 9:89 28
    Visions 1.4 29
    Visions 2.5–6 28
    Revelation 5.1–2 29
    Similitude (Parable) 9.12.2 28
    Visions 1–4 28
    Visions 1.2–3 28
    Visions 1.4 29
    Visions 2.4.1 181
    Visions 2.5 28

Visions 3 28, 29
Visions 4 182
Visions 6.2–3 28
Shorter Roman Martyrology (Ado of
    Vienne)
  XII KL Iulii 15
Sirach (Ecclesiasticus)
  24 362, 363
  24:1 361, 362
  50:5–21 363
  51:1 361
  51:13–17 361
Song of Songs
  4:8 369
Statuta ecclesiae antiqua (Gennadius of
    Marseilles)
  Canon 37 142
  Canon 41 142
Studia Patristica
  F.1 82
Syriac Bible (Paris, B. N.)
  ms. syr. 113, 111r-112v 250
  ms. syr. 341, 118r 249

Testamentum Domini
  1.19 131
  1.23 131
1 Timothy
  1:2 16
  1:18 16
  2:9–15 114, 115, 116
  2:11–12 115
  2:12 115, 206
  2:13–14 116
  3:8–10 136
  3:8–14 277, 283
  3:11 130, 136
  3:12–13 136
  4:14 257, 365
  5:2 152
  5:3–8 129
  5:3–15 130
  5:3–16 132

  5:9–10 129
  5:11 126, 129
  6:20 16
2 Timothy
  1:2 16
  1:6 257, 365
  1:17 16
  4:19 356
  4:21 16, 356
Titus
  2:3 152
  2:3–5 116
Tours, Council of
  Canon 14 (13) 159

Vatican Library Manuscripts
  lat. 1145
    50r-59v 305
    59v 305
    59v-62r 305
    61r 305
  lat. 1191
    90r-93v 367
    96v-101v 368
    98r-v 368
    98v 368, 369
    99r 369
    100r 369
    100v-101r 369
    101r 369
    101v 369
    101v-105r 370
    103v 370
    104v 371
    105r 371
    182v-183r 367
  lat. 3764
    2v 17
  lat. 6839
    104v 291
    109v 291
  lat. 8701
    102v 87, 89

Vatican Library Manuscripts (*Cont.*)
    103 89
    103v 87
    104r-105r 87
    104v 87
    114r-115r 89
    179v 82
    188v 82
    189v 86
    190v 86
Veronensis (Leonine sacramentary)
    XXVIII 264

Wisdom
  7:30b 361

Worms, Council of
    Canon 73 148
Würzburg epistles
    114 78
    214–255 89
    CCLIIII 90

Pope Zacharias
    De monachis ancillis Dei, de quibus flagitatum
    Canon 5 216
    Letter 5, "Against Nuns' Proclamation or Singing." 155

Index of Subjects

Aachen, Council of, 2
Abbacus, burial of, 336
abbesses, 223
    Atto of Vercelli and, 211–218, 211n128–217n148
    as canonesses, 161–162, 161n186–162n192
    confession and, 164, 164n196, 166, 166–167n203
    as diaconas, 148, 161
    as episcopas, 160–164, 161n186–164n199
    ordination of, xii–xiii, 148, 289–299
    as presbyteras, 180
    as *sacerdotes* (priests), 161
Abraham, in works of art, 43
absolute ordination, 245, 245n16
M. Acilius Glabrio, 25, 25n83
Acta SS. Pudentianae et Praxedis, 18, 32, 260
Acta Sanctorum, 18–19, 369
Acts of Paul and Thecla, 126, 126n48
Acts of the Apostles, 20, 59, 69, 77, 103, 118–135 *passim*, 243, 257, 359
    Pudens clan and, 13–14
    virginity and, 123
    women as leaders and, 120, 120n25, 122

Acts of Thomas, 126
Adam and Eve, 104, 116
Admonitio generalis, 275
Ado of Vienne (archbishop), martyrology of, 2–5, 15, 16n50, 17, 85, 365
"Against Nuns' Proclamation or Singing" (Zacharias), 155, 155n163–164
agape meal, 185
Agathe (diacona/abbess), 223
Age of Martyrs, 20–26, 124–125n40, 124–127
Agnes, 80n83, 101, 177, 201
    Paschal I and, 317–318
    in works of art, 67, 105, 106 (photo)
S. Agnes, catacomb of, 34, 201–202, 201n96
S. Agnes ad Duo Furna, 42n144, 101, 101n141
Alaric I (Visigoth king), 66
Alcuin epistles, 75–100 *passim*, 75n69, 79n82, 361
Alcuin of York, 75, 75n69, 84–86, 84n90, 85n92
Alexander VII (pope), 170
All Saints feast, 76–78, 78n79, 84–87, 84n90–86n97

Aloisi, Benigno (prior), 344, 347–349
altar of S. Prassede, 43 (figure), 48, 331, 339 (figure), 348 (photo); see also relic translation
  dedication of, xiii, 1, 1n1, 337–343
Alvisinda (diacona/abbess), 223
Amantius, burial of, 336
Ambrose (archbishop of Milan), 127, 129, 178
Ambrose (presbyter), 212
Ambrosiaster (commentator), 132
the Anastasis, 109
Andrew (apostle), in works of art, 101–105, 102n144–106n156
Andronicus (relative of Paul), 120
angels, Revelation and, 74–82 passim
Anicetus (pope), 26n86, 27
Anna (diacona), 219, 269
Anna daughter of Phanuel (prophetess), 117–118, 368
Anna of Dalmatia (diacona), 148
annular crypt of S. Prassede, 43 (figure), 48, 339 (figure)
anti-prophets, women as, 118, 118n16
Antoninus of Pisca, 44n148
Antoninus Pius (Roman emperor), 4, 11, 11n31, 12, 12n36, 23, 189, 319, 369
Antony the Great, 128–129
annulment of ordination, 141–142
Apelles (early Christian), 120
S. Apollinare Nuovo, 109
Apollos (early Christian), 121
apostles; see also specific names
  woman as, 120, 120n22
  in works of art, 44, 46, 50, 50n163, 63n37, 67, 69, 70n55, 95, 96n125, 197
Apostolic Constitutions, 137, 139, 172, 204, 244, 245, 247, 252
"Apostolic Office: Sacrament of Christ" (Kilmartin), 376

Apostolic Tradition, 128–139 passim, 158, 158n174, 174, 191, 243–244, 243n12
Apphia (early Christian), 122
apse of S. Prassede, 40–50 passim, 41 (photo), 43 (figure), 49n161–50n164, 57 (photo), 233, 339 (figure)
  decorative cycles of, 52
  descending christology and, 58, 58n20
  iconography of mosaics of, 60–64, 85–86
  Lateran triclinium and, 55n12
  mosaics of, xii
apse of S. Pudenziana, 203, 207
  mosaics of, 7, 8 (photo)
  presbyteras and, 192–195
apsidal arch of S. Prassede, 43 (figure), 44, 47–48, 48–49n159–160, 57 (photo), 79, 339 (figure)
  decorative cycles of, 52
  descending christology and, 58, 58n20
  iconography of mosaics of, 64–66, 83–84
  Lateran triclinium and, 55n12
Aquilla (early Christian), 20, 20n64, 20n65, 24–25n81, 34–35, 34n117, 35n120, 120–122, 120n25, 121n27, 356; see also Prisca
Archiepiscopal Palace, Ravenna, 233–234
Archippus (early Christian), 122
arcosolia (tomb type), 24
Argyrius, 6
Arles Pontifical (Paris, B. N.), 303–304
Armagh, Book of, 147
ascending christology, 58, 58n20, 91–95
Asia Minor, churches of, 27–28
atrium of S. Prassede, 43 (figure), 339 (figure)

Atto of Vercelli (bishop), 170, 211–218, 211n128–217n148
Audifax, burial of, 336
Augustine of Canterbury, 274
Augustine of Hippo, 66, 71, 127, 129, 151, 175, 290
S. Augustine's basilica, 154
Augustinian Rule, 151
Aurelian (emperor), 23
Aventius (presbyter), 6, 9

baptism, 12, 12n35
   diaconas and, 140–142, 140n107, 170
   freeing of slaves and, 11, 11n32
   Pascha annotina and, 87
   at S. Prassede, 20n63
   Priscilla cemetery and, 25
   of Pudens clan members, 10–11n29, 13, 13n39, 171
baptistry, 11, 12, 12n35
   Lateran, 12n35, 200, 200n94, 229–231, 230 (photo)
   at S.-Maximin La-Sainte-Baume, 143, 146
   at S. Prassede, 324
   of S. Prassede, 78n76
Barnabus (early Christian), 122
Barozzi, Giovanni (bishop of Bergamo), 304–305
Bartholomew (apostle), 172
basilica, 8n20
Basilica Euphrasiana, 110, 231–233
basilica Sancti Laurentii de palatio, 353
Basilla, burial of, 336
Bede, the Venerable, recensions of, 1, 2n3, 15, 15n42, 371
Benedict VIII (pope), 222
Benedict XIII (pope), 48, 314, 344, 346
Benedict XIV (pope), 5, 5n12, 175, 316, 351
Benedict XVI (pope), 310
Benedicta (patron), 236

Benedict Biscop, 274
Benedictine Rule, 149, 150
Benedict of Aniane, 149, 265, 278
Benedict of Nursia, 150
Bibliotheca hagiographica latinae, 319, 321, 326, 370
Bibliotheca Sanctorum (Vanmaele), 372
bishops
   duties of, 241
   as rulers, 21, 30–31, 31n107
   wives of, 159, 159n177, 159n181
bishop's chair of S. Prassede, 43 (figure), 339 (figure)
the Bollandists, 8–9, 10n27, 18, 321, 369
Bonosus (father of Paschal I), 228
Borromeo, Charles (cardinal), 87, 343, 345
Brigid of Kildare (Mary of the Gaels), 160, 160n182
burial practices, 23–26, 24n79, 329–351 *passim. See also* catacomb; mausoleum-chapel; Priscilla cemetery; relic translation; *specific locations*
   caskets and, 197–200, 197 (photo)
   crypt-altars and, 332–334
   funeral banquets and, 185–186
   hypogea and, 183
   loculus and, 15, 24
   sarcophagi and, 142–146, 143n115–146n122, 144–145 (photos), 195–196, 196 (photo)

Caesarius of Arles, 150, 175–176
Callistus catacomb, 80n83, 186
Cambrai copy of the Gregorian *Hadrianum*, 265–266
Candida, burial of, 336
canonesses, 149–151, 150n141, 151n144
   abbesses as, 161–162, 161n186–162n192
   as *sacerdotes* (priests), 156–157, 157n171, 161

Canons of Hippolytus, 132, 132n72, 139
"The Carolingian Revival of Early
    Christian Architecture"
    (Krautheimer), 329
Carolingian rulers, xiii, 37, 38, 38n134,
    47, 51, 86; *see also* specific
    monarch
  art under, 55
  foundation myth of S. Pudenziana
    and S. Prassede and, 18–20
  Roman church and, 53–54
  Rome during, 32
  women office holders under, 149–150,
    150n140, 155–156
Carthage, Council of, 215
Castulus, burial of, 336
catacomb, 333; *see also* burial practices;
    Priscilla cemetery
  S. Agnes, 34, 201–202, 201n96
  art in, 14, 24
  Callistus, 80n83, 186
  Domitilla, Veneranda at, 224–226,
    225 (photo)
  S. Valentine, 34
Cecilia, 34, 50n163, 317–318
S. Cecilia, 34, 40, 40n140, 50n163,
    55, 62
Celestine I (pope), 321
celibacy, 123–129, 124n38–127n50, 138;
    see also virginity
Celtic church, 147
cemeteries; *see* burial practices;
    Priscilla cemetery
Chalcedon, Council of, 139, 148
Chalons-sur-Saône, Council of, 149
chancel barrier at S. Prassede,
    350–351
"Chapel of the Sacraments" at the
    Callistus catacomb, 186
Charlemagne (Charles the Great),
    xiii, 54, 265, 275, 298; *see also*
    Carolingian rulers

cheirotonia, 245–247, 246n19–20, 250,
    252n38, 256n50, 262
Chloe (early Christian), 130
Christian liturgy; *see* liturgy
Christology; *see* ascending christology;
    descending christology
Chrodegang of Metz (bishop), 274
Chronographer of 354, 16, 21, 27
Chrysanthus, burial of, 336
Chrysostom, John (archbishop of
    Constantinople), 78, 127–139
    passim, 133n79
church; *see* Eastern churches, women's
    place in; Roman church,
    women's place in; stational
    churches; *specific church*
"Church from the Circumcision" figure
    at S. Sabina's, 194, 204, 207
"Church from the Gentiles" figure at S.
    Sabina's, 194, 204, 207
Church of the Holy Apostles, 16
City of God (Augustine), 66, 71
classical illusionism, 35, 35n123
Claudia, 15n42, 16
Claudius (emperor), 20, 120
Clement (presbyter-bishop), 181
Clement VIII (pope), 308
S. Clemente, 370
Clementine pontifical, 308
Clement of Alexandria, 139
1 Clement to the Corinthians, 123, 240
Colossians, 59, 116, 122, 130, 135
Columban, rule of, 150
column of flagellation, 44–45,
    44n148–45n149
communion; *see* Eucharist
communion ecclesiology, 242–243
confession, women office holders
    and, 164, 164n196, 166,
    166–167n203
confessio of S. Prassede, 43 (figure),
    339 (figure)

Congregation of the Lateran, 162
consecration of virgins, 177–179
Constantia (diacona), 223, 236
Constantina (daughter of Constantine), 177, 201, 201n96
Constantine (emperor), 33, 41n143, 42, 60, 98n132, 173, 177, 197, 320, 329
   Lateran Baptistery and, 200, 200n94
   in works of art, 198
Constantinian Peace, 242, 319
Constantinople, First Council of, 137
Corbie lectionary, 75n70, 80, 82, 84, 100
1 Corinthians, 114–130 *passim*, 201, 229, 283, 300, 362; *see also* 1 Clement to the Corinthians
   limitations on women in, 113–117
   on remarriage, 126
   virginity/celibacy and, 123
   women as prophets and, 118, 118n15
2 Corinthians, 127, 134
Cornelius (pope), 32n112, 174, 257
SS. Cosma e Damiano, 49, 55n12, 62, 62n29, 64, 65
councils of the Church; *see* location of council
S. Crisogono, 331
"Crispina" sarcophagus, presbyteras and, 195–196, 196 (photo)
Crispus, 13n39
cross-reliquary of Paschal, 93–95, 94n122, 94 (photo)
crypt-altars, 332–334; *see also* altar of S. Prassede; relic translation
cubicula (tomb type), 24, 333
Cyprian (bishop of Carthage), 128
Cyriac, burial of, 336
Cyrinus, burial of, 336

Dafne (widow), 218
Damasus I (pope), 7, 180, 319, 320–321

Daniel (prophet), 1, 15, 143
Daria, burial of, 336
daughters of Philip, 118, 123, 123n134
Davanzati, Benigno (prior of S. Prassede), 170–172, 171n6–172n12, 343, 350, 366
David (king of Israel), 104
deacons; *see* diaconas
Decentius of Gubbio (bishop), 260
Decius (emperor), 23
De civitate Dei (Augustine), 66, 71
decorative cycles of S. Prassede, 52–111; *see also* mosaics
   apse and, 52
   apsidal arch and, 52
   mausoleum-chapel and, 54, 98–100, 98n132, 100n137
   presbytery and, 54–73
   transept and, 56–73 *passim*
   triumphal arch and, 52, 54
   Zeno Chapel and, 52, 54–56
deesis, 98, 98n133
De locis sanctis martyrum, 35
De monachis ancillis Dei, de quibus flagitatum (Zacharius), 216
S. Denis, 54
descending christology, 58, 58n20
Deusdedit (presbyter), 6, 9
diaconas, 119, 119n19, 130, 133n79, 173; *see also* diaconiae (social service centers)
   abbesses as, 148, 161
   annulment of, 141–142
   Atto of Vercelli and, 211–218, 211n128–217n148
   baptism and, 140–142, 140n107, 170
   canonesses and, 149–151, 150n141, 151n144
   celibacy and, 138
   comparison of male and female ordination rites and, 281–289
   Benigno Davanzati on, 172

diaconas (*Cont.*)
  defining, 134–136
  duties of, 139–140, 250
  in early Christianity, 133n79, 134–151, 134n82–150n142
  in Eastern churches, 136–140
  hierarchy and, 137
  Fioravante Martinelli on, 170
  S.-Maximin La-Sainte-Baume and, 142–146, 143n115–146n122, 144–145 (photos)
  nuns and, 303–306
  ordination of, xiii, 139–142, 148, 172, 247–256, 269–299 *passim*
  S. Paul's Outside the Walls and, 200, 219–220
  prohibition of, 141–142
  requirements for, 138, 138n97
  in the Roman church, 218–224, 218n149–223n168, 269–274
  Romano-Germanic Pontifical of the Tenth Century and, 279–299
  textual evidence for, 220–224, 220n155–223n168
  widows as, 138, 140–141
diaconiae (social service centers), 6, 33, 33n114, 34, 37, 37–38n131
Dialogues (Gregory I), 328
Dictionnaire d'archeologie chrétienne et de liturgie, 145
Didascalia Apostolorum, 88, 136–137
Diocletian (emperor), 21, 23, 80n83, 331
Dionysius (pope), 326
Dionysius Exiguus, 153
Dometius (deacon), 219, 269
Dominica in natale sanctorum, 77–80
Dominic de Guzman (Friars Preachers founder), 237
Domitilla catacomb, Veneranda at, 224–226, 225 (photo)
Domna Odocia (diacona/abbess), 223
domus ecclesiae; *see* house-church

Donatism, 147
Durand, William, 301–306

early Christianity, women's place in, 112–168 *passim*; *see also* Eastern churches, women's place in; Roman church, women's place in; *specific offices*
  as apostles, 120, 120n22
  as canonesses (*see* canonesses)
  celibacy and (*see* celibacy)
  confession and, 164, 164n196, 166, 166–167n203
  as diaconas (*see* diaconas)
  ecclesiastical widows and, 129–133, 129n61–133n77
  as episcopas (*see* episcopas, *episcope* and)
  Eucharist and, 118, 118n18
  as evangelists, 119–123
  Gelasius I and, 154–156
  hierarchy of positions and, 137
  house-churches and, 119–123, 322–324
  limitations on, 113–117, 114n5, 116n11, 139–142
  liturgy and, 163–165, 163n193–164n199
  Council of Laodicea and, 152–153, 152n151, 153–154n157
  as office holders (*see* office holders, women as; *specific offices*)
  official rites and, 243–244
  ordination rites and, 244–256, 244n15–256n50
  Potentiana's *vita* and, 318–329
  Praxedes' *vita* and, 318–329
  as presbyteras (*see* presbyteras)
  as prophets, 117–118
  as *sacerdotes* (*see* *sacerdotes* (priests))
  virginity and (*see* virginity)
  widows and (*see* widows)
  Zacharias and, 155, 155n163–164

Easter, 27–28n94, 27–32, 27n91, 28n95. *see also* Paschaltide
   Ambrose of Milan and, 178
   Hermas and, 27
   mosaic iconography and, xii, 70, 110
   Paschal I and, 351–363 *passim*
   paschal Triduum and, 356–358
   Pius I and, 27, 110
   propitiatorium and, 351–353
   sancta sanctorum and, 351–353
   stations of Holy Week and, 353–356
Eastern churches, women's place in
   All Saints feast and, 78
   celibacy and, 128–129
   diaconas in, 136–140
   iconoclastic movement and, 52–53, 53n3
   ordination rites in, 244–256, 244n15–256n50
   papacy and, 32–33
   widows and, 131–132, 132n71
   women's feasts and, 83
Easter week, 359–360
ecclesia (congregation/place of assembly), 7n20, 12, 42n145
ecclesia Pudentiana, 16, 19, 321
Ecclesiastes, 71
Ecclesiastical Canons of the Apostles, 139
ecclesiastical widows, 129–133, 129n61–133n77, 175
Ecclesiasticus (Sirach), 361–363
ecclesiology, 58, 58n20
Edict of Milan, 320
Egbert of York (archbishop), 272
Elect Lady of 2 John, 122
Eleuther (pope), 28, 28n95
Elijah, in works of art, 69–71, 70n54–55, 96–97n127
Elizabeth (cousin of Mary), 118, 232, 368
Elvira, Synod of, 179
Emerentiana, 201
enculturation of liturgy, 76

Enoch, in works of art, 70n55, 96.97n127
enrolled widows, 174–176, 174n16–176n23
entry stair of S. Prassede, 43 (figure), 339 (figure)
Ephesians, 116, 135
Epiphanius (bishop of Salamis), 153, 153n54
Epiphany, 178
Episcopa Q, 226–227
episcopas, *episcope* and, 21, 30, 157–162, 158n173–162n192
   abbesses as, 160–162, 161n186–162n192
   Archiepiscopal Palace, Ravenna and, 233–234
   Basilica Euphrasiana and, 231–233, 231 (photo), 232 (photo), 233 (photo)
   Benigno Davanzati on, 172
   duties of, 157–158, 158n173
   Lateran Baptistry's Chapel of S. Venantius and, 229–231, 230 (photo)
   monarchical episcopacy and, 21, 30, 157–158, 158n174
   S. Paul's Outside the Walls and, 226–227
   in the Roman church, 224–236, 224n170–236n198
   as *sacerdotes* (priests), 158
   Vatican, Pinacoteca, Universal Judgment and, 234–236
   Veneranda, Domitilla catacomb and, 224–226, 225 (photo)
   wives of bishops and, 159, 159n177, 159n181
   Zeno Chapel at S. Prassede and, 227–229
episcope (oversight); *see* episcopas, *episcope* and

Epistolarum Ordinis Vallombrosani, 76–91 *passim,* 372
epistolary; *see also* lectionary
   Alcuin, 75–100 *passim,* 75n69, 79n82, 361
   Family A, 75–76, 75–76n70, 86
   Family B, 75–76, 75–76n70, 79
   Würzburg, 75–104 *passim,* 79n82, 147, 361, 372
   Zeno Chapel and, 101–105, 102n144–106n156
Escrivá, Jose María (founder, Opus Dei), 167
etimasia, 102
Eucharist, 118, 118n118, 185–189
Eufrosina (diacona/abbess), 223
Eugene II (pope), 39
Euphemia (diacona), 148
Euphrasia (widow of Bishop Namatius), 159
Euphrasius (bishop), 231
Eusebius (historian), 36n125, 174, 329
Eustochium (friend of S. Jerome), 206–207
Evacrius (husband of Theodora Magistra), 202
evangelists, women as, 119–123
Eve, 104, 116
Exodus, 297, 351
Ezekiel, 36, 100

Fabian (bishop of Antioch), 174
Fabian (pope), 21, 32n112
façade of S. Prassede, 43 (figure), 339 (figure)
Family A epistolary, 75–76, 75–76n70, 86
Family B epistolary, 75–76, 75–76n70, 79
family funerary banquets, 186
Felicula, burial of, 336
Felix (pope), 326, 336

SS. Felix and Philip, basilica of, 25
female imagery in *The Shepherd,* 28–29
fermentum, 260–261, 260n61–62, 261–262n66, 323n29
Ferrandus (deacon of Carthage), 154
Fini (Finij) (cardinal), 346
First Apology (Justin Martyr), 369
flagellation, column of, 44–45, 44n148–45n149
Flavia Arcas (ecclesiastical widow), 175
Flavia Vitalia, 241
Florus of Lyons, martyrology of, 85
foundation myth
   iconography of mosaics and, 54
   of S. Prassede, xii, 10, 18–20, 29–31, 54
   of S. Pudenziana, 10, 18–20, 29–31
   topographical record and, 18–20
Fractio panis fresco at the Priscilla cemetery, 183–189, 183n47–189n61, 184 (photo)
frescoes at Priscilla cemetery, 183–192, 183n47–192n73
funeral banquet, 185–186

Gabriel (angel), 65n42, 81, 232
Gaius, 13n39
Galatians, 117, 117n13, 194
Galla Placidia, Aelia, 98n132, 99–100
Gallienus (emperor), 326
Old Gelasian Sacramentary, 179
Gelasius I (pope), 32, 32n111, 154–156, 173, 178, 207–211, 216, 237, 263, 299, 321, 328
gender parity
   in family funerary banquets, 186
   at S.-Maximin La-Sainte-Baume, 142–146, 143n115–146n122, 144–145 (photos)
   in mosaic imagery, xi, xii, 44, 95–110 *passim*

in ordination rites, 281–289
in Priscilla cemetery frescoes, 183–192 passim, 183n47–192n73
Genesis, 44, 61, 63, 97, 105, 242
Gennadius of Marseilles, 142
gesta martyrum, 9, 321
Giovanni (Scuola Romana painter), 234
S. Giovanni in Laterano, 230
Giulia Runa (presbytera), 154
Gordian, burial of, 336
Greek Chapel, Priscilla cemetery, 183–189, 183n47–189n61
Gregorian *Hadrianum*, 265–277 passim, 339, 355
Gregorian Leofric Missal, 272–273
Gregorian *Paduensis* recension, 266–267, 266n80, 273–274, 291
Gregorian *Tridentinum* recension, 220, 266–274 passim, 269–270n90, 270n93, 293
Gregory I (Gregory the Great) (pope), 33, 42, 48, 48n160, 62, 62n28, 93, 103, 180, 237, 264, 315, 328–334, 370
Gregory II (pope), 221
Gregory III (pope), 345
Gregory IV (pope), 62n32, 85
Gregory VII (pope), 271, 274, 364
Gregory IX (Hugolino of Ostia) (pope), 237, 237n202
Gregory of Nyssa, 153
Gregory of Tours, 159

Habacuk, burial of, 336
Hadrian (emperor), 23, 319
Hadrian I (pope), 6, 6n16, 13n38, 24–25n81, 24–56 passim, 41n143, 53n3, 265, 314, 378
Hadrianum. see Gregorian *Hadrianum*
Hagia Sophia, 138, 139, 256
hagiography, 9–10
  decorative cycles and, 56
  intent of, 8
  women's feasts and, 81, 83
heavenly liturgy, 64–66
Hebrews, book of, 240, 363
  in the epistolary, 76–77, 87–91
  iconography of mosaics and, 56–73 passim, 76, 87–91
  women as leaders and, 121–122, 122n29
Helena (empress), 98n132, 198, 320
Helisachar (chancellor to Louis the Pious), 75n69
Hellemo, 36n124, 36n125, 36n127, 62n28, 63n37
Herford, abbess of, 162
Hermas, 16–17, 16n50, 26–29, 26n88, 27n91, 28n96, 126, 181, 369
Hieronymian martyrology, 7, 15
Hilary (diacona), 147
Hildegard of Bingen (abbess), 163, 164n98
Hildoard, Sacramentary of, 265–266
Hippolytus, 131–132
Hippolytus and the Roman Church in the Third Century (Brent), 30
historical romance, 8–9, 10n26
History of the Franks (Gregory of Tours), 159
holy communion; see Eucharist
Holy Innocents, sanctoral cycle and, 82
Holy Spirit, 137
Holy Week, 353–356
Honorius I (pope), 75n69, 80n83, 202, 220, 264, 266, 331, 378
Honorius III (pope), 237
Hormisdas (pope), 210
house-churches, 30–31, 51, 322–324
  foundation myth and, 29–31
  Potentiana and, 16
  Praxedes as presbytera of, xi–xii, 16
  Prisca and Aquilla and, 20, 20n65
  Pudens clan and, 11
  women as leaders of, 119–123, 130

household codes, 29–30, 117n13
house-schools, 30
Hrotsvitha of Gandersheim (secular canoness), 163
Las Huelgas, abbess of, 167
Hyacinth, burial of, 336
Hyginus (pope), 26n86
hypogea, 183

iconoclastic movement, 52–53, 53n3
iconography of mosaics at S. Prassede, 49–51, 50n163, 56–73 *passim*
  apse and, 60–64, 85–86
  apsidal arch and, 64–66, 83–84
  Easter and, xii, 70
  foundation myth and, 54
  Hebrews and, 76, 87–90
  Revelation and, xii, 56–75 *passim*, 76–90 *passim*
  transept and, 56–73 *passim*
  triumphal arch and, xii, 66–73, 70n53–55, 83–84, 88
  Zeno Chapel and, xii, 54–56, 70, 70n54, 95–110, 95n124–110n163, 96 (photo), 99 (photo), 103 (photo), 106 (photo), 107 (photo)
Ignatius of Antioch, 124, 124n38, 130, 137, 157–158, 158n173
imagery
  gender parity in, xi, 28–29, 44, 95–110 *passim*
  at S. Prassede mosaics, 61–73, 62n30–72n61, 85, 105, 108–109
  in *The Shepherd*, 28–29
imaginative romance, 9
indiction defined, 41n143
Innocent I (pope), 7, 260, 262
Innocent III (pope), 166, 236
S. Ippolito, cemetery of, 6
Irenaeus (bishop of Lyon), 32, 59n22, 336
Irene (Byzantine empress), 53, 53n3

"The Irish Life of Brigit," 160, 160n182
Irvin, Dorothy, 187–188, 191–192, 224, 228
Isaac, in works of art, 143, 189

Jacques de Vitry (bishop), 236
James (apostle), 8
  James the Less *vs.* James the Greater and, 102–103, 102n147
  in works of art, 101–105, 102n144–106n156
Jerome (priest and translator), 127, 128, 175, 193, 194, 206, 262
Joan (legendary pope), 229
John, gospel of, 63, 93, 146, 183, 229, 284, 300, 357, 359, 371
John (apostle), 71n56, 74, 102–105, 102n144–106n156
1 John (epistle), 103, 359
2 John (epistle), 122
John IV (pope), 229, 229n188–300n189
John VII (pope), 55
John XIX (pope), 222
John XXIII (pope), 378
S. John Lateran, 33
John Paul I (pope), 378
John Paul II (pope), 310
John the Baptist, 69, 69n52, 70n53, 81n84–85, 98, 98–99n135, 98n133
Joshua, in works of art, 70n55
Julian (emperor), 320
Junia (relative of Paul), 120, 120n22
Justinian (emperor), 139
Justin Martyr, 126, 176, 189, 369

3 Kingdoms, 84
1 Kings, 84, 351
2 Kings, 97

laity, separation of clergy from, 131
Laodicea, Council of, 152–153, 152n151, 153–154n157, 170

Lateran Baptistry, 12n35, 200, 200n94, 229–231, 230 (photo)
Lateran Council IV, 164
Lateran triclinium, 55, 55n12, 65
Laurentian schism, 31–32, 31n109, 32n112
Laurentius (anti-pope), 31, 31n109, 318
Laurenziana, 18
Lawrence of Rome, 79, 81n84, 98n132
S. Lawrence's Outside the Walls, 53
laying on of hands, 128, 132, 139, 172, 243–299 passim, 308
Lazarus, 109
leadership, 239–243 passim; see also office holders, women as; specific office
  in early Christianity, 119–123, 133, 322
  in the Roman church, 28–33
Leclercq, Henri, 145–146, 177, 185, 190, 225
lectionary, 74–77, 74n65–74n72; see also epistolary
  Corbie, 75n70, 80, 82, 84, 100
  Murbach, 75n70, 76–104 passim, 85n92
  sanctoral cycle of, 80–87, 80n83–86n97
  use of Revelation in, 74, 74n65
  Verona, 75–76n70, 80–100 passim, 87n100
Leo I (Leo the Great) (pope), 33, 55n12, 66, 88, 263
Leo II (pope), 270, 378
Leo III (pope), 24–25n81, 38, 39, 39n137, 42n145, 53–56, 65, 70n54, 221–222, 315, 337, 345, 353
Leo V (emperor), 56
Leo IX (pope), 223
Leofric Missal, 272–273
LePin, Jean, 306
Leviticus, 352
Liberian Catalogue, on Hermas, 16, 16n50

Liberius (pope), 178
Liber Pontificalis, 3, 17, 26–28, 38–42, 40n140, 41n143, 92, 101, 221, 228, 317–353 passim
limitations on women, 141–142
  in early Christianity, 139–140
  in the New Testament, 113–117, 114n5, 116n11
Linus, 15n42, 16
liturgy; see also evangelists
  decorative cycles of S. Prassede and, 57–73 passim
  enculturation of, 76
  heavenly, 64–66
  pontificals and, 274–278
  Praxedes and, 360–363
  Revelation in, 73–90 passim, 74n64–85n96
  stational, 58n18
  women as office holders and, 163–165, 163n193–164n199
loculus (shelf-grave), 15, 24
Leofric of Exeter (bishop), 273
Louis the Pious (emperor), 39n135, 39n137, 75n69, 85, 86, 155
love feast (agape meal), 185
Lucca, canonical institute at, 162
Luke, gospel of, 70, 117, 118, 134, 195, 213, 229, 356, 370
Lydia of Thyatira (early Christian), 122, 130

Magdelene, Mary, apocrypha and, 8
Maineri, Giovanni de', 372
Malachi, 71
Marcella (friend of S. Jerome), 206–207
Marcellianus (martyr), 82, 336
Marcellina (sister of Ambrose of Milan), 129, 178
SS. Marcellino e Pietro, 185
Marcellinus, 82, 98n132

Index of Subjects

Marcion of Sinope (heretic), 26
Marcus (martyr), 82, 336
Marcus Aurelius (emperor), 11n31, 17, 23, 319
S. Maria ad Martyres, 78, 273
S. Maria Antiqua, 108
S. Maria in Domnica, 40, 55, 70n53, 316, 352
S. Maria in Via Lata, 171, 223
S. Maria Maggiore, basilica of, 5–7, 6n14, 10, 40–52 passim, 192, 273, 316, 334
Marian devotion, 273–274
Mariano oratory, 364–366, 365 (photo)
S. Maria of Kapitol, Cologne, 156
Marina (Margaret of Antioch), 366–367, 368 (photo)
Marius, burial of, 336
Mark, gospel of, 70, 189, 229, 370
marriage law, Roman, 125
Martha of Bethany, 134, 134n82, 146n124, 336
S. Martin, 236
Martina (diacona), 220
martyrology, 10, 10n27, 15–17, 21–22, 22n71, 22n72; see also Age of Martyrs
  of Ado of Vienne, 2–5, 15, 16n50, 17, 85, 365
  of the Venerable Bede, 1, 2n3, 15, 15n42, 371
  under Benedict XIV, 5, 5n12
  defined, 2n3
  De locis sanctis martyrum, 35
  of Florus of Lyons, 1–2, 2n3, 85
  gesta martyrum and, 9, 321
  Hieronymian, 7, 15–16
  of Rabanus Maurus, 4–5
  of Usuard of Saint-Germain des Prés, 5, 5n11–12, 15, 17
Mary (friend of Paul), 120
Mary (mother of John Mark), 122, 130

Mary Magdalene, 129, 146, 146n124
  vita of, 370–371
Mary of Bethany, 134, 146, 146n124, 355–357, 370
Mary of Egypt, 129
Mary of Rome, 130
Mary Theotokos (Virgin Mary), 44, 94–95, 94n122, 94 (photo), 368
  feast of the Virgin, 81, 83, 83n88
  Holy Spirit and, 137
  S.-Maximin La-Sainte-Baume and, 142–146, 143n115–146n122, 144–145 (photos)
  women as prophets and, 117–118
  in works of art, 68–110 passim, 69n52, 70n55, 95n123, 98n133, 98n135–99n136, 107n157–110n163, 107 (photo), 190, 227, 230, 232, 234–235, 249, 366
Matrona (diacona), 221
Matthew, gospel of, 32, 70, 71, 73, 93, 105, 113, 126, 134, 189, 195, 213, 229, 294, 297, 355, 361, 370, 375
Matthias (apostle), 68
mausoleum-chapel; see also burial practices
  of Constantina, 201, 201n96
  of S. Prassede, decorative cycles of, 54, 98–100, 98n132, 100n137
Maxentius, 320
S.-Maximin La-Sainte-Baume, sarcophagi at, 142–146, 143n115–146n122, 144–145 (photos), 371
Medard (bishop of Noyon), 147
Medici, Alessandro de' (cardinal), 317
Meditations (Marcus Aurelius), 23
Mel the bishop, 160
Merovingian rulers, 149
Michael (angel), 65n42, 74–82 passim, 81n84, 104, 104n151

Milan, Edict of, 320
Minicius Felix (Christian apologist), 126, 126n49
monarchical episcopacy, 21, 30, 157–158, 158n174
Montanism, 147, 208
Morimond, abbot of, 166
mosaics; *see also* decorative cycles of S. Prassede
  classical illusionism in, 35, 35n123
  foundation myth and, 54
  hiatus in, 55
  iconoclastic movement and, 52–53, 53n3
  iconography of (*see* iconography of mosaics)
  imagery in (*see* imagery)
  positional orientation of, 45–46, 45–46n152
  Potentiana in, 36–37, 37n128
  at S. Prassede, xi, xii, 40–51 *passim*, 41 (photo), 42n144–50n164, 52–73 *passim*
  Praxedes in, 36–37, 37n128
  at S. Pudenziana, 7, 7–8n20, 8 (photo), 35–37, 192–195
  Revelation and, 73–74
  Theodora *episcopa* and, xii
Moses, 68–70, 69–71n53–56
Muratorian Fragment, 16, 26
Murbach lectionary, 75n70, 76–104 *passim*, 85n92
Museo Archeologico, the Pola casket at, 197–200, 197 (photo)
Museo Pio-Cristiano, Vatican, "Crispina" sarcophagus at, 195–196, 196 (photo)

Namatius (bishop of Vienne), 159
Natalia, Nazaria Nita (abbess), xii, 310–311
nave of S. Prassede, 2 (photo), 50

SS. Nereus and Achilleus, 6, 6n16, 55, 70n53–54
Nero (emperor), 21, 21n67, 329
New Testament, limitations on women in, 113–117, 114n5, 116n11; *see also* specific books
Niccolò (Scuola romana painter), 234
Nicea, First Council of, 138
Nicea II, Council of, 52, 53n3, 100
Nicholas of Tusculum (cardinal), 237
Nicodemes, burial of, 336
Nicolò V (pope), 343
Nimes, Second Council of, 141
Notitia ecclesiarum urbis Romae (pilgrim guide), 34
Novatian (presbyter), 32n112, 170, 170n, 173
Novatus, 27n90, 32n112, 170–173, 170n, 325, 369
  foundation myth of S. Pudenziana and S. Prassede and, 18–19, 19n61
  in martyrology, 4, 4n9, 15, 15n45
  property of, 11–12
  Pudens clan genealogy and, 14
  in works of art, 67, 365
Novellae Constitutiones (Justinian), 139
nuns, 303–307; *see also* abbesses
Nympha of Laodicea (early Christian), 122, 130

Octavia (ecclesiastical widow), 175, 218
office holders, women as, xii; *see also* specific office
  annulment of, 141–142
  celibacy and, 138
  confession and, 164, 164n196, 166, 166–167n203
  duties of, 139–140
  in early Christian church, 133–162, 133n79–162n192
  in Eastern churches, 136–140

office holders, women as (*Cont.*)
   Gelasius I and, 154–156
   hierarchy and, 137
   Council of Laodicea and, 152–153, 152n151, 153–154n157
   limitations on, 113–117, 114n5, 116n11, 139–142
   liturgy and, 163–165, 163n193–164n199
   requirements for, 138, 138n97
   vestments and, 40, 151, 155–156
   Zacharias and, 155, 155n163–164
Old S. Peter's; *see* S. Peter's basilica
Olympias (patron), 138, 139
Optatus (bishop of Milevi), 147
Opus Dei, 167
Orange, Council of, 141–142
oratory
   dedication of, 83–84
   Mariano, 364–366, 365 (photo)
ordinals of Christ, 240, 240n2
ordination, 169, 239–312 *passim*; *see also* rites/rituals
   of abbesses, xii–xiii, 148, 289–299
   absolute, 245, 245n16
   annulment of, 141–142
   comparison of male and female, 281–289
   of diaconas, xii–xiii, 139–142, 148, 172, 247–256, 269–274
   in the Eastern churches, 244–256, 244n15–256n50
   gender parity and, 281–289
   Fioravante Martinelli on, 170
   pontificals and, 274–278
   prayers re, 264–268
   of presbyteras, 152–156, 153n152–156n167, 172, 251–252
   regulations for, 262–264
   Romano-Germanic Pontifical of the Tenth Century and, 278–299
   sacramentaries and, 264–268
   texts and, 264–268

Ordines Romani, 265, 274–278, 338–342
orientation, positional
   of S. Peter's basilica, 198n88
   of S. Prassede, 45–46, 45–46n152, 98, 98n133
Origen (early Christian theologian), 139, 181
Otto I (emperor), 279
Ottonian rulers, 149–150
oversight *(episcope)*; *see* episcopas, *episcope* and

Paduensis recension, 266–267, 266n80, 273–274, 291
S. Pancrazio, 331
papacy, early history of, 21, 26, 32–33n113, 32–35
Paris, Council of, 155–156
Parvum romanum (Ado of Vienne), 3, 3n7
Pascha annotina, 87
Paschal I (pope), 15, 378; *see also* Theodora *episcopa*
   Agnes and, 317–318
   art commissions of, 315–318
   Cecilia and, 317–318
   cross-reliquary of, 93–95, 94n122, 94 (photo), 335–336
   death of, 38–39, 39n137
   Easter and, 351–363 *passim*
   iconoclastic movement and, 53, 56
   life of, 38–41, 38n132–40n140
   rebuilding program of, xii, 1, 1n1, 5, 10, 26–56 *passim*, 38n134–50n165, 43 (figure), 76, 84–111 *passim*, 101n141, 105n154, 227–233, 313–314, 331–360 *passim*
   small-scale art commissions and, 91–95, 92n111, 93n119
   in works of art, 40–41, 41 (photo), 60–62, 61 (photo), 97
   world view of, xiii, 51, 315–318

Index of Subjects

Paschaltide, 74, 74n64, 77, 88–90, 104, 110, 164, 310; *see also* Easter
paschal Triduum, 356–358
Paschasius Radbertus (abbot of Corbie), 93n119
Pastor (presbyter), 26, 26n88, 127, 171, 181, 323, 325
   acts of Pudentiana and Praxedes and, 10–13
   house-church named for, 11, 11n30
   Laurentian schism and, 32
   in martyrology, 3, 16–17, 16n49
   Pudens clan genealogy and, 14
   in works of art, 67, 190
The Pastoral Letters, 16
"St. Pastor the martyr" (oratory), 17
patronus, 128
Paul (apostle), xii, 15n42, 194, 204, 277
   Benigno Davanzati on, 171
   death of, 21, 21n67, 81
   as *diakonos*, 134
   episcope and, 157
   Hebrews and, 87, 87n102
   Hermas and, 26
   limitations on women and, 113–117, 114n5, 116n11, 117n13
   Fioravante Martinelli on, 170
   in martyrology, 3
   Natale S. Pauli and, 81, 81n84
   papacy and, 32–33, 32–33n113
   The Pastoral Letters and, 16, 16n47
   Phoebe and, 135, 135n85, 218, 223
   Prisca and Aquilla and, 20, 20n64, 20n65, 24–25n81
   Pudens clan and, 10–11n29, 13–14, 13n39
   on remarriage, 126, 126n48
   Roman church and, 20–21, 20n64, 20n65, 21n67
   slavery and, 11n32
   virginity/celibacy and, 123–129 *passim*
   in works of art, 40, 41 (photo), 49, 60–62, 61 (photo), 69, 70n55, 71n57, 86–105 *passim*, 102n144–106n156, 192–203 *passim*, 364
Paul I (pope), 53, 334
Paul VI (pope), 310
Paula (friend of S. Jerome), 206–207
Pauline mission, 20n64, 241
S. Paulinus of Nola, 66n44
S. Paul's Outside the Walls, 13, 32–33n113, 44, 269
   archdeaconess at, 200
   design of S. Prassede and, 64n39
   diaconas and, 219–220
   Episcopa Q and, 226–227
   Revelation and, 48
Pelagia of Antioch, 367, 367n178
Pelagius II (pope), 330
Pepin the Short (king of the Franks), 53–54, 155, 155n163–164, 211, 275
Persis (early Christian), 120, 130
Peter (apostle), 15n42, 16–17, 16n49, 98n132, 100, 194, 204, 329, 370
   apocrypha and, 8
   cemetery of Priscilla and, 25
   Benigno Davanzati on, 171
   death of, 21, 21n67, 80–81, 81n84
   papacy and, 26, 32–33, 32–33n113
   Petronella and, 225
   Pudens clan and, 10, 13–14, 17
   Punicus Pudens and, 194
   Roman church and, 20–21, 21n67
   sanctoral cycle and, 82
   in works of art, 40, 49, 60–62, 61 (photo), 62n28, 70n55, 71n57, 86–105 *passim*, 102n144–106n156, 187–203 *passim*
1 Peter, 30, 103, 104, 240, 358, 359
Peter of Silva Candida (cardinal bishop), 222
S. Peter's basilica, 31n109, 33n113, 34, 40, 54, 55n12, 61, 236, 267, 315
   chapel of SS. Processus and Martinian in, 39, 39n136
   crypt-altar of, 333–335

S. Peter's basilica (*Cont.*)
   design of S. Prassede and, 1, 42, 44, 48, 48–49n160, 64n39, 65, 329–330
   the Pola casket and, 197–200, 198n88, 198n90
   positional orientation of, 198n88
   Revelation and, 48, 73
   "St. Pastor the martyr" and, 17
Petronella (martyr-patron), 225–226
Pfalzel bei Trier, 157
Phanuel (angel), 65n42, 81
Philemon (early Christian), 122
Philip, daughters of, 118, 123, 123n34
Philip (early Christian), 135
Philippians, 134–135, 157
Phoebe (diacona), 119, 119n19, 130, 135, 170, 172, 218, 223, 256
Pico della Mirandola, Ludovico (Cardinal of S. Prassede), 48, 64, 343–345
pilgrimages, 33–35, 48n160
Pimenius, 16n49
Pinius, Johannes, 306
Pippin III; *see* Pepin the Short
Pius I (pope), 11–13, 26–27, 26n86, 27n90, 27n92, 170, 319, 324–325, 378
   death of, 17
   Easter and, 27, 110
   foundation myth of S. Pudenziana and S. Prassede and, 18, 18n59
   Hermas and, 16–17, 16n50
   in martyrology, 3, 15
   Pudens clan genealogy and, 14
   slavery of Hermas and, 27
   in works of art, 67, 190
Pius XII (pope), 377
Pliny the Younger, 136
the Pola casket, presbyteras and, 197–200, 197 (photo)
politics of the Roman church, 31–32, 31n109, 32n112, 38–39, 39n135, 39n137, 53–54
Polycarp of Smyrna, 27, 124
Pontian, burial of, 336
Pontifical of Egbert, Archbishop of York, 272
pontificals, 270–308 *passim*
positional orientation
   of S. Peter's basilica, 198n88
   of S. Prassede's, 45–46, 45–46n152, 98, 98n133
Potentiana/Pudentiana, xii, 1, 1n2, 7, 15, 34, 314; *see also* S. Pudenziana, basilica of
   acta SS. Pudentianae et Praxedis, 18, 32, 260
   baptism of, 10–11n29, 13, 13n39, 171
   burial of, 336
   Benigno Davanzati on, 171–172
   feast of, 81, 83, 83n87
   genealogy of, 14
   Laurentian schism and, 31–32, 31n109, 32n112
   Fioravante Martinelli on, 170
   in martyrology, 3–5, 4n9, 5n12
   Pastor and, 29
   pilgrimage and, 34–35, 35n120
   virginity and, 127–128
   vita of, 9–30, 11n33, 12n34, 110–111, 123, 176, 193, 210, 262, 318–329, 367–369
   in works of art, 36–37, 37n128, 40, 41 (photo), 50, 60–62, 61 (photo), 86, 105–110, 106 (photo), 107 (photo), 190–194, 227, 235, 347–349, 348 (photo), 365
S. Prassede; *see* Praxedes; structure of S. Prassede; *specific area, e.g.* apse of S. Prassede; *specific topic, e.g.* decorative cycles of S. Prassede
Praxedes, xii, xiii, 7, 15, 34, 44, 227
   acta SS. Pudentianae et Praxedis, 18, 32, 260
   baptism of, 10–11n29, 13, 13n39, 171

burial of, 336
Benigno Davanzati on, 171–172
death of, 12–13, 13n37, 171, 319
feast of, 1n2, 81, 83, 83n87
genealogy of, 14
Laurentian schism and, 31–32, 31n109, 32n112
liturgy and, 360–363
Fioravante Martinelli on, 170, 173
in martyrology, 1–5, 1n2, 3n7, 4n9, 5n12
Mary Magdalene and, 372–373
Pastor and, 29
pilgrimage and, 34–35, 35n120
as presbytera, xi–xii, 170–173, 327–328, 343–350
S. Pudenziana and, 363–366
Vatican ms. lat 1191 and, 366–371
virginity and, 127–128
vita of, 9–30, 12n34, 32n112, 78n76, 110–111, 123, 176, 193, 210, 262, 318–329, 367–369
in works of art, 36–37, 37n128, 40, 41 (photo), 50, 60–62, 61 (photo), 68, 69, 70n55, 86, 105–110, 106 (photo), 107 (photo), 190–194, 227–228, 235, 347–349, 348 (photo), 365
prayer-graffiti, 24
preaching; *see* evangelists; liturgy
presbyteras, 30–31, 31n107, 151–157, 152n147–157n171
abbesses as, 180
Atto of Vercelli and, 211–218, 211n128–217n148
"Crispina" sarcophagus and, 195–196, 196 (photo)
Benigno Davanzati on, 172
defined, xi
duties of, 241
Gelasius I and, 154–156, 207–211
hierarchy and, 137
Council of Laodicea and, 152–153, 152n151, 153–154n157

ordination of, 152–156, 153n152–156n167, 172, 251–252
the Pola casket and, 197–200, 197 (photo)
Praxedes as, xi–xii, 6, 170–173, 327–328
Priscilla cemetery and, 182–192, 182n43–192n73
in the Roman church, 179–200, 179n33–200n94
in works of art, 182–200, 182n43–200n94
Zacharias and, 155, 155n163–164
presbyter-bishops, 21, 257
presbyterial council, 21, 29
presbytery of S. Prassede, 2 (photo), 43 (figure), 45–50, 45n151–50n164 *passim*, 57 (photo), 73, 339 (figure)
priests; *see sacerdotes* (priests)
Primo trofeo della Sma Croce eretto in Roma nella Via Lata da S. Pietro Apostolo (Martinelli), 170, 172n4
Prisca (early Christian), 20, 20n64, 20n65, 24–25n81, 34–35, 34n117, 35n120, 81n86, 120–122, 120n25, 121n27, 356
S. Prisca, 10n28, 25n81, 26, 34, 34n117
Priscilla, 10n28, 13, 24, 323; *see also* Priscilla cemetery
baptism of, 171
genealogy of, 14
in works of art, 187, 190
Priscilla cemetery, 4, 7, 10n28, 12–13, 24–25n81, 24–26, 25n83, 34, 325, 336, 356, 369; *see also* burial practices; Priscilla
catacomb art of, 14
excavation of, 13
Fractio panis fresco at, 183–189, 183n47–189n61, 184 (photo)
frescoes at, 183–192, 183n47–192n73

Priscilla cemetery (*Cont.*)
  Greek Chapel in, 183–189,
    183n47–189n61
  loculus in, 15, 15n42
  presbyteras and, 182–192,
    182n43–192n73
  Velatio fresco at, 177, 178 (photo),
    189–192, 189n63–192n73
Priscillian (lay evangelist), 141
prophets, women as, 117–118
propitiatorium, 351–353
Protoevangelium of James, 8
Proverbs, 29, 201, 249, 362
Psalms, 89, 91, 283, 309, 357
Pudens clan, 7–20, 10–11n29, 169–173,
    169n1–172n10, 363, 368. *see also*
    specific family members
  genealogy of, 14
  The Pastoral Letters and, 16
  Priscilla cemetery and, 24–26, 25n81,
    25n83
  2 Timothy and, 171
  in works of art, 190
Pudens "Junior," 10–11n29, 10–15, 15n42,
    120n25, 190, 193, 322–323,
    368–369
  death of, 16, 323–324
  genealogy of, 14
  in martyrology, 3–4, 4n9, 5n12
  The Pastoral Letters and, 16
  in works of art, 67, 365
S. Pudenziana, basilica of, 7, 7–8n20,
    8 (photo), 25n81, 27n90, 260,
    363–366. *see also* Potentiana/
    Pudentiana
  apse of, 203, 207
  chapel of S. Peter in, 14
  foundation myth of, 10, 18–20, 29–31
  Peter and, 17
  presbyteras and, 192–195
  Punicus Pudens and, 10n28
  rebuilding of, xii, 35–37, 35n121

Punicus Pudens, 10, 10n28, 13, 17, 323
  baptism of, 171
  Benigno Davanzati on, 171
  genealogy of, 14
  Peter and, 194

Quintus Cornelius Pudens, 13; *see also*
  Punicus Pudens

Rabanus Maurus (archbishop of
  Mainz), martyrology of, 4–5
Radegonde (queen of the Franks), 147
Raphael (angel), 65n42, 81
refrigerium (funeral banquet), 185–186
Regina (ecclesiastical widow), 175, 218
relic translation, xiii, 1, 1n1, 16, 42, 47,
    47n156, 48, 48n160, 85, 313–314,
    329–351 *passim*; *see also* altar of
    S. Prassede
  Praxedes as presbytera and, 343–350,
    348 (photo)
  relic-list of S. Prassede and, 335–337
  reliquary of Paschal and, 93–95,
    94n122, 94 (photo), 335–336
Remigius (bishop of Reims), 147
resurrection scenes, 91–95,
    92n111–112
Revelation, 29, 47–108 *passim*, 118,
    332, 368
  in the epistolary, 73–90 *passim*,
    74n64–85n96
  iconography of mosaics and, xii, 52,
    56–90 *passim*
  use of in lectionary, 74, 74n65
rites/rituals
  consecration of virgins, 177–179
  in early Christianity, women and,
    243–244
  ordination (*see* ordination)
Romana of Jerusalem (diacona), 367
Roman Carolingian renaissance,
    38, 38n134

Index of Subjects

Roman church, women's place in, 169–238 *passim*; *see also* early Christianity, women's place in; *specific office*
- as abbesses (*see* abbesses)
- "Age of Martyrs" and, 20–26
- Atto of Vercelli and, 211–218, 211n128–217n148
- as canonesses (*see* canonesses)
- Carolingian rulers and, 53–54
- dedication of, 83–84
- as diacona (*see* diaconas)
- early history of, 21–31, 174–207, 174n16–207n117
- enrolled widows in, 174–176, 174n16–176n23
- Gelasius I and, 207–211
- iconoclastic movement and, 52–53, 53n3
- Laurentian schism and, 31–32, 31n109, 32n112
- leadership models in, 28–33
- offices of (*see* office holders, women as; *specific office*)
- ordination in (*see* ordination)
- ordination prayers of, 264–268
- pilgrimages and, 33–35
- politics of, 31–32, 31n109, 32n112, 38–39, 39n135, 39n137, 53–54
- pontificals and, 270–307 *passim*
- as presbyteras (*see* presbyteras)
- sacramentaries and, 264–268
- secular sphere and, 33
- stational churches and, xiii, 5–6n13, 6, 20, 34–35, 58n18, 77–88 *passim*, 265, 314–315, 353–363
- as teachers, 200–207, 201n95–207n117
- texts and, 220–224, 220n155–223n168, 264–268
- *tituli* (*see tituli* (immovable church property))
- virgins in, 176–179, 176n25–179n31
- works of art and, 182–200, 182n43–200n94

Roman epistolary; *see* epistolary
Roman lectionary; *see* lectionary
Roman liturgy; *see* liturgy
Roman marriage law, 125
Roman martyrology, 17
Romano-Germanic Pontifical of the Tenth Century, 270–299 *passim*, 307
Roman Pontifical of William Durand, 301–306
Roman Pontifical of the Twelfth Century, 299–301
Romans, book of, 20, 119–135 *passim*, 181, 201, 212–223 *passim*, 256, 257, 375
- Hermas and, 26
- women as leaders and, 119, 119n19, 322
Roman synod of 499, 6, 9, 31
Roman synod of 595, 6, 9, 31
Rome, Council of, 150
Rossellino, Bernardo, 343
Rufus (early Christian), 120

Sabina (diacona), 223
S. Sabina, 34, 34n117, 175
- "Church from the Circumcision," 194, 204, 207
- "Church from the Gentiles," 194, 204, 207
- women as teachers and, 201–202, 201n96, 203 (photo), 205 (photo)
sacerdotes (priests)
- abbesses as, 161
- canonesses as, 156–157, 157n171, 161
- duties of, 241
- episcopas as, 158
- sacramentaries, 264–268

Sacramentary of Hildoard, 265–266
sainthood, history of, 21–22
sancta sanctorum, 351–353
sanctoral cycle of the lectionary, 80–87, 80n83–86n97
the Sanctus, 66, 66n43
San Sisto (enclosure), 237
Sav(b)inella, 10, 15, 323
   baptism of, 10–11n29, 13, 13n39, 171
   genealogy of, 14
Schuster, Ildefonso (abbot, S. Paul's Outside the Walls), 13
secular canonesses, 150–151
Sergia (diacona/abbess), 223
Sergius (archbishop of Ravenna), 148
Sergius I (pope), 83, 83n88, 273
The Shepherd (Hermas), 16, 16n50, 26–29, 26n88, 27n91, 28n96, 126, 181, 182, 218, 369
Shorter Roman Martyrology (Ado of Vienne), 15
Silvester I, 61, 320
Simmetrius (presbyter), 2, 34–35, 35n120, 319, 327
   death of, 12, 12n36
   in martyrology, 4, 17
   Pudens clan genealogy and, 14
   in works of art, 67
Sion church, 44n148
Sirach, 361–363
Siricius (pope), 7, 178, 180, 226, 228, 237, 320–321
San Sisto (enclosure), 237
Sixtus II (pope), 12n36
Sixtus III (pope), 6n14
slaves, 11, 11n32, 27
small-scale art commissions, 91–95, 92n111, 93n119
social service centers; *see diaconiae* (social service centers)
social status, 29, 122, 202, 243, 258n55, 322n22

Solomon (king of Israel), 104, 204
Song of Songs, 127, 369
Sophia, 249
S. Sophia's, Benevento, 163
spiritual marriage, 128
Le ss. Prassede e Maria Maddalena (Maineri illustration), 372
stational churches, xiii, 5–6n13, 6, 20, 34–35, 58n18, 77–88 *passim,* 265, 314–315, 353–363
Statuta ecclesiae antiqua (Gennadius of Marseilles), 142
SS. Stefano e Cassiano, 53
S. Stephano, as model for S. Prassede, 38n132
Stephanus, 13n39
Stephen (martyr), 50, 50n164, 135, 298
Stephen II (pope), 54
Stephen IV (pope), 38, 337
Stephen V (pope), 41n143
Stephen of Fossanova (papal chamberlain), 237
Stratonicus, burial of, 336
structure of S. Prassede, 41–50, 42n144–50n165, 43 (figure), 339 (figure)
Studia Patristica, 82
"Sunday of the Birthday Saints," 76–80, 77n73–79n82
S. Susanna, 55
Symmachus (pope), 31, 31n109, 318, 330
syneisaktism, 127
Syriac Bible (Paris, B. N. ms. syr. 113), 249–250

Tabitha (early Christian), 130
Tacitus, on Nero, 21
teachers, women as
   catacomb of S. Agnes and, 201–202, 201n96, 203 (photo), 205 (photo)
   in the Roman church, 200–207, 201n95–207n117

S. Sabina's and, 201–202, 201n96, 203 (photo), 205 (photo)
Tertullian, 21, 21n67, 126, 126n47, 136, 208n118
Testamentum Domini, 131, 132n72, 154, 154n158
Theodora (Magistra), 202
Theodora *episcopa*, 45, 97, 99, 99n136, 111, 227–229, 317
    Archiepiscopal Palace, Ravenna and, 233–234
    Basilica Euphrasiana and, 231–233, 231 (photo), 232 (photo), 233 (photo)
    Lateran Baptistry's Chapel of S. Venantius and, 229–231, 230 (photo)
    mosaic bust of, xii
    Vatican, Pinacoteca, Universal Judgment and, 234–236
    in works of art, 106–110, 107n157–110n163, 107 (photo)
Theodora of Sihla, 312
Theodore (abbot of Stoudite monastery), 53
Theodore I (pope), 78, 229
Theodore the Studite, 101n141
Theodosian classicism, 35, 35n122
Theodosius (emperor), 98n132
Theodosius (pilgrim), 44n148
Theodosius I (pope), 44
Theophilus (bishop of Alexandria), 27n92, 28
Theosebia (presbytera), 153
Tiburtius, 98n132
Timothy (presbyter), 50, 50n164, 170–173, 325
    acts of Pudentiana and Praxedes and, 10–13
    in martyrology, 15
    Novatus and, 11–12
    The Pastoral Letters and, 16, 16n47
    Pudens clan genealogy and, 14
    shrine to, 33
    in works of art, 365, 365 (photo)
1 Timothy, 16, 114–136 *passim*, 152, 206, 243, 257, 277, 283, 365
    limitations on women in, 113–117
    on remarriage, 126
    on widows, 129–130, 132
2 Timothy, 16, 29, 243, 257, 365
    Pudens clan and, 13, 171
tituli (immovable church property), 5–6n13, 30–31, 34, 259–262, 326–327
    female ownership of, 31, 31n107
    Laurentian schism and, 32
titulus Pastorus, 11, 11n30, 16, 127
titulus Praxedis, 5–6, 6n16, 12, 12n35, 19, 19n61, 31n109, 34–37, 37n129, 110, 314, 327–328, 360
titulus Prisca, 8n86
titulus Pudentis, 7, 16, 110, 323
titulus sanctae Praxedis, 6, 9
Titus, book of, 29, 116, 152
topographical record, foundation myth and, 18–20
Tours, Council of, 159
Trajan (emperor), 136
transept of S. Prassede, iconography of mosaics of, 56–73 *passim*
translation; *see* relic translation
Tridentinum recension, 220, 266–274 *passim*, 269–270n90, 270n93, 293
triumphal arch of S. Prassede, 41–47, 42n144, 43 (figure), 47n154–156, 57 (photo), 339 (figure)
    decorative cycles of, 52, 54
    descending christology and, 58, 58n20
    iconography of mosaics of, xii, 66–73, 70n53–55, 83–84, 88
    Lateran triclinium and, 55n12

Trullo III, Council of, 63
Tryphaena (early Christian), 120, 130
Tryphosa (early Christian), 120, 130
Tychicus (early Christian), 135

Universal Judgment, Vatican, Pinacoteca, 234–236
Uota of Niedermünster (abbess), 161
Urbanus (early Christian), 120
Usuard of Saint-Germain-des Prés, martyrology of, 5, 5n11–12, 15, 17
Uta Codex, 161

S. Valentine, catacomb of, 34
Valentinus (heretic), 26
Valerian (emperor), 12n36, 322n22
Vallombrosan epistolary, 76–91 *passim*, 372
Vanmaele, Basile (Christian archeologist), 372
Varatec, Basilian Orthodox community of, xii, 140n106, 310–311
Vatican, Pinacoteca, Universal Judgment, 234–236
Vatican codex Barberini gr. 336, 252, 252n37
Vatican Library Manuscripts
  Chigi ms. C V 148, 304
  lat. 1145, 304–305
  lat. 1191, 366–371
  lat. 3764, 17–18
  lat. 6839, 17–18, 291
  lat. 8701, 76–91 *passim*, 372
Velatio fresco at the Priscilla cemetery, 177, 178 (photo), 189–192, 189n63–192n73
Veneranda, Domitilla catacomb, 224–226, 225 (photo)
Verona lectionary, 75–76n70, 80–100 *passim*, 87n100
Veronensis (Leonine sacramentary), 264, 309

Vestel virgins, 176
vestments
  women office holders and, 40, 155–156
  in works of art, 80, 97, 105, 143–145, 144 (photo), 145 (photo), 151, 191–206 *passim*, 205 (photo), 235–236, 249
Victor (pope), 27n92, 28
vicus (city district), 7n17
"Viérge, virginité" (H. Leclercq), 190
virginity, 368; *see also* celibacy
  consecration of, 177–179
  in early Christianity, 123–129, 124–125n40, 124n38, 126n47–127n50
  in the Roman church, 176–179, 176n25–179n31
  unmarried woman and, 123
  vestals and, 176
  widows and, 130
  in works of art, 190–191
Virgin Mary; *see* Mary Theotokos
Vita sanctarum virginum Praxedis et Pudentiana, et Pius Papa, 367–368; *see also* Potentiana/Pudentiana; Praxedes
Vogel, Cyrille, 246–247, 278, 280

weekday temporal cycle, 87–90
welfare; *see diaconiae* (social service centers)
widows, 123–135 *passim*, 126n47, 135n86, 368
  ecclesiastical, 129–133, 129n61–133n77, 175
  enrolled, 174–176, 174n16–176n23
  requirements for diaconas and, 138–141
Widukind (Benedictine of Corvey), 156
Wilpert, Joseph (priest-archeologist), 183, 185, 187, 193
wisdom, personification of, 28, 195
Wisdom, books of, 104, 249, 361

wives of bishops, 159, 159n177, 159n181
woman-church, 28–29
women; *see* early Christianity, women's place in; Eastern churches, women's place in; gender parity; Roman church, women's place in; woman-church; *specific names; specific offices*
Women Officeholders in Early Christianity (Eisen), xii
Worms, Council of, 148
Würzburg epistles, 75–104 *passim*, 79n82, 147, 361, 372

Zacharias (pope), 78, 155, 155n163–164, 211, 212, 216
Zeno (presbyter), 50, 50n164, 97, 105, 105–106n156, 105n154, 109
Zeno Chapel of S. Prassede, xi, 42–45, 42n144, 43 (figure), 44n148–45n150, 46n152, 73–74, 233, 315–318, 335, 339 (figure), 373
  column of flagellation in, 44–45, 44n148–45n149
  decorative cycles of, 52, 54–56
  epistola catholica and, 101–105, 102n144–106n156
  iconography of mosaics of, xii, 54–56, 70, 70n54, 95–110, 95n124–110n163, 96 (photo), 99 (photo), 103 (photo), 106 (photo), 107 (photo)
  Theodora *episcopa* and, 227–229
Zerubbabel, in works of art, 70n55
Zoticus, burial of, 336